ROUTLEDGE HAND
SECUI

The *Routledge Handbook of Arctic Security* offers a comprehensive examination of security in the region, encompassing both state-based and militarized notions of security, as well as broader security perspectives reflecting debates about changes in climate, environment, economies, and societies.

Since the turn of the century, the Arctic has increasingly been in the global spotlight, resulting in the often invoked idea of "Arctic exceptionalism" being questioned. At the same time, the unconventional political power which the Arctic's Indigenous peoples hold calls into question conventional ideas about geopolitics and security. This handbook examines security in this region, revealing contestations and complementarities between narrower, state-based and/or militarized notions of security and broader security perspectives reflecting concerns and debates about changes in climate, environment, economies, and societies.

The volume is split into five thematic parts:

- Theorizing Arctic Security
- The Arctic Powers
- Security in the Arctic through Governance
- Non-Arctic States, Regional and International Organizations
- People, States, and Security.

This book will be of great interest to students of Arctic politics, global governance, geography, security studies, and International Relations.

Gunhild Hoogensen Gjørv is Professor at the Centre for Peace Studies at UiT – The Arctic University of Norway.

Marc Lanteigne is an Associate Professor of Political Science at UiT – The Arctic University of Norway.

Horatio Sam-Aggrey has been interning at the Centre for Peace Studies, as well as the Centre for Sámi Studies, at UiT – The Arctic University of Norway. He is additionally a Project Assessment Analyst with the Government of Northwest Territories, Canada.

ROUTLEDGE HANDBOOK OF ARCTIC SECURITY

Edited by Gunhild Hoogensen Gjørv, Marc Lanteigne and Horatio Sam-Aggrey

Routledge
Taylor & Francis Group
LONDON AND NEW YORK

First published 2020
by Routledge
2 Park Square, Milton Park, Abingdon, Oxon OX14 4RN

and by Routledge
605 Third Avenue, New York, NY 10017

First issued in paperback 2022

Routledge is an imprint of the Taylor & Francis Group, an informa business

Publisher's Note
The publisher has gone to great lengths to ensure the quality of this reprint but points out that some imperfections in the original copies may be apparent.

British Library Cataloguing-in-Publication Data
A catalogue record for this book is available from the British Library

Library of Congress Cataloging-in-Publication Data
Names: Hoogensen Gjørv, Gunhild, 1966- editor. | Lanteigne, Marc, editor. |
Sam-Aggrey, Horatio, editor.
Title: Routledge handbook of Arctic security / edited by Gunhild Hoogensen
Gjørv, Marc Lanteigne and Horatio Sam-Aggrey.
Other titles: Handbook of Arctic security
Description: London ; New York : Routledge/Taylor & Francis Group, 2020. |
Includes bibliographical references and index.
Identifiers: LCCN 2019043155 (print) | LCCN 2019043156 (ebook) |
ISBN 9781138227996 (hardback) | ISBN 9781315265797 (ebook)
Subjects: LCSH: Arctic Regions–Strategic aspects. |
Arctic Regions–Politics and government. | Geopolitics–Arctic regions. |
Human security–Arctic regions. | National security–Arctic regions. |
Security, International.
Classification: LCC UA880 .R68 2020 (print) | LCC UA880 (ebook) |
DDC 355/.0330113–dc23
LC record available at https://lccn.loc.gov/2019043155
LC ebook record available at https://lccn.loc.gov/2019043156

ISBN: 978-1-03-240078-5 (pbk)
ISBN: 978-1-138-22799-6 (hbk)
ISBN: 978-1-315-26579-7 (ebk)

DOI: 10.4324/9781315265797

Typeset in Bembo
by Swales & Willis, Exeter, Devon, UK

CONTENTS

ILLUSTRATIONS

Figures

Tables

Maps

CONTRIBUTORS

Adele Airoldi received a Master's in Environmental Sciences (1979, ULB Brussels), an M.Phil. in Polar Studies (1989, University of Cambridge), and was a Fellow for the EU at CFIA, Harvard University (1994–5) She was also an administrator in the General Secretariat of the Council of the European Union, principally for research and environment policies, including international negotiations on environment and development and on climate change. Since retirement, she is active as an independent expert on EU–Arctic relations, and is the author of *The European Union and the Arctic: Policies and Actions* (2008), commissioned by the Nordic Council of Ministers, along with subsequent editions (2010 and 2014).

Rasmus Gjedssø Bertelsen is Professor of Northern Studies and the inaugural Barents Chair in Politics at UiT – The Arctic University of Norway. Originally from Denmark, he grew up in Reykjavík and has a deep personal and professional commitment to the North Atlantic and the Arctic. Rasmus studied in Copenhagen, Reykjavík, Geneva, Lausanne, and Amsterdam. His PhD is from the University of Cambridge with a year at Sciences Po. He was a postdoc at Harvard, United Nations University (Yokohama) and Aalborg University. His main research interests include transnational flows of knowledge, talent, and resources between East and West.

Andrew Chater is a Fellow at the Polar Research and Policy Initiative and an Assistant Professor at Brescia University College. He was the 2018–19 Fulbright Visiting Research Chair in Arctic Studies at the University of Washington. He completed his doctorate at the University of Western Ontario. His dissertation, "Explaining the Evolution of the Arctic Council," examines reasons for contemporary changes in the role of the Arctic Council. His research interests include Arctic politics, global governance, and foreign policy. Outside of academic life, Andrew plays music and has taught guitar in Iqaluit, Nunavut, as part of the Iqaluit Music Camp.

Gordon B. Cooke is Associate Professor of Industrial Relations within the Faculty of Business Administration at Memorial University of Newfoundland, Canada. He studies the changing nature of "work," meaning the growth and prominence of various "non-standard work arrangements" like fluctuating work schedules, long or short work weeks, casual/on-call /non-permanent employment, and unusual work locations (e.g. telework). He conducts research focusing on Northwest Ireland, Northern Norway, the Faroe Islands, Shetland, and especially rural Newfoundland. His research has been published in journals such as *Human Relations, International Journal of Human Resource Management, Relations Industrielles, Community Work & Family*, and *Island Studies Journal*.

Michael T. Corgan was Associate Professor of International Relations at the Frederick S. Pardee School of Global Studies at Boston University. He served in the US Navy, including two tours in Vietnam and several teaching assignments at the US Naval Academy, the National War College, and the United States War College. He authored multiple scholarly works in the field of security studies, particularly related to the Nordic and Arctic region, and was widely sought after by the media as a security commentator. His 2002 book, *Iceland and Its Alliances: Security for a Small State* has been used as a briefing guide for officers at the NATO headquarters of the Supreme Allied Commander – Atlantic. He taught at the University of Iceland in 2001 on a Fulbright fellowship, and returned in 2006 and 2014. He was associated faculty at the University of Lapland, Finland and was a member of the University of the Arctic Thematic Network.

Magnus DeWitt is a doctoral student at the School of Science and Engineering at Reykjavík University. He graduated with a Master's degree in sustainable energy engineering from the Iceland School of Energy hosted at Reykjavík University. Magnus also holds a bachelor's degree in mechanical engineering. His research interest is focused on energy-related issues in the Arctic. A major research area is the energy transition in remote villages. This includes issues such as energy security, energy policy, technologies, and involvement of communities.

Klaus Dodds is Professor of Geopolitics and Director of Research for the School of Life Sciences and Environment at Royal Holloway University of London. He is co-author with Mark Nuttall of *The Arctic: What Everyone Needs to Know* (Oxford University Press, 2019). He was a recipient of a Major Research Fellowship from the Leverhulme Trust 2017–20 for a project on the Global Arctic, and is a Fellow of the Academy of Social Sciences in the UK.

Niklas Eklund is Senior Lecturer and Associate Professor in Political Science at the Department of Political Science, Umeå University, specializing in public administration, security, leadership, and crisis management. He is also Vice-Director of the Arctic Research Centre at Umeå University (Arcum). Among his publications on Arctic affairs is "Refracting (Geo-) political choices in the Arctic" (2017) with Lize-Marié van der Watt in *The Polar Journal* and the book chapter "The Swedish Chairmanship: Foresight and Hindsight in Arctic Activism" (2019) in *Leadership for the North – The Influence and Impact of Arctic Council Chairs,* edited by Douglas C. Nord (Springer Polar Sciences).

Heather Exner-Pirot is a Research Associate at the Observatoire de la politique et la sécurité de l'Arctique (OPSA) and the managing editor of the *Arctic Yearbook*. She has held positions at the University of Saskatchewan, the International Centre for Northern Governance and Development and the University of the Arctic. She is a regular contributor to Radio Canada's *Eye on the Arctic* website, a Board member for The Arctic Institute (TAI) and Saskatchewan First Nations Economic Development Network, and Chair of the Canadian Northern Studies Trust. She completed her PhD in Political Science at the University of Calgary in 2011, and has published extensively on Arctic and northern governance, human security, and development.

Gail Fondahl is Professor of Geography at the University of Northern British Columbia, Canada. Her research focuses on the legal geographies of Indigenous territorial rights in the

Russian North, where she has carried out fieldwork since 1992, and on the cultural and governance dimensions of Arctic sustainability. She served as Canada's representative to the International Arctic Science Committee's Social & Human Sciences Working Group from 2011–18, and as president of the International Arctic Social Sciences Association (2011–14). She co-edited the second Arctic Human Development Report (AHDR-II).

Piotr Graczyk is a Research Scientist at the NORCE Norwegian Research Centre and a PhD Research Fellow at UiT – The Arctic University of Norway, both located in Tromsø, Norway. His research interests centre on roles of the Arctic Council in Arctic governance, international institutions, ocean and shipping governance, and Arctic shipping. He published several peer-reviewed papers and book chapters on the Arctic Council and Arctic shipping. He worked as a policy assistant at the Arctic Council Secretariat and has been a member of Poland's observer delegations to various Arctic Council meetings, with a focus on the Protection of the Arctic Marine Environment (PAME) Working Group.

Wilfrid Greaves is Assistant Professor of International Relations at the University of Victoria, British Columbia. His research examines intersections between global politics, security studies, and Canadian foreign policy, with focuses on climate change, energy extraction, Indigenous peoples, and the circumpolar Arctic. He has co-edited two books on Arctic politics, and authored more than 20 peer-reviewed articles and book chapters. He holds a PhD in Political Science from the University of Toronto, and was previously a Visiting Scholar at the Centre for Sámi Studies at UiT The Arctic University of Norway.

Gunhild Hoogensen Gjørv is Professor of Critical Peace and Conflict Studies with a specialization in Security Studies and International Relations at UiT The Arctic University of Norway. Hoogensen Gjørv's research addresses the interactions between perceptions of state and human security in a variety of contexts, particularly focusing on civil–military interaction and Arctic perceptions of security. She was awarded a Fulbright Arctic Initiative fellowship (2015–16), after which she was awarded the Nansen Professorship at the University of Akureyri (2017–18). Her previous edited volume (lead editor and contributor) was *Environmental and Human Security in the Arctic* (Routledge, 2014).

Lassi Heininen is a Research Director at the Institute for Atmospheric and Earth System Research (INAR) at the University of Helsinki, and Emeritus Professor at the Faculty of Social Sciences, University of Lapland. Among his other academic positions are Professor at Northern (Arctic) Federal University (Russia), Editor of *Arctic Yearbook*, and Head of UArctic Thematic Network on Geopolitics and Security Studies. His research fields include international relations, geopolitics, security studies, environmental politics, and Arctic studies. He lectures, supervises and speaks regularly abroad, and actively publishes in international academic publications.

Alan K. Henrikson is the Lee E. Dirks Professor of Diplomatic History Emeritus and founding Director of Diplomatic Studies at The Fletcher School of Law and Diplomacy at Tufts University, where he has taught American diplomatic history, contemporary US–European relations, global political geography, and the history, theory, and practice of diplomacy. During 2010–11 he was Fulbright Schuman Professor at the College of Europe in Bruges. He has taught at the Diplomatic Academy of Estonia and at MGIMO University in Russia. His writings have included studies in the history of transatlantic relations and also of Nordic/Arctic security.

Thora M. Herrmann is Associate Professor at the Department of Geography at the Université de Montréal, Canada. Her research interests include the study of impacts of socio-environmental change on animal and plant species, and on the lifestyles, cultures, and traditions of Indigenous peoples in the sub-polar and polar regions, as well as the protection of endangered species by integrating geographic, ecological, and sociocultural aspects. Her research has been published in journals including *Polar Geography*, *Écoscience*, and the *Polar Journal.*

Kara K. Hodgson is a PhD. candidate and Research Fellow in the Centre for Peace Studies at UiT – The Arctic University of Norway. She has studied and worked extensively in Russia, and her research interests include politics and governance in the Arctic, with a particular emphasis on exploring the dynamics of human security in the Russian Arctic.

Kamrul Hossain is a Research Professor and the Director of the Northern Institute for Environmental and Minority Law at the Arctic Centre of the University of Lapland. By training, he is a researcher in the field of international law, and has been working on a diverse range of Arctic issues for over a decade. The main focus of his research currently lies in international environmental law which applies to the Arctic as well as in human rights law, in particular the rights of Indigenous peoples with a focus on the Arctic.

Rob Huebert is an Associate Professor of Political Science at the University of Calgary. He also served as the associate director of the Centre for Military and Strategic Studies, and was a member of the Canadian Polar Commission during 2010–15. He is also a research fellow with the Canadian Global Affairs Institute, publishes on the issues of Canadian Defence and Arctic Security, and his work has appeared in numerous Canadian and international affairs journals. He is the author (with Whitney Lackenbauer and Franklyn Griffiths) of *Canada and the Changing Arctic: Sovereignty, Security, and Stewardship* (2011). He regularly comments on Canadian security and Arctic issues in the Canadian and international media.

Auður H. Ingólfsdóttir holds a joint PhD. degree in international relations and gender studies from University of Lapland and University of Iceland. Her doctoral dissertation focused on climate change and security in the Arctic, where she used a feminist perspective to analyse norms and values shaping climate policy in Iceland. She was an Assistant Professor at Bifröst University, Iceland for eight years (2010–17). She worked as a researcher at the Icelandic Tourism Research Centre (2017–19), before starting her own consulting business, Transformia, focusing on issues related to sustainability and social responsibility.

Aytalina Ivanova is a Research Docent at the North Eastern Federal University, Yakutsk, Russia. She specializes in legal anthropology, Arctic Indigenous peoples' law, and environmental governance. Her publications have focused on the relations between Indigenous and rural livelihoods, processes of Arctic industrialization, and the governance of the Arctic. Ivanova has worked in a project on Indigenous territorial governance at the Arctic University of Norway (UiT) (2016–18), and is currently leading a Russian–Finnish research project on the legal anthropology of Arctic Youth (2018–20).

Rauna Kuokkanen is Research Professor of Arctic Indigenous Studies at the University of Lapland, Finland. Before that, she was Associate Professor at the Department of Political Science and Indigenous Studies Program at the University of Toronto (2008–18). Her main areas of research include comparative Indigenous politics, Indigenous feminist theory, Indigenous women's rights, Arctic Indigenous governance, legal, and political traditions. Professor Kuokkanen's most recent book, *Restructuring Relations: Indigenous Self-Determination, Governance and Gender* from Oxford University Press (2019), is an Indigenous feminist investigation of the theory and practice of Indigenous self-determination, governance, and gender regimes in Indigenous political institutions.

Marc Lanteigne is an Associate Professor of Political Science at UiT The Arctic University of Norway, and has also taught international relations and Asian politics in Britain, Canada, China, and New Zealand. His research interests include Chinese and East Asian foreign policy, including China's relations with Europe and the polar regions. He is the author of *China and International Institutions: Alternate Paths to Global Power* (2005) and *Chinese Foreign Policy: An Introduction* (fourth edition 2019), and the co-editor of *China's Evolving Approach to Peacekeeping* (2012) as well as numerous articles and chapters on Asian politics. He is also the editor of the Arctic news blog *Over the Circle* and a regular commentator on Asia–Arctic diplomacy.

Bjarni Már Magnússon is Professor at Reykjavík University School of Law and chair of Reykjavík University's Institute of International and European Law. He received his PhD. in law from the University of Edinburgh in 2013, and is a Fulbright and Chevening alumnus.

Charles H. Norchi is the Benjamin Thompson Professor of Law in the University of Maine School of Law. He directs the Center for Oceans and Coastal Law, Graduate Law Programs and serves on the faculty of the Climate Change Institute of the University of Maine. He teaches and writes on the Arctic, public international law, law of the sea, maritime law and geopolitics, and has served as the Fulbright Ministry of Foreign Affairs Arctic Scholar in Iceland. He is co-chair of the Arctic Futures Institute (Maine), and a contributing editor to *Global Geneva*. He holds university degrees from Harvard, Case Western Reserve University School of Law and Yale Law School.

Embla Eir Oddsdóttir has experience in research, project management, and policy-relevant issues in the Arctic, including in shipping, risk, climate change, resilience, and gender. Embla is Director of the Icelandic Arctic Cooperation Network and Polar Law Institute and has lectured on northern issues at various universities and venues. Her educational background is interdisciplinary, including socio-economic development, anthropology, cultural geography, international relations, international law, Indigenous and gender studies, rural development, and Political Science. She holds an MSc in Law, Anthropology, and Society from the London School of Economics and has completed diploma-level courses in Polar Law.

Barbora Padrtova is an Assistant Professor at the Department of International Relations and European Studies at the Faculty of Social Studies at Masaryk University in Brno, the Czech Republic. In 2018–19, she also worked as a Research Scholar affiliated with the Arctic Futures Initiative at the International Institute for Applied Systems Analysis (IIASA), based in Laxenburg, Austria. She is a Czech delegate to the Social & Human Working Group of the International Arctic Science Committee (IASC). Her research interests focus on geopolitics and security in the Arctic region, securitization theory, US–Russia relations, and NATO–Russia relations.

Tobjørn Pedersen is Professor of Political Science at Nord University, Norway. He holds a PhD. degree in Political Science from UiT – The Arctic University of Norway and received a Master of Arts degree in International Relations and International Economics while a Fulbright fellow at SAIS Johns Hopkins University, Washington, DC. Pedersen specializes in international relations and security policy in the Arctic. He is also a former journalist and has worked for media outlets such as Reuters, Aftenposten and the Norwegian Broadcasting Corporation (NRK).

Bui K. Petersen is a Postdoctoral Fellow at Memorial University of Newfoundland. His varied cross-disciplinary research has examined issues related to labour and employment, negotiation and conflict management, management education, rural employment, industrial relations, as well as innovation and technology. He has a particular research interest in how technological changes affect the nature of and access to work and employment, especially in regions dependent on resource-based industries. His research has been published in *Business & Society*, *Canadian Journal of Administrative Sciences*, and *Island Studies Journal*.

Jon Rahbek-Clemmensen is an Associate Professor at the Royal Danish Defence College's Institute for Military Operations, where his research interests include Arctic politics, European security, Danish foreign and defense policy, and civil–military relations. His Arctic-related publications include *Greenland and the International Politics of a Changing Arctic* (Routledge, 2017), which he edited with Kristian S. Kristensen. He holds a PhD in International Relations from LSE and has previously been affiliated with several research institutions including Columbia University and CSIS.

Dele Raheem received his doctoral degree in Food Sciences from the University of Helsinki. He also obtained the Post Graduate Certificate in Education from the University of Greenwich, London, UK and a certificate on Vocational Teachers Pedagogy from Haaga-Helia University of Applied Science, Helsinki. His research interest is in food bioprocessing, preservation, and crosscutting issues related to food security and safety. He has gained extensive research and industrial experience in the last three decades. Currently, he is affiliated to the Northern Institute for Environmental and Minority Law, Arctic Centre, at the University of Lapland, as a Senior Researcher.

Svein Vigeland Rottem is a Senior Research Fellow at the Fridtjof Nansen Institute, Norway. Rottem's research interests are within the fields of Arctic security, Arctic governance, and the Arctic Council. His PhD. (Political Science) was on the Norwegian defence establishment's encounter with new post-cold-war realities, emphasizing, among other things, security in the Arctic. In recent years, his research focus has been on Arctic governance, maritime safety issues in the Arctic, science-policy influence, and the Arctic Council. Rottem has published a number of books, articles in academic journals, and reports on these issues.

Horatio Sam-Aggrey has been conducting research on various northern and Indigenous issues for over six years, most recently interning at the Centre for Peace Studies and the Centre for Sámi Studies at UiT The Arctic University of Norway. He has worked on Aboriginal engagement to facilitate the deployment of various power facilities in Canada's north, and an assessment of the governance triangle in Norway involving the Sámi of Norway, the Norwegian government, and the mining industry. His educational background is in Indigenous and northern studies and sociology. Sam-Aggrey has additionally been a consultant on Arctic issues at the University of Saskatchewan, Saskatoon, Canada.

Leah Sarson is Assistant Professor of International Relations in the Department of Political Science at Dalhousie University in Halifax, Canada. Her work explores Indigenous global politics in the extractive resource sector, while her broader research interests focus on Canadian foreign policy, international relations, gender, and the Arctic. Before joining Dalhousie, she was a Fulbright researcher and SSHRC postdoctoral fellow at Dartmouth College in

Hanover, New Hampshire where she remains a fellow at the Dickey Centre for International Understanding and a visiting Arctic fellow at the Institute of Arctic Studies.

Benjamin Schaller is a PhD. candidate and Research Fellow at the Centre for Peace Studies at UiT – The Arctic University of Norway. His research focuses on NATO–Russia relations in Europe and the Arctic region as well as on the roles of trust and distrust in the defence and security relations between Norway, Sweden, Canada, and Russia. From 2015–17, he was a desk officer at the German Federal Foreign Office, responsible for policies in the area of arms control and military security, in connection with the German chairmanship of the OSCE in 2016.

Alexander Sergunin is Professor of International Relations, Moscow State Institute of International Relations and St. Petersburg State University, Russia. He holds a PhD. (History) from the Moscow State University (1985) and Habilitation (Political Science) from the St. Petersburg State University (1994). His research interests include Arctic politics and Russian foreign-policy thinking and making. His most recent book-length publications include: *Russia in the Arctic. Hard or Soft Power?* (Stuttgart, 2016) (with Valery Konyshev), *Explaining Russian Foreign Policy Behaviour: Theory and Practice* (Stuttgart, 2016), and *Russian Strategies in the Arctic: Avoiding a New Cold War* (Moscow, 2014) (with Lassi Heininen and Gleb Yarovoy).

Florian Stammler is a Research Professor of Social Anthropology at the University of Lapland. He specializes in Arctic anthropology, particularly the Russian Far North, and his research interests lie in the human role in reindeer-herding systems, Arctic economics, nomadism, Indigenous knowledge, resource extraction, native populations, industrial migration, and centre–periphery relations.

Hlynur Stefánsson is an Associate Professor at the School of Science and Engineering at Reykjavík University in Iceland, and co-director of Reykjavík University Sustainability Institute and Forum (SIF). Hlynur received his PhD. degree in engineering from Imperial College London and MSc degree from the Technical University of Denmark, and is an expert in analytics and data-driven decision-making. He has worked on research related to energy, sustainability and climate change, and published research articles in academic high-impact journals such as *Journal of Energy, Energy Policy, Journal of Renewable Energy, Journal of Natural Resource Modeling, Transport Reviews, Technological Forecasting and Social Change*, and *Journal of Cleaner Production*. Hlynur has also worked on various applied research projects in collaboration with industry and has served as a consultant.

Victoria Sweet JD, MA, serves as a program officer for Indigenous Communities at the NoVo Foundation. She is White Earth Ojibwe. Victoria graduated from Michigan State University Law with a certificate in Indigenous Law and Policy. She has researched and published about violence against Indigenous women, human trafficking, and the links between climate change, extractive industries, and human security. She has been traveling to Alaska since 2013, visiting Alaska Native villages and learning about regional security issues. She serves on several advisory boards for organizations working to improve the lives of Indigenous peoples and survivors of violence and exploitation.

Ágúst Valfells is a Professor in the Department of Engineering at Reykjavík University. He received his PhD. in nuclear engineering from the University of Michigan, and a C.S. in mechanical engineering from the University of Iceland. His main areas of research are in physical electronics and energy systems. Before joining Reykjavík University, he worked at the National Energy Authority of Iceland/Orkustofnun on alternative energy carriers, and at the University of Maryland on electron beam devices.

Fern Wickson currently works as Scientific Secretary for the North Atlantic Marine Mammal Commission (NAMMCO), based in Tromsø, Norway. She holds an interdisciplinary PhD. in biology and political science and her work is focused on environmental conflicts, ecological management,and good governance. Working across the science/policy interface, she is particularly committed to experimenting with how to effectively integrate environmental science, values, indigenous knowledge, and stakeholder views in environmental decision-making. She has previously worked as a Senior Scientist and Research Professor of environmental governance at the GenØk Centre for Biosafety, and has served as an expert delegate to the Intergovernmental Panel on Biodiversity and Ecosystem Services (IPBES) working group on the diverse conceptualization of values in nature. She has also been a member of the Norwegian Biotechnology Advisory Board and is a former President of the International Society for the Study of New and Emerging Technologies (S.Net).

Page Wilson is an Associate Professor at the University of Iceland. She was admitted as a solicitor and barrister of the Supreme Court of Victoria, Australia, in 2002, and received her PhD. in International Relations from the London School of Economics in 2007. Her research interests include questions of international security, (particularly Arctic security and governance), and the politics of international law. Her first book, *Aggression, Crime and International Security* was published by Routledge in 2009, and subsequent works have appeared in journals such as *International Affairs, Cooperation and Conflict, Global Society* and *Polar Record*.

Wrenn Yennie-Lindgren is a Research Fellow at the Norwegian Institute of International Affairs (NUPI) and an Associate Fellow at the Swedish Institute of International Affairs. She was also a 2018 Japan Foundation fellow at Meiji University and visiting researcher at Waseda University in Tokyo. Yennie-Lindgren's research focuses on the politics and foreign policy of Japan, international relations in East Asia, East Asian states' interests in the Arctic, and traditional and non-traditional security issues in the Asia-Pacific region. Her work has been published in *Polar Geography, The Hague Journal of Diplomacy* and the *Japanese Journal of Political Science*. She also co-edited the volume *China and Nordic Diplomacy* (Routledge, 2018).

Kristian Åtland is a Senior Research Fellow at the Norwegian Defence Research Establishment (FFI). He holds a PhD. in Political Science from UiT – The Arctic University of Norway and an MA degree in Russian studies from the University of Oslo. He is a former diplomat and has worked as a defence researcher since 2002, specializing on Russia and security issues in the High North. During the 2019–20 academic year he was a Visiting Scholar at the Institute of Slavic, East European, and Eurasian Studies (ISEEES), University of California, Berkeley.

Andreas Østhagen is a Senior Fellow at the Fridtjof Nansen Institute in Oslo; a world leading research institute concerned with international relations, Arctic affairs, and resource management. His research looks at Arctic geopolitics and ocean governance, hereunder maritime disputes and resource management. He is also a Senior Fellow at The Arctic Institute and an Advisor at the High North Centre for Business and Governance at Nord University. He has previously worked for the Norwegian Institute for Defence Studies and the North Norway EU Office in Brussels. Østhagen holds a PhD from the University of British Columbia, and an MSc from the London School of Economics.

ACKNOWLEDGMENTS

Security studies is truly a multidisciplinary field. This *Handbook* was the result of extensive research by the contributors within the numerous areas of security studies, Arctic regional anthropology, comparative politics, economics, history, international relations and diplomacy, political science, sociology, and strategic studies as well as fieldwork and data-gathering from all parts of the Arctic and beyond. The editors would like to warmly thank all of the chapter contributors for their hard work and diligence in making this book; the first of its kind to address the complex issue of modern Arctic security from a myriad of angles and approaches.

Great thanks, as well, to Andrew Humphrys at Routledge for his invaluable assistance in the shepherding of this project from its tentative beginnings; to Tom Mowle at Rampart Solutions for providing excellent independent reviews and editing assistance; and also to the Centre for Peace Studies (CPS) at UiT – The Arctic University of Norway for providing a central hub for the gathering and organising of the materials which would eventually form this volume.

Funding for the research and logistics of the *Handbook* was provided by and through a number of important research projects and their funding institutions. They are:

The Research Council of Norway (NRC), "Challenges in Arctic Governance: Indigenous Territorial Rights in the Russian Federation." (2015–19).

Norwegian Agency for International Cooperation and Quality Enhancement in Higher Education (DIKU), "Security, Geopolitical, and Governance Challenges in relation to Arctic Extractive Industries" (2013–18).

NordForsk Nordic Centre of Excellence project (award 76654) Arctic Climate Predictions: Pathways to Resilient, Sustainable Societies (ARCPATH).

Finally, we would like to dedicate this book to the late Professor Michael T. Corgan, who wrote the chapter in this volume on American security policy in the Arctic and who passed away in November 2018. He was a leading light in studies of the Arctic, including security studies, and his work was essential to improving our understanding of this extraordinary part of the world.

Gunhild Hoogensen Gjørv
Marc Lanteigne
Horatio Sam-Aggrey

Map 0.1 Arctic administrative areas

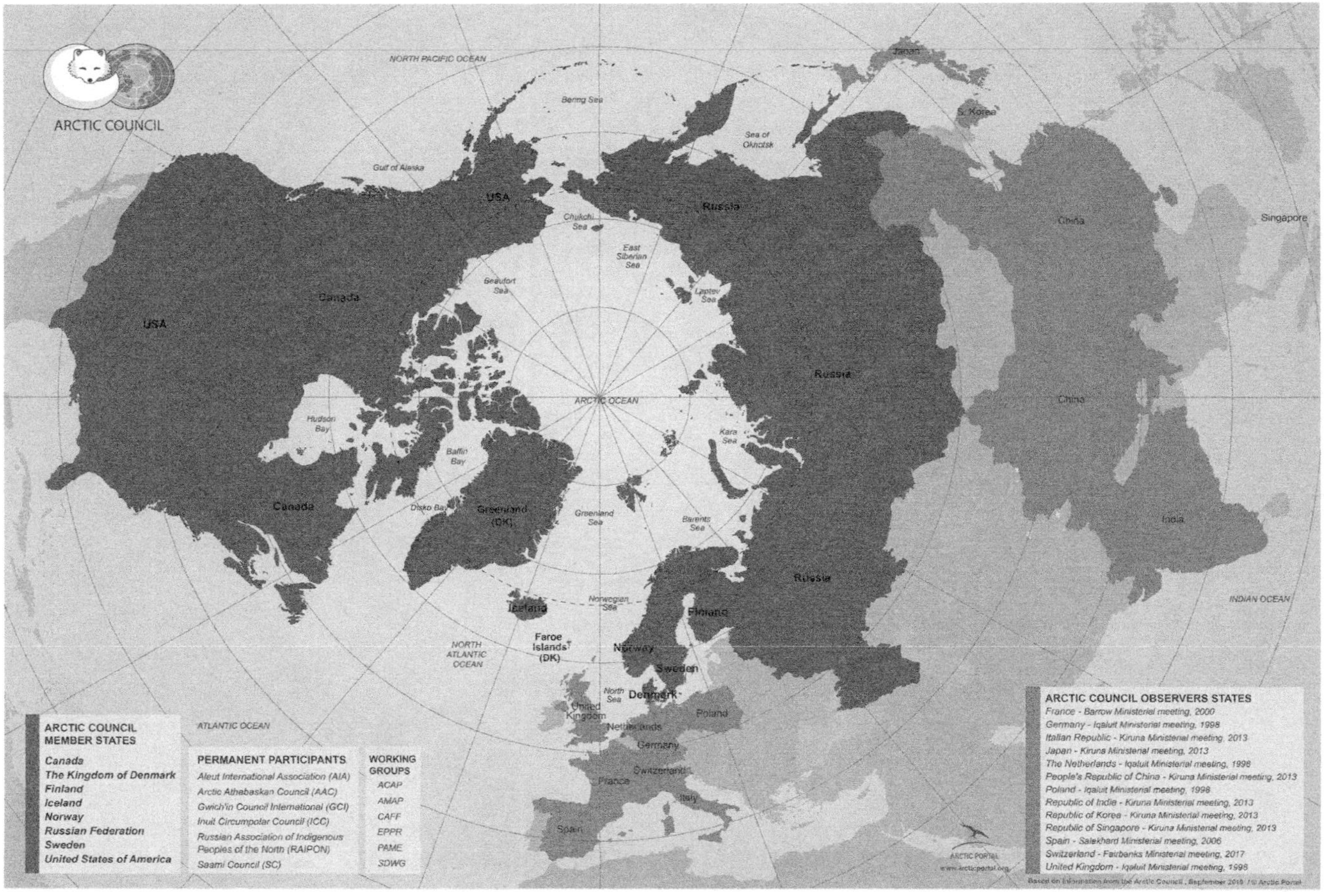

Map 0.2 Arctic Council members

1

UNDERSTANDING ARCTIC SECURITY

What has changed? What hasn't?

Gunhild Hoogensen Gjørv, Marc Lanteigne, and Horatio Sam-Aggrey

Introduction

> Security is a concept about power, as well as a powerful concept. Invoking the concept is a political act. It makes a claim to power. The debate around what the concept means is itself a practice in power. It is a concept that has been, and continues to be, invoked to draw attention to "something" that is or should be valued above all other things.
>
> *(Hoogensen Gjørv et al. 2014, 1)*

This handbook is the result of research in a wide array of disciplines relating to politics and international relations. It presents diverse perceptions of Arctic security, with various scholars coming from different vantage points and traditions to understand the idea of security in the northernmost regions of the world. As a handbook, the volume does two things. First, based on a range of empirical data and case material, it provides a snapshot of various security perceptions about the Arctic in the second decade of the twenty first century. These snapshots allow scholars to reflect upon the degree to which security perceptions have changed or remained the same over time, as well as get a better understanding of which issues dominate the high-politics arena, which is often equated with security matters, and why. Cases and empirical data are always a moving target, however, so what appear to be the most important security considerations today may not have the same priority tomorrow. Therefore, the handbook also provides insights into different security analysis tools and practices, which can help scholars reflect upon how our understanding of security – what we do to protect that which we value most, and who decides – changes over time. The Arctic is a vast, dynamic, and diverse region that has come under increasing attention as it becomes ever more important to the rest of the world. This handbook provides many insights into why that is.

Although the Arctic occupies about one-sixth of the globe and is home to approximately four million people, depending where one chooses to draw the region's borders (Wheeler 2010, 4–11), the Arctic Ocean and the lands encircling it have only very recently been subject to a serious, comprehensive debate about security, either in policy or in research circles. Strategic matters, including military issues, have never been wholly absent from the Arctic, given that the region was a buffer zone between the United States and the Soviet

Union during the Cold War. For many reasons, however, there has been a widely held perception that many of the security concerns that occupy most of the world are not widely found in the Far North.

First, the climate and geography of the Arctic have been seen as too hostile for large-scale state-centric security activity, except in rare cases, and as not suitable as a milieu for military conflict (although exceptions can be noted, including the Aleutian campaign during the Pacific Theater of World War II and the 1939 Winter War between Finland and the Soviet Union) (Garfield 1995; Naske and Slotnick 2014; Trotter 1991). The advent of longer-range missiles during the Cold War raised the profile of the Arctic as an arena for superpower rivalry, but it was seen primarily as a space where missiles could traverse a shorter distance between the United States and the Soviet Union. The widely held perception of the Arctic as a land of few (accessible) resources and impassable corridors added to a widely held view that the region was largely excluded from mundane state-based security interests.

Second, since the end of the Cold War there has been a concerted effort among the eight states that have Arctic borders, namely Canada, Denmark, (via the Faroe Islands and Greenland), Finland, Iceland, Norway, Russia, Sweden, and the United States, to create a space often described as "high north, low tension" (Stavridis 2013), a region where security concerns have been set aside in favor of issues related to building mutual cooperation, human development, addressing environmental change, and scientific diplomacy. Indeed, the most prominent regional organization in the circumpolar north, the Arctic Council, with the eight Arctic states listed above as members, specifically decided to eschew debates on military security matters in the regime's founding document, the 1996 Ottawa Declaration (Arctic Council 2019). It has been widely assumed that the specific physical conditions of the Arctic make zero-sum thinking within the region unviable, and thus the Arctic should be considered an area of exceptionalism in international security studies because of the strong regional preference for cooperation over competition. Should the Arctic be viewed as a region of *asecurity* (Wæver 1998), where security is simply not present in studies of it?

It is argued in this book that the concept of the Arctic as separate from the world's security discourses was never matched by reality, and the idea of Arctic exceptionalism itself has also begun to be challenged on many fronts and for a variety of reasons, many of which can be traced back to the single most prominent change in the region: the effects of global climate change. The melting of the polar ice cap and the Greenland ice sheet, as well as glaciers and sea ice in the region, are all having profound effects on not only the region's environment but also its economy, development, and politics (Jouzel et al. 2008). The traditional customs, histories, and vocations of the citizens of the Far North, especially Indigenous peoples, have already started to be greatly affected by the changed climate conditions all over the Arctic. In many cases governments, businesses, and the Arctic populations themselves are still struggling to understand and adjust to these new circumstances.

It has been a long-standing tradition in Arctic discourse, including within the Arctic Council, to check one's politics at the door, so to speak. This concept implies that non-Arctic disputes, including those in the security realm, should not spill over into the Arctic. That practice was rarely challenged during much of the early post-Cold War period, not least due to the atmosphere of cooperation and collaboration that followed the fall of the Berlin Wall (Græger 1996). However, worsening relations between Russia and the West have placed strains on Arctic states' abilities to compartmentalize their northern and southern policies, especially after the 2014 Crimea/Donbas crises in Ukraine drove a deeper wedge between Moscow and many other Arctic governments. Much current discourse about Arctic security focuses on Russian interest in rearming its Arctic lands in anticipation of increased sea traffic through the Northern Sea Route (NSR) and its engaging in renewed air and sea incursions into the Nordic Arctic region (Astrasheuskaya and Foy 2019). In response, US President Donald Trump, after spending much of the beginning of his tenure ignoring the Arctic, has now begun to weigh the possibility of a greater American military presence in the Far North (Kesling 2019; Lemothe 2019). In the meantime, the Arctic and Russian military actions in that region have started playing a greater role in NATO planning. This is illustrated by the organization's *Trident Juncture* military exercises, involving more than 50,000 personnel, which took place in Norway and the Atlantic-Arctic region in October–November 2018 (Norwegian Armed Forces 2018). Thus, it seems that hard security is making a comeback to levels not seen since the Cold War.

With the melting of Arctic ice, resources that were once unreachable and shipping lanes considered impractical are now being eyed not only by the Arctic Eight but also many international actors. The Arctic Council includes observer states, such as France, Germany, Great Britain, Italy, Japan, Netherlands, South Korea, and Switzerland, which have developed Arctic policies based on histories of regional interest in the region and current economic priorities that include engagement in the Arctic. Even states not normally associated with the Arctic, like India and Singapore, have joined the Arctic Council's observer cohort and are carving out their own policies in the region. The largest of the non-Arctic observer states, China, has taken the lead in proposing new forms of scientific and economic cooperation, calling for an Ice Silk Road and a greater role for non-Arctic states in regional affairs (Hongjian 2018; Lanteigne 2019a; PRC State Council Information Office 2018). This development has caused some consternation among some Arctic actors, especially the United States, which has begun to look at a possibly closer Sino–Russian partnership in the Arctic as a direct challenge to its own status in the region.

As both Arctic and non-Arctic states look at the developing economic opportunities in the region, ranging from oil and gas development in Siberia, to potential mines in Greenland, to new shipping lanes drastically cutting transit times between Asia and Europe, debate about a resource scramble or a de facto Arctic gold rush, appeared in earnest a decade ago, along with the possibility of disagreements or even conflicts over the emerging riches of the Far North (Emmerson 2010; Kuersten 2015). This despite the fact that many of these so-called new resources rest well within the land and sea boundaries of Arctic states. This has led to further questions about the rights and responsibilities of Arctic and non-Arctic states in the region and about who is an Arctic stakeholder, given that many southern countries are not only developing interests in Arctic resources but also facing climate change challenges that in some cases can be traced directly back to the Arctic itself.

It is tempting, when looking at the dominant debates surrounding the current rethinking of Arctic security, to simply restrict ourselves to the classic geopolitical/hard security questions and issues raised above. To do that, however, would be falling into the black box or billiard ball traps that international relations specialists warn about when describing the limitations of only looking at security from the state or governmental levels (Bull 1977; Singer 1961). This in turn reifies the idea of "trickle down" security whereby the security of the state and its borders automatically translates into security for those living within those states (Hoogensen and Rottem 2004). Despite classic characterizations of the Arctic as remote and desolate with "little international relevance" (Young 1989), the region is a compilation of diverse states which are home to even more diverse peoples. It is thus crucial to look at security challenges on the individual level, known as "human security" to better understand the ways in which different peoples experience insecurities and/or provide for their own security. Some human insecurities have always been present in the region, while others have appeared as a result of the dramatic change in the Arctic's geographies. These have included security challenges related to economic development, gender, health, mobility, non-state organizations, social norms, and various forms of cooperation beyond the state (Hoogensen Gjørv et al. 2014). What is the interplay between these areas of security and between various levels ranging from individuals and communities to governments, sub-regions, and the Arctic as a whole?

As part of the blank-space/desolatation rhetoric about the Arctic, there has also been the impression that the legal regimes that are plentiful throughout the rest of the world are either missing or irrelevant in the Far North. The truth is quite the opposite, given that many aspects of international law, including the UN Convention on the Law of the Sea (UNCLOS) and other forms of international maritime law are hardly absent from the region: the Arctic Ocean is, after all, an ocean. Moreover, new forms of governance have begun to appear as a result of changes in the region. A Polar Code came into operation in 2017 to better regulate civilian maritime traffic in the Arctic, and a fishing ban in the Central Arctic Ocean (CAO) was approved in October 2018 to ensure that as the waters surrounding the North Pole become ice-free in the coming decades, a race for the region's seafood resources does not cause further damage to the center of the Arctic (IMO 2019; Independent Barents Observer/Radio Canada 2018). There has also been a growth in Track II (sub-governmental) organizations that discuss numerous scientific, economic, political, and strategic subjects related to the Far North. These include the Arctic Circle, founded in 2013, which meets every year in Reykjavík and has since produced spin-off forums in places ranging from Québec City to Shanghai, as well as the Arctic Frontiers meeting in Tromsø and the US-based Arctic Encounter Symposium. While there is certainly more talk in and about the Arctic over the past decade, how much of it is actually contributing to the region's overall security?

Then, of course, there are the security challenges that are directly tied to Arctic climate change itself. Although environmental security is still a relatively new discipline compared to traditional materialist schools (i.e., those that look almost exclusively at weapons and wealth), it is becoming further understood that the warming conditions and changed weather patterns in the region are creating threats to security from many directions. Will traditional ways of life have to be abandoned? Will new resource extraction projects further harm the environment and displace local communities? Will environmental threats bring Arctic states together or divide them? Attendees at the May 2019 Arctic Council Ministerial in Rovaniemi, Finland, received an unwelcome wake-up call to the possibility of inaction on Arctic climate change: the US delegation, deferring to Trump's obstructionist climate change denial, refused to sign any policy document that included the term "climate change" (Lanteigne 2019b). Instead, the United States sought to focus on the growing challenges posed by Russia and China to Arctic security and rule of law, moves that may further divide the region politically.

Given all of these significant changes in the realm of Arctic security, this book unpacks and deconstructs the various concepts of security that have appeared in the Arctic in recent decades. It argues that the concept has become more complex not only because of the vagaries associated with climate change but also because of the human responses to it.

Chapter summaries

This handbook opens with an overall view of the Arctic from a historical perspective, written by historian and law professor emeritus Alan Henrikson, in Chapter 2. This overview sets the stage for subsequent sections of the book, which cover different themes relevant to Arctic security.

Theoretical perspectives

Part I describes theoretical perspectives that are relevant to our understanding of Arctic security. It is clear from this section that there is not just one way to understand security in the Arctic. This section commences with an examination by Padrtova of typical approaches to Arctic security – that is, military and state security approaches. This third chapter complements the first two chapters in the handbook – the introduction and historical perspective – as it offers a platform for thinking beyond state-based perceptions of security in the Arctic and also expands the discussion to understanding Arctic security as a regional security complex. Padrtova distinguishes the traditional approach of security, based on realism, from the nontraditional approach, based on liberalism. The author discusses the factors that led to the extension of the concept of security from being solely based on military and state security to incorporating other areas, such as environmental, economic, food, health, and societal security. This shift in the perception of danger also marked the beginning of a fundamentally different political environment, both in a real and a theoretical sense.

In the book's fourth chapter, Chater, Greaves, and Sarson examine how security issues in the Arctic are managed through a multilayered regional governance system. The complex web of governance institutions that provide fora for problem-solving and cooperation includes the Arctic Council, the Barents Euro-Arctic Council, and the Northern Forum. The authors also examine alternative or unconventional security institutions related to the emergence of nonmilitary security challenges and non-state forms of regional governance, focusing on the role of Indigenous autonomous governance arrangements. The authors conclude that strong state and sub-state governments exist alongside long-standing international regimes and organizations, creating a region where the rule of domestic and international law is strong and respected.

Continuing with the theme of Arctic security, Bertelsen explores the impact of international security events and factors on Arctic security. Employing a historical perspective, the author outlines how regional and international conflicts such as the Napoleonic Wars, Crimean War, the two World Wars, and the Cold War had geostrategic implications for security in the Arctic. The author concludes that, similarly, contemporary international security events and factors impact Arctic security.

In Chapter 6, Hoogensen Gjørv widens the scope of theorizing about security, arguing for a comprehensive approach to understanding security in the Arctic. She sets the stage by examining how the concept of security has developed historically, and how the concept was narrowed or reduced to state security concerns, rather than being a concept that included people. She discusses the advent of the human security concept and the relevance it has for the Arctic. She concludes that the complexity of the Arctic demands a complex understanding of security – comprehensive security – which integrates multiple security perspectives that operate simultaneously in the Arctic.

The following chapter, by Kuokkanen and Sweet, "Indigenous security theory: intersectional analysis from the bottom up," argues for a more comprehensive conception of Indigenous security in the Arctic. The authors note that the core elements of Arctic Indigenous security – food, shelter, and personal/community safety – are intertwined and informed by complex environmental, political, social, and cultural concerns. They contend that future Indigenous security research should involve an intersectional analysis that simultaneously accounts for indigeneity and gender. Kuokkanen and Sweet also maintain that it is not possible to consider security in Indigenous communities without addressing interpersonal physical and sexual violence, both of which are fundamentally gendered.

In Chapter 8 by De Witt, the importance of a reliable and uninterrupted electricity supply in the rural Arctic to energy security in the region is highlighted. The author notes that electricity is used for a wide variety of applications: not only productivity and personal entertainment, but also ones that have health and safety implications. Therefore, a reliable electricity supply is critical to the security of people living in cold and harsh conditions in remote Arctic communities.

Lanteigne and Sam-Aggrey opine that although environmental security has begun to mature as an important branch of strategic studies, its application in the Arctic region is very new. This is especially the case with attempts to link climate change and ice erosion to evolving Arctic politics. The authors highlight close links between environmental issues and human security that can be observed in many parts of the Arctic. Areas discussed include environmental security, Indigenous livelihoods, and the role of climate change in Arctic governance. With a particular focus on the role of China in Arctic issues, the authors also discuss the non-Arctic states that are seeking a greater diplomatic role in the Far North.

Cooke and Petersen then note in the next chapter that economic security is a necessary component of positive security and that the most basic building block of economic security is access to paid local work. This chapter is based on primary research conducted with respondents from northern Norway, the Faroe Islands, Newfoundland, and Labrador (2011–18). The authors distinguished among approaches to labor markets and the provision of social services by liberal market economies and coordinated market economies in the Arctic and North Atlantic. They argue that these differences in approaches have implications for labor market outcomes in the respective countries. Cooke, Hoogensen Gjørv, and Petersen point out that if opportunities for paid work are insufficient, then the resulting economic hardships could lead to short-sighted decision-making and the pursuit of projects that jeopardize the social and environmental security of remote communities. In order to strengthen economic security, the authors advocate strong government intervention in the labor market, substantial investments in human capital and infrastructure, and the sustenance of local businesses.

Perspectives of Arctic countries

Part II, which focuses on formal security perspectives from Arctic countries, starts with a chapter by Sergunin on Russian Arctic perceptions. The author argues that in contrast to the Cold War era, when the Arctic was a zone of global confrontation between the Soviet Union and the US/NATO, there has been a significant shift in Russia's threat perceptions and security policies in the High North. Moscow now envisions this region as a platform for international cooperation. According to the author, Russia now believes that no serious hard security threats emanate from the region; rather, Moscow is convinced that soft security agenda issues such as climate change mitigation, environmental protection, maritime safety, Arctic research, Indigenous peoples, cross- and trans-border cooperative projects, and culture could form the basis of regional cooperation. In light of this shift in threat perceptions, Sergunin argues that Russia's military power in the region is now focused on protecting the country's sovereignty over its exclusive economic zone and continental shelf, protecting Moscow's economic interests, and performing other symbolic functions.

In Chapter 12, on Canadian Arctic views, two regional specialists, Exner-Pirot and Huebert, provide a comprehensive review of the issues and events that have shaped Canadian perspectives on Arctic security. The authors highlight the unique nature of Canada's Arctic security perspective, which is fueled by a long-standing preoccupation with sovereignty; the rise of a Russian threat, real and imagined; and a growing emphasis on human security, while still building on traditional security.

Continuing on the theme of Arctic security in North America, Corgan's chapter on American Arctic security policies notes that historically the American Arctic region has not been a focus of the country's security policymaking – even when nearby Aleutian Islands were captured during the Second World War. US national security policies did not even mention the Arctic until President Bush, and then President Obama, included the region in their National Security Strategies in the post-9/11 flurry of homeland security activity. Corgan argues that despite the inclusion of the Arctic in official national security policy, there is little specific guidance from above, only a token commitment of resources and no provision for coherent direction. Corgan believes that this situation is unlikely to change under the Trump administration.

Åtland then discusses the impact of the European Arctic on Norwegian security policy in Chapter 14. The author highlights changes in the security situation in the Barents Sea region that have been precipitated by climate change and growing human activity, Russia's military modernization, and the post-2014 deterioration of Russia's relationship with the West. Åtland emphasizes the important geostrategic position of Norway vis-à-vis Russia and notes that despite a freeze in military-to-military cooperation and the continued presence of mutually restrictive measures in the economic sphere due to Russia's 2014 intervention in Ukraine, Norway and Russia have been able to preserve much of their stability-enhancing cooperation in the High North in the new geopolitical environment. Nevertheless, the author emphasizes the need for increased attention to confidence-building measures and enhanced soft security cooperation.

Next, continuing the theme of formal Arctic security perspectives, Rahbek-Clemmensen comments on the evolving relationship between Denmark and Greenland in the Arctic, arguing that regional (subnational) security dynamics are not felt uniformly throughout the Arctic. The author illustrates how local political forces and authority structures in Greenland – a regional entity within the Kingdom of Denmark that has extensive autonomy – affect security dynamics. Rahbek-Clemmensen notes that whereas Cold War civilian security challenges were primarily consequences of the American military presence on the island and the Danish modernization project, current civilian security challenges in Greenland are fueled by increased industrial and commercial activity, encouraged primarily by the local government in Nuuk.

Turning to Iceland, Wilson and Ingólfsdóttir argue that the country's security perspective can be understood through the lens of two competing security identities. The first identity emphasizes Iceland's position as a small state with limited resources and clout, while the second identity focuses on Iceland's big impact capability, noting its disproportionate influence and strategic significance at key moments in international affairs. The author believes that while Iceland's first national security policy (NSP), released in 2016, can be explained by reference to changes in both the domestic and international security landscapes, an analysis of the NSP reveals that the tensions between these two security identities remain preserved in its text. Then to Finland, as Heininen notes that, given the country's geographical and geopolitical situation, Finnish Arctic and security policies focus on promoting geopolitical stability, security cooperation in the Arctic region, and playing a leadership role in solving the grand, mostly environmental challenges of the Arctic.

In Chapter 17 Heininen offers insights into the Finnish Arctic security perspective by emphasizing the importance of so-called nontraditional approaches to security, in particular environmental security. Heininen demonstrates the ways in which cooperation, confidence-building, and stability measures have all played significant roles in creating a security environment that is not overly dominated by classic geopolitical considerations. Indeed, he argues that the core, if not "grand," security concern is deeply embedded within ongoing and future environmental challenges.

Eklund's analysis of Sweden's security policy in the Arctic in Chapter 18 concludes the second section. The author discusses some of the core ideas underpinning Swedish security policy in an effort to tease out whether or not these ideas also have an Arctic dimension. Eklund argues that Sweden's chairing of the Arctic Council between 2011 and 2013 was a unique opportunity to shift security perceptions towards the Arctic, but this did not happen: Swedish security perceptions remained firmly rooted in the Baltic Sea region. The author concludes that, short of a military conflict, Swedish membership in NATO could be a game-changer in facilitating a shift in Swedish security perceptions toward the Arctic.

Security through Arctic governance

In the first chapter in Part III, Gracyzk and Rottem explore the role of the Arctic Council (AC) in security governance in the region. The authors note that the AC is the Arctic's central intergovernmental forum, handling a wide range of issues revolving around the environment and sustainable development, with special focus on the effects of climate change and globalization. The two authors argue that although military security is explicitly excluded from its mandate, through its work on environmental and other issues, the Council plays an important role in indirectly strengthening security and stability in the Arctic.

Bertelsen continues with Chapter 20, discussing the importance of Arctic science diplomacy in maintaining Track II dialogue during the diplomatic crisis over Ukraine and facilitating regional governance in light of global change caused by China's economic rise. Bertelsen argues that the Arctic region is characterized by relatively high levels of scientific activity, which can be expensive; this warrants strong international cooperation. According to the author, Arctic international politics and security reflect the international system both historically and in the contemporary period.

In the following chapter, Magnússon and Norchi explore the role of international law in the geopolitics of the Arctic. The authors argue that the public order of the Arctic – a function of geopolitics and international law – is currently optimal and that stakeholder interactions are stable. Participants pursue common interests utilizing codified and customary law within dedicated mechanisms and institutions. The interplay of interests, power, and law ensures that any "Scramble for the Arctic" is controlled and managed, in contrast to the unfettered nineteenth-century "Scramble for Africa."

In Chapter 22, Dodds explores the intersection between regional geopolitics, security, and governance. The author notes that the content and scope of all three terms are contested, imagined, and operationalized in varied Arctic contexts. The Arctic is dominated by the eight Arctic states; their own particular security agendas shape governance at a variety of spatial and social scales. However, Dodds notes that Arctic governance is not the exclusive preserve of Arctic states, as an array of actors, practices, and interests (ranging from Indigenous peoples' organizations and extraterritorial players to material practices such as science and resource mapping) make their presence felt in the Arctic governance landscape.

In the next chapter, Pedersen argues that security challenges in the Svalbard area relate to both traditional geopolitics and the exploitation of natural resources in and around the archipelago. Svalbard presents a strategic challenge to Russia, due to its proximity to the

Northern Fleet's bases on the Kola Peninsula and vital sea-lanes of communication. In the maritime areas surrounding Svalbard, security challenges also relate to the exploitation of natural resources, especially the islands' fisheries. The author argues that the United States and other NATO allies must delicately balance potential economic interests and security concerns, since any actions that undermine Norway's legal position in Svalbard vis-à-vis Russia may affect stability in the region, and ultimately have wider security implications.

In a bid to better understand why the role of coast guards is on the rise in northern waters, Østhagen's Chapter 24 explores whether pan-Arctic coast guard cooperation is a result of states' desire to cooperate to solve a number of pressing concerns in the Arctic or whether cooperation is an independent variable that affects the states and shapes outcomes between them. Østhagen concludes that multilateral pan-Arctic coast guard cooperation was not developed to serve an immediate demand that states could not deal with on their own or through bilateral modes of cooperation. Instead, the coast guards and their respective states seem to have realized the benefits of cooperation for its own sake and avoid focusing on contentious issues.

Chapter 25 by Ivanova and Fondahl, is the last in Part III and looks at the complex subject of international law in the Arctic. In exploring the relationship between political change and legislative change, the authors discuss how different post-Soviet legislative reforms impact the trajectory of hard and soft security for the Russian Federation as a whole and for its Arctic inhabitants. After analyzing different legal initiatives, the authors identify a period of increased concern for environmental and human security in the 1990s and early 2000s, while more recent legislative changes mirror the increased political tensions between the Russian Federation and other Arctic and non-Arctic countries. Ivanova and Fondahl note that the trajectory of this legal change is manifested in legislation concerning Russia's northern Indigenous minorities and the extraction of subsurface resources. The authors also highlight the importance of regional governance in filling the gaps left by federal law in strengthening the human security of local populations. However, the authors also note that the more the federal state tightens the screws in governing its regions, the less leverage regional governance actors have for adopting legislation that suits the needs of local people.

Interactions between local and international actors in the Arctic

In the first chapter of Part IV, Lanteigne discusses the rising level of Chinese involvement in environmental, economic, and political issues in the region, including the role of Russia in these issues. The author argues that China is trying to become an Arctic insider through a multilayered policy approach aimed at creating an Arctic identity, regardless of geography. The author also discusses the impact of China–Russia cooperation on Arctic security, highlighting that it was confirmed in early 2018 that the Northern Sea Route would form part of China's expanding "Belt and Road" trade networks. Lanteigne argues that increasing cooperation between Russia and China is contributing to the debate about the securitization of the Arctic and asks whether it is proper to consider the Arctic to be a security region.

Yennie-Lindgren's chapter postulates that Japan's Arctic engagement has developed at a faster and more integrated pace than ever before, especially in the political arena. The author states that Japan's inaugural Arctic Policy came to fruition in 2015. A year later, the Arctic trilateral dialogue with China and South Korea was established, further indicating how Japan perceives that challenges and opportunities in the polar and East Asian regions will unfold. While Japan acknowledges its status as a non-Arctic state, it still manifests interest and involvement in the security and safety of the High North. Yennie-Lindgren unpacks how security, on traditional and nontraditional, and on national and international levels, factors in and demonstrates the synergy between Arctic security issues and broader foreign policy issues such as freedom of the seas, peaceful coexistence, and environmental sustainability.

In the following chapter, Airoldi pinpoints security issues originating from climate change, together with the enlargement of the European Union (EU) to northern European countries bordering Russia, as the main factors driving EU involvement in the Arctic region. However, she laments the slow elaboration of an EU Arctic Policy since 2008, and notes that the EU has refrained from taking a strong explicit position on security in the Arctic because the Arctic remains of peripheral interest to the EU. Thus, an EU role has yet to be fully and unconditionally accepted in the Arctic context. Despite this state of affairs, the organization has repeatedly expressed both support for and the will to contribute to the existing cooperative order in the Arctic. It has focused its involvement in the Arctic on research, climate issues, environment preservation, maritime safety, and cross-border cooperation.

In the last chapter of Part IV, Schaller and Sam-Aggrey argue that despite the increasing importance of the Arctic, and the region being a mirror of security dynamics across the globe, neither NATO nor the OSCE have a dedicated Arctic strategy or collective approach to addressing traditional or nontraditional security issues in the region. According to the authors, the main reasons for this are the general hesitancy of Arctic states to open up the region to third parties and a concern among some Arctic states that stronger involvement by either organization could strain the long-lasting history of regional cooperation. As other actors continue to push into the High North and regional developments have an increasing impact on the core mandates of NATO and the OSCE, it remains to be seen to what extent Arctic states will be able to continue keeping both organizations in the observer's seat.

People, states, and security

In the first chapter of Part V, Greaves discusses the relationship between Indigenous peoples and the fields of international relations and security studies. Greaves highlights the unequal relations of power and authority that exist between Indigenous peoples and the institutions of the states in which they reside, as well as the ontological relationship between Indigenous peoples and land. According to Greaves, these two factors – possession of a non-dominant identity within their respective political contexts and having their identities and well-being inherently tied to specific ecological systems – produce unique security issues for Indigenous peoples and particular challenges in adequately responding to issues that threaten their survival and well-being. The chapter also discusses security issues facing Indigenous peoples in diverse contexts across the circumpolar region.

In the following chapter, Stammler, Hodgson, and Ivanova explore the nexus between the human security of the people resident in the Russian North and the development of extractive industries in the region. The authors contend that the most significant threat to peoples' security lies in the cumulative effects of industrial developments, yet current efforts to mitigate the detrimental impacts of extractive industries on Indigenous groups are compartmentalized, focusing solely on quantifiable damage from specific projects and operators. Other threats to the human security of Indigenous people in the region include anxieties arising from an inner alienation of Indigenous peoples from their land and cultural roots and a systemic problem of decisions regarding Indigenous livelihoods being made by sedentary and urbanized people (some of them being Indigenous) who are out of touch with the realities of people at the grassroots.

With a focus on resource development and the sustainability of traditional livelihoods, the next chapter by Sam-Aggrey examines the role of Indigenous local knowledge (ILK) in the environmental governance of diamond mines by co-management boards in the Mackenzie Valley. The author discusses the importance of caribou to the security of the Dene people in the Mackenzie Valley and the potential role of ILK in enhancing Indigenous security. Sam-Aggrey concludes that while there is evidence of substantial incorporation of ILK about caribou in environmental governance, a careful analysis of the process suggests that the inclusion of ILK is restricted to aspects of ILK that are compatible with Western scientific knowledge and processes. This lends credence to the claims made by some researchers that ILK is often used to fill science gaps rather than used in its cultural or spiritual context as an alternative way of knowing.

In the following chapter, Hoogensen Gjørv, Oddsdóttir, and Wickson address some of the ways gender and identity security has been imagined and reimagined in the Arctic context and how the concept of human security potentially translates into an Arctic context. They discuss how human security has been and continues to be problematic as the human dimension enters into conflict with the concept of state security. However, feminist and gender security studies have been useful in informing human security debates. They have opened up the concept as a site of intersectional engagement for local, national, and international actors and practices. Human security in the Arctic necessitates an understanding of local practices, the role of institutions of patriarchy, and ways of resisting oppression and colonialism or violence in relation to local communities.

In Chapter 34, Hossain, Herrmann, and Raheem argue that climate and socioeconomic and environmental changes in the Arctic alter the diversity, abundance, and distribution of key traditional food sources. The authors contend that for Indigenous and local communities in the Arctic, food is not just a commodity for physical consumption: it also offers social, spiritual, and cultural sustenance. Hence, the scarcity of nutritious, healthy, and fulfilling dietary options results in numerous risks and security concerns. The chapter also discusses the right to food and food sovereignty and the broader context of governance in the Arctic. It suggests a better cooperation mechanism among local communities, government, business, and other relevant institutions that integrates food security and sovereignty in the region. The concluding chapter by Ketkina et al. looks at environmental security via the case study of the Komi Republic in Russia to see how issues such as pollution and climate change affect security thinking on the local level.

The final chapter in this section, and concluding the handbook, explores the senses of security people in two different communities in Komi Republic, Russia. The authors, Ketina, Loginova, Popov, Istomin, Mikkelsen, Hoogensen Gjørv, and Bojko, combine a wide range of disciplines from physiology to political science, to provide an analysis of comprehensive security based on initial empirical data gathered in the Izhma and Ezhva regions of Komi Republic. Surveys were conducted with people living in these two communities to ask about their perceptions of and relationships to the impacts of environmental pollution in their communities. The chapter shows how we can begin to understand comprehensive security perspectives through the intersections of economic security brought by industry, environmental insecurity brought by various sources of pollution, and which values people prioritize when thinking of their community and individual survival in the Arctic.

References

Arctic Council. 'Ottawa Declaration (1996),' 2019, http://hdl.handle.net/11374/85.

Astrasheuskaya, Nastassia and Henry Foy, 'Polar Powers: Russia's Bid for Supremacy in the Arctic Ocean,' *Financial Times*, 28 April 2019.

Bull, Hedley. *The Anarchical Society: A Study of Order in World Politics* (London: Macmillan, 1977).

Emmerson, Charles. *The Future History of the Arctic* (New York: PublicAffairs, 2010).

Garfield, Brian. *A Thousand Mile War: World War II in Alaska and the Aleutians* (Fairbanks, AK: University of Alaska Press, 1995).

Græger, Nina. (1996). 'Environmental Security?' *Journal of Peace Research* 33(1): 109–116.

Hongjian, Cui. 'Arctic Corridor Makes "Ice Silk Road" a Reality,' *China Institute of Strategic Studies*, 21 March 2018, www.ciis.org.cn/english/2018-03/21/content_40259486.htm.

Hoogensen, Gunhild and Svein Vigeland Rottem. (2004). 'Gender Identity and the Subject of Security,' *Security Dialogue* 35(2): 155–171.

Hoogensen Gjørv, Gunhild, Dawn R. Bazely, Marina Goloviznina and Andrew J. Tanentzap. eds. *Environmental and Human Security in the Arctic* (London and New York: Routledge, 2014).

Independent Barents Observer/Radio Canada International. 'Nine Countries and EU Set to Sign "Historic" Agreement to Protect Central Arctic Ocean,' 3 October 2018, https://thebarentsobserver.com/en/arctic/2018/10/nine-countries-and-eu-set-sign-historic-agreement-protect-central-arctic-ocean.

International Maritime Organisation. 'Shipping in Polar Waters: Adoption of an International Code of Safety for Ships Operating in Polar Waters (Polar Code),' 2019, www.imo.org/en/MediaCentre/HotTopics/polar/Pages/default.aspx.

Jouzel, Jean, Claude Lorius and Dominique Rynaud. *The White Planet: The Evolution and Future of Our Frozen World* (Princeton, NJ and Oxford: Princeton University Press, 2008).

Kesling, Ben. 'US Navy Plans to Extend Its Reach in the Arctic,' *Wall Street Journal*, 1 May 2019.

Kuersten, Andreas. 'The Arctic Race that Wasn't: Hyperbole, Imaginaries, and the North Pole,' *Foreign Affairs*, 20 August 2015, www.foreignaffairs.com/reviews/2015-08-20/arctic-race-wasnt.

Lanteigne, Marc. 'China's Emerging Strategies in the Arctic,' *High North News*, 24 April 2019a, www.highnorthnews.com/en/chinas-emerging-strategies-arctic.

Lanteigne, Marc. The US Throws Down the Gauntlet at the Arctic Council's Finland Meeting,' *Over the Circle*, 7 May 2019b, https://overthecircle.com/2019/05/07/the-us-throws-down-the-gauntlet-at-the-arctic-councils-finland-meeting/.

Lemothe, Dan. 'Trump Administration's New Arctic Defense Strategy Expected to Zero in on Concerns About China,' *Washington Post*, 15 March 2019.

Naske, Claus M. and Herman E. Slotnick. *Alaska: A History* (Norman, OK: University of Oklahoma Press, 2014).

Norwegian Armed Forces. 'Trident Juncture 18,' 27 October 2018, https://forsvaret.no/en/exercise-and-operations/exercises/nato-exercise-2018.

Singer, J. David. (October 1961). 'The Level-of-Analysis Problem in International Relations,' *World Politics* 14(1): 77–92.

The State Council Information Office of the People's Republic of China. 'China's Arctic Policy,' 28 January 2018, http://english.gov.cn/archive/white_paper/2018/01/26/content_281476026660336.htm.

Stavridis, James. 'High North or High Tension?' *Foreign Policy*, 21 October 2013, https://foreignpolicy.com/2013/10/21/high-north-or-high-tension/.

Trotter, William R. *A Frozen Hell: The Russo-Finnish Winter War of 1939–40* (Chapel Hill, NC and New York: Algonquin Books of Chapel Hill, 1991).

Wæver, Ole. 'Insecurity, Security and Asecurity in the Western European Non-War Community,' *Security Communities*, eds. Emanuel Adler and Michael Barnett (Cambridge and New York: Cambridge University Press, 1998), 69–118.

Wheeler, Sara. *The Magnetic North: Travels in the Arctic* (London: Vintage, 2010).

Young, Oran R. (1989). 'The Politics of Regime Formation', *International Organization* 34(3): 349–375.

2

THE ARCTIC PEACE PROJECTION

From Cold War fronts to cooperative fora[1]

Alan K. Henrikson

Introduction: a diplomatic-historical approach

The global Arctic region has long had a symbolic role, illustrated by its centrality in United Nations flag—a world map surrounded by conventionalized branches of the olive tree. The High North itself has been an inspirational region for an even longer period. For many, it represents the future—a *peaceful* future. The concept of the North Pole as the "pole of peace," as Mikhail Gorbachev called it in his speech at Murmansk on 1 October 1987, is a political projection of this idea (Gorbachev 1987a).

The policy content of the Arctic-as-peace concept is not easy to identify or understand. Regional stabilization in the Arctic is a complex multilayered process that involves many parties. Presenting some of the remarkable story of Arctic cooperation against occurrences of confrontation in the region demonstrates ways in which peace and security at the top of the world can be preserved and even strengthened.

Explanatory lenses: concept, power, organization, and their interplay

How might we better understand, and thus be able to safeguard, peace in the Arctic, in ways that may contribute to a wider sense of security? Three main approaches exist, all of which can be assessed from a historical perspective. The first approach, which might be classified as constructivist, emphasizes the determinative role of *concept*—the influence of a unifying idea, including the very goal of achieving *Arctic peace*, the theme of the 2017 Arctic Frontiers conference at The University of Tromsø. The suggestion of Gorbachev and others to declare the Arctic to be a "zone of peace"—more specifically, making it an Arctic Nuclear Weapons-Free Zone (ANWFZ)—is a prominent example of how that idea might be realized (Teeple 2017). *Sanctuary* is another concept that has been applied to the Arctic. It is offered from a naturalist and environmentalist perspective (Hamilton 2014). The broader, somewhat legalistic concept of the Arctic Ocean as a *global commons* also has been advanced, mainly from outside the region (Gautam 2011).

A second approach emphasizes the role of *power*. The reasoning here, put forward from a realist perspective, is that peace depends on stability. The surest way to establish stability is through an equilibrium of forces, a more or less equal power balance and distribution, in a region. In practical terms, this means that the Arctic littoral states and perhaps others with interests in the region establish their presence there, appropriate to their size and commensurate with their interests and strengths, so as not to leave a void; a power vacuum that could be suddenly and disruptively filled by competitors. The calculus of such balancing, given the interaction of regional and extra-regional factors, is complex, as attempts to systematically define a more geographically limited *Nordic balance* have demonstrated (Brundtland 1966; Noreen 1983).

A third approach stresses the role of *organization*. This reflects an institutionalist point of view. Organization does not necessarily mean a formal body like the United Nations or one of its specialized agencies, programmes, and conferences. Clearly, however, something more than occasional, ad hoc meetings or side conversations at large organizational sessions, is called for. The word to be used to indicate this intermediate, interstitial, yet institutionally relevant modality is *forum*. This suggests that dialogue, including diplomatic dialogue, needs to have a shaped space that has some continuity of participants and into which others with genuine interest and serious purpose can enter. A forum is a place of open discussion; a site of deliberative interchange. It can be moderated by a presiding officer or other impartial facilitator and at the same time allow free expression as a basis for possible consensus.

In what follows, concept, power, and organization will be referred to in reviewing the working through of the peace theme in the Arctic. Some might hypothesize, along with the Copenhagen School, that in order to truly understand peace in the Arctic and increase chances of sustaining it, the region must be *de-securitized* (Buzan, Wæver, and de Wilde 1998). In other words, one must examine how the perception of threats emanating from or to the Arctic, either from dangerous physical changes in the natural condition of the region itself or from deployments of military forces in and around it, generates a sense of *emergency*, which can then lead to the taking of *extraordinary measures*, and possibly to war. The risk is that the perceived and emphasized peril may prove to be unreal, but the proof of its nonexistence comes too late, if ever. The resources committed would, at best, be wasted. A policy goal, therefore, should be to make Arctic relationships, including Arctic politics and diplomacy, as normal as possible.

The difficulty is that, over the years, there have been grounds for judging the crises that have arisen in the North to be not just serious but objectively real. These events gave almost literal meaning to the term Cold War. The North became a global front during that conflict that in retrospect was also paradoxically The Long Peace (Gaddis 1987). The ironies are many. For instance, the very concern of the United States and other Western powers about Soviet and Russian militarization in the North motivated not only counterbalancing military efforts but also Arctic-focused scientific research activities and the formation of a peace-oriented community of scientists and other researchers around them. That community, and the processes of science diplomacy that have been developing, are themselves a kind of forum, if a somewhat self-contained one. Scientists can and do contribute their knowledge, including their familiarity with each other, in a positive and influential way. They might now be able to more directly and publicly contribute to the formation of a broader Arctic peace community. Should such a science-inspired goal be achieved, however, might not the resulting de-securitization of the Arctic weaken the will of governments to continue to finance the very scientific work and transnational collaboration that helped to bring it about?

The interplay of security-motivated and peace-oriented processes relating to the Arctic is very complicated. The two processes are distinct and have moved in different phases, but they are also aspects of the same developments and events. In reviewing the security side of the Arctic story during the Cold War years and afterward, attention will be paid to the peace side of it—including the involvement of the scientific-community, Indigenous communities, corporate communities, and even countries' militaries. The last of these includes coast guards, which in the American and other national cases have a regulatory and enforcement role as well as a protective function. This combination of responsibilities could be a key to Arctic peace and security.

Security first: Arctic defense and diplomacy

At the end of the Second World War, air power was considered vital not only to the security of the United States but also to global stability. Wartime advances in aviation led to suggestions that the United Nations have its own internationally managed air force to maintain peace and security around the world (Russell 1958: 470–72). General Henry H. "Hap" Arnold, head of the Army Air Forces, raised the specter of an atomic Pearl Harbor, warning: "A surprise attack could readily come from across the roof of the world unless we were in possession of adequate airbases outflanking such a route of approach." Countries from which such an attack could come were identified by Arnold only as lying "north of the 30th parallel." In effect, Arnold was declaring the Arctic to be a new geostrategic front vis-à-vis Soviet Russia (Arnold 1946). Although it did not test an atomic weapon until 1949, the Soviet government did possess long-range bombers.

The influential Russian-born American aviator and inventor Alexander de Seversky asserted that long-range aircraft would be strategically decisive in any future conflict, and thus a "key to survival" (de Seversky 1950). Given the increased speed and range of American and Russian bombers, no longer were the United States and the Soviet Union militarily distant from one another. Each had vast areas of extended air dominance that overlapped across the Arctic region. The areas of decision would be where their air operations might collide, perhaps above Alaska or Norway (de Seversky 1950). In order to defend the United States, it would be necessary to defend Canada too. This realization led to the creation of the North American Air Defense Command (NORAD) with headquarters at Ent Air Force Base in Colorado and a command center under Cheyenne Mountain in the same state. The continent was covered for surveillance purposes by Distant Early Warning (DEW) Line radar stations from Alaska to Greenland. These were backed up by the Mid-Canada and Pine Tree Lines. Today's North Warning System (NWS), a joint US–Canadian undertaking, is based on these antecedents.

When Norwegian Defense Minister Jens Christian Hauge read the report of the US President's Air Policy Commission, *Survival in the Air Age* (Finletter Report), he called in the American military, naval, and air attachés and inquired how Norway might fit into the strategic picture that planners in the United States government were forming (Bay 1948). That was consequential, conceptually as well as geo-strategically. Because of the inclusion of Norway, Denmark, and Iceland, the incipient alliance, which might otherwise have been only a narrow "Atlantic approaches" pact of the United States with the United Kingdom, France and the Benelux countries, encompassed all of the North Atlantic above the Tropic of Cancer, including a large part of the Arctic (Henrikson 1980; Njølstad 2008: 405–25). In 1950, the Atlantic alliance became an international organization, NATO (Kaplan 1984).

The perceived threat of a surprise attack was not removed. In 1955 at the Four-Power Geneva Conference, US President Dwight D. Eisenhower put forward an ambitious proposal for the mutual exchange of maps of military installations, supplemented by aerial surveillance, in order to assure compliance with arms control agreements that he hoped might be reached (Rostow 1982). The Soviet side was unwilling, however, to allow such close observation of its territory and military facilities and rejected this Open Skies scheme, describing it as an "espionage" plot. The idea of increasing security through mutual aerial observation nonetheless persisted, and during the presidency of George H.W. Bush a Treaty on Open Skies was negotiated between the members of NATO and the now-dissolved Warsaw Pact. This was signed in Helsinki, in neutral Finland, on 24 March 1992. Canada and Hungary, the two treaty-depository countries, conducted the first test flights using unarmed aircraft. The Open Skies Treaty, with 34 countries now party to it, operates to this day and contributes to cross-border transparency and international confidence (US Department of State n.d.). It remains a positive example of military-to-military peacebuilding. The Treaty covers the entire national territories of the signatory states, and thus verges on the central Arctic area. Were the Open Skies Treaty to be extended in geographical scope and modernized in its photographic precision, it could offer close surveillance of the entire Arctic zone in support of Arctic peace as well as military stability.

A good deal of basic science and engineering lay behind the Open Skies proposal and its treaty-based technical operations. Even more scientific work of a broader nature, as well as direct participation by scientists, was involved in the series of International Polar Years (IPY). Going back to 1882–1883 and 1932–1933, the series continued through the International Geophysical Year (IGY) of 1957–1958 and to the fourth IPY of 2007–2008. Even Operation Sunshine, the long underwater journey of the nuclear submarine USS *Nautilus* (SSN-571) that broke through the ice at the North Pole on 3 August 1958, had a scientific function: to explore the subsurface of the Arctic basin. It also had a politically related purpose—to provide a boost to American technological prestige following the USSR's placing of the artificial satellite *Sputnik 1* in orbit around the earth the year before. Nonetheless, the polar transit by the USS *Nautilus* was basically an IGY operation. Although the project was the brainchild of the secretive Admiral Hyman Rickover, some of its findings were internationally shared.

The monitoring of Soviet industrial and military activity was a constant American government preoccupation during the 1950s, especially in the absence of arms control cooperation with the USSR. In these circumstances, security took precedence over peace. The Eisenhower Administration, at a considerable risk of failure and embarrassment, implicitly acknowledged by its preparing a cover story in case of exposure, repeatedly from 1956 sent an ultra-high-altitude aircraft, the U-2, on secret reconnaissance missions over Soviet territory. On 1 May 1960, the Soviet Air Force shot down a plane piloted by Francis Gary Powers high over Sverdlovsk. The flight had begun in Peshawar, Pakistan and was to have ended at Bodø in Norway. Powers survived, but the cover story—that the aircraft was a weather plane that somehow had lost its way—did not (Powers with Gentry 2004). An East–West summit meeting between Eisenhower and Soviet leader Nikita Khrushchev that had been scheduled for Paris collapsed almost as soon as it began. Eisenhower's insistence, as well as that of French President Charles de Gaulle and British Prime Minister Harold Macmillan, that the U-2 flights were defensive rather than aggressive, was not convincing.

A similar event occurred during the Cuban missile crisis of October 1962 during the presidency of John F. Kennedy. Although the main foci of international tension were the Caribbean and Berlin, an episode near the Bering Strait caused sudden concern. On 27 October, a U-2 plane flown by US Air Force Captain Charles Maultsby, on a mission to the North Pole to collect samples from Soviet nuclear testing at Novaya Zemlya, strayed far off course. Kennedy said, with a brief laugh despite the grim situation, that "There is always some so-and-so who doesn't get the word" (Schlesinger 1965: 828). Magnetic compasses do not work well in the polar region, so Maultsby was using celestial navigation. The aurora borealis, however, blinded him. Unknowingly, he flew westward over the Chukotka

Peninsula. Soviet interceptors tried, but failed, to shoot down his plane. Maultsby finally realized where he was and, although rapidly running out of fuel, managed to glide back safely to Alaska (Dobbs 2008).

Despite this further U-2 intrusion into Soviet airspace, which under the circumstances might well have appeared to the Russians as the start of a pre-emptive attack, the Soviet government, when confronted by the American declaration of a quarantine (naval blockade) of Cuba, announced the next day that it would withdraw its missiles from the island. A showdown was thus averted—but just barely. Crisis management required sober decision-making, and careful implementation control, on both sides (Khrushchev 2000: 533–662; May and Zelikow 1997). In order to reduce the very real risk that a nuclear war could be caused accidentally by such operational mistakes as Captain Maultsby's, Washington and Moscow established a Direct Communications Link—the *hotline*. The connection in its physical form was a duplex radiotelegraph system; it was represented symbolically as a red telephone.

As a further measure, even an explicitly peace-making one, the United States and the Soviet Union agreed to limit their open-air nuclear testing. The Partial Test Ban Treaty (PTBT)—formally, the Treaty Banning Nuclear Weapons Tests in the Atmosphere, in Outer Space and Under Water—was signed in Moscow on 10 October 1963 by representatives of the United States, the United Kingdom, and the Soviet Union. Each of the signatory governments undertook to prohibit, prevent, and not carry out nuclear explosions "at any place under its jurisdiction or control"—which could be construed to cover the high Arctic's sea and air space as well as land-based test sites. The PTBT was the beginning of practical arms control between East and West.

The PTBT did not preclude the further build-up of military strength, particularly by the Soviet Union which, under Admiral of the Fleet Sergei Gorshkov, expanded its navy in both size and range until it became a global operating force—a blue-water navy (Gorshkov 1979). Soviet naval and air operations increasingly challenged the defensive–offensive lines of Western strategy, including the Greenland–Iceland–United Kingdom (GIUK) Gap—the choke point between the Norwegian Sea and the North Atlantic Ocean. For the Soviet navy, with its submarines based on the Kola Peninsula, the passages of the GIUK Gap were critical outlets—just as they were, for NATO, avenues for obstructing Soviet egress and maritime access to the rest of the globe.

KAL 007, UNCLOS III, *Arktika* 2007, and GIUK-N

Despite the failure of Reykjavík, which in retrospect can be seen as the meeting that ended the Cold War (Adelman 2014), the Gorbachev period of Soviet politics, with its liberalizing *glasnost* and *perestroika* policies opened up new prospects of cooperation (Gorbachev 1987b). One of the most important of these is the often-overlooked sphere of transpolar civil aviation (Henrikson 1990). Due to the military realities of the Cold War, and the closure during that time of Russian and Chinese air spaces, long-distance flights between Europe and Northeast Asia had to take circumventing routes via Alaska, with Anchorage as the transit point. Scandinavian Airlines (SAS), using Douglas DC-7Cs, was the first, in February 1957, to fly the northern route from Europe to Tokyo through Anchorage.

A disaster occurred in September 1983 when a Korean Air Lines Boeing 747 aircraft, KAL 007, flying from New York via Anchorage to Seoul erroneously passed over the Kamchatka Peninsula and the southern tip of Sakhalin and was shot down by a Soviet Su-15 interceptor over the Sea of Japan (Dallin 1983). Considered a test of world aviation comity, the incident was taken up by the International Civil Aviation Organization (ICAO) whose Council, by vote of 22–2 (with the Soviet Union and Czechoslovakia opposing) condemned the Russian action. A positive diplomatic result of the KAL 007 crisis was the 1985 negotiation of the US–Japanese–Soviet North Pacific Air Safety Agreement. The KAL incident also brought to light the potential civil use of the sophisticated satellite navigation system, NAVSTAR Global Positioning System (GPS), in development for the American armed forces. The Soviet Union was working on its own system, GLONASS. Both systems since have become indispensable for guidance and tracking in the Arctic as well as for navigation of all kinds throughout other regions. The ICAO has come to accept GLONASS on the same footing as GPS in its overall Global Navigation Satellite System (GNSS).

In another organizational-diplomatic setting, the United Nations Law of the Sea Conference (UNCLOS), the United States and the Soviet Union found that they, though rivals, had much in common, particularly their interest in preserving the right of *innocent passage* on, under, and above international straits. For the US government, the principle of *freedom of navigation* has put it at odds even with its next-door neighbor and ally, Canada, over ship movement through the Northwest Passage. Canada considers the Passage to be an internal waterway. During the Third UN Law of the Sea Conference (UNCLOS III), under the chairmanship of Ambassador Tommy Koh of Singapore, a comprehensive Convention was negotiated in 1982 that balanced the interests of naval powers, coastal states, and even land-locked countries (Koh 1986). With general acceptance of the new concept of the "common heritage of mankind," all states could share in the exploitation of sea-floor resources outside the limits of national jurisdiction under a regime and tribunal to be established. Norway's delegate, the jurist Jens Evensen, led an expert negotiating group that proposed innovative solutions to some of the most complicated problems, including the creation of exclusive economic zones (EEZs). The US representative, Elliot Richardson, firmly defended American strategic interests while participating constructively in the wider deliberations that produced a final consensus. He signed the resulting Convention on behalf of the United States which, although it has yet to ratify it, recognizes much of it as a codification of general international law. The US government remains unable, nonetheless, to submit a claim under UNCLOS to an extended continental shelf beyond its 200-nautical mile EEZ north of Alaska—a major continuing issue in American Arctic policy.

A balance between national interests, focused on the sea floor, and common interests, focused on the water column, in the Arctic Ocean cannot easily be worked out (Berkman and Young 2009). The Russian Federation is contesting control of the Lomonosov Ridge with Denmark and Greenland. A Russian expedition, *Arktika* 2007, led by the explorer Artur Chilingarov, planted a titanium Russian flag on the seabed at the North Pole and took soil samples there in order to prove a natural connection with the Russian landmass. This was done ostensibly within the scientific framework of the 2007–2008 International Polar Year: a global undertaking, but it clearly had a national purpose.

It is noteworthy that Russian leader Vladimir Putin stated at the first Arctic Forum in Moscow in September 2010: "We think it is imperative to keep the Arctic as a zone of peace and cooperation," echoing Gorbachev. "We have heard futuristic predictions threatening a battle for the Arctic," he acknowledged. However, "the majority of scary scenarios about the Arctic do not have any real basis" (Putin 2010). After the *Arktika* 2007 expedition to the North Pole and Putin's presumed support for Chilingarov's flagging of it, the Russian Federation mapped out a claim to an extensive part of the sea floor beyond the 200-mile zone in its Arctic sector. At the international Arctic: Territory of Dialogue forum in Arkhangelsk in March 2017, Putin outlined an extensive economic program for the development of Russia's Arctic zone. Again stating that "there is no potential for conflict in the Arctic region," he explained:

> International law clearly specifies the rights of littoral and other states and provides a firm foundation for cooperation in addressing various issues, including such sensitive ones as the delineation of the continental shelf in the Arctic Ocean and the prevention of unregulated high seas fishing in the Central Arctic Ocean, which is surrounded by the exclusive economic zones of the United States, Canada, Denmark, Norway, and Russia.

Russia, he emphasized, "is open to constructive cooperation" in the Arctic and "does its utmost to create a proper environment for its effective development" (Putin 2017). Presumably in that spirit, Russia in December 2017 joined other Arctic nations in a provisional moratorium on fishing in newly ice-free areas of the High Arctic (Kramer 2017). The opening of Arctic waters represents for Russia a future as a global maritime trading state (Antrim 2010).

While denying any potential for conflict, and in support of its polar assertion and economic ambitions, the Russian government under Putin has embarked upon a major expansion of its military facilities in its Arctic zone. It has carried out provocative naval and air operations in the Norwegian Sea, in the Baltic Sea region, and farther south in the North Atlantic. Again, there is concern among the Atlantic allies about the porousness of the strategic GIUK gap—or now the GIUK-N gap, with Norway's maritime domain being included (Nordenman 2016). Accordingly, plans were made within NATO to upgrade the military facilities at Iceland's Keflavík Air Base and to enhance other northern Atlantic defenses. Security imperatives are being felt once more.

Stakeholders in the Arctic and their diplomatic arrangements

Current military developments in the North Atlantic, and the North Pacific as well, have occurred against a background of multilayered, though not yet truly strong, institutionalization covering all or some parts of the Arctic region. Many countries and organizations are now considered stakeholders there. The stakeholder notion is a complicated and somewhat elusive one. There are primary and secondary stakeholders, as well as parties without recognized stakes that nonetheless may be materially or otherwise affected by what might occur there. The concept implies that all who possess or declare interests in the Arctic should be consulted, or at least have their concerns taken into account, when meetings are held and decisions are contemplated that might affect them. Within what has been described by Paul Berkman as a System of Arctic Stakeholders, there are now 20 or more states as participants, along with Arctic-sensitive organizations such as NATO. This notional system also includes less-structured *information networks* such as the 1973 Agreement on the Conservation of Polar Bears (Berkman 2015). The issues addressed within this diverse assemblage, an imputed rather than formal system, have their own identities and histories. Changing interests in changed contexts, however, can alter said issues.

Russia, with privileged economic access to the Norwegian territory of Svalbard under the 1920 Spitsbergen Treaty (Østhagen 2018), has settled its long-standing fisheries-related maritime border dispute with Norway in the Barents Sea, permitting cooperation in the development of oil and gas resources in the area. The agreement, signed by the Norwegian and Russian foreign ministers at Murmansk on 15 September 2010, was negotiated bilaterally following UNCLOS guidelines but without adjudication by a tribunal (Nilsen 2010). The settlement could be a model for future boundary delimitation in other Arctic area waters, perhaps in the Beaufort Sea where Canada and the United States have a jurisdictional disagreement or between Canada and Denmark over ownership of tiny Hans Island between Ellesmere Island and Greenland.

The Norway–Russia maritime delimitation agreement was, in part, a manifestation of the comity that had developed among four countries of the Barents region, including those with a Baltic orientation (Sweden and Finland), regarding common problems of their northernmost districts and peoples. In Kirkenes in January 1993, under the leadership of Norway's Foreign Minister Thorvald Stoltenberg, the Barents Regional Council (BRC) was created as a forum for Norwegian, Swedish, Finnish, and Russian exchange. During the same period, with representatives of Iceland and the European Commission also participating, the Barents Euro-Arctic Council (BEAC) was formed. The BRC and the BEAC, although different in composition and scope, coordinate some of their activities through a common organ, the International Barents Secretariat (IBS), located in Kirkenes. The Barents Program of 2014–2018 reflects the shared conviction of all participants that "Barents cooperation remains a successful model for peaceful international and interregional cooperation, and can be replicated in other parts of the world" (Barents Euro-Atlantic Council 2013).

The Inuit Circumpolar Council (ICC), a nongovernmental organization of Indigenous peoples spanning the whole Arctic area with offices in four Inuit nations (ICC Chukotka, ICC Alaska, ICC Canada, ICC Greenland), also espouses the ethos of Arctic peace. Although only founded in 1997, the ICC claims a longer lineage through the "sovereign" human basis of "living in the Arctic from time immemorial" and also of its inhabitants' occupying and using its lands and waters sustainably. While being citizens of Russia, the United States, Canada, or Denmark, the Inuit with their status as a recognized Indigenous people have rights and responsibilities "under international law." Among these declared rights, besides that of participation in decision-making in matters relating to themselves, is "the right to peace and security" (Inuit Circumpolar Council 2009).

The Arctic Council (AC), established by the eight Arctic countries with the 1996 Ottawa Declaration, has come to be accepted as the principal intergovernmental forum for the discussion of Arctic issues, with the express exclusion of military security. The word *peace* was also initially avoided as its use could be understood to imply demilitarization. Reference to peace began to appear, however, in Arctic Council communications in 2009. In the preamble of the Tromsø Declaration of 29 April 2009, for instance, the signatories joined in "*Confirming* that in international relations the rule of law is a prerequisite for peaceful regional development." In the Nuuk Declaration of 12 May 2011, the signatories joined in "*Recognizing* the importance of maintaining peace, stability and constructive cooperation in the Arctic" (Arctic Council 2017). The pacific intent and hoped-for pacifying influence of the Arctic Council and its activities have not gone unnoticed (Byers 2016; US Department of State 2016).

The Arctic Council is a composite organization, combining Member States with Permanent Participants. It also accepts Observers. The ICC is one of its six Permanent Participants, which have "full consultative rights" but do not have the right to join in Council decision-making. This is reserved for the eight Member States acting on the basis of consensus. Permanent Participants have the administrative support of an Indigenous Peoples Secretariat (IPS) that is sponsored by Denmark and located in Copenhagen. Despite the inherent limitation of their role, Indigenous peoples participating in the Arctic Council have opportunities to speak and are respectfully heard. The forum nature of the Council is a distinct advantage for them, as it gives them an integral position within its structure. This is in contrast with the Observer countries and organizations which, although many are large, wealthy, and powerful, must watch and listen as the Council deliberates.

At the level of the AC working groups on projects and task forces dealing with issues ranging from climate conditions and biodiversity to human development, Observers can and do contribute their knowledge and make their presence felt. The Observer roster now includes China, which has characterized itself as a "near-Arctic state" (Brady 2017; Lanteigne 2017). The UN is present through three of its specialized agencies: the United Nations Development Programme (UNDP), the United Nations Environment Programme (UNEP), and most recently the International Maritime Organisation (IMO). So, also are, among others, the Arctic Parliamentarians, the International Red Cross Federation, and the Nordic Council.

The Arctic Council's Declarations, which are issued at ministerial-level meetings at the end of a Member State's rotating chairmanship, are nonbinding. The Council has, however, generated three significant agreements that are legally binding: the Agreement on Cooperation on Aeronautical and Maritime Search and Rescue in the Arctic (concluded in 2011 at Nuuk, Greenland), the Agreement on Cooperation on Marine Oil Pollution Preparedness and Response in the Arctic (concluded in 2013 at Kiruna, Sweden), and, in May 2017 at the ministerial meeting in Fairbanks, Alaska, at the conclusion of the US Arctic Council chairmanship, an Agreement on Enhancing International Arctic Scientific Cooperation (Berkman et al. 2017).

The Arctic Council has its origins in scientific cooperation. Its founding in 1996 was premised on the Arctic Environmental Protection Strategy (AEPS), which was agreed upon by the eight Arctic countries in 1991. Scientific assessments that have been conducted under Arctic Council auspices have contributed both directly and indirectly to positive undertakings such as the International Maritime Organization's Polar Code, finalized in 2017. Future effectiveness of the Council's scientific and other work remains somewhat in doubt, however. Not the least of the reasons for this is the uncertainty of international support for the 2015 Paris Climate Accord, from which the United States government under President Donald Trump withdrew in 2017.

Despite everything, a general lesson of Arctic experience has been the necessity of working together, however difficult that may be. As Putin, like the explorer Vilhjalmur Stefansson and other early northern visitors, has observed: "If you stand alone you can't survive in the Arctic. Nature makes people and states to help each other" (Harding 2010). Mutual assistance in the challenging Arctic context requires organized cooperation. Organization, if it is to be effective, requires implementation. In practical terms, because of the extreme physical difficulty of action in the Arctic environment, that means coordinated if not actual joint operations by willing military services of the Arctic states. Unfortunately, inter-military cooperation between the Russian Federation and the West, including the United States and other Arctic Council states, is today mostly frozen. There is very little high-level contact between their militaries at present. The reasons are well known: major policy differences that exist over the situation in Ukraine, from which Russia seized Crimea in 2014 and incorporated it into its Federation; and also the crisis in Syria. There are also disagreements over adherence to the 1998 Intermediate-Range Nuclear Forces (INF) Treaty.

The NATO–Russia Council (NRC), established at the NATO–Russia Summit in Rome in May 2002, still exists and meets periodically, but practical cooperation within it is very limited (North Atlantic Treaty Organization 2018). The NRC serves as a venue for discussing transparency and risk reduction, including notification of military exercises, such as, in 2018, Russia's huge *Vostok* exercise in Siberia and NATO's *Trident Juncture* exercise in and around Norway. Within the Arctic regional context, there was a security-related arrangement: the Arctic Chiefs of Defense Staff (CHOD), which met at Goose Bay, Newfoundland, in 2012. It no longer functions, however. The Arctic Security Forces Roundtable, which was convened in Reykjavík in 2015, met in Halifax, Nova Scotia, but no participant from Russia was present (Ellis 2018).

One bright light is the Arctic Council's October 2015 establishment of the Arctic Coast Guard Forum. Coastal and border guard services, with their combined domestic and international roles, have a unique capacity for diplomatic engagement owing to their nonthreatening presence and their concern for overall domain awareness. In the words of US Coast Guard Commandant Admiral Paul Zukunft, the Arctic Coast Guard Forum "represents a critical step forward in our collective efforts to promote safety, security and environmentally-responsible activity in the Arctic" (Braynard 2015). At a meeting of the Forum in Boston in March 2017, the chairmanship of the eight-country group was handed over to Lieutenant General Jaakko Kaukanen, chief of the Finnish Border Guard. "When we first started meeting," Zukunft reflected, "we were strangers. Now, we're working together for the common good" (Grant 2017).

The results of the Boston Arctic Coast Guard meeting included recognition of the need for a common doctrine as well as agreements on tactics, procedures, and information-sharing protocols for Arctic operations. An early live exercise was planned. While emphasizing cooperation over competition, Admiral Zukunft was mindful of the power factor: the large gap in capabilities he had to deal with as the officer-in-charge of the Coast Guard of the United States. He had only two functional icebreakers at his disposal, one of them more than four decades old. He needed and was strongly advocating for the construction of three heavy and three medium icebreakers. "If we are not up there operating as a show of sovereignty," as he testified, other nations, in support of their claims, will be there. If the United States did not ratify the UN Convention on the Law of the Sea, on basis of which it could register its own legal claim to the continental shelf beyond its EEZ, he further warned, it might find the area included in the "global commons." President Trump, responding rhetorically to the Coast Guard's request, offered, when speaking at the commencement exercises of the Coast Guard Academy on 17 May 2017, that under his administration "we will be building the first heavy icebreakers the United States has seen in over 40 years. We're going to build many of them," (Lamothe 2017).

Conclusion: factors and facilitators of New North cooperation

A fundamental factor in understanding Arctic peace and security, in addition to the concept of Arctic distinctiveness or exceptionality, is the mutual recognition by the eight governments and peoples of the region that cooperation in the Arctic is a necessity, and that they need each other to protect their own interests and common future. The maintenance of a power equilibrium, differentiated but roughly even, is an important factor as well, if kept at low levels. So, too, are organizational factors, including universal technical ones such as ICAO and region-specific ones including, most centrally, the Arctic Council.

Skillful diplomacy, including American and Russian co-chairmanship of well-focused Arctic policy meetings, such as the White House Arctic Science Ministerial that took place in September 2016 during the presidency of Barack Obama, can make a difference. So might, even, in a more salient and creatively disruptive way, the Trump–Putin summit meeting that was held in Helsinki on 16 July 2018, if it leads, beyond deconfliction, to eventual collaboration for positive purposes. Diplomacy has long been manifest among

Arctic scientists in their research cooperation, in distinct counterpoint to the role that scientists played in building their respective national security states during the Cold War era. The Arctic Science Agreement signed by foreign ministers, including those of the Russian Federation and the United States, at the Arctic Council meeting in Fairbanks is particularly promising.

People-to-people exchanges, of course, matter as well. This has been demonstrated in the direct contacts that have developed between neighboring Indigenous groups, including those of the ICC. Joint educational undertakings such as the University of the Arctic (UArctic) and the Fulbright Arctic Initiative network carry promise for the future. Even major corporate ventures such as the interrupted Rosneft–Exxon Mobil partnership have a pacific potential. A comprehensive forum for consideration of Arctic matters is the Arctic Circle, an Icelandic nonprofit and nonpartisan initiative begun during the presidency of Ólafur Ragnar Grímsson (1996–2016). The forum describes itself as "the largest network of international dialogue and cooperation on the future of the Arctic" (Arctic Circle n.d.).

Diplomacy, including the supportive involvement of these and other groupings with serious interests in the Arctic, can modify the adverse politics of the present historical period. It can help to make the New North Cooperation, as it has been characterized, a steady, progressive reality. Thus may diplomacy in all its aspects and with its many official and unofficial participants, contribute still further to Arctic peace and security, which, if well understood and widely explained, can contribute to the peace of the world.

Note

1 Based on a keynote address given at the conference *Understanding Peace in the Arctic*, organized by the Centre for Peace Studies of The University of Tromsø—The Arctic University of Norway, Tromsø, 13–15 June 2017.

References

Adelman, Ken. 2014. *Reagan at Reykjavík: Forty-Eight Hours That Ended the Cold War*. New York: HarperCollins.

Antrim, Caitlyn L. 2010. 'The Next Geographical Pivot: The Russian Arctic in the Twenty-first Century', *Naval War College Review* 63, no. 3 (Summer): 15–37.

Arctic Circle. n.d. 'The Largest International Gathering on the Arctic'. www.arcticcircle.org/about/about

Arctic Council. 2017. 'All Arctic Council Declarations 1996–2017'. https://oaarchive.arctic-council.org/handle/11374/94

Arnold, Henry H. 1946. 'Air Power for Peace', *The National Geographic Magazine* 89, no. 2 (February): 137–194.

Barents Euro-Atlantic Council. 2013. 'The Barents Programme 2014–2018'. www.barentsinfo.fi/beac/docs/Barents_Programme_2014_2018_adopted_2_2013.pdf

Bay, Charles Ulrich. 1948. 'The Ambassador in Norway (Bay) to the Secretary of State', Oslo, 19 February, *Foreign Relations of the United States 1948, Volume III, Western Europe*: 24–26. Washington, DC: United States Government Printing Office, 1974.

Berkman, Paul Arthur. 2015. 'Institutional Dimensions of Sustaining Arctic Observing Networks (SAON)', *Arctic* 68, SUPPL. 1: 1–11.

Berkman, Paul Arthur, Lars Kullerud, Allen Pope, Alexander N. Vylegzhanin, and Oran R. Young. 2017. 'The Arctic Science Agreement Propels Science Diplomacy', *Science* 358, no. 6363 (3 November): 596–598.

Berkman, Paul Arthur, and Oran R. Young. 2009. 'Governance and Environmental Change in the Arctic Ocean', *Science* 324, no. 5925 (17 April): 339–340.

Brady, Anne-Marie. 2017. *China as a Polar Great Power*. Cambridge: Cambridge University Press.
Braynard, Katie. 2015. 'Establishment of the Arctic Coast Guard Forum', *Coast Guard Compass*, 30 October. http://coastguard.dodlive.mil/2015/10/establishment-of-the-arctic-coast-guard-forum/
Brundtland, Arne Olav. 1966. 'The Nordic Balance: Past and Present', *Cooperation and Conflict* 1, no. 4 (1 June): 30–63.
Buzan, Barry, Ole Wæver, and Jaap de Wilde. 1998. *Security: A New Framework for Analysis*. Boulder, CO: Lynne Rienner.
Byers, Michael. 2016. 'The Arctic Council Maintaining Peace through Cooperation', *Shared Voices Magazine*, Special Issue, UArctic. www.uarctic.org/shared-voices-magazine-2016-special-issue/the-arctic-council-maintaining-peace-through-cooperation
Dallin, Alexander. 1983. *Black Box: KAL 007 and the Superpowers*. Berkeley, CA: University of California Press.
de Seversky, Alexander P. 1950. *Air Power: Key to Survival*. New York: Simon & Schuster.
Dobbs, Michael. 2008. 'One Minute to Midnight: Kennedy, Khrushchev and Castro on the Brink of Nuclear War', *The National Security Archive*, posted 11 June. https://nsarchive.gwu.edu/nsa/cuba_cris/dobbs/maultsby.htm
Ellis, Lucy. 2018. 'Partners in the North: Canada Hosts the Arctic Security Forces Roundtable in Halifax', *The Maple Leaf—Defence Stories*, 10 May. https://ml-fd.caf-fac.ca/en/2018/05/
Gaddis, John Lewis. 1987. *The Long Peace: Inquiries into the History of the Cold War*. New York: Oxford University Press.
Gautam, Pradeep Kumar. 2011. *The Arctic as a Global Common*. IDSA Issue Brief. New Delhi: Institute for Defence Studies and Analysis, 2 September.
Gorbachev, Mikhail. 1987a. Mikhail Gorbachev's Speech in Murmansk at the Ceremonial Meeting on the Occasion of the Presentation of the Order of Lenin and the Gold Star to the City of Murmansk, Murmansk, 1 October. www.barentsinfo.fi/docs/Gorbachev_speech.pdf
Gorbachev, Mikhail. 1987b. *Perestroika: New Thinking for Our Country and the World*. New York: Harper and Row.
Gorshkov, Sergei Georgievich. 1979. *The Sea Power of the State*. Annapolis: Naval Institute Press.
Grant, Andrew. 2017. 'US, Other Nations Gather to Work on Arctic Issues', *The Boston Globe*, 24 March.
Hamilton, Neil T.M. 2014. *Arctic Sanctuary: Global Commons, Environmental Protection & Future-Proofing*. Amsterdam: Greenpeace International, June.
Harding, Luke. 2010. 'Vladimir Putin Call for Arctic Claims to Be Resolved under UN Law', *The Guardian*, 23 September.
Henrikson, Alan K. 1980. 'The Creation of the North Atlantic Alliance, 1948–1952', *Naval War College Review* 32, no. 3/seq. 279 (May-June): 4–39.
Henrikson, Alan K. 1990. 'A World 'Arctic Mediterranean'? Open Skies and Transpolar Civil Aviation', in Tertu Utriainen (ed.), *Legal Problems in the Arctic Regions*, Juridica Lapponica 6: 24–64. Rovaniemi: The Institute for Nordic Law, University of Lapland.
Inuit Circumpolar Council. 2009. 'A Circumpolar Inuit Declaration on Sovereignty in the Arctic', April 2009. Iccalaska.org/wp-icc/wp-content/uploads/2016/01/Signed-Inuit-Sovereignty-Declaration-11x17.pdf
Kaplan, Lawrence S. 1984. *The United States and NATO: The Formative Years*. Lexington, NC: The University Press of Kentucky.
Khrushchev, Sergei N. 2000. *Nikita Khrushchev and the Creation of a Superpower*. University Park, PA: The Pennsylvania State University Press.
Koh, Tommy T.B. 1986. 'Negotiating a New Order for the Sea', in Alan K. Henrikson (ed.), *Negotiating World Order: The Artisanship and Architecture of Global Diplomacy*: 33–45. Wilmington, DE: Scholarly Resources Inc.
Kramer, Andrew E. 2017. 'Russia, US and Others Join to Limit Arctic Fishing', *The New York Times*, 11 December.
Lamothe, Dan. 2017. 'Trump Pledges to Build Coast Guard Icebreakers, but It's Unclear How Different His Plan is from Obama's', *The Washington Post*, 17 May.
Lanteigne, Marc. 2017. '"Have You Entered the Storehouses of the Snow?" China as a Norm Entrepreneur in the Arctic', *Polar Record* 53, no. 2 (March 2017): 117–130.
May, Ernest R., and Philip Zelikow. 1997. *The Kennedy Tapes: Inside the White House during the Cuban Missile Crisis*. Cambridge, MA: The Belknap Press of Harvard University Press.

Nilsen, Thomas. 2010. 'Norway and Russia Sign Maritime Delimitation Agreement', *Barents Observer*, 15 September. http://barentsobserver.com/en/sections/spotlights/norway-and-russia-sign-maritime-delimitation-agreement

Njølstad, Olav. 2008. *Jens Chr. Hauge—fult og helt*. Oslo: Archehoug & Co.

Nordenman, Magnus. 2016. 'Russian Subs Are Reheating a Cold War Chokepoint', *Defense One*, 4 March. www/defenseone.com/ideas/2016/03/russian-subs-are-reheating-cold-war-chokepoint/126428/

Noreen, Erik. 1983. 'The Nordic Balance: A Security Concept in Theory and Practice', *Cooperation and Conflict* 18, no. 1 (1 March): 43–56.

North Atlantic Treaty Organization. 2018. 'NATO-Russia Council', 13 November. www.nato.int/cps/en/nato/hq/topics_50091.htm

Østhagen, Andreas. 2018. 'Managing Conflict at Sea: The Case of Norway and Russia in the Svalbard Zone', *Arctic Review on Law and Politics* 9, no. 2018: 100–123. doi:10.23865.v9.1084.

Powers, Francis Gary, with Curt Gentry. 2004. *Operation Overflight: A Memoir of the U-2 Incident*. Washington, DC: Potomac Books.

Putin, Vladimir. 2010. 'Arctic Must Remain Zone of Peace: Putin', 24 September. www.sbs.com.au/news/article/2010/09/24/arctic-must-remain-zone-peace-putin

Putin, Vladimir. 2017. 'The Arctic: Territory of Dialogue International Forum', 30 March. http://en.kremlin.ru/events/president/news/54149

Rostow, Walt Whitman. 1982. *Open Skies: Eisenhower's Proposal of July 21, 1955*. Austin, TX: University of Texas Press.

Russell, Ruth B. 1958. *A History of the United Nations Charter: The Role of the United States 1940–1945*. Washington, DC: Brookings Institution.

Schlesinger, Arthur M., Jr. 1965. *A Thousand Days: John F. Kennedy in the White House*. Boston, MA: Houghton Mifflin Company.

Teeple, Nancy Jane. 2017. *Arms Control on the Eve of Destruction? The Prospects for an Arctic Nuclear Weapons-Free Zone in an Age of Counterforce Dominance*. Burnaby, British Columbia: Simon Fraser University.

US Department of State. 2016. 'The Arctic Council: A Forum for Peace and Cooperation', 20 September. www.state.gov/e/oes/ocns/opa/arc/uschair/262197.htm

US Department of State. n.d. 'Treaty on Open Skies (OS)'. www.state.gov/t/avc/cca/os/

PART I

Theorizing Arctic security

3

APPLYING CONVENTIONAL THEORETICAL APPROACHES TO THE ARCTIC

Barbora Padrtova

Introduction

Traditionally, state-based perceptions of security have fluctuated in a combined response to the emergence of new types of threats to the state's existence as well as ongoing political decisions about security priorities. Since the Treaties of Westphalia, the international system has been largely characterized by conflicts between states, rather than within them. This international system primarily recognized external dangers as legitimate, and this perception dominated during the Cold War. Security in the Arctic was thus associated with a classical military/political rivalry between the two superpowers, the United States and the Soviet Union. The region was frozen, not only climatically, but also politically. Following the dissolution of the Soviet Union and the cessation of the nuclear arms race, however, the international political focus reoriented itself towards other significant internal threats, as newly recognized (though ever-present) areas crucial for human survival and welfare like the economy, environment, food, and health were identified. This shift in the perception of threats also marked the beginning of a fundamentally different political environment, both in a real and in a theoretical sense. This change initiated an academic debate on whether the concept of security (confined to a military understanding) was sufficient or whether a broader definition would constitute a more accurate depiction of reality in a new international system.

This chapter focuses on the development and transformation of security through various theoretical lenses with an illustration of a case study about the Arctic region. The chapter opens with an elaboration of the theoretical development of security concepts, followed by a comparison of traditional and nontraditional theoretical approaches. Second, the chapter explores the non-traditionalist "widening" and "deepening" perspectives, which include a broader range of new threats in four nontraditional sectors of security: political, economic, societal, and environmental. Third, the chapter discusses the Regional Security Complex Theory and the possibility of applying this concept to the Arctic region. Fourth, it summarizes the perception of Arctic security from a historical perspective. Finally, the chapter concludes with a discussion of current perceptions of security in the Arctic, particularly in light of the exclusion of military security in the Arctic Council framework.

Concepts of security reflected in theories – traditionalists vs. non-traditionalists

Though the concept of security has a long and complex history (Rothschild, 1995; Hoogensen Gjørv, 2017), a narrower, state-based focus has dominated since the Napoleonic wars, thereafter characterized as "traditional" or "classical" security. Since the 1990s, however, various security perspectives have re-emerged. These range from Stephen Walt's very narrow interpretation of security in strictly military and state-centric terms (traditionalist), moving through the (more issues-based areas) view taken by Mohammed Ayoob, Barry Buzan, Ole Wæver, and Jaap de Wilde, which examines a wider variety of issue areas, to the nontraditional conception of security promoted by Ken Booth or V. Spike Peterson, which uses a deeper level of analysis (a nontraditional line of thought). While traditionalists favor the maintenance of a state-based conception of security reminiscent of the Cold War, the non-traditionalists argue that other issues, such as economic, environmental and social threats, endanger the lives of individuals rather than strictly the survival of states. Hence, a broader definition of security is necessary (Tarry, 1999).

Disagreement between the traditional and nontraditional approaches can be said to reflect the classical ideological cleavage in international relations between two schools of thought – realism and liberalism. Non-traditionalists are not united either, with a key difference illustrated in the approaches of two groups of scholars: the so-called "wideners" and the "deepeners." "Wideners" focus on a broader range of security issues and argue that the greatest threats to state survival may not be military, but environmental, social, and economic. The "deepeners," on the other hand, ask the question of whose security is being threatened and support the construction of a definition that allows for individual or structural referent objects, as opposed to solely the state (Figure 3.1) (Tarry, 1999).

Traditional approach

A traditionalist understanding of security is firmly rooted in realism, extensively discussed by one of the most prominent security studies scholars, Stephen Walt (1991). The approach is state-centric and restricts the application of security predominantly to military-related threats. The military serves as a means of preventing or countering conflict and the resulting

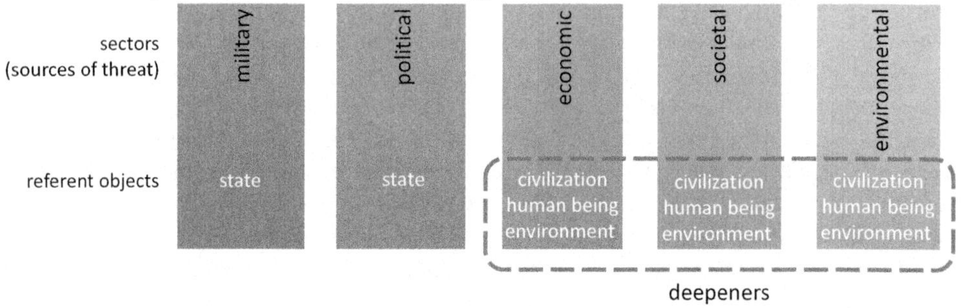

Figure 3.1 Five sectors (sources of threats) and different understandings of security

security (an absence of conflict) is understood as the equivalent of peace. In addition, the state is considered the most important actor in the international system (Tarry, 1999). The international system is anarchic due to the absence of world government. The system is dominated by sovereign states pursuing their own self-interests to maximize power in order to survive in a competitive state system (Hough, 2013).

Classical realist tradition was later transformed into neorealism, first introduced by Kenneth Waltz (1979). Although the main realist ideas were preserved, neorealists see the world as less chaotic, with some order coming from the cooperation of states. However, even this cooperation is driven by states pursuing their own interests. The traditional approach thus expects Arctic politics to be dominated by rivalry between the most powerful Arctic states seeking to advance their national interests (Hough, 2013).

Nontraditional approach: "wideners"

The new generation of scholars, so-called "wideners," redefined the concept of security beyond the military sector. One of the key proponents of the group of wideners is Mohammed Ayoob (1997), who argued that the predominant source of the emergence of intrastate conflicts is political-institutional underdevelopment. Ayoob contends that national security is a function of state building, which requires that a state possesses more than simply "security hardware" (control of coercive force) but also "security software" (legitimacy and integration). However, Ayoob admits that not all issues have the same influence over time and among specific countries; thereby, he avoids attaching issues like environmental degradation, pollution, or migration to a definition of security. In his understanding, these issues are not national security matters. In addition, like Walt, Ayoob's focus is clearly state-centric and excludes threats to individual and global security (Ayoob, 1997).

In contrast to Ayoob, Michael Klare and Daniel Thomas (1994) argued that the concept of security must be expanded because of the declining significance of geographical boundaries. In their view, state actors are not capable of responding to global problems like ecological threats, rights abuses, negative demographic trends, or economic crises. Through the inclusion of such varied global problems, Klare and Thomas view global security as equivalent to human security. In their view, all actors of international systems need to collectively respond to global threats (Tarry, 1999).

Besides Ayoob, Klare, and Thomas, another well-known proponent of the "wideners" is Ole Wæver (1995). Wæver, together with his colleagues from the Conflict and Peace Research Institute of Copenhagen, Barry Buzan and Jaap de Wilde, are known as the "Copenhagen School." They proposed nonmilitary threats in four other sectors: political, economic, environmental, and societal. The Copenhagen School further contributed various concepts to the field of security studies, most importantly those of securitization. The securitization theory goes beyond the state as the only securitizing actor and referent object. This enables the identification of new securitizing actors like political leaders, NGOs, pressure groups, or media and referent objects, such as ecosystems, industry, ethnic groups, and collective identity (Buzan et al., 1998; Emmers, 2013; Does, 2013).

The broadened security concept, with new referent objects, is particularly suitable for the Arctic. First, the increased focus on the region has been largely framed within the context of the extraction of natural resources, being mainly oil and gas. Thus, the Arctic is seen as a resource base that is relevant to the economic sector (economic security). Second, at the same time, the fragile natural environment is endangered by global warming and the negative impacts of rapid climate change, and by intensified economic development (environmental security). Third, an increase in industrial development, complemented by climate change and its impacts, also poses threats to the traditional livelihoods of Indigenous peoples in the Arctic. The resilience of Arctic communities and the ability of future generations to adapt, live, and prosper in the Arctic are in jeopardy (societal security). Finally, on the political-military level, the Arctic is perceived as an area where the interests of world powers meet, and every Arctic state tries to protect its national interests (political and military security) (Padrtova, 2018).

Regional security complex?

In addition to the securitization theory, the Copenhagen School also focused on regional security. The School introduced the Regional Security Complex Theory (RSCT), which provided a comprehensive framework for the analysis of regional security dynamics. The theory introduced 12 different regional security complexes (RSCs) covering almost the whole world; however, the theory did not include the Arctic or polar territories as RSCs. The Arctic was considered a "leftover" region without any significant security dynamics. One of the possible explanations for this exclusion could be the School's understanding of the Arctic as a region of low intensity of regional security interactions. Another reason could be the Mercator projections of maps and illustrations used in the work of Buzan and Wæver (2003). With Mercator projections, the world is distorted and both the northernmost and southernmost peripheral territories are not shown. The geographical distortion could then be a cause of failure to identify the precise northern boundaries for any Arctic-rimmed security complex (Padrtova, 2017).

The essential idea of the RSCT is based on the presumption that a comprehensive analysis of one isolated object (e.g. the security of Norway) must be studied in a wider context (Buzan et al., 1998). The School argued that most states fear their neighbors more than distant powers, because most threats travel more easily over short distances than over long ones. Security interdependence is therefore normally patterned into regionally based clusters. The classical approach to regional security analysis looks for patterns of security interdependence that are strong enough to mark a group of units from its neighbors. The RSC is defined as "a set of units whose major processes of securitization, de-securitization, or both are so interlinked that their security problems cannot reasonably be analyzed or resolved apart from one another" (Buzan and Wæver, 2003). The essential structure of an RSC is comprised of four variables: boundary, anarchic structure, polarity, and social construction.

Boundary

First, a boundary differentiates the RSC from its neighbors and determines the dynamics inside the RSC. When identifying the borders of the RSC, it is no different from identifying the borders of any other artificially created geographical entity. Inside the RSC, there are visible features of security interdependence (the intensity/relative strength of security interactions) among individual states/units, while security relations with others outside the RSC are weaker (Buzan et al., 1995). In some regions, these features are more visible and stronger (for example, between Taiwan and the People's Republic of China) while in other regions they can be relatively weak (as between states within the European Union) (Gibbs, 2011).

According to Buzan and Wæver (2003), boundaries of the complex are identical to the external borders of the states. This can be a problematic element of the theory in the case of the Arctic because the region does not consist of whole states, but rather northern territories of individual states. Thus, if the classic version of RSCT were strictly applied, the classification of the

Arctic as an RSC fails because the original theory explicitly operates with states as the exclusive building block of the RSC. The revised definition, however, has replaced the term "state" with a more general term "unit", which enables a substate entity (e.g. a substate region as an administrative unit of the state). From this perspective the Arctic, as a geographically coherent set of units, may be classified as a distinct RSC. The possible demarcation line for the Arctic RSC could be defined as all territories that lie closely around and north of the Arctic Circle.

Anarchic structure

The second element of the RSC's essential structure is anarchy. Based on the theory, the RSC is a small version of the international system, which exhibits the characteristics of plurality of actors and the absence of a central superior authority. The fact that four out of five Arctic-rim states are founding members of NATO is not an expression of lack of anarchy in the region, but rather the existence of a mature form of international organization on a regional level. From this point of view, the Arctic region fulfills the condition of an anarchic structure, as it is composed of more than five units, which are subdivided into sub-units within each country's sovereign territory. Thus, according to the RSCT, only water and ice extend beyond the northern territories of coastal states and the Arctic Ocean might be categorized as an unstructured region.

Polarity

Third, polarity covers the distribution of power among the units. The RSCT differentiates between three types of complexes: unipolar/hegemonic, bipolar, and multipolar. Unipolarity in this case originates from the superiority of one regional actor, not the intervention of a global power or superpower. Moreover, Buzan and Wæver (2003) argued that the presence of a global power in the specific RSC suggested stronger interregional ties between individual RSCs and neighboring RSCs. Despite the fact that the United States is the only current global superpower, it does not hold a superpower position in the Arctic because its presence in the region is geographically conditioned and thus modified. Therefore, the Artic RSC could not be described as unipolar.

Moreover, given that the majority of security relations in the Arctic region relate primarily to the area of the Arctic Ocean (demarcation of the continental shelf, maritime limitations, exploration and exploitation of natural resources, and usage of new shipping routes), the United States might in some respect even be considered a weaker player. One of the reasons for this might be the non-ratification of the United Nations Convention on the Law of the Sea (UNCLOS 1982) by the United States, which precludes the country from formally raising any claim regarding the continental shelf, unlike other Arctic states. This limitation puts the United States in a weaker bargaining position in the debate about the future of the Arctic. Although the Arctic RSC is composed of two nuclear powers (the United States and Russia), they both play the role of regional powers. Neither of them dominates Arctic regional security relations to the extent that it could be described as a bipolar RSC. Thus, the Arctic RSC is best described as a multipolar complex.

Social construction

Finally, the last variable includes patterns of amity and enmity among the units. Relations between the countries within the complex range of a scale that spans from real rapprochement, expectations of protection, or support on the one hand, to openly hostile relations motivated by suspicion and fear on the other hand. There can be two distinct opposite extremes of relations, ranging from total chaos where all units are enemies, to mutual trust and a generally accepted commitment to solve any conflicts peacefully. In addition, between these two poles is a relatively wide space of indifference or neutrality (Buzan and Wæver, 2003).

The Arctic is generally considered a peaceful region with pragmatic/cooperative relations among actors. However, with the increasing geopolitical importance of the region, interactions among actors are on the rise and thus the current status quo might be threatened. The character of mutual relations among the Arctic states is to some extent related to their individual foreign policy traditions and orientations. Mutually friendly relations among Arctic states (conditioned historically and culturally) can be observed, as well as antagonisms and unresolved disputes in the Arctic Ocean, such as the status of the Lomonosov Ridge in the central Arctic Ocean.

Criticisms

The RSCT has faced criticisms, largely from Christopher Freeman (2001), Matt McDonald (2008), and Thierry Balzacq (2005, 2008, 2010, 2011), among others. The three major shortcomings of the theory are as follows. First, the outdated argument that "states fear their neighbors more than distant powers" was criticized mainly by Freeman (2001), who argued that the argument does not reflect the contemporary world and current global threats such as international terrorism and cyber threats arising from globalization, economic interdependence, and the new world order, where distance between states does not play any role.

Second, the exclusiveness of membership in RSCs appears to be problematic. For example, in the case of the Arctic, the region crosses three different RSCs: "European" (arranged around the European Union), "post-Soviet/Russian" (centered on the Russian Federation), and "North American" (centered on the United States and Canada). Thus, the Arctic could not be identified as a distinct RSC if the classical RSCT, which excluded plurality of memberships, were strictly applied.

Finally, the RSC's state-centric orientation is strictly limited to national borders. Again, in the case of the Arctic, the RSC is not formed by five states' entire territories, but the sovereign states constitute the basic units of this complex as they represent portions of the Arctic territories. Therefore, in order to classify the Arctic as a regional security complex, the three above-mentioned points of criticism would need to be taken into consideration (Padrtova, 2017).

Nontraditional approach: "deepeners"

One of the first advocates for a deepened conception of security was Ken Booth (1997), who argued that war is actually a cultural phenomenon, which implies that it has a potential for change. Booth combined the concepts of emancipation and (in)security while locating them at the individual level (Tarry, 1999). This approach was largely criticized by Ayoob, who argued against Booth's assumption that emancipation decreases insecurity of individuals and groups. Ayoob discussed the example of how the emancipation of Kurds from Northern Iraq may increase rather than decrease their insecurity (Ayoob, 1997).

Another group within the "deepeners" strongly promotes the role and rights of women in international systems and argues that the narrow concept of security with the preeminence of state sovereignty is a primary source of insecurity for women, because it limits and then decreases the security of women (Tarry, 1999). Spike Peterson (1992), one of the main proponents of this perspective, advocated a move toward the perception of security in global terms. In contrast to the other perspectives reviewed earlier, for the "deepeners," feminism is not simply a theoretical discourse, but something that is manifested in practice. In the Arctic, particularly in rural areas, the feminist approach is even more important given that the society is governed with a bias towards White men holding leadership positions (local governments, communities, and industry). Therefore, women are in a more vulnerable position.

Perceptions of Arctic security from a historical perspective

During the era of bipolar world politics, international relations were managed on the global level and the rivalry between two world powers blocked development of regional security dynamics. In this period, the Arctic was at the center of a conflict between two hostile superpowers – the United States and the USSR. Starting in the 1950s, the Arctic region became increasingly militarized and played a crucial role as a geostrategic and geopolitical playground. The main factors behind the strategic importance of the Arctic were geography and technology. The shortest distance for nuclear bombers and missiles between the heartlands of the United States and the Soviet Union was over the North Pole. The Arctic Ocean served as both a hiding place for their own missile submarines and a hunting ground to seek out and destroy enemy missile submarines.

As the Cold War heated up, the United States, facing potential nuclear attacks, relied heavily on a previously established airspace monitoring system. The North American Aerospace Defence Command (NORAD) was established in 1957[1]. However, Washington pushed for stronger defense cooperation with Canada. The United States and Canada agreed to establish a series of radar stations, known as the Distant Early Warning Line (DEW Line), across the Canadian Arctic. The purpose of the DEW Line was to monitor the Arctic airspace, and to deter and provide advance notice of potential attacks. Additionally, bomber and fighter bases were built from Greenland to Alaska. The United States built an air force base in Keflavik in exchange for protection and considerable economic benefits provided to Iceland (Tamnes and Holtsmark, 2014).

Following the end of the Cold War, international security began to take on a more regionalized character. The regional relationships transformed from confrontation to cooperation. Sources of challenges and security threats, resulting mostly from globalization and climate change, transformed from purely military to nonmilitary issues, such as economic or environmental concerns. At the same time, military investment and activity in the Arctic declined, although there were large regional variations.

In many places, the ties between civil society and military were very close, while in other places – especially in the Russian Arctic – militarized areas were kept isolated and local people were banned from using former military infrastructure, including roads. The Arctic played a central role in Soviet identity and economic development. On the naval-strategic level, the most important objectives for Moscow were the maintenance of the credibility of its nuclear deterrence and securing open access for its strategic submarines to the world's seas. In case of war, the Soviet Navy's strategic objective would be to cut the connection between Europe and North America (Padrtova, 2014).

With a significant militarization of the Russian Arctic, projects for exploration and exploitation of rich mineral deposits were accelerated. The Kola Peninsula became one of the most heavily militarized areas in the world. In the 1990s, the small city of Murmansk transformed into by far the largest city north of the Arctic Circle, with a population of almost 470,000 people. The military build-up of the Arctic was a major source of wealth and employment. However, to a large extent it ignored the rights of Indigenous populations, leading to a loss of their territories (Tamnes and Holtsmark, 2014).

The first cooperation initiatives – both among states in the region and between the states and nonstate actors – focused mainly on environmental protection, particularly for nuclear safety, in order to eliminate a potential environmental catastrophe. In 1996, technological cooperation on nuclear safety was institutionalized between Norway, Russia and the United States through the Arctic Military Environmental Cooperation (AMEC)[2] (Heininen, 2016). In 2002, the Arctic Monitoring and Assessment Program (AMAP) report was published. The report warned the states about the potential disastrous consequences of radioactivity on the Arctic's fragile ecosystem, and urged Arctic states to speed up cooperation for the safe disposal of the nuclear waste from installations throughout the Arctic (Heininen, 2016).

Besides the above-mentioned nuclear safety, environmental cooperation for prevention and mitigation of pollution is a high priority for Arctic stakeholders. In addition to oil spills, carbon dioxide, and greenhouse effects, toxic threats to human health and the environment come from another group of serious pollutants: persistent organic pollutants (POPs) and mercury pollutants. Even though these pollutants do not originate in the Arctic, their accumulation in dangerous quantities threatens the regional food chain. In particular, these pollutants pose a serious threat to the well-being of all northern people, especially the Indigenous populations who are dependent on food caught in the wild (Huebert, 2014).

Arctic security today: between theory and practice

For the last two decades, the Arctic has been a peaceful region with low tension and low potential for conflict. Despite some remaining unresolved boundary disputes, the Arctic states have taken a pragmatic approach. The cooperative environment reflects the number of interests shared by the different states and how much they have in common (Offerdal, 2014). The prevailing liberal approach considers cooperation to be a core prerequisite for regional stability and security in the Arctic. Liberals envisage cooperative and pluralistic politics emerging in the Arctic, with international law regulating any potential disputes that do occur (Hough, 2013).

Since pollution does not respect borders, both regional and global impacts of pollution can only be dealt with when all stakeholders in the region cooperate. Security in the Arctic can be understood through three analytical levels: local, regional and global (Figure 3.2). Local-level cooperation includes security threats that are directly connected to the life of people living in the Arctic. Areas of cooperation between communities and Indigenous populations include mitigating threats to food security, environmental security, and information security. In this case, security stems from the individual/society, a so-called bottom-up approach.

On the regional level, cooperation is fostered by the state and intends to intensify positive relations between the states in the Arctic region. The character of the threats is too massive to be dealt with by a single state, and they all have important shared interests. Therefore, all coastal states cooperate in order to address environmental and societal security challenges, such as oil spills, sabotage, smuggling, illegal fishing, illegal migration, and cruise ship accidents (Tamnes and Offerdal, 2014).

On the global scale, security challenges influence states in and outside the region. For example, the impact of climate change and global warming does not remain in the Arctic; it has become a global problem. Cooperation is required between Arctic states and non-Arctic states

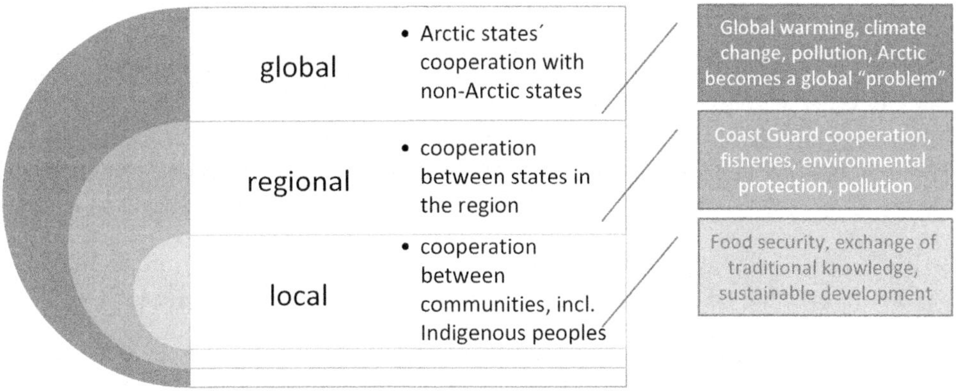

Figure 3.2 Understanding of security on three levels

in order to address these global challenges. Moreover, at this level, international institutions and nonstate actors like NGOs, business corporations, and the media play a crucial role.

Since the start of the post-Cold War era, all Arctic states have respected international law and the sovereignty of other states in the region. Most importantly, they are committed to respect the law of the sea – UNCLOS – as embedded in the 2008 Illulisat Declaration and followed by all Arctic Council members and observers. The UNCLOS provides a basis for the handling of a large bundle of issues involving territorial jurisdiction, resource extraction, navigation, and environment protection. The Convention established the Exclusive Economic Zone (EEZ), which defines coastal states' sovereign rights over natural resources in the 200 nautical miles (375 nautical kilometers) zone, calculated from the baselines, and including territorial waters. Coastal states also have obligations to manage resources sustainably and to cooperate with other countries to this end (Holtsmark and Smith-Windsor, 2009).

One successful example of cooperative relations is the existence of regional organizations with membership of almost all Arctic states. The first Arctic organization created for the purpose of strengthening cooperation in the field of "soft security" among regional actors was the Barents Euro-Arctic Council (BEAC) in 1993. However, the United States and Canada were not members of this platform. Thus, in 1996 all eight Arctic states signed the Ottawa Declaration as a founding document of the Arctic Council (AC). Currently, neither the BEAC nor the AC, the two major high-level intergovernmental regional institutions, officially handles military and security policy issues (Heininen, 2016).

The Arctic Council provides a means for promoting cooperation, coordination and interaction among the Arctic states, with the involvement of the Arctic Indigenous communities and other Arctic inhabitants, on common Arctic issues, and in particular, issues of sustainable development and environmental protection in the Arctic. The AC is the most important circumpolar cooperation forum, consisting of the eight Arctic nations. As a high-level forum, it relies on building consensual knowledge and understanding (Holtsmark and Smith-Windsor, 2009). A special feature of the cooperation is the role given to six groups of Indigenous peoples that participate in decision-making processes along with the eight states as Permanent Participants. However, in comparison to member states they have a limited status. Additionally, the AC is a platform where non-Arctic states are invited to participate as Observer States. There are 12 non-Arctic countries that have been approved as Observers to the AC.

Current challenges and risks

One of the most important geopolitical issues in the Arctic is the existence of long-standing and still unresolved sovereignty questions such as maritime limitations, questions of the delimitation of EEZs, and limits of continental shelves. Moreover, there are different interpretations of the conditions for passage of ships in some Arctic waters. Most of the security challenges in the Arctic are cross-sectorial and require close cooperation between civilian and military authorities. The seabed of the Arctic Ocean lies outside the jurisdiction of the coastal states. Neither the sea areas nor the seabed, which lie outside the exclusive jurisdiction of the coastal states, can be regulated by individual coastal states. The International Seabed Authority is responsible for the regulation of extraction activities from the Arctic seabed (a future possibility in the case of the Arctic).

The Arctic region faces many unresolved challenges. There are two developments in particular that are often presented as potential drivers for future conflict in the Arctic. The first includes climate change and its implications for (1) increased offshore oil and gas exploration, and (2) opening of new Arctic Sea Lines of Communication (SLOCs) and trans-Arctic shipping, which will pose (3) serious environmental risks and (4) will have an effect on natural resources, especially Arctic fisheries. The second development includes (5) the resolution of bilateral issues between countries in the region regarding boundaries between their marine areas and (6) the response of Arctic countries to the national interests of a plethora of non-Arctic actors.

The Arctic has often been presented as the new frontier of global oil and gas production, the "next Gulf," with incredible amounts of hydrocarbon resources. Many of the political disputes concerning the Arctic are motivated by these resource-exploitation expectations (Mitrova, 2014). However, these predictions of increased interest in natural gas and oil extraction from the Arctic will depend greatly on factors such as oil price, political framework conditions, technological developments, global demand, and developments in other energy regions. Although climate change could alter the equilibrium over the coming years in the race for exploitation of more readily accessible natural resources, for now the disputes have been dealt with peacefully.

Recently, the Arctic has been at the center of several security-related political and academic discussions regarding its uniqueness with respect to the absence of military conflict. Arctic relations to date have been mostly diplomatic and respectful of international law. Since four of five Arctic 5 states are NATO members, the potential for the destabilization of the region is mainly associated with Russia and its engagement in the region. Russian policy is likely to focus on international stability and on the development of regional relations as long as they support Russian interests. However, Russian diplomatic and military actions (including Russian military intervention in Georgia in 2008 and the ensuing occupation of two-thirds of its territory – Abkhazia and South Ossetia – as well as Russia's engagement in the Ukrainian crisis and its military intervention and illegal annexation of Crimea in 2014) decreased her trustworthiness, stepping up conflict dynamics and potentially undermining Russia's own key economic interest in maintaining regional stability (Kristensen and Sakstrup, 2016).

On the one hand, it is in the interests of all Arctic states not to allow their disagreements over Ukraine and conflicts elsewhere around the globe to spread to the region. On the other hand, the behavior of the actors in the international security environment in one region cannot be decoupled from the other regions. As a result of aggressive Russian foreign policy and an isolationist government in the United States, current relations between the

United States and NATO, and the United States and Russia have deteriorated to their lowest level since the end of the Cold War. Even though there are different perceptions of the Kremlin's foreign policy by the individual Alliance members, there is a general condemnation of Russian military activities in Ukraine (Warsaw Summit Communiqué, 2016; Wales Summit Declaration, 2014). Thus, there are risks associated with the future development of Russia's policy in the Arctic (Kristensen and Sakstrup, 2016).

In contrast to other areas in Ukraine or Georgia, the Arctic is the only strategically important region where Russia has not thus far violated the internationally recognized borders and status quo. For the time being, Moscow respects international law in the Arctic. All its claims (including teh Arctic Ocean seabed and an area under the North Pole) have been addressed by means of international law when presented to the United Nations. It is not in Russia's interests to have any kind of military conflict in the Arctic. However, the question is whether the Kremlin will also respect the boundaries set by international law once the status quo is seen as unsuitable by the Russian side.

As a consequence of the current security changes in Europe, keeping the Arctic region as a zone of peace and cooperation has been a great challenge. Since 2013, Russia has been restoring its old Soviet military airfields and ports in the Russian Arctic. This was followed by numerous military exercises, increased in number and scale, such as frequent maneuvers of bombers or fighter aircraft in the proximity or edge of Arctic states' airspace, modernization of military equipment, and the deployment of two brigades with special training for operations in the Arctic environment. This very significant increase in the military deployment of Russian forces, combined with Russia's controversial statements, nontransparent sources of capabilities, and military plans, raises security concerns in other states in the region. These developments inevitably led to the improvement of US-Canadian capabilities (NORAD) as well as those of Norway and Denmark. In turn, this leads to increasing Russian perceptions of insecurity and creates an unavoidable classical security dilemma while intensifying the securitization of the whole region (Hoogensen Gjørv et al., 2014; Padrtova, 2014). Even though the level of military tension in the region is higher at the time of this writing, it is still much lower than it used to be, and lower still than in other parts of the world.

Concluding remarks

The traditional theoretical approaches share an understanding of security that rests largely with the state. This understanding of security is too narrow and incapable of reflecting the current security challenges and threats in the Arctic region. As discussed in this chapter, focusing solely on military security in the Arctic is outdated. During the last 20 years, a need to broaden the concept of security to other sectors naturally emerged and developed. Nontraditional approaches incorporate other sources of threat and attempt to address newly emerged challenges in four sectors: political, economic, societal, and environmental. Non-traditionalists also find support for their understanding of security in reality, as the most important international platform for regional cooperation – the Arctic Council – does not include military issues in its agenda.

The Arctic is a significant security region with the longest direct border between NATO and Russia. At the same time, the relationships between states in the region are dominated by dialogue and cooperation. Despite some occasional bellicose rhetoric, major actors in the region have more shared than conflicting interests. One of the reasons why the Arctic is a region of high stability and peaceful relationships could be the above-mentioned Arctic

Council's intentional omission of controversial military matters. This enables states to focus on other areas, particularly soft security challenges – e.g., human and societal security, environmental issues – that concern them all and must be dealt with by cooperation. Furthermore, Arctic states recognize the important role of international institutions, nongovernmental organizations and forums that further enhance regional stability and security. The Arctic's exceptionally peaceful character of interstate relations is also demonstrated by the tendency of states to find pragmatic solutions and solve potential conflicts within the limits of international law, despite disagreements and unresolved territorial disputes.

The future security of the Arctic is inseparably connected to the response of Arctic states to new challenges. These include conflicts outside the region, as well as increased interest in the Arctic manifested by countries that are geographically not directly linked to the region, such as China, India, Japan, or Singapore. Although behavior of actors in the international security environment in one region cannot be separated from their actions in other regions, Arctic states should be able to prevent their disagreements on Ukraine and conflicts elsewhere from spreading to their region. As the geopolitical importance of the Arctic is likely to increase in the future, strong cooperation will be a fundamental prerequisite for long-term peaceful developments.

Notes

1 In May 2006, this agreement was expanded to incorporate maritime warning mission, reflecting the US emphasis on maritime security (Lackenbauer, P.W., 2011. Polar Race or Polar Saga? in: Kraska, J. (Ed.), *Arctic Security in an Age of Climate Change*. Cambridge University Press).

2 The same year, the Arctic Council was established.

References

Ayoob, M., 1997. Defining Security: A Subaltern Realist Perspective, in: Krause, K. and Williams, M.C. (Eds.), *Critical Security Studies*, 121–146. Minneapolis, MN: University of Minnesota Press.

Bailes, J.K.A., 2015. Wider Security Angles, in: Jokela, J. (Ed.), *Arctic Security Matters*, 69–74. European Union Institute for Strategic Studies (EUISS), Paris, Report No. 24.

Balzacq, T., 2005. The Three Faces of Securitization: Political Agenda, Audience and Context. *European Journal of International Relations*. SAGE Publications and ECPR- European Consortium for Political Research, Vol. 11 (2), pp. 171–201.

Balzacq, T., 2008. The Policy Tools of Securitization: Information Exchange, EU Foreign and Interior Policies. *JCMS*, Vol. 46 (1), pp. 75–100.

Balzacq, T. (Ed.), 2010. *Securitization Theory: How Security Problems Emerge and Dissolve*. London: Routledge.

Balzacq, T., 2011. A Theory of Securitization: Origins, Core Assumptions, and Variants, in: Balzacq, T. (Ed.), *Securitization Theory: How Security Problems Emerge and Dissolve*, 1–30. London: Routledge.

Booth, K., 1997. Security and Self: Reflections of a Fallen Realist, in: Krause, K. and Williams, M.C. (Eds.), *Critical Security Studies*, 83–120. Minneapolis, MN: University of Minnesota Press.

Buzan, B. and Wæver, O., 2003. *Regions and Powers: The Structure of International Security*. Cambridge: Cambridge University Press.

Buzan, B., Wæver, O., and de Wilde, J., 1995. Environmental, Economic and Societal Security. Paper for pan-European Conference in Paris 13–16 September 1995. Copenhagen: Centre for Peace and Conflict Research.

Buzan, B., Wæver, O., and de Wilde, J., 1998. *Security: A New Framework for Analysis*. London: Boulder Lynne Rienner Publishers.

Does, A., 2013. Securitization Theory According to the Copenhagen School, in: Does, A. (Ed.), *The Construction of the Maras: Between Politicization and Securitization*. eCahiers de l'Institut. Graduate Institute Publications. Available from http://books.openedition.org/iheid/719

Emmers, R., 2013. Securitization, in: Collins, A. (Ed.), *Contemporary Security Studies*, 168–182. Oxford: Oxford University Press.

Freeman, C., 2001. The European Security Complex – Fait Accompli? A Critique of the Copenhagen School. *Peacekeeping and International Relations*, Vol. 30 (5/6).

Gibbs, D.R., 2011. MacKinder Meets Buzan: A Geopolitical Extension to Security: Complex Theory with an Emphasis on the Polar Regions (Unpublished doctoral thesis). The University of Waikato, New Zealand. Available from http://researchcommons.waikato.ac.nz/handle/10289/5966

Heininen, L., 2016. Security of the Global Arctic in Transformation – Potential for Changes in Problem Definition, in: Heininen, L. (Ed.), *Future Security of the Global Arctic: State Policy, Economic Security and Climate*, 12–34. Basingstoke: Palgrave Macmillan.

Holtsmark, S.G. and Smith-Windsor, B.A., 2009. Security Prospects in the High North: Geostrategic Thaw or Freeze? Forum Paper 7, NATO Defense College – Research Division. Available from www.files.ethz.ch/isn/102391/fp_07.pdf

Hoogensen Gjørv, G., 2017. Tensions between Environmental, Economic, and Energy Security in the Arctic, in: Fondahl, G. and Wilson, G. (Eds.), *Northern Sustainabilities: Understanding and Addressing Change in a Circumpolar World*. Cham: Springer International Publishing.

Hoogensen Gjørv, G., Bazely, D., Goloviznina, M., and Tanentzap, A. (Eds.), 2014. *Environmental and Human Security in the Arctic*. Earthscan Research Editions. London: Routledge.

Hough, P., 2013. *International Politics of the Arctic. Coming in from the Cold*. London: Routledge.

Huebert, R., 2011. Canada and the Newly Emerging International Arctic Security Regime, in: Kraska, J. (Ed.), *Arctic Security in an Age of Climate Change*, 193–217. Cambridge: Cambridge University Press. doi:10.1017/CBO9780511994784.013

Klare, M.T. and Daniel, C.T. (Eds.), 1994. *World Security: Challenges for a New Century*. New York: St. Martin's Press.

Kristensen, K. S., Sakstrup, C., 2016. *Russian Policy in the Arctic after the Ukraine Crisis*. Center for Militære Studier, Københavns Universitet. 68 pp. https://cms.polsci.ku.dk/english/publications/russian-policy-in-the-arctic/Russian_Policy_in_the_Arctic_after_the_Ukraine_Crisis.pdf

McDonald, M., 2008. Securitization and the Construction of Security. *European Journal of International Relations*, Vol. 14 (4), pp. 563–587. Available from http://wrap.warwick.ac.uk/1232/1/WRAP_McDonald_0671572-pais-270709-mcdonald_securitisation_and_construction_of_security_ejir_forthcoming_2008.pdf

Mitrova, T., 2014. Commentary: Global Role of Arctic Oil And Gas, in: Young, O.R., Kim, J.D., and Kim, Y.H. (Eds.), *North Pacific Arctic Conference Proceedings*. Korea: Maritime Institute and East-West Center.

NATO, 2014. Wales Summit Declaration. 5 September 2014. Available from www.nato.int/cps/en/natohq/official_texts_112964.htm

NATO, 2016. Warsaw Summit Communiqué. 9 July 2016. Available from www.nato.int/cps/en/natohq/official_texts_133169.htm

Offerdal, K., 2014. Interstate Relations, in: Tamnes, R. and Offerdal, K. (Eds.), *Geopolitics and Security in the Arctic. Regional Dynamics in a Global World*. London: Routledge.

Padrtova, B., 2014. Russian Military Build-up in the Arctic: Strategic Shift in the Balance of Power or Bellicose Rhetoric Only? in: Heininen, L. (Ed.), *Arctic Yearbook 2014*, 415–433. Available from www.arcticyearbook.com

Padrtova, B., 2017. Securitization of the Arctic: The US Securitizing Actors and Their Strategies. PhD Dissertation. Department of International Relations and European Studies, Masaryk University, Czech Republic.

Padrtová, B., 2019. Frozen Narratives: How Media Present Security in the Arctic. *Polar Science*. doi:10.1016/j.polar.2019.05.006 (Elsevier, 2019. ISSN 1873-9652).

Peterson, V.S. (Ed.), 1992. *Feminist (Re)Visions of International Relations Theory*. Boulder, CO: Lynne Rienner.

Rothschild, E., 1995. What is security? *Daedalus*, Vol. 124 (3), pp. 53–98.

Tamnes, R., and Offerdal, K. (Eds.). (2014). *Geopolitics and Security in the Arctic: Regional Dynamics in a Global World*. London and New York: Routledge.

Tamnes, R. and Holtsmark, S.G., 2014. The geopolitics of the Arctic in historical perspective, in: Tamnes, R. and Offerdal, K. (Eds.), *Geopolitics and Security in the Arctic. Regional Dynamics in a Global World*, 12–48. London: Routledge.

Tarry, S., 1999. 'Deepening' and 'Widening': An Analysis of Security Definitions in the 1990s. *Journal of Military and Strategic Studies*, Vol. 2 (1), Fall/Winter.

Wæver, O., 1995. Securitization and Desecuritization, in: Lipschutz, R. (Ed.), *On Security*, 46–86. New York: Columbia University Press.

Walt, S.M., 1991. The Renaissance of Security Studies. *International Studies Quarterly*, Vol. 35 (2) (Jun., 1991), pp. 211–239. Blackwell Publishing on behalf of The International Studies Association.

Waltz, K.N., 1979. *Theory of International Politics*. Addison-Wesley series in political science. Clinical Practice Series. Boston, MA: Addison-Wesley Pub. Co. Michigan University.

4

ASSESSING SECURITY GOVERNANCE IN THE ARCTIC

Andrew Chater, Wilfrid Greaves, and Leah Sarson

Introduction

The circumpolar Arctic remains a region undergoing an extended period of interrelated political, economic, social, and ecological changes that are equal to or greater than any other region of the world. Such sweeping changes inevitably implicate a range of questions pertaining to issues of security. Given such changes, what does security mean? How has it changed, and what are the effects of economic and cultural modernization, globalization, and global warming? The circumpolar Arctic constitutes a regional security complex, in that it comprises "a group of states or other entities [that] possess a degree of security interdependence sufficient both to establish them as a linked set and to differentiate them from surrounding security regions" (Buzan and Wæver 2003: 47–8). Given the ecological holism and environmental interdependence that characterize the circumpolar region, and the specific significance of the natural environment for conditions of security and well-being ranging from the local to the regional scales, the post-Cold War Arctic has been characterized as a regional environmental security complex in which ecological factors constitute security issues in their own right (Greaves 2016a; Hoogensensen Gjørv et al. 2014), and mediate the emergence and severity of other security issues, including those in the military and political sectors (Chater and Greaves 2014; Exner-Pirot 2013).

Many observers frame issues of Arctic security in bleak, even dire, terms. In light of the many challenges confronting the region, some pessimism is warranted. A plethora of issues within and beyond the region pose severe challenges to people, states, and governance institutions, requiring transnational, international, or even global cooperation to effectively resolve them. Most notably, climate change threatens to fundamentally change the basic character of the region and endangers existing ways and systems of life for its inhabitants. Warming temperatures mean reduced sea ice, which significantly affects both people and marine animals, while enabling increased maritime traffic through the region as a result of both global shipping and an increase in "destination" tourism. More ships mean an increased risk of nautical accidents in challenging, isolated, and often poorly charted Arctic waters.

While extractive industries such as mining generate employment and promote the development of much-needed regional infrastructure, they also create significant local environmental damage as well as unintended social consequences with significant adverse effects for local communities. Taken together, these many changes threaten the traditional ways of life and modern livelihoods of the Arctic's Indigenous peoples. Meanwhile, unresolved maritime boundary disputes, the as-yet-incomplete process of determining the extent of Arctic states' extended continental shelves under the United Nations *Convention on the Law of the Sea*, and the deteriorated relations between Russia and the Western Arctic states, particularly those that are members of the North Atlantic Treaty Organization (NATO), have generated high political tensions that have persisted for over a decade and increased significantly since 2014. Thus, human security for residents of the Arctic is tenuous, with concerns over potential military conflict existing alongside more quotidian issues such as insecure or prohibitively expensive access to food, difficulties providing education, limited or inadequate health care services and employment opportunities, substandard and overcrowded housing, and many other local concerns.

On the other hand, as most Arctic experts are quick to observe, the region possesses a complex web of governance institutions that provide fora for problem-solving and cooperation, such as the Arctic Council, the Barents Euro-Arctic Council, and the Northern Forum. Strong state and sub-state governments exist alongside longstanding international regimes and organizations to create a region where the rule of domestic and international law is strong and respected. The active interest of many nongovernmental organizations, such as Greenpeace and the Worldwide Fund for Nature, help ensure a strong degree of outside interest in developments within the Arctic and provide further resources for activities such as environmental conservation and education. In all these ways, the Arctic is neither lawless nor a wilderness, but it is a system where changes that affect conditions of security are managed through a multilayered network of regional governance.

In this chapter, we frame the relationship between security and governance in the Arctic around two questions and sections: How are security issues in the Arctic governed? And how do regional governance institutions contribute to security within the Arctic region? In the first section, we outline the traditional institutions of Arctic security governance, highlighting the key features of post-Cold War Arctic politics that have dynamically altered the region over the last 25 years. In the second section, we examine alternative/unconventional security institutions related to the emergence of nonmilitary types of security challenges and non-state forms of regional governance, outlining in particular the role of Indigenous autonomous governance arrangements and paradiplomacy. In the final section, we reiterate Chater and Greaves' argument (2014) that the Arctic suffers from three distinct pathologies of security governance that serve to undermine the efficacy of regional institutions and contribute negatively to conditions of security in the region.

Traditional governance institutions in the Arctic

Historically, the Arctic has had a weak network of institutions and an underdeveloped framework for regional governance. During the twentieth century, Arctic states disagreed over a variety of issues, including the legal status of Arctic waters, the appropriate legal regime for the Arctic region, and even the validity of international law. The Cold War generally stifled cooperative governance of the entire Arctic region, even on seemingly nonstrategic issues such as environmental protection. In the absence of strong institutions, circumpolar cooperation was pursued on an ad hoc basis, primarily between the Western capitalist democratic neighbors in the Arctic. International law and regulations governing the Arctic were often by-products of other legal or political regimes, or resulted from the unilateral actions of Arctic states. Only since the early 1990s, with the end of the Cold War, have pan-regional institutions begun to develop, and new governance structures emerged to provide opportunities for political agency to state and non-state actors from across and beyond the circumpolar region.

The most important governance institution for the Arctic region is the Arctic Council, a regional body that grew out of the Arctic Environmental Protection Strategy (AEPS), which was tasked with facilitating environmental research in the wake of the thawing of relations between the West and the Soviet Union as the Iron Curtain began to fall. The AEPS consisted of four working groups: the Arctic Monitoring and Assessment Programme (AMAP), the Conservation of Arctic Flora and Fauna group (CAFF), the Protection of the Arctic Marine Environment (PAME), and the Emergency Prevention, Preparedness and Response group (EPPR). To these, the Council added the Sustainable Development Working Group (SDWG) and later the Arctic Contaminants Action Program (ACAP). Its members are Canada, Denmark (Faroe Islands/Greenland), Finland, Iceland, Norway, Russia, Sweden, and the United States, as well as six Permanent Participants representing Indigenous peoples. The Council is the only international institution that consists of all of the Arctic states and specifically promotes cooperation in the Arctic region.

There is no treaty that establishes the role of the Council; instead, the 1996 *Ottawa Declaration* established that the Council

> provide a means for promoting cooperation, coordination and interaction among the Arctic States, with the involvement of the Arctic indigenous communities and other Arctic inhabitants on common Arctic issues, in particular issues of sustainable development and environmental protection in the Arctic.
>
> *(Arctic Council 1996)*

It is a forum that facilitates cooperation to create environmental research and technical projects. A footnote in the *Ottawa Declaration* specified, "The Arctic Council should not deal with matters related to military security." The institution has grown more robust in recent years, adding a permanent secretariat in Tromsø in 2011. It is also the major forum for all interested Arctic actors to meet and converse; currently, the Council incorporates 39 Observers, including non-Arctic states such as Britain, China, France, Germany, Japan, and South Korea.

A second regional organization is the Barents Euro-Arctic Council, formed in 1993 by Denmark, Finland, Iceland, Norway, Russia, and Sweden. It also allows an observer role for other states, including the rest of the Arctic states (Canada and the United States) as well as sub-state regions within member states (which form the Barents Regional Council). It includes a sister organization for individual sub-state regions that includes 14 from Finland, Norway, Russia, and Sweden (Barents Regional Council 2018). The goal of the Barents Euro-Arctic Council is to facilitate cooperation regarding sustainable development specifically within the Barents region (Barents Council 2018), such as its 2009 joint search and rescue strategy for the Barents Sea (Plouffe 2017). The Barents Euro-Arctic Council plays a similar role in governance as the Arctic Council by focusing on the environment, and to a lesser extent economic development, but it confines its activities to the Barents Sea and those states that possess territory in this region.

A less formal, weaker institution of environmental governance is the Arctic Science Ministerial meeting, a biannual meeting initiated by the United States in 2016. Twenty-five governments took part, including all eight Arctic countries and non-Arctic countries such as China, Germany, India, Japan, and New Zealand, as well as Indigenous representatives. Science ministers, representatives, or equivalents met to share and coordinate activities in

Arctic science. The United States held the event as part of its Arctic Council chair, but it was not an official Arctic Council event. It was successful enough that Germany – which was not selected as host – planned to independently host the second meeting in October 2018, which was held in Berlin and co-hosted by Finland.

Several regional organizations are implicated in Arctic security governance, including the Nordic Council, European Union, and NATO. The Nordic Council comprises Denmark, Iceland, Norway, Sweden, and Finland, as well as regions of the Nordic countries, including Åland, the Faroe Islands, and Greenland. Its main activities are information exchange and to serve as a venue for joint projects related to cultural promotion, sustainability, economic development, and social welfare. The Council contributes to Arctic governance by sending representatives to the Arctic Council, Baltic Sea Parliamentary Cooperation, and Standing Committee of Parliamentarians of the Arctic region. The European Union only includes the Arctic states of Denmark, Finland, and Sweden, but remains an important Arctic institution. The EU facilitates cooperation on a wide variety of issues, such as trade, commerce, currency, and military security. The Union's policy limits its goals to promoting cooperation on environmental protection and sustainable development (European Union 2016) and it has completed a variety of environmental assessments and technical projects related to the Arctic region. Finally, among NATO's 29 member states are the Arctic countries of Canada, Denmark, Iceland, Norway, and the United States. NATO's collective security obligations extend to Arctic security governance, which has recently produced tensions between NATO members and Russia.

Less institutionalized are two venues that appear to have stalled. In 2012 and 2013, Denmark and Greenland hosted meetings of Arctic defense chiefs focused on search and rescue that included all eight Arctic states, including non-NATO members Sweden and Russia (Ljunggren 2012). However, these meetings have not resumed following Russia's annexation of Crimea and the subsequent deterioration in relations between NATO allies and Moscow. Lastly, in 2008 and 2010, the five Arctic states that border the Arctic Ocean – Canada, Denmark, Norway, Russia, and the United States – participated in the Arctic Oceans Conference to discuss residual boundary disputes and the legal status of the ocean. It saw the release of the 2008 Ilulissat Declaration, which saw states pledge to resolve differences peacefully and multilaterally. The meetings attracted controversy for not including the other three Arctic countries or Indigenous peoples, notably from then-US Secretary of State Hillary Clinton (Blanchfield 2010).

States rely on international law to manage maritime issues in the Arctic and Arctic states have generally complied with existing international laws. The United Nations' Convention of the Law of the Sea (UNCLOS) dictates how states can control maritime territory. Although the Convention is voluntary, states comply with the Convention in the Arctic region, including the United States. Currently, states do not have any serious territorial disputes in the Arctic region. States have relied on the UN Commission on the Limits of the Continental Shelf to help settle the question of overlapping continental shelves, following the law closely and even collaborating to help each other make claims (Riddell-Dixon 2017).

There are also two sub-state regional organizations that contribute to security governance, broadly defined, within the Arctic. The Northern Forum came together in 1991, made up of 13 Arctic regional governments: Akureyri (Iceland), Alaska (United States), Chukotka (Russia), Gangwong (South Korea), Kamchatka Krai (Russia), Khanty-Mansi (Russia), Krasnoyarsk Krai (Russia), Lapland (Finland), Magadan Oblast (Russia,) Nenets (Russia), Primorsky Krai (Russia), Sakha Republic (Russia), and Yamalo-Nenets (Russia). It provides information sharing in the areas of environmental, sustainable development and culture for the

Arctic sub-state governments (Northern Forum 2018), such as zoos or water. The forum does not, however, represent all Arctic sub-state governments and it no longer lists members from Canada or Japan. Alaska's membership lapsed from 2011 until 2016 (Rosen 2016).

Meanwhile, the Conference of Parliamentarians of the Arctic Region, also referred to as the Standing Committee of the Parliamentarians of the Arctic Region, consists of all members of parliament or equivalent from the eight Arctic countries. It is a biannual meeting to discuss regional issues, which started in 1993. While it initially formed to encourage the creation of the Arctic Council, it evolved to become a forum for parliamentarians to discuss the Council's activities and is now focused on environmental and economic topics more generally (Conference of Parliamentarians of the Arctic Region 2018).

There are three main institutions that non-state actors can utilize to represent their views. First, many of these organizations participate in the Arctic Council as observers. Second, Iceland has held an international conference for international institutions, governments, researchers, and nongovernmental organizations since 2013, called the Arctic Circle Assembly. Third, the Arctic Economic Council (AEC) is a business organization founded in 2014. Each Arctic Council member state and Permanent Participant selects three representatives. It is an organization of economic representatives to advise the Arctic Council and states of the business perspectives of the Arctic region. The AEC has working groups on marine transportation, telecommunications, "responsible resource development" and "stewardship in the Arctic" (Arctic Economic Council 2015). It was an Arctic Council initiative, but it now exists as an independent institution. The AEC has a secretariat and headquarters in Tromsø, Norway, which is the same location as the Arctic Council. These organizations participate in activities typical of nongovernmental organizations, attempting to influence government by providing quality information that alerts states to interests and issues, as well as provide pressure by harnessing the power of their membership. Examples include the Association of World Reindeer Herders, Circumpolar Conservation Union, the International Union for the Conservation of Nature, or the World Wildlife Fund.

Representation for Indigenous peoples at the international level comes from the Arctic Council Permanent Participants. This group includes six organizations founded between 1956 and 2000. They are the Aleut International Association (AIA), the Arctic Athabaskan Council (AAC), the Gwich'in Council International (GCI), the Inuit Circumpolar Council (ICC), the Russian Association of Indigenous Peoples of the North (RAIPON), and the Sámi Council (SC). The Arctic Council is the only international institution that includes Indigenous representative organizations as members alongside states. They need not apply to attend Council meetings and states cannot block their participation if policymakers wish; the rules of procedure give Permanent Participants the right to attend Council meetings, participate fully in those meetings and sponsor projects (Arctic Council 2013, specifically sections 4, 12, 13, 19, 20, 21, 24, 26, 24–38, 44, and 46). Together, they represent the interests of every major Indigenous group in the Arctic region. However, they cannot vote on Council decisions. The following section discusses the relationship between sub-state and Indigenous governments, and how governance and security reaches far beyond mere political representation and poses various challenges to state-centric approaches and institutions.

Sub-state governance in the Arctic

The Arctic can be considered "a governance barometer in the sense that it is an area generating early indications of the growing need for innovation in governance systems" (Arctic Governance Project 2010). This is particularly true as the boundaries between the domestic and the international become increasingly blurred and sub-state governments become more involved in policymaking areas that were once considered the exclusive purview of the state, such as security. Moreover, policy areas that were once considered exclusively the domain of the domestic – such as fisheries, transportation, or health care – are now understood in a global context. The international engagement of sub-state actors is particularly important in the Arctic, where the priorities of Indigenous governments may not coincide with those of states, and there is often a sizable gulf between policymakers in the South and the peoples of the North. While the Northern Forum is dedicated to the international relations of the sub-state actors of the region, it is hampered by decreasing interest in the organization.

Exner-Pirot (2016) described the overlapping governance structures and institutions of the Arctic as a web, an image that aptly illustrates the messy, overlapping authorities engaged in international relations that are at the center of the paradiplomacy literature on the international activities of sub-state actors. The paradiplomacy literature draws on work that emphasizes shifting boundaries between inside and outside the state. Tavares, for instance, describes paradiplomacy as "Janus-faced – facing inward and outward at the same time" (2016: 41). Such conceptualizations of sub-state governments that operate neither inside nor outside the state are salient to security priorities and preferences described in this section. Not only do these governments engage in policy areas once considered the exclusive purview of states, they also pursue their objectives using unconventional diplomatic practices such as track-two diplomacy and science diplomacy. This section explores the ways in which sub-state or noncentral governments in the Arctic – such as Greenland, the Sápmi territory of the Sámi of Scandinavia, or Nunavut – affect security governance in the Arctic, demonstrating the ways in which sub-states, and particularly Indigenous governments, engage in policymaking that might not coincide with the preferences and interests of states. With a focus on border control, infrastructure, and socioeconomic policy, this section demonstrates how the noncentral governments of the Arctic are changing understandings of and policymaking related to security.

Borders

Borders – and the ability to control them – are among the most tangible elements of the state's security apparatus. Yet, borders are also among the most tangible signs of the tension between the state's inherent need to control its territory and the rights of Indigenous peoples and nations. The territories and relationships of Indigenous peoples often transcend imposed state borders. Typically, colonial borders were arbitrary imposed, often in ways that disrupted Indigenous nations and continue to prevent them from freely exercising their rights to lands, water, resources, services like education or health, and traditional trading relationships (Bennett et al. 2016). The nascent institutionalized global Indigenous rights regime has begun to recognize these obstacles to Indigenous peoples' use of their lands. Article 36 of the United Nations Declaration on the Rights of Indigenous Peoples (UNDRIP), for instance, states that

> Indigenous peoples, in particular those divided by international borders, have the right to maintain and develop contacts, relations and cooperation, including activities for spiritual, cultural, political, economic and social purposes, with their own members as well as other peoples across borders.

Although states that have acceded to the UNDRIP are obligated to support the implementation of this right, these provisions run-up against the state's security governance as it struggles to balance its domestic and international obligations to Indigenous peoples with the need to control its international affairs.

Along the Canada/US Arctic borders, for instance, the 1794 Jay Treaty between the British Crown and the United States affects many Indigenous communities' relations with the state and its borders. The Treaty states that Great Britain and the United States would allow Indigenous peoples to live on either side of the newly established border and to freely cross the border. Although Canada never signed the Treaty, Indigenous communities along the border regularly hold ceremonies to assert their sovereignty over their lands and the Treaty right to cross the border freely. The Gwich'in Tribal Council is one such government that regularly engages in diplomatic activities to ensure that its citizens can freely move through its territory despite what it deems an artificial border. In its recent submission to the Government of Canada's consultations for a new Arctic framework, the Council emphasized the "the implementation of the Jay Treaty to facilitate mobility amongst Gwich'in and Gwich'in communities" over all other priorities (2018a: 13). Gwich'in peoples continue to cross the border as part of overall political diplomacies (Fox 2017), leaving governments – particularly the Canadian government – struggling to control the flow of people, harvests, and other goods across borders.

In Scandinavia, the Sámi peoples have similarly engaged in diplomatic activities – both inadvertent and blatant – that serve to undermine state borders. State borders divided their traditional lands in the 1700s and they have been gradually pushed to the far north of Finland, Norway, and Sweden. Reindeer herding was and remains an important cultural activity, although declining numbers of people are living off the land in traditional ways. When the borders of these states were imposed and closed to Sámi reindeer herding, ways of life that had been in place for thousands of years were disrupted. In 2017, Finland, Norway, and Sweden signed the Nordic Sámi Convention after more than ten years of negotiation and many more of activism. The Convention is meant to provide a cooperative trilateral framework to protect Sámi rights, including the right to self-determination. It's also the first regional treaty concerning Indigenous peoples. However, the Convention is not yet law and Sámi peoples are still restricted in their traditional pursuits of hunting, fishing, and reindeer herding.

Infrastructure

In many ways, Indigenous governments drive infrastructure projects in the Arctic. These governments have long struggled to engender understanding from central governments about local needs and priorities and in many cases are looking to the private sector to commit the massive investment necessary for infrastructure development in the region. Inuit in Canada, for instance, have billions in trust funds as a result of land claim agreements with the federal government that are essentially Inuit sovereign wealth funds. These governments are partnering with foreign and domestic private firms to realize infrastructure development beyond central government leadership. These relationships between Indigenous governments and private firms can be understood as challenging the control of the central government in the areas of transportation, shipping, telecommunications, and other critical entities. No government is more implicated in these discussions than China, which claimed in its January 2018 White Paper that Indigenous peoples would benefit from Chinese engagement in the region. In Canada, the security questions emerging from issues about Chinese control of infrastructure projects in the north are less about Chinese incursions on Canadian sovereignty, and much more about the relationships between Beijing and Indigenous governments in Canada.

In May 2018, the Canadian government prevented a takeover of Canadian construction giant Aecon Group Inc. by China's CCCC International Holdings Inc. worth C$1.5 billion (US$1.12 billion) in the name of national security. Innovation Minister Navdeep Bains justified the decision, arguing,

> [...] we listened to the advice of our national security agencies throughout the multi-step national security review process under the Investment Canada Act. Based on their findings, in order to protect national security, we ordered CCCI not to implement the proposed investment.

Yet, Chinese interests are heavily involved in infrastructure projects in the far north, where climate, cost, and labor, among other challenges, make such large-scale projects prohibitively expensive for states even as the smaller governments of the north demand them. The growing literature on Chinese engagement in the Arctic highlights this tension between local and regional infrastructure demands and state-level security concerns, and while China is the main actor in this conversation, particularly in light of its desired "polar silk road," other states are also implicated.

While recent commentary such as that by Adam Lajeunesse argues that "Chinese money as part of this Polar Silk Road, if properly managed, can go to establishing the infrastructure that we have been trying as a nation to establish since John Diefenbaker in the 1960s" (Sevunts 2018), history suggests that there is reason to be concerned about the developing relationships between the Indigenous governments of the region and Beijing. In June 2016, the Canadian Broadcasting Corporation (CBC) reported that they had obtained, via an access to information request, an internal communication prepared by Canada's Ambassador to China, Guy Saint-Jacques, that was circulated in Global Affairs Canada and Natural Resources Canada in the autumn of 2015 (Beeby 2016). Saint-Jacques warned that some Chinese mining companies were complaining about difficulties they encounter when working in Canada, particularly in remote areas, with others noting that there is a "blanket unhappiness" coming from Chinese companies dealing with Canada. Former Canadian ambassador to China, David Mulroney, dismissed those concerns. He claimed that China does not need to be reminded that Canada's climate is harsh and suggested that "China would like to do in Canada what it does with investment projects in the developing world, namely to ship in its own workforce and run the project as a Chinese enclave" (ibid.).

Relationships between Indigenous governments and China have also sparked questions related to Canadian security. According to one United States' media report, Canadian Security Intelligence Service (CSIS) officials have also raised concerns about provincial politicians being subject to Chinese influence (MacDonald 2012). These concerns piggyback on several Canadian and Hong Kong media outlet reports in 2012 that stated that CSIS was investigating possible links between Indigenous peoples and China (Barrera 2014; Gerson 2012; MacDonald 2012). At the center of these stories was a lawyer who had worked with the Kaska Nation and claimed that he had been approached by CSIS agents in 2010 and 2011 (Gerson 2012). Additionally, in the spring of 2016, Canadian mining giant Teck Resources elected a sitting member of China's National People's Congress to its board of directors, a move that instigated debate over foreign influence in Canada's resource sector (Penner 2015).

These dynamics are playing out across the Arctic. Denmark, for instance, is increasingly concerned about the security and defense implications of Chinese investment in key infrastructure projects in Greenland. China Communications Construction Company was a finalist to invest in three airport projects on the island. For its part, Copenhagen has expressed concern about how such changes would impact the Denmark–United States security relationship, with one "high-ranking Danish official" stating, "We are deeply concerned. China has no business in Greenland" (Matzen and Daly 2018). In the same Reuters article, Greenlandic politician Aaja Chemnitz Larsen is quoted: "In Greenland we don't suffer from China anxiety, like they obviously do in the government in Copenhagen [...] They lack an understanding for Greenland's need for investments, and we can sense a big interest in China for our projects." While Greenland's self-rule agreement demarcates its jurisdiction over domestic issues and Denmark's control over issues of security and defense, these issues demonstrate how these sub-state governments continue to blur traditional boundaries around security.

Socioeconomic determinants

Militarized and state-based understandings of security in the Arctic neglect primary threats to the security of Arctic peoples at the socioeconomic level, which are generally confronted by sub-state levels of government, particularly in the context of community-based approaches. Across the Arctic, Northern, and particularly Indigenous peoples face dramatic disparities in socioeconomic and public health outcomes. Moreover, in some jurisdictions, Indigenous governments administer many policy sectors that other similarly sized governments do not, such as health, education, and housing. These issues demonstrate that security in the Arctic is broadly defined, an understanding that has been documented in the literature (Greaves 2016c; Huebert et al. 2012; Smith 2010). Indeed, the Inuit Circumpolar Council's *Circumpolar Inuit Declaration on Sovereignty in the Arctic* states, "The foundation, projection, and enjoyment of Arctic sovereignty and sovereign rights all require healthy and sustainable communities in the Arctic." Northern communities and governments, however, often lack the capacity to generate and implement policy responses to these issues. Such issues include lack of designated funding for such intergovernmental approaches, incongruent policy objectives and other political silos between governments, and ingrained colonial approaches from the central government.

Understanding the socioeconomic challenges as security issues is not new. The purpose in reviewing them is to reiterate the argument that security governance in the Arctic reaches far beyond states and state-centric approaches. Sub-state governments, especially Indigenous governments, will need to be at the center of meaningful regional solutions to security challenges. Movement towards such revised governance and jurisdictional approaches to overcoming public health challenges is exemplified by the Sámi Norwegian National Advisory Unit on Mental Health and Substance Use (SANKS) and the Sámi Council's 2017 *Plan for Suicide Prevention Among the Sámi People in Norway, Sweden, and Finland*. The plan highlighted self-determination beyond state-based boundaries as necessary for overcoming the health challenges of the Sámi people. The following section identifies three pathologies of security governance that dilute the utility of regional institutions and the engagement of Indigenous and other sub-state governments in the Arctic.

Pathologies of Arctic security governance

As Exner-Pirot (2013: 122) noted, the Arctic's distinctiveness as a security region is derived from its being centered around a (historically) frozen ocean; its political and institutional underdevelopment, particularly as related to fundamental issues of territorial boundaries, sovereign claims and economic activity; and the formalized incorporation of Indigenous peoples into its regional governance structures. Previously, Chater and Greaves (2014) argued that the contradictions that arise from these factors within a globalizing Arctic have produced three pathologies of Arctic security governance: regional (re)militarization in the absence of a specific military threat; hydrocarbon resource exploration and extraction in the context of global climate change; and constrained inclusion of Arctic Indigenous peoples in regional security governance. While each of these pathologies remains relevant, they are also subject to change as a result of factors external and internal to the Arctic region.

The first pathology refers to the seeming paradox that, pre-2014, Arctic states were engaging in a significant remilitarization of their Arctic regions and capabilities in the absence of a clearly defined military threat. In the last decade, circumpolar states have reinvested in Arctic military capabilities and infrastructure to support military operations, renewed Cold War-era military activities, such as long range bomber patrols and "buzzing" of neighbors' airspace; asserted, sometimes belligerently, their territorial boundaries, including delimitation of the Arctic seabed and continental shelves; and sought to deter non-Arctic states from asserting claims in the region (Åtland 2014; Chater and Greaves 2014; Huebert et al. 2012). While actual spending has often fallen short of rhetorical commitments, military reinvestment has nonetheless contributed to widespread media coverage and public perception of a militarized race for Arctic territory and resources, particularly as they pertain to the North Pole and the as-yet undetermined extent of Arctic states' extended continental shelves.

All eight Arctic states, as well as increasingly active non-Arctic states such as China, have unanimously affirmed their commitments to a peaceful and rule-governed Arctic order based on international law and the peaceful negotiation of disputes. Beyond mere assertions, the official policies of the Arctic all state that there is no prospective military threat in or to the region (Heininen 2012); however, the subtext of this renewed Arctic militarism was the lingering tension between Russia and the other Arctic states. Notwithstanding a clear improvement in military relations compared to the Cold War era, and important recent areas of cooperation such as the negotiated settlement of the Norwegian Russian maritime boundary in the Barents Sea in 2010, persistent suspicion arising from long-held patterns of enmity between Russia and the West appeared to fuel a pattern of remilitarization.

Alongside other analysts (Charron et al. 2012), Chater and Greaves (2014) argued that Russia is not the rogue actor it is sometimes portrayed as, and that recognizing it as the single most significant actor in the region does not mean it has hostile or aggressive intent towards other Arctic states. The sum of Arctic security policies is thus contradictory: Arctic states strenuously emphasize the absence of military threats in the region and note the cooperative relations among all circumpolar neighbors, yet at the same time increase military activities and investment in the region. Unfortunately, since we first made this argument, circumstances have changed and the suspicions among Arctic states have increased significantly.

In spring 2014, following the overthrow of the pro-Russian president of Ukraine in an American-backed popular revolution, the Russian Federation invaded and illegally annexed the Ukrainian region of Crimea. It then launched an unconventional conflict in the eastern regions of Ukraine involving support for secessionist militias and proxy forces supported by the Russian military. This conflict has claimed more than 10,000 lives, including nearly 300 people killed when Malaysian Airlines Flight 17 was shot down, allegedly by Russian forces, in July 2014. As a result, relations between Russia and the five Arctic states that are members of NATO (Canada, Denmark, Iceland, Norway, and the United States) are the worst they have been since the end of the Cold War. Russia, NATO, and the European Union all increased military activities in northern Europe, and the five Nordic states announced unprecedented military cooperation with each other and with the neighboring Baltic states (Fjeldsbø 2014). Though Norwegian officials dismiss prospects of a Russian invasion, Norway's military establishment reinvigorated much of the Northern defense apparatus that became moribund after the Cold War due to the improvement in relations with Russia (Higgins 2015). Sweden, which was neutral during the Cold War to help preserve the strategic "Nordic balance," has seriously contemplated NATO membership, and the government issued a manual to every household in the country with guidelines for how citizens should respond in case of a national crisis, including war.

The diplomatic deterioration has had direct effects on Arctic governance. On the one hand, Russia continues to cooperate in all of the relevant institutions, such as the Arctic Council and Northern Forum. On the other hand, there have not been any defense meetings or oceans conferences as there were prior to 2014. There have been outward signs of disagreement, such as boycotting of some Arctic Council events in 2014 and 2015 (Exner-Pirot 2015), though Russia did participate in the 2016 Arctic Science Ministerial meeting. Thus, while the case for military conflict within the Arctic itself still appears to be unlikely, political relations within the Arctic remain sensitive to geopolitical events that occur beyond the region. While it remains to be seen whether the effects of the conflict in Ukraine on governance and security within the Arctic will remain over the long term, militarization in the region is now less ambiguous than it was.

The second pathology of Arctic security governance is the continued emphasis on fossil fuel extraction in the circumpolar region, particularly the enthusiasm for offshore oil and gas drilling generated by the US Geological Survey's 2008 estimates that the region may contain up to 13% of the world's undiscovered oil reserves and 30% of undiscovered natural gas (Gautier et al. 2009). Such enthusiasm is at odds with the global political consensus that climate change must be limited to less than 2°C, reflected in the 2015 Paris Agreement, and the scientific assessment that doing so requires "that all Arctic [energy] resources should be classified as unburnable" and must remain unexploited (McGlade and Ekins 2015). On balance, the policies pursued by Arctic states are inconsistent with this goal. In his final year in office, US President Barack Obama did make two joint announcements with Canadian Prime Minister Justin Trudeau that appeared to signal a deeper commitment by both countries to act on climate change, including the December 2016 *United States-Canada Joint Arctic Leaders' Statement* that instituted a near-total moratorium on new offshore oil and gas drilling in the coastal Arctic waters of both Canada and the United States. However, the moratorium was reversed soon after Donald Trump's accession to the presidency in 2017, and the prospects for further US-Canadian cooperation are negligible in light of the ensuing deterioration in their bilateral relationship. Elsewhere in the region, Norway has opened new blocks of the Barents Sea to oil and gas exploration, and Russia, though limited by sanctions imposed following the Ukraine crisis, continues to pursue fossil fuel extraction as the backbone of its national economy. Its massive US$27 billion project on the Yamal Peninsula in Siberia began exporting natural gas to China in December 2017, an undertaking that will export 16.5 million tons of liquefied natural gas per year by 2019 (Foy 2017). Greenland has also reopened bidding for oil and gas drilling on its western coast for 2021, after a brief pause.

Thus, despite continued rhetorical emphasis on the importance of addressing climate change, Arctic governments fail to identify the contradiction between their pursuit of oil and gas extraction and climate-related security imperatives. Disregarding the many assessments of the damage that climate change is already inflicting upon the region and the severe effects predicted to occur (ACIA 2004; AHDR 2004; Larsen and Fondahl 2014), circumpolar states remain focused on the economic benefits to be gained by exploiting Arctic resources. Instead of restricting further hydrocarbon development, Arctic states emphasize instead regional cooperation emergency response through the Arctic Council's 2013 Oil Spill Agreement and the reduction of industrial particulates that aggravate ice-melt. The brief momentum that global and regional climate change negotiations appeared to have in 2015–2016 has all but vanished in the face of dramatic policy reversals by the Trump Administration, the various political and economic crises precipitated by the new president, and the continued tensions between Russia and the West.

The third pathology that we identified also persists, namely the constrained inclusion of Arctic Indigenous peoples in regional governance arrangements and their contestation of how "Arctic security" is defined and pursued. While a defining feature of the modern Arctic has been the prominent and formalized role of Indigenous peoples within regional governance, nonetheless there is ample evidence suggesting that Indigenous peoples' views with respect to Arctic security have been marginalized or excluded within the policies of Arctic states. This marginalization results from the fact that many Indigenous peoples have publicly challenged the Arctic states' military and resource-based conceptions of regional security, and sought instead to situate the continued social, economic and cultural well-being of Indigenous peoples and other Northern residents at the center of what is meant by "Arctic security" (Greaves 2016b, 2016c; Nickels 2013). Since Indigenous well-being is intimately connected to the natural environment, this in turn implicates state inaction on climate change. The second and third paradoxes of Arctic security are thus linked, since greater empowerment of Indigenous peoples would result in greater action to mitigate the environmental changes that are so dramatically undermining the capacity for Indigenous peoples to practice their traditional ways of life on their traditional territories (Larsen and Fondahl 2014).

Conclusion

There is a robust security governance complex in the Arctic to address environmental issues, sustainable development, human security, and economics, including oil production as well as shipping. Despite the Arctic Council's proviso to abstain from military security issues, expanded definitions of security mean that the Arctic Council remains the primary security governance institution in the region. Along with Barents Euro-Arctic Council, the European Union, and the Nordic Council (2018), among others, these organizations address issues of economic and human security. Sub-state governments, and particularly Indigenous governments, continue to affect the security governance of the region and contribute to amorphous definitions of security, although their international agency is devalued by states. Non-state actors engage regularly with these governments and institutions, encouraging the evolution of international norms related to the region. The efficacy of these actors, however, is undermined by three pathologies of Arctic security governance: the uncertain trajectory of militarization; the contradiction of hydrocarbon resource exploration and climate change imperatives; and constrained inclusion of Arctic Indigenous peoples in regional security governance. Thus, evolving governance structures and expanding understandings of security collide with the dismal predictions of Arctic observers.

References

ACIA. 2004. *Impacts of a Warming Arctic: Arctic Climate Impact Assessment. ACIA Overview Report*. Cambridge: Cambridge University Press.

AHDR. 2004. *Arctic Human Development Report*. Akureyri: Steffanson Arctic Institute.

Arctic Council. 1996. *The Ottawa Declaration*. Ottawa: Arctic Council Ministerial Meeting.

Arctic Council. 2013. *Rules of Procedure*. Tromsø: Arctic Council Secretariat.

Arctic Council. 2015. "Arctic Economic Council." September 1. www.arctic-council.org/index.php/en/our-work2/8-news-and-events/195-aec-2.

Arctic Governance Project. 2010. "Arctic Governance in an Era of Transformative Change: Critical Questions, Governance Principles, Ways Forward." www.arcticgovernance.org/getfile.php/1219555.1529.wyaufxvxuc/AGP+Report+April+14+2010%5B1%5D.pdf.

Åtland, Kristian. 2014. "Interstate Relations in the Arctic: An Emerging Security Dilemma?" *Comparative Strategy* 33 (2): 145–166.

Barents Council. 2018. "About Us: Cooperation in the Barents Euro-Arctic Region." www.barentscooperation.org/en/About.

Barents Regional Council. 2018. "The Barents Regional Council." www.barentscooperation.org/en/Barents-Regional-Council.

Barrera, Jorge. 2014. "CSIS Watchdog Chair Lobbying for FN Energy Firm with Links to China." *APTN National News*, January 1. http://aptn.ca/news/2014/01/07/csis-watchdog-chair-lobbying-fn-energy-firm-links-china/.

Beeby, Dean. 2016. "Chinese Mining Companies Feel Misled by Canada, Report Says." *CBC News*, June 7. www.cbc.ca/news/politics/china-mining-ambassador-investors-infrastructure-1.3619228.

Bennett, Mia, Wilfrid Greaves, Rudolf Riedlsperger, and Alberic Botella. 2016. "Articulating the Arctic: Contrasting State and Inuit Maps of the Canadian North." *Polar Record* 52 (6): 630–644.

Blanchfield, Mike. 2010. "Clinton Rebukes Canada and Leaves Arctic Summit." *Canadian Press*, 30 March.

Buzan, Barry and Ole Wæver. 2003. *Regions and Powers: The Structure of International Security*. Cambridge: Cambridge University Press.

Charron, Andrea, Joël Plouffe, and Stephane Roussel. 2012. "The Russian Arctic Hegemon: Foreign Policy Implications for Canada." *Canadian Foreign Policy Journal* 18 (1): 38–50.

Chater, Andrew and Wilfrid Greaves. 2014. "Arctic Security Governance." In *Handbook on Governance and Security*, ed. James C. Sperling, 133–147. Cheltenham: Edward Elgar.

Conference of Parliamentarians of the Arctic Region. 2018. "About." www.arcticparl.org/about.aspx.

European Union. 2016. "European Union External Action: EU Arctic Policy." April 27. https://eeas.europa.eu/arctic-policy/eu-arctic-policy_en.

Exner-Pirot, Heather. 2013. "What is the Arctic a Case of? The Arctic as a Regional Environmental Security Complex and the Implications for Policy." *Polar Journal* 3 (1): 120–135.

Exner-Pirot, Heather. 2015. "The Canadian Arctic Council Ministerial – What to Expect." *Eye on the Arctic*, April 15. www.rcinet.ca/eye-on-the-arctic/2015/04/15/the-canadian-arctic-council-ministerial-what-to-expect/.

Exner-Pirot, Heather. 2016. "Why Governance of the North Needs to Go beyond the Arctic Council." *Open Canada*, October 14. www.opencanada.org/features/why-governance-north-needs-go-beyond-arctic-council/.

Fjeldsbø, Tore Andre Kjetland. 2014. "The Nordic Countries Extends Military Cooperation." *Nora Region Trends*, April 13. www.noraregiontrends.org/news/news-single/article/the-nordic-countries-extends-military-cooperation/87/.

Fox, Lori. 2017. "Gwich'in Prepare for Another Battle to Stop Drilling in Caribou Calving Grounds." *Yukon News*, October 11. www.yukon-news.com/news/gwichin-prepare-for-another-battle-to-stop-drilling-in-caribou-calving-grounds/.

Foy, Henry. 2017. "Russia Ships First Gas from $27bn Arctic Project." *Financial Times*, December 8. www.ft.com/content/515d451c-dc11-11e7-a039-c64b1c09b482.

Gautier, Donald L., Kenneth J. Bird, Ronald R. Charpentier, Arthur Grantz, David W. Houseknecht, Timothy R. Klett, Thomas E. Moore, Janet K. Pitman, Christopher J. Schenk, John H. Schuenemeyer, Kai Sørensen, Marilyn E. Tennyson, Zenon C. Valin, and Craig J. Wandrey. 2009. "Assessment of Undiscovered Oil and Gas in the Arctic." *Science* 324 (5931): 1175–1179.

Gerson, Jennifer. 2012. "CSIS Said to Be Probing Financial Links between First Nations, China." *National Post*, July 25. http://nationalpost.com/news/canada/csis-said-to-be-probing-financial-links-between-first-nations-china.

Greaves, Wilfrid. 2016a. "Securing Sustainability: The Case for Critical Environmental Security in the Arctic." *Polar Record* 52 (6): 660–671.

Greaves, Wilfrid. 2016b. "Arctic In/Security and Indigenous Peoples: Comparing Inuit in Canada and Sámi in Norway." *Security Dialogue* 47 (6): 461–480.

Greaves, Wilfrid. 2016c. "Environment, Identity, Autonomy: Inuit Perspectives on Arctic Security." In *Understanding the Many Faces of Human Security: Perspectives of Northern Indigenous Peoples*, eds. Kamrul Hossain and Anna Petrétei, 35–55. Leiden: Brill.

Gwich'in Council International. 2018a. "Home." https://gwichincouncil.com/.

Gwich'in Council International. 2018b. "Submission to the Government of Canada's Arctic Policy Framework." March 21. www.eia.gov.nt.ca/sites/eia/files/content/2018-03-21_gwichin_tribal_council_arctic_policy_framework_submission.pdf.

Heininen, Lassi. 2012. "State of the Arctic Strategies and Policies – A Summary." In *Arctic Yearbook 2012*, ed. Lassi Heininen, 2–47. Akureyri: Northern Research Forum.

Higgins, Andrew. 2015. "Norway Reverts to Cold War Mode as Russian Air Patrols Spike." *The New York Times*, April 1. www.nytimes.com/2015/04/02/world/europe/a-newly-assertive-russia-jolts-norways-air-defenses-into-action.html?mwrsm=Email&_r=0.

Hoogensen Gjørv, Gunhild, Dawn R. Bazely, Maria Goloviznina, and Andrew Tanentzap, eds. 2014. *Environmental and Human Security in the Arctic*. New York: Routledge.

Huebert, Rob, Heather Exner-Pirot, Adam Lajeunesse, and Jay Gulledge. 2012. *Climate Change and International Security: The Arctic as a Bellwether*. Arlington: Center for Climate and Energy Solutions.

Larsen, Joan Nymand and Gail Fondahl, eds. 2014. *Arctic Human Development Report: Regional Processes and Global Linkages*. Akureyri: Steffanson Arctic Institute.

Ljunggren, David. 2012. "Arctic Generals Agree Closer Ties at Historic Meet." *Reuters*, April 13. https://ca.reuters.com/article/domesticNews/idCABRE83C1DE20120413.

MacDonald, Alistair. 2012. Inside Canada, China Asserts Itself. *Wall Street Journal*, 16 July. www.wsj.com/articles/SB10001424052702303933704577530870461914202.

Matzen, Erik and Tom Daly. 2018. "Greenland's Courting of China for Airport Projects Worries Denmark." *Reuters*, March 22.

McGlade, Christopher and Paul Ekins. 2015. "The Geographical Distribution of Fossil Fuels Unused When Limiting Global Warming to 2° C." *Nature* 517 (7533): 187–190.

Nickels, Scot, ed. 2013. *Nilliajut: Inuit Perspectives on Security, Patriotism, and Sovereignty*. Ottawa: Inuit Tapiriit Kanatami.

Nordic Council. 2018. "Nordic Co-Operation." www.norden.org/en.

Northern Forum. 2018. "About the Projects." www.northernforum.org/en/projects.

Penner, Derrick. 2015. "Province Approves Silvertip Mine in B.C.'s Far North." *Vancouver Sun*, June 30. www.vancouversun.com/province+approves+silvertip+mine+north/11176358/story.html.

Plouffe, Joël. 2017. "The Arctic Council and the Barents Region: Mutually Reinforcing Partners." *Interview with Florian Vidal*, May 24. https://worldpolicy.org/2017/05/24/the-arctic-council-and-the-barents-region-mutually-reinforcing-partners/.

Riddell-Dixon, Elizabeth. 2017. *Breaking the Ice: Canada, Sovereignty and the Arctic Extended Continental Shelf*. Toronto: Dundurn Press.

Rosen, Yereth. 2016. "After Hiatus, Alaska Returns to Northern Forum." *Alaska Dispatch News*, July 28. www.rcinet.ca/eye-on-the-arctic/2016/07/28/after-hiatus-alaska-returns-to-northern-forum/.

Sevunts, Levon. 2018. "China's Arctic Ambitions No Threat to Canada, Say Experts." *Radio Canada International Eye on the Arctic*, April 18. www.rcinet.ca/eye-on-the-arctic/2018/04/18/china-not-threatening-canada-in-arctic-say-experts/.

Smith, Heather A. 2010. "Choosing Not to See: Canada, Climate Change, and the Arctic." *International Journal* 65 (4): 931–942.

Tavares, Rodrigo. 2016. *Paradiplomacy: Cities and States as Global Players*. New York: Oxford University Press.

5

ARCTIC SECURITY IN INTERNATIONAL SECURITY

Rasmus Gjedssø Bertelsen

Introduction: Arctic security at the international system level

This chapter argues that Arctic security, defined within the framework of war and peace between states, has historically reflected security at the global level: a trend likely to continue. Thus, local and regional factors are unlikely to determine war and peace in the Arctic in the future. This "international systemic" argument runs counter to much of the contemporary popular and scholarly commentary and analysis, which warns of potential conflict in the Arctic driven by improved access to natural resources because of climate change and diminished ice on sea and land. This argument also runs counter to the oft-cited notion of "Arctic exceptionalism," meaning a peaceful and cooperative Arctic today is cordoned off from most security pressures facing other parts of the world. A peaceful and cooperative Arctic reflects the position of this region in the international system as much as hypothetical conflict or mass militarization of the Arctic would. The arguments here focus on security at the level of war and peace between states, also known as "traditional" national security. Concurrently, system-level great-power conflict and Arctic state national security policy have had strong effects on regional human security in multiple dimensions. High intensity conflict, or excessive levels of militarization have adversely affected local and Indigenous Arctic communities, families, and individuals. These effects include forced displacement, cultural and linguistic intrusion, assimilation policies, crime, corruption, and pollution (Gjørv et al. 2014)

The focus of this chapter argues, via historical cases followed by analyses of the current and evolving international system, that war and peace in the Arctic are determined at the systemic rather than local and regional levels. It focuses on the place of the Arctic in a Eurocentric and, since WWII, a US-centric, international system. The historical focus is therefore on the European and North Atlantic Arctic, rather than the Eurasian and Pacific Arctic. These regions were later integrated because of systemic developments. The systemic forces at play in the international system today are the twin power transitions from Western states to Eastern states and from state to non-state actors (Nye 2011). The other force is the return of Russia as a more typical great power, after two decades of artificial relative weakness (Mearsheimer 2014). There is a popular scholarly argument that the Arctic in recent decades has gained the world's attention primarily because of climate change and its environmental, political, and economic effects. According to this assertion, the Arctic was previously much more isolated from outside attention and influences. This line of thinking is well illustrated by the shopworn refrain: "what happens in the Arctic, does not stay in the Arctic." This saying refers to the effects of climate change in the Arctic on other regions of the world, but the saying ignores the strong external influences on the Far North, especially in the social, economic, and political spheres (Borgerson 2008.

For centuries, if not millennia, the Arctic has been a part of larger social systems. The Nordic and North Atlantic Arctic has been a part of European affairs since the Viking Age between the 800s and 1100s CE. Indigenous peoples migrated and traded in and out of the Arctic much earlier, but this is beyond the scope of this chapter. European society, economy and politics spread to the White Sea and across the North Atlantic via the Faroe Islands, Iceland, Greenland, and North America, through Viking migration and early state formation in Iceland and Norway. Russian state formation and transcontinental colonization, and eventually North American (Alaskan) colonization, integrated the Russian Arctic and Alaska into the international system. British and French North American colonization brought the rest of the North American Arctic into this Eurocentric international system. France colonized Canada as New France (Nouvelle-France), followed by British North America, (including Rupert's Land in what is now north-central Canada), while the Hudson's Bay Company was set up in 1670 to bring Canadian furs, an extractive industry, to markets in Europe (Heininen and Southcott 2010).

The Arctic in great-power geostrategy for 250 years

Anglo-French great-power competition is a good starting point for illustrating how war and peace in the Arctic has time and again reflected great-power conflict at the systemic level, rather than reflecting local and regional factors. The Seven Years' War/*La guerre de la Conquête* (1756–1763) was perhaps the world's first truly "global" conflict, since it involved European great powers and was fought on all continents except Antarctica. The war also affected the Arctic directly, with profound long-term social, economic, political, cultural, and linguistic consequences. In the end, France was forced to cede New France to Britain; a move that continues to shape Canadian socio-political life today in many ways.

The geostrategic role of the Arctic was also illustrated in the aftermath of the Seven Years' War. In 2005, the University of Iceland, the Icelandic government, and City of Reykjavík celebrated the 75th birthday of the former President of Iceland, Vigdís Finnbogadóttir, with the international conference titled Dialogue of Cultures. There, Dr Anna Agnarsdóttir presented, from archival work in the French Ministry of Defense, a secret memo that was sent by the French navy to the Duc de Choiseul – minister of foreign affairs and for the navy and close confidant of monarch Louis XV – after the war. In this memo, the French navy was extremely concerned about having lost most of its access to the North Atlantic (via Canada). Therefore, the navy recommended that the King of France propose to the King of Denmark–Norway that he exchange Iceland for Louisiana, then a vast North American territory. Iceland would thereby serve as a naval strongpoint to threaten both British Canada and Scotland (Agnarsdóttir 2005; Einarsson 2005). The memo from the French navy is an excellent illustration of the geostrategic importance of Iceland. Either the offer was never made from the King of France, who may have valued Louisiana's economic interest higher, or it was not accepted in Copenhagen. However, in the nineteenth and twentieth centuries, the geostrategic history of the North Atlantic also clearly demonstrated that Britain would never have accepted Iceland as a French naval rampart in the North Atlantic, in Britain's backyard. Such a French-Danish–Norwegian exchange would have immediately caused war with Great Britain and likely British *de jure* or *de facto* control over Iceland.

The ideas of the American and French Revolutions and the road to North Atlantic microstates

Today, the most politically dynamic societies of the Arctic are the Faroe Islands and Greenland, which are relentlessly pursuing independence from the Kingdom of Denmark. As a result, these two societies in the Arctic are the only ones with governments with a political status that could be considered fluid. These societies are inspired by the ideas of the American and French Revolutions of national identity, national sovereignty, and also Indigenous rights. The French Revolution and the Napoleonic Wars shaped the current North Atlantic Arctic. Denmark–Norway was a major seafaring nation with one of the world's strongest navies of its time. Denmark–Norway sought to stay neutral in the Napoleonic Wars but ultimately failed. The strategic genius of British Admiral Lord Horatio Nelson was to defeat the three peer-competitor navies of the time in three separate battles: the French navy at the Battle of the Nile (Aboukir Bay) in 1798, the Danish–Norwegian navy at the Battle of Copenhagen in 1801, and the French–Spanish navy at Trafalgar in 1805. The remaining Danish–Norwegian Navy was subsequently dispatched by the Royal Navy in 1807, after the terrible bombardment of Copenhagen (Glenthøj and Rasmussen 2007; Munch-Petersen 2007). The loss of the Danish–Norwegian Navy in 1801 and 1807 meant the immediate loss of Danish–Norwegian access to and control of its North Atlantic possessions, the Faroe Islands, Iceland, and Greenland, which Denmark has *de facto* never regained. Greenlandic society was cut off from Western supplies, and had to revert to pre-contact harvesting techniques (Markussen 2017). A Danish adventurer and revolutionary, Jørgen Jürgensen, took power in Reykjavík, declaring an independent Iceland and imprisoning the Danish governor, Count Trampe. Jürgensen's rule continued for 100 days until he was arrested and removed by the Royal Navy (Mentz 2018). This *de facto* British sphere of influence in the North Atlantic continued until WWII, when it was replaced by an American sphere of influence that continues to this day.

National liberalism, the ideational effect of the American and French Revolutions, continues to influence the world and the North Atlantic today. The revolutions proposed the ideas of national identity and national sovereignty vested in the people. In the 1830s, like the Danish intellectuals around them, Icelandic students and intellectuals in Copenhagen became captivated by these ideas. The Old Danish (Danish–Norwegian until 1814) kingdom was a multi-ethnic, multilingual state of Danes, Norwegians, and Germans in the Duchies of Schleswig-Holstein; and citizens of Iceland, the Faroe Islands, the colony of Greenland, and some small tropical colonies. This absolutist state could exist regardless of identity, language, and common identity. Ideas of national identity and sovereignty will eventually dissolve such a state, either peacefully or violently. The creation of the Danish democratic nation-state through the 1849 constitution immediately led to the first Schleswig War (1848–1850), when Germans in Schleswig-Holstein rebelled. Denmark won this war, but it laid the foundations for the catastrophic Danish defeat in the Second Schleswig War of 1864 against Bismarck's Prussia.

In 1845, the Viking-Age Icelandic *Althingi* assembly had been reconstituted as one of the consultative assemblies of the absolutist Danish king. In 1851, the Danish governor of Iceland, Count Trampe (a relative of Count Trampe arrested by Jørgen Jürgensen), tried to make the *Althingi* adopt the new Danish constitution for Iceland, making Iceland an integral part of Denmark. The leader of the Icelandic independence movement, Jón Sigurðsson, a lifelong scholar in Copenhagen, successfully opposed this. This set the stage for Iceland's political struggle for independence, a separate constitution in 1874, home rule in 1904, sovereignty as the Kingdom of Iceland, (in union of shared monarchy with the Kingdom of Denmark), in 1918, and the founding of the Republic of Iceland in 1944. The declaration of the Republic was in accordance with the 1918 union law, but was opposed by Denmark, which was under German occupation at the time.

The next great-power conflict to affect the Arctic was the Crimean War (1853–1856), which is thought-provoking in light of the post-2014 Ukraine and Crimea crisis between the West and Russia. The Crimean War included an oft-overlooked dimension of British–French naval forces operating against Russia in the White Sea and the Baltic Sea (Rath 2015). In the aftermath of the Crimean War, Russia decided in 1867 to sell its North American colony of Alaska to the United States rather than Britain (Canada), its recent enemy in the Crimean War. This transaction between Russia and the United States, which at the time was highly controversial in American policy circles, naturally transformed the United States into an Arctic state (Office of the Historian n.d.).

The geostrategic position of the North Atlantic and Arctic in two World Wars

The twentieth century is the story of the key geostrategic position of the North Atlantic and the Arctic, as set out by the French navy after the Seven Years' War. This position led to high intensity combat at sea, on land, and in the air, with excessive levels of militarization even in peace time, and profound effects on local and Indigenous Arctic local communities, families, and individuals. World War I was the first industrialized "total war," where the polities of great powers fought for life and death and where four such polities – the German, the Austro-Hungarian, the Russian, and the Ottoman Empires – succumbed. This total war and associated upheavals profoundly affected the Arctic. Germany and Britain as part of the total war imposed naval blockades on each other. The British naval blockade of Germany meant that Denmark again lost its connection to the North Atlantic, the Faroe Islands, Greenland, and Iceland. The North Atlantic visibly became a British sphere of interest. During World War I, Faroese and Icelandic fish exports and trade became much more oriented towards Britain, which contributed to the dissolution of political and economic ties between Denmark and the North Atlantic (Jensdóttir 1980, 1986; Thorhallsson and Joensen 2015, 187–206; Bjarnason 2016).

Tsarist Russia, pounded into eventual collapse and revolution by Germany and Austro-Hungary, founded the port city of Murmansk in 1916 to ensure shipping connections to its Western allies. The 1917 October Revolution would later affect the Soviet Arctic profoundly. The revolution also had Arctic and Barents dimensions, in that North Norwegian ports became hotbeds of revolutionary publication activity being distributed in Russia through historical Pomor trading and shipping networks between Northern Norway and Northwest Russia (Nielsen 2015, 136–172). The Bolshevik Revolution sparked the Russian Civil War, where Western allies intervened. American and British forces intervened in the White Sea region and fought Red forces there between 1918 and 1920 (Hudson 2004). World War II would affect the Arctic even more than previous global great-power wars. When Nazi Germany invaded Poland in September 1939, Britain again imposed a naval blockade on Germany, sealing off the English Channel and the North Sea. This unraveling security order reached the Arctic when the USSR attacked Finland in late 1939 and the two fought the Winter War on their common border from the Arctic coastline to the Baltic. After this conflict, Finland lost its corridor to the Arctic Ocean, Petsamo, which it had had since its independence in the aftermath of the October Revolution.

German, British, and French competition over the strategically important northern Swedish iron ore resources around Kiruna brought World War II to the Nordics and the Barents Arctic. During winter, the Bay of Bothnia and parts of the Baltic Sea are ice covered, making shipping difficult or impossible. Therefore, the iron ore railroad was constructed in 1904 across the mountains from northern Sweden to the Northern Norwegian port of Narvik, which is always ice-free. Germany was dependent on shipments of the Swedish iron ore for its armaments industry. In the spring of 1940, Britain and France tried to stop these shipments by laying mines in Norwegian waters, despite the protest of the then-neutral Norwegian government.

The British–French–German struggle over these seaways led Germany to invade Denmark and Norway on 9 April 1940. The Norwegian government resisted the German invasion, and quickly British, French, and Free Polish forces intervened in the war in Norway. The German forces around Narvik were cut off because of British naval superiority in the North Atlantic and were near defeat by the Allied land forces. Germany pressured neutral Sweden into allowing covert resupply of the encircled German forces by Swedish rail and the iron ore railroad. This Swedish acquiescence caused long-term Norwegian resentment towards Sweden after World War II, but it reflected Sweden's highly exposed geostrategic position towards Germany, which dominated the Baltic Sea region. The successful German invasion of the Low Countries and France in May 1940 and the rapidly deteriorating situation for the allies there forced them to withdraw from Norway, ensuring the German conquest of the whole of Norway. With Germany capturing the Norwegian coastline, British control of the North Atlantic was deeply threatened, and Britain moved quickly and decisively in its North Atlantic *de facto* sphere of influence by occupying the Faroe Islands on 11 April and Iceland on 10 May 1940.

Greenland was again cut off from Denmark, and Danish colonial legislation authorized the two governors of North and South Greenland to govern Greenland independently in such circumstances. These two comparatively young Danish civil servants divided the task between them, so that Eske Brun stayed in Greenland as overall governor and Aksel Svane went to the United States to represent Greenland there and secure supplies for Greenland in exchange for cryolite minerals mined on the island. Cryolite was important in aluminum production and crucial for airplane manufacturing; another example of an Arctic natural resource of strategic importance in a given technological context (Brun 1985). Danish ambassadors in Allied capitals, most notably Henrik Kauffmann in Washington, DC and Count Reventlow in London, declared their temporary independence from their king under Nazi occupation in Copenhagen. On 9 April 1941, one year after the German occupation of Denmark, Kauffmann and the American government entered a defense agreement concerning Greenland, which gave the United States the means to establish an enormous strategic infrastructure of airfields and other military installations in Greenland (Lidegaard 1996).

On 7 July 1941, the United States replaced Britain as the protective occupier of Iceland, five months before Pearl Harbor and US entry into WWII (Corgan 2002). The British occupation from May 1940 and the United States' occupation of Iceland from July 1941 had a profound social, economic, political, technological, cultural, and linguistic impact on Icelandic society, which is still felt today. Newly independent and sovereign Iceland had been very adversely affected by the Great Depression of the 1930s. British (and later American) construction and other activities injected an enormous stimulus into the Icelandic economy.

German occupation of Norway, and the subsequent use of Northern Norway as the staging ground for attacks on Russia, is another example of how great-power systemic conflict acted forcefully on the Arctic, affecting community, family, and individuals. When Germany attacked the USSR, the Soviet Union became an ally of Britain and soon the United States. Against the onslaught of German military and industrial might, the USSR became deeply dependent on supplies from Britain and the United States. This supply by convoy was delivered across the North Atlantic to Murmansk. The convoys stopped in Hvalfjörður or Seyðisfjörður on the west and east coasts of Iceland, respectively. The allies created large supplies and protective infrastructures in these locations. German planes flying from occupied Norway attacked Seyðisfjörður regularly to bomb Allied ships.

The Battle of the Atlantic between German submarines and Allied convoys throughout the war was the struggle to cut off or maintain these crucial strategic supply lines from North America to Britain and to Murmansk. Germany and the USSR were equally aware that if German forces attacking the Kola Peninsula and the northwestern USSR from Finnmark in Northern Norway and from Lapland in northern Finland were to capture or cut off the Kola Peninsula, it would also halt Allied convoys as effectively as sinking them out at sea. Two other supply routes existed between the Western Allies and the USSR during World War II: one via the Persian Gulf and Iran; and the other via Alaska and the Soviet Far East across the Bering Strait. The United States delivered aircraft to the USSR via Alaska. When Japan attacked the United States at Pearl Harbor as well as other American protectorates in the Pacific on 7 December 1941, the Empire of Japan subsequently invaded the westernmost Aleutian Islands of Alaska. The US military and Japan fought the brief Aleutian Campaign under Arctic conditions. Afterwards, Washington built up Alaska, which officially became a state in 1959, as a strategic base aligned towards the Pacific region.It has new importance today because of the rise of Asia (Altunin 1997).

The Cold War and the Arctic

The defeat of Nazi Germany, principally by the industrial might of the United States and the strength and size of the Soviet Red Army, founded the bipolar Cold War international system. The Cold War deeply affected the Arctic, again for geostrategic reasons that had little to do with local or regional factors in the Arctic. The Cold War led to the most extreme and prolonged militarization of the Arctic. Although no combat occurred in the Arctic, the military build-up in the region had profound consequences on the culture, languages, health, and environment of local and Indigenous communities (Gjørv et al. 2014). The bipolar rivalry between the two superpowers also engendered intense scientific and technological competition. The world was caught in a "balance of terror," and the Arctic was center stage in this balance, given that the transpolar route across the geographic North Pole is the shortest flightpath for long-range bombers or ICBMs between North America and Eurasia. From a NATO perspective, looking at the Warsaw Pact in Europe, Norway was the northern flank, Central Europe was the central front and the Mediterranean was the southern flank. Looking strategically at the USSR from the United States, Alaska was the western flank, Greenland was the central front, and Norway and the United Kingdom were the eastern flank.

Washington built a large strategic distant early-warning infrastructure, aka the DEW Line, based on radar stations from the Cobra Dane radar in the Aleutians via Canada, to the central Thule station in Northern Greenland, to radars in Britain and the Vardø facilities in Northern Norway. The USSR built a similar warning and air-defense system across the Soviet Arctic. The USSR/Russia has very limited all-year open-sea access, principally through the Kola Peninsula. Therefore, the Soviet Union was, and Russia today remains, dependent on ballistic-missile submarines carrying nuclear weapons (SSBNs) as deterrents operating from the Kola Peninsula and, to a lesser extent, the Russian Far East. The United States, Britain, and France have practically unlimited access to the open ocean for their SSBNs. America and its NATO allies expended significant resources tracking and possibly countering these Soviet (Russian) submarine forces (Barnes 2017; Office of the Historian n.d.).

The Cold War geostrategic role of the Arctic between the United States and the Soviet Union deeply affected Alaska and the Soviet Arctic. For instance, the "Ice Curtain" across the Bering Strait separated Indigenous people from family members on the other side (Ramseur 2017). The Cold War also affected the other Arctic nations deeply. The Cold War geostrategic role of the Arctic shaped the relationship between the United States and its three small NATO allies in the Arctic: the Kingdom of Denmark (the Thule radar in Greenland), Iceland (the Keflavík base) and Norway (Vardø radar and signal and electronic intelligence in Northern Norway). Finland and Sweden, which link the Baltic and Barents Sea regions over land, jealously guarded their nonaligned status. This dynamic was part of the Nordic balance, where Denmark, Iceland, and Norway were critical NATO members, Sweden and Finland were nonaligned, and the USSR showed restraint, especially towards Finland.

The unexceptional post- and post-post-Cold War Arctic

For close to 30 years, we have enjoyed an Arctic of circumpolar cooperation (including with Russia). This cooperation has given rise to an argument about Arctic exceptionalism: that the Arctic is decoupled from the international system and conflicts in that realm. It is useful to critically re-evaluate such a claim of Arctic exceptionalism, in order to better understand the place and role of the Arctic in the international system. The foundation for post-Cold War circumpolar cooperation was laid in the last years of the Cold War and the USSR, when Soviet President Mikhail Gorbachev gave his keynote speech in Murmansk in 1987 calling for the Arctic to be a zone of peace, environmental protection, and scientific cooperation. This speech was a part of Gorbachev's *perestroika* (restructuring) and *glasnost* (openness) policies of domestic reform and external opening-up, not least motivated by the extremely dangerous nuclear balance of terror (Issaraelian 1989).

Finland, as a small, nonaligned state with a difficult and dangerous relationship with the USSR "caught the ball" and initiated the Rovaniemi Process in 1989, leading to the formulation of the Arctic Environmental Protection Strategy (AEPS), which was adopted by the eight Arctic states in 1991. The Rovaniemi and subsequent AEPS processes occurred in the context of the fall of the Berlin Wall, the fall of Communist one-party regimes in Central and Eastern Europe, and the disintegration of the Soviet Union. The Finnish initiative was the first in a line of small states or medium powers using the opportunities of fewer systemic constraints to use "softer" policies such as environmental cooperation to pursue foreign and security policy goals. Norway founded its own Barents Euro-Arctic

Council initiative in 1993. This initiative traces its roots to the successful management of Barents cod fishing by the Norwegian–Soviet Fisheries Commission from 1974 (Jørgensen and Hønneland 2013. The middle power, Canada, took the Finnish process further by facilitating the foundation of the Arctic Council via the Ottawa Declaration of 1996 (English 2013). This harmonious Arctic circumpolar cooperation reflected an international system where the United States was the unipolar hegemon and smaller Western states, even bordering Russia, had greater freedom of action. In the 1990s, Russia was in an unprecedented social and economic crisis, which greatly diminished its power-projection capabilities everywhere, including the Arctic.

Russia and Arctic security today and in the future

Today, the most important systemic international processes for the Arctic are twin power transitions from Western states to Eastern states and power diffusion from state to non-state actors (Nye 2011); and the return of Russia as a more typical great power (Mearsheimer 2014). What is striking when speaking with Russian colleagues and students is the stark differences in the memory of the 1990s. For Westerners, the 1990s was an exceptionally positive era of European reunification, peace dividends, economic growth under the presidency of Bill Clinton, and the rise of the Internet. For Russians, the 1990s was a decade of catastrophic social and economic crisis, rampant organized crime at all levels of society, and withdrawal of the state and its services in many areas, not least the Russian Arctic. The current crisis between Russia and the West could perhaps be formulated as: the West cannot have the 1990s back, and Russia cannot have the USSR back.

The rule of President Vladimir Putin, after the chaotic tenure of President Boris Yeltsin, together with higher oil prices, strengthened the Russian state and economy. This transformation in Russian fortunes had widespread effects on Russia's behavior in multiple regions of the world. Because of Russian economic weakness and absence of soft power (due to an unattractive political and economic system), Russia lost its entire Cold War Central and Eastern European sphere of influence to European unification in the European Union and NATO membership. Before 2008, Russia was helpless to respond, but it took decisive action against Georgia in 2008, crushing Georgian NATO aspirations. The Ukraine crisis from 2014 is a similar example of competition over spheres of influence between Russia and the EU and NATO, where Russia took military action because it lacked the soft power or attractiveness of the EU or NATO (Mearsheimer 2014).

The deep Russian–Western crisis over Ukraine, (and the post-2011 civil war in Syria, where Russia maintains military facilities), has raised the question of the potential effects of this deterioration in the relations of the Arctic. Superficial analysis has asked whether Russia would act as assertively in the Arctic as in the Caucasus and Eastern Europe. That is a misguided question, since Russian action against Georgia and Ukraine was motivated by specific regional factors that are not relevant in the Arctic. When there is a proxy war in Eastern Ukraine and peace and cooperation in the Arctic, there is also a tendency to see the Ukraine crisis as the general situation, and the Arctic cooperation as the exception. This misperception may be more widespread in the small Nordic Arctic states and may reflect a small-state foreign and security policy experience. The Nordic small states are relatively very highly developed societies, but they are small states because of their smaller absolute capabilities in comparison with larger countries. The Nordic small states have limited engagements, interests, and responsibilities, whereas great powers and the US superpower have myriad engagements, interests, and responsibilities around the world.

Great powers continuously consider whether to link or delink questions across functional and geographic domains. In the case of the Arctic and the Ukraine crisis, Russia has decided not to link the Ukraine crisis with the Arctic, which is to be expected, since Russia has no similar strategic problems in the Arctic as it has in Eastern Europe or the Caucasus. Russia is building up military capabilities in the Arctic, but here the great strategic and economic importance of the Arctic to Russia must be kept in mind, and this build-up must not be overestimated, particularly when compared with an artificial low in the 1990s. On the other hand, the West linked the Ukraine crisis and the Arctic through targeted financial and technological sanctions against Russian Arctic offshore oil and gas activities. From a Western point of view, these actions made sense because they targeted a vital sector of the Russian domestic political economy (Farchy and Mazneva 2017; Konyshev, Sergunin, and Subbotin 2017).

Before jumping to conclusions about Arctic exceptionalism in the current Ukraine and Syrian crises, it is important to keep in mind how Russia and Western great powers compete and cooperate across different functional and geographic domains. The all-important US–Russian relationship is dependent on keeping a stable and secure strategic balance of nuclear deterrence, nuclear non-proliferation, and space cooperation around the International Space Station (ISS), where the United States and everybody else depend on Russian rockets to reach the ISS. Russia remains dependent on a submarine-based strategic nuclear deterrent for its great-power status, since the Russian economy, roughly the same size as Spain's, is nowhere near great-power status and is unlikely to reach such a level. The Kola Peninsula will therefore remain the base of a large proportion of Russian strategic nuclear weapons, with large conventional forces to protect them. Russia will continuously seek to make these submarines quieter and quieter, and the United States, Norway and other NATO allies will continue to expend significant resources to track these submarines at all times and to counter them in wartime (Barnes 2017). The Arctic may become an area of Russian–Western conflict, but that will only occur if the conflict elsewhere escalates to a level which forces both sides to use the Arctic in the conflict, or if either side decides to move towards an overall conflict and competition in the Arctic area. There are no local or regional Arctic factors that can be expected to ignite a Russia–West conflict.

The return of Asia and its effects on Arctic security

The most important systemic development in international politics today is the return of Asia, led by China, to its relative historical importance in the world economy. This development is also affecting comprehensive Arctic security today. Asia is predicted to represent more than half of the world economy by 2050 (Asian Development Bank 2011). This gigantic economic shift drives the power transition from Western to Eastern states. Other great shifts are the diffusion of power from state to non-state actors, and the proliferation of technology between states and from state to non-state actors (Nye 2011). Asian interests in the Arctic make sense in this larger context. Very large economies have global political, economic, scientific, and security interests. Great Western powers have had that for centuries, and those interests did not face the level of scrutiny that Asian interests have faced. Today we must realize that very large Asian economies also have such global interests, including in the Arctic. The security dimensions of Asian interest and interests in the Arctic fall in the following areas: deterrence and missile defense, the Northern Sea Route, and Sino-Western competition in Greenland.

American Arctic strategic infrastructure from the Cold War has new important roles shaped by a new international system and new technology. Alaska's geostrategic position towards the Asia-Pacific is today shaped by proliferation of nuclear and ballistic-missile technology to North Korea. Alaska plays a central role in US ballistic-missile defense regarding Northeast Asia (Mitchell 2018). The Thule radar in Greenland is today a part of US missile defense (Kile 2004; Kristensen 2004; The Associated Press 2004), and Norway's Vardø installation may also assume this role (Sellevåg 2000, 26–29; Higgins 2017).

Russian energy and natural resources along the Northern Sea Route (NSR) are being developed for the Chinese market, and with Chinese capital, as is clear from the Yamal LNG project (Farchy and Mazneva 2017). The NSR, as the Polar Silk Road, is also the northern dimension of China's grand strategy of the Belt and Road Initiative, where China as the continental power counters the United States as the maritime power (Johnson and Standish 2018). There seems to be much uncertainty, especially in Western shipping circles, about Russian regulation of the NSR. There is a unique maritime strategic aspect to the NSR, which is at the basis of this unease, but never acknowledged explicitly. The developing NSR is the only major international waterway that is not controlled to some degree by the US Navy, representing a major change in international maritime power.

The Faroe Islands and Greenland are moving towards eventual independence from Denmark. China is also becoming engaged in Greenland via investments in potential mining projects. The Sino-Greenlandic relationship is causing concern in Denmark (Shi and Lanteigne 2018), especially over the question of whether China will have a negative effect on Greenland's economic sovereignty. There have been stereotypical paternalistic, postcolonial voices fearing that China as a great power will cheat or corrupt the small Greenlandic population without the parental, postcolonial oversight of Denmark. The great importance of Greenland to the United States since at least World War II was explained earlier in this chapter, but more recently the US is also expressing concern about Beijing's economic interests in Greenland. The United States and China are competing on a global scale, and the US military is heavily present and close to China and Chinese core interests in the East and South China Seas. China may decide to respond by seeking an economic, political, scientific, and cultural presence close to the United States and where America has important strategic interests, such as in Greenland. All societies around the world, including Greenland, are rapidly developing political, economic, scientific, and cultural relations with China, which is soon to be the largest economy in the world. Thus, Greenland, Denmark, the United States, and China must avoid unintended conflicts in this process (Sørensen 2018).

Conclusion: Arctic security was never about the Arctic and will not be in the future

This chapter asserts that Arctic security has historically been driven by forces at the international system level, particularly the rise and fall of great powers and the wars between them. In the future, Arctic security as war and peace between states is likely to be driven at the international systemic level. This argument counters the idea of Arctic exceptionalism and the idea that Arctic peace and cooperation is cordoned off from the ongoing Ukraine crisis between Russia and the West. Armed conflict and previous militarization of the Arctic have had highly detrimental effects on the human security of local and Indigenous Arctic communities, families, and individuals. The small Nordic Arctic states and local and Indigenous populations have been powerless against such forces. Perhaps a better understanding of how collapses in the international order, and outbreaks of great-power wars far from the Arctic have spread to the Arctic, can contribute to the understanding of resilience and human security within Arctic local and Indigenous communities.

References

Agnarsdóttir, Anna. 2005. "Ísland Og Versalir: Frakkar Við Íslandsstrendur á 18. Öld [Iceland and Versailles: French in Icelandic Seas in 18th Century]." Háskoli Íslands, 04/13-15.

Altunin, Evgenii. 1997. "ALSIB: On the History of the Alaska-Siberia Ferrying Route." *The Journal of Slavic Military Studies* 10 (2) (06/01): 85–96. doi:10.1080/13518049708430292.

Asian Development Bank. 2011. *Asia 2050: Realizing the Asian Century*. Singapore: Asian Development Bank.

Barnes, Julian E. 2017. "A Russian Ghost Submarine, its U.S. Pursuers and a Deadly New Cold War." *The Wall Street Journal*, last modified 2017/10/20, accessed 11/12, 2017, www.wsj.com/articles/a-russian-ghost-submarine-its-u-s-pursuers-and-a-deadly-new-cold-war-1508509841.

Bjarnason, Gunnar Þór. 2016. *Þegar Siðmenningin Fór Fjandans Til: Íslendingar Og Stríðið Mikla 1914–1918 [When Civilization Went to Hell: Icelanders and the Great War 1914–1914]*. Reykjavík: Mál og Menning.

Borgerson, Scott G. 2008. "Arctic Meltdown: The Economic and Security Implications of Global Warming." *Foreign Affairs* 87 (2 March/April): 63–77.

Brun, Eske. 1985. *Mit Grønlandsliv* [*My Greenland Life*]. København: Gyldendal.

Corgan, Michael T. 2002. *Iceland and its Alliances: Security for a Small State*. Scandinavian Studies; v. 8. Lewiston, NY: Edwin Mellen Press.

Einarsson, Guðni. 2005. "Frakkar Vildu Skipta Við Dani á Íslandi Og Louisiana [France would Exchange Louisiana for Iceland with Denmark]." *Morgunblaðið*, 2005/04/19.

English, John. 2013. *Ice and Water: Politics, Peoples, and the Arctic Council*. Toronto: Allen Lane.

Farchy, Jack and Elena Mazneva. 2017. "Russia Wins in Arctic after U.S. Fails to Kill Giant Gas Project." *Bloomberg*, last modified 2017/12/14, accessed 05/20, 2018, www.bloomberg.com/news/articles/2017-12-14/russia-dreams-big-as-u-s-fails-to-kill-27-billion-gas-project.

Gjørv, Gunhild Hoogensen, Dawn R. Bazely, Marina Goloviznina, and Andrew J. Tanentzap, eds. 2014. *Environmental and Human Security in the Arctic*. London, New York: Earthscan.

Glenthøj, Rasmus and Jens Rahbek Rasmussen, eds. 2007. *Det Venskabelige Bombardement: København 1807 Som Historisk Begivenhed Og National Myte [The Friendly Bombardment: Copenhagen 1807 as Historical Event and National Myth]*. København: Museum Tusculanum Press.

Heininen, Lassi and Chris Southcott, eds. 2010. *Globalization and the Circumpolar North*. Fairbanks, AK: University of Alaska Press.

Higgins, Andrew. 2017. "On a Tiny Norwegian Island, America Keeps an Eye on Russia." *The New York Times*, last modified 06/13, accessed 07/24, 2018, www.nytimes.com/2017/06/13/world/europe/arctic-norway-russia-radar.html.

Hudson, Miles. 2004. *Intervention in Russia 1918-1920: A Cautionary Tale*. Barnsley: Leo Cooper.

Issaraelian, Evgenia L. 1989. "L'initiative de Gorbatchev à Mourmansk et les mesures de restauration de la confiance dans l'Arctique [Gorbachev's Initiative in Murmank and Confidence-Building in the Arctic]." *Études internationales* 20 (1): 61–70.

Jensdóttir, Sólrún B. 1980. *Ísland á Brezku Valdsvæði 1914–1918 [Iceland in the British Sphere of Influence 1914–1918]*. Studia Historica. Reykjavík: Sagnfræðistofnun og Menningarsjóður.

Jensdóttir, Sólrún B. 1986. *Anglo-Icelandic Relations during the First World War*. Outstanding Theses from the London School of Economics and Political Science. New York: Garland Pub.

Johnson, Keith and Reid Standish. 2018. "Putin and Xi are Dreaming of a Polar Silk Road." *Foreign Policy*, last modified 03/08, accessed 07/24, 2018, https://foreignpolicy.com/2018/03/08/putin-and-xi-are-dreaming-of-a-polar-silk-road-arctic-northern-sea-route-yamal/.

Jørgensen, Anne-Kristin and Geir Hønneland. 2013. "In Cod we Trust: Konjunkturer i Det Norsk-Russiske Fiskerisamarbeidet [In Cod we Trust: Trends in Norwegian-Russian Fisheries Cooperation]." *Nordisk Østforum* 27 (4): 353–376.

Kile, Shannon N. 2004. "Ballistic Missile Defence." In *SIPRI Yearbook 2004: Armaments, Disarmament and International Security*, 647–658. Oxford: Oxford University Press.
Konyshev, Valery, Alexander Sergunin, and Sergei Subbotin. 2017. "Russia's Arctic Strategies in the Context of the Ukrainian Crisis." *The Polar Journal* 7 (1) (01/02): 104–124. doi:10.1080/2154896X.2017.1335107.
Kristensen, Kristian Søby. 2004. *Greenland, Denmark, and the Debate on Missile Defense: A Window of Opportunity for Increased Autonomy*. Copenhagen: Danish Institute for International Studies.
Lidegaard, Bo. 1996. "I Kongens Navn: Henrik Kauffmann i Dansk Diplomati 1919–1958." ["In the Name of the King."] Københavns Universitet.
Markussen, Inga Dóra. 2017. "West-Nordic Security: From the Cold War to Present Time." Reykjavík University, 2017/ 05/10.
Mearsheimer, John J. 2014. "Why the Ukraine Crisis is the West's Fault: The Liberal Delusions that Provoked Putin." *Foreign Affairs* 93 (5 September/October): 77–89.
Mentz, Søren. 2018. *Den Islandske Revolution [The Icelandic Revolution]*. Aarhus: Aarhus Universitetsforlag.
Mitchell, Justin. 2018. "In Alaska, Soldiers Relish Role in U.S. Missile Defense." *Reuters*, last modified 04/27, accessed 07/24, 2018, www.reuters.com/article/us-north-korea-missiles-alaska/in-alaska-soldiers-relish-role-in-u-s-missile-defense-idUSKBN1HY0FD.
Munch-Petersen, Thomas. 2007. *København i Flammer: Hvordan England Bombarderede København Og Ranede Den Danske Flåde i 1807 [Copenhagen in Flames: How England Bombarded Copenhagen and Stole the Danish Navy in 1807]*. København: Gyldendal.
Nielsen, Jens Petter. 2015. "Sovjetunionen Og Norsk Arbeiderbevegelse [The USSR and the Norwegian Labor Movement]." In *Naboer i Frykt Og Forventning: Norge Og Russland 1917–2014 [Neighbors in Fear and Expectation: Norway and Russia 1917–2014]*, edited by Sven Holtsmark, 136–172. Oslo: Pax Forlag.
Nye, Joseph S., Jr. 2011. *The Future of Power*. New York: PublicAffairs.
Office of the Historian. n.d. "Purchase of Alaska, 1867." United States Department of State, last modified nd, accessed 07/18, 2018, https://history.state.gov/milestones/1866-1898/alaska-purchase.
Ramseur, David. 2017. *Melting the Ice Curtain: The Extraordinary Story of Citizen Diplomacy on the Russia-Alaska Frontier*. Fairbanks, AK: University of Alaska Press.
Rath, Andrew C. 2015. *The Crimean War in Imperial Context, 1854–1856*. New York: Palgrave MacMillan.
Sellevåg, Inge. 2000. "Vardø Exposed." *Bulletin of the Atomic Scientists* 56 (2): 26–29.
Shi, Mingming and Marc Lanteigne. 2018. "The (Many) Roles of Greenland in China's Developing Arctic Policy." The Diplomat, 30 March. https://thediplomat.com/2018/03/the-many-roles-of-greenland-in-chinas-developing-arctic-policy/.
Sørensen, Camilla Tenna Nørup. 2018. *China as an Arctic Great Power. Potential Implications for Greenland and the Danish Realm*. Copenhagen: Royal Danish Defence College. http://pure.fak.dk/portal/files/7392648/Policy_Brief_2018_01_februar_UK.pdf.
The Associated Press. 2004. "Greenland Base to be Upgraded as Part of Missile Shield Plan." *The New York Times*, last modified 08/07, accessed 07/24, 2018, www.nytimes.com/2004/08/07/world/greenland-base-to-be-upgraded-as-part-of-missile-shield-plan.html.
Thorhallsson, Baldur and Tómas Joensen. 2015. "Iceland's External Affairs from the Napoleonic Era to the Occupation of Denmark: Danish and British Shelter." *Icelandic Review of Politics and Administration* 11 (2): 187–206. doi:10.13177/irpa.a.2015.11.2.4.

6

SECURITY AS AN ANALYTICAL TOOL

Human and comprehensive security approaches to understanding the Arctic

Gunhild Hoogensen Gjørv

> The concept of security has for too long been interpreted narrowly: as security of territory from external aggression, or as protection of national interests in foreign policy or as global security from the threat of a nuclear holocaust. It has been related more to nation-states than to people.
>
> *(UNDP 1994: 22)*

Security in the Arctic is a combination of (a) multiple complex social, political, economic, and environmental processes; and (b) the power to determine which of these processes warrant prioritizing as a security issue. As such, understanding security requires us to interrogate who the actors are (both the *securitizer* and the *referent*, as well as who has power and who does not); the values being secured (what is prioritized and why); the practices (how to secure these); the ways in which these values are linked to the survival of one or more actors or referents (existential threat); and the relevance of the threat over time (future) (Hoogensen Gjørv 2017). Perceptions of security are often still dominated by a state-centric orientation in which the state is both the security actor and the referent of security. Despite increasing rhetoric claiming that relations between Arctic states have begun to replicate the chill of the Cold War days (Rasmussen 2015, Kuzmarov and Marciano 2017), it is apparent that perceptions of security in the Arctic are complex and include more than just state-level perspectives. Environmental, energy, economic, and (not least) human security perspectives are demonstrating their continued, if not increasing, relevance across the diversiform region called the Arctic (Hoogensen Gjørv and Bazely 2014).

Environmental, economic, energy, human, and state security are often closely linked and are not always easy to distinguish. Indeed, each of these categories can influence the weight and power of the others, depending on the actors who claim the power of defining them. This is very often the case in the Arctic context; for example, there is a steady stream of proposed initiatives regarding energy and mineral resource development in the Arctic region as a result of ice erosion and the expansion of accessible land and sea space. Even with the 2014 downturn in prices for oil and gas and the subsequent United Nations Framework Convention on Climate Change (UNFCCC) COP21 Paris agreement in 2015 (BBC News

2015), some analysts claim that oil and gas, particularly in the Arctic, still have a role to play in reducing dependency on coal (Topdahl and Stokka 2015). Fossil fuel development due to rapidly melting ice – allowing greater access to suspected oil and gas reserves – is also seen as a source of increased geopolitical tensions, raising the specter of the Cold War again (Brzozowski 2019).

The tensions between state and human security, economic security, energy needs, energy security, and environmental security have been heightened by the increasing global attention to and scrutiny of offshore drilling and other extractive industries, including their potential impact on global climate change, habitat degradation, and community health and welfare. Continued oil and gas exploration in the Arctic has local as well as global implications: climate change and environmental contamination of territories occupied by Indigenous peoples impact their food and health security as well as the ability of Indigenous communities to continue traditional economic and social activities such as hunting marine mammals (whale, seal) and reindeer herding (Huntington et al. 2016, Stammler and Ivanova 2017). The influence of state and regional security interests on oil and gas extraction cannot be divorced from its economic, environmental, and human security impacts. Therefore, a comprehensive analytical approach to security is required.

This chapter provides an overview of a human security approach in the Arctic that is not limited to state-based perspectives. Human security is an analytical tool that is still relatively new to the Arctic milieu. It was largely introduced, and actively promoted, as a potential approach in 2004 at the University of Tromsø (UiT), Norway (Hoogensen 2004, Hoogensen Gjørv and Bazely 2014). By 2006, it was featured in the International Polar Year (IPY) initiative of 2007–2008, and was employed as the core analytical lens in an international project that examined the impacts of oil and gas extraction practices on peoples of the Arctic (Hoogensen Gjørv et al. 2016). Since then, interest in a human security analysis in the Arctic has expanded; it is the focus of a small but growing number of researchers (Hoogensen 2009, Hoogensen et al. 2009, Stuvøy 2009, 2011, Tanentzap et al. 2009, O'Brien et al. 2010, Dale 2011, Greaves 2012, Hoogensen Gjørv and Bazely 2014, Cassotta et al. 2016, Hoogensen Gjørv et al. 2016, Hossain and Petrétei 2016, Goes 2017, Hossain and Zojer 2017, Hossain et al. 2017).

However, human security is often still treated as disconnected from so-called *traditional* security issues, relegating it to a side issue that in little or no way impacts geopolitical and hard security interests. The Arctic, insofar as it can be referred to as a unified region, demonstrates how this disconnect is neither warranted nor practical.

The borders of the eight Arctic states are not able to confine the varied and continuously changing impacts of climate change that are affecting environmental, human as well as national security; the lands and rights of Indigenous peoples are intimately connected to resource use and development by both Indigenous and non-Indigenous peoples, crossing local, regional and national interests; and "Arctic" states are also "global" states, engaged with and impacted by migration of peoples from other insecure parts of the world. All of these issues make a comprehensive security approach that is informed by human security extremely relevant to the Arctic of today.

This chapter argues that state-based approaches are insufficient and calls for a comprehensive security approach that moves beyond a narrow, exclusive, and arguably deficient analytical perspective, which includes multiple security perspectives not the least of which is environmental, and has a bottom-up or human security focus. What follows is a brief discussion of the concept of *security* itself, noting that the state has not always been the primary focus. This is followed by an in-depth discussion of human security as a concept and analytical tool, including its strengths and weaknesses. The chapter concludes by discussing a comprehensive approach to security that of necessity incorporates human security and environmental security perspectives and throws an analytical spotlight on how security can be understood within complex and diverse Arctic settings.

Security: not just about states

The concept of *security* is a concept of power, both in its content as well as in who gets to decide that content. The distinctions between human or state security, for example, are historically contingent, reflecting the values of those who have had the power to define security at a given time. It therefore bears repeating that the concept of security is not a purview of the state. It is simply about reducing or eliminating fear but *whose* fear – state, societies, individuals – is not predetermined. The work of Cicero (106–43 BCE) is cited frequently as the departure point for our understanding of the concept of security. Cicero coined the word *securitas* to reflect a state of calm undisturbed by passions like fear, anger, and anxiety (Liotta and Owen 2006, Hamilton 2013). The concept also included the acknowledgement that without security, one was "incapable" (Hamilton 2013: 62). As such, the condition of security ensures that an individual has the capacity to pursue tasks and ambitions with as little fear as possible. The concept was grounded in the individual experience, although Cicero recognized its relevance for larger political communities (Hamilton 2013). Even after the creation of states within Europe via the 1648 treaties of Westphalia, Western political philosophers continued to theorize security from the standpoint of the individual, focusing on the tensions between individual and state responsibilities for security (Rothschild 1995, Hoogensen 2005).

Not until the Napoleonic wars in the 19th century was the individual replaced by the state as the central referent object of security (Rothschild 1995). In this vision of security, as long as the state was secure, human beings were assumed to be secure via a form of trickle-down security (Hoogensen and Rottem 2004). The idea of the state as the sole security actor became increasingly prevalent throughout the 20th century, particularly during the Cold War. Nuclear annihilation and the security of individuals were largely viewed as an irrelevant contrast. Even so, attempts to widen and deepen the concept of security continued throughout this period, including environmental issues as well, opposing the concepts of society or nation to the state (Buzan 1983, Ullman 1983, Mathews 1989).

A narrower version of security still suited some scholars after the end of the Cold War, however. They claimed that security was only relevant in a select few circumstances, arguing for the continuance of a primarily state-based concept of security that followed realist traditions of international relations theory, but also the idea that to allow for other actors and issue areas would be to water down the concept and make it far less rigorous (Walt 1991). Including nonmilitary and non-state-based threats, such as pollution, disease, or economic recessions, as part of security studies was viewed as counterproductive because it "runs the risk of expanding 'security studies' excessively" and "destroy[s] its intellectual coherence" (Walt 1991: 213). This special relationship of security to the state and military, or *high politics* concerns, prompted many in the traditional security community to argue against widening the concept. Environmental security was nevertheless a front runner breaking through the barrier between high and low politics even before the end of the Cold War, and it had "indeed become part of the 'high politics' sphere in Western countries" (Græger 1996: 111).

By the early 1990s, in an atmosphere of cooperation after the end of the Cold War, it was clear that the narrow definition of security as a militarized and elite notion reserved for the state, bound within an anarchic international system regulated by superpowers, was insufficient for making sense of key international political concerns (Walt 1991, Hough 2008). Since the late 1970s, many analysts had been noting that security referred to issues that went well beyond using military power to protect the state (Ullman 1983, Rothschild 1995). Early advocates of human security, including the United Nations Development Programme (UNDP), were arguably attempting to redefine security precisely because it was considered high politics (Hough 2008) and thus commanded both political attention and funding. Including poverty and inequality as fundamental threats to (human) security, as the UNDP sought to do, would help ensure the attention, funding, and broader prioritization for these issues that had been absent during the Cold War.

The concept of human security came into popular use through its introduction in the 1994 UNDP *Human Development Report* (UNDP 1994). This report and the associated concept of human security had a substantial impact on debates about the theory and practice of security. The dominance of the state as the referent object and actor of security remains; it is regularly referred to as *traditional* or *classical* security. The human security concept, however, returns to the earlier assumption that there is nothing about security that necessitates a focus on states or precludes a focus on individuals. The chosen focus may reflect what a particular actor, value, and practice considers relevant to interpretations of future survival, but the essential meaning of security is not reduced to just one such actor, value, or practice. The concept of security includes diverse and multiple actors and multiple referent objects. Yet the security concept has often reflected the interests of those who have the power to define it. It embodies a competition of values: which values should be prioritized, and who decides (Wolfers 1952, Wibben 2008).

Human security

The 1994 UNDP report on human security was intended to generate "another profound transition in thinking – from nuclear security to human security" (UNDP 1994: 22) and against the narrow definition that dominated international relations theory discourse during the Cold War. Indeed, the notion of human security contributes to *deepening* the concept of security from the Cold War focus on military defense of the state down to the individual and to *widening* the concept from state and military security to include economic, environmental, and other domains (Buzan and Hansen 2009). It had become increasingly clear that the state was by no means the sole security actor, particularly in weak or failed states; where states chose to exclude select populations (i.e., Indigenous peoples); or where civilians had to rely on other sources, including themselves, to establish some semblance of security to manage their day-to-day existence. The UNDP report acknowledged the role of more "traditional" security threats, such as the large-scale physical violence understood as "ethnic and other conflicts," and "military spending" (UNDP 1994: 38). However, these indicators cannot be seen as the only aspects of security that take individuals into account. Human insecurity is equally severe under conditions of food insecurity, job or income insecurity, human rights violations and inequality, political insecurity, or gross environmental degradation.

Thus, at its core, human security is concerned with how people themselves experience security and insecurity. The UNDP report highlighted four essential characteristics of human security: it is "universal," "interdependent," "easier to ensure through early prevention," and "people centred" (UNDP 1994: 22–23). Human security has often been defined as "freedom from fear and freedom from want" (Winslow and Eriksen 2004, Vietti and Scribner 2013), which the UNDP report claimed were the "two major components of human security"

(UNDP 1994: 24). The 1994 UNDP report further defined seven main categories of threats to human security: political, personal, food, health, environment, economic, and community.

The Commission on Human Security (CHS), founded by the government of Japan, defined human security as the means "to protect the vital core of all human lives in ways that enhance human freedoms and human fulfilment" (CHS 2003: 4). The CHS further widened the possibility of understanding human security from the viewpoint of individuals rather than states. Both the UNDP and CHS reports are clear about the important role of the individual. Individuals are not just a security "referent," nor are state actors expected to address all manner of human security threats. Rather, the concept of human security is also a call to action and a recognition of people's agency. It acknowledges the capacities of individuals to address their own security and the barriers they face, stating that "people are the most active participants in determining their well-being" (ibid.) and are security actors in their own right, able to "meet their own essential needs and to earn their own living" (UNDP 1994: 24). As such, human security:

> Is achieved when individuals and/or multiple actors have the freedom to identify risks and threats to their well-being and values … the opportunity to articulate these threats to other actors, and the capacity to determine ways to end, mitigate or adapt to those risks and threats either individually or in concert with other actors.
>
> *(Hoogensen Gjørv et al. 2016: 186)*

The concept of human security thus draws attention to security dynamics at the level of civilians or non-state actors. Understanding the needs and capacities of persons and how they understand and manage their security needs, is crucial for both academics and policymakers. People, particularly those with marginalized voices (women, people of color, Indigenous peoples, and the poor, etc.), need to be included in any equation that helps us understand security from the local to the global level. Policymakers need to be aware of how policy may decrease human security or work against the initiatives of non-state security actors operating in the same environment.

Challenges remain

Twenty-five years after the UNDP report, human security continues to have varying relevance and application in both policy and academic worlds. The concept opened up possibilities of power, whereby actors other than states could define the parameters of security and ask whose security counted, why, and who decided.

Human security provides a framework for discussing a wide range of issues, including war and peace, humanitarian intervention, and the responsibility to protect (R2P) (ICISS 2001, Orford 2013). It is relevant to diverse disciplines, including health and medicine, criminology, gender and feminist studies, security studies, and international relations (Wibben 2008, Anand 2012, Roses Periago 2012, Newman 2016). The concept has thus gained attention in the context of nonviolent conflict, with analysts using it to make sense of intersections between challenges of identity, health, food, and environmental security, particularly in Arctic contexts (Greaves 2012, Hoogensen Gjørv and Bazely 2014, Cassotta et al. 2016). At the same time, however, human security has been subjected to sustained critique.

Some saw this as inevitable, given the absence of a clear theoretical foundation or even definition (Breslin and Christou 2015). Critics have suggested that the human security concept is everything and nothing, constituting the international relations (IR) equivalent of "motherhood and apple pie" (Paris 2001, Hoogensen and Rottem 2004: 158). The definition of "freedom from fear, freedom from want" has been criticized for being either too vague or too all-encompassing: everything in life becomes a potential human security issue so it is a "shopping list" of a wide range of otherwise disconnected issues (Krause 2004: 367). Paris (2001) noted that it was unclear whether advocates of human security saw it operating as a new security paradigm for theorists or as a progressive policy agenda for practitioners. As a conceptual framework, it is claimed that human security fails to provide a resource for either understanding global security politics or the processes through which political communities give meaning to security (McDonald 2002). It has also been accused of failing to alter the security considerations and practices of key actors – states – and of serving as a tool used by neoliberal power brokers to perpetuate Western interests, particularly through the use of military intervention (Booth 2007, Chandler 2012).

Though the UNDP report placed human security into a global perspective, it was operationalized with a predominantly Global South orientation, focusing on sources of people's insecurity such as violent conflict or extreme poverty and inequalities. The Global South orientation was clear in the adoption of the human security agenda as part of the foreign policy portfolios of northern states such as Canada, Norway, and Japan (Owen and Martin 2010, Hoogensen Gjørv and Bazely 2014). The human security policies of states like Canada and Norway were criticized for perpetuating ahistorical claims that strong states provide better security (Tadjbakhsh and Chenoy 2007, Wibben 2011). The Global North is assumed to be composed of strong states, devoid of human insecurities, that could assist the perceived insecure Global South, and by doing so support northern state security (McRae and Hubert 2001).

This co-opted approach to human security was nothing less than a form of virtuous imperialism, whereby Global North states engage in humanitarian interventions or other human security measures for the purposes of ensuring that unrest in the Global South does not reach northern states through migration or terrorism (Hoogensen Gjørv 2014). Furthermore, including human insecurities within the Global North was seen by some scholars a coopting a concept that was intended to focus on more extreme and precarious human insecurities in the Global South. They feared that including Global North human insecurities would redirect resources back to northern states that were considered more adroit in handling human insecurity (ibid.).

Comprehensive security

The end of the Cold War by the early 1990s opened the floodgates for discussions about the complexity of security, from feminist and gender security perspectives to human security. Perceptions of environmental security had been pushing their way into security discourses for a couple of decades (Greaves 2016), as had the concept of *comprehensive* security. Asian states took the lead in developing the comprehensive security concept. Dewitt discussed the advent of comprehensive or *overall* security, noting that it was coined in Japan as an alternative to the military-dominated concept of national security (Dewitt 1994). This concept did not wholly reject militarized security but instead "was meant to give a new and wider basis for Japan's international role and to rationalise its defence effort" (ibid: 2). Comprehensive security included multiple levels, from the domestic and bilateral to the regional and global (ibid: 3). The Association of Southeast Asian States (ASEAN) defined comprehensive security with a more inward-looking understanding of security; one that focused less on military aspects of security and more on the importance of "economic and social development, political stability and a sense of nationalism" (ibid.). Stability and prosperity were crucial to comprehensive security and the overall resilience of a society as well as of the ASEAN region itself: as each "part" (state) in the region strengthened itself internally, this contributed to the strength of the region as a whole. Arifi, drawing on experiences in the Balkans, linked the evolution of "new wars" theory and trends in asymmetrical warfare "from the state aspect to local context" (Arifi 2011: 21) to the relevance of comprehensive security. Threats can be local as well as transnational, transcending the boundaries of traditional national security approaches. The focus on political stability, economic growth and prosperity, and social harmony promoted an approach to security that found its roots within society – in a sense, from the bottom up.

Arifi equated the widening of the security concept by Buzan and others at the Copenhagen School (Buzan 1991, Buzan, Wæver and de Wilde 1998) with comprehensive security, as it expanded the concept across the political, military, economic, environmental, and social sectors (Arifi 2011). Though it is difficult to attribute the notion of comprehensive security to the Copenhagen School, its adherents did acknowledge a comprehensive security analysis, "requiring that one take particular care to investigate how the regional level mediates the interplay between states and the international system as a whole" (Buzan 1991: 158) and further acknowledged that the Japanese approach – credited with coining the term comprehensive security – "influence[d] positively the overall international environment, to cope unilaterally with threats, and to act in solidarity with 'countries sharing the same ideals and interests'" (Buzan, Wæver, and de Wilde 1998: 173).

At the same time, the scholars associated with the Copenhagen School are cautious about arguing that linkages across sectors can be innumerable. One example is the way in which the environmental sector is frequently linked to other sectors – including societal, economic, and military – to strengthen a security claim (ibid: 175). These claims are further strengthened when linked regionally, across states. An important point, however, is that most of this discussion still takes place at the state and interstate levels, reinforcing the dominance of state perspectives. To a degree this is mitigated by societal security approaches (Greaves). The Copenhagen School does not embrace, however, the human security perspective that is somewhat present in the Japanese approach.

Comprehensive security is broad, inclusive, and difficult to grasp, particularly with respect to a region. Each part of a region may operationalize and balance the factors relevant to security in different ways, which may not always complement regional strengths. Comprehensive security "recognises the continuing problems associated with military conflict, but argue that other factors also increasingly threaten the survivability and coherence of the state, but not only the state" (ibid: 9). Comprehensive security is more than state-based national security with a regional and global applicability, but rather emanates from and is relevant to the local community (Arifi 2011). How does this translate to the Arctic?

Heininen argued for the application of comprehensive security "so as to include the perspectives of human beings, societies and regions, rather than just states" (Heininen 2014: 38). He noted that the goal was a broader agenda of security "*including* the traditional military sector and also social, economic, and environmental sectors" (Ibid: 39, italics mine). Heininen took the Japanese concept further by explicitly noting the relevance of human security perspectives (that is, the security of non-state actors) as well as the importance of both human and environmental security perspectives in an Arctic comprehensive security constellation. Otherwise, his development of the concept resembles the thread of thinking since the 1970s, albeit with a stronger human security focus:

> Implementation of comprehensive security requires consideration of practical issues pertaining to an individual's life, such as ensuring shelter, good health, social and economic well-being, as well as life in peace without conflict, war and violence. In addition, however, comprehensive security also includes more immaterial values like political freedom, democracy, human rights and freedom from a range of threats and risks, such as disasters, pollution and other environmental problems, hunger and starvation, diseases or other illness and terrorism. It can also be interpreted to include cultural survival, freedom of expression and security of communication ... this extended definition and comprehensive interpretation of security is based on the idea that there are a vast number of threats and risks to national security, besides traditional military threats, trans-border crime and international terrorism.
>
> (*Ibid.: 40–41*)

Heininen's definition thus follows and speaks to what has become a long tradition of thinking about comprehensive security. Linkages to environmental security are crucial in this formulation. Human well-being is intricately linked to the condition of the environment. Deforestation, overgrazing, and poor conservation methods have led to environmental degradation, such as, for example, desertification, leaving the land no longer sustainable or usable for agriculture. A central area of focus has become climate change: human activities exacerbate the warming of the planet, which is predicted to have dire consequences on individuals, communities, and states (IPCC 2014).

Human security as a central feature of comprehensive security

Contrary to what was originally envisioned in the UNDP and CHS reports, a state orientation, domination, and implementation of human security interprets non-state actors as passive and renders invisible numerous human insecurities and vulnerabilities that are not identified by states. This approach assumes that community and individual voices are represented and attended to by a state actor, and it disguises and prevents shared human security concerns and experiences between peoples across communities and regions, or even states. The result is an imbalance in perceptions and explanations of what occurs within and across regions and the globe; a tendency that also disguises the contributions and competencies of different actors in providing security at different levels. While individuals clearly have a role in providing their own human security, there are many instances in which individual action is insufficient: for example, responding to interstate violence, structural threats, or issues requiring transnational cooperation. States are powerful actors in the international system that have considerable resources and capabilities; the best way to advance progressive ends within that system is to work with them.

At the same time, however, a state's embrace of human security may not necessarily be consistent with the ultimate goals of the approach. If human security emerges as a necessary response to the failure of the state system to serve the interests of people, can we realistically expect those same institutions to protect the rights of others? State leaders prioritize the rights and needs of their own population over others, which does not necessarily serve the interests of suffering populations abroad (Hataley and Nossal 2004). Moreover, states may co-opt a human security agenda to add legitimacy to business-as-usual practices or even to help justify illiberal ends.

Conclusion

Human security is a complex concept that will continue to play an integral and ongoing role in the field of security studies. It continues to be subject to debate. Is it co-opted by states, which use humanitarian rhetoric to perpetuate measures and policies that in fact may not be conducive to the security of individuals? Or is it a revolutionary and radical concept that opens up the security debate to allow room for marginalized voices?

Critical approaches to human security expose the activities and processes that are taking place on the ground. Individuals are creating spaces of security that are often fragile but in constant development. Local efforts by women and men can influence perceptions of security beyond the individual and community level. Sometimes, the powers behind competing geopolitical interests understand that local community perceptions and experiences of security can be decisive for their own purposes. This is clear when looking at the design of the Arctic Council (see Chapter 19) and its inclusion of a selection of Arctic Indigenous peoples' representatives. The lessons learned thus far are that human security perspectives emanating bottom-up from the community and individual levels are not irrelevant or side issues compared with the so-called traditional or state security perspectives articulated by governments. Particularly where state authorities are weak, fragile, or virtually nonexistent, community needs and interests can be even more crucial to security at multiple levels.

References

Anand, S. (2012). "Human Security and Universal Health Insurance." *The Lancet* 379(9810): 9–10.

Arifi, D. Q. (2011). "The Concept of «Comprehensive Security» as a Draft for Reconstructing Security in a System of International Relations." *Iliria International Review* 1(1): 19–32.

BBC News. (2015). "COP21: Paris Climate Deal is 'Best Chance to Save Planet'." *BBC Science and Environment* 13.01.16.

Booth, K. (2007). *Theory of World Security*. Cambridge, Cambridge University Press.

Breslin, S. and G. Christou. (2015). "Has the Human Security Agenda Come of Age? Definitions, Discourses and Debates." *Contemporary Politics* 21(1): 1–10.

Brzozowski, A. (2019). "Faul-tlines Surface in Arctic as Region Turns into Gepolitical Hotspot." Arctic Agenda. www.euractiv.com/section/arctic-agenda/news/fault-lines-surface-in-arctic-as-region-turns-into-geopolitical-hot-spot/.

Buzan, B. (1983). *People, States, and Fear. The National Security Problem in International Relations*. Brighton, Wheatsheaf Books.

Buzan, B. (1991). *People, States and Fear: An Agenda for International Security Studies in the Post-Cold War Era*. Dorchester: Pearson-Longman.

Buzan, B. and L. Hansen. (2009). *The Evolution of International Security Studies*. Cambridge, Cambridge University Press.

Buzan, B., Wæver, O. and De Wilde, J. (1998). *Security: A New Framework for Analysis*. Boulder and London: Lynne Rienner Publishers.

Cassotta, S., M. E. Goodsite, J. Ren and K. Hossain. (2016). "Climate Change and Human Security in a Regulatory Multilevel and Multidisciplinary Dimension: The Case of the Arctic Environmental Ocean." In *Climate Change Adaptation, Resilience, and Hazards*, W. e. a. Leal (Ed.). Switzerland, Springer International Publishing, 71–91.

Chandler, D. (2012). "Resilience and Human Security: The Post-interventionist Paradigm." *Security Dialogue* 43(3): 213–229.

CHS. (2003). *Human Security Now*. New York, Commission on Human Security.

Dale, B. (2011). Securing a Contingent Future. How Threats, Risk and Identity Matter in the Debate over Petroleum Development in Lofoten, Norway. PhD, University of Tromsø.

Dewitt, D. (1994). "Common, comprehensive, and cooperative security". *The Pacific Review* 7(1): 1–15.

Goes, M. (2017). Extracting Human Security from the Shtokman Gas Field: Security Assemblage in the Murmansk Region (2007–2012). PhD, UiT The Arctic University of Norway.

Græger, N. (1996). "Environmental Security?" *Journal of Peace Research* 33(1): 109–116.
Greaves, W. (2012). "For Whom, from What? Canada's Arctic Policy and the Narrowing of Human Security." *International Journal* 2011(12): 219–241.
Greaves, W. (2016). "Arctic (in) security and Indigenous peoples: Comparing Inuit in Canada and Sámi in Norway". *Security Dialogue* 47(6): 461–480.
Hamilton, J. T. (2013). *Security: Politics, Humanity, and the Philology of Care*. Princeton, Princeton University Press.
Hateley, T.S. and K. R. Nossal (2004). "The Limits of the Human Security. Agenda: The Case of Canada's Response to the Timor Crisis." *Global Change, Peace and Security* 16(1): 5–17.
Heininen, L. (2014). "A new northern security: Environmental degradation and risks, climate change, energy security, trans-nationalism and flows of globalization and governance". In *Environmental and Human Security in the Arctic*, G. Hoogensen Gjørv, D. R. Bazely, M. Goloviznina and A. J. Tanentzap (eds.). London and New York: Routledge, 37–57.
Hoogensen, G. (2004). *Human Security in the North: Is It Relevant? IHDP Update*. Bonn, International Human Dimensions Programme on Global Environmental Change (IHDP), 8–9.
Hoogensen, G. (2005). *International Relations, Security and Jeremy Bentham*. London and New York, Routledge.
Hoogensen, G. (2009). *Human security and Oil and Gas development in the North. V Northern Social and Environmental Congress*. Moscow, Russian Academy of Sciences, Russian Federation.
Hoogensen Gjørv, G. (2014). Virtuous Imperialism or a shared global objective? The relevance of human security in the global North. In *Environmental and Human Security in the Arctic*, G. Hoogensen Gjørv, D. R. Bazely, M. Goloviznina and A. J. Tanentzap (eds.). London and New York: Routledge, 58–79.
Hoogensen, G., D. R. Bazely, A. J. Tanentzap, J. Christensen and E. Bojko. (2009). "Human Security in the Arctic – Yes, It Is Relevant!" *Journal of Human Security* 5(2): 1–10.
Hoogensen, G. and S. V. Rottem. (2004). "Gender Identity and the Subject of Security." *Security Dialogue* 35(2): 155–171.
Hoogensen Gjørv, G. (2017). "Tensions between Environmental, Economic, and Energy Security in the Arctic." In *Northern Sustainabilities: Understanding and Addressing Change in a Circumpolar World*, G. Fondahl and G. Wilson (Eds.). Cham, Springer International Publishing, 35–46.
Hoogensen Gjørv, G. and D. Bazely, Eds. (2014). *Human and Environmental Security in the Arctic*. London, Routledge.
Hoogensen Gjørv, G., B. Dale, M. Lvova, K. A. Bråthen, V. T. González, D. Bazely, J. Christiensen, A. J. Tanentzap and E. Bojko. (2016). "Human Security in the Arctic: The IPY GAPS Project." In *Implications and Consequences of Anthropogenic Pollution in Polar Environments*, R. Kallenborn (Ed.). Berlin, Springer-Verlag, 181–202.
Hossain, K. and A. Petrétei, Eds. (2016). *Understanding the Many Faces of Human Security: Perspectives of Northern Indigenous Peoples. Studies in International Minority and Group Rights 13*. Leiden and Boston, Brill Nijhoff.
Hossain, K. and G. Zojer. (2017). "Rethinking Multifaceted Human Security Threats in the Barents Region: A Multilevel Approach to Societal Security." *Juridica Lapponica* 2 (University of Lapland).
Hossain, K., G. Zojer, W. Greaves, J. M. Roncero and M. Sheehan. (2017). "Constructing Arctic Security: An Inter-disciplinary Approach to Understanding Security in the Barents Region." *Polar Record* 53(1): 52–66.
Hough, P. (2008). *Understanding Global Security*. London, Routledge.
Huntington, H. P., L. T. Quakenbush and M. Nelson. (2016). "Effects of Changing Sea Ice on Marine Mammals and Subsistence Hunters in Northern Alaska from Traditional Knowledge Interviews." *Biology Letters* 12(20160198): 1–4.
ICISS. (2001). *The Responsibility to Protect: Report of the International Commission on Intervention and State Sovereignty (ICISS)*. Ottawa, International Development Research Centre.
IPCC (2014). *Impacts, Adaptation, and Vulnerability*. Cambridge: Cambridge University Press.
Krause, K. (2004). "The Key to a Powerful Agenda, if Properly Delimited." *Security Dialogue* 35(3): 367–368.
Kuzmarov, J. and J. Marciano. (2017). "The Russians are Coming, Again." *Monthly Review* 69(4): 15–23.
Liotta, P. H. and T. Owen. (2006). "Sense and Symbolism: Europe Takes on Human Security." *Parameters* Autumn 2006: 85–102.
Mathews, J. T. (1989). "Redefining Security." *Foreign Affairs* 68(2): 162–177.
McDonald, M. (2002). "Human Security and the Construction of Security." *Global Society* 16(3): 277–295.

McRae, R. and D. Hubert, Eds. (2001). *Human Security and the New Diplomacy: Protecting People, Promoting Peace*. Montreal and Kingston, McGill-Queen's University Press.
Newman, E. (2016). "Human Security: Reconciling Critical Aspirations with Political 'Realities'." *British Journal of Criminology* 2016(56): 1165–1183.
O'Brien, K., A. L. St. Clair and B. Kristoffersen, Eds. (2010). *Climate Change, Ethics and Human Security*. Cambridge, Cambridge University Press.
Orford, A. (2013). "Moral Internationalism and the Responsibility to Protect." *European Journal of International Law* 24(1): 83–108.
Owen, T. and M. Martin. (2010). "The Second Generation of Human Security: Lessons from the UN and EU Experience." *International Affairs* 86(1): 211–224.
Paris, R. (2001). "Human Security: Paradigm Shift or Hot Air?" *International Security* 26(2): 87–102.
Rasmussen, A. F. (2015). "A Place Apart: A Peaceful Arctic No More?" *Harvard International Review* 36 (3): 45–48.
Roses Periago, M. (2012). "Human Security and Public Health." *Pan American Journal of Public Health* 31 (5): 355–358.
Rothschild, E. (1995). "What is Security?" *Daedalus* 124(3): 53–98.
Stammler, F. and A. Ivanova. (2017). "Resources, Rights, and Communities." *Europe-Asia Studies* 68(7): 1220–1244.
Stuvøy, K. (2009). Security Under Construction: A Bourdieusian Approach to Non-state Crisis Centres in Northwest Russia. PhD, University of Tromsø.
Stuvøy, K. (2011). "Human Security, Oil and People: An Actor-based Security Analysis of the Impacts of Oil Activity in the Komi Republic, Russia." *Journal of Human Security* 7(2): 5–19.
Tadjbakhsh, S. and A. M. Chenoy. (2007). *Human Security. Concepts and Implications*. London and New York, Routledge.
Tanentzap, A. J., D. R. Bazely, P. A. Williams and G. Hoogensen. (2009). "A Human Security Framework for the Management of Invasive Nonindigenous Plants." *Invasive Plant Science and Management* 2(2): 99–109.
Topdahl, R. C. and M. Stokka (14 December 2015). "Oljeindustrien er løysinga, ikkje problemet (The oil industry is the solution, not the problem)". NRK Rogaland. Accessed 11 november 2019 at www.nrk.no/rogaland/klimaavtalen-kan-gi-konkurransefortrinn-1.12704062.
Ullman, R. H. (1983). "Redefining Security." *International Security* 8(1): 129–153.
UNDP. (1994). *Human Development Report 1994: New Dimensions of Human Security*. New York, United Nations Development Programme.
Vietti, F. and T. Scribner. (2013). "Human Insecurity: Understanding International Migration from a Human Security Perspective." *Journal on Migration and Human Security* 1(1): 17–31.
Walt, S. M. (1991). "The Renaissance of Security Studies." *International Studies Quarterly* 35(2): 211–239.
Wibben, A. (2011). *Feminist Security Studes: A Narrative Approach*. London, Routledge.
Wibben, A. T. R. (2008). "Human Security: Toward an Opening." *Security Dialogue* 39(4): 455–462.
Winslow, D. and T. H. Eriksen. (2004). "A Broad Concept That Encourages Interdisciplinary Thinking." *Security Dialogue* 35: 361–362.
Wolfers, A. (1952). "'National Security' as an Ambiguous Symbol." *Political Science Quarterly* 67(4): 481–502.

7

INDIGENOUS SECURITY THEORY

Intersectional analysis from the bottom up

Rauna Kuokkanen and Victoria Sweet

Conventional understandings of state security that are maintained through the military and characterized by protecting borders, institutions, and people from external aggressors are not only largely irrelevant, but often antithetical, to Indigenous conceptions of security. For some Arctic Indigenous peoples, the language of security is relatively new, but there are a number of issues that have long been considered a threat to their collective survival, including environmental protection, preservation of Indigenous identities and economies, as well as restoring political autonomy and Indigenous rights (Deiter and Rude 2005; EKOS 2011; Exner-Pirot 2012; Greaves 2012, 2016). Arctic Indigenous peoples who have employed security discourse have established the connection between (ongoing) colonialism and the creation of insecurities, including environmental change (Nickels et al. 2013). More recent concerns deal specifically with climate change, food security, and related issues of traditional knowledge, traditional ways of life, and health (Cameron 2012; Greaves 2012; ICC Canada 2012; Kuhnlein et al. 2014; Sejersen 2015).

This chapter is informed by "a bottom-up" human security theory that defines security "from the position of those who are most insecure" (Hoogensen Gjørv 2014: 59). In the Arctic, Indigenous women are among the least secure. Drawing on existing literature, this chapter conceptualizes Indigenous security by taking its cue from Indigenous women in the Arctic who have articulated the key aspects of security as food, shelter, and individual and collective safety. According to Rosemary Kuptana, former president of Inuit Tapiirit Kanatami, "[S]ecurity to Inuit was, and is, having food, clothing and shelter" (Kuptana 2013: 11–12). This chapter also conceives Indigenous security as necessarily informed by feminist analysis. Surveys have shown that in the Arctic, women and men not only experience security differently but also consider different issues a priority when identifying security (EKOS 2011). It has been suggested that "[T]o talk about security without thinking about gender is simply to account for the surface reflections without examining what is happening deep down below the surface" (Booth 1997: 101). Without a feminist analysis of gender, the understanding of relations of power and domination remains weak and incomplete.

Notably, however, a gendered human security analysis does not imply a sole focus on women. Gendered human security analyses expose relations of domination that otherwise are frequently rendered either insignificant or invisible. It enables us "to identify the ways in which insecurities develop as a result of relationships of dominance/nondominance, [and] how they manifest themselves according to context" (Hoogensen and Stuvøy 2006: 219). The intersection of feminist and Indigenous approaches to human security will deepen the discourse, highlight the voice of the least heard but most greatly impacted group in the Arctic, and increase the likelihood that Arctic security discussions will lead to definitive steps to promote well-being for all.

This chapter consists of four sections. The first considers existing research on Indigenous security. The second examines three interrelated concerns of Indigenous security: food, shelter, and individual/collective safety. The third examines the relationship between Indigenous security and self-determination, arguing that without addressing gender in general and violence against Indigenous women specifically, Indigenous self-government arrangements do not advance Indigenous security. In conclusion, the chapter identifies future directions in Indigenous security research in the Arctic.

Indigenous security studies and human security in the Arctic

Human security challenges conventional definitions of state security as being too narrow, elitist, masculinist, and state-centered.[1] A more robust conception of human security has drawn attention to the silencing and exclusion of gendered forms of violence in the mainstream security discourse. It has exposed the asymmetric relations of power and domination of security, and shown how security itself is gendered (Hoogensen and Stuvøy 2006). While many feminist scholars applaud the bottom-up approach, others maintain that human security is still patriarchal and military-focused because of the implications associated with the term security, the power structures within societal structures, and the tendency to focus on institutions and organizations instead of human relationships and human needs (McKay 2004). Despite these reservations, arguments have been made that the Arctic is a particularly appropriate place to transition security discussions to the human security framework because of the unique conditions and needs that exist: particularly climate-related insecurities (Goloviznina and Hoogensen Gjørv 2014; Sweet 2014a).

For example, many of the emerging security concerns are directly related to climate change. These changes are dramatically impacting the circumpolar Arctic region, but may not be as noticeable in other parts of countries with Arctic territory. Using only a state-centered approach, the leadership of each country might overlook the needs of the peoples living in the Arctic regions because their needs are so different from the rest of the country. The only way to ensure that these concerns are given proper weight is to apply a human-centered approach and allow the citizens to effectively address concerns distinct to their region (Sweet 2014a). Also, the Arctic is fairly politically stable. This creates the perfect circumstances for focusing security discussions on human-centered concerns (Hoogensen Gjørv et al. 2009).

In addition to the gendered arguments, questions have been raised about the cultural appropriateness of a human security approach. Notably absent in most of the Arctic human security discourse is the voice of Indigenous peoples. The perspective of Indigenous women on security is particularly under-studied. This is especially concerning when discussing human security in the Arctic, since the circumpolar Arctic region is home to many Indigenous communities.

Significance of Indigenous voices in security discourse

The Arctic is home to more than 400,000 Indigenous people who belong to 50 different nations, including the Inuit, Sámi, Athabaskan, Dene, Chukchi, Nenets, and others. These groups have historically enjoyed political autonomy and for generations have practiced their subsistence economies, such as hunting, trapping, fishing, and reindeer herding. Several authors have made the case that only by including Indigenous voices in security conversations will true security in the Arctic be realized. Slowey made the assertion that Indigenous people will not be fully secure until their environmental as well as social, personal, and community needs are fulfilled, and this can only occur with self-governance structures that allow for a strong voice in all discussions (Slowey 2014). A similar position was taken by Hossain when he explained that no country is truly secure when any portion of the population remains insecure, and that the one way to provide this security is through acknowledging the right to environment and the right to development and addressing these rights by guaranteeing self-determination for Indigenous peoples in the Arctic (Hossain 2015). The discourse of Indigenous self-determination, however, needs to be gendered in order to understand and further analyze the positions of domination and nondomination and how they manifest in Indigenous communities. We will discuss this at the end of the chapter.

Others have pointed out the relevance of Indigenous voices in security discourses (Simon 1989; Stern 2006; Zellen 2009) and how including community voices in these conversations empowers individuals and communities to make informed choices and act on their own behalf (Indian Law and Order Commission 2013; Ogata and Cels 2003). Greaves compared the different approaches of the Inuit and the Sámi and theorized why one group chose to phrase environmental concerns as a security issue and the other group does not discuss environmental concerns in this manner (Greaves 2016). This serves as an important reminder that not all Indigenous perspectives will be aligned and no single approach to incorporating Indigenous voices will be sufficient. No single approach to Indigenous security in the Arctic will ever be appropriate.

In addition to focusing on engaging community voices, a number of scholars have made an effort to discuss concerns related specifically to Indigenous women, including gendered violence and political participation (Irlbacher-Fox et al. 2014; Stuvøy and Sinevaara-Niskanen 2009; Sweet 2014a, 2014b). Reports have noted the lack of governmental and societal response to these concerns (Amnesty International 2004; Indian Law and Order Commission 2013). Some literature related to extractive industry development explores safety concerns beyond personal safety. Many extractive industry projects have polluted or destroyed the environment. This contamination impacts Indigenous women more dramatically than the men from the same communities (Archibald and Crnkovich 1999; Cariño 2002; Collins and Fleischman 2013; Czyzewski et al. 2014; Deiter and Rude 2005; Hall 2013).

Unfortunately, very little scholarly work has been published from the personal perspective of Indigenous women in the Arctic. While it is necessary to continue the general dialogue to remind policymakers that Indigenous voices must be at the table in security discussions, in order to fully understand how Indigenous women might define security from their own perspectives, Indigenous women's concerns and needs must be expressed and heard. In recent years, a few examples of such expressions have begun to appear. Inuit leader Sheila Watt-Cloutier expressed that the fight to protect the environment is about more than environmental security: it is a fight to protect her people's way of life and culture (Watt-Cloutier 2015). While the environmental security approach has been a useful vehicle for raising awareness, the Indigenous perspective goes beyond the idea of existing on the Earth to include the idea of being part of their surrounding territories. Thus, it could be argued that security from the perspective of Indigenous women goes deeper and is more personal than someone who does not share this worldview might understand.

Food security in the Arctic

Food security is a concept that refers to a broad set of social, economic, and physical conditions related to access to sufficient, safe, and nutritious food (FAO 2004). Food security was identified as a critical area for concern by the World Economic Forum's 2012 Global Risks Report (WEF 2012). The food system is characterized by systemic power inequities in a multitude of ways, all of which are deeply gendered and have gendered consequences. Worldwide, women and girls experience greater poverty, undernourishment, and have less access to decision-making, land and capital (Patel 2012).

Food security is a critical component of Indigenous security in the Arctic. It consists of a complex set of social, economic, cultural, political, and physical conditions, all of which are deeply gendered. These include questions of sovereignty, traditional knowledge and skills, access and availability of resources and traditional food sources, environmental change and degradation, and geography (Duhaime and Bernard 2008; ICC Canada 2012; Kuhnlein et al. 2014). Significantly, Indigenous rights play a critical role in having access to traditional territories and natural resources, including traditional foods (Kuhnlein et al. 2014).

As elsewhere, the disruption of the food systems in Arctic Indigenous communities was a result of processes of colonialism and neoliberal economic globalization and has far-reaching health, social, and cultural consequences (Robidoux and Mason 2017). Growing food insecurity has fueled food sovereignty movements that seek to attain food self-sufficiency, restore local food systems and practices, and establish control and authority over them. Some have suggested that food sovereignty is a form of decolonization and continuation of anticolonial struggles (Grey and Patel 2015), while others point out that food self-sufficiency is not necessarily a realistic option for all communities (Agarwal 2014). In the Arctic, the Inuit have been at the forefront in calling for attention to the growing problem of food security in Indigenous communities. The Inuit Circumpolar Council Canada 2012 report noted:

> Remoteness, limited transport infrastructure, difficult climatic conditions, high global prices for food commodities and oil all combine to make the cost of food and its distribution a significant driver of food insecurity for many Inuit communities. … At the same time, families living in these remote communities also have to deal with the high cost of other essential commodities.
>
> *(ICC Canada 2012: 5)*

Considerations of Indigenous food security in the Arctic are predominantly either gender-blind or biased, focusing on male practices of hunting, harvesting, and herding in spite of the fact that many women have, for generations, hunted or played other important roles in hunting (Bodenhorn 1990; Parlee 2016; Parlee et al. 2005). Gendered caretaking roles extend to animal species upon which Indigenous communities rely on in the Arctic. For example, "Inuvialuit, Gwich'in, and Sahtú women alike have responsibilities for 'taking care' of caribou that reflect women's spiritual power and their ability to influence the appearance or disappearance of caribou" (Parlee 2016: 186). Research has demonstrated that traditional knowledge and skills related to harvesting food on the land are critical factors enabling food security (e.g., Duhaime and Bernard 2008; Gombay 2010). Existing data prevents us from getting a comprehensive picture of the gender and other dynamics and structural inequalities of Indigenous food security in the Arctic.

However, there is evidence to suggest that the role of women in subsistence activities and traditional economies might be changing. For example, according to one study, young

Inuit women in Canada between the age of 15 and 24 participated the least (55%) in harvesting of traditional foods (compared to 74% of men in the same age group) (Tait 2001; see also Kuhnlein et al. 1995). What is more, income and employment play a role in accessing traditional food as money is required to purchase and operate the equipment needed to procure it (Duhaime et al. 2002; Lawn and Harvey 2001). The labor force and wage economy in the Arctic are often patterned along gender lines; more women are educated than men and they hold more permanent jobs, especially in service and public sectors (Nahanni 1992; Parlee 2016; Poppel 2005, 2014; Tróndheim 2001). It may be theorized that more women are looking for less traditional means to support food acquisition. Yet, what happens when a woman is left alone to provide for children with no willing or competent male relatives? In most Arctic areas, it takes the combination of both male and female efforts, and without male support it appears that these women suffer the most. Studies indicate that in some Arctic Indigenous communities, gendered division of labor, such as the availability and skills of a male hunter in the household, plays a large role in having access to traditional foods (Duhaime et al. 2002; Lawn and Harvey 2001).

Gendered access to traditional foods might be mitigated by food-sharing practices and community networks of reciprocity, which remain important for food security as well as cultural and intergenerational well-being in many Arctic Indigenous communities (McMillan 2011; Kuhnlein et al. 2014: 75). These practices and networks are not gender-neutral and to understand the significance of the different roles and responsibilities that men and women play vis-à-vis food security, more research needs to be done.

As elsewhere, socioeconomic and political factors have gendered consequences on food systems and food security. Access to and consumption of traditional foods remains central to security of Indigenous peoples in the Arctic. As an example, although Indigenous women hold specific land management practices and have deep, complex knowledge and skills related to gathering, using and taking care of plants and animals (Turner 2003), they "largely lack a voice in co-management decision making, and their role in household economies has been neglected in research and rarely informs policy" (Parlee 2016: 186).

Further, food insecurity is closely connected to housing insecurity, which in some Arctic Indigenous regions is particularly severe. The provision of food is among the greatest challenges faced by people with housing insecurity. This is an especially critical concern for women with children, who may have to choose to go hungry themselves in order to feed their children. Women with children are also gravely impacted by the lack of housing because without adequate accommodation, children are at risk of being apprehended (Bopp et al. 2007).

Homelessness and housing insecurity

In many Arctic communities, homelessness is an urgent problem that remains inadequately addressed. The rates of homelessness are commonly higher among Indigenous peoples than other populations. A recent report of the Standing Senate Committee on Aboriginal Peoples revealed that due to substandard homes, severe overcrowding, and a lack of adequate housing, many families in Inuit communities in Canada are "one step away from homelessness" (Dyck and Patterson 2017). A study from Nunavut identified the housing crisis, together with poverty, lack of education, and limited employment, as one of the main contributing factors in making Inuit more susceptible to human trafficking and "being lured by traffickers to move to the south to escape challenging living conditions and limited options" (Roos 2013: 40).

Severe overcrowding also results in a lack of privacy and quiet spaces for children to study, which compounds family tensions and may lead to domestic violence and child abuse (Dyck and Patterson 2017; Meyer 2005; Roos 2013). Community services, shelters or transitional housing are extremely limited or nonexistent and as a result victims are often forced to stay in abusive situations (Dyck and Patterson 2017; Enoksen 2005; Roos 2013; Schmidt et al. 2015).[1] Those who leave their communities due to violence and go into shelters in more urban areas are often faced with homelessness in the new setting.

Studies have illustrated how the complex web of interlocking vicious cycles can make it extremely challenging for Indigenous women to get out of housing and food insecurity. There are regional differences; for example, in Nunavut, rapid population growth, and, in the Northwest Territories, unprecedented economic growth, play a role in creating housing insecurity and homelessness (Christensen 2017; Dyck and Patterson 2017). More structural, systemic factors such as paternalistic colonial policies combined with often aggressive resource extractive practices have profoundly transformed life in many Arctic Indigenous communities and are frequently overlooked when assessing and analyzing housing insecurity (Christensen 2017: 4–5).

Housing insecurity in the Arctic is illustrative of the intersections of race and gender oppression and the ways in which inadequate housing conditions compound the vulnerability of Indigenous women and their children to violence and abuse. In most regions of the Arctic, research or statistics on violence against Indigenous women remains scant (United Nations Permanent Forum on Indigenous Issues (UNPFII) 2019). In regions where studies exist, gendered violence is considerably higher than average (see Eriksen et al. 2015; Mcgrath 2014; Naalakkersuisut 2013; Pauktuutit 2006; Statistics Canada 2006). When seeking assistance, experiences of racism, sexism, and stigmatization are common. Further, some women are faced with abandonment "by their families and friends for a variety of reasons including leaving their home communities, being blamed for abuse and assault and for their lifestyles (i.e. being homeless and using substances)" (Schmidt et al. 2015: np). Without a gender analysis, the different factors and consequences of housing insecurity between men and women in Arctic Indigenous communities are made invisible.

Indigenous security and self-determination

It has been suggested that Arctic Indigenous communities are more secure if they have greater self-determination. Drawing on research in Indigenous communities, Slowey argued that negotiating and settling land claims simultaneously with self-government agreements (rather than negotiating land claims alone) significantly contributes to the collective decision-making authority and the community's ability to take control over political affairs. Specifically, in Arctic Indigenous communities with intensified extractive industry activities, self-government significantly strengthens the community's ability to "address their human security issues" (Slowey 2014: 188). However, strong self-government alone will not be sufficient to alleviate safety concerns related to extractive industry development projects.

The negative impacts of development projects on Northern Indigenous communities, particularly on Indigenous women, have been addressed by a number of authors who discussed the physical violence and exploitation that already has been or could potentially be perpetrated on Indigenous women (Cox and Mills 2015; Hall 2013; Koutouki and Lofts 2018; Little 2007; Nightingale et al. 2017; Sweet 2014a, 2014b). Risk factors that increase the likelihood of violence include the large numbers of transient male workers entering an area, the inability of rural communities (most Arctic development projects will likely be located in rural areas) to absorb and address infrastructure needs (including policing to keep community members safe), and the history of prejudice and violence against Indigenous communities (Sweet 2014a). Even a community with strong self-government will require new funding and proactive community and organizational actions in order to effectively respond to the first two identified factors, and there are no quick solutions to systemic and societal biases.

What is more, existing self-governing institutions in the Arctic have largely failed to address the prevalent problem of violence against Indigenous women and children. According to research, there is a general consensus among Indigenous women in Canada, Scandinavia, and Greenland that the interpersonal dimension of gender violence must be an inextricable part of the process and implementation of Indigenous self-determination. Gender violence is a relation and structure of domination that prevents not only Indigenous women from participating in advancing the collective self-determination of their communities, nations, and societies, but ultimately prevents Indigenous communities, nations, and societies from achieving self-determination (Kuokkanen 2019).

In order for Indigenous self-government to truly advance the human security of Indigenous peoples in the Arctic it needs to pay attention to gendered violence. It is not possible to discuss security in Indigenous communities without addressing interpersonal physical and sexual violence, both of which are fundamentally gendered. Self-government may increase decision-making authority and jurisdiction, but in and of itself it does not advance human security in Indigenous communities. Gender violence negatively impacts entire communities, not just women and girls, often creating cycles of violence and intergenerational trauma, as well as causing the breakdown of family and kinship relations, including the removal of children to the child-welfare system. This impacts community cohesion and the community's ability to control its collective affairs. The Indigenous human security discourse needs to pay specific attention to the silencing and exclusion of gendered forms of violence at a number of levels, including research, self-government institutions, and at the grassroots level in Indigenous communities.

Conclusion

This chapter established the core elements of Indigenous security as food, shelter, and personal/community safety. It demonstrated that these elements are intertwined with and informed by complex environmental, political, social, and cultural concerns. We argued that in addition to acknowledging the complexity of these elements, a comprehensive conception of Indigenous security in the Arctic and future Indigenous security research must comprise an intersectional analysis that simultaneously accounts for Indigeneity and gender. As our examination has shown, without an intersectional approach both the analysis and subsequent solutions remain inadequate. Conceptualizing Indigenous security in gender-neutral terms obfuscates the dynamics and power relations involved in the security discourse, resulting in analyses and policies that are partial at best, or misguided at worst. What need to be addressed are gender-specific social and economic factors and institutionalized structures of domination and control.

Existing scholarship on Arctic Indigenous security is limited and tends to homogenize Indigenous communities in non-gendered terms. There is little recognition that the approach that works with one group may not be appropriate for a different group. Examining the core elements of Indigenous security without a gender analysis obfuscates critical aspects such as how intimate-partner violence contributes to housing insecurity of many Indigenous women. In turn, housing insecurity frequently increases food insecurity, with far-reaching consequences for women with children.

Moreover, an intersectional analysis incorporates an examination of the structural inequalities of Arctic Indigenous security. It considers the relations of domination ranging from the intimate micro-level to the macro-levels of state and global geopolitics with a specific Indigenous gendered analytic. It recognizes not only that elitist militaristic security discourses are a central part of the relations of domination and a form of structural violence, but also that state-centered conceptions of security are irrelevant and inappropriate for Indigenous peoples.

Indigenous intersectional security theory interrogates how the structural violence of state and state institutions, including patriarchal and patronizing colonial policies, and more recent neoliberal economic development agendas, have wreaked havoc with the social, political, and cultural security of Arctic Indigenous communities. The intersection of all these aspects requires more detailed empirical research and theoretical considerations in order to set an agenda for future Indigenous security research and policymaking in the Arctic and beyond.

Acknowledgment

The authors thank Frances Abele for her helpful comments.

Notes

1 For a discussion on strengths and weaknesses of the concept of human security, see the special issue of *Security Dialogue* 2004 35(3): 347–387.

2 For example, only seven of the 53 communities in Nunavut have shelters (Mcgrath 2014). In Greenland, there are fewer than 10 crisis centers in the entire country for victims of domestic violence (Enoksen 2005).

References

Agarwal, Bina (2014). "Food Sovereignty, Food Security and Democratic Choice: Critical Contradictions, Difficult Conciliations." *Journal of Peasant Studies* 41(6): 1247–1268.

Amnesty International (2004). *Stolen Sisters: A Human Rights Response to Discrimination and Violence against Indigenous Women in Canada*. Ottawa, Amnesty International.

Archibald, Linda and Mary Crnkovich (1999). "If Gender Mattered: A Case Study of Inuit Women, Land Claims and the Voisey's Bay Nickel Project." Ottawa, Status of Women Canada. 40 pp.

Bodenhorn, Barbara (1990). "I'm Not the Great Hunter, My Wife Is': Inupiat and Anthropological Models of Gender." *Études/Inuit/Studies* 14(1–2): 55–74.

Booth, Ken (1997). "Security and Self: Reflections of a Fallen Realist." *Critical Security Studies*. Krause, Keith and Michael C. Williams eds. Minneapolis, University of Minnesota Press: 83–120.

Bopp, Judie, Rian van Bruggen, et al. (2007). *You Just Blink and It Can Happen: A Study of Women's Homelessness North of 60. Pan-Territorial Report*. Cochrane, Four Worlds Centre for Development Learning, Qulliit Nunavut Status of Women Council, YWCA Yellowknife, Yellowknife Women's Society and Yukon Status of Women's Council.

Cameron, Emilie S. (2012). "Securing Indigenous Politics: A Critique of the Vulnerability and Adaptation Approach to the Human Dimensions of Climate Change in the Canadian Arctic." *Global Environmental Change* 22(1): 103–114.

Cariño, Jill (2002). "Women and Mining in the Cordillera and the International Women and Mining Network." *Tunnel Vision: Women, Mining and Communities*. Macdonald, Ingrid and Claire Rowland Eds. Victoria, Australia, Oxfam Community Aid Abroad: 16–19.

Christensen, Julia (2017). *No Home in a Homeland: Indigenous Peoples and Homelessness in the Canadian North*. Vancouver, UBC Press.

Collins, Ben and Lesley Fleischman (2013). *Human Rights and Social Conflict in the Oil, Gas, and Mining Industries: Policy Recommendations for National Human Rights Institutions*. Boston and Washington, DC, Oxfam America.

Cox, David and Suzanne Mills (2015). "Gendering Environmental Assessment: Women's Participation and Employment Outcomes at Voisey's Bay." *Arctic* 68(2): 246–260.

Czyzewski, Karina, Frank Tester, et al. (2014). "The Impact of Resource Extraction on Inuit Women and Families in Qamani'tuaq, Nunavut Territory: A Qualitative Assessment." Toronto, Canadian Women's Foundation.

Deiter, Connie and Darlene Rude (2005). *Human Security and Aboriginal Women in Canada*. Ottawa, Status of Women Canada.

Duhaime, Gérard and Nick Bernard, eds. (2008). *Arctic Food Security*. Edmonton, Canadian Circumpolar Institute Press & Centre interuniversitaire d'études et de recherches autochtones.

Duhaime, Gérard, Marcelle Chabot, et al. (2002). "Food Consumption Patterns and Socioeconomic Factors among Inuit of Nunavik." *Ecology of Food and Nutrition* 41(2): 91–118.

Dyck, Lillian Eva and Dennis Glen Patterson (2017). *We Can Do Better: Housing in Inuit Nunangat*. Ottawa, Standing Senate Committee on Aboriginal Peoples.

EKOS (2011). *Rethinking the Top of the World: Arctic Security Public Opinion Survey*. Toronto, Walter and Duncan Gordon Foundation & Canada Centre for Global Security Studies at the Munk School of Global Affairs.

Enoksen, Regine (2005). "Arbejdet På Krisecentre Og Klientellet." *Køn Og Vold I Grønland*. Poppel, Mariekathrine Ed. Nuuk, Forlaget Atuagkat: 327–331.

Eriksen, Astrid M. A., Ketil Lenert Hansen, et al. (2015). "Emotional, Physical and Sexual Violence among Sámi and Non-Sámi Populations in Norway: The Saminor 2 Questionnaire Study." *Scandinavian Journal of Public Health* 43(6): 588–596.

Exner-Pirot, Heather (2012). "Human Security in the Arctic: The Foundation of Regional Cooperation." *Working Papers on Arctic Security No. 1*. Toronto, Walter and Duncan Gordon Foundation.

FAO (2004). *The State of Food Insecurity in the World 2004: Monitoring Progress Towards the World Food Summit and Millennium Development Goals*. Rome, Food and Agriculture Organization of the United Nations.

Goloviznina, Marina and Gunhild Hoogensen Gjørv (2014). "Conclusion: Revisiting Arctic Security." *Environmental and Human Security in the Arctic*. Hoogensen Gjørv, Gunhild, Dawn Bazely, Marina Goloviznina and Andrew Tanentzap Eds. London & New York, Routledge: 269–274.

Gombay, Nicole (2010). "Community, Obligation, and Food: Lessons from the Moral Geography of Inuit." *Geografiska Annaler Series B-Human Geography* 92B(3): 237–250.

Greaves, Wilfrid (2012). "Turtle Island Blues: Climate Change and Failed Indigenous Securitization in the Canadian Arctic." *Working Paper on Arctic Security No. 2*. Toronto, Walter and Duncan Gordon Foundation.

——— (2016). "Arctic (in)Security and Indigenous Peoples: Comparing Inuit in Canada and Sámi in Norway." *Security Dialogue* 47(6) (December 2016): 461–480.

Grey, Sam and Raj Patel (2015). "Food Sovereignty as Decolonization: Some Contributions from Indigenous Movements to Food System and Development Politics." *Agriculture and Human Values* 32(3): 431–444.

Hall, Rebecca (2013). "Diamond Mining in Canada's Northwest Territories: A Colonial Continuity." *Antipode* 45(2): 376–393.

Hoogensen Gjørv, Gunhild (2014) "Virtuous Imperialism or a Shared Global Objective? The Relevance of Human Security in the Global North." *Environmental and Human Security in the Arctic*. Hoogensen Gjørv, Gunhild, Dawn Bazely, Marina Goloviznina and Andrew Tanentzap eds. London, Routledge: 58–80.

Hoogensen Gjørv, Gunhild, Dawn Bazely, et al. (2009). "Human Security in the Arctic – Yes It Is Relevant!" *Journal of Human Security* 5(2): 1–10.

Hoogensen, Gunhild and Kirsti Stuvøy (2006). "Gender, Resistance and Human Security." *Security Dialogue* 37(2): 207–228.

Hossain, Kamrul (2015). "Securing the Rights: A Human Security Perspective in the Context of Arctic Indigenous Peoples." *Yearbook of Polar Law* 5: 493–522.

ICC Canada (2012). *Food Security across the Arctic. Background Paper of the Steering Committee of the Circumpolar Inuit Health Strategy*. Ottawa, Inuit Circumpolar Council - Canada.

Indian Law and Order Commission (2013). "Reforming Justice for Alaska Natives: The Time Is Now." *A Roadmap for Making Native America Safer: Report to the President & Congress of the United States*. 55–61.

Irlbacher-Fox, Stephanie, Jackie Price, et al. (2014). "Women's Participation in Decision Making: Human Security in the Canadian Arctic." *Environmental and Human Security in the Arctic*. Hoogensen Gjørv Gunhild, Dawn Bazely, Marina Goloviznina and Andrew Tanentzap Eds. London & New York, Routledge: 203–230.

Koutouki, Konstantia and Katherine A. Lofts. Available at SSRN: (2018). "A Rights-Based Approach to Indigenous Women and Gender Inequities in Resource Development in Northern Canada."

Kuhnlein, Harriet V., Fikret Berkes, et al. (2014). *Aboriginal Food Security in Northern Canada: An Assessment of the State of Knowledge*. Ottawa, Council of Canadian Academies.

Kuhnlein, Harriet V., R. Soueida, et al. (1995). "Baffin Inuit Food Use by Age, Gender and Season." *Journal of the Canadian Dietetic Association* 56(4): 595–626.

Kuokkanen, Rauna (2019). *Restructuring Relations: Indigenous Self-Determination, Governance and Gender*. New York, Oxford University Press.

Kuptana, Rosemary (2013). "The Inuit Sea." *Nilliajut: Inuit Perspectives on Security, Patriotism, and Sovereignty*. Scot Nickels, Karen Kelley, Carrie Grable, Martin Lougheed, James Kuptana Eds. Ottawa, Inuit Tapiriit Kanatami: 10–13.

Lawn, Judith and Dan Harvey (2001). *Change in Nutrition and Food Security in Two Inuit Communities, 1992 to 1997*. Ottawa, Indian and Northern Affairs Canada.

Little, Lois (2007). "Securing Our Place in Northern Society - Women, Global Industries and the Power of Stories." Athabasca University.

Mcgrath, Melanie (2014). *Endemic Rape, Sex Trafficking and Appalling Levels of Domestic Violence: Why the Us and Canadian Arctic Is One of the World's Most Dangerous Places to Be a Woman*. MailOnline. 1 Sept. www.dailymail.co.uk/femail/article-2737814/Why-US-Canadian-Arctic-one-worlds-dangerous-places-woman.html-ixzz4nB4sPpvo (accessed 18 Jul. 2017).

McKay, Susan (2004). "Women, Human Security, and Peace-Building: A Feminist Analysis." *Conflict and Human Security: A Search for New Approaches of Peace-Building*. Shinoda, Hideaki and How Won Jeong Eds. Hiroshima, IPSHU: 152–175.

McMillan, Roger (2011). "Resilience to Ecological Change: Contemporary Harvesting and Food-Sharing Dynamics in the K'asho Got'ine Community of Fort Good Hope, Northwest Territories." *Department of Resource Economics and Environmental Sociology*. Edmonton, University of Alberta.

Meyer, Jørgen (2005). "Køn of Vold - Udviklingen Set Med Politiets Øjne." *Køn Og Vold I Grønland*. Poppel, Mariekathrine Ed. Nuuk, Forlaget Atuagkat: 56–62.

Naalakkersuisut (2013). *Bryd Tavsheten! Stop Volden. Naalakkersuisut's Handlingsplan Mod Vold 2014–2017*. Nuuk, Naalakkersuisut (Government of Greenland).

Nahanni, Phoebe (1992). "Dene Women in the Traditional and Modern Northern Economy in Denendeh, Northwest Territories, Canada." *Dept. of Geography*. Montreal, McGill University. MA.

Nickels, Scot, Karen Kelley, et al., Eds. (2013). *Nilliajut: Inuit Perspectives on Security, Patriotism, and Sovereignty*. Ottawa, Inuit Tapiriit Kanatami.

Nightingale, Elana, Karina Czyzewski, et al. (2017). "The Effects of Resource Extraction on Inuit Women and Their Families: Evidence from Canada." *Gender and Development* 25(3): 367–385.

Ogata, Sadako and Johan Cels (2003). "Human Security: Protecting and Empowering the People." *Global Governance* 9(3): 273–322.

Parlee, Brenda (2016). "Gender and the Social Dimensions of Changing Caribou Populations in the Western Arctic." *Living on the Land: Indigenous Women's Understanding of Place*. Kermoal, Nathalie and Isabel Altamirano-Jimenez Eds. Edmonton, Athabasca University Press: 169–190.

Parlee, Brenda, Fikret Berkes, et al. (2005). "Health of the Land, Health of the People: Case Study on Gwich'in Berry Harvesting in Northern Canada." *Eco Health* 2: 127–137.

Patel, Raj (2012). "Food Sovereignty: Power, Gender, and the Right to Food." *PLoS Medicine* 9(6): e1001223. https://doi.org/10.1371/journal.pmed.1001223.

Pauktuutit (2006). *National Strategy to Prevent Abuse in Inuit Communities, and Sharing Knowledge, Sharing Wisdom: Guide to the National Strategy*. Ottawa, Pauktuutit Inuit Women of Canada.

Poppel, MarieKathrine (2005). "Barrierer for Grønlandske Mænd På Arbejdsmarkedet." *Arbejdsmarkedet I Grønland*. Carlsen, A. V. Ed. Nuuk, Ilisimatusarfik: 125–140.

——— (2014). "Citizenship of Indigenous Greenlanders in a European Nation State: The Inclusionary Practices of *Iverneq*." *Reconfiguring Citizenship: Social Exclusion and Diversity within Inclusive Citizenship Practices*. Dominelli, Lena and Mehmoona Moosa-Mitha. Surrey & Burlington, Ashgate: 127–136.

Robidoux, Michael A. and Courtney W. Mason (2017). *A Land Not Forgotten: Indigenous Food Security and Land-Based Practices in Northern Ontario*. Winnipeg, University of Manitoba Press.

Roos, Helen (2013). "Phase I – Service and Capacity Review for Victims of Sexual Exploitation and Human Trafficking in Nunavut." Gatineau, Roos-Remillard Consulting Services.

Schmidt, Rose, Charlotte Hrenchuk, et al. (2015). "Trajectories of Women's Homelessness in Canada's 3 Northern Territories." *International Journal of Circumpolar Health* 74. DOI: 10.3402/ijch.v74.29778

Sejersen, Frank (2015). *Rethinking Greenland and the Arctic in the Era of Climate Change. New Northern Horizons*. New York and London, Routledge.

Simon, Mary (1989). "Security, Peace and the Native Peoples of the Arctic." *The Arctic: Choices for Peace and Security*. Berger, Thomas R. Ed.. West Vancouver, Gordon Soules: 31–36.

Slowey, Gabrielle (2014) "Aboriginal Self-Determination and Resource Development Activity: Improving Human Security in the Canadian Arctic?" *Environmental and Human Security in the Arctic*. Hoogensen Gjørv, Gunhild, Dawn Bazely, Marina Goloviznina and Andrew Tanentzap Eds.. London, Routledge: 187–202.

Statistics Canada (2006). *Measuring Violence against Women. Statistical Trends 2006*. Ottawa, Statistics Canada.

Stern, Maria (2006). *Naming Security- Constructing Identity: 'Mayan-Women' in Guatemala on the Eve of Peace*. Manchester, Manchester University Press.

Stuvøy, Kirsti and Heidi Sinevaara-Niskanen (2009). "Agencies of Human Security in the North." *Journal of Human Security* 5(1): 32–48.

Sweet, Victoria (2014a). "Extracting More Than Resources: Human Security and Arctic Indigenous Women." *Seattle University Law Review* 37: 1221–1224.

——— (2014b). "Rising Waters, Rising Threats: The Human Trafficking of Indigenous Women in the Circumpolar Region of the United States and Canada." *MSU Legal Studies Research Paper* 12(1): np.

Tait, Heather (2001). *Harvesting and Country Food: Fact Sheet. Inuit in Canada: Findings from the Aboriginal Peoples Survey – Survey of Living Conditions in the Arctic*. Ottawa, Statistics Canada.

Tróndheim, Gitte (2001). "The Flexibility of Greenlandic Women." *Indigenous Affairs*. Copenhagen, IWGIA. 1–2, 58–66.

Turner, Nancy J. (2003). "Passing on the News: Women's Work, Traditional Knowledge and Plant Resource Management in Indigenous Societies of North-Western North America." *Women and Plants. Gender Relations in Biodiversity* Management *and Conservation*. Howard, Patricia L. Ed. London, Zed Books: 133–149.

'United Nations Permanent Forum on Indigenous Issues (UNPFII),' *United Nations Department of Economic and Social Affairs – Indigenous Peoples*, 2019.

Watt-Cloutier, Sheila (2015). *The Right to Be Cold: One Woman's Story of Protecting Her Culture, the Arctic and the Whole Planet*. London, Allen Lane.

WEF (2012). *Global Risks Report*. Geneva, World Economic Forum.

Zellen, Barry Scott (2009). *On Thin Ice: The Inuit, the State, and the Challenge of Arctic Sovereignty*. Lanham, Lexington Books.

8
ENERGY SECURITY IN THE ARCTIC

Magnus DeWitt, Hlynur Stefánsson, and Ágúst Valfells

Arctic energy systems

There are many different definitions of energy security. The International Energy Agency (IEA) defines energy security as the "uninterrupted availability of energy sources at an affordable price" (IEA 2018b). The IEA split energy security into short-term and long-term parts. The short-term part concerns the ability of the system to react to sudden changes on the demand and supply side, and how to balance the electricity system. On the other hand, the long-term part focuses on timely investment and long-term development in terms of the economy and environment.

Energy security plays an important role in the Arctic. The most important part of energy security in rural Arctic areas concerns the uninterrupted availability of energy, or the security of supply. There is a special focus on electricity, which is in use for several matters that are related to safety and public health rather than just for productivity, personal convenience or entertainment (Allen et al. 2016, 24). If a failure were to occur, it would be dangerous for the population under the cold and harsh Arctic conditions in such remote areas (Government of Canada 2011, 12). Due to the remoteness of many of these communities, it can take some time to bring the needed spare parts and technicians on site if they are not already in place. The difficult weather conditions can also make transportation impossible. The need for electricity for public security and health makes an uninterrupted supply under the harsh Arctic weather conditions very important. The supply chain, generation, and utility system must operate reliably under the given circumstances. Since diesel-fueled generators have proven reliable for electricity production under Arctic conditions, more than 80% of the remote communities in the Arctic are exclusively dependent on fossil fuels as a primary energy source (Bhattarai and Thompson 2016, 710). In larger communities, hydropower is often in use if it is locally available (Naalakkersuisut 2018, 11). Other sources such as wind and solar can be found as substitutional energy sources (Boute 2016, 1030). However, locally based diesel-driven electricity generation has some downsides in terms of energy security and social and environmental impacts, as underlined in the following sections.

Critical issues for energy security in the Arctic areas

Connected and unconnected communities

In terms of energy systems, Arctic communities can be divided into two categories: connected and unconnected communities. Connected communities have access to a continental electricity grid or natural gas grid. The connection to a continental grid allows them to trade electricity with the grid, to sell or purchase electricity to match their demands, and secure the electricity supply. Furthermore, a continental electricity grid has the ability to reroute the electricity flow if a failure were to occur in a part of the system. This is possible due to the large scale and the redundancy of components and possibilities to bypass broken transmission sections in a larger electricity grid. That means, for connected communities, the energy security is substantially the same as in temperate areas, with the addition of risks created by the harsh Arctic weather conditions, such as icing of transmission lines, challenging construction, and adaption of technology (Baring-Gould and Corbus 2007, 10; Sullivan et al. 2003, 49). On the other hand, unconnected communities have no access to a continental grid. They have to fulfill the demand with locally generated electricity. If a failure occurs, it is very likely that the whole system will crash. In some cases, communities in close proximity build a so-called regional grid where they can distribute electricity among themselves.

The map in Figure 8.1 shows that most areas in the Arctic are unconnected. In Scandinavia and a few parts of Russia, one can see an extension of the continental grid above the Arctic Circle. The Arctic has a population of around four million inhabitants (Fondahl, Filipova and Mack 2015, 8). A look further south shows that unconnected communities and regional grids dominate the sub-Arctic area as well. For example, in Russia 10 to 15 million people live in unconnected communities (Lombardi et al. 2016, 3). The map shows that the area of unconnected communities in Russia goes far south, stopping above the line of the Trans-Siberian railway. The area of unconnected communities in Russia represents about 60% of the Russian landmass (Susulov 2012, 1).

Short-term energy security

As mentioned before, the International Energy Agency (IEA) defines energy security from short-term and long-term perspectives. Specific characteristics in the Arctic also give rise to a mid-term perspective which deals with issues related to unconnected Arctic communities. In the following sections, energy security will be discussed in terms of the three different perspectives.

Short-term energy security deals with the responsiveness of the grid to rapid changes and the ability to ensure operation in a stable manner. Currently, diesel power is by far the main energy source for electricity generation in unconnected Arctic communities. The share of communities that are exclusively dependent on diesel is above 80% (Bhattarai and Thompson 2016, 710). The use of diesel for electricity generation has a long history in that region; the technology is well proven and established to work under the harsh Arctic conditions (Allen et al. 2016, 14). One of the advantages of diesel generators is their constant performance in terms of frequency and voltage (Muhando, Keith, and Holdmann 2010, 9). This allows a secure electricity supply without additional regulation equipment. As the serial chain of equipment gets longer and more complex it is likely that the system gets weaker. Several serious blackouts were caused by improperly maintained diesel generators (Government of Canada 2011, 12). To ensure a secure electricity supply, it is vital to have a secondary system as backup in the case of emergency. Even in small settlements, a second generator is needed as

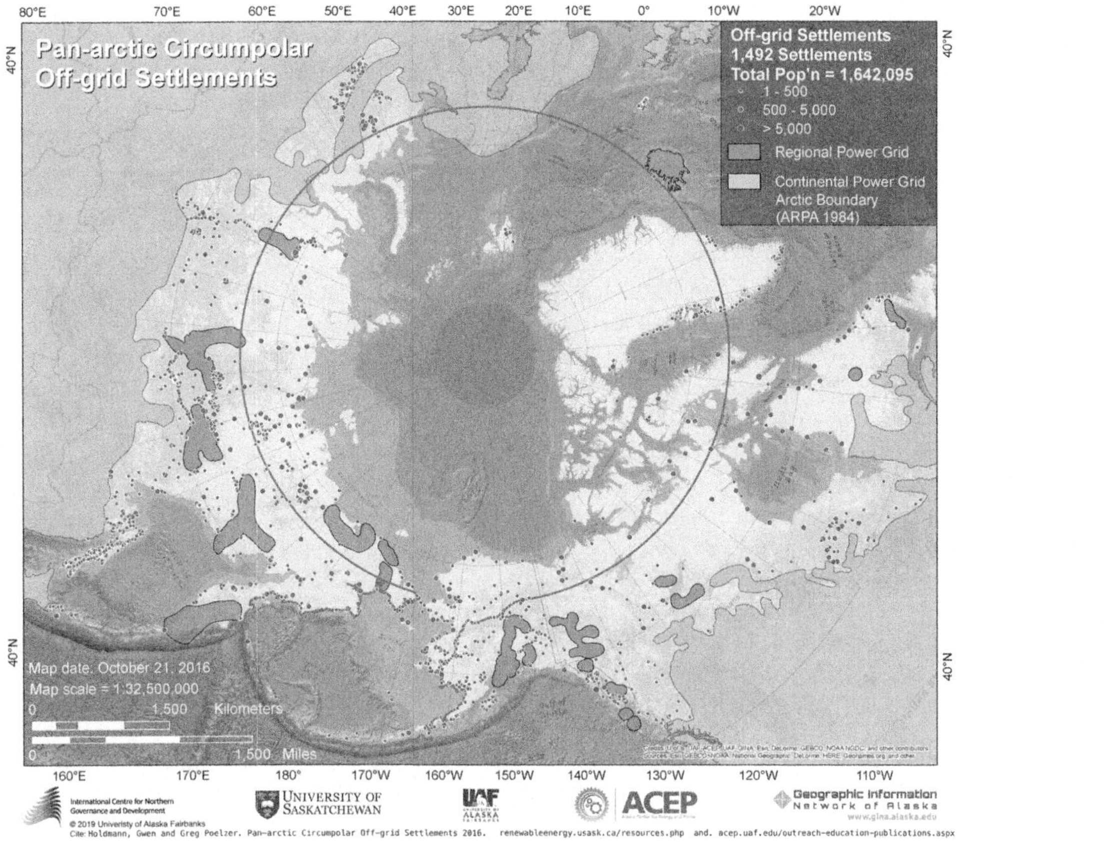

Figure 8.1 Pan-Arctic circumpolar off-grid settlements. Holdmann, Gwen, and Greg Poelzer. Pan-Arctic Circumpolar Off-grid Settlements [map]. 1: 32,500,000.

Source: Fairbanks, Alaska: Alaska Center forEnergy and Power. 2016. https://renewableenergy.usask.ca/resources.php and http://acep.uaf.edu/outreach-education-publications.aspx.

backup (WWF 2017, 5). In many cases the constant production is split over several generators, which lowers the amount of required reserve capacity. If one generator breaks down, a standby generator can take over. Furthermore, the backup generators can be used to cover peak loads, which can occur in cold winter times. In Arctic areas the backup capacity is on average 50% of the installed capacity for normal production as an ongoing study shows.[1]

An investigation of more sustainable resources for electricity generation identified two different types of resources: dispatchable and non-dispatchable energy sources (Tester et al. 2012, 101–102). The dispatchable energy resources, like hydropower and geothermal, have very specific requirements on the location or the availability of the resources. The capacity of hydro and geothermal resources varies considerably depending on the size of the resources. Geothermal power plants in most cases provide a stable base load for electricity and heat demand. The output from hydropower plants is usually more seasonal, depending on rain and snow melting, but can be regulated with reservoir lakes if geographical conditions allow. The non-dispatchable energy resources such as wind and solar are easily adjusted to the desired output. Yet the output is, as the name implies, not able to be regulated and depends on the current availability of resources that can change rapidly. For example, the wind blows and a few minutes later there is no wind at all. This pattern of the wind flow can be translated directly to performance output. This requires energy storage for a secure supply if a large amount of non-dispatchable resources is used (Tester et al. 2012, 102).

Another option is to penetrate an existing diesel generator with non-dispatchable renewable sources. A system that combines diesel generators with renewables, such as wind and solar, is called a "hybrid system" (Boute 2016, 1030). Diesel generators have the capability to be penetrated with up to 20% renewables (depending on the generator) and still be able to regulate the system's frequency and voltage (Muhando, Keith, and Holdmann 2010, 12). An increase in the renewable fraction requires additional regulation equipment, which increases the system's complexity and creates additional expenses (Baring-Gould and Corbus 2007, 6). The control system must manage the different power sources. The fluctuation in performance has to be smoothed and coordinated to create a stable voltage and frequency (Hu et al. 2015, 68). To achieve a constant performance, flywheels or super-capacitors can be used (Pedrasa and Spooner 2018, 1).

An advantage of hybrid systems is that different resources are connected to the system. The diversification of resources increases the electricity generation security such that if one source fails the others still work and an essential energy supply can be secured. Another advantage of renewable sources is that they are in a relatively close proximity to the customer. The use of local resources gives independence to the community and thereby higher levels of security. Also, if local resources can reduce the use of diesel then there will be less need for fuel deliveries, which can be vulnerable as discussed in the next section (Muhando, Keith, and Holdmann 2010, 12).

Mid-term energy security

Mid-term energy security is applicable to unconnected communities that are dependent on fuel deliveries for diesel generators. In many cases, the delivery takes place just once a year and must cover the demand for the whole of next year. Depending on the location of the community, the fuel is shipped on barges during the summertime. This is common for coastal communities or communities located on navigable rivers. Another option is to ship it with trucks on ice roads during the wintertime if the community is located on non-navigable rivers or inland. Ice roads are frozen rivers which are used as roads over the winter; often these rivers are too shallow for the use of barges.

Fuel transportation (most often diesel) has a huge influence on the price of energy, which is relatively high. The fuel is used for heating, transportation, fishing and electricity generation (Boute 2016, 1030). The affordability of energy is an important part of energy security and has a key role in the definition of energy security (IEA 2018b). The high transportation costs are created by the long distances transport has to travel (Susulov 2012, 2). Another cause is the short timeframe available for shipment. After the fuel has been transported it has to be stored, and the storage has to be large enough to supply the community for one year plus reserves (Bhattarai and Thompson 2016, 710). The storage cost is reflected in the price as well. If it is not possible to deliver enough fuel within the shipment period it must be flown in to secure the supply (Government of Canada 2011, 12).

Transportation of fuel on barges has become easier due to climate change, as the ice-free period extends. That opens a wider window for long shipments. This allows one to find a good window in the harsh weather conditions, which reduces the risk of accidents and fuel spills (Government of Canada 2011, 11; Boute 2016, 1030). In contrast, transportation on ice roads is becoming more complicated. The increase in temperature leads to a shorter opening time for the ice roads that are needed to deliver the fuel to these communities. The ice gets thinner, which makes the ice roads unstable (Bhattarai and Thompson 2016, 710). Furthermore, during wintertime the harsh weather can be a huge risk on the long drive (Boute 2016, 1030). Transporting with trucks has a negative impact on the environment, due to high greenhouse gas emissions compared to the amount of fuel that is transported (Government of Canada 2011, 11). Diesel spills are a common problem in those areas (McDonald and Pearce 2012, 466). Sometimes diesel spills happen during storage as well (Government of Canada 2011, 11). The diesel spills have a huge impact on the local environment. There is a strong connection between diesel spills and the degradation of land and wildlife (McDonald and Pearce 2013, 96). This impact has severe consequences for the surrounding communities. Many of them are dominated by Indigenous peoples who have a strong cultural connection to the land (McDonald and Pearce 2013, 96). The impact of oil spills can transfer from the wildlife into the food chain. The environmental impact can even be recognized years after an incident took place (McDonald and Pearce 2012, 466).

The long-lasting use of diesel as a primary energy source for transportation, heat, fishery, and electricity has led to a strong dependency on this fuel (McDonald and Pearce 2013, 95). The local infrastructure is completely adapted for the use of diesel. This dependency makes any potential changes in fuel technology more complicated. Use of local resources could, however, help to solve or minimize problems related to transportation (Susulov 2012, 1–2).

Long-term energy security

Emissions and climate change

Long-term energy security involves aspects such as investment in securing the supply and consequences of the resource-use over time. There are several environmental problems associated with CO_2 and black carbon emissions. The focus of this section is on the political challenges related to environmental issues and financing, which are closely related. For example, the construction of wind turbines can lower the carbon footprint. The construction cost of a wind turbine in the Arctic is two to three times more expensive than a comparable project in lower latitudes (Baring-Gould and Corbus 2007, 12). This leads to the question: would it be better to put the money and effort into projects that are located in lower latitudes? There it would be possible to build more wind turbines with the same amount of money, which would result in higher electricity production. The higher electricity production would lead to greater reduction of CO_2 emissions. The CO_2 emissions of the Arctic countries are approximately 5% of total global emissions; this number includes the whole of Russia and Denmark (Greenland) (EIA 2015; EDGAR 2017). Even if the Arctic produces such a small fraction of global emissions, it is essential to cut down emissions there since the climate change impact in the Arctic is in general more severe than in temperate regions, and the temperature increases two to three times faster than elsewhere on the planet (Perez and Yaneva 2016, 443; Skinner and Murck 2011, 597–598).

Black carbon has a huge effect on the climate. Unlike greenhouse gases (GHGs), black carbon is the solid form of carbon with a particle size of a few micrometers. The effect of black carbon can be seen to have two seemingly opposite effects: in high altitudes it blocks the sunlight from entering the atmosphere, which leads to a cooling of the atmosphere; in lower altitudes it absorbs radiation, which leads to a warming of the atmosphere (EPA 2016, 5). Compared to GHGs such as CO_2, black carbon has a short lifetime as an aerosol, on average lasting between one and two weeks (Cape, Coyle, and Dumitrean 2012, 257; Ling et al.

2017, 1037). A huge problem in the Arctic can arise from black carbon emissions after its lifetime as an aerosol. If the particular matter settles down on ice or snow, these particles lower the albedo effect. The albedo effect reflects sunlight, and the particles absorb the radiation and accelerate the melting of snow or ice (EPA 2016, 5). The aforementioned short lifetime of black carbon is one reason why it is important to stop burning fossil fuels in Arctic regions. Studies have shown that the range of distribution of black carbon is more regionally distributed (EPA 2016, 5). Therefore, it is more important to focus on the Arctic and nearby regions to lower the effect of heating due to black carbon emission.

Climate change mitigation

Due to increasing environmental awareness, there have been developments in climate change mitigation, starting in 1992 with the founding of the UNFCCC (United Nations Framework Convention on Climate Change) (Duyck 2015, 2). Later, in 1997, the Kyoto Protocol was announced as a first step to reduce greenhouse gas emission and climate-related issues (Duyck 2015, 2). In 2015, the Paris Agreement was the next step; 187 countries supported the agreement. These countries produce 97% of the world's greenhouse gas emissions (NRDC 2015, 1). These countries agreed on a long-term goal of reducing CO_2 and other pollutants in the energy sector and other industries. The aim is to keep the global warming under 2°C on average compared to preindustrial levels (NRDC 2015, 2).

Political effects in the Arctic can be observed as a result of global processes to cut down on emissions. Some Arctic countries have already introduced policies to lower their carbon footprints. A goal of the Arctic Council is to cut down black carbon emissions to mitigate the dangerous effects in the Arctic. The Arctic states emitted approximately 720 kilotons of black carbon in 2013 (Arctic Council 2017, 37–38). The recommendation of the Arctic Council Experts Group was to reduce black carbon emission by 25%–33% in 2025 compared to 2013 (Arctic Council 2017, 5). The individual Arctic countries have different political strategies to lower their carbon footprints. The strategies are in most cases related to the introduction of renewables and increasing the efficiency of existing infrastructure. The following paragraphs give a glimpse of activities and targets in different countries.

Russia used 20% renewables for electricity generation in 2015 (Gielen and Saygin 2017, 1). Large-scale hydro dominates by far, with approximately 97.4% of all renewables (Gielen and Saygin 2017, 1). The remaining 2.6% are solar, wind, biomass, and geothermal, among others. In official reports large-scale hydropower is excluded from renewables, which results in a share of renewables of slightly over 0.5%. The aim of the Russian government is to increase the share of renewables, excluding large-scale hydropower, to 4.5% by 2020 (Boute 2016, 1031; Lombardi et al. 2016, 1).

Alaska also aims to increase the share of renewable energy sources in the energy sector. The state's government announced a goal of 50% renewables by 2025 (Allen et al. 2016, 7). A look at net generation levels reveals that Alaska is already close to that target, with 48% renewables in May 2018 (EIA 2018). Hydropower is the largest renewable energy source and only 7% of all renewables are from sources other than hydropower (EIA 2018).

The current share of renewables in Greenland is around 70%, mainly consisting of hydropower (Bawa 2015, 23; WWF 2017, 5). The aim of the electricity sector is to increase the portion of renewables. The formulation of the Greenlandic government is quite vague: "By 2030, the goal is that the public energy supply must be, to the fullest extent possible, delivered from renewable energy sources" (Naalakkersuisut 2018, 4). Another target is to increase the public heat supply to reduce the dependency on oil (Naalakkersuisut 2018, 9).

Centralized water boilers can be installed that are powered by electricity during daily periods of electricity surplus. The boiler stores the electricity, which would have been wasted, in the form of heat and provides the heat to customers via a district-heating grid.

In Canada, the government aims to reduce greenhouse gas emissions by 30% of the 2005 level, which was 738 Mt CO_2 equivalent (Environment and Climate Change Canada 2018a, 5–6). This would lead to a reduction of nearly 220 Mt CO_2 equivalent. In 2017, the CO_2 emission was 716 Mt, which indicates that Canada is only 10% of the way to its target (Departmental Plan 2019 to 2020 Report, Environment and Climate Change Canada,' *Government of Canada*, 11 April 2019, www.canada.ca/en/environment-climate-change/corporate/transparency/priorities-management/departmental-plans/2019-2020.html and 'Canada's Official Greenhouse Gas Inventory,' *Government of Canada*, 29 April 2019, www.canada.ca/en/environment-climate-change/services/climate-change/greenhouse-gas-emissions/inventory.html). A detailed look shows that the energy sector is the biggest emitter, followed by the transportation sector (Environment and Climate Change Canada 2018b, 7–8). One of the incentives is to phase out subsidies for inefficient fossil fuels for electricity generation by 2025 (Environment and Climate Change Canada 2017, 16).

To make electricity affordable in the Arctic, subsidies have been introduced. In Nunavut in Canada, the government spends 20% of its annual budget on energy (McDonald and Pearce 2012, 466). In the period of 2010–2011, around $7.4 million was spent on electricity subsidies and in total nearly $40 million on energy in Nunavut (McDonald and Pearce 2012, 466). The problem of financing renewables is elaborated by the example of hydropower plants. The introduction of renewable energy sources such as hydropower plants requires high investment. Cost estimations show that the price per kilowatt installed capacity is between 4.000–6.500 $/kW for hydropower plants below 20MW (Tester et al. 2012, 637). For medium-sized hydropower plants of the size 20 to 250MW, there is a significant drop in price. The estimates assume 2.000–4.000 $/kW installed capacity (Tester et al. 2012, 637). Large-scale hydropower plants would be even cheaper. The high cost of smaller power plants can make it difficult for smaller communities to use hydropower. The advantage of hydropower plants is, however, the long lifespan of 50 to 100 years and the low operation costs (Tester et al. 2012, 637). That can make the high investment profitable over the long term (expected payback after 20 years on average).

Affordability of energy

As stated in the definition of energy security, electricity should be available for an affordable price to the consumer. As already mentioned, electricity is essential for people's health in the harsh Arctic environment, which adds more importance to the affordability of electricity. Electricity is, however, expensive in the Arctic. In Alaska, electricity is on average 3.5 times higher than the US average cost (Allen et al. 2016, 12). In Nunavut, in extreme cases the price can be up to ten times more expensive (McDonald and Pearce 2012). The high cost of electricity is a huge problem in regions with high unemployment rates and poverty. This can also be found among small remote northern Indigenous communities (Coates and Poelzer 2014, 26; Koivurova, Tervo, and Atepien 2008, 9). This and other factors create high living costs in remote northern communities.

Heating is very important in the Arctic and there are plans for improved district-heating systems. To increase the efficiency of fossil fuel use, the waste heat from diesel power plants can be used for residential heating (Karanasios and Parker 2016, 54). Another heat source can be heat recovery from waste-burning facilities (Statistics Greenland 2017, 24). More negative side effects of the use of diesel are the greenhouse gas emissions, which can have a negative influence on the population's health (Government of Canada 2011, 12). Furthermore, the noise of the generators can be very disruptive in remote and quiet communities (Government of Canada 2011, 12). These factors all lower the quality of life in those remote areas.

Towards a sustainable and secure energy future

To ensure energy security in the future, the two points of the IEA definition, "affordability" and "reliability," have to match. As discussed before, there are problems in many regions with affordability, and the dependency on a single energy source such as diesel can lead to insecurity. An option to increase the energy security in unconnected Arctic communities is the use of renewable energy resources. Renewable resources would give communities more independence from fossil fuels and all the related risks like transportation, global oil prices, and environmental impacts. Furthermore, integration of renewables leads to a diversification of primary energy resources. The advantage of diversification is that if one source breaks down the other sources still can cover the supply (Lombardi et al. 2016, 10). For example, if in a hybrid system, the wind turbine fails, the solar cells, energy storage, and diesel generator can cover the supply. This helps to increase energy security.

To realize such a transition to supply systems that have a low- or no-fossil-fuel demand, a few problems have to be tackled. These problems include financing renewables, adapting renewable energy generation technologies to Arctic conditions, and improving grid stability under high penetration of non-dispatchable energy sources. To accomplish the last two points, further research and development are needed. To give a few examples, foundations must be adapted for construction on permafrost and be prepared for its decline, which results in higher costs for construction and maintenance (Benkert 2015, 20; Lewkowicz 2015, 3). Other adaptions are related to icing. To protect wind turbine blades from icing, different solutions can be found; for example, black blades that absorb solar radiation, or simply heated blades (Holdmann 2015, 8; Verret 2015, 12).

Another common problem related to icing is the collapse of transmissions lines due to the weight of the ice. A solution could be a method which breaks the ice on transmission lines by the use of a high frequency (Sullivan et al. 2003, 49). Another point is that providing constant energy with a high penetration of renewables in small communities can require proportionally large energy storage. The storage should have the capacity to supply the community with anything from just a couple of hours up to several days of energy (Baring-Gould and Corbus 2007, 2). All the required technologies are in early stages of development and further development should be undertaken to solve problems related to the harsh conditions and to make the technology more cost competitive (McDonald and Pearce 2012, 469). To accomplish such innovations, education at all levels is required. Education can also help to solve unemployment and poverty-related problems, which are common issues among northern communities (Coates and Poelzer 2014, 26; Koivurova, Tervo, and Atepien 2008, 9). Energy companies have also found it difficult to find suitably educated employees in Arctic regions (McDonald and Pearce 2012, 469). On another level, education can raise people's awareness of how to best use energy under the harsh Arctic conditions (Koivurova, Tervo, and Atepien 2008, 10).

Another aspect to consider is the financing of renewable energy projects. As stated, all the Arctic countries have targets to increase the share of renewables. For communities to do so, the problem of financing the high upfront cost must be solved (McDonald and Pearce 2013, 99).

Nowadays, fuel subsidies lower the price of energy artificially; this money would be better used to introduce renewable sources. The use of renewables would lower electricity prices after the payback period.

Not enough is yet known about energy security and reliability of energy systems in the Arctic. The data that is available highlights common key performance indicators (KPI), such as the system average interruption duration index (SAIDI) and the system average interruption frequency index (SAIFI). These KPIs are in use around the world to measure and compare the reliability of electricity supplies, but are rarely used in the Arctic. KPIs could be identified only for very few communities; in other cases only approximations regarding the downtime of the supply system were available, as a current ongoing study indicates.[2] SAIDI is a calculation of the duration of outages (usually in minutes or hours) in a given time frame (year) per customer (Kornatka 2017, 1). SAIFI is a measurement of the frequency of outages in a given time frame (year) per customer (Kornatka 2017, 1). In small communities it should be easier to calculate KPIs because if the grid fails then the supply for the whole community fails (Bhattarai and Thompson 2016, 710). This means it is not necessary to check how many customers would be affected by the outage – it would be the whole community. The KPIs can help to benchmark the performance and reliability of the systems. If the electricity system becomes more complex as a consequence of additional renewable energy sources, it is important to know how the systems perform to keep it operational in the most efficient way. Furthermore, if a KPI exceeds its limits it can be the starting point for a cost-effective improvement process by helping to identify where to improve things and which improvements are most important.

Notes

1 Magnus DeWitt, unpublished paper.
2 Magnus DeWitt, unpublished paper.

References

Allen, Riley, Donna Brutkoski, David Farnsworth, and Peter Larsen. 2016. *Sustainable Energy Solutio for Rural Alaska.* Montpelier, VT: RAP.

Baring-Gould, I., and D. Corbus. 2007. *Satus of Wind-Diesel Applications in Arctic Climates.* Anchorage: NREL.

Bawa, Harmeet. 2015. "Clean Sustainable Energy for Greenland." *The Circle - Renewable Energy in the Arctic* No. 3: 22–23.

Benkert, Bronwyn. 2015. "Shifting Sands - Living on Permafrost." *The Circle - Permafrost Slow-motion Meltdown* 10: 20–22.

Bhattarai, Prasid Ram, and Shirley Thompson. 2016. "Optimizating an Off-Grid Electrical Systemin Brochet, Manitoba, Canada." *Renewable and Sustainable Energy Review* 53: 709–719.

Boute, Anatole. 2016. "Off-grid Renewable Energy in Remote Arctic Areas: An Analysis of the Russian Far East." *Renewable and Sustainable Energy Reviews* 59: 1029–1037.

Cape, J. N., M. Coyle, and P. Dumitrean. 2012. "The Atmospheric Lifetime of Black Carbone." *Atmospheric Environmet* 59: 256–263.

Coates, Ken, and Greg Poelzer. 2014. "A Work in Progress – Completing the Devolution Revolution in Canada's North." *MacDonald-Laurier Institute* (April 2014): 38.

Arctic Council. 2017. *Expert Group on Black Carbon and Methane - Summary of Progress and Recommendations 2017.* Fram Centre, NO-9296 Tromsø, Norway: Arctic Council Secretariat.

Duyck, Sebastien. 2015. "What Role for the Arctic in the UN Paris Climate Conference (COP-21)?" In *Arctic Yearbook 2015.* Lassi Heininen and Joël Plouffe eds. Akureyri, Iceland: Northern Research Forum.

EDGAR. 2017. *Emissions Database for Global Atmospheric Research.* 10 30. Accessed 08 21, 2018. http://edgar.jrc.ec.europa.eu/overview.php?v=CO2ts1990-2015.

EIA. 2015. *EIA - Ranking: Total Carbone Dioide Emission*. Accessed 08 21, 2018. www.eia.gov/state/rankings/?sid=AK#series/226.

EIA. 2018. *Alaska's Net Electricity Generation by Sources May 2018*. 5. Accessed 08 22, 2018. www.eia.gov/state/?sid=AK#tabs-4.

Environment and Climate Change Canada. 2017. *Achieving a Sustainable Future*. Gatineau: Environment and Climate Change Canada.

Environment and Climate Change Canada. 2018a. *Canadian Environmental Sustainability Indicators - Progress towards Canada's Greenhouse Gas Emissions Reduction Target*. Gatineau: Environment and Climate Change Canada.

Environment and Climate Change Canada. 2018b. *National Inventory Report 1990–2016 Greenhouse Gas Sources and Sinks in Canada*. Gatineau: Environment and Climate Change Canada.

EPA. 2016. "Methane and Black Carbone Impacts on the Arctic: Communicating the Science." https://19january2017snapshot.epa.gov/sites/production/files/2016-09/documents/arctic-methane-blackcarbon_communicating-the-science.pdf

Fondahl, G., V. Filipova, and L. Mack. 2015. "Indigenous Peoples in the New Arctic." In *The New Arctic*, 7–23. Cham, Heidelberg, New York, Dordrecht, London: Springer.

Gielen, Dolf, and Deger Saygin. 2017. *REMAP 2030 Renewable Energy Prospects for the Russian Federation*. Abu Dhabi: IRENA.

Government of Canada. 2011. *Status of Remote/Off-Grid Communities in Canada*. Ottawa, ON, Canada: Government of Canada.

Statistics Greenland. 2017. *Greenland in Figures 2017*. Edited by Bolatta Vahl and Naduk Kleemann. Nuuk: Statistics Greenland.

Holdmann, Gwen. 2015. "Alaska - the Microgrid Frontier." *The Circle - Renewable Energy in the Arctic* No 3: 6–9.

Hu, Jingwei, Tieyan Zhang, Shipeng Du, and Yan Zhao. 2015. "An Overview on Analysis and Control of micro-Grid System." *International Journal of Control and Automatisation* 8 (6): 65–76.

IEA. 2018b. *IEA - What is Energy Securit*. Accessed 08 09, 2018. www.iea.org/topics/energysecurity/whatisenergysecurity/.

Karanasios, Konstantinos, and Paul Parker. 2016. "Recent Development in Renewable Energy in Remote Aboriginal Communities, Nunavut, Canada." *PCED* 16: 54–64.

Koivurova, Timo, Henna Tervo, and Adam Atepien. 2008. *Indegenous Peoples in the Arctic*. Arctic Transform. www.arctic-transform.eu/download/IndigPeoBP.pdf

Kornatka, Miroslaw. 2017. "Distribution of SAIDI and SAIFI Indices and the Saturation of the MV Network with Remotly Controled Switches." IEEE Conferences.

Lewkowicz, Antoni. 2015. "It's not Permanent." *The Circle - Permafrost Slow-motion Meltdown* 10: 3.

Ling, Qi, Li Qinbin, Li Yinrui, and He Cenlin. 2017. "Factors Controling Black Carbon Distribution in the Arctic." *Atmospheric Chemistry and Physics* 17(2): 1037–1059. doi:10.5194/acp-17-1037-2017.

Lombardi, Pio, T Sokolnikova, K. Suslov, N. Voropai, and Z. A. Styczynski. 2016. "Isolated Power Systems in Russia. A Chance for Renewable Energies?." *Renewable Energy* 90: 532–541. DOI: 10.1016/j.renene.2016.01.016.

McDonald, Nicole C., and Joshua M. Pearce. 2012. "Renewable Energy Policies and Programs in Nunavut: Perspectives from the Federal and Territorial Government." *Arctic* 65 (4): 465–475.

McDonald, Nicole C., and Joshua M. Pearce. 2013. "Community Voices: Perspectives on Renewable Energy in Nunavut." *Arctic* 66 (1): 94–104.

Muhando, Billy, Kat Keith, and Gwen Holdmann. 2010. *Power Electronics Review - Evaluation of the Ability of Inverters to Stabilize High-Penetration Wind-Diesel Systems in Diesel-Off Mode Using Simulated Components in a Test Bed Facility*. Fairbanks: Alaska Center for Energy and Power.

Naalakkersuisut. 2018. "Cheap, Modern and Green Energy and Water for Everyone," Nuuk.

NRDC. 2015. "The Paris Agreement on Climate Change." www.nrdc.org/sites/default/files/paris-climate-agreement-IB.pdf

Pedrasa, Michael Angelo, and Ted Spooner. 2018. *Researchgate*. 01. Accessed 02 01, 2018. www.researchgate.net/publication/225183496_A_Survey_of_Techniques_Used_to_Control_Microgrid_Generation_and_Storage_during_Island_Operation.

Perez, Elena Conde, and Zhaklin Valerieva Yaneva. 2016. "The European Arctic Policy in Progress." *Polar Science* 10: 441–449.

Skinner, Brian J., and Barbara W Murck. 2011. *The Blue Planet - an Introduction to Earth System Science*. New York: John Wiley & Sons, Inc.

Sullivan, Charles R., Viktor F. Petrenko, Joshua. D. McCurdy, and Valeri Kozliouk. 2003. "Breaking the Ice: De-Icing Power Transmission Lines with High-frequency, High-voltage Excitation." *IEEE Industry Applications Magazine* 9 (5): 49–54.
Susulov, K. V. 2012. "A Microgrid Concept for Isolated Territories of Russia." In *Innovative Smart Grid Technologies (ISGT Europe), 2012 3rd IEEE PES International*, pp. 1–5. IEEE, 2012. DOI: 10.1109/ISGTEurope.2012.6465614.
Tester, Jefferson W., Elisabeth M. Drake, Michael J. Driscoll, Michael W. Golay, and William A. Peters. 2012. *Sustainable Energy – Choosing Among Options*. 2. Cambridge: MIT Press.
Verret, Jean-Francois. 2015. "Raglan Mine's Wind Power." *The Circle* No 3: 10–12.
WWF. 2017. "Renewable Energy Across the Arctic: Greenland Report." http://awsassets.wwfdk.panda.org/downloads/Greenland_RE_Report_July_2017_v2.pdf

9

ENVIRONMENTAL SECURITY IN THE ARCTIC

Shades of grey?

Horatio Sam-Aggrey and Marc Lanteigne

Ice and iron cannot be welded.

– Robert Louis Stevenson, *Weir of Hermiston* (1896)

Introduction: the environment in Arctic security discourse

The push to understand the overlap in emerging studies of the environment – including the effects of climate change – and traditional security analyses has so far been erratic at best, echoing divisions over what is and is not a security issue, and over who determines that distinction. Nonetheless, compared with 20 years ago when the study of environmental security arguably first hit its stride, today it is much more widely accepted in academic and policy circles that there is a considerable array of connections between environmental affairs and different types of security, including on the global, state, and individual (or human security) levels. Those who point to these links have frequently found the Arctic to be a readily identifiable case study of why environmental concerns feed into insecurity, and often vice versa (Stokke 2011). This is due to the mounting evidence of ongoing ice erosion and altered weather conditions in the Far North, and growing questions about the political, in addition to the physical. effects of these changes. Examples include the potential for resource and fossil fuel extraction and possible contests over access; the legal status of the Central Arctic Ocean (CAO) in light of the possibility that the North Pole may be surrounded by open water in a few short decades (The Arctic 2017); and the spillover effects of Arctic climate change on lands much further south. To use the shopworn saying: "What happens in the Arctic, no longer stays in the Arctic."

Many studies of environmental security on the international and regional levels have looked at how changes in climate affect access to the necessities of life (food, water, and shelter) as well as economic development in a given area. Connections have also been made between green issues and human security, including health threats, poverty, and in extreme cases the growing issue of climate refugees, such as in the Pacific Islands region (Anderson 2017). There have also been questions about the contributions of environmental changes to resource scarcity and conditions that may spiral into open conflict: an area of great concern in regions such as the Middle East. These concerns may be less overt in the Arctic, due to its distinct geography, relative isolation, and comparatively smaller populations, as well as the limited prospects of overt militarization of the Arctic, even under current political conditions such as the deteriorated post-2014 diplomatic relationship between Western governments and Russia. "High north, low tension" is another saying that frequently finds its way into regional meetings (Sevunts 2018).

However, environmental security issues have appeared in the Arctic in many forms and on multiple levels, ranging from the effects of climate change on local populations to the growing attractiveness of the Arctic to non-Arctic states as a result of the numerous economic opportunities that are appearing in the circumpolar north due to the ongoing erosion of the polar ice cap. The questions, therefore, are:

1) What is the Arctic region contributing to the study of environmental security?
2) Does the Arctic have a specific set of environmental security concerns?
3) How will the ongoing opening up of the Arctic, in many forms, further affect the connections between the environment and various types of the security thinking?

The idea of the Arctic as a region of *asecurity*, meaning a space where actors feel neither secure nor insecure and therefore where security is downgraded as a consideration (Wæver 1998), is a concept that was never matched by reality and is being further eroded along with Arctic Ocean ice. As climate change continues to affect the region, and the attention paid to the circumpolar north increases among the Arctic Eight states[1] as well as among a growing list of non-Arctic governments, the study of environmental security in the region is set to widen and deepen. It is only a question of which actors will be most responsible for setting that agenda.

Identifying environmental security and where the Arctic fits

For several decades, especially during the Cold War era, environmental issues were relegated to subaltern status in favour of high-politics matters: those that directly affected a given state's national security and survival. However, even during the height of the Cold War, arguments had begun to emerge that even so-called low-politics issues, including economics, social issues, and the environment, can be used effectively to promote cooperation and increase overall security by spilling over into the high political realm (Auer 2000; Haas 1964). This concept of spillover would prove to be highly relevant to the Arctic, given that environmental changes account for some of the numerous reasons why the region is coming under such increased global scrutiny.

Environmental security itself has often been defined as the measurement of how various political actors can mitigate, or adapt to, environmental changes without acute negative effects. However, the widening of the overall study of links between green politics and security, as well as the end of the Cold War and of a near-exclusive focus on high politics in strategic studies, has led to some variation in how to explain the idea of environmental security. Hard security approaches have focused on the possibility of conflicts over sparser resources due to environmental changes, or other forms of national security threat which can be traced to changes in a given ecosystem. The approach can also be turned on its head via the measurement of how human agency is disturbing the environment, or more specifically how environmental change affects the security of individuals as opposed to states. While environmental security has been defined at times as the addition of green political concerns to national security and grand strategy, including in areas such as economic development and political stability, in many cases the security of the individual is also greatly dependent on the prevention of environmental insecurity in various forms (Allenby 1998, Barnett 2001; Ullman 1983).

Thus, environmental security is not only a product of the greater movement in the past two decades towards comprehensive security (reflecting both military and nonmilitary variables), but also a consequence of the emancipation of security studies beyond materialist and statist viewpoints (Booth 1991). At the same time as it is made apparent that environmental effects are rarely confined within the boundaries of a single state, there is also the growing acknowledgement that addressing environmental security concerns is best accomplished via a multilateral approach, including global and regional levels. With the end of superpower rivalry and the perceived decline of ideology as a major force for competition, especially among great powers, a space also opened up in which to address strategic issues brought forward by various types of globalization as well as the specific security concerns in developing regions (Allenby 2000; Floyd 2008). In short, the shared space between environmental and security policies has grown rapidly in recent years, and that process has had a significant impact on how these two areas have been grafted into the study of Arctic politics.

Climate change in the Arctic is now measurable from several directions, with the most prominent being the erosion of the ice cap in the Arctic Ocean on a year-by-year basis with associated effects (Briggs 2014). Even during the winter months, there has been a marked reduction in the ice pack in many parts of the Arctic Ocean, with reports in March 2018 (National Snow and Ice Data Centre (NSIDC) 2018) suggesting that the extent of winter sea ice was the second-lowest on record, narrowly beating the figure for 2017. Reports in March 2019 suggested a slight recovery, but that month represented the seventh-lowest winter ice levels to be recorded. These conditions took place at a time when winter 2017–2018 temperatures in the Arctic region were up to 7°C higher than average, with warm spots centred in the Bering Sea region and the Atlantic-Arctic, including Greenland, according to the National Snow and Ice Data Centre (Doyle and Gardner 2018; NSIDC March 2019). During the summers of 2018 and 2019, record high temperatures were also recorded in some parts of the Arctic, including in the Nordic region (Nilsen 2018). In July 2019, Alert in the Canadian territory of Nunavut, and the northernmost permanent settlement in the Arctic (latitude 82° 30' 6" N), recorded a record temperature of 21°C (AFP 16 July 2019). By the middle of that year, Greenland was experiencing extremely high summer temperatures which accelerated the melting of the island's vast ice sheet, with figures from July 2019 suggesting that the island had lost 197 billion metric tonnes of ice in just that month (Rising 2019).

Moreover, there is now a debate over whether the international community can successfully achieve a global temperature-rise limit of 1.5°C above preindustrial levels, as outlined by the 2015 Paris Agreement, or whether a 2°C limit was more viable. According to an April 2018 report in the journal *Nature Climate Change*, a 1.5°C limitation would reduce the chances of an ice-free Arctic Ocean in the summer months by 70% as opposed to a limitation of a half degree more (Jahn 2018). In addition to concerns over ice coverage, there has also been a marked decrease in multiyear ice (ice that lasts beyond a single year), as opposed to first-year ice, which represents only a single year's growth and is traditionally thinner than older ice packs (Stroeve, Serreze, Holland, Kay, Malanik and Barrett 2012; Monastersky 2016). This has led to the question of whether a tipping point, or a so-called "Arctic death spiral" has been surpassed, meaning the continuous diminishment of sea ice in the Arctic Ocean until the entire region becomes sporadically or even permanently ice-free is now inevitable. The past decade has seen longer stretches of open water in that ocean during the summer months, with the argument that ice-free summers will soon become the norm in more and more parts of the Arctic (Wadhams 2016).

These effects have been further magnified by other contributing factors in Arctic climate change, including air and sea pollution originating both from the Arctic region and also from southern areas. One major example of external maritime pollution is plastic waste, which has become endemic in the world's oceans and has drifted northwards to the Arctic region according to a 2018 study by the Norwegian Polar Institute. Soot from south of the Arctic Circle has also begun to settle in Arctic lands, with black carbon being blamed for reducing the reflectivity (or albedo) of regional ice, thus causing magnified radiative forcing and ice-melt at faster rates, creating a vicious cycle (Byers 2014; Dou and Xiao 2016). Added to this are concerns about the possibility of a large-scale release of methane gases from permafrost and other ice erosion that could accelerate global climate change trends. Related to that threat has been the controversial "clathrate gun" hypothesis, which suggests that a mass release of methane into the atmosphere could result in a cascade effect of atmospheric warming in the space of less than a century (Hong, Torres, Carroll, Crémière, Panieri, Yao and Serov 2017; Mathiesen 2015). The erosion of the Greenland ice sheet (GrIS) could also produce widespread effects on the local climate as massive amounts of fresh water are channelled into the North Atlantic. A March 2018 study suggested that parts of the ice sheet are melting at rates not seen for centuries. Given the sheer size of the GrIS in total – approximately 1.7 million km^2 in area and on average 2 km in thickness, and representing about a 7 m rise in sea level if fully melted – the effects of its erosion may be profound in places well beyond the European Arctic (Kintisch 2017; Mooney 2018).

The impacts of these changes on Arctic environmental security, as one 2016 study explained, include detrimental effects on wildlife and traditional hunting practices, rising sea levels affecting coastal communities, changed weather patterns, and changed iceberg distribution. Additionally, communities and communications/transportation links built on permafrost are affected by melting, with one notorious example taking place in Churchill, Manitoba, which was cut off by land due to flooding of the only railway link into the town during much of 2017, prompting the construction of an alternative ice road that was completed in December of that year. Many communities that are less developed are finding it more difficult to address the economic, and in some cases, human security threats inherent in these environmental changes (Bailes 2016; Hoye 2017). While some new economic activities might appear as a result of climate change, including resource extraction and shipping, there remain the questions of cost/benefit, as well as who specifically does and does not benefit, as these transformations continue.

Arctic communities are affected by interacting environmental and socioeconomic changes. Some of these impacts create new challenges, while others present opportunities. The multiple and interacting climatic and socioeconomic changes happening in the Arctic are likely to lead to more intense conflicts over land use as new activities such as wind farm developments, increased natural resource extraction, and traditional activities like reindeer herding, come into competition (Arctic Monitoring and Assessment Program/AMAP 2017). Such conflicts place communities in a situation where they have to balance economic security concerns with environmental security concerns. In certain cases, people have to prioritize one type of security over another based on their socioeconomic circumstances.

It is also important to postulate that environmental security is "value laden" (i.e., it means different things to different people). The relationship of Indigenous peoples to specific lands makes degradation of the environment through industrial pollution, land use changes, and other modern practices directly threatening to Indigenous culture and identity. Wilfrid Greaves noted that Inuit peoples have framed environmental and social challenges as security issues, and emphasized environmental protection, preservation of cultural identity, and maintenance of Indigenous political autonomy. In contrast, the Sámi generally do not employ securitizing language to discuss environmental and social issues, rarely characterizing them as existential issues threatening their survival or well-being (Greaves 2016). Hence, not all Indigenous perspectives on security will be aligned, and no single approach to incorporating Indigenous points of view will be adequate.

While there is no unitary Indigenous conception of what security means, there is agreement among different Indigenous peoples that the ecological vitality and survival of Indigenous peoples' traditional territories is threatened. Even where disagreement exists over the relative "securityness" of some of these claims, the potential severe effects of climate change on the survival of most Indigenous people is indisputable. The cultural survival and identity of Indigenous societies depends to a considerable degree on the maintenance of environmental quality (Cocklin 2002). For Indigenous people, the fight to protect the environment is important not only to ensure environmental security but also to ensure the survival of their culture (Watt-Cloutier 2015).

Environmental security is a multidimensional phenomenon that cuts across a range of topics, namely food security, energy security, economic security, and access to natural resources. Consequently, environmental insecurity is not uniformly felt within a community or across communities in the Arctic. For example, within Indigenous communities, Indigenous women are among the least secure. Hence, these women are likely to have different perceptions of environmental security from men (EKOS 2011). It is pertinent for these gender differences in perceptions of environmental security to be studied, in order to fully understand how Indigenous women might define environmental security from their own perspectives. Also, geographical and geopolitical conditions differ between different parts of the Arctic region; thus, perceptions of environmental security may differ across the region. Additionally, differences in local political conditions, especially the empowerment of Indigenous peoples, are also likely to shape the trajectory of environmental security trends.

Environmental security is a dynamic phenomenon, as factors impacting it evolve over time, and the way its various components interact with each other also changes over time. Thus, how societies deal with the dynamic nature of this threat is bound to impact environmental security trends. Socioeconomic and political factors will determine to a large extent who has a seat at the table to define environmental security issues and solutions to these problems. As matters stand in the Arctic region, Indigenous and northern communities (and women) would point out that they are excluded from defining what counts as environmental security as government, extractive industries, and men impose their definitions of environmental security. The socioeconomic and cultural implications of this top-down imposition of the definition of environmental security for individuals and communities is of considerable importance and has consequences for locals in the Arctic. Nevertheless, competing definitions of environmental security and the knowledge needed to stem the problem create avenues for effective stakeholder dialogue and participatory governance mechanisms.

Multilateral cooperation on environmental protection

Part of the explanation as to why the Arctic has often been seen as a region where security is less of a consideration as opposed to other parts of the world is that there are comparatively fewer institutions in the Far North, none of which are specifically dedicated to security issues. Unlike the Antarctic Treaty System (ATS) at the opposite pole, there is no overreaching legal structure across the Arctic, and no equivalent of Article 1 of the original 1959 Antarctic Treaty which called for the continent to be used for peaceful purposes and for military activity to be prohibited (National Science Foundation n.d.). Of course, the North American Treaty Organization (NATO) is well represented in the region, but Russia is not a member (and is very unlikely ever to be so), and Finland and Sweden are also outside NATO despite ongoing debates about their future membership, given the growing concerns about Russian military expansionism under the Vladimir Putin government (NATO 2016). However, security concerns have started to enter the Arctic through various other regional and sub-regional regimes, along with dialogues in relation to environmental security matters.

The initial Ottawa Declaration in 1996, which led to the founding of the Arctic Council, included the recognition of the importance of environmental affairs in the region and a commitment to the protection of the Arctic environmental and regional ecosystems, as well as a commitment to maintaining local biodiversity and conservation measures. The Council itself was an offshoot of previous multilateral attempts by the eight Arctic states to develop a means for joint protection of the local environment, including the 1989 Rovaniemi Process and the subsequent Arctic Environmental Protection Strategy (AEPS) (Arctic Council 1991). The Council was dedicated to five specific regional goals: the protection of the overall Arctic ecosystem including human inhabitants; protection and improvement of the local environment in tandem with the responsible and sustainable use of resources; accommodation of the customs and needs of Indigenous persons; review of the state of the Arctic environment; and the identification and reduction of pollution (Arctic Council 1996; Tanaka 2013).

However, under the terms of the Ottawa agreement, it was decided that military security issues would not be under the Council's purview. Environmental security was another matter, even though the Council took care not to stress any sort of hard security dimensions to that approach. For example, within the Arctic Council mechanisms, there are six working groups that address various areas of regional environmental concerns, including pollution, threat monitoring, flora and fauna protection, emergency responses to environmental emergencies, marine environmental protection, and methods for sustainable development (Arctic Council 2015; Rottem 2015). In addition to the eight member states, the 13 state observers within the Council, as well as potential future observers, are also required to engage with the working groups, including supporting environmental initiatives in the region, as outlined in the 2013 Observer Manual for Subsidiary Bodies (Arctic Council 2013).

It is therefore not surprising that several of the 13 observer nations within the Council that have released Arctic policy papers have also stressed a commitment to protecting the Arctic environment as part of their engagement with the regime. For example, Germany's Arctic policy paper stressed the need to set the highest possible environmental standards for the Arctic in addition to recognizing the region's economic potential, including the areas of biodiversity and protection of marine environments. Japan's Arctic policy document noted the potential for research cooperation on environmental issues with governmental and nongovernmental actors, and also the importance of the Arctic to Japan's national security interests, especially as a maritime trading state (Germany (Federal Foreign Office) 2013; Japan (The Headquarters for Ocean Policy) 2015).

The most recent Arctic strategy by the government of the United Kingdom, published in April 2018, illustrated UK attempts to address four major environmental hazards in the region: threats to marine conservation, marine litter, pollution (including from mercury), and dangers to local bird populations (United Kingdom (Foreign and Commonwealth Office) 2018). The newest member of the Council's observer roster, Switzerland (joined in 2017), also stressed not only its history of Arctic exploration but its commitment to studying changes in ice patterns based on previous work in what was called the "vertical Arctic," specifically the Alps (Lanteigne 2017a). In a Swiss policy paper published as the country was preparing its application for Council observer status, specific research projects on ice erosion in Greenland, the effects of Arctic environmental changes on European weather patterns, and polar atmospheric research were all cited as proof of Swiss commitment to environmental security issues and potential contributions to the working groups (Swiss Federal Department of Foreign Affairs, 2015) In many of these cases, adherence to the principles of environmental protection was a necessary component of building an Arctic identity, one that would be acceptable to the Arctic Eight and the Arctic Council itself.

The largest of the Arctic Council observers, China, was arguably under a comparatively greater degree of pressure to not only prove its Arctic credentials before being added to the observer list in 2013, but also to affirm its commitment to environmental responsibility in the region, given concerns about the country's own record regarding green policies (Shapiro 2012) as well as its growing economic interests in the Arctic. Although scientific diplomacy has been seen in Beijing as the vanguard of Chinese Arctic interests, endeavours ranging from oil and gas cooperation with Russia, free trade with Iceland, and emerging mining projects in Greenland have underscored China's interests in not being left behind in a potential economic renaissance in the Arctic (Lanteigne 2017b). Moreover, China has been especially vocal about stressing certain aspects of Arctic development as international in nature, such as those involving sea lanes and resource extraction, as opposed to remaining just within the mandate of the Arctic Eight. After a long gestation period, Beijing's first governmental Arctic White Paper was published in January 2018, which included a description Beijing's commitment to protecting the regional environment and confirming that China "respects the environmental protection laws and regulations of the Arctic States and calls for stronger environmental management and cooperation" (People's Republic of China 2018; Lanteigne and Shi 2018) The paper also specified Chinese concerns about the state of Arctic fauna, the state of the region's cryosphere, and the need to take the effects of climate change seriously.

With the withdrawal of the United States from the Paris Agreement on climate by the Donald Trump government in mid-2017, China found itself as the great-power banner holder for international efforts to combat climate change and environmental degradation (Gowen and Denyer 2017; Volcovici 2017). The government of Xi Jinping has frequently referred to its new status as a central advocate for international environmental cooperation, including during the Chinese president's opening speech at the April 2018 Boao Forum in Hainan. The presentation included China's growing support for protecting global ecosystems and promoting sustainable development, promising that "we will leave the blue sky, the blue sea and the green mountains for our children and grandchildren" (Sina 2018). As China's Arctic interests continue to expand, including in the areas of resources and shipping in emerging sea lanes, including the Northern Sea Route between Asia and Europe, and possibly even the Central Arctic once conditions permit, Beijing will continue to be under the proverbial microscope to continually demonstrate its commitments to regional environmental protection and security.

Beyond the Arctic Council, environmental security concerns in the region have also been a frequent topic at Track II sub-governmental bodies, including annual conferences such as the Arctic Circle in Reykjavík, Arctic Frontiers in Tromsø, and the China–Nordic Arctic Research Council (CNARC) forum. In some cases, including the Arctic Circle, these mechanisms perform functions closer to that of a Track 1.5 organization, considering the frequent participation of governmental actors in these conferences. These forums allow for a wider array of environmental-political issues to be openly debated, with ideas often drifting upwards towards the governmental level, or Track I.

From a legal standpoint, the UN Convention on the Law of the Sea (UNCLOS) is active in the Arctic Ocean region, including laws regarding exclusive economic zones (EEZs). Even as more of the Arctic region opens to potential maritime activity, ranging from shipping to tourism, it is unlikely that UNCLOS provisions would be directly challenged in the region. However, other Arctic specific initiatives have begun to appear in order to address the changing ecosystem in the circumpolar north and to potentially get ahead of emerging economic activities in the Arctic that, if mishandled, could add to the already considerable list of environmental threats facing that part of the world.

For example, the International Code for Ships Operating in Polar Waters, or simply the Polar Code, was designed by the International Maritime Organization (IMO) to regulate civilian maritime activity at both poles (International Maritime Organization 2018). This activity is expected to grow considerably in the Arctic as new shipping lanes appear that promise faster transit times between Asia, Europe, and North America. The Polar Code, which formally came into effect in January 2017 and evolved from the IMO's maritime safety guidelines in the Arctic drawn up in 2009, recognized the distinct geographic conditions of the Arctic Ocean and designated specific measures, including proper modifications to vessels, which must be undertaken for any civilian ships to operate in regions defined by the code. However, there have been calls for a widening of the region covered by the Polar Code, given that current boundaries do not include the Icelandic and Norwegian coasts as well as parts of northwestern Russia, such as Murmansk. Also, there are concerns about enforcement, especially since a larger number of vessels are expected to operate within the Arctic Circle, there is no enforcement mechanism beyond state governments, and there is the question of whether the regulations are stringent enough to prevent accidents and dangers to the local environment (Sevunts 2017; Williams 2017). Thus, it remains to be seen whether the Polar Code can withstand an upcoming "acid test" as regional maritime shipping grows in the coming years.

A similar trial may await another regional legal agreement designed to be a preemptive measure against overfishing in the emerging CAO region, also colloquially known as "the doughnut hole" (Bennett 2015), as it represents the part of the Central Arctic which lies outside of the various EEZs of the Arctic littoral states, namely Canada, Denmark/Greenland, Norway, Russia, and the United States. In 2008, the five governments released the Ilulissat Declaration that recognized their distinct responsibility for the protection of the Arctic Ocean and the peaceful settlement of disputes. However, despite the specific status of the littoral states, the Central Arctic area is likely to see increased sea traffic, and possible commercial traffic, in the coming years as a Central Arctic Route through the region may become open for longer periods each summer. For example, in mid-2017, the Chinese icebreaker *Snow Dragon* (*Xuelong* 雪龙) traversed the Central Arctic region in its circuit of the region amid announcements by Beijing's then-State Oceanic Administration (*Guojia Haiyang Ju* 国家海洋局) that China was seeking to make future use of the CAO for commercial purposes (People's Daily 2017).

China joined Northeast Asian neighbours Japan and South Korea, along with the five littoral Arctic states, Iceland, and the European Union, in signing an agreement to establish a moratorium on fishing in the Central Arctic: a statement that was hoped would set the tone for future international regulations involving regional resources as well as cooperation between Arctic and non-Arctic states. The November 2017 agreement, struck in Washington, would cover 2.8 million km^2 of the Arctic Ocean and ban fishing in that region until at least 2033 (Canada NewsWire 2017; Ocean Conservancy 2017). These agreements provide further evidence that environmental security concerns are being discussed with greater regularity in the Arctic, and that various agreements and more formal legal structures are being created to address different types of environmental security concerns. One question that has emerged from these developments, however, is whether a convergence of these regimes will eventually form some sort of treaty mechanism covering all aspects of Arctic environmental security, or whether this issue will be addressed through the current constellation of different-sized and shaped organizations.

Conclusion

It is now much more widely accepted in academic and policy circles that there are a considerable array of connections between environmental affairs and different types of security, including on global, state, and individual levels. It is also now commonly known that ongoing climate change is continuing to make its impact felt on Arctic sea ice, permafrost, and the livelihoods of human and nonhuman communities in the Arctic. While the conceptual widening and deepening of security has allowed for the inclusion of human and environmental security issues that are of significance to local and Indigenous peoples to be finally recognized within Arctic security discourse, there are still many areas that need academic and policy attention. These issues include the intersection of gender and indigeneity within the climate change regime and environmental security discourse, the connection between ongoing projects (resource development) and the creation of insecurities, including environmental change, and the effects of increased demand for natural resources on Arctic natural and social environments.

Conscious of the fact that the region is on the verge of transformational environmental change, Arctic states and observer nations have sought to ensure environmental security through multilateral cooperation. These efforts to develop a cooperative multilateral governance regime, mainly through the Arctic Council, have been based on goodwill and mutual interest in environmental conservation. The adoption of the Polar Code and the legal agreement designed to prevent overfishing in the emerging CAO region represent important steps in enhancing environmental security; however, these regimes face upcoming "acid tests" in the wake of increased activities in this region of the world.

The economic rise of Asia (particularly China) is one of the reasons why Arctic environment and natural resource issues are becoming more and more important to international relations in the Arctic. Melting polar ice, wildlife, resource projects, and ships traversing through the Arctic sea also play their part in raising awareness about Arctic environmental issues and the urgency of action to mitigate climate change. While we expect Arctic and non-Arctic states to be key actors in setting the agenda for environmental security, it is unclear which other actors will be most responsible for setting that agenda. What is clear is that the meaning of Arctic environmental security is evolving rapidly due to the intersection of globalization, expanded Indigenous rights, and climate change. Arctic communities will continue to experience unique forms of environmental insecurity, as environmental security in the future remains tied both to developments within, and far beyond, the Arctic region.

Note

1 The Arctic Eight states are Canada, Denmark (Faroe Islands, Greenland), Finland, Iceland, Norway, Russian Federation, Sweden, and the United States.

References

AFP. 2019. "Red Alert: record temperatures in world's northernmost settlement," *Agence France Presse*. 16 July. www.afp.com/en/news/826/red-alert-record-temperatures-worlds-northernmost-settlement-doc-1iu4f51.

Allenby, Brad. 1998. "Environmental Security as a Case Study in Industrial Ecology." *Journal of Industrial Ecology* 2(1): 45–60. doi:10.1162/jiec.1998.2.1.45

Allenby, Braden R. 2000. "Environmental Security: Concept and Implementation." *International Political Science Review* 21(1): 5–21. www.jstor.org/stable/1601426.

Anderson, Charles. 2017. "New Zealand Considers Creating Climate Change Refugee Visas," *The Guardian*. 31 October 2017. www.theguardian.com/world/2017/oct/31/new-zealand-considers-creating-climate-change-refugee-visas.

The Arctic. 2017. "Russia and Canada to Begin Talks on Arctic Shelf Borders in Late November," *Arctic.ru*. 22 November. Accessed on July 10 2018. https://arctic.ru/international/20171122/687957.html.

Arctic Council. 1991. "Declaration on the Protection of Arctic Environment," *Arctic Council*. 14 June 1991. http://library.arcticportal.org/1542/1/artic_environment.pdf.

Arctic Council. 1996. "Declaration of the Establishment of the Arctic Council," Ottawa, Canada. 19 September 1996. https://oaarchive.arctic-council.org/bitstream/handle/11374/85/EDOCS-1752-v2-ACMMCA00_Ottawa_1996_Founding_Declaration.PDF.

Arctic Council. 2013. "Observer Manual for Subsidiary Bodies." 15 May 2013. http://hdl.handle.net/11374/939.

Arctic Council. 2015. "Working Groups." 10 September. www.arctic-council.org/index.php/en/about-us/working-groups.

Arctic Monitoring and Assessment Program (AMAP). 2017. Adaptation Actions for a Changing Arctic: Perspectives from the Barents Area. Oslo, Norway: AMAP.

Auer, Matthew R. 2000. "Who Participates in Global Environmental Governance? Partial Answers from International Relations Theory." *Policy Sciences* 33(2): 155–180. doi:10.1023/A:1026563821056

Bailes, Alyson J.K. 2016. "Security in the Arctic: Definitions, Challenges and Solutions." In *The New Arctic Governance*, edited by Linda Jakobsen and Neil Melvin, 24–25. Oxford: Oxford University Press/SIPRI.

Barnett, Jon. 2001. *The Meaning of Environmental Security: Ecological Politics and Policy in the New Security Era*. London: Zed Books.

Bennett, Mia. 2015. "The Donut Hole at the Center of the Arctic Ocean," *Cryopolitics*. 23 June 2015. www.cryopolitics.com/2015/06/23/the-donut-hole-at-the-center-of-the-arctic-ocean/.

Booth, Ken. 1991. "Security and Emancipation." *Review of International Studies* 17: 313–326. www.jstor.org/stable/20097269.

Briggs, Chad Michael. 2014. "Arctic Environmental Security and Abrupt Climate Change." In *Environmental and Human Security in the Arctic*, edited by Gunhild Hoogensen Gjørv, Dawn R. Bazely, Marina Goloviznina, and Andrew J. Tanentzap, 98–112. London and New York: Routledge.

Byers, Michael. 2014. *International Law and the Arctic*. Cambridge: Cambridge University Press. 197–199.

Canada (Department of Fisheries and Oceans (DFO)). 2017. "Statement – Minister LeBlanc Commends Historic International Agreement to Prevent Unregulated Fishing in the High Seas of the Central Arctic Ocean," *Canada NewsWire*. 1 December 2017. www.newswire.ca/news-releases/statement—minister-leblanc-commends-historic-international-agreement-to-prevent-unregulated-fishing-in-the-high-seas-of-the-central-arctic-ocean-661136543.html.

Cocklin, Chris. 2002. "Water and 'Cultural Security.'" In *Human Security and the Environment: International Comparisons*, edited by Edward A. Page and Michael Redclift, 154–176. Northampton: Edward Elgar.

Dou, Ting-Feng and Cun-De Xiao. 2016. "An Overview of Black Carbon Deposition and its Radiative Forcing over the Arctic." *Advances in Climate Change* 7(3): 115–122.

Doyle, Alister and Gardner, Timothy. 2018. "Arctic Ocean Ice Near Record Low for Winter, Boost for Shipping," *Reuters*. 24 March 2018. www.reuters.com/article/us-climatechange-arctic/arctic-ocean-ice-near-record-low-for-winter-boost-for-shipping-idUSKBN1GZ2UK.

EKOS. 2011. *Rethinking the Top of the World: Arctic Security Public Opinion Survey*. Toronto: Walter and Duncan Gordon Foundation & Canada Centre for Global Security Studies at the Munk School of Global Affairs.

Floyd, Rita. 2008. "The Environmental Security Debate and its Significance for Climate Change." *International Spectator* 43(3): 51–65. doi:10.1080/03932720802280602

Germany (Federal Foreign Office). 2013. "Guidelines of the Germany Arctic Policy Assume Responsibility, Seize Opportunities." September 2013. www.bmel.de/SharedDocs/Downloads/EN/International/Leitlinien-Arktispolitik.pdf?__blob=publicationFile.

Gowen, Annie and Denyer, Simon. 2017. "As US Backs Away From Climate Pledges, India and China Step Up," *Washington Post*. 1 June 2017. www.washingtonpost.com/world/asia_pacific/as-us-backs-away-from-climate-pledges-india-and-china-step-up/2017/06/01/59ccb494-16e4-4d47-a881-c5bd0922c3db_story.html?utm_term=.87eabccbafb1.

Greaves, Wilfred. 2016. "Arctic (in)security and Indigenous peoples: Comparing Inuit in Canada and Sámi in Norway." *Security Dialogue* 47(6): 461–480. doi:10.1177/0967010616665957

Haas, Ernst. 1964. *Beyond the Nation-State: Functionalism and International Organization*. Stanford: Stanford University Press.

Hong, Wei-Li, Marta E. Torres, Jo Lynn Carroll, Antoine Crémière, Giuliana Panieri, Haoyi Yao, and Pavel Serov. 2017. "Seepage From an Arctic Shallow Marine Gas Hydrate Reservoir is Insensitive to Momentary Ocean Warming." *Nature Communications* 8(15745). doi:10.1038/ncomms15745

Hoye, Bryce. 2017. "With Ice Road Complete, 1st Haul of Goods Set to Arrive in Churchill Before Christmas," *CBC News*. 15 December 2017. www.cbc.ca/news/canada/manitoba/churchill-ice-road-1.4451279.

International Maritime Organisation (IMO). 2018. "International Code for Ships Operating in Polar Waters (Polar Code)." www.imo.org/en/MediaCentre/HotTopics/polar/Documents/POLAR%20CODE%20TEXT%20AS%20ADOPTED.pdf.

Jahn, Alexandra. 2018. "Reduced probability of Ice-free Summers for 1.5°C Compared to 2°C Warming." *Nature Climate Change*. 2 April 2018. doi:10.1038/s41558-018-0127-8

Japan (The Headquarters for Ocean Policy). 2015. "Japan's Arctic's Policy," 15 October 2015. http://library.arcticportal.org/1883/.

Kintisch, Eli. 2017. "The Great Greenland Meltdown," *Science*. 23 February 2017. www.sciencemag.org/news/2017/02/great-greenland-meltdown.

Lanteigne, Marc. 2017a. "Switzerland and the Arctic Council: The New Kid on the Block," *Over the Circle*. 26 September 2017. https://overthecircle.com/2017/09/26/switzerland-and-the-arctic-council-the-new-kid-on-the-block/.

Lanteigne, Marc. 2017b. "Have You Entered the Storehouses of the Snow? China as a Norm Entrepreneur in the Arctic." *Polar Record* 53(2): 117–130.

Marc Lanteigne, and Mingming Shi, "China Stakes its Claim to the Arctic," *The Diplomat*, 29 January 2018, https://thediplomat.com/2018/01/china-stakes-its-claim-to-the-arctic/

Mathiesen, Karl. 2015. "Permafrost 'Carbon Bomb' May be More of a Slow Burn, Say Scientists," *The Guardian*. 9 April 2015. www.theguardian.com/environment/2015/apr/09/arctic-carbon-bomb-may-never-happen-say-scientists.

Monastersky, Richard. 2016. "Incredibly Thin Arctic Sea Ice Shocks Researchers." *Nature*. 14 December 2016. doi:10.1038/nature.2016.21163

Mooney, Chris. 2018. "Ice Cores Show Greenland's Melting is Unprecedented in at Least Four Centuries," *Washington Post*. 28 March 2018. www.washingtonpost.com/gdpr-consent/?destination=%2fnews%2fenergy-environment%2fwp%2f2018%2f03%2f28%2fgreenland-is-melting-faster-than-at-any-time-in-the-last-450-years-at-least%2f%3f&utm_term=.aae640758a02.

National Science Foundation. n.d. "The Antarctic Treaty." Accessed on June 1 2018. www.nsf.gov/geo/opp/antarct/anttrty.jsp.

National Snow and Ice Data Centre (NSIDC). 2018. "Winter Arctic Sea Ice: Bering Down." 4 April. http://nsidc.org/arcticseaicenews/2018/04/2018-winter-arctic-sea-ice-bering-down/.

NATO. 2016. "'Nordic Duo Should Stay Together' – Study on NATO Membership," *NATO Review*. 19 May 2016. www.nato.int/docu/review/2016/Also-in-2016/nato-membership-finland-sweden/EN/index.htm.

Nilsen, Thomas. 2018. "A Heat Wave under the Midnight Sun," *The Independent Barents Observer*. 13 July 2018. https://thebarentsobserver.com/en/ecology/2018/07/heatwave-under-midnight-sun.

NSIDC. 2019. "Arctic Sea Ice Maximum Ties for Seventh Lowest in Satellite Record," *National Snow and Ice Data Center*. 20 March. http://nsidc.org/arcticseaicenews/2019/03/.

Ocean Conservancy. 2017. "Meeting on High Seas Fisheries in the Central Arctic Ocean, Washington DC, 28-30 November 2017," *Chairman's Statement*. https://oceanconservancy.org/wp-content/uploads/2017/11/Chairmans-Statement-from-Washington-Meeting-2017.pdf.

People's Daily. 2017. "China to Further Active Engagement in Arctic Affairs." 25 August 2017.

The People's Republic of China (*The State Council of the People's Republic of China*). 2018. "China's Arctic Policy." 26 January 2018. http://english.gov.cn/archive/white_paper/2018/01/26/content_281476026660336.htm.

Rising, David. 2019. "Greenland Lost 217 Billion US Tons of Ice Amid July Heat Wave," *Boston Globe/Associated Press*, 1 August.

Rottem, Svein Vigeland. 2015. "A Note on the Arctic Council Agreements." *Ocean Development & International Law* 46: 50–59. doi:10.1080/00908320.2015.988940

Sevunts, Levon. 2017. "New Polar Code Takes Centre Stage at Arctic Shipping Summit in Montreal," *Barents Observer*. 15 March 2017. https://thebarentsobserver.com/en/arctic/2017/03/new-polar-code-takes-centre-stage-arctic-shipping-summit-montreal.

Sevunts, Levon. 2018. "NATO Wants to Keep the Arctic an Area of Low Tensions, Stoltenberg," *Radio Canada International*. 4 April 2018. www.rcinet.ca/en/2018/04/04/nato-wants-to-keep-the-arctic-an-area-of-low-tensions-stoltenberg/.

Shapiro, Judith. 2012. *China's Environmental Challenges*. Cambridge and Malden, MA: Polity Press.

Sina. 2018. '习近平博鳌亚洲论坛开幕演讲(全文),' (speech by Xi Jinping at the Boao Forum for Asia) 10 April 2018. http://news.sina.com.cn/c/xl/2018-04-10/doc-ifyvtmxe8682980.shtml.

Stokke, Olav Schram. 2011. "Environmental Security in the Arctic: The Case for Multilevel Governance." *International Journal* 66(4): 835–848. doi:10.1177/002070201106600412

Stroeve, Julienne C., Mark C. Serreze, Marika M. Holland., Jennifer E. Kay, James Malanik, and Andrew P. Barrett. 2012. "The Arctic's Rapidly Shrinking Sea Ice Cover: A Research Synthesis." *Climatic Change* 110: 1005–1027.

Switzerland (Swiss Federal Department of Foreign Affairs). 2015. "Swiss Polar Research: Pioneering Spirit, Passion and Excellence." https://naturalsciences.ch/service/publications/33404-swiss-polar-research-pioneering-spirit-passion-and-excellence.

Tanaka, Yoshifumi. 2013. *The International Law of the Sea*. Cambridge and New York: Cambridge University Press. 306.

Ullman, Richard H. 1983. "Redefining Security." *International Organization* 8(1): 129–153. doi:10.2307/2538489

United Kingdom (Foreign and Commonwealth Office). 2018. "Beyond the Ice: UK Policy Towards the Arctic," April 2018. https://assets.publishing.service.gov.uk/government/uploads/system/uploads/attachment_data/file/697251/beyond-the-ice-uk-policy-towards-the-arctic.pdf.

Volcovici, Valerie. 2017. "US Submits Formal Notice of Withdrawal from Paris Climate Pact," *Reuters*. 5 August 2017. www.reuters.com/article/us-un-climate-usa-paris/u-s-submits-formal-notice-of-withdrawal-from-paris-climate-pact-idUSKBN1AK2FM.

Wadhams, Peter. 2016. *A Farewell to Ice: A Report from the Arctic*. London: Allen Lane. 82–91.

Wæver, Ole. 1998. "Insecurity, Security and Asecurity in the West European Non-War Community." In *Security Communities*, edited by Emmanuel Adler and Michael Barnett, 69–118. Cambridge and New York: Cambridge University Press. doi:10.1017/CBO9780511598661

Watt-Cloutier, Sheila. 2015. *The Right* to be C*old*: *One Woman's Story* of P*rotecting her Culture*, the *Arctic*, and the *whole Planet*. Toronto: Allen Lane.

Williams, Laura C. 2017. "An Ocean Between Us: The Implications of Inconsistencies Between the Navigational Laws of Coastal Arctic Council Nations and the United Nations Convention on the Law of the Sea for Arctic Navigation," *Vanderbilt Law Review*. 27 January 2017. www.vanderbiltlawreview.org/2017/01/an-ocean-between-us-the-implications-of-inconsistencies-between-the-navigational-laws-of-coastal-arctic-council-nations-and-the-united-nations-convention-on-the-law-of-the-sea-for-arctic-navigation.

10

ECONOMIC SECURITY

Employment policy needs for rural and remote communities

Gordon B. Cooke and Bui K. Petersen

Introduction

Economic security is central for the sustainability of rural and remote communities. As these communities are located far from financial (and intellectual) centers, their economic viability is tied to the economic assets locally available, which typically means a dependence on resource-based industries such as oil, gas, mining, agriculture/agrifoods, or fishing. As extractive industries have been the main sources of industrial development in the Arctic since the 1970s (Hoogensen et al. 2009), sustainability of remote and Arctic communities has become intrinsically tied to global markets. The result is that while international investments, often from multinational corporations (MNCs), have provided a much needed influx of money into local communities, these communities have had to contend with some of the challenges of such resource industries, including the impact on the natural environment, health, local identities, traditional livelihoods, and income dispersion (Deiter and Rude 2005).

In this chapter, we argue that active labor market policies and government intervention are essential for ensuring the economic security of rural and remote communities. By *rural and remote*, we simply mean communities that are small and situated beyond the range of daily commuting to work in an urban center. Simply speaking, residents have three options: find work within the community (or nearby), be unemployed, or migrate out for work opportunities elsewhere. Needless to say, this means that the quantity, quality, and breadth of jobs within these communities are of critical importance.

Economic security refers to the (subjective) degree to which an individual has sufficient financial means at present, and confidence in maintaining it in the future (see Cooke et al. 2013). There is an argument that economic security is a necessary component of positive security and that the security (i.e., viability and quality) of a remote community cannot be achieved unless its people, collectively, are at least reasonably economically self-reliant. Yet, for the people in these communities to be fully secure, economic opportunities need to be balanced with environmental protection, as well as with the consideration of social and cultural implications. Our expertise is in North Atlantic jurisdictions, including Nordic countries as well as Newfoundland and Labrador in Eastern Canada. While it is accepted that there is much that is unique to Arctic communities and Arctic peoples, it is also suggested that they have many economic and public policy similarities with sub-Arctic and other remote northern locations. In these regions, communities tend to have transportation and weather/climate related challenges that hamper the movement of people and goods traveling in or out, and that also hamper industries such as tourism, manufacturing, and agriculture/agrifoods.

Government intervention into local economies means that, rather than leaving economic activity to private sector organizations, governments enter the marketplace and take an active role in coordinating the production of goods and services. In turn, economically vibrant communities can retain more of their populations, which leaves more people and resources for social and other lifestyle endeavors.

Review of the literature

This chapter emerged out of collaborations across academic disciplines, and with the express goal of sharing and comparing analyses from different perspectives.[1] Academic disciplines are frequently criticized for having a "siloed" mentality that inhibits the cross-fertilization of knowledge and impedes a broader dialogue on important social issues (Jacobs 2014; Stirling 2014). However, taking an interdisciplinary approach necessarily means that only a sampling of research from different fields can be reviewed in one short book chapter. Below, literature is interweaved from a variety of academic traditions that explore two subthemes: (a) the economic component of human security, and (b) modern employment conditions, especially as they pertain to rural and remote northern communities. Finally, active labor market policies and direct public sector investment are examined as policy responses.

Economic component of human security

Human security is an elusive concept because different people define it in different ways. One way is to view human security as being free, or protected, from a military or geopolitical threat. Certainly, being secure includes being protected from those sorts of threats, but that definition misses the point as to what *having security*, as opposed to *avoiding insecurity*, means. Protection from insecurity is one element, but positive security is *enabling* – it means having good and just outcomes, and not just the avoidance of negatives (see Hoogensen et al. 2009; Hoogensen Gjørv 2012). Once the focus shifts to access these attractive options, the question becomes: what should local people living in remote northern areas have? According to the United Nations, it means having "an equitable share of market opportunities" (United Nations Development Programme [UNDP] 1994, 6).

Again, the issue is not what should they be able to avoid, but what they can expect. Certainly, access to clean water, air, and land is a starting point, and political power or self-governance is key. However, to what end? For true individual security, a certain level of financial well-being and financial independence is essential. So, for example, when resource developments are being planned, local people have a right to expect serious considerations of environmental and social implications to be respected, but further, these people have a right to share in the economic gains in terms of royalties, tax revenues, commercial relationships, and especially employment opportunities (see Hoogensen Gjørv 2012; UNDP 1994).

If positive security depends upon "relations," or cooperation, between actors, as Hoogensen Gjørv (2012) suggests, then positive *economic* security depends on cooperation between economic stakeholders in a given region. In any such cooperation, corporations are going to want clarity on investment size, possible returns, and timelines for such. Communities will instead be concerned with the potential financial benefits, how these will be distributed, and the environmental, social, and other costs that are likely to occur, as well as the efforts made to reduce, if not minimize, these costs. In other words, the communities will be concerned with the distribution of the net benefits.

Conceivably, there can and should be an overlap between corporate financial interests and the economic security needs of local communities. Indeed, there are strong business voices that argue that the most effective way to address social concerns is by taking an inward look and trying to integrate corporate practice and operation with social and environmental goals, rather than seeing corporate social responsibility or social development initiatives as something external to corporate strategy (Harvey 2014; Porter and Kramer 2006).

In modern welfare-capitalist countries, governments are expected to assist vulnerable members of society to reduce or mitigate the gaps in income, wealth, and power. Without government intervention, people with relatively little labor market power (e.g., women, Indigenous peoples, immigrants, lesser skilled people, etc.) are at risk of having unfairly poor employment opportunities (Saunders 2003). Because they also tend to lack labor market power, similar challenges face people in rural and remote locations who have few local employment opportunities. Without policy intervention, these people will similarly have insufficient security.

Modern employment conditions and rural and remote communities

The industrial relations systems framework (Dunlop 1958) provides a theoretical lens for studying labor market outcomes like conditions of work, industrial conflict, and worker satisfaction levels. These outcomes are shaped by broad influences such as technological advances or changes in political, social, legal, or economic environments, but also by the way that stakeholders respond to those environmental changes when they interact with each other. In other words, conditions of work for a particular group of workers are shaped by the broader economic, political, and social contexts, but also by choices made by stakeholders in response to those external environments.

Two decades ago, Betcherman and Lowe (1997) correctly predicted that employment conditions would become increasingly polarized, with a lucky minority able to acquire a job with a high level of pay, benefits, security, and control over working conditions. They also predicted that working conditions would deteriorate for the majority of others, and that there would be growing casualization of work within the labor market. In brief, that means more temporary, contract, on-call, and/or casual employment, as employers pass business risk onto workers by matching labor levels more closely to production levels. A key factor is employer-driven changes to satisfy operational, profit, or strategic reasons (see Zeytinoglu et al. 2009). Employers facing low-cost global competition frequently choose to respond by reducing labor wages, benefits, and hours (Chaykowski and Gunderson 2001). On the other hand, employers could choose the opposite strategy of differentiating themselves by outcompeting others via producing high quality goods and services by increasing employee skills and engagement levels.

There are also changes occurring to the social environment, as a demand for decent work has emerged. At its core, a right to decent work means having a chance at income opportunities that are meaningful, financially rewarding, sufficiently secure, and facilitating work–life balance (Boulin et al. 2006; Saunders 2003). For people in rural locations, the ability to find and maintain decent employment can be especially difficult due to narrower (i.e., less diverse) economies, and a reliance on cyclical resource-sector jobs. On average, lower education and skill levels tend to lead to correspondingly lower income and advancement opportunities (Cooke et al. 2015; OECD 2012, 2015). The challenge for public policymakers is to try to alter labor markets to make them stronger, more equal, and more inclusive. That is, governments need to help ensure economic security for all individuals, their families, and their communities.

Active labor market policies and direct government involvement in markets

Countries vary in how much governments actively intervene in the regulation of labor markets. In their influential work *Varieties of Capitalism*, Hall and Soskice (2001) categorized capitalist economies into two main types, *liberal market economies* (LMEs) and *coordinated market economies* (CMEs). Hall and Soskice (2001) identified five coordination problems in capitalist societies: (a) industrial relations, (b) vocational training and education, (c) corporate governance, (d) inter-firm relations, and (e) relations between firms and their employees. LMEs rely more on market mechanisms to resolve these coordination problems, and typically it is left more to individual firms to resolve these problems. CMEs, on the other hand, rely much more on nonmarket mechanisms such as greater government involvement in coordinating economic and labor market issues, and more cooperation between economic and labor market actors, including tripartite negotiations between government, industry, and labor unions. In essence, CMEs and LMEs represent different macro-level *institutional logics* (Thornton et al. 2012) that are embedded in history, culture, and political and institutional practices.

With the greater active government engagement in the economy and labor markets, CMEs typically have higher government cost structures. Nordic countries, which are prototypical CMEs, have managed to simultaneously have productive, competitive, and successful economies by embracing innovation and social inclusion (Economist 2013a). That is, people are adaptive and open to change because everyone (in theory) has access to training and social supports to be able to respond to labor market fluctuations. In other words, Nordic countries tend to invest more heavily than others in developing their collective human capital.[2] Norway, for example, has coordinated how resource development income is managed by setting aside resource development royalties and taxes in a sovereign wealth fund that enables Norway to share the benefits with future generations and encourage diversification by investing heavily in infrastructure and in other sectors of the economy (Economist 2013b; Recknagel 2014). This has involved direct investments (through share purchase) in private sector organizations and an expansion of the mandates of public sector organizations (Economist 2013b). Through active labor market policies, Norway has also managed to achieve high labor market participation rates and low unemployment rates (Statistics Norway 2016). In this way, Norway has extended positive security for its citizens across all geographic regions, including those living north of the Arctic Circle.

An example of how labor market coordination can balance individual economic security with the need for global industry competitiveness is the *flexicurity* system in Denmark (Madsen 2006). This system involves a set of policies that provide industry with increased flexibility in hiring and firing, at the same time providing generous unemployment benefits and programs (including retraining) to help people move quickly into new jobs. The flexicurity program is an example of how CME countries try to coordinate the need for economic development and job creation.

The provision of and funding of education is an important factor distinguishing CMEs from LMEs. In contrast to LMEs, where education is seen more as an individual responsibility, CME countries typically have low (or no) postsecondary tuition fees and often have relatively generous student grants as education is not seen as an individual's investment into future employability, but rather as a public investment into a skilled and educated workforce.

In contrast, LME governments accept less responsibility, and the labor market policies that exist are typically much more fragmented. Canada is an example of an LME country with some labor market programs, such as unemployment insurance, individual job creation and business creation support, and some access to retraining. However, these programs are relatively limited in scope, offering low benefit amounts (e.g., 55% of pay) and very limited access to retraining. Furthermore, there is a considerable lack of coordination between the programs. For example, the federal government provides unemployment benefits, but when the maximum benefit period has expired (maximum 45 weeks; Government of Canada 2017), people have to apply for social assistance from the provincial government. In either case, there is very little in terms of coordinated services for helping people get back into work. In most cases, the services are bare bones and consist of a small amount of job search guidance and some career counseling. While labor market policies will be idiosyncratic from country to country, the Canadian example illustrates that while LME countries sometimes will have some active labor market policies, these will frequently be undermined by lack of coordination and overall strategy.

To be fair, there is some debate around the effectiveness of active labor market policies. The question is whether the investment in such policies results in sufficiently beneficial outcomes. In the literature evaluating the effectiveness of such policies, Card et al. (2010) found in a meta-analysis that not all active labor market programs are equally effective, but did find that training is particularly associated with medium to longer-term positive effects. It is important, however, to note that most of these labor market policies, including those evaluated by Martin and Grubb (2001), focus on individual level services and not overall long-term labor market strategy. Active labor market policies can, if properly supported, pay off in terms of getting people back into the workforce. It is more effective, however, if the overall labor market strategy takes a more long-term perspective in managing a jurisdiction's human resources, by identifying current and future needs (at both collective and individual levels), and if it includes a strategy for how to address those needs through training, education, and investment to build capabilities and experience.

The empirical context

In this chapter, summary findings are examined from a collection of research projects undertaken in rural and remote locations within North Atlantic jurisdictions between 2011 and 2018. The objectives of these projects involved exploring the employment and life experiences of individuals, especially those in, or from, remote locations, with a focus on showing the effects of different government policy approaches. The project involved semi-structured interviews of more than 75 people in northern Norway, the Faroe Islands (including some who were students in Denmark at the time), and Newfoundland and Labrador. Participants were a mix of men and women, young adults and older adults, and local government, community, and business representatives.

A look at employment in northern Norway

Troms is the second most northerly county within Norway and is situated entirely north of the Arctic Circle. It has a population of little more than 150,000 people spread out over 500 kilometers from south to north, and with circuitous transportation routes due to the water, islands, and topography. The only urban area is Greater Tromsø, which has half of the county's population. Due to the low population density and sheer distance between communities, the remainder of the population can be described as rural and remote (and in the low Arctic), even for those living in other communities like Harstad or Narvik.

Tromsø, as the regional education, health, and transportation center of the region, has many good quality jobs at its university, hospital, and airport. Also, as a regional hub, it has a large number of civil service jobs within a variety of government agencies and departments. Moreover, Tromsø has become a tourism destination for international visitors interested in the midnight sun (or polar night/Northern Lights) seasons, Sámi culture and traditions, or other northern/Arctic experiences. In contrast, the smaller, rural and remote communities, too far for daily commuting to Tromsø, are much more reliant on fishery, aquaculture, agriculture/agrifood production, and spinoffs from the oil and gas sector.

Interviews were primarily conducted in Harstad, which, as mentioned above, can be considered to be at the large end of "rural and remote," notwithstanding Norwegian classifications.[3] Several of the young interview participants were from surrounding villages or further away, and in the process of deciding where they wished to live in the near future.[4] What was striking was the ranking of factors in the decisions of these individuals. Instead of bracing to relocate to wherever employment opportunities might materialize, it was common for these individuals to be looking at lifestyle factors, such as whether they wished to continue to live in the more rural and remote Norwegian north, or whether they wanted to try a "southern city" like Oslo or Bergen. This often involved the degree of privacy that a person preferred, or their choice of hobbies. Several also mentioned the preference (or not) to be near friends or family. Each of these recurring themes is entirely reasonable. What is surprising is the number of these lifestyle factors. Implicitly, the Norwegian participants foresaw having the choice to live in a variety of places and being able to find suitable employment in each of them. This contrasts with the typical responses in other rural and remote places in which locals speak of the need to be grateful for finding any local work (i.e., paid employment).

One person at a mid-career stage admitted that she had studied and worked in Tromsø for many years while waiting for an opportunity to move home. She had finally found one, and was even willing to accept a fixed-term contract and leave a permanent job to be able to return to her preferred community. Another woman, at an early career stage, expressed exasperation at Norway's "Master's disease," which she described as the situation in which people had to acquire extra education to get a desirable job, even if that training was not needed to be able to do that job. In other words, because Norway promotes education so heavily, a negative side effect is that job applicants need significant credentials simply because other applicants have them, as opposed to needing them for a given job. This places remotely located citizens at a disadvantage, since they need to move to larger communities that have at least one postsecondary institution.

It was also noted that some young people were reliant on social payments, and had little financial incentive to find paid employment. Notwithstanding these unfortunate side effects, it was noted that even citizens living in rural and remote locations in northern Norway typically had some local employment opportunities, and also had access to funding to acquire more education and training, and to social payments if unemployed. As a result of these generous social policies, it was found that, consistent with the stereotype of Norway, economic insecurity was uncommon, and the individuals spoken to generally had favorable life experiences to share.

A look at employment in the Faroe Islands

The Faroe Islands (or Faroes) are a group of islands in the North Atlantic, in-between Norway and Iceland. They are part of the Kingdom of Denmark but essentially operate autonomously. Although there are people living on about 17 different islands in the Faroes, the vast majority live on one of the four middle islands, or one of the two southern ones. In terms of distance, it is approximately 100 kilometers from the bottom of the southern island to the top of the northernmost one. The population is about 50,000 in total, with about half living in the centrally located capital of Tórshavn (Hagstova Føroya 2016). Notwithstanding that it is the capital of the Faroes, its location and modest size mean that it can be described as rural and remote.

The low population total is problematic because it is difficult to retain a wide range of expertise in a small base of people. However, significant public funds have been invested in physical infrastructure (like roads, subsea tunnels, and public transportation) as well as in healthcare, education, and culture. So, despite the low population and ongoing outmigration from rural communities and outer islands, the population of the Faroes is stable and even inching upwards.

The Faroese people have been able to maintain their culture, which is similar to, and yet unique from, other nearby Nordic nations. Collectively, Faroese people have been passionate enough to protect their own language. The economy, being reliant on commercial fishing and other ocean- and shipping-related industries, is subject to cyclical swings, and yet has been diversifying into newer service industries as well, including a growing tourism sector. One problem is a geographic divide in terms of economic diversity and opportunity. The employment, entertainment/culture, service, and retail options are much greater in the capital region than in other parts of the Faroes, and that partially accounts for the ongoing migration of the population towards Tórshavn. Overall, though, the economy of the Faroes can be described as vibrant, and the per capita income level is fairly high but somewhat lower than most Nordic nations. Although subsea tunnels and public transportation options can help those seeking leisure or recreational pursuits, it is noted that such infrastructural developments also open up labor market options for those who, without moving, find themselves in a commuter location rather than a remote location relative to Tórshavn. In other words, a well-funded societal infrastructure can boost economic security without requiring a person to move from their social connections.

About half of the young Faroese people (typically 20–29 years of age) interviewed were originally from Tórshavn and the other half were from one of the rural communities. Of these, several were interviewed in Copenhagen, where they had chosen to attend postsecondary institutions because of the administrative ease of studying in Denmark, and because it allowed them to experience life in a different culture and in a metropolitan center. Several of these young Faroese individuals had adapted well to life "away," and were enjoying the anonymity, privacy, and lifestyle of a large city, including the variety of employment, educational, and recreational options available. Several also commented on the cheaper cost of living in Copenhagen compared to the Faroes, notwithstanding Denmark's relatively high price levels by international standards. That said, almost all of these expat Faroese participants articulated a common set of reasons as to why they hoped and planned to return to live and work in the Faroes "at some point."

Similarly, most of the local citizens interviewed in and around Tórshavn expressed some worry about their ability to find a good enough job to have sufficient income to be able "to buy a house and raise a family here." A few also admitted that they would want to live in

Tórshavn or surrounding areas in the future, even if they were originally from a rural village in the Faroe Islands. In contrast, a few others were keen to return to live (eventually) in a rural village, even if it meant commuting daily to work in the capital region. While this would cost them extra time and money to commute, it would allow them to enjoy the family, social, and lifestyle benefits more fully than living in Tórshavn.

The views and experiences of these young Faroese individuals are an interesting case study in economic security. These views reinforce the trade-offs that sometimes have to be made when an individual is (a) rural and remotely located, and (b) trying to prioritize lifestyle, proximity to family and friends, and employment opportunities. As mentioned above, the Faroese, collectively as a community of people and via their government, have chosen to invest in local trade colleges and a university, and have invested in other physical and cultural infrastructure so that Tórshavn is an attractive place to live and so that more rurally located citizens can also benefit and utilize those amenities and seek employment.[5] While the Faroese government cannot make its land less remote in a physical and absolute sense, it has implemented policies so that its wealth and employment opportunities are spread across its population base. As a result, despite its small size and remote location, almost all individuals interviewed thought that they could have enough economic security if they lived in the Faroes. They might choose to move or live elsewhere for lifestyle or other reasons, and they might migrate out for more or different employment opportunities, but they do not *have to* move away to seek economic security.

A look at employment in Newfoundland

The eastern Canadian province of Newfoundland and Labrador has a population of about 525,000 people, with half living in or around the capital of St. John's. The other half is spread out over about 1,000 kilometers, from east to west or from south to north. Thus, the population density is very low, as is typical of sub-Arctic regions.[6] Residents in St. John's are urban. Also, those within an hour's drive can be considered to be in a suburban commuter zone because they have access to the capital region's labor market, assuming that they own a reliable vehicle, since there are effectively no intercity public transportation options. The only other (arguably) urban area is the Corner Brook-Deer Lake area in western Newfoundland, with a combined population of 35,000. The remainder of Newfoundlanders live in villages or small towns scattered across the island, often with significant distances between them.

Individuals in rural Newfoundland typically describe the various steps needed to survive with a seasonal full-time, or even seasonal part-time job, often coupled with social payments during the employment gaps. The exceptions are the lucky ones who have a public sector job like a police officer, teacher, nurse or healthcare worker, or civil servant. Even a number of those jobs feature a schedule (and payment) of less than full-year, full-time employment. Individuals in rural Newfoundland tend to be reliant, directly or indirectly, on the health of primary sector industries like the fishery, forestry, mining, and especially oil and gas. Industries like tourism, aquaculture, and manufacturing only exist on a small scale and in a limited number of areas. On the whole, the local labor markets are narrow (lacking diversity) and relatively weak. People who have high financial wants or needs face tough choices if they cannot acquire a well-paid local job. Either they migrate out (i.e., move away) or enter into a long-distance commuting arrangement such as a fly in, fly out (FIFO) job, or move away for a season (or more) of work before returning. These arrangements are known to pay far higher annual incomes, but they can wreak havoc on one's physical and mental health and social relationships. The residents who remain are the ones with a full-time, full-year job, or are able to manage on seasonal or part-time employment, or enter into a long-distance commuting arrangement with all of its pros and cons, to be able to enjoy the social and lifestyle benefits within their chosen community.

Due to the low population density, and the cyclical and limited local labor markets, some rural residents have become reliant on employment insurance (EI) schemes that require a worker to reach a threshold of paid hours, whether that occurs over a year or only part of a year.[7] Once the threshold is reached, the worker is eligible for EI payments for several months, but earned income is clawed back if receiving EI payments. As a result, workers have more incentive to find seasonal full-time work (and then be off work receiving EI benefits) than to find one or more part-time jobs throughout the year (thereby not qualifying for EI, or having earnings clawed back). To go further, the provincial government implements *make-work* programs when necessary, in years and regions in which local workers are struggling to reach the threshold of paid hours to qualify for EI benefits. That is, local workers in need end up on a short-term make-work project to reach the minimum threshold to qualify for unemployment benefits. This is not to suggest that all, or most, rural Newfoundlanders rely on these social schemes directly. But, it is accurate to say that the people of rural and remote communities, collectively, are reliant upon these programs because private sector economic activity generates insufficient income opportunities to sustain the current population level. Not surprisingly, populations have aged and declined in numbers steadily over the past two decades as harvesting and processing jobs in the commercial fishery have fallen.

These rural Newfoundlanders were likely to discuss the lifestyle benefits that they enjoyed in terms of hobbies, family and social networks, and quality of life. Yet, they also tended to fall into one of two economic categories. A minority held permanent full-time, secure jobs. However, the majority faced varying degrees of uncertainty about their employment and income prospects because they could only access seasonal or part-time employment, with variable weeks and hours of work. As such, they endured a higher degree of economic insecurity because of inadequate local employment opportunities. In turn, this leads to more migration, which exacerbates problems with public finances at a community and provincial level.[8]

Discussion and policy recommendations

The importance of local employment is about more than mere economics. Factors such as value preferences and lifestyle choice can be equally, if not more, important than simply having a source of income. Furthermore, for many people it is critical that they find meaningful and professionally challenging jobs, and that the communities they live in are sufficiently rich culturally and in terms of infrastructure and services. Yet, having local earning opportunities is a key foundation of economic security, and remote communities need to have a diverse range of economic activities that will provide for a broad range of jobs. If a community becomes too dependent on just one employer or project, the community sustainability will become too dependent on the global forces affecting a singular industry. Additionally, a single industry town is likely to have a narrower range of infrastructure, services, and cultural activities, making it less likely that people will want to settle and more likely that workers will settle for a FIFO work arrangement: something that is not conducive to building diverse and culturally rich communities. Similarly, reliance on social payments is inherently economically insecure since governments and public policy priorities are subject to change.

While remote-location jobs are always likely to be resource-dependent and therefore often require the investment of a large (usually multinational) corporation, our argument is that a coordinating logic, as demonstrated in CMEs, is necessary to truly address issues of economic security. One reason that coordination is important is that the lack thereof leaves the management of different stakeholder interests in the hands of individual corporations. Although corporations within LMEs will have to negotiate access and "social license" with communities and other stakeholders, with the likely imbalance in bargaining power, such negotiations are likely to focus on immediate shareholder and employee interests much more than long-term community wants and needs.

For corporations, social and environmental goals will often be in tension with profitability goals and shareholder demands. A lack of coordination leaves the corporations to manage these tensions themselves. Even if some corporations may be inclined to be very proactive in supporting local communities – such as through progressive human resource (HR) procurement, infrastructure, asset management practices (Harvey 2014), and other social initiatives – relying on individual corporations is likely to lead to inconsistencies from place to place, and from development to development. In addition, even with progressive HR practices, corporations will rarely be in a position to coordinate labor markets outside of their own HR needs. Thus, any corporation-initiated labor market strategies are more likely to be associated with the single main employer, "company town" structure (i.e., a narrow labor market), which is not as conducive to the development of a broader and more diverse labor market. Once a development project is finished, there could be many jobs lost at once, as has been the case with the completion of the construction of the Hebron oil platform and other resource development projects in Newfoundland and Labrador (Roberts 2015). There are similar examples of mining towns that have become ghost towns after mines have been closed.

Instead of corporations needing to think of how social initiatives fit within their corporate development strategies, it is suggested that the relationship be flipped so that government authorities take a leading role in putting social and economic long-term sustainability first and only then consider how any individual development proposal fits within this overall social strategy. In doing so, it is important to think beyond the few (or many) local jobs that are created. It is also essential to consider the types of jobs, the longevity/tenure of those jobs, who is likely to take those jobs, and the social and cultural implications. For instance, will the jobs be filled by locals, or will there be a need to fly in people with particular skills? Will these people be likely to settle and contribute to community life, or just continue in a FIFO arrangement?

If local employment is the goal, then there has to be a strategy for having a local skilled workforce. While corporations can provide some training, longer-term education needs a longer-term strategy that will often be beyond the temporal scope of a corporate project. At the very least, the corporations will not have the time to wait for many people to gain multi-year postsecondary education before starting the project. Furthermore, for locals to acquire the right kind of necessary training and education, they need to know that the training and education they take will be needed in their communities in the future. If governments take an active role in anticipating future educational skills and development needs, there is a greater likelihood that corporate investment interests will intersect with the needs of local communities, and with the locally available human resources. The public policy choice is therefore clear. Underinvesting in the physical, technological, educational, and economic infrastructure is likely to lead to a lack of jobs and to outmigration for rural and remote communities. How can governments in the Faroes and northern Norway possibly afford to spend public funds in their remote communities? Because wise investments were made, more rural populations were retained and employed, which meant local businesses had more customers, and the tax base was preserved, which meant social, educational, and leisure pursuits were likewise maintained. In other words, if public funds are not used to maintain the economic vibrancy of a remote community, then a downward spiral is more likely to develop.

Overall, an argument can be made that active government coordination of labor markets will lead to a much greater benefit to remote and rural communities and individual inhabitants. This chapter explored the experiences of some contrasting jurisdictions representing different labor market logics and found that the active government coordination of otherwise capitalist economies leads to much better outcomes. While some liberal market economies, such as Canada, have adopted, to a certain degree, active labor market policies, the small scale and lack of coordination and overall strategy has severely limited their effectiveness. In the end, economic security is a necessary component of positive security, and the most basic building block of economic security is access to paid *local* work. If those opportunities are insufficient, then the resulting economic hardships could lead to short-sighted decision-making and the pursuit of projects that jeopardize the social and environmental security of remote communities.

Funding sources

This chapter is partially based on research funded by a Norwegian SIU High North grant used by the first author, and by a Faroese Research Council grant held by the third author.

Notes

1 The UArctic Extractive Industries Thematic Network is an international interdisciplinary network fostering research collaboration and education on the social, cultural, economic, and environmental impacts of extractive industries in the Arctic.
2 See Becker (1962) for a seminal study advocating investing in human capital (i.e. skills upgrading).
3 While Norwegian communities of 10,000+ are classified as "cities," we categorize Harstad as relatively "rural and remote," given its northern location, modest population, and lack of proximity to a metropolitan area.
4 A large proportion of the Norwegian interview participants were under 30 and attending, or considering attending, a rural postsecondary institution, because they were the focus of the particular research study undertaken in that jurisdiction.
5 Due to its investment in subsea tunnels, and ongoing migration towards the capital, more than 90% of Faroese citizens are now within an hour's drive of Tórshavn.
6 Our interviews were conducted in Newfoundland and not in Labrador. The latter is commonly defined as sub-Arctic, while the former is not. Our point is that the rural and remote parts of Newfoundland are similar, in many ways, to sub-Arctic regions.
7 The threshold to qualify for employment insurance in rural Newfoundland is usually 420 paid hours.
8 While the causes of outmigration are multifaceted, Cooke et al. (2013) and Cooke (2012) showed that insufficient local employment and education options can lead to outmigration even among those strongly preferring to stay.

References

Becker, Gary S. 1962. "Investment in Human Capital: A Theoretical Analysis". *Journal of Political Economy* 70, no. 5, Part 2: 9–49.

Betcherman, Gordon, and Graham S. Lowe. 1997. *The Future of Work in Canada: A Synthesis Report.* Ottawa, Canada: Canadian Policy Research Networks.

Boulin, Jean-Yves, Michel Lallement, and François Michon. 2006. "Decent Working Time in Industrialized Countries: Issues, Scopes, and Paradoxes" in Jean-Yves Boulin, Michel Lallement, Jon Messenger, and François Michon (Eds.) *Decent Working Time, New Trends New Issues*. Geneva, Switzerland: ILO: 13–40.

Card, David, Jochen Kluve, and Andrea Weber. 2010. "Active Labour Market Policy Evaluations: A Meta-Analysis". *The Economic Journal* 120, no. 548: F452–F477.

Chaykowski, Richard P., and Morley Gunderson. 2001. "The Implications of Globalization for Labour and Labour Markets" in Richard P. Chaykowski (Ed.) *Globalization and the Canadian Economy: The Implications for Labour Markets, Society and the State*. Kingston, Canada: School of Policy Studies, Queen's University: 27–60.

Cooke, Gordon B. 2012. "High Fliers versus Upstream Swimmers: Young Rural Workers in Canada and Ireland" in Alfredo Sanchez-Castaneda, Lavinia Serranii, Francesca Sperotti (Eds.) *Youth Unemployment and Joblessness: Causes, Consequences, Responses*. Association for International and Comparative Studies in the field of Labour Law and Industrial Relations (ADAPT). Newcastle, UK: Cambridge Scholars Publishing: 151–168.

Cooke, Gordon B., Jimmy Donaghey, and Isik U. Zeytinoglu. 2013. "The Nuanced Nature of Work Quality: Evidence from Rural Newfoundland and Ireland". *Human Relations* 66, no. 4: 503–527.

Cooke, Gordon B., Deidre Hutchings, Jimmy Donaghey, and Isik U. Zeytinoglu. 2015. "Beyond Deprivation Theory: Examining Rural Experience" in Ray Griffin and Tom Boland (Eds.) *The Sociology of Unemployment*. Manchester, UK: Manchester University Press: 90–106.

Deiter, Constance, and Darlene Rude. 2005. *Human Security and Aboriginal Women in Canada*. Ottawa, Canada: Status of Women Canada.

Dunlop, John T. 1958. *Industrial Relations Systems*. New York, NY: Henry Holt and Company.

Economist. 2013a, February 2. "Northern Lights." *The Economist*. Accessed August 30, 2016. www.economist.com/news/special-report/21570840-nordic-countries-are-reinventing-their-model-capitalism-says-adrian.

Economist. 2013b, February 2. "Norway the Rich Cousin." *The Economist*. Accessed August 30, 2016. www.economist.com/news/special-report/21570842-oil-makes-norway-different-rest-region-only-up-point-rich.

Government of Canada. 2017. "Regular Benefits – How Much Could You Receive." Accessed July 10, 2018. www.esdc.gc.ca/en/ei/regular_benefit/benefit_amount.page.

Hagstova Føroya. 2016. "Fólkatal." Accessed June 30, 2018. www.hagstova.fo/fo/hagtalsgrunnur/ibugvar-og-val/folkatal.

Hall, Peter A. and David W. Soskice. 2001. *Varieties of Capitalism: The Institutional Foundations of Comparative Advantage*. Oxford, UK: Oxford University Press.

Harvey, Bruce. 2014. "Social Development Will Not Deliver Social Licence to Operate for the Extractive Sector". *The Extractive Industries and Society* 1, no. 1: 7–11.

Hoogensen Gjørv, Gunhild. 2012. "Security By Any Other Name: Negative Security, Positive Security, and a Multi-Actor Security Approach". *Review of international Studies* 38, no. 4: 835–859.

Hoogensen, Gunhild, Dawn Bazely, Julia Christensen, Andrew Tanentzap, and Evgeny Bojko. 2009. "Human Security in the Arctic-Yes, It Is Relevant!". *Journal of Human Security* 5, no. 2: 1–10.

Jacobs, Jerry. A. 2014, January 24. "Critique of Disciplinary Silos – Chicago Scholarship." Accessed May 9, 2017. http://chicago.universitypressscholarship.com/view/10.7208/chicago/9780226069463.001.0001/upso-9780226069296-chapter–2.

Madsen, Per Kongshøj. 2006. "How Can It Possibly Fly? The Paradox of a Dynamic Labour Market in a Scandinavian Welfare State" in John L. Campbell, John A. Hall, and Ove Pedersen (Eds.) *National Identity and the Varieties of Capitalism the Danish Experience*. Montreal, Canada: McGill-Queen's University Press: 323–355.

Martin, John, and David Grubb. 2001. "What Works and for Whom: A Review of OECD Countries' Experiences with Active Labour Market Policies". *Swedish Economic Policy Review* 8: 9–56.

Organisation for Economic Co-operation and Development [OECD]. 2012. *Better Skills. Better Jobs. Better Lives. The OECD Skills Strategy Executive Summary*.

Organisation for Economic Co-operation and Development [OECD]. 2015. *New Rural Policy: Linking Up for Growth. Background Document for National Prosperity through Modern Rural Policy Conference*.

Porter, Michael E., and Mark R. Kramer. 2006. "Strategy & Society: The Link Between Competitive Advantage and Corporate Social Responsibility". *Harvard Business Review* 84, no. 12: 78–92.

Recknagel, Charles. 2014. "What Can Norway Teach Other Oil-Rich Countries?" Radio Free Europe Radio Liberty. Accessed August 31, 2016. www.rferl.org/a/what-can-norway-teach-other-oil-rich-countries/26713453.html.

Roberts, Terry. 2015, August 25. "N.L. to Lose 24,000 Jobs Over Next Three Years." Accessed May 10, 2017. www.cbc.ca/news/canada/newfoundland-labrador/n-l-to-lose-24-000-jobs-over-next-three-years-1.3202703.

Saunders, Ron. 2003. *Defining Vulnerability in the Labour Market.* Ottawa, Canada: Canadian Policy Research Networks (CPRN).

Statistics Norway. 2016. Accessed August 31, 2016. www.ssb.no/en/arbeid-og-lonn/statistikker/akumnd/maaned.

Stirling, Andy. 2014, June 11. "Disciplinary Dilemma: Working across Research Silos Is Harder than It Looks." *The Guardian.* www.theguardian.com/science/political-science/2014/jun/11/science-policy-research-silos-interdisciplinarity.

Thornton, Patricia H., William Ocasio, and Michael Lounsbury. 2012. *The Institutional Logics Perspective: A New Approach to Culture, Structure, And Process.* Oxford, UK: Oxford University Press.

United Nations Development Programme [UNDP]. 1994. *Human Development Report 1994.* New York, NY: Oxford University Press.

Zeytinoglu, Isik U., Gordon B. Cooke, and Sara L. Mann. 2009. "Flexibility: Whose Choice Is It Anyway?". *Relations Industrielles/Industrial Relations* 64, no. 4: 555–574.

PART II

The Arctic powers

"Arctic Five" and "Arctic Eight"

11
ARCTIC SECURITY PERSPECTIVES FROM RUSSIA

Alexander Sergunin

Introduction

Russia's security strategies in the Arctic are a matter of controversy in both the mass media and the academic community. The outbreak of the 2014 Ukrainian crisis and Moscow's military intervention in the Syrian conflict that began in 2011 have spurred new accusations of Russia being an aggressive and militarist power, not only in Eastern Europe and the Middle East but also in the Arctic (Lakshmi 2015; Poulin 2016; Tayloe 2015). According to some Western analysts, its economic weakness and technological backwardness leads Russia to resort to military-coercive instruments to protect its national interests in the Arctic. This, they say, will inevitably lead to a regional arms race, remilitarization of the High North, and military conflicts there. In the wake of the Ukrainian and Syrian crises, it was expected that Moscow would dramatically increase its military activities and presence in the High North, as well as accelerate its military modernization programs (Lakshmi 2015; Stratfor 2015; Tayloe 2015).

However, these concerns did not materialize. Instead of the expected significant military build-up and increased military activities in the region, the Kremlin prioritized the socioeconomic development of the Arctic Zone of the Russian Federation (AZRF). In parallel, Moscow managed to separate Arctic cooperation from its current tensions with the West and to keep its relations with other regional players on a cooperative track.

This chapter discusses whether Russia really is a revisionist power in the Arctic or whether Russia's actions can be evaluated more positively as those of a country that is interested in the region's security and stability and is open to international cooperation in the High North. However, before addressing this main research question, this chapter analyzes Russian threat perceptions and the doctrinal underpinnings of Moscow's military strategy in the region.

Threat perceptions and security doctrines

After the collapse of the Soviet Union, the Kremlin paid little attention to the Arctic prior to the early 2000s. When the Cold War ended, the region lost its military-strategic significance as a zone of potential confrontation with NATO and the United States. During the Boris Yeltsin era, the economic potential of the region was underestimated. Moreover, Russia's Arctic regions were perceived by the federal government in the 1990s as a burden or source of various socioeconomic problems, rather than as an economically promising region. The far northern regions were almost abandoned by Moscow and had to rely on themselves or foreign humanitarian assistance for sustenance.

The situation started to slowly change in the early 2000s, when the general socioeconomic situation in Russia improved and the Vladimir Putin government, with its ambitious agenda of Russia's revival, came to power. However, it was President Dmitry Medvedev who approved the first Russian post-Soviet Arctic strategy: *Foundations of the State Policy of the Russian Federation in the Arctic Up to and Beyond 2020* (*Strategy – 2008*) (Medvedev 2009). Moscow was one of the first Arctic states to adopt such a document. Only Norway, in 2006, was ahead of Russia in shaping its official doctrine for the North.

This document listed Russian national interests in the region as follows: develop the resources of the Arctic, turn the Northern Sea Route (NSR) into a unified national transport corridor and line of communication, and maintain the region as a zone of peace and international cooperation. According to the plan, the multifaceted development of the northern territories was expected to culminate in the Arctic becoming Russia's "leading strategic resource base" between 2016 and 2020.

The strategic security goal was defined at the time as "maintenance of the necessary combat potential of general-purpose troops (forces)," strengthening the Coast Guard of the Federal Security Service (FSS) and border controls in the AZRF, and establishing technical control over straits and river estuaries along the whole NSR. Thus the Russian armed forces deployed in the AZRF, which were to be organized under a single command – the Arctic Group of Forces (AGF) – were charged not simply with defending territory but also with protecting Russia's economic interests in the region. This in turn required increasing the capacity of the Northern Fleet, which was (and still is) seen as an important instrument for demonstrating Russia's sovereign rights in the High North and protecting its economic interests in the region.

Although the document was mostly designed for domestic needs (in particular, it aimed at setting priorities for development in the AZRF), many foreign analysts tended to interpret *Strategy – 2008* as "solid evidence" of Russia's revisionist aspirations in the region (Huebert 2010). For them, the Russian plans to "define the outer border of the AZRF," create the AGF, and build a network of border guard stations along the coastline of the Arctic Ocean were evidence of Moscow's expansionism in the region. The Kremlin's assertions about the purely defensive nature of these initiatives were received with great skepticism.

Because *Strategy – 2008* was of a rather general nature, its content needed to be made more concrete and specific. Its provisions also needed to be outlined in detail and updated regularly in other documents. On 20 February 2013, President Putin approved *The Strategy for the Development of the Arctic Zone of the Russian Federation* (*Strategy – 2013*) (Putin 2013). This document was both a follow-up to and update of *Strategy – 2008*. This document could not be considered Russia's full-fledged Arctic doctrine because it covered only the AZRF rather than the whole Arctic region. In this sense, the document was comparable to the Canadian and Norwegian strategies for the development of their northern territories.

Strategy – 2013 had some international dimensions. One of these was Moscow's intention to legally define Russia's continental shelf in the Arctic Ocean and file a revised application to the UN Commission on the Limits of the Continental Shelf. Another was expressing the need for international cooperation in areas such as exploration and exploitation of natural resources, environmental protection, and preservation of Indigenous peoples' traditional economy and culture. However, the main objective of the document was to provide a doctrinal/conceptual basis for the sustainable development of the AZRF. In other words, it was designed for domestic rather than international consumption.

The new Russian strategy was much more open to international cooperation to address numerous Arctic problems and ensure the sustainable development of the region at large. Like the 2008 document, *Strategy – 2013* emphasized Russia's national sovereignty over the AZRF and NSR and called for the protection of the country's national interests in the area. However, along with this rather traditional stance the new strategy had an impressive list of priorities for cooperation with international partners. This endowed *Strategy – 2013* with a more positive international image than the previous document.

The purely military aspects of *Strategy – 2013* included the following tasks:

- Ensuring a favorable operating regime for the Russian troops deployed in the AZRF so they could adequately meet military dangers and threats to Russia's national security;
- Providing the AGF with military training and combat readiness to protect Russian interests in its exclusive economic zone (EEZ) and deter potential threats to and aggression against the country;
- Improving the AGF's structure and composition, as well as providing these forces with modern armaments and infrastructure;
- Improving air and maritime space-monitoring systems;
- Applying dual-use technologies to ensure both the AZRF's military security and sustainable socioeconomic development; and
- Completing hydrographic work to more precisely define the external boundaries of Russia's territorial waters, EEZ, and continental shelf (Putin 2013).

In summary, *Strategy – 2013* was more an invitation to further discussions on Russia's Arctic policies than a comprehensive and sound doctrine. To become an effective national strategy for the region, it needed to be further clarified, specified, and instrumentalized in a series of federal laws, regulations, and task programs. The Russian Arctic strategy also need to be better designed for international consumption. Even though the Russian Arctic doctrine of 2013 clearly addressed soft security, some foreign audiences – by virtue of inertia – continued to perceive such Russian documents as manifestations of Moscow's expansionist plans in the High North.

The Ukrainian crisis prompted a full revision of Russian national security policies' conceptual/doctrinal basis. This began with Russia's military strategy. On 26 December 2014, a new version of Russia's military doctrine was approved by President Putin (Putin 2014). Although the Arctic was mentioned only once in the document, for the first time the protection of Russia's national interests in the Arctic in peacetime was assigned to the Russian armed forces. Even though the new military doctrine generally retained its defensive character, Russia's neighbors, including those in the High North, remained concerned about Moscow's intentions in the region.

In July 2015, President Putin approved a new version of Russia's maritime doctrine (Putin 2015a). The Arctic was identified as one of two regions (the other was the North Atlantic), where NATO activities and international competition for natural resources and sea routes continued to grow and required Russia's "adequate response." According to the document, naval forces and the nuclear icebreaker fleet should be modernized by 2020. A new national security strategy was approved by President Putin in late December 2015

(Putin 2015b). The Arctic was mentioned three times in this document. First, the region was identified as an area where international competition over the natural resources of the world's oceans could increase. Second, the Arctic was described as an important transport/ communication corridor; one that was crucial for Russia's economic security. Finally, the High North was depicted as a region of international cooperation, peace, and stability.

In November 2016, a new version of the Russian Foreign Policy Concept (Putin 2016) was signed by President Putin. The Arctic was mentioned twice in this document. First, it was described as a region where cooperation with Canada was possible. Second, it was mentioned in the special section on the High North. This document underlined the importance of cooperation between regional players in areas such as sustainable development of natural resources, transport systems (including the NSR), environmental protection, and the preservation of peace and stability. The concept also emphasized the need to strengthen regional multilateral institutions, such as the Arctic Council (AC) and the Barents Euro-Arctic Council (BEAC). The document particularly insisted on the need to isolate the Arctic from the current tensions between Russia and the West and to prevent any military confrontation in the region.

To summarize, the Ukrainian crisis affected Moscow's threat perceptions in the region to some extent, but did not significantly change the Kremlin's general attitude about the Arctic. According to Russian leadership, the Arctic should remain a zone of peace and security: cooperation should be the dominant paradigm in the region.

Hard security strategy

As mentioned above, a radical shift in Russia's threat perceptions in the Arctic region has taken place over the last quarter-century. This shift has clearly focused on the increasing role of soft rather than hard security-related concerns. These soft security concerns include ensuring Russia's access to and control of the region's natural resources and transport routes, climate change mitigation, and cleaning up environmental hot spots. At the same time, some Russian strategists believe there are a number of security threats and challenges in the region that require the preservation and further development of a certain military capability and presence in the North. They note that the ongoing Ukrainian crisis has negatively affected Russia's relations with NATO and its member states, with NATO unilaterally suspending several cooperative projects with Russia. These suspended activities include military-to-military contacts and the development of confidence- and security-building measures.

In contrast to some pessimistic expectations, there has been no substantial change in Russia's perceptions of the role of military power in the Arctic. As before, Moscow's military strategies are geared towards the attainment of three major goals: first, to demonstrate and ascertain Russia's sovereignty over the AZRF, including the EEZ and continental shelf; second, to protect its economic interests in the High North; and third, to demonstrate that Russia retains its great-power status and has world-class military capabilities (Konyshev and Sergunin 2014). In a sense, Russian military strategies are comparable with those of other coastal states, especially the United States and Canada.

Because the Soviet-era military machine in the Arctic had significantly degenerated in the 1990s and early 2000s, Russian nuclear and conventional forces badly needed modernization in order to effectively meet new challenges and threats. The main idea behind the modernization plans is to make the Russian armed forces in the Arctic more compact and better equipped and trained. The Russian armed forces' modernization started well before the outbreak of the Ukrainian crisis, namely with the launch of the third State Rearmament Program (2007–2015), which covered both nuclear and conventional components.

The modernization programme of Russia's strategic forces in the North, which was not influenced by the Ukrainian crisis, includes the renewal of its fleet of eight strategic nuclear submarines. Only six Delta IV-class submarines will undergo the process of modernization. It is planned that the Typhoon- and Delta IV-class submarines will be replaced with the new Borey-class fourth-generation nuclear-powered strategic submarines. The first Borey-class submarine, the *Yuri Dolgoruky,* has been in operation with the Northern Fleet since January 2013. Three other Borey-class submarines designed for the Northern Fleet, the *Prince Vladimir,* the *Prince Oleg,* and the *Prince Pozharsky,* will become operational between 2018–2020 (Dimmi 2017).

In contrast with the strategic component, Russia's conventional forces' composition and posture were affected by the Ukrainian crisis. As part of efficiently reorganizing Russian land forces in the AZRF, there had been plans to transform the motorized infantry and marine brigades located near Pechenga (Murmansk Region) into the Arctic special force unit. Soldiers in this unit were to be trained in a special program and equipped with modern personal equipment for military operations in the Arctic. The Arctic brigade was expected to be operational by 2016. As mentioned above, all conventional forces in the AZRF were to be organized into the AGF, which would be led by the joint Arctic command that was to be established in 2017 (Sergunin and Konyshev 2016, 152).

However, the Ukrainian crisis and NATO's reaction to Russian actions precipitated some adjustments to this military planning. While two Pechenga-based brigades were left in place, the Arctic brigade was created ahead of schedule (in January 2015) and deployed in Alakurtti, which is close to the Finnish border. In another move precipitated by an "increased NATO military threat" in the North, President Putin accelerated the creation of a new strategic command "North," which was established in December 2014, three years ahead of schedule. It was also announced that the second Arctic brigade would be formed and stationed in the Yamal-Nenets autonomous district (east of the Ural Mountains in the Arctic Circle) (Sergunin and Konyshev 2016, 152, 153).

Russian Defense Minister Sergei Shoigu also announced that two new Arctic coast defense divisions would be established by 2018 as part of an effort to strengthen security along the NSR. One of them was to be stationed on the Kola Peninsula (in addition the existing military units) and the other in the eastern Arctic (Chukotka Peninsula). The new forces would be tasked with anti-assault, anti-sabotage, and anti-aircraft defense duties along the NSR (Staalesen 2017). They would both interact closely with law-enforcement authorities like the Ministry of Interior, the National Guard, and the Border Guard Service (BGS).

Growing Russian tensions with NATO have forced Russia to pay more attention to the air-defense force units that are stationed in the AZRF on the Kola Peninsula, near Severodvinsk (Arkhangelsk region), Chukotka, and on a number of Russian islands in the Arctic (Novaya Zemlya, Franz Josef Land, the New Siberian Islands, and Wrangel Island). Some of these units have re-established old Soviet airfields and military bases in the Arctic. These units, which are equipped with, among other things, RS-26 Rubezh coastal missile systems, S-300 air-defense missiles, and the Pantsyr-S1 anti-aircraft artillery weapon system (Klimenko 2016, 21), were merged into a joint task force in October 2014. Another measure to increase Moscow's military potential in the region was the creation of a new air force and air-defense army, including regiments armed with MiG-31 interceptor aircraft, S-400 air-defense missile systems (to replace the S-300 systems), and radar units (International Institute for Strategic Studies 2016, 165, 166). Another goal is to restore continuous radar coverage along Russia's entire northern coast, which had been lost in the 1990s. To that end, a total of 13 airfields, an air-force test range, and ten radar sites and direction centers will be established in the Arctic in the coming years.

The strengthening of the BGS is among the top priorities of Russia's national security policy in the High North. An Arctic border guard unit tasked with monitoring the circulation of ships and poaching at sea was created in 1994 and reorganized in 2004–2005. In 2009, it was announced that new Arctic units had been established at border guard stations in Arkhangelsk and Murmansk. Furthermore, two new border guard commands – one in Murmansk for the western AZRF regions, and one in Petropavlovsk-Kamchatsky for the eastern Arctic regions – were established. The border guards were assigned the task of dealing with new soft security threats and challenges, such as the establishment of reliable border-control systems, the introduction of special visa regulations to certain regions, and the implementation of technological controls over fluvial zones and sites along the NSR. The NSR is monitored from the air by border guard aircraft and on land and sea by the North-Eastern Border Guard Agency. The Russian border guards plan to establish a global monitoring network from Murmansk to Wrangel Island. All in all, Moscow plans to build 20 border guard stations along the Arctic Ocean coastline (Klimenko 2016, 14, 15; Zagorsky 2013).

Another structural change is an ongoing reorganization of the Russian Coast Guard, which is part of the BGS. The Coast Guard now has a wider focus in the Arctic: in addition to the traditional protection of biological resources in the Arctic Ocean, the agency's new top priorities include oil and gas installations and shipping along the NSR. There are plans to equip the Coast Guard in the AZRF with the brand new vessels of Project 22100. The Okean-class ice-going patrol ship, the *Polyarnaya Zvezda* (Polar Star), is currently undergoing sea trials in the Baltic Sea. Vessels of this class can break up to 31.4-inch-thick ice. They have an endurance of 60 days and a range of 12,000 nautical miles at 20 knots. They are equipped with a Ka-27 helicopter and can be supplied with Gorizont drones (Staalesen 2015).

The attention Russia now gives to the Coast Guard is in line with other coastal states, especially Norway and Denmark. Moreover, Russia actively participated in the creation of an Arctic Coast Guard Forum, which was established by the coastal states in November 2015. Moscow argues that this build-up is defensive in nature, and that the number of armed forces added is small. The Kremlin asserts that these activities are prudent, given the importance of the North to Russia's future economic development plans, the increasing permeability of Russia's vast northern borders, and the anticipated increase in commercial shipping along Russia's North as Arctic sea ice melts.

A soft security agenda

The Kremlin has a busy domestic security agenda, which has been prioritized over the international problems in the region. Russia's leadership realizes that most of the threats and challenges to the AZRF originate inside rather than outside the country. These problems are rooted in a confluence of factors, including the degradation of Soviet-era economic, transport, and social infrastructure in the region; the resource-oriented model of the Russian economy; numerous ecological problems generated by the Soviet model of industrialism and military activities; and the lack of funds and managerial skills in Russia to properly develop the AZRF.

Economic dimension

The economic dimension of Russia's soft security strategy has the following priorities for the AZRF: sustainable economic activity and increasing prosperity of Arctic communities; sustainable use of natural, including living, resources; and the development of transport infrastructure (including aviation, marine and surface transport), information technologies, and modern telecommunications (The Government of the Russian Federation 2014, 11–17). Russian economic strategic priorities were slightly revised in the aftermath of the Ukrainian crisis. First and foremost, Moscow had to adjust its energy policy priorities. In view of the lack of Western technologies and investment, offshore projects were slowed down or postponed. Liquefied natural gas (LNG) production was emphasized because it was seen as a more promising export-oriented project than oil-related ones (a case in point: the Yamal LNG plant in Sabetta, established in 2017). To counter Western sanctions, Russia invited China, South Korea, India, and Vietnam –countries that did not impose sanctions on Russia – to support its Arctic projects through funding, the provision of technology, and participation in joint development projects.

Environmental dimension

The environmental dimension of Russia's AZRF strategy includes monitoring and assessing the state of the Arctic environment; preventing and eliminating environmental pollution in the Arctic; protecting the Arctic marine environment; conserving biodiversity in the Arctic; assessing climate change impact in the Arctic, and preventing and eliminating ecological emergencies in the Arctic, including those relating to climate change (The Government of the Russian Federation 2014, 9–11).

Moscow is very concerned about the environmental situation in the AZRF. As a result of intensive industrial and military activity in the region, many AZRF areas are heavily polluted and pose serious health hazards. Russian scientists have identified 27 so-called "impact zones," where pollution has led to environmental degradation and increased morbidity among the local population. The main impact zones are the Murmansk region (10% of the total pollutants in the 27 impact zones), the Norilsk urban agglomeration (over 30%), the West Siberian oil and gas fields (over 30%), and the Arkhangelsk region (approximately 5%) (Dushkova and Evseev 2011). In total, some 15% of the AZRF territory is polluted or contaminated (Kochemasov et al. 2009).

In 2011, the Russian Government launched a 2.3 billion ruble program to clean the AZRF, including the Franz Joseph Land and Novaya Zemlya archipelagos. By the end of 2016, some 42,000 tons of waste had been removed from these archipelagos and 349 hectares of insular land had been cleaned (RIA Novosti 2016a). In 2015, another AZRF cleaning program was launched, this time with 21 billion rubles of funding. By the end of 2016, the cleaning of Wrangel Island – including the removal of 36,477 barrels and 264 tons of scrap metal by the Russian military (Neftegaz.ru 2016) – was nearly complete. A comprehensive analysis of the environmental situation in another seven major AZRF areas had been planned, but the federal government was unable to find reliable contractors for that purpose. Similarly, the cleaning of Russian mining villages on Spitsbergen, planned for 2011–2013, was never implemented.

Nuclear safety in the High North is also an area where Russia and other Arctic states cooperate. More than 200 decommissioned nuclear reactors from submarines and icebreakers from the Soviet period are stored on the Kola Peninsula – a Soviet "legacy" that is especially problematic for neighboring countries like Norway, Finland, and Sweden. The US–Russian Cooperative Threat Reduction Program (Nunn-Lugar) of 1991–2012 (Nikitin and Woolf 2014) and the 2003 Multilateral Nuclear Environmental Program in the Russian Federation (Framework Agreement on a Multilateral Nuclear Environmental Program in the Russian Federation 2003) played a significant role in nuclear waste treatment.

The Russian Government's program on nuclear and radiological safety for the 2008–2015 period succeeded in dismantling 195 retired nuclear submarines (97% of the total), removing 98.8% of radioisotope thermoelectric generators from service, and dismantling 86% of these generators. Centralized long-term storage facilities for spent nuclear fuel were constructed. Moreover, 53 hazardous nuclear facilities were decommissioned, 270 hectares of contaminated land were remediated, and open-water storage of radioactive waste was ended (Rosatom 2017).

Russia has supported and vigorously participated in developing all UN-related environmental initiatives, from the Intergovernmental Panel on Climate Change report (2014) to the International Maritime Organization's Polar Code (2014–2015) and the Paris agreement on climate change (2015). Moscow has also actively participated in the AC's working and expert groups involved in environmental research and assessment.

Social dimension

The social dimension of Moscow's soft security strategy focuses on the health of the people living and working in the Arctic, education and cultural heritage, prosperity and capacity building for children and youth, gender equality, enhancing well-being, and the eradication of poverty among Arctic peoples (Putin 2009; The Government of the Russian Federation 2014, 8–9). Even though good ideas have been articulated, implementation remains problematic – something true of many areas of Russian public policy. The path to the AZRF's modernization and innovation charted by the Russian Government must begin to move from policy declarations to the actual implementation of specific, realistic projects in the region.

The Kremlin appears to understand the need for constructive dialogue and deeper political engagement with all of Russia's AZRF regions, municipalities, Indigenous people, and nongovernmental organizations (e.g., the Russian Association of Indigenous Peoples of the North, environmental groups, and human rights activists). Moscow generally encourages these actors to work with international partners – unless, of course, such engagement assumes a separatist character or involves attempts to challenge Moscow's foreign policy prerogatives. In practice, however, the federal bureaucracy's policies and approaches are often confrontational towards the projects of subnational actors and civil society groups. Instead of using the resources of these actors in a creative way, Moscow tries to control them. In so doing, the state undermines their initiative, making them passive, both domestically and internationally.

Conclusions

There has been a significant shift in Russia's threat perceptions and security policies in the High North since the 1990s. In contrast with the Cold War era, when the Arctic was a zone for global confrontation between the USSR and the US/NATO, this region is now seen by Moscow as a platform for international cooperation. The Kremlin now believes that there are no serious hard security threats to the AZRF and that the soft security agenda is much more important.

While some media, politicians, and strategic analysts portray the changes in Russia's military capabilities as a significant military build-up and even a renewed arms race in the region, the real picture is far from that apocalyptic scenario. It is more accurate to characterize these military developments as a limited modernization along with increases or changes in equipment, force levels, and force structure. Some of these changes – for example, the creation of new Russian Arctic units, commissioning more sophisticated and better-armed warships, and the establishment of new command structures in the Far North – have little or nothing to do with projecting power into the potentially disputed areas where the Arctic coastal states' claims overlap or the region at large. Instead, they are for patrolling and protecting recognized national territories that are becoming more accessible, including monitoring for illegal activities such as overfishing, poaching, smuggling, and uncontrolled migration. Other changes – such as the modernization of Russian strategic nuclear forces – have more to do with maintaining a deterrent potential than with developing offensive capabilities.

In other words, these programs need not provoke an arms race or undermine regional cooperation. Moscow is mostly concerned with soft security challenges to the AZRF, such as dependence on extractive industries and the export of energy products, socioeconomic disparities between Russia's northern regions, degradation of urban infrastructure, debilitating ecological problems, and threats to Indigenous peoples' traditional economies and way of life.

In its foreign policy, Russia has clearly demonstrated that it prefers soft power instruments (diplomatic, economic, and cultural) in the Arctic region, as well as activity and discourse via multilateral institutions. Moscow has developed a pragmatic international strategy that aims at using Arctic cooperative programs and regional institutions to solve Russia's specific problems rather than address abstract challenges. Russia's pragmatism should be taken into account by other regional players and should not be misinterpreted by them. Currently, there is no Russian "hidden agenda" in the Arctic. Moscow insists that its strategy in the region is predictable and constructive rather than aggressive or improvised. The Kremlin is quite clear about its intentions in the region, saying that Russia does not want to be a revisionist power or troublemaker in the Arctic. Russia will achieve its national goals in the region by using peaceful diplomatic, economic and cultural means, and by acting through international organizations and forums rather than unilaterally.

Russian leadership believes that the Arctic cooperative agenda could include the following areas: climate change mitigation, environmental protection, emergency situations, air and maritime safety (including the Polar Code implementation, charting safe maritime routes, and cartography), search and rescue operations, Arctic research, Indigenous peoples, cross- and trans-border cooperative projects, and culture, etc. In order to prevent potential conflicts, avoid misunderstandings, and facilitate regional cooperation, Russia suggests that the Arctic states should be clear about their military policies and doctrines and should include arms-control initiatives and confidence- and security-building measures as part of bilateral and multilateral relations in the Arctic. Solid institutional support is needed to make this ambitious agenda concrete. For this reason, regional (the AC and BEAC) and global (International Maritime Organization, UN Environment Program, UN Development Program, etc.) governance institutions, which have slowed down their activities in the Arctic because of the recent tensions between Russia and the West, should be revived.

References

Dimmi, 2017, *Project 955 – Borey/Dolgorukiy*, 19 March, http://militaryrussia.ru/blog/topic-338.html (in Russian).

Dushkova, D., and A. Evseev, 2011, 'Analiz Techogennogo Vozdeistviyana Geosistemy Evropeiskogo Severa Rossii' [Analisys of Technogenic Impact on Geosystems of the European Russian North], *Arktika i Sever* [The Arctic and the North], no. 4, 1–34, http://narfu.ru/upload/iblock/673/16.pdf (in Russian).

Framework Agreement on a Multilateral Nuclear Environmental Program in the Russian Federation, 2003, 28 October, www.pircenter.org/media/content/files/11/13613597850.pdf.

The Government of the Russian Federation, 2014. 'Sotsial'no-Ekonomicheskoe Razvitie Arkticheskoy Zony Rossiyskoi Federatsii na Period do 2020 Goda [Socio-Economic Development of the Arctic Zone of the Russian Federation for the Period up to 2020],' http://government.ru/media/files/AtEY gOHutVc.pdf (in Russian).

Huebert, Rob, 2010, *The Newly Emerging Arctic Security Environment*, Calgary: Canadian Defence & Foreign Affairs Institute (CDFA Paper, March), www.cdfai.org/PDF/The%20Newly%20Emerging%20Arctic%20Security%20Environment.pdf (accessed June 28, 2013).

The International Institute for Strategic Studies, 2016, *The Military Balance 2016*, London: The International Institute for Strategic Studies.

Klimenko, Ekaterina, 2016, *Russia's Arctic Security Policy. Still Quiet in the High North?* Stockholm: SIPRI (SIPRI Policy Paper No. 45).

Kochemasov, Y.V., Morgunov, B.A., and V.I. Solomatin. 2009. Ekologo-Ekonomicheskaya Otsenka Perspectivy Razvitiya Arktiki [Ecological-Economic Assessment of Perspectives of the Arctic's Development] www.ecoenergy.ru/Article54.html (in Russian).

Konyshev, Valery, and Alexander Sergunin, 2014, 'Is Russia a revisionist military power in the Arctic?' *Defence and Security Analysis* 30, no. 4, 323–335.

Lakshmi, Aiswarya, 2015, 'Is Russia militarizing the Arctic?' *MarineLink.com*, 20 August, www.marine link.com/news/militarizing-russia396525.aspx.

Medvedev, Dmitry, 2009, *Osnovy Gosudarstvennoi Politiki Rossiiskoi Federatsii v Arktike na Period do 2020 Goda i Dal'neishuiu Perspektivu* [Foundations of the State Policy of the Russian Federation in the Arctic Up to and Beyond 2020], 2008, www.rg.ru/2009/03/30/arktika-osnovy-dok.html (accessed June 30, 2013).

Neftegaz.ru, 2016, 'Usiliyami Rossiyskih Voennyh s Ostrova Vrangelya Bylo Vyvezeno 36,477 Bochek i 264 tons Metalloloma' [The Russian Military Removed 36,477 Barrels and 264 Tons of Scrap Metal from the Wrangel Island], *Neftegaz.ru*, 2 November, http://neftegaz.ru/news/view/154946-Usiliyami-rossiyskih-voennyh-s-ostrova-Vrangelya-bylo-vyvezeno-36-477-bochek-i-264-tmetalloloma (in Russian).

Nikitin, Mary Beth D., and Amy F. Woolf, 2014, *The Evolution of Cooperative Threat Reduction: Issues for Congress*, Washington, DC: Congressional Research Service, https://fas.org/sgp/crs/nuke/R43143.pdf.

Poulin, Andrew, 2016, '5 ways Russia is positioning to dominate the Arctic,' *International Policy Digest*, 24 January, https://intpolicydigest.org/author/andrew-poulin/.

Putin, Vladimir, 2009, *Kontseptsiya Ustoychivogo Razvitiya Korennykh Malochislennykh Narodov Severa, Sibiri i Dal'nego Vostoka Rossiyskoi Federatsii* [The Concept for the Sustainable Development of Small Indigenous Population Groups of the North, Siberia and the Far East of the Russian Federation], 4 February, http://docs.cntd.ru/document/902142304 (in Russian).

Putin, Vladimir, 2013, *Strategiya Razvitiya Arkticheskoi Zony Rossiyskoi Federatsii i Obespecheniya Natsional'noi Bezopasnosti na Period do 2020 Goda* [The Strategy for the Development of the Arctic Zone of the Russian Federation and Ensuring National Security for the Period up to 2020], Approved by President Vladimir Putin on 20 February 2013, http://правительство.рф/docs/22846/ (accessed June 28, 2013) (in Russian).

Putin, Vladimir, 2014, *Voennaya Doktrina Rossiyskoy Federatsii* [The Military Doctrine of the Russian Federation], 26 December, http://static.kremlin.ru/media/events/files/41d527556bec8deb3530.pdf (in Russian).

Putin, Vladimir, 2015a, *Morskaya Doktrina Rossiyskoy Federatsii* [Maritime Doctrine of the Russian Federation], July, http://statc.kremlin.ru/media/events/files/ru/uAFi5nvux2twaqjftS5yrIZUVTJan77L.pdf (in Russian).

Putin, Vladimir, 2015b, *O Strategii Natsional'noi Bezopasnosti Rossiyskoi Federatsii* [On the National Security Strategy of the Russian Federation], 31 December, www.scrf.gov.ru/documents/1/133.html (in Russian).

Putin, Vladimir, 2016, *Kontseptsiya Vneshnei Politiki Rossiyskoi Federatsii* [The Foreign Policy Concept of the Russian Federation], 30 November, http://publication.pravo.gov.ru/Document/View/0001201612010045?index=0&rangeSize=1 (in Russian).

Rekord Dal'nosti, 2011, 28 August, www.arms-expo.ru/049057054048124050052056054051.html (in Russian).

RIA Novosti, 2016a. *Likvidatsiya Nakoplennogo Ekologicheskogo Usherba v Arktike* [Elimination of accumulated environmental damage in the Arctic], 21 November, https://ria.ru/infografika/20161121/1481781022.html (in Russian).

Rosatom, 2017, *Back-end*, www.rosatom.ru/en/rosatom-group/back-end/index.php?sphrase_id=11699.

Sergunin, Alexander, and Valery Konyshev, 2016, *Russia in the Arctic: Hard or Soft Power?* Stuttgart: Ibidem.

Staalesen, Atle, 2015, 'Navy fills up with new ships,' *The Independent Barents Observer*, 28 December, https://thebarentsobserver.com/en/security/2015/12/navy-fills-new-ships.

Staalesen, Atle, 2017, 'New Russian forces to protect Arctic coast,' *The Independent Barents Observer*, 20 January, https://thebarentsobserver.com/en/security/2017/01/new-russian-forces-protectarctic-coast.

Stratfor, 2015, *Russia's Plans for Arctic Supremacy*, 16 January, www.stratfor.com/analysis/russias-plans-arctic-supremacy.

Tayloe, Shane C., 2015, 'Projecting power in the Arctic: The Russian scramble for energy, power, and prestige in the high North,' *Pepperdine Policy Review* 8, article 4 (Spring), 1–19. http://digitalcommons.pepperdine.edu/ppr.

Zagorsky, Andrei, 2013, *Arkticheskie Ucheniya Severnogo Flota* [The Arctic exercises of the Northern Fleet], www.imemo.ru/ru/publ/comments/2013/comm_2013_053.pdf (in Russian).

12
ARCTIC SECURITY
The Canadian context

Heather Exner-Pirot and Rob Huebert

Introduction

The Arctic has more than just geographical significance in Canada: it has also played an outsized role in contemporary and historical domestic security discussions. The prominence of the North in the Canadian identity has often made these discussions political in nature. This chapter provides a comprehensive review of the events, issues, and characteristics that have shaped Canadian perspectives on Arctic security. Long-standing preoccupations with sovereignty; the rise of a Russian threat, real and imagined; and a growing emphasis on human security, while still building on traditional security, make Canada's Arctic security context unique within the region.

Demographics and geography of the Canadian Arctic

Although the Arctic is often conceived as homogenous – white, icy, and cold – to southern dwellers, there are important distinctions between different parts of the region. Fennoscandia[1] enjoys relatively warm ocean currents, which cause the region to experience higher temperatures than its northerly latitude would predict. This has led to higher population density and industrial activity in the Barents region, which crosses Norway, Sweden, Finland, and Russia, than in any other part of the Arctic.

Northern Canada is much more similar to Alaska, Greenland, and Northeastern Russia in terms of geographic and demographic characteristics, including sparseness, remoteness, and a large Indigenous population. Yet even there, Canada is unique. It lacks the industrial activity, largely driven by oil, gas and mining, of Alaska and Russia, and thus does not have large urban areas and services. Northern Canada also lacks the accessibility that Greenland enjoys by virtue of all its communities being situated on an ice-free coast. In many ways, the Canadian Arctic is the least accessible, least developed, and least populated part of the Arctic Ocean region.

These facts have shaped security concerns in interesting ways. Most political attention, dating back to Confederation, has been directed at exercising sovereignty. Was Canada able to provide effective stewardship and control of its vast and remote Arctic territory? Were the United States or Russia going to exploit its limited capacities by challenging that sovereignty?

Attention has inevitably focused on the fact that it has been difficult for the Canadian state to secure the region as a result of its inhospitable geography, yet few have reached the logical conclusion that the situation would be equally challenging for others.

Importance of the Arctic to Canadian identity

Canada's approach to Arctic security has been strongly influenced by its sense of national identity. "True North, strong and free" is the refrain from its national anthem, complemented by popular associations of Canadian-ness with cold, ruggedness, and wilderness. This, despite more than four out of five Canadians living in urban areas, and about three out of four Canadians living within 100 miles, or 160 kilometres, of the United States border. Only 5% of Canadians have been to Yukon or the Northwest Territories (NWT), and only 1% to Nunavut (Historica Canada & IPSOS, 2016).

Canada's Arctic foreign policy has drawn on a conception that its Arctic sovereignty is threatened. This concept has been used for domestic political purposes by politicians of all stripes, from Prime Ministers William Lyon Mackenzie King and Stephen Harper, the latter of whom described the Canadian Arctic as "so beautiful that it can readily inspire that romantic patriotism which is one of the most priceless assets of a people" (as quoted in Williams, 2011: 117), to the government of Justin Trudeau. This makes it very difficult politically to take a soft, or, as some experts would describe it, moderate, approach to Arctic security. A lack of icebreaking power, a cooperative stance towards Russia in the region, or a conciliatory stance on border disputes (for example over Hans Island or the extent of Canada's continental shelf into the Arctic Ocean) can earn a rebuke in the media or from the parliamentary opposition (Byers, 2013).

Generations of Canadian politicians have needed to demonstrate concern and action to protect the vast Canadian Arctic from external threats. The following section provides an overview of these efforts.

History of Canadian Arctic security strategies and responses

One of the greatest challenges of addressing the history of Canadian Arctic security is that in many ways the core issues are not about the Arctic itself. Canadian political leaders first experienced this in 1904 when they found themselves caught in the middle of a greater geopolitical exercise involving the delineation of the Alaska/Yukon border. For Canada, the issue was about determining its northwestern border. For both the United Kingdom and the United States, the issue was really about the larger context (Sands, 2009–10). While the end result was not as bad as some commentators claimed, the basis of the settlement was largely determined by the interests of an increasingly powerful United States and a United Kingdom that needed the Americans' support as the German threat grew in the years before the First World War (Haglund and Onea, 2008).

The next major Arctic security challenge facing Canada came during the Second World War. Both the Japanese and Germans either used or attacked locations in or near the North American Arctic. The Japanese attacked and occupied two of the Aleutian Islands, Attu and Kiska. Canada found itself working closely with the Americans to defend against further incursions and assisted in the effort to recover the islands (Grant, 2010). German U-boats brought secret landing parties that built weather stations along the northern Labrador coast (Dege, 2004). Both incidents were peripheral to the greater conflict, but they demonstrated that the Arctic region was no longer isolated from international politics.

The Cold War forced Canada to engage upon a wholesale effort to defend its Arctic region (Sutherland, 1966). By the middle of the 1940s it had become apparent that the Grand Alliance of the Second World War had broken down. Furthermore, the development of new military technologies – long-range bombers and a missile-based delivery system, combined with nuclear weapons – meant the geography of the Arctic took central importance in the developing conflict between the USSR and the Western powers (Eayrs, 1972). Canada worked closely with the United States to develop a means of detecting and defending against the rising Soviet bomber threat and deterring the missile threat through the creation of the North American Aerospace Defense Command (NORAD) (Jockel, 1987) and construction of the Distant Early Warning (DEW) Line (Lackenbaurer, 2005). In the following years, as the USSR introduced nuclear-missile-carrying and nuclear-powered submarines into the Arctic, the United States and Canada continued to cooperate to meet this new element of the Soviet threat – albeit in a much more secretive manner (Lajeunesse, 2016).

Throughout the 1970s and 1980s, the Arctic remained central to Canadian security. The defense policies of successive Liberal and Conservative governments listed the defence of North America as the second most important priority, behind only the defence of Canada itself. This in turn meant defence against the USSR focused on ensuring that Canada played a meaningful role in defending against and then deterring the Soviet threat, primarily in the North, through NORAD (Bland, 1987).

At the same time, it was also recognized that there was a need to demonstrate to the Americans that Canada was "doing its part." Referred to as the "defense against help," academic observers noted that regardless of what Canadians believed about the Soviet threat, they still needed to act as long as the Americans perceived a threat (see e.g. Ørvik, 1983). There was a fear that if American officials thought Canada was not doing enough, the United States would act on its own within Canadian Arctic territory, as it deemed necessary.

This fear of an American threat to Canadian sovereignty has been one of the most significant themes associated with Canadian Arctic security. Sharing a continent with the United States has prompted sensitivity among Canadian policymakers to American actions in the Arctic region since the Alaskan boundary dispute. Both during and immediately after the Second World War, Prime Minister Mackenzie King was deeply suspicious of American actions and intent in the Arctic, regardless of the fact that the Americans were always very proper in their treatment of the Canadian Arctic (Coates et al., 2008: 59).

These concerns were only a backdrop until 1969, when an American flagged supertanker – the USS *Manhattan* – was sent through the Northwest Passage (Dosman, 1976). The purpose of this voyage was to determine whether it was more economical to transport oil that had been discovered on the North slope of Alaska by tanker through the Passage or by a pipeline to a southern Alaskan port and then by ship from there (Kirton and Munton, 1992). The Americans viewed the Passage as an international strait that did not require Canadian permission to transit. The Canadian position remains that the Northwest Passage is part of Canada's internal waters and therefore all foreign vessels – American ships included – must seek Canadian permission to enter and transit (Pharand, 2007). In 1985, a similar crisis occurred when another American vessel, the Coast Guard icebreaker *Polar Sea*, transited the Passage without seeking permission (Huebert, 1995). Both voyages were seen as direct challenges to Canadian Arctic sovereignty and created widespread public concern in Canada.

This ongoing suspicion about American motivations and the ongoing disagreement regarding the international status of the Northwest Passage created a perception among some elements of the Canadian public and some policymakers (especially within the Liberal Party), that the greatest threat to Canadian Arctic sovereignty was the Americans. In the 1970s and 1980s, there were more concerns about American violations of Canadian Arctic sovereignty than there were about Soviet threats to Canadian Arctic security.

In the 1980s, the Brian Mulroney government attempted to address the challenges and threats to Canada's Arctic sovereignty and security with a series of policies intended to strengthen Canadian military capabilities in the Arctic. Following the voyage of the *Polar Sea*, Secretary of State for External Affairs (a post now referred to as Foreign Minister) Joe Clark introduced a number of policy options to defend Canadian Arctic sovereignty (Canada, Department of External Affairs, 1985). At the same time, the government released a defence policy that called for the construction of a fleet of nuclear-powered submarines, primarily for the protection of North Atlantic and Arctic waters (Ferguson, 2014). However, the end of the Cold War resulted in a move away from traditional Arctic sovereignty and security concerns, and the government abandoned most of the initiatives that would have strengthened Canadian Arctic security capabilities. At this point, the regional focus of successive Canadian governments shifted towards a closer association with elements of human security.

Contemporary threats to Canadian Arctic security

Discussions about Arctic security primarily revolve around the potential for conflict between the Western Arctic states and a resurgent Russia. There are two competing understandings in Canada. One set of observers sees the Russians as a real and rising threat.[2] Following the end of the Cold War, Russia was increasingly seen as a partner in the Arctic region rather than as an adversary. This was bolstered by the realization that the implosion of the Soviet Union had left its successor state, the Russian Federation, economically destitute. This meant that the former Soviet submarine fleet no longer sailed; it was instead left to rust in northern Russian ports. The United States and Norway, and subsequently Canada, came to see the precarious state of the former Soviet submarine force as a major environmental threat to the Arctic. The fleet's deteriorating condition could lead to major radionuclide contamination if its reactors, which remained on board, failed. Canada recognized the environmental threat posed by the submarines, but did not initially join the American and Norwegian effort to provide what amounted to tens of millions of dollars in technical and monetary assistance (United States Government Accountability Office, 2004). Ultimately, Canada did join this effort through the G8 Global Partnership against the Spread of Weapons and Materials of Mass Destruction in 2002 under the Liberal government of Jean Chrétien (Canada, Foreign Affairs and International Trade, 2011).

However, new concerns about the Russian government's approach to Arctic cooperation began to develop in the mid-2000s. Some observers noted a return of Russian military activity to the region. This included the resumption of long-range bomber patrols and nuclear-powered nuclear-missile-carrying submarines (SBBNs) (BBC News, 2007; Russian Strategic Nuclear Forces [blog], 2012; Schmitt, 2016). While some suggested this was simply Russia engaging in standard military action as its economy recovered thanks to high oil prices, others were concerned that this represented a Russian effort to reassert military power in the region.

Towards the end of the 2000s, many of Russia's neighbours, including Norway (Smith, 2017b), Sweden (Adams, 2016), and Finland (Writte, 2014), began to publicly report increased Russian military activity near their northern borders and, in some instances, incursions into their sovereign territories. The Canadian government under Stephen Harper began to take a more critical public position regarding Russian behaviour in the Arctic (Robinson, 2014).

Throughout the 2010s, there have also been rising concerns about other aspects of increasing Russian military activity in the Arctic region. This includes the modernization of a number of sites along the Northern Sea Route, which the Russian government insists are intended to improve search and rescue capabilities in the region (Hoyle, 2013). However, the issue that has provoked the greatest concern is Russian military activity outside the Arctic. The consequences for Arctic security of military actions taken by the Russian government outside the Arctic region is one of the more challenging aspects of Canadian Arctic security Policy.

Under President Vladimir Putin, the Russian government, supported by the high price of oil in the mid-to-late 2000s, moved to reassert its power in the international system. This resulted in a growing number of disputes with the West. Successive Canadian governments attempted to downplay the impact they had on Arctic cooperation. The Harper government, however, became more critical of Russian actions, including Foreign Affairs Minister Peter MacKay's 2007 rebuke of the planting of a titanium Russian flag beneath the ice at the North Pole by Duma member Artur Chilingarov (Coates et al., 2008: 137). Even so, the Harper government moderated its criticism of the Russian government for a time after this event and in most of their subsequent statements focused on cooperation with Russia in the Arctic.

This changed in 2014 when Russia used military force to seize the Crimean Peninsula and then continued to use covert operations to foment military opposition to the Ukrainian government. In response, Canada joined other Western nations, including the United States and Norway, in imposing a series of sanctions against Russia, many of which affected Russian companies with an interest in the development of Arctic oil and gas (Chase and Mackinnon, 2015). The Russian government reacted by increasing military activity near and often over the territory of its Arctic neighbors, including Canada (Oliphant, 2015).

The Harper government also began to connect Russian actions elsewhere in the world to activities in the Arctic. For example, it cancelled participation in an Arctic Council Task Force meeting in Moscow that was scheduled for April 14, 2014 (CBC News, 2014; Mackrael, 2014). With the defeat of the Conservatives in 2015, there were signs that the connection between Russia's aggressive actions elsewhere and cooperation in the Arctic would be reversed. As leader of the Department of Global Affairs (renamed from the Department of Foreign Affairs), Foreign Minister Stéphane Dion initiated a reset to the Russian–Canadian relationship, hosting a conference on "Canada–Russia Dialogue and Co-operation in the Arctic" in Ottawa on November 24, 2016 (Blanchfield, 2017).

At the time of writing, the Liberals have begun to share many Conservative concerns about the increasing danger posed by Russian international behaviour. Foreign Minister Chrystia Freeland has been outspoken in her concerns about Russian actions worldwide (Kassam, 2017). Canada's most recent Defence Policy, released in June 2017, reiterates that Canada has been able to cooperate with Russia on economic, environmental, and safety issues in the Arctic, (National Defence Canada, 2017). But that policy also makes clear that in terms of political and strategic issues, Russia has increasingly been taking actions that threaten international peace and security: "Russia has proven its willingness to test the international security environment. A degree of major power competition has returned to the international system" (National Defence Canada, 2017: 50).

The Defence Policy also reaffirms the Liberal government's commitment to completing a number of Arctic-focused defence capital programs that had been initiated by the former Conservative government. This includes completing construction of five or six Arctic Offshore Patrol Vessels and opening the Nanisivik refuelling site in Nunavut. The new policy adds a commitment to rebuilding a number of Arctic-specific Canadian defence capabilities, such as modernizing the North Warning System (formally the DEW Line), one of the most important elements of NORAD (National Defence Canada, 2017:79). It explains:

> While the current NWS is approaching the end of its life expectancy from a technological and functional perspective, unfortunately the range of potential threats to the continent such as that posed by *adversarial cruise missiles* and ballistic missiles has become more complex and increasingly difficult to detect.
>
> *(National Defence Canada, 2017; emphasis added)*

The reference to adversarial cruise missiles is about Russia.

In a break from Conservative government policy, the Liberal Defence Policy also calls for greater cooperation with NATO in the Arctic. For reasons that have never been publicly released, the Harper government had resisted NATO efforts to increase its activities in the Arctic (Clark, 2011). The Liberal Defence Policy explicitly states that "among the challenges at home is the need to operate in the Arctic, alongside the Canadian Coast Guard, and alongside *allied* partners" (Clark, 2011; emphasis added). Furthermore, the Policy states:

> NATO has also increased its attention to Russia's ability to project force from its Arctic territory into the North Atlantic, and its potential to challenge NATO's collective defence posture. Canada and its NATO Allies have been clear that the Alliance will be ready to deter and defend against any potential threats, including against sea lines of communication and maritime approaches to Allied territory in the North Atlantic.
>
> *(Clark, 2011: 79)*

Thus, the Liberal government makes it clear that it sees increased Russian military action in the Arctic as a new form of power projection that must be matched by closer cooperation with its NATO allies. This has included expanded traning missions with NATO in more northern waters (Naval-technology.com, 2017).

Alongside those who see Russia as a real and rising danger are those who see little threat of an actual "hot" conflict in the Arctic, with Canada's Arctic being particularly safe from outside incursion (Lackenbauer, 2010). If a potential conflict is predicated on expropriating hydrocarbon resources, then it would make more sense for Russia to do so in the waters off the coasts of Norway, Alaska, or even Greenland because there is relatively little hydrocarbon potential in Canadian Arctic waters. Furthermore, Russia has the largest untapped Arctic oil and gas reserves: its problem is not running out of oil and gas but rather getting it to market profitably (Roberts, 2010). With regard to strategic positioning for shipping and navigation, Russia is intent on promoting its Northern Sea Route as a fast and well-serviced alternative to more southerly options (Brigham, 2013). Canada's Northwest

Passage, in comparison, is ice-infested, less predictable, and lacks adequate infrastructure. There would be no reason for Russia to use or promote traverses through Canadian Arctic waters. Finally, with regard to potential overlaps in claims to extended continental shelf in the central Arctic Ocean, Russia, Canada, and the other Arctic coastal states have publicly committed in the 2008 Ilulissat Declaration to settling any disputes peaceably and under existing international legal frameworks. Based on its behaviour during the past nine years, there is no reason to expect otherwise.

Perhaps most tellingly, Canadian Armed Forces reports and strategies over the past decade, including the latest Defence Policy, have highlighted the predominantly cooperative atmosphere in the region and minimized the potential of any conventional military threat in the Canadian Arctic. They focus instead on safety issues arising from increased human activity (Lackenbauer and Lajeunesse, 2016).

Analysis: unique aspects of Canadian Arctic security

During the past 11 years, each of the Arctic states has proffered a public Arctic policy – an interesting and rare convergence. The consistency in themes and goals among the eight Arctic states has been called an Arctic consensus; one that is marked by priorities around security and sovereignty, international cooperation, climate change and environmental protection, sustainable economic and social development, the rights of Indigenous peoples, and scientific cooperation. Canada's Arctic security and policy goals are broadly consistent with these. Yet Canada's Arctic security and policy goals stand apart in several ways. This section outlines those aspects that are more or less unique to Canada.

A preoccupation with sovereignty

Canada has long viewed Arctic security through a lens of sovereignty, with the 1969 voyage of the *Manhattan* recognized as a catalyst for such thinking (Lajeunesse, 2008).[3] This occurred at a time when Canada was particularly concerned with differentiating itself as a nation and as a state from its southern neighbour, so nationalist passions were easily provoked.

The Conservatives took this narrative to new heights in the late 2000s, encapsulated by the turn of phrase adopted by Prime Minister Harper in August 2007, that Canada must "use it or lose it" with respect to its Arctic territory: a legally nonsensical but memorable statement. Harper made the defence of Arctic sovereignty a central campaign pillar in the 2006 election, and subsequently the number one priority of the government's 2010 Statement on Canada's Arctic Foreign Policy. Harper visited the Arctic every summer during his tenure as prime minister, securing photo ops with Canadian Rangers, icebreakers, or other projections of power, as well as ensuring that the relevant departments were delivering on the government's policies. The annual trips also focused media attention on the Canadian North in a manner that quickly dissipated when the Trudeau government discontinued them. The Harper government's policies were met with broad agreement among the Canadian population: in a 2009 Environics survey commissioned by the Department of National Defence, 54% of Canadians believed that the country faced a threat to its Arctic sovereignty and to the security of its northern border (Landriault, 2016).

Arctic sovereignty became associated with the Conservative brand between 2006–15, to the point that the Trudeau Liberals began dissociating themselves from the language, choosing to emphasize instead "stewardship" and "control." Yet the narrative is fairly will locked in for a generation of Canadians, which could impede policy decisions for fear of the government looking "soft" on Arctic security and sovereignty. When Liberal Foreign Minister Dion was shuffled out of the portfolio, for example, one commentator observed that he was a good man but naïve when it came to Russia: "Stéphane wanted to re-engage with Russia but didn't understand that when you talk to Putin you need to carry a big stick. Stéphane talked about common interests in the Arctic but Russia is militarizing the Arctic" (Marcus Kolga as quoted in Ivison, 2017).

The Arctic as homeland: self-determination of Canadian Indigenous peoples

More so than any other Arctic nation, Canada's relationship with its Indigenous people has defined its Arctic foreign and security policy. With few exceptions, Northerners have had real influence in the development of Canada's Arctic policy during the past three decades, which has thus leaned towards greater self-determination and economic development.[4]

Although this orientation is more visible in multilateral and diplomatic endeavours, especially as it relates to Canada's participation in the Arctic Council, it has veered into Indigenous issues from time to time. The Canadian government has frequently identified historic Inuit use and occupation of frozen Arctic waters as a legal argument in support of its sovereignty claims. Subsequently, many Inuit and other Indigenous groups have used that argument as leverage for additional federal support.

The Canadian Rangers – a part of the Canadian Armed Forces reserve drawn from remote and Indigenous regions to conduct patrols, perform sovereignty and national security duties, and assist in search and rescue efforts (Canadian Army, n.d.) – is a perfect convergence of Canadian Arctic interests, and therefore receives considerable support and good will from the federal government.

Environmental security on the margins

As mentioned previously, Canada's Arctic is underdeveloped and sparsely populated. It hosts limited economic activity, even by Arctic standards. While some mining occurs, there is no oil and gas development, no large-scale commercial fishing, and minimal trans-Arctic shipping. While there are concerns with mitigating climate change, and efforts to establish effective land and marine management regimes to protect food sources (e.g., caribou, whale, and salmon), the greatest threats to Canadian Arctic communities are social and economic (Conference Board of Canada, 2017).

As such, environmental security and mitigation of climate change is a less prominent issue in Canada than it is in most of the other Arctic states, and certainly less than in the Nordic states.

Traditional security: not about the Arctic, but from the Arctic

Since the end of the Cold War, most Canadian documents and officials have adopted the mantra that the Arctic region is a stable and rules-based region of the globe that has avoided the tensions and conflicts associated with so many other parts. There is little question that there is not much risk of a conflict breaking out over a region of the Arctic. However, Canadian concerns regarding military security in the Arctic have never focused on a war about the Arctic. Instead, concerns have always been rooted in the reality that Russia's geography and modern weapons systems mean that it will place a significant element of its forces in the Arctic. As long as relations remain good between Canada and Russia, there is little need for Canada to be concerned with traditional military concerns in the region. However, when relations deteriorate, as they did after the Second World War or the Russian intervention in the Ukraine, then Canada needs to concern itself with meeting and responding to Russian forces.

Conclusion

Canada's perspectives and actions with regard to security in its Arctic region underlie its complicated and at times contradictory relationship with its own North. It faces minimal threats to its Arctic sovereignty, yet still struggles to exercise it. Canada is wary of Russia's actions in the region, yet the countries have complementary interests and cooperate well in the Arctic. It is often insular and focused on how its actions are received domestically, yet has led and continues to promote multilateral circumpolar cooperation. Canada treats the Arctic as exotic and distant, while celebrating it as a homeland for Northern and Indigenous Canadians.

Although the Canadian Arctic is often securitized, it has enjoyed a remarkable run of peace and stability. This can be seen as a success of government policy over the decades. But a different kind of public and political understanding about the nature of Canadian Arctic security will be required if more modern threats – economic, environmental, and safety – are to be tackled effectively.

Notes

1 Fennoscandia is a geographical region that comprises the Scandinavian Peninsula, Finland, Karelia, and the Kola Peninsula.

2 Prior to Russian intervention in the Ukraine, the number of such observers were quite small and included one of the co-authors of this chapter. After the intervention there have been an increasing number of proponents, including Andrea Charron (June 2015), "Canada, the Arctic and NORAD: Status Quo or New Ball Game?" in *International Journal* 70(2), pp. 215–231; Ekaterina Klimenko (March 15, 2015), "Russia and the Arctic: an end to Cooperation?" *Stockholm International Peace Research Institute*, [www.sipri.org/media/newsletter/essay/mar-15-russia-and-the-arctic]; and Alexander Sergunion, and Valery Konyshev (2015), *Russia in the Arctic: Hard or Soft Power*. Stuttgart: Ibidem Press.

3 The Canadian government's first explicit mention of Canadian sovereignty over Arctic waters came in 1946, when Ambassador to the United States Lester Pearson (later Foreign Minister And Prime Minister) called all water and ice in the Canadian sector national territory.

4 Concrete examples include Canada's advocacy for the Permanent Participant category, support for strengthening Indigenous inclusion and traditional knowledge in the Arctic Council and other Arctic fora, and the prioritization of northern peoples in its Arctic Council Chairmanship agenda.

References

Adams, Paul (February 4, 2016). "Russian Menace Pushes Sweden towards NATO," *BBC News*. Accessed August 13, 2017 from www.bbc.com/news/world-europe-35456535.

BBC News (August 17, 2007). "Russia Restarts Cold War Patrol," Accessed June 29, 2017 from http://news.bbc.co.uk/2/hi/europe/6950986.stm.

Blanchfield, Mike (May 12, 2017). "Freeland Praises Tillerson's Work on Arctic Council Climate Change Statement," *CBC News*. Accessed March 23, 2018 from www.cbc.ca/news/politics/freeland-tillerson-arctic-council-1.4111883.

Bland, Douglas (ed.) (1987). *Canada's National Defence, Volume 1 Defence Policy*. Kingston: School of Policy Studies.

Brigham, Lawson W. (2013). "Russia Opens its Maritime Arctic," in *The Fast Changing Arctic: Rethinking Arctic Security for a Warmer World*, Barry Zellen (ed.), Calgary: Calgary University Press, pp. 297–306.

Byers, Michael (2013). *International Law and the Arctic*. Cambridge: University of Cambridge Press, pp. 10–16.

Canada, Department of External Affairs (September 10, 1985), "Policy on Canadian Sovereignty," *Statements and Speeches* No. 85/7. Statement by the Right Honourable Joe Clark, Secretary of State for External Affairs, in the House of Commons.

Canada, Foreign Affairs and International Trade Canada (2011) *Dismantling of Nuclear Submarines*. Accessed August 13, 2017 from www.international.gc.ca/gpp-ppm/info_nuclear_submarines-sous marins_nucleaires.aspx?lang=eng&view=d.

Canadian Army [website] (n.d.). "Canadian Rangers," Accessed July 18, 2017 from www.army-armee.forces.gc.ca/en/canadian-rangers/index.page.

CBC News (April 16, 2014), "Canada Boycotts Arctic Council Moscow Meeting over Ukraine," Accessed August 13, 2017 from www.cbc.ca/news/canada/north/canada-boycotts-arctic-council-moscow-meeting-over-ukraine-1.2611964.

Chase, Steven and Mark MacKinnon (March 24, 2014). "Harper Leads Charge to Expel Russia from G8, Ramp Up Sanctions," *Globe and Mail*. Accessed July 17, 2017 from www.theglobeandmail.com/news/politics/harper-leads-charge-to-expel-russia-from-g8-ramp-up-sanctions/article17631725.

Circumpolar Inuit Declaration on Resource Development Principles (May, 2011). Accessed June 20, 2017 from www.inuitcircumpolar.com/uploads/3/0/5/4/30542564/declaration_on_resource_developmen t_a3_final.pdf

Clark, Campbell (May 12, 2011). "Harper's Tough Talk in the Arctic Less Stern in Private," *Globe and Mail*. Accessed August 13, 2017 from www.theglobeandmail.com/news/politics/harpers-tough-talk-on-the-arctic-less-stern-in-private/article579749/.

Coates, Ken S., P. Whitney Lackenbauer, William R. Morrison and Greg Poelzer (2008). *Arctic Front: Defending Canada in the Far North*. Toronto: Thomas Allen Publishers.

Conference Board of Canada (2017). *Social Outcomes in the Territories*. Accessed August 13, 2017 from www.conferenceboard.ca/hcp/provincial/society/territories.aspx

Dege, Wihelm (2004). Translated by William Barr. *The Last German Arctic Weather Station of World War II*. Calgary: University of Calgary Press.

Dosman, Edgar (1976). "The Northern Sovereignty Crisis 1968–70," in Edgar Dosman (ed.), *The Arctic in Question*. Toronto: Oxford University Press, pp. 35–57.

Eayrs, James (1972). *In Defence of Canada – Peacemaking and Deterrence*. Toronto: University of Toronto Press.

Ferguson, Julie (2014). *Through a Canadian Periscope: The Story of the Canadian Submarine Service*. (2nd ed.) Toronto: Dundurn, pp. 343–361.

Grant, Shelagh (2010). *Polar Imperative: A History of Arctic Sovereignty in North America*. Vancouver: Douglas & McIntyre, pp. 31–33.

Haglund, David G. and Tudor Onea (2008). "Victory without Triumph: Theodore Roosevelt, Honour, and the Alaska Panhandle Boundary Dispute," in *Diplomacy & Statecraft* 19(1), pp. 20–41.

Historica Canada & IPSOS (June 29, 2016). "Majority of Canadians Say There's Something for Everyone in Canada, So Why Go Anywhere Else?" Toronto. Accessed July 18, 2017 from www.historicacanada.ca/sites/default/files/PDF/polls/Historica%20Canada%20Day%20Poll%20Factum%202016.pdf.

Hoyle, Ben (September 17, 2013). "Russia Ready for a Colder War in Arctic; Russia: Military Base Reopens as Melting Ice Frees Sea Route," *The Times*.

Huebert, Rob (July, 1995). "Polar Vision or Tunnel Vision: The Making of Canadian Arctic Waters Policy," in *Marine Policy* 19(4), pp. 343–363.

Ilulissat Declaration (May 29, 2008). Accessed June 19, 2017 from www.oceanlaw.org/downloads/arctic/Ilulissat_Declaration.pdf.

Ivison, John (May 19, 2017). "Chrystia Freeland's Homespun take as Trudeau's Minister for Everywhere," *National Post*. Toronto.

Jockel, Joseph (1987). *No Boundaries Upstairs: Canada, the United States, and the Origins of the North American Air Defence, 1945–1958*. Vancouver: University of British Columbia Press.

Kassam, Ashifa (January 10, 2017). "Canada Names Chrystia Freeland, Leading Russia Critic as Foreign Minister," *The Guardian*. Accessed August 13, 2017 from www.theguardian.com/world/2017/jan/10/canada-chrystia-freeland-foreign-minister-russia-critic.

Kirton, John and Don Munton (1992). "Protecting the Canadian Arctic: The Manhattan Voyages, 1969–1970," in *Canadian Foreign Policy: Selected Cases*, John Kirton and Don Munton (eds.), Toronto: Prentice-Hall, pp. 206–221.

Lackenbauer, P. Whitney (ed.) (2005). *The Distant Early Warning (DEW) Line: A Bibliography and Documentary Resource List*. Calgary: Arctic Institute of North America.

Lackenbauer, P. Whitney (2010). "Mirror Images? Canada, Russia, and the Circumpolar World," in *International Journal* 65(4), pp. 879–897.

Lackenbauer, P. Whitney and Adam Lajeunesse (2016). "The Canadian Armed Forces in the Arctic: Building Capabilities and Connections," in *Journal of Military and Strategic Studies* 16(4), pp. 7–66.

Lajeunesse, Adam (2008). "Lock, Stock and Icebergs? Defining Canadian Sovereignty from Mackenzie King to Stephen Harper." *Calgary Papers in Military and Strategic Studies*. Accessed July 18, 2017 from https://journalhosting.ucalgary.ca/index.php/cpmss/article/view/36345/29298.

Lajeunesse, Adam (2016). *Lock, Stock and Icebergs: A History of Canada's Arctic Maritime Sovereignty*. Vancouver: University of British Columbia Press.

Landriault, Mathieu (2016). "Public Opinion on Canadian Arctic Sovereignty and Security," in *Arctic* 69 (2), pp. 163–164.

Mackrael, Kim (April 15, 2014). "Ottawa Upbraids Russian Envoy, Skips Arctic Council Meeting over Ukraine," Toronto: Globe and Mail.

National Defence Canada (2017). *Strong, Secure, Engaged: Canada's Defence Policy*. Accessed July 14, 2017 from http://dgpaapp.forces.gc.ca/en/canada-defence-policy/docs/canada-defence-policy-report.pdf

Naval-technology.com (June 29, 2017), "NATO Begins Dynamic Mongoose 2017 Anti-Submarine Warfare Exercise in Iceland," Accessed August 13, 2017 from www.naval-technology.com/news/newsnato-submarine-surveillance-exercise-dynamic-mongoose-2017-begins-in-iceland-5855663.

Oliphant, Roland (May 15, 2015). "Mapped: Just How Many Incursions into NATO Airspace has Russian Military Made?" *The Telegraph*. Accessed August 13, 2017 from www.telegraph.co.uk/news/worldnews/europe/russia/11609783/Mapped-Just-how-many-incursions-into-Nato-airspace-has-Russian-military-made.html

Ørvik, Nils (May/June, 1983). "Canadian Security and 'Defence against Help'," in *International Perspective*, pp. 26–31.

Pharand, Donat (2007). "Arctic Waters and the Northwest Passage: A Final Revisit," in *Ocean Development and International Law* 38, pp. 3–69.

Roberts, Kari (2010). "Jets, Flags, and a New Cold War? Demystifying Russia's Arctic Intentions," in *International Journal* 65(4), pp. 957–976.

Robinson, Belinda (September 19, 2014). "US and Canadian Fighter Jets are Scrambled to Intercept Six Russian Military Airplanes Near the Western Coast of Alaska and Canadian Coastline, Say Authorities," *Mail Online*. Accessed August 13, 2017 from www.dailymail.co.uk/news/article-2763056/US-Canadian-jets-intercept-8-Russian-aircraft.html.

Russian Strategic Nuclear Forces (March 7, 2012). "Russian Strategic Submarines to Resume Regular Patrols in June 2012," Accessed June 27, 2017 from http://russianforces.org/blog/2012/03/russian_strategic_submarines_t.shtml.

Sands, Christopher (Winter 2009–10). "Canada's Cold Front: Lessons of the Alaska Boundary Dispute for Arctic Boundaries Today," in *International Journal* 65(1), pp. 209–219.

Schmitt, Eric (April 20, 2016). "Russia Bolsters its Submarine Fleet, and Tensions with US Rise," *New York Times*. Accessed August 13, 2017 from www.nytimes.com/2016/04/21/world/europe/russia-bolsters-submarine-fleet-and-tensions-with-us-rise.html.

Smith, Duane (2017a). *Letter in Response to US-Canada Joint Arctic Leaders' Statement*. Accessed March 3, 2017 from https://assets.documentcloud.org/documents/3318896/IRC-Letter-to-PM-1.pdf

Smith, Leah (February 16, 2017b). "Fear of Invasion? Norway and Russia's Rocky Relationship," *thepolitic.org*. Accessed August 13, 2017 from http://thepolitic.org/a-rocky-relationship-norway-russia-and-fear-of-invasion/.

Sutherland, R. J. (1966). "The Strategic Significance of the Canadian Arctic," in R. St. J. Macdonald (ed.), *The Arctic Frontier*. Toronto: University of Toronto Press, pp. 256–278.

United States Government's Accountability Office (September, 2004). "Russian Nuclear Submarines: U.S. Participation in the Arctic Military Environmental Cooperation Program Need Better Justification," *Report to Congress*. GAO-04-924. Accessed August 13, 2017 from www.gao.gov/assets/250/243985.pdf.

Williams, Lisa (2011). "Canada, the Arctic and Post-National Identity in the Circumpolar World," in *Northern Review* (33), pp. 113–131.
Writte, Griff (November 23, 2014). "Finland Feeling Vulnerable amid Russian Provocations," *Washington Post.* Accessed August 13, 2017 from www.washingtonpost.com/world/europe/finland-feeling-vulnerable-amid-russian-provocations/2014/11/23/defc5a90-69b2-11e4-bafd-6598192a448d_story.html.

13

US SECURITY POLICY IN THE AMERICAN ARCTIC

Michael T. Corgan

Introduction

This consideration of United States security policy in the American Arctic deals with US territory in Alaska north of the Arctic Circle and the surrounding waters. Since World War II, US Arctic security policies have encompassed much more of the Arctic region via North American Treaty Organization (NATO) alliance responsibilities with Canada, Greenland (as part of Denmark), Iceland, and Norway. Most of the American commitment of assets and organization for Arctic security deals with that High North area, which has a great impact upon how the United States sees security in its own Arctic area. However, for the most part this chapter focuses on traditional security measures for American national territory.

The part of the United States that is in the Arctic has never been, nor is it now, anywhere near the highest priority for American national security, whether among the defense establishment, most politicians, or the public at large – even for many Alaskans. Thus, any study of US Arctic security policy must keep in mind that the Arctic region is a "stepchild" to the more pressing concerns of defense planners and strategists. The reasons for this relative neglect are the obvious ones of distance – until relatively recently Alaska, like Hawaii, was only reachable from the contiguous United States by sea or air – and population. Alaska, with just a little over two-tenths of 1% of the nation's population (738,000 persons as of 2018), does not command a great deal of attention in national politics. The unique realities of arduous Arctic terrain and climate also inhibit political engagement.

When looking at security policy in a large country like the United States, it must be kept in mind that there can be, and usually are, numerous articulations of policies by actors from the White House to the Pentagon to the floor of Congress. Quite often, these are merely articulations of yet-to-be achieved directions or of best outcomes. Furthermore, with any policy one must look at the actual allocation of resources resulting from budget appropriations rather than just authorizations. Sometimes a policy statement is nothing more than an acknowledgment that there needs to be a policy in the first place. A prime example of this is a term that has been frequently used in the 2010s: "domain awareness" for the Arctic. With these caveats in mind, looking at American Arctic security policy over the years since World War II reveals a decided lack of sustained attention for the US Arctic from faraway Washington.

Hot war to Cold War

For the first 75 years after the United States purchased Alaska from Imperial Russia in 1867, there was virtually no thought about security measures for such a remote place, secluded from Washington, DC, and equally remote from any other power center. The only matter that could have involved protection of territory was confrontations between the hordes of American treasure seekers in the gold rush years of the late 1890s and Canadian authorities trying to establish identifiable and agreed-upon boundaries between the Alaskan Territory and the Canadian Yukon Territory, which had been founded in 1898. It wasn't until World War II that a serious threat to, and eventual capture of, territory in the region by Japanese forces focused attention on Alaskan defense. Three Aleutian Islands, (Agattu, Attu and Kiska), fell under Japanese occupation in 1942–3, before being retaken by American forces (Immerwahr 2019, 178–9). It is instructive that even under these circumstances, with this likely attack on US territory in North America having been foreseen, Alaska and the Arctic remained a low priority for actual defense planning and activity.

A study of such security forces as there were in Alaska before the onset of the Pacific war, *The Western Hemisphere*, maintains that the US Army "had taken little more than an academic interest in [Alaska]" and the Navy "ignored Alaska to all intents and purposes … on the belief that Alaskan waters were secure as long as the Japanese abided by the terms of the Washington Naval Treaty of 1922" (Conn et al. 1959, 223). What was necessary, planners estimated, was to keep raiding parties from seizing locations that could be used as air or sea bases for attacking targets in the United States proper. In the years leading up to the war, 1939–41, the Army and Navy worked together with limited resources to provide some protection for naval bases that were being constructed, but the Army Air Force placed stationing of aircraft in Alaska well below needs in Panama, Hawaii, and the Philippines (ibid., 239). Alaska was the last US overseas department to receive combat aircraft, in late 1940. On 3 June 1942, the Japanese attacked Dutch Harbor in the Aleutians and the Americans began to marshal forces for counterstrikes. A month later, Brigadier General Laurence Kuter of the Army Air Force staff told local defenders that "the War Department considered the Aleutian situation of little consequence and Alaska a minor theatre of operations"(ibid., 365). This sentiment illustrates the sort of inattention to Alaska that was common in the high command of the American military. Eventually, enough attention was paid and after some of the bloodiest fighting in the Pacific, the 7th Infantry Division, with naval and air support, retook the Aleutian Islands in early August 1943. After that, strategic operations in Alaska and near the Arctic quickly receded from the thoughts of US military commanders for the rest of the war. This wartime episode illustrates the characteristic lack of attention that matters in the Arctic received in American security thinking.

This inattention to the Arctic continued even after the Cold War began. The US Army had only vestigial garrison forces in the region. The newly independent US Air Force sent its oldest operable aircraft to a few air bases (the last of its propeller-driven fighters were retired from Alaska in 1953). The Navy largely ignored the seas beyond the Bering Strait. However, this indifference changed dramatically in 1949 when the United States entered its first military alliance since its 1778 Treaty of Amity and Commerce with France, namely the North American Treaty Organization (NATO). The United States was now inextricably bound up in global affairs, and NATO forced American planners and security thinkers in the newly established Department of Defense, in the emerging think tanks dealing with international security, and in a Congress hitherto characterized by isolationism, to think globally. Central Europe was the focus, but now the High North and the Arctic itself were also relevant (Add (Conn, Engelman and Fairchild 1959).

Three NATO members, Norway, Denmark, and Iceland, are Arctic states, and all three had important strategic locations vis-à-vis the Soviet Union. Along with Canada, these three countries were essential to forming a line of radar surveillance posts, most notably the Distant Early Warning (DEW) Line, to detect transpolar aircraft and missile strikes. The radar surveillance network extended from the North Cape of Norway to the northern United Kingdom to Iceland to Greenland to Canada and finally to northern Alaska. Submarine-detecting cables, many radiating from Iceland, were the sentries of the Greenland–Iceland–UK (GIUK) Gap. These could detect Soviet submarines deploying from the only Soviet naval ports that could access the open Atlantic without going through a NATO member's waters. This widespread and sophisticated submarine-detection system was not repeated in Alaska. The United States looked at security in Alaska, given its proximity to the Soviet Pacific Fleet, but this theatre remained secondary to others in planning and resources. In the early 1950s, the Army spent considerable effort developing procedures and tactics for operating in the harsh conditions of Arctic Alaska. At the Detroit Tank Automotive Command, much work was done with Canadian forces to discover what would and would not work in the unforgiving environment.[1] In January 1959, Alaska was formally granted the status of the forty-ninth state of the United States (Cole 2010).

The US Navy dramatically increased American focus on the Arctic around Alaska through its spectacular submarine activity. The USS *Nautilus* made the first submerged transit of the waters of the North Pole in 1958, and the USS *Skate* surfaced at the Pole itself in 1959. Both the United States and the Soviets sought ways to take advantage of Arctic ice cover to make ballistic-missile submarines almost impossible to detect. While the US Army and Air Force maintained a presence and some infrastructure on Alaskan bases, it was the Navy operating in Arctic waters that played the main role in Arctic security.

In the security planning and policies promulgated by the US defense establishment during the Cold War, the Arctic was not singled out for particular consideration. There was a brief flurry of activity when National Security Advisor[2] Henry Kissinger issued National Security Decision Memorandum (NSDM) 144, *United States Arctic Policy and Arctic Policy Group*, on 22 December 1971. This document said the United States:

> will support the sound and rational development of the Arctic, guided by the principle of minimizing any adverse effects to the environment; will promote mutually beneficial international cooperation in the Arctic; and will at the same time provide for the protection of essential security interest in the Arctic, including preservation of the principle of freedom of the seas and superjacent airspace.
>
> *(US National Security Decision Memorandum 144. 1971)*

The memorandum was classified SECRET. There were no public statements concerning US Arctic policy pending the president's review. A follow-on document, 1973's NSDM 202, used virtually the same language. Little was done in reaction to these NSDMs because the Vietnam War had a far higher priority than matters in Alaska and the Arctic.[3] NSDM 90, issued by the Ronald Reagan administration in 1983, used quite similar language to the two Richard Nixon NSDMs (Osherenko and Young 1989, 222). These NSDMs merely represented statements of desired outcomes: there was no assignment of responsibilities, allocation of resources, or shaping of an integrated structure to realize the objectives. The Arctic never figured notably, if at all, in subsequent Cold War NSDMs. There were no presidential-level national security policy statements specifically on the Arctic for the remainder of the Cold War. As in the hot war of World War II, the Arctic received only fitful mention in US strategic thinking and planning.

US Arctic security after the Cold War

With the ending of the Cold War, American attention to matters of security and national strategy rapidly shifted from Europe to areas of greater immediate concern, particularly the Middle East. Moreover, the very concept of security was enlarging to include more than just defense of national territory. The rapidly changing environment in the Arctic and the threat posed by substate actors had become far more important than they had been. Many of what one might call the "Arctic-aware" community in the United States called attention to melting polar ice as portending a sea change in how the Arctic would factor in international affairs, including traditional national security, environmental degradation, and impact upon Indigenous populations. However, no serious and sustained national efforts to fund the many well-considered proposals of social welfare advocates, scientists, or security think tanks materialized.

Operating below the radar, as it were, was the one American armed service that had always maintained a keen interest and played an advocacy role in Arctic affairs: the Coast Guard. The Coast Guard, founded in 1790, was responsible for providing security, albeit not the defense of national territory. Rather, the security role of this service was at the level of constabulary efforts: search and rescue, anti-pollution actions, control of smuggling, illegal entry, and so on. One of the most telling indications of the gap between articulated and actual policies has long been proclamation versus appropriation. Nowhere in US Arctic affairs is this more pronounced or telling than in the matter of icebreakers for the Coast Guard.

Washington's strategic thinking immediately after the Cold War focused on the role of the United States as the world's lone superpower. President George H.W. Bush's "New World Order" speech to a joint session of Congress in September 1990 exemplified this (Bush, George H.W.). The United States was now to assume global strategic responsibilities in a unipolar world. Yet little if any of this thinking involved the Arctic. Only a few National Security Strategies, even though required annually, were actually produced; none featured the Arctic. However, Presidents Bill Clinton, George W. Bush, and Barack Obama did produce specific Arctic strategies of various types.

Arctic strategies emerge: Clinton and George W. Bush

The first specific US Arctic strategy came in 1994, during the Clinton administration (Presidential Decision Directive 26 (PDD 26)). It combined the Arctic and Antarctic in its scope, but was never circulated (Corgan 2014). With no publicity, its impact on public awareness and possible support for Arctic strategic enhancement was negligible. The attacks on US territory in September 2001 turned attention to direct threats to the US homeland, but this was almost entirely toward what Alaskans frequently call the "Lower 48." The first major public statement about the Arctic strategy of the United States after the Cold War came in the 9/11 attacks' aftermath, during the administration of George W. Bush. It was simultaneously issued as National Security Presidential Directive NSPD-66 and Homeland Security Presidential Directive HSPD-25, Arctic Region Policy (The White House 2009).

The document begins with a declaration that the United States is an Arctic nation and notes that in view of the 9/11 attacks, "altered national policies on homeland security and defense" have prompted the Directive. Other developments enumerated are climate change, the work of the Arctic Council, fragility of the region, and its resource potential. Lest there be any doubt that the policy was formulated in the aftermath of the 9/11 attacks, the Policy section on National and Homeland Security Interests in the Arctic begins with an assurance found later in the National Security Strategy documents issued in 2002 (*Arctic Region Policy*) and 2006 (National Security Strategy 2006). "The United States ... is prepared to operate either independently or in conjunction with other states to safeguard these interests." The section on International Governance asserted that "The geopolitical circumstances of the Arctic region" meant that, unlike the Antarctic, a broad-scope Arctic treaty "is not appropriate or necessary." The United States and the other seven members of the Arctic Council agreed that the UN Convention on the Law of the Sea (UNCLOS) was governance enough because the Arctic was, unlike the Antarctic, primarily an ocean area. Indeed, the document urged that the "Senate should act favorably on US accession to the UN Convention on the Law of the Sea promptly." (*Arctic Region Policy*). UNCLOS came into effect in 1994, but the United States has yet to ratify the agreement.

This nod to the international community in Arctic legal affairs, which was at variance with the "go it alone" slant of the National Security Strategy, only makes sense when one realizes that the NSPD-66/HSPD-25 was issued on 9 January 2009, when this Bush administration had only days left and there was no chance of political challenge or recrimination from the party base. The rest of the document outlined, at greater length, proposed actions in the areas of scientific cooperation, transport, and economic and energy issues. All this was to be "subject to the availability of appropriations." Although issued in the waning moments of the administration, with no discussion of how any initiatives were to be funded, this Directive led to a flurry of bureaucratic activity that outlasted the administration.

Responses to the Bush strategy

To judge how this George W. Bush Directive on the Arctic, although issued by a very lame-duck president, had changed things, one may observe that the Navy's 2007 document on maritime strategy made only fleeting references to NATO, the Arabian Gulf/Indian Ocean, and the Western Pacific; it did not mention the Arctic at all (*A Co-operative Strategy for 21st Century Seapower* 2007). One of the first commentaries on the NSPD-66 observed: "The new directive results from the first comprehensive reassessment of US Arctic Policy in many years and seems likely to provide a framework for action by the Obama administration" (*Comprehensive New Statement* 2009). This proved to be so for the military services in the new administration, particularly the Navy and the Coast Guard.

Later in 2009, Margaret Blunden observed that while the United States had not increased its Arctic operations, other states had, and their policies envisioned more bellicose possibilities (Blunden 2009, 144). She argued that the Russian Security Strategy through 2020 maintained that "rivalry for resources will be a condition that does not exclude the possibility of military confrontation." She also noted that Norway had moved its Operational Command Headquarters to Bodø, north of the Arctic Circle. She identified a period of "sustained inattention" to the Arctic following the end of the Cold War because the United States had "only reluctantly joined the Arctic Council" and had unilaterally withdrawn its military forces from Keflavík in 2006 (ibid., 131). Explanations for this inattention to Arctic matters, especially security, may be found in the state of the American economy and its political climate. However, by 2016 the US armed forces had begun a process of returning to Keflavík, given the growing challenge of Russian military air and submarine activity in the Nordic Arctic region.

Economic and political realities: Senator Murkowski's hearings

In the aftermath of the 2008 Global Financial Crisis, any new American Arctic strategy that required new assets such as base infrastructure, icebreakers, additional personnel, surveillance equipment, and so on was bound to compete with and likely lose to the demands of fighting two actual wars in the Middle East. The phrase, "Acquiring the right capability at the right cost and right time" appeared in the Navy's *2009 Roadmap* and was a way of recognizing this economic reality. Domain awareness meant that nothing was going to happen soon, despite the growing understanding that the environment in the region was changing and that economic activity was increasing.

Politicians from Alaska tried to direct some of the American public's attention to the Arctic. Republican Lisa Murkowski, the senior (and Alaska-born) senator from Alaska, held hearings on the "Strategic Importance of the Arctic in US Policy" in August 2009 in Anchorage, Alaska, before the Senate Subcommittee on the Department of Homeland Security, which is under the Senate Committee on Appropriations, of which she was a member (*Strategic Importance*). Alaska Governor Sean Parnell argued that "Alaska is America's Arctic guardian" and noted that the threat "from the north to our oil production" was real (ibid., 8). Governor Parnell's statement was one of the first by a prominent politician to introduce the idea of protection of a key resource into Arctic strategic discourse. Mead Treadwell, chair of the US Arctic Research Commission, pointed out that the Bush NSPD-66 was "the first public security policy ever issued for this region" (ibid., 8).

The term that Senator Murkowski used to give identity and focus to the proceedings: an "ice-diminished" Arctic, reflected the political reality that her Republican Party did not view climate change as a serious problem. By not using either "global warming" or "climate change," she avoided a possible challenge from her fellow Republicans, for many of whom such language was anathema. Even Admiral Thad Allen, Commandant of the US Coast Guard, acknowledged her astuteness in using this term (ibid., 48). The subject of climate change in the Arctic and in general became an even-more unassailable political taboo in the United States after the election of President Donald Trump, an unabashed climate change denier. American reluctance to acknowledge the phenomenon prevented the issuing of a formal Arctic Council declaration in May 2019 after the American delegation refused to support any paper with "climate change" included. Admiral Allen further observed that it was unlikely that the United States would add to its fleet of three icebreakers. The United States has only one operational heavy icebreaker, the *Polar Star*, which was commissioned in 1976. Only in early 2019, after a long period of legal wrangling, were funds finally committed to the building of new icebreakers for the Coast Guard.

The best summary of the likely impact of these hearings and other attempts to focus American attention on the Arctic came in a response to a question Senator Murkowski asked of those present. Mayor Edward S. Itta, of a township facing the Arctic Ocean on Alaska's north coast, gave the most poignant and revealing answer. The senator wondered,

"How we can better promote the importance of the Arctic." The mayor of North Slope Borough answered:

> So many in America did not realize Alaska was a part of the United States and that we are US citizens. I think this is a part of our challenge. How does what goes on in the Arctic relate to … life in Des Moines, Iowa?[4]

These hearings resulted in no significant changes in Congressional appropriations or reallocation of military resources. The Department of Defense *Quadrennial Defense Review Report 2010* (QDR), in the section on rebalancing force in the Arctic, introduced the term "domain awareness," which hardly suggests the detailed commitment of resources or the restructuring of already existing strategic thinking.

Action on the Bush strategy

In May 2011, the US Department of Defense released *Report to Congress on Arctic Operations and the Northwest Passage*. This report summarizes what had and had not been done since the Bush 2009 Arctic Policy, NSPD-66. It began by noting, "Uncertainty about the rate and linearity of climate change makes resource commitment difficult … The challenge is to balance the risk of being late-to-need with the opportunity cost of making premature investments" (Report to Congress 2011). This assessment made it easy to do nothing. Also noted were overlapping authorities, missions, responsibilities, and timeliness among the Department of Defense and the Department of Homeland Security in the Arctic. This problem was not addressed then or later. Most telling, however, was this acknowledgment: "The near-term fiscal and political environment will make it difficult to support significant new US government investments" (ibid., 12).

A January 2012 report from the Center for Strategic and International Studies (CSIS) observed that, with regard to security matters, the United States "has a woeful lack of Arctic Military capabilities" (Conley et al. 2012) In reviewing the Bush Arctic policy (NSPD-66) and succeeding government statements, the authors argued that the time to develop the capabilities envisioned in the 2011 Department of Defense (DoD) *Report to Congress on Arctic Operations* had already arrived. Coast Guard capabilities were such that it, now relocated from the Treasury to the Homeland Security Department, remained suited more for constabulary and not war-fighting tasks. Little substantive action was taken on the Bush NSDM.

Obama's Arctic strategy

Obama was the first president to visit the Arctic while in office; many expected that his administration would take more decisive action about and in the Arctic than his predecessors. On 10 May 2013, Obama's *National Strategy for the Arctic Region* was issued. The president's introductory letter referred to the Arctic region as "peaceful, stable, and free of conflict" and concluded that "we will partner with the State of Alaska, and Alaska Natives, as well the international community and the private sector." While this shows a newly heightened concern for Indigenous people, it seems remarkable that the federal government should be partnering with one of its own states. This language meant that Alaska was to bear the burden of much of the development. The document outlined three lines of effort: (a) advance United States security interests, (b) pursue responsible Arctic region stewardship, and (c) strengthen international cooperation. Security interests included three things the government would attempt: *evolve* [emphasis added] Arctic infrastructure and strategic capabilities, enhance Arctic domain awareness, and preserve Arctic region freedom of the seas.

Soon after, in May 2013, the Coast Guard produced its own strategy, which had three specific objectives: improving awareness, modernizing governance, and broadening partnerships. *(US Coast Guard Arctic Strategy)*. The latter two objectives included concern for tribal input. In November 2013, the Department of Defense *Arctic Strategy* outlined a more tangible set of actions or at least approaches to action than the Obama document. Its two key objectives were preserving a conflict-free region and preparing for a wide range of challenges. This latter goal was prompted by a recognition that "projections about future access to and activity in the Arctic may be inaccurate" (*Arctic Strategy* 2013). *Arctic Strategy* explained that the idea was to avoid "making premature and/or unnecessary investments," thereby reducing "the availability of resources for other pressing priorities, particularly in a time of fiscal austerity." As if to underscore how low level an "evolving" Arctic infrastructure might be, its example of modification to existing bases was "the addition of a new hangar." Only one hangar was foreseen for all of Alaska.

In January 2014, the National Security Council issued the *Implementation Plan for the National Strategy for the Arctic Region*, repeating the emphasis on incorporating the ideas and inputs of natives of the region (Crook 2009). It again called for the United States to accede to the Law of the Sea Convention III. However, The Arctic Institute/Center for Circumpolar Security Studies came out with a critical and even scathing interpretation of the Obama strategy (White House 2014). First, the Bush Arctic strategy was dismissed by the Institute as "rather brief and vague." What they saw from President Obama, who was famously on record as calling for "a pivot to Asia" in US policy after 2011, was a document that effectively told Alaskans they were on their own. The Institute's assessment of what was missing from the Obama strategy included lack of specificity, no plan to upgrade an inadequate and outdated icebreaker fleet or deep-water ports, no budget information, failure to assign tasks, and many other plan shortcomings. Because no details were offered on what "domain awareness," still in the discourse, might entail, the conclusion was that "US Arctic strategy remains as elusive as a mirage on the Arctic ice-sheet" (ibid.). In February 2014, the Navy came out with a comprehensive update of 2009's *Arctic Roadmap* that attempted to forecast needs and activities several decades hence with considerable specificity (*US Navy Arctic Roadmap for 2014 to 2030*). This update acknowledged that "ice conditions in the Arctic are changing more rapidly than first anticipated" and called for more investment and accession to UNCLOS III.

Trump and the Arctic

To judge by the presidential campaign between Hillary Clinton and Trump, it seemed as if it would be bad news for Arctic interests if Trump won. Clinton campaigned on continuing Obama's legacy; Trump essentially campaigned on undoing just about everything Obama had done at home and abroad. This meant leaving the Trans-Pacific Partnership trade agreement, the Paris climate accord, and the 2015 Iran nuclear agreement. Trump did the first two immediately and the third a year later. His campaign literature did not mention the Arctic, the environment, or climate change. The only specific Arctic-related matter mentioned during the early days of the Trump administration concerned the number of Coast Guard icebreakers that might now be built. At the Inaugural Parade, as Coast Guard

Academy cadets marched by the reviewing stand, the Coast Guard Commandant was verbally promised six icebreakers by the new president. That number shrank to zero in subsequent appropriations bills, although it then seemed to recover back to six, at least in Senate Defense Authorization bills. After Trump was elected but before he was sworn in, the DoD in December 2016 issued a revised Arctic Strategy to Congress (Report to Congress). This strategy was meant to be a follow-on to and improvement upon earlier strategic statements, especially the 2013 National Strategy for the Arctic Region. Although only 17 pages long, the document clarified the many interlocking and overlapping military command responsibilities in the US Arctic region. The DoD definition of the US Arctic region was reaffirmed as including the Aleutian Islands.

The junior Republican senator from Alaska, Dan Sullivan, expressed great satisfaction with the report, calling it "a much more serious strategy for the Arctic region" (Martinson 2017). A little over a month later, in March 2017, both he and senior senator Lisa Murkowski visited Trump in the Oval Office to make a case for the new administration to do more for Alaska, which had one of the highest unemployment rates in the nation. Although economic matters were foremost, security issues were also raised. Murkowski brought a number of maps with her because, as she said, "He's just a very visual person" (ibid.) Regarding defense and security matters, Sullivan gave a pitch for strengthening military presence, inviting the president to review the troops as Commander in Chief. Murkowski used one of her maps to show the president how close Russia was. Both brought up the US–Russia icebreaker discrepancy and Sullivan reminded Trump about the updated Air Force presence, with F-22s already in Alaska and F-35s on the way.

In December 2017, Trump became the first US president to issue a National Security Strategy during his first year in office (by law they are required each year) (The White House 2017). This NSS was only the second one to mention the Arctic, though it did so rather obliquely. The section titled Achieve Better Outcomes in Multilateral Forums included the statement: "The United States will prioritize its efforts in those organizations that serve American interests," including the Arctic in the listing of areas with relevant organizations and thus, by implication, the Arctic Council. The Trump NSS did not mention climate change as a security threat but did argue for "energy dominance." It was during his subsequent efforts to get a major tax overhaul bill passed, however, that the Arctic came to the fore. It was a matter of achieving energy dominance. Needing every vote, the administration overturned decades of practice and allowed oil drilling in the Alaska National Wildlife Refuge. Even a president not known for his environmental concerns was reluctant to allow drilling in this protected environmental sanctuary until, needing Senator Murkowski's vote to pass the tax bill, he relented and allowed the exploratory drilling. For this presidency there had emerged on the Arctic coast of Alaska a major security need: to protect a vital and vulnerable resource, one essential to energy dominance.

The concern for protection of US oil resources in the Arctic prompted the Navy Department to promise a revised Arctic strategy in summer 2018. When asked in April by the Senate Armed Services Committee what had prompted a new strategy, Secretary of the Navy Richard V. Spencer replied, "the Arctic triggered it, the damn thing melted" (Eckstein 2018). However, a meeting in June organized by lawmakers from the House of Representatives and senior Navy officials cast a less favorable light on DoD actions. Rep. John Garamendi (D-CA) said, "The Navy has no interest … the Navy has simply abandoned the Arctic Ocean other than submarines" (Aton 2018). Essentially agreeing with this unfavorable assessment, the Secretary of Defense told a gathering at a stopover at Alaska's Eielson Air Force Base while on the way to East Asia: "Certainly America has got to up its game in the Arctic" (*Voice of America News* 2018). He even added for emphasis "that Alaska is, in many ways, the absolute center of the defense of our country, for the Indo-Pacific region and certainly over the polar ice cap" (KUAC TV 2018). Perhaps the best assessment of US security efforts in the Arctic belongs to Admiral James Stavridis, now retired, who had been the first naval officer chosen as NATO's Supreme Allied Commander for Global Operations: "What is lacking, unfortunately, is a sense of a coherent focused national effort despite the nascent efforts of the disparate interagency organizations" (Stavridis 2017, 257).

As with other domestic and foreign policy matters, President Trump, during his first few years in office, characteristically displayed a bewildering tendency to shift positions on major matters of policy, often reversing himself once and then again. However, two of his most often-voiced themes showed a remarkable durability: "America first" and energy dominance. The oil fields in Alaska, particularly those on the shores of the North slope facing the Beaufort Sea are seen more than ever before as essential to energy dominance and their protection as an inextricable part of the "America first" policy that had been proclaimed in his Inaugural Address. However, as noted above, the Trump administration has faced legal head winds in opening up Alaska to expanded fossil fuel extraction; a situation not helped by the unpredictable nature of global energy prices (Brehmer 2019).

By the end of 2018, however, another element of US Arctic Policy began to coalesce, namely that of hard security concerns centered on Russia's growing military presence in its Arctic lands and waters, and the growing Arctic interests of China, which began to move closer to Moscow in developing an "Ice Silk Road" trade route connecting China with northern Europe. In October–November 2018, US forces joined with NATO allies in a military simulation, Trident Juncture, which took place in Norway and parts of the Atlantic-Arctic region (NATO 2018). During that year, the US Coast Guard published an updated Arctic policy which called for improved Arctic operations, cooperation with regional partners, and strengthening of the "rules-based order" in the Arctic (US Coast Guard 2019). These concepts were echoed in a June 2019 document issued by the US Department of Defense which also cited Russian and Chinese activities in the Arctic as detrimental to peace and stability, with Beijing being accused of attempting to "alter Arctic governance" by developing an intensified economic presence in the region. Both the 2019 USCG and DoD papers studiously avoided mentioning climate change, instead making only vague references to changed environmental conditions in the Arctic.

This turn towards a US unilateralist approach in the Arctic was underscored at the aforementioned May 2019 Arctic Council Ministerial meeting in Rovaniemi, Finland, where the US not only found itself at odds with the other seven members of the Council over climate change, but also in other areas related to regional security. The keynote speech by US Secretary of State Mike Pompeo at the event was poorly received by many delegates due to its pugnacious tone, stressing the looming threats of China and Russia in the region while ignoring climate change and other pressing areas of Arctic human security (Lanteigne 2019, BBC News 2019). It remained unclear whether the speech signaled a looming break with US friends and allies in the Arctic over security policies, or simply a rough patch in the ongoing process of Arctic political cooperation.

Conclusion

Security for the US Arctic region has never been a significant priority for governmental action, even when the Aleutian Islands were invaded and briefly captured in war. The first specific inclusion of security for the US Arctic region occurred during the Nixon administration a little over 100 years after the acquisition of Alaska. That embryonic attention to Arctic security came to naught when US involvement in Vietnam ended because the Watergate imbroglio then seized all of Washington's attention. The next articulation of an Arctic security posture came over 20 years later, but Clinton's NSS was never circulated. The NSS from George W. Bush regarding the Arctic was brief and vague on key points and was issued in his last week in office when he was the lamest of lame-duck presidents. The National Security Strategy for the Arctic issued by Obama was more vague, and placed much of the burden of doing anything substantive on Alaska.

Up to now the United States has maintained Arctic security in the Atlantic area through alliances covering the High North. How well this arrangement will stand up is now questionable. Many observers discern a growing US withdrawal of commitment to long-established agreements and alliances, even those involving security. Notably, Trump continues to complain that most allied countries in NATO are not paying the 2% of their GDP for defense they had agreed to (although not until 2024). Indeed, none of the other NATO countries in the Arctic, Canada, Denmark, Iceland, or Norway, does. Given Trump's America First posture, all US security commitments are in question. It may well be that after a not unlikely withdrawal of commitment to NATO and its role in the High North, the United States will focus inward and, in the absence of stronger security arrangements, at last develop a continuing and robust security policy for its own Arctic regions. Construction of new icebreakers could well be the first sign of this outcome (Axe 2019).

Notes

1 The author's father was much involved with these design efforts in Detroit and subsequent field testing in Alaska from 1950–53

2 Technically, this position is the Special Assistant to the President for National Security Affairs, thus not a Constitutionally specified "Officer of the Government" and therefore not subject to Senate approval.

3 As an indicator of priorities, during this period the author, as a naval advisor in Vietnam, noted that much of the shipping to the region was done by the Alaska Barge and Tug Co.

References

Adam Aton. (2018) "US Still Lags Behind in Preparing for a Changing Arctic," *Scientific American*, 8 June 2018, www.scientificamerican.com/article/u-s-still-lags-behind-in-preparing-for-a-changing-arctic/.

Arctic Strategy. 2013. The Department of Defense: Washington, DC. www.defense.gov/Portals/1/Documents/pubs/2013_Arctic_Strategy.pdf.

Axe, David. 2019. "43 Years in the Making: The US Coast Guard Finally Gets New Icebreakers," *The National Interest*, 25 February. https://nationalinterest.org/blog/buzz/43-years-making-us-coast-guard-finally-gets-new-icebreakers-45572.

BBC News. 2019. 'US Climate Objections Sink Arctic Council Accord in Finland.' 7 May. www.bbc.com/news/world-europe-48185793.

Blunden, Margaret. 2009. "The New Problem of Arctic Stability." *Survival*, Vol. 51, pp. 121–142.

Brehmer, Elwood. "Economists say Alaska recession likely to end in 2019," *Anchorage Daily News*, 27 January. www.adn.com/business-economy/2019/01/27/economists-say-alaska-recession-likely-to-end-in-2019/.

Bush, George H. W. 1990. *New World Order*. [speech to Congress]. https://en.wikipedia.org/wiki/New_world_order_(politics).

Cole, Terrence. 2010. *Fighting for the Forty-Ninth Star: C. W. Snedden and the Crusade for Alaska Statehood*. Fairbanks: University of Alaska Foundation.

Conley, Heather A. Terry Toland With and Jamie Kraut. "A New Security Architecture for the Arctic: An American Perspective," *Report of the CSIS Europe Program*.

Conn, Stetson and Rose C. Engelman, and Byron Fairchild. 1959. *The Western Hemisphere: Guarding the United States and Its Outposts*. Washington, DC: Center of Military History United States Army.

"*A Co-operative Strategy for 21st Century Seapower*." 2007. Department of the Navy: Washington DC. www.navy.mil/local/maritime/150227-CS21R-Final.pdf.

Corgan, Michael T. (2014) The USA in the Arctic: Superpower or Spectator?. In Heininen, Lassi. (ed.) *Security and Sovereignty in the North Atlantic*. London: Palgrave Macmillan, pp. 62–79.

Crook, John R. 2009. "Comprehensive New Statement of US Arctic Policy." *The American Journal of International Law*, Vol. 103, No. 2. pp. 342–349.

Immerwahr, Daniel. 2019. *How to Hide an Empire: A Short History of the Greater United States*. London: Bodley Head/Vintage.

Implementation Plan for the National Strategy for the Arctic Region. 2014. Washington, DC: The White House (National Security Council). https://obamawhitehouse.archives.gov/blog/2016/03/09/advancing-implementation-national-strategy-arctic-region.

'Implementation Plan For The National Strategy for the Arctic Region.' (2014). The White House, January 2014, www.iarpccollaborations.org/uploads/cms/documents/implementation-plan-for-the-national-strategy-for-the-arctic-region-executive-office-of-the-president-2014.pdf

KUAC TV. 2018. http://fm.kuac.org/post/defense-secretary-affirms-alaska-s-role-homeland-defense-pacific-and-arctic-regions.

Lanteigne, Marc. 2019. "The United States' Hardening Stance on Arctic Security," *Over the Circle*, 5 May. https://overthecircle.com/2019/05/05/the-united-states-hardening-stance-on-arctic-security/.

Martinson, Erica. 2017. *Alaska Dispatch News*. www.arcticnow.com/arctic-news/2017/02/02/heres-whats-in-the-us-defense-departments-new-arctic-strategy/.

"Mattis: 'America's Got to Up Its Game in the Arctic,'" (2018) *Voice of America News*, 25 June 2018, www.voanews.com/usa/mattis-americas-got-its-game-arctic.

Megan Eckstein. (2018). "Navy to Release Arctic Strategy This Summer, Will Include Blue Water Arctic Operations," *US Naval Institute (USNI) News*, 19 April 2018, https://news.usni.org/2018/04/19/navy-to-release-arctic-strategy-this-summer-will-include-blue-water-arctic-operations.

National Security Presidential Directive 66/Homeland Security Presidential Directive 25. 2009. "*Arctic Region Policy*." www.nsf.gov/geo/opp/opp_advisory/briefings/may2009/nspd66_hspd25.pdf.

"National Security Decision Memorandum 144 – December 22, 1971", (2019), Federation of American Scientists, 2019, https://fas.org/irp/offdocs/nsdm-nixon/nsdm-144.pdf.

National Security Strategy. 2002. https://georgewbush-whitehouse.archives.gov/nsc/nss/2002/.

National Security Strategy. 2006. https://georgewbush-whitehouse.archives.gov/nsc/nss/2006/.

"National Security Strategy of the United States of America – December 2017," (2017), *The White House*, www.whitehouse.gov/wp-content/uploads/2017/12/NSS-Final-12-18-2017-0905.pdf.

Navy to Release Arctic Strategy This Summer Will Include Blue Water Arctic Operations. 2018. "Naval Institute News." https://news.usni.org/2018/04/19/navy-to-release-arctic-strategy-this-summer-will-include-blue-water-arctic-operations.

Obama, Barack. May 2013. *National Strategy for the Arctic Region*. Washington, DC: The White House. https://obamawhitehouse.archives.gov/sites/default/files/docs/nat_arctic_strategy.pdf.

Osherenko, Gail and Oran R. Young. 1989. *The Age of the Arctic*. Cambridge and New York: Cambridge University Press.

"*PDD-26* 'U.S. Policy on Arctic and Antarctic Regions'." 1994. https://clinton.presidentiallibraries.us/items/show/12750.

"*Quadrennial Defense Review Report 2010*." Washington, DC: Department of Defense. www.defense.gov/Portals/1/features/defenseReviews/QDR/QDR_as_of_29JAN10_1600.pdf.

"*Report to Congress Department of Defense Arctic Strategy*." 2019. Office of the Under Secretary of Defense for Policy: US Department of Defence (June). https://media.defense.gov/2019/Jun/06/2002141657/-1/-1/1/2019-DOD-ARCTIC-STRATEGY.PDF.

"*Report to Congress on Arctic Operations and the Northwest Passage*." 2011. Department of Defense: Washington, DC. www.defense.gov/Portals/1/Documents/pubs/Tab_A_Arctic_Report_Public.pdf.

"*Report to Congress on Strategy to Protect United States National Security Interests in the Arctic Region*." 2016. Washington, DC: Department of Defense.

Stavridis, James. 2017. *Sea Power: The history and Geopolitics of the World's Oceans*. New York: Penguin Press.

Strategic Importance of the Arctic in U.S. Security Policy. 2009. "[Hearings] Senate Subcommittee on the Department of Homeland Security. Sen. Lisa Murkowski, Chair." https://fas.org/irp/congress/2009_hr/arctic.pdf.

The White House, Office of the Press Secretary, (2009). www.nsf.gov/geo/opp/opp_advisory/briefings/may2009/nspd66_hspd25.pdf.

Trident Juncture. 2018. "NATO." www.nato.int/cps/en/natohq/157833.htm.

US Coast Guard Arctic Strategic Outlook. 2019. https://assets.documentcloud.org/documents/5973939/Arctic-Strategic-Outlook-APR-2019.pdf.

US Coast Guard Arctic Strategy. 2013. Washington, DC: Department of Homeland Security. www.uscg.mil/Portals/0/Strategy/cg_arctic_strategy.pdf.

"*US National Strategy for the Arctic Re: Strong Foothold or Thin Ice?*" 2013. Washington, DC: The Arctic Institute/Center for Circumpolar Security Studies. www.thearcticinstitute.org/us-national-strategy-for-arctic-region/.

"*US Navy Arctic Roadmap for 2014 to 2030*." 2014. Washington, DC: Department of the Navy. www.dtic.mil/docs/citations/ADA595557.

"US Still Lags Behind in Preparing for a Changing Arctic." 2018. *Scientific American*. www.scientificamerican.com/article/u-s-still-lags-behind-in-preparing-for-a-changing-arctic/.

14
SECURITY PERSPECTIVES FROM NORWAY

Kristian Åtland

The purpose of this chapter is to shed some light on the role of the Arctic, particularly the European Arctic, in Norwegian security policy.[1] The Barents Sea region has traditionally been an important meeting place for Norwegian and Russian cultural, environmental, economic, and security interests. Even in today's geopolitical environment, which is marked by growing tension and mistrust between Russia and the West, Norwegian and Russian authorities, organizations, and individuals continue to interact on a daily basis. This is the case on the mainland, where the two countries share a 196-kilometer land border, as well as in the Barents Sea and on the remote archipelago of Svalbard, located halfway between the North Cape and the North Pole.

In order to get a better understanding of the role of the Arctic – including the Euro-Arctic region – in contemporary Norwegian security thinking and policy, it is necessary to put recent changes into historical perspective. This chapter explores not only how and how much the security situation in the Barents Sea and other parts of the Arctic has changed in recent years, but also how interstate relationships in this region have evolved since Mikhail Gorbachev's watershed 1987 speech in Murmansk, which marked the beginning of the end of the Cold War in the Arctic. In approaching this topic, it is also necessary to distinguish between "hard" and "soft" security. As this chapter argues, the dynamics within different spheres of security vary greatly, as do the prospects for successful Russian–Western cooperation in dealing with the identified challenges.

The chapter is divided into five parts. The first part discusses the nature of the emerging security challenges in the Arctic, as seen from a Norwegian perspective. The second part sheds light on major trends and important developments in Norway's security relationship with Russia since the Cold War. This is followed, in part three, by a discussion of current and possible future implications of Russia's 2014 intervention in Ukraine for interstate relations and regional security dynamics in the Arctic. The fourth part discusses possible measures that may be taken to preserve political, military, and ecological stability in the Arctic. The fifth and final part contains a brief summary of findings and some concluding remarks.

The nature of the emerging challenges: a Norwegian perspective

Speaking at the Arctic Circle Conference in Reykjavik in November 2014, Norway's deputy foreign minister, Bård Glad Pedersen, noted that "security policy in the Arctic needs to be based on a modern and comprehensive understanding of security," one that includes "territorial, ecological, social and political dimensions." At the same time, he emphasized that "security policy – in the traditional sense – also needs to be part of the mix" (Ministry of Foreign Affairs of Norway 2014). Thus, the emerging environmental, societal, and human security challenges in the Arctic have not *replaced* military security challenges. Rather, the nontraditional and nonmilitary security challenges come *in addition* to the traditional and military ones, and they will require approaches and strategies that are different from – and more comprehensive than – those applied in the sphere of military and territorial security.

Following this line of reasoning, the use of concepts such as hard security and soft security may add to our understanding of the increasingly complex security challenges that are emerging in the Arctic. The term *hard security* usually refers to the military security of states, whereas the term *soft security* typically refers to the nonmilitary dimensions of security – environmental, economic, societal, human, and so on. Both dimensions of security are, in various forms, included and represented in contemporary threat perceptions and security policy strategies for the Arctic.

Norway's (and NATO's) ability to deter and defend against external threats, pressures, and military aggression is, for instance, a recurring theme in Norway's recently adopted Long-Term Defense Plan for the period up to 2020 (Ministry of Defense of Norway 2016). In Norway, just as in Russia, military means are still seen as playing an important role in the preservation of regional stability and the maintenance of situational awareness. Norway's traditional role as NATO's "eyes and ears" in the European Arctic has not become less relevant. As outlined in the Defense Plan, investments will be made in new maritime patrol aircraft, submarines, and other capabilities suited for this purpose (ibid.).

Russia's military modernization, which has been in steady progress since 2008, and Russia's growing military activity in northern waters and airspace, does not in itself represent a threat to the country's northwestern neighbors. What makes it challenging from a security perspective is the increasingly nontransparent and sometimes outright provocative nature of the activity. Russia's anti-Western rhetoric and military muscle-flexing, not to mention Russia's violations of its southern neighbors' borders, sovereignty, and territorial integrity, have raised legitimate security concerns among the country's neighbors in Northern Europe and rendered practical military cooperation with Russia virtually impossible. This is, unfortunately, part of "the new normal" in Europe (Ministry of Defense of Norway 2015).

The growing scope, scale, and frequency of Russia's military exercises in the Barents Sea, which often include missile launches and live-fire training, also present a challenge to civilian stakeholders, such as the fishing industry. Norwegian trawlers operating in the eastern part of the Barents Sea do not always receive prior notice of Russian exercises, and they are often forced to cancel fishing or leave the fishing grounds at short notice. The negative economic consequences of unforeseen interruptions can, in some cases, be significant. In fall 2016, the Norwegian Fishing Vessel Owners Federation described the situation as "unacceptable" and urged Norwegian authorities to help find a solution (Hjul 2016).

At the same time, it is recognized in Oslo as well as in Moscow that the states that surround the Arctic Ocean face a number of severe and long-term soft security challenges, which are mainly brought about by outside influences. Warming air and water temperatures are changing the physical geography of the Barents Sea and other parts of the Arctic. The retreat of the ice cap is opening previously inaccessible parts of the region to fisheries, resource exploration, and ship traffic; this is creating new environmental hazards and marine safety concerns for the coastal states. The emerging soft security challenges in the region will require an increased degree of interstate cooperation and coordination at the bilateral and regional levels.

The post-Cold War period: from desecuritization to resecuritization

Soviet leader Mikhail Gorbachev's Murmansk speech in October 1987 became the starting point for a wide-ranging desecuritization of interstate relations in the Arctic. Efforts were made to overcome the old East–West divide and replace the logic of Cold War antagonism with a new logic that would be based on common values and shared interests. Some of these efforts were quite successful, others perhaps less so (Åtland 2008). In any event, cross-border interaction on the level of institutions, organizations, and individuals in the northeastern part of Norway and the northwestern part of Russia grew rapidly throughout the 1990s and early 2000s. Security-related restrictions on commercial and industrial activities in the Barents Sea region were lifted, and new patterns of civil-military relations started to emerge. By the early 2000s, the Barents Sea and other parts of the Arctic, which had been seen primarily as a theatre of military operations, were increasingly seen as an arena for economic activities such as fisheries, marine transportation, and offshore petroleum exploration.

In the 1990s and 2000s, Norway's bilateral cooperation with Russia in the High North was not merely limited to joint endeavors in nonmilitary fields, such as fisheries management, environmental protection, and nuclear safety. Starting in the first half of the 1990s, cooperative relations were also established between the two countries' armed forces. In 1994, Norwegian and Russian naval forces conducted their first joint exercise in the Barents Sea, called Pomor. Similar exercises were held intermittently until spring 2013, and they increasingly had a hard security profile (Pettersen 2013). Some of the joint military activities, such as the Northern Eagle exercises, also involved American naval forces. The purpose of the latter exercises, which were held for the first time in 2004, was to promote trilateral military cooperation between the United States, Russia, and Norway in the High North (O'Dwyer 2012).

A major concern in Norway's bilateral relationship with the Soviet Union, and later the Russian Federation, had been the two countries' inability to reach agreement on a maritime boundary in the Barents Sea and the Arctic Ocean. In 2010, after more than four decades of negotiations, a compromise solution to this issue was finally reached. The Norwegian–Russian treaty on Maritime Delimitation and Cooperation in the Barents Sea and the Arctic Ocean established a 1,700-kilometer boundary line between the two countries' northern economic zones and continental shelves. The 2010 agreement entered into force in July 2011 and seems to be working well.

Today, the Norwegian Coast Guard cooperates closely with its Russian counterpart, which is part of the FSB's Border Guard Service, in the management of commercially important living marine resources. Largely as a result of these joint efforts, illegal, unreported, and unregulated (IUU) fishing seems to be much less of a problem in the northern waters than in many other regions, and IUU fishing in this region is significantly less extensive today than it was in the 1990s and early 2000s (Hønneland 2012, 75). However, climate change and rising water temperatures have led to northward movement among many fish stocks, causing additional management and enforcement challenges for Norway and other Arctic coastal states. Anticipating the possibility that some fish stocks might migrate into maritime areas located outside the coastal states' 200-nautical-mile Exclusive Economic Zones (EEZs), the Arctic coastal states signed a 2018 declaration temporarily banning commercial fisheries in the central Arctic Ocean until a proper regulatory regime is in place.

Russia's growing military presence in the Arctic started well before the Ukraine conflict, but it has intensified since 2014. Most likely, the level and scope of Russia's military activity in the High North will continue to increase, particularly at sea and in the air. In 2007, Russia resumed the practice of conducting strategic bomber patrols in the international airspace over the Barents, Norwegian, and Greenland Seas; this has since become a routine occurrence. In 2013, the first of Russia's new Borei-class submarines, the *Yuri Dolgorukiy*, entered service in the Northern Fleet. The class is planned to consist of at least eight submarines, each carrying between 16 and 20 ballistic missiles. The *Severodvinsk*, which is Russia's first nuclear-powered attack submarine of the Yasen class, was commissioned in December of the same year. More submarines and surface vessels, with increasingly sophisticated weapons systems, will enter service with the Russian Northern Fleet in the coming years. Currently, some 55 percent of Russia's more than 750 sea-based strategic nuclear warheads are based in the country's northwestern corner, with the remaining 45 percent deployed in Kamchatka.

If the Gorbachev and Yeltsin years (late 1980s and 1990s) were a period of desecuritization in the Arctic, the Putin years (2000–2008 and since 2012) have been, to a large extent, a period of resecuritization. The military dimension is certainly more prominent in Russia's Arctic policies today than it was in the 1990s. Military exercises in the region are larger and more frequent, and Russia's relationship with the West has taken a dramatic turn for the worse. Cold War-era limitations on civilian and commercial activities in the region, which were lifted or relaxed in the 1990s, are now being reintroduced or tightened.

Transparency is increasingly being replaced by secrecy. Several Norwegian journalists, scholars, and NGO representatives have had their Russian visas cancelled,[2] and the climate for cross-border interaction and cooperation is less favorable than it was in the 1990s. Thus, there are many indications that Norway's security situation, and the general political climate in the High North, has been negatively affected by the post-2014 deterioration of Russia's relationship with the West, although maybe not as much as in NATO's eastern frontier regions. The region continues to be "Norway's most important foreign policy priority" (Office of the Prime Minister of Norway 2017).

The Ukraine conflict and its implications in the European Arctic

The security situation in Northern Europe and the nature of Norway's bilateral relationship with Russia are to a significant degree shaped, or at least influenced, by developments in other parts of the world and the dynamics of the NATO–Russia relationship. The negative effects of Russia's 2014 intervention in Ukraine have been most strongly felt within the military sphere. Shortly after Russia's intervention in Crimea, the Norwegian government decided in March 2014 to put its military cooperation with Russia on hold, including all planned visits, exchanges, and joint military exercises (Ministry of Defense of Norway 2014). The trilateral (Norwegian–Russian–American) Northern Eagle exercise planned for spring 2014 was also called off. In April of the same year, NATO's foreign ministers agreed to suspend all of NATO's practical cooperation with Russia, military as well as civilian (NATO 2014). The EU and Norway have also imposed individual travel restrictions, in the form of a Schengen visa ban on several high-ranking military officers who are believed to have played a role in the planning or execution of the Russian intervention in Ukraine.

If the lack of dialogue, interaction, and cooperation between military commanders and military forces in northern Norway and northwestern Russia becomes permanent, this may contribute to a climate of reduced military transparency and increased suspicion and mistrust. Incidents and episodes in the northern waters, including incidents involving Russian actors, may escalate more easily than in the past. Given the growing economic and strategic significance of the Arctic region and Russia's new assertiveness in international affairs, Russia may be more inclined to engage in brinksmanship in defense of its rights and interests in this and other border regions (cf. Frear, Kulesa & Kearns 2014, 9–11).

The fishing grounds off the archipelago of Svalbard, located in the northwestern part of the Barents Sea, have traditionally had a significant Russian presence. Russia has on many occasions questioned the legal basis for Norway's establishment of the Svalbard Fisheries Protection Zone in 1977. The Norwegian Coast Guard's enforcement measures vis-à-vis Russian trawlers operating there have on occasion lead to fierce reactions from Russian state and nonstate actors. In this geopolitical climate, fishery disputes in this and other parts of the Barents Sea may be more prone to escalation than in the past. The same holds for interstate disagreements regarding the legal status of the continental shelf around the archipelago (Åtland 2014b, 146–153).

As in the Cold War period, routine military activities on the Norwegian side – on land, at sea, and in the air – are likely to be interpreted in Russia as an expression of NATO's allegedly "aggressive intentions" in the Arctic. Despite being of a relatively small scale, exercises that take place in the far northeast, in the county of Finnmark, are often portrayed in Russia as deliberate "NATO provocations." This was the case with the 2015 and 2017 editions of the Joint Viking exercise that were held in Finnmark and involved, respectively, 5,000 and 8,000 personnel, mainly Norwegian. The short-term presence of a Norwegian frigate in the border town of Kirkenes during the 2015 exercise was seen as particularly problematic, according to Russian media reports (Khrolenko 2015).

The participation of troops, vessels, and aircraft from other NATO countries in military training activities in northern Norway, such as the Cold Response exercises, has also been a source of Russian complaints. The Cold Response exercises, which have been held on a more or less regular basis since 2006, are usually held further south than in Finnmark, mainly in the county of Troms. These exercises are increasingly being interpreted in context with NATO's deteriorating relationship with Russia. Cold Response 2016, which involved some 15,000 troops from 14 NATO member and partner countries, including Sweden and Finland, was not well received by the Russian political and military establishment (RIA Novosti 2016), nor was Trident Juncture, a 40,000-troop high-visibility NATO exercise held in mid-Norway in fall 2018.

In a somewhat similar manner, Russia's military exercises in the region, which have grown in size and frequency over the past decade, seem to be causing new security concerns in the West. This is particularly the case with so-called snap exercises, which are unannounced and often large in scale. Despite generally good intelligence, Russia's Western neighbors have no way of knowing for sure whether such exercises are only for military training purposes or are a cover for the preparation of armed aggression. During the 2014 intervention in Ukraine, Russia demonstrated that its modernized and highly mobile forces could use the element of surprise to their advantage. At the same time, Norwegian security policy analysts and defense planners acknowledge that the European Arctic is not Ukraine, and that the security dynamics in the High North are different from those on Russia's southern frontier.

Norway's security situation in the High North may have certain features in common with the security situation of Norway's neighbors to the east and south, that is, Sweden, Finland, Estonia, Latvia, and Lithuania, but there are also a number of significant differences. The ethnic composition of the population along the eastern border of the Schengen region varies greatly. In the Norwegian border town of Kirkenes, the Russian population constitutes less than 10 percent of the town's total population. Most of the ethnic Russians living in this and other parts of Norway are well integrated and few if any of them claim to be discriminated against. Thus, it is difficult to envision a Crimean scenario materializing on Norwegian soil or in Finland's eastern border regions. In these regions, there is little room for the use of local political, ethnic, or linguistic tensions as a pretext for military intervention.

Such scenarios are probably more likely to occur in Estonia or Latvia, both of which have large Russian minorities within their borders – in many cases located in areas close to the Russian Federation. One of the things Norway and the Baltic states have in common, though, is that they are relatively small countries located on the periphery of Europe, and that their armed forces are relatively small, at least compared to those of Russia. Therefore, they depend heavily on NATO for their national security. Together with other northern European allies, Norway has in recent years tried to direct NATO's attention towards the re-emerging hard security challenges on the northern flank of the alliance and the need to reinforce NATO's defense and deterrence posture in the North Atlantic. At the same time, efforts have been made to preserve the High North's traditional character as a region of low tension.

The way forward: reducing risk, restoring trust?

The emerging hard and soft security challenges in the Arctic are anything but trivial. The challenges will require the development of functional military, constabulary, and emergency response capabilities; a consistent and sustainable maritime presence; enhanced maritime domain awareness; and an improved ability to respond rapidly and effectively to crises and emergencies. Due to their geographical location, the eight Arctic Council member states, including the five Arctic coastal states, have a special role to play in joint efforts to preserve ecological, political, and military stability in the northern part of the globe.

Judging from the way in which the Arctic rim states formulate their visions and priorities for the region, they do have significant goals and interests in common. Since 2008, all five Arctic coastal states, as well as Sweden, Finland, Iceland, and the European Union, have adopted strategy or policy documents for the Arctic region. These documents overlap and coincide in a number of areas. All of the Arctic nations, as well as the European Union, emphasize the importance of international law, particularly the Law of the Sea Convention (UNCLOS), in settling unresolved maritime disputes in the region. Moreover, they stress the need to protect the region's vulnerable coastal and marine environment, the need to ensure that living marine resources are managed in a responsible and sustainable manner, and the need to strengthen existing regional cooperation arrangements such as the Arctic Council.

In recent years, the Arctic Council's eight member states have been able to expand and deepen their cooperation within a number of fields. The Agreement on Cooperation on Aeronautical and Maritime Search and Rescue in the Arctic, which was signed in 2011 and entered into force in 2013, was the first legally binding agreement negotiated under the auspices of the Arctic Council. Also in 2013, the Arctic Council member states signed an agreement enhancing marine oil pollution preparedness and response capabilities in the Arctic; this entered into force in 2017. Since 2014, the Arctic Council has largely been able to refer concerns and disagreements relating to the Russia–Ukraine conflict to other and more appropriate forums, thus preventing much of the negative political spillover effect that many anticipated at the outset of the conflict.

In fall 2014, the Arctic Coast Guard Forum (ACGF) was established during a ceremony at the US Coast Guard Academy in New London, Connecticut (Braynard 2015). Based on agreed-upon procedural guidelines, the eight Arctic coast guards will be able to use this forum to enhance their operational capabilities through extensive information sharing, the development of best practices, the identification of future training needs, and the organization and conduct of combined exercises and operations (Sevunts 2016). In the absence of military-to-military cooperation between Russia and its Arctic neighbors, the ACGF may turn out to be an important arena for East–West dialogue and cooperation regarding the Arctic. This and other regional and bilateral cooperation arrangements within the sphere of soft security (e.g., air and maritime search and rescue, oil-spill preparedness, resource management, and constabulary presence), may contribute to an increased level of trust in Arctic interstate relations.

This is not to say that there is no potential for interstate conflict in the region. Unlike Antarctica, the Arctic is not a demilitarized area. The region still plays an important role in the nuclear deterrence strategies of Russia and the United States, and all of the Arctic coastal states attach great importance to their economic and national security interests in the region. If challenged by their neighbors or outside actors, they may be willing to go to great lengths to defend their rights and interests in the northern maritime and shelf areas.

The fact that four of the five Arctic coastal states (Norway, Denmark, the United States, and Canada) are members of the same military alliance (NATO) seems to be a source of particular concern for the fifth one (Russia). Russian media and policymakers have recently tended to portray any foreign military presence in the Arctic – particularly that of NATO – as hostile and provocative, even when such activity has not infringed on recognized Russian rights. According to the secretary of the Russian Security Council, Nikolay Patrushev, "the United States, Norway, Denmark, and Canada are pursuing a common and coordinated policy aimed at denying Russia access to the riches of the Arctic continental shelf" (Gazeta 2009, my translation). Obviously, such statements are often intended for domestic audiences and should not necessarily be taken at face value. At the same time, there are many indications that Russia's military security concerns related to the region are genuine.

The Kola Peninsula's role as the primary basing area for Russia's sea-based strategic deterrent is clearly an important factor in this regard. In February 2012, General Nikolai Makarov, the chief of the Russian General Staff, stated: "We will not accept that US vessels equipped with the Aegis Ballistic Missile Defense System to operate in our part of the Arctic." He added that Russia had "matching measures ready" to counter such a turn of events (Staalesen 2012). Russian civilian authorities, including the embassy in Oslo, have also on numerous occasions warned Norway against participating in, or contributing to, NATO's missile defense system (Embassy of the Russian Federation in Norway 2017). Whether and how Norway will participate in this project is still an open question.

The United States, for its part, maintains that its antiballistic-missile (ABM) measures, including efforts to equip a growing number of US Navy cruisers and destroyers with ABM-capable Aegis missile defense systems, are directed against not Russia but rather the missile threat from rogue states such as Iran and North Korea. In December 2011, US

Secretary of State Hillary Clinton noted: "We have explained through multiple channels that our planned system will not and cannot threaten Russia's strategic deterrent. It does not affect our strategic balance with Russia and is certainly not a cause for military countermeasures" (Northam 2011).

These examples illustrate how the Arctic security dilemma plays out in the field of nuclear deterrence and how action–reaction dynamics may contribute to an unintended and often unforeseen increase in military presence and tension in the region (Åtland 2014a, 146). Part of the problem seems to be that Russia and the other Arctic coastal states do not have a proper forum in which to discuss military security issues such as the ones mentioned above. Russia is neither a member of NATO nor part of the Western security community. The Arctic Council, which Russia is a prominent member of, is not seen as a forum in which hard security issues can or should be discussed. In the Arctic, as in other maritime border regions, military relations between Russia and the West are increasingly marked by fear, lack of communication, and mutual distrust. Restoring trust and confidence is a challenging task.

The 1990 Incident at Sea Agreement (INCSEA) between Norway and Russia, which regulates how the two countries' naval forces signal, navigate, and communicate when they meet outside their own territorial waters, is still in force. The agreement contains important rules of conduct not only for naval vessels but also for military aircraft, particularly with respect to how they should behave in the vicinity of the other party's air and naval vessels. Key provisions for avoiding mishaps include maintaining a safe distance and refraining from provocative or dangerous maneuvers or simulated attacks. General or episode-specific concerns relating to the other side's compliance with the provisions of the agreement may be raised and discussed in high-level meetings between the two countries' military authorities. Such meetings are still held on a regular basis, including in Oslo in November–December 2016.

The duty officer at the Norwegian Joint Headquarters, located at Reitan, outside Bodø in northern Norway, also has a direct communication channel to his counterpart at the Russian Northern Fleet's staff in Severomorsk on the Kola Peninsula (High North News 2016). This working-level hotline offers an around-the-clock channel for communicating concerns, formulating questions and answers, and thus preventing misunderstandings and unintended escalation of incidents and episodes in the region.

In addition to Norway and the United States, ten other NATO members have bilateral INCSEA agreements with Russia, and four NATO members have bilateral agreements with Russia on the prevention of dangerous military activities (DMAs). There are also other agreements, such as the Vienna Document (Organization for Security and Co-operation in Europe 2011), which regulates important military aspects of confidence and security, particularly on land. In the current international climate, it is important that all parties abide by existing agreements on incident management and actively work towards the common goal of greater military transparency, in the High North as well as in other Russian–Western frontier regions (Kulesa, Frear & Raynova 2016, 59–62).

Conclusion

The security environment in the Arctic has undergone significant changes in recent years, as have the dynamics of Russia's relationship with its Western neighbors. Since 2008, Russia has invested heavily in the modernization of its military forces. The country's military presence and activity in the Arctic has grown in scope, scale, and geographic reach. On top of that, Russia's actions in Ukraine since 2014 have had a distinctly negative impact on Russia's relations with the West and created new security concerns for the country's northern neighbors.

Within NATO, renewed attention is being paid to "the Russia factor" and to the emerging hard security challenges on the northern flank of the alliance. It is being emphasized that NATO's Article 5 commitments apply to all of the member states and all parts of their land, sea, and air territory, including such remote areas as the archipelago of Svalbard. NATO's contingency plans for the North Atlantic and the European Arctic are being revised and updated, and interoperability is being boosted through exercises and training.

As for NATO's relations with Russia, it is important to have realistic ambitions. A "strategic partnership" between the two, as outlined in NATO's 2010 Strategic Concept (NATO 2010), is currently not feasible; mostly because Russia sees NATO as its main military adversary. Instead, Russia and NATO should try to agree on some basic steps to rebuild mutual trust and confidence. Such steps may include measures to increase the transparency and predictability of military activity, as well as other measures aimed at reducing the likelihood and/or escalation risk of incidents at sea or in the air.

Despite the negative impacts of Russia's 2014 intervention in Ukraine, including the freeze in military-to-military cooperation and the continued presence of mutual restrictive measures in the economic field, Norway and Russia have been able to preserve much of their stability-enhancing cooperation in the High North. This includes, among other things, the Norwegian and Russian Coast Guards' generally successful joint efforts to combat illegal fishing in northern waters, cooperation between the two countries' maritime search and rescue services, and cooperation between the two countries' local police and border authorities. Similarly, Russian–Western cooperation in regional or intergovernmental forums such as the Barents Euro-Arctic Council and the Arctic Council has been largely unaffected by the negative fallout from the Ukraine conflict. These cooperation efforts make important contributions to the common goal of preserving regional stability in the Arctic.

Norway and Russia share significant interests in the High North, particularly in the sphere of soft security. Norwegian–Russian efforts to jointly address the emerging nonmilitary security challenges in the region have largely been successful, and cooperation between the two countries' coast guards, border guards, and maritime search and rescue services constitutes a significant part of the current interaction between the two countries. As Norway's experience in the High North has demonstrated, it is possible, even in the current security environment, to maintain cordial relations and a significant degree of practical cooperation with Russia on nonmilitary security issues, despite continued economic sanctions and despite the suspension of military-to-military cooperation. In a political climate marked by growing fear, suspicion, and mistrust between Russia and the West, joint endeavors within the sphere of soft security can contribute to the preservation of regional stability and the easing of East–West tensions within the sphere of hard security.

Notes

1 The opinions and views expressed in this chapter are those of the author and should not be attributed to the Norwegian Government. Parts of the chapter are based on a research paper entitled "East–West Relations in the High North: Challenges and Opportunities," which was presented at the Kiel Maritime Security Conference in June 2016.

2 Recent examples include Thomas Nilsen of the Independent Barents Observer, Bjørn Engesland of the Norwegian Helsinki Committee, and Julie Wilhelmsen of the Norwegian Institute of International Affairs.

References

Åtland, Kristian. 2008. "Mikhail Gorbachev, the Murmansk Initiative, and the Desecuritization of Interstate Relations in the Arctic." *Cooperation and Conflict* 43(3): 289–311.

Åtland, Kristian. 2014a. "Interstate Relations in the Arctic: An Emerging Security Dilemma?" *Comparative Strategy* 33(2): 145–166.

Åtland, Kristian. 2014b. "The Status of Svalbard and its Consequences for International Politics." In Eckart D. Stratenschulte (ed.) *Heilsame Vielfalt? Formen differenzierter Integration in Europa*, 143–164. Baden-Baden: Nomos.

Braynard, Katie. 2015. "Establishment of the Arctic Coast Guard Forum." *The Coast Guard Compass*, 30 October, http://coastguard.dodlive.mil/2015/10/establishment-of-the-arctic-coast-guard-forum/.

Embassy of the Russian Federation in Norway. 2017. "Commentary from the Embassy of the Russian Federation in Norway to 'Dagbladet' in Connection with the Joint Norwegian-US Development of Parameters for the Norwegian Contribution to the Missile Defense System of NATO." 9 March, www.norway.mid.ru/en/press_17_010.html.

Frear, Thomas, Lukasz Kulesa & Ian Kearns. 2014. "Dangerous Brinkmanship: Close Military Encounters between Russia and the West in 2014." Policy Brief, European Leadership Network, November.

Gazeta. 2009. "Patrushev: protiv Rossii v Arktike vedut skoordiniovannuyu politiku" ["Patrushev: A Coordinated Policy against Russia is Pursued in the Arctic"]. 30 March, www.gazeta.ru/news/lenta/2009/03/30/n_1346529.shtml.

High North News. 2016. "Norwegian Joint Headquarters: – We Talk to Russia over Skype." 17 June, www.highnorthnews.com/norwegian-joint-headquartes-we-talk-to-russia-over-skype/.

Hjul, Jenny. 2016. "Fishermen Angered by Russian Naval Exercises." *FISHupdate*, 19 October, www.fishupdate.com/fishermen-angered-by-russian-naval-exercises/.

Hønneland, Geir. 2012. *Making Fisheries Agreements Work: Post-Agreement Bargaining in the Barents Sea.* Cheltenham: Edward Elgar Publishing.

Khrolenko, Aleksandr. 2015. "Ucheniya NATO v Severnoy Norvegii: razvedka ili provokatsiya" ["NATO's Exercises in Northern Norway: Espionage or Provocation"]. *RIA Novosti*, 17 March, http://ria.ru/authors/20150317/1053024319.html.

Kulesa, Lukasz, Thomas Frear & Denitsa Raynova. 2016. "Managing Hazardous Incidents in the Euro-Atlantic Area: A New Plan of Action." Policy Brief, European Leadership Network, November.

Ministry of Defence of Norway. 2014. "Norway Suspends All Planned Military Activities with Russia." Press Release, 25 March, www.regjeringen.no/en/aktuelt/Norway-suspends-all-planned-military-activities-with-Russia-/id753887/.

Ministry of Defence of Norway. 2015. "State Secretary Øystein Bø's Speech on Norwegian Security and Defense Policy at MSPO 2015 in Poland." 3 September, www.regjeringen.no/no/aktuelt/state-secretary-oystein-bos-speech-on-norwegian-security-and-defense-policy-at-mspo-2015-in-poland/id2438200/.

Ministry of Defence of Norway. 2016. "Long Term Defence Plan Adopted." 18 November, www.regjeringen.no/en/topics/defence/ltp/ny-langtidsplan-for-forsvarssektoren/langtidsplanen-for-forsvarssektoren-er-vedtatt/id2520659/.

Ministry of Foreign Affairs of Norway. 2014. "Security in the Arctic – A Norwegian Perspective." Speech by State Secretary Bård Glad Pedersen at the Arctic Circle Conference in Reykjavik, 2 November, www.regjeringen.no/no/aktuelt/security-arctic/id2351274/.

NATO. 2010. "Active Engagement, Modern Defence: Strategic Concept for the Defence and Security of the Members of the North Atlantic Treaty Organisation." adopted in Lisbon on 19 November, www.nato.int/cps/en/natohq/official_texts_68580.htm.

NATO. 2014. "Statement by NATO Foreign Ministers." Press Release, 1 April, www.nato.int/cps/en/natohq/news_108501.htm

Northam, Jackie. 2011. "Clinton, Russia Spar over Missile Defense System." *NPR*, 8 December, www.npr.org/2011/12/08/143386914/clinton-russia-spar-over-missile-defense-system.

O'Dwyer, Gerald. 2012. "Norway Hails Northern Eagle as Bridge-Builder." *Defense News*, 24 August.
Office of the Prime Minister of Norway. 2017. "A Strategy to Promote Peaceful, Innovative and Sustainable Development in the Arctic." Press Release, 21 April, www.regjeringen.no/en/aktuelt/en-nordomradestrategi-for-et-fredelig-skapende-og-barekraftig-nord/id2550095/.
Organization for Security and Co-operation in Europe. 2011. "Vienna Document on Confidence- and Security-Building Measures." adopted in Vienna on 30 November, www.osce.org/fsc/86597?download=true.
Pettersen, Trude. 2013. "Norwegian-Russian POMOR-2013 Naval Exercise Starts This Week." *BarentsObserver*, 7 May, http://barentsobserver.com/en/security/2013/05/norwegian-russian-pomor-2013-naval-exercise-starts-week-07-05.
RIA Novosti. 2016. "Mnenie: v peshcherakh Norvegii mozhet khranit'sya ogromnoye kolichestvo oruzhiya" ["Opinion: Enormous Amounts of Military Equipment May be Stored in Norway's Caves"]. *RIA Novosti*, 19 February, http://ria.ru/radio_brief/20160219/1377317332.html.
Sevunts, Levon. 2016. "Arctic Nations Deepen Coast Guard Cooperation." *Radio Canada International*, 10 June, www.rcinet.ca/en/2016/06/10/arctic-coast-guar-forum-nations-deepen-cooperation/.
Staalesen, Atle. 2012. "Russian General Sends Arctic Warning to USA." *Barents Observer*, 16 February, www.barentsobserver.com/russian-general-sends-arctic-warning-to-usa.5021760.html.

15

DENMARK AND GREENLAND'S CHANGING SOVEREIGNTY AND SECURITY CHALLENGES IN THE ARCTIC

Jon Rahbek-Clemmensen

Introduction

The Arctic has undergone significant changes during the post-Cold War period. Climate change and globalization are opening up the region for more human activity, which in turn has led to new civilian and political–military security challenges. New human activity obviously increases civilian security threats, such as accidents with implications for individuals and the environment, but political–military security is also changing throughout the Arctic, as great powers eye new opportunities and threats in a changing region. Adding to this complexity, the security transformation is not uniformly felt throughout the region. Not only do geographical and geopolitical conditions differ between different parts of the region, but local political conditions, especially Inuit empowerment, shape both political–military and civilian security trends.

Greenland, a regional entity within the Kingdom of Denmark, illustrates the importance of local political conditions for both civilian and political–military security. Greenland has more autonomy than any other subnational actor in the Arctic and, unlike other Inuit polities, it has a clear path to independence codified in the 2009 Self-Government Act. This makes it the most likely place to see the impact of Inuit empowerment and local authority structures on security dynamics.

This chapter examines how civilian and political–military security dynamics in and around Greenland have changed since the onset of the Second World War and how changing sovereignty structures and shifts in the relationship between Denmark and Greenland have altered these dynamics. Applying the sector framework of the Copenhagen School, this chapter uses the term *political–military security* to mean political or military threats against the long-term survival of the state and uses *civilian security* to mean threats against individuals (individual security), the economy (economic security), the environment (environmental security), or the identity of social groups (societal security) (Buzan, Wæver, and de Wilde 1998).

Sovereignty has always been fluid and challenged in Greenland. Its interaction with other large-scale trends, such as the end of the Cold War and the opening of the Arctic for human activity due to climate change and globalization, has changed the nature of both civilian and political–military security challenges. Whereas Cold War civilian security challenges were primarily consequences of the American presence on the island and the Danish modernization project, current civilian security challenges stem from the increased commercial activity in the region, which is pushed primarily by the local government in Nuuk. While Cold War political–military security dynamics were mainly a bilateral Danish–American affair, Greenland has gained a say in these matters, which makes it more difficult to secure American interests and opens a sliver of maneuvering room for other great powers, the most important of which is China.

This chapter has three sections. The first section examines the geopolitical and strategic importance of Greenland for the great powers, especially the United States. The second section tracks security dynamics in Greenland during the Second World War and the Cold War. The final section examines changes that have occurred since the end of the Cold War.

Greenlandic geopolitics

Greenland lies at North America's northeastern periphery, as a geostrategically important steppingstone between the Western Hemisphere, Europe, and northern Asia. The island has historically caught the eye of American geostrategists who understood the Americans' need to close off its northern flank. Greenlandic geopolitics is therefore intimately linked to American global strategy and the threat posed to it by other great powers, most importantly Russia. This was particularly clear during the Second World War and the Cold War, when Greenland at times hosted significant American troop contingents and base facilities, but this has become less obvious since the fall of the Soviet Union, as Washington's attention has been more focused on other regions (Lidegaard 1996; Danish Institute for International Affairs 1997; Danish Institute for International Studies 2005; Berry 2016; Doel 2016; Henriksen and Rahbek-Clemmensen 2017).

Since the beginning of the Cold War, the United States has had three fundamental geopolitical interests in Greenland: detection of cross-polar attacks by strategic missiles and bombers, control of the Greenland–Iceland–United Kingdom gap (the GIUK gap), and, to a lesser extent, access to Greenlandic minerals. Though the importance of these interests has fluctuated along with changes in technology, the international system, and general American priorities, they remain fundamental for US regional strategy. As other great powers seek to gain geopolitical advantages or counter American influence, they also have an interest in Greenland, albeit less interest than the United States.

First, the American air base in Thule (Pittufik) in northwestern Greenland (established 1951–1952) is the US military's most northern installation and an important node in its ballistic missile defense system (Wilkening 2004, 31; Petersen 2011). During the Cold War, the purpose of Thule and other bases in Greenland, such as Narsarsuaq and Kangerlussuaq (Søndre Strømfjord), fluctuated with changes in technology and East–West relations. In the 1950s, the bases were important refueling stops for American offensive operations with strategic bombers. However, when the USSR gained second-strike capability and the United States began to rely on long-range bombers and missiles, the purpose of the bases became defensive: detection of a Soviet cross-polar attack (Archer 1988, 2003; Danish Institute for International Affairs 1997; Petersen 2011). The end of the Cold War meant that Thule became less important for US strategy, but it regained prominence after the turn of the millennium following the Bush administration's renewed focus on missile defense (Archer 2003; Kristensen 2005).

Second, the GIUK gap, being the waters between Greenland, Iceland, the Faroe Islands, and the British Isles, are a chokepoint where NATO can detect and block the Russian Northern Fleet's passage into the North Atlantic. In the event of a military confrontation between NATO and Russia, the Northern Fleet would most likely try to move through the GIUK gap and into the North Atlantic, where it could launch nuclear and conventional missiles against Europe and North America in support of operations in other theaters (such as the Baltic Sea), cut underwater cables, and block American reinforcements from reaching Europe (Gramer 2016). Greenland can provide bases and ports for NATO aircraft and ships patrolling the GIUK gap. NATO countries can also install sophisticated listening stations off the coast of Greenland, akin to the Sound Surveillance System (SOSUS) used during the Cold War (Howard 2011; Stashwick 2016).

Finally, several great powers, including the United States, view some of the resources found in Greenland as critical, although this dimension is less important than other interests. The open global resource market ensures a steady supply of most resources at reasonably market-effective prices, but some resources gain strategic importance because they serve an essential economic or military purpose and because they can suddenly be in short supply as they are difficult to substitute, extracted in low quantities, or controlled by a few countries that can disrupt supply during a crisis (Rasmussen 2013; Rosing, Hanghøj, and Kalvig 2014). For instance, during the Second World War, cryolite from Ivigtut in Southwestern Greenland was essential for the aluminum industry and thus for the war effort (Lidegaard 1996, 647; Berry 2012; Sejersen 2014). Uranium, perhaps the most controversial mineral in Greenland, is not a critical resource; neither is oil or gas. Instead, Greenland may contain significant quantities of niobium, platinum-group metals, and rare earth elements (REEs), all of which are viewed as critical resources by the US Department of Energy. The Geological Survey of Denmark and Greenland estimates that Greenland contains several other minerals that the European Union views as critical resources, such as tantalum, fluoride, and graphite (Boersma and Foley 2014, 37–38; Rosing, Hanghøj, and Kalvig 2014, 24; Steensgaard et al. 2017, 9). However, none of these resources are currently being mined in Greenland and no projects seem feasible in the short term.

The Second World War and the Cold War: the impact of modernization and great-power competition

Great-power interests in Greenland have historically created security problems on the island and challenged Danish sovereignty, over which the Greenlandic population and authorities had limited influence. Danish sovereignty has changed over the course of the 20th century. Copenhagen has had to accommodate the great powers, most often the United States, to secure its sovereignty over the island. In 1917, Denmark secured American acceptance of the Danish presence in Greenland as part of the American purchase of the Danish West Indies (US Virgin Islands). Danish sovereignty over the island was only fully settled after the Permanent Court of International Justice in The Hague ruled against a Norwegian claim to eastern Greenland in 1933.

Since the onset of the Second World War, American security interests in Greenland have posed both a challenge and an opportunity for Denmark. On the one hand, the United States has been keen to gain a foothold on the island, which challenged Danish sovereignty. On the other hand, the American interest in Greenland meant that the United States has protected the island and has given Denmark leverage it could use to achieve other political goals vis-à-vis the United States. During the war, with Denmark occupied by Nazi Germany, the United States made an agreement with the Danish ambassador in Washington – without the consent of the Danish government – to gain de facto control of Greenland to prevent Germany from using it as a steppingstone to North America. Although Copenhagen protested at the time, the agreement was later viewed as a Danish contribution to the Allied war effort and it was one of the few arguments that the Danish government could later use to claim status as an Allied power. After the war, Washington used the agreement to maintain a military presence on the geostrategically important island, much to the concern of the Danish government, which wanted to avoid hosting a foreign power in Greenland (Lidegaard 1996; Danish Institute for International Affairs 1997; Danish Institute for International Studies 2005). The American presence in Greenland complicated Denmark's relationship with the Soviet Union and meant that Denmark struggled to maintain its neutrality, while mainland Denmark was left unprotected (Danish Institute for International Affairs 1997, 562; Danish Institute for International Studies 2005, vol. 1, 297).

The Greenland question was one of the reasons Denmark became a founding member of NATO in 1949. Moving Danish–American relations into a multilateral setting meant that the American interest in Greenland could be used to ensure an American commitment to the protection of mainland Denmark as well. In other words, the American presence went from being a liability to an asset. After 1949, Denmark therefore changed course and no longer worked towards an American withdrawal from Greenland, instead facilitating US interests in Greenland and using the so-called Greenland Card in NATO negotiations. Greenland thus came to play an important political role for Denmark. Copenhagen could free-ride on the American security guarantee, maintaining a low NATO-force contribution and resisting certain NATO initiatives, while using the US interest in Greenland, along with Denmark's relatively large development aid to countries in the Third World, to limit American criticism (Lidegaard 1996; Danish Institute for International Affairs 1997).

Thus the Cold War also became a period of fluid sovereignty in Greenland. A division of competences was created, where Denmark maintained de jure sovereignty and control over social and economic life on the island, but the United States got, de facto, a free hand to operate militarily in Greenland as long as its activities were isolated from Greenlandic society (Lidegaard 1996, 444–501; Danish Institute for International Affairs 1997). For example, American forces secretly used Thule Air Base for flights with nuclear weapons, even though the Danish government had decided that nuclear weapons should not be stored on Danish soil. The Danish government refrained from protesting against the American activities, thus tacitly accepting the American activity in Greenland. The practice was abandoned in 1968 after a nuclear-armed B-52 bomber crashed near Thule. The crash made the public aware of the presence of American nuclear weapons in Greenland, even though the full extent of American activities was concealed by the American and Danish governments (Danish Institute for International Affairs 1997).

During the early Cold War, the Danish government used its control over social and economic life to pursue a rapid modernization and integration program that aimed to make Greenland self-sustaining through economic reform, Danish-focused education, and centralization. Although spearheaded by Denmark, this program was supported by large parts of the Greenlandic elite, which viewed it as an opportunity to create equality between Danes and Greenlanders. Only in the second half of the Cold War did most of the Greenlandic elite come to view modernization and Danification as threats to Greenlandic identity (A. K. Sørensen 2009; Beukel, Jensen, and Rytter 2010; K. H. Nielsen 2016; Heinrich 2017).

Of course, the American presence in Greenland and Danish policies both created environmental, individual, and societal civilian security challenges for the local population.

Some American activities had environmental consequences that only surfaced decades later. For instance, in the late 1950s and early 1960s, the American authorities built Camp Century, a large nuclear-powered research installation under the ice near Thule, which functioned as a cover for Project Iceworm, a secret plan to build a 135,000 square kilometer subglacial base and nuclear-missile launch facility (H. Nielsen and Nielsen 2016). However, when Project Iceworm was deemed to be infeasible, Camp Century was closed and stocks of hazardous materials were left to be sealed off under the ice. Climate change may unfreeze the facilities and lead to leakage of these materials (J. S. Nielsen 2016). Similarly, the aforementioned B-52 bomber crash contaminated the Thule area with low levels of radioactive material and exposed the clean-up crew and perhaps the local population to unusually high doses of radiation. Subsequent analyses have concluded that the radiation did not lead to health issues (Danish Institute for International Affairs 1997; Juel, Engholm, and Storm 2005).

The American presence and Danish policies also led to threats against individual security. For instance, in 1953, the Danish government decided to relocate people from the Uummannaq settlement away from their traditional hunting grounds near Thule to facilitate the American base. The roughly 100 inhabitants were given only four days' notice before being moved 160 kilometers to an incomplete settlement in Qaanaaq: circumstances that were ruled to be illegal by the Danish Eastern High Court in 1999 (Christensen and Kristensen 2009). Similarly, in the 1950s, as part of Denmark's general modernization policy in Greenland, Danish authorities attempted to create a cadre of Danish-speaking elite Greenlandic students by moving 22 Greenlandic children from their families to Denmark, where they were educated in Danish. The experiment was a failure, as the students lost touch with their roots and became alienated from Greenlandic society, which in many instances had severe psychological repercussions (Bryld 1998).

Finally, American activities and Danish policies also threatened Greenlandic identity. Many of the aforementioned violations of individual rights, such as moving people from their traditional hunting grounds or failing to educate them in Greenlandic language and customs, obviously had negative consequences on Greenlandic identity. Furthermore, some critics argue that Danish modernization and integration policies weakened Greenlandic identity – a claim that downplays the explicit support that these programs had from parts of the Greenlandic elite. The large-scale presence of foreign troops was also at times viewed as a threat to local society. For instance, Danish elites feared that the several thousand American troops stationed in Greenland during the Second World War would erode the local population's attachment to Denmark (Heinrich 2017).

New security challenges in the post-Cold War era

In the post-Cold War era, the character and origins of security threats have changed significantly. New types of civilian activity are coming to Greenland, pushed by globalization and climate change, and these pose new civilian security challenges. Unlike during the Cold War, when most civilian security challenges originated in Danish modernization programs or the American presence, many of the new challenges are furthered by the Greenlandic government. Similarly, Greenland's enhanced autonomy complicates political–military security dynamics and may weaken the American presence on the island.

The end of the Cold War lowered military tensions in the Arctic, and the region became a marginal issue in the 1990s and early 2000s. Decreased American interest in the polar region meant that Denmark could no longer use Greenland diplomatically in an alliance context. Denmark instead became perhaps the most active European nation in American stability operations in the Global South, most importantly in the wars in Afghanistan, Iraq, and Libya, and its armed forces underwent a large-scale transformation from a territorial defense force to a small and agile expeditionary force (Mouritzen 2007; Ringsmose and Rynning 2008; Henriksen and Rahbek-Clemmensen 2017).

While interest in the Arctic decreased in the 1990s, climate change and globalization began to open the Arctic for human activities, such as shipping, energy and minerals industries, and tourism. This has slowly pushed the region back onto the global agenda since the middle of the 2000s. From around the turn of the millennium, more or less simultaneously with the opening up of the Arctic, the Greenlandic government began to push for increased autonomy. This led to the 2009 Self-Government Act, which codified new boundaries of authority between Copenhagen and Nuuk and gave the latter a roadmap to independence (Government of Denmark 2009; Gad 2016).

Greenland has used this autonomy to develop a separate foreign policy and forge bilateral and multilateral relations with other actors. It has established its own diplomatic representation as part of the Danish embassies in Washington and Brussels, and engaged with other Inuit organizations as well as the Arctic Council (Gerhardt 2011; Ackrén and Jakobsen 2015; Olsen and Shadian 2016). Greenland's long-term goal is to achieve full independence – a goal that is supported by almost all parties in the Greenlandic parliament – but its weak economy means that the island remains dependent on the annual block grant (DKK 3.7 billion (USD 530 million), excluding services, in 2015) received from Denmark. The 2009 Self-Government Act froze the block grant at its 2009 real level, which has made economic stability a new security threat facing the Greenlandic government.

Greenland pursues two short-to-medium-term goals: carving out as much autonomy as possible without losing the block grant and attracting foreign investments to strengthen its ailing finances (Rahbek-Clemmensen 2020). Although attracting new investments may help solve the fiscal challenges facing the Greenlandic government, more activity will also lead to new environmental, societal, and individual security problems.

New activity entails environmental threats. Although attempts to find oil and gas off the coast of Greenland have proved futile, a future offshore oil and gas industry would increase the risk of environmental hazards, such as oil spills. Similarly, certain types of mining, especially of uranium, place the surrounding population and environment at risk from airborne radioactive dust or chemical fumes and leakage or seepage of liquid waste (Hansen et al. 2016, 46–47).

New commercial activity in the Arctic may lead to more traffic, increasing the risk of accidents in Greenlandic waters. Projecting future traffic is fraught with uncertainty, because even one project or event can change patterns significantly. But most recent analyses expect a moderate traffic increase in the short-to-medium term, especially in the cargo and tourism sectors (DNV GL AS DNV GL Oil & Gas 2015, 18; Jakobsen and i Dali 2016). Increased traffic may increase the risk of accidents and therefore the need for Danish search-and-rescue (SAR) capabilities. Cruise traffic around Greenland is especially risky, as it could lead to a mass-casualty accident that would require capabilities beyond those of the Danish and Greenlandic authorities (Public Accounts Committee 2013; Jakobsen and Kern 2016).

Enhanced Greenlandic autonomy and the possibility of new commercial opportunities have also transformed the whole way that threats to Greenlandic identity are understood. Unlike during the Second World War and the Cold War periods, when Denmark largely controlled social conditions in Greenland and the main identity threats came from the American presence on the island and the Danish-driven modernization project, authority has moved to the Greenlandic government. Most societal threats now result from commercial developments that are furthered by the government in Nuuk. For instance, large-scale mining projects are at times framed as a threat to social coherence, as thousands of imported workers, most likely from China, will make up a significant percentage of the Greenlandic population (Mortensen 2013, 114–20). Similarly, some critics view the development of Greenland as a Faustian bargain, where fiscal sustainability and independence are bought at the price of ecological and democratic ruin: traditional activities that define Greenlandic identity, such as hunting and fishing, become impossible and democratic processes are set aside to hurry along the exploitation of mineral wealth (Nuttall 2013; Kristensen and Rahbek-Clemmensen 2017).

As a rule of thumb, most of the challenges related to activity on the mainland and within three nautical miles off the coast are the responsibility of the Greenlandic government, while the Danish authorities typically deal with challenges related to the Exclusive Economic Zone (EEZ) beyond three nautical miles. However, these boundaries shift from one issue-area to another (Danish Ministry of Defence 2016, 109–10). Furthermore, in practice, these boundaries are fluid, and Danish and Greenlandic authorities cooperate to handle incidents (Jørgensen and Rahbek-Clemmensen 2009).

The Danish Ministry of Defense has responded to these challenges by reorganizing and expanding its maritime capabilities. Its two North Atlantic maritime commands – Faroe Islands Command and Greenland Command – have merged into a Joint Arctic Command with its headquarters moved from Tórshavn (Faroe Islands) and Kangilinnguit (southern Greenland) to a joint headquarters in Nuuk (Thorsen 2011). Other branches of the armed forces have become part of the Arctic Preparedness Force, an organizational structure that prepares different units for an Arctic emergency by, for instance, organizing annual live or table-top exercises (Danish Ministry of Defence 2016, 200). New capabilities and resources have been allocated to the Arctic. For instance, the aging Agdlek-class cutters are being replaced with the more formidable Knud Rasmussen-class patrol vessels. A 2016 defense review recommended that an additional DKK 120 million (USD 17 million) be spent on Arctic capabilities, including increased surveillance flights, increased Arctic presence by one of Denmark's Ivar Huitfeldt-class frigates, voluntary schemes for Greenlandic citizens, and increased use of surveillance satellites. The report also recommended that Denmark strengthen its cooperation with other nations, most importantly Canada, Iceland, Norway, and the United States (Danish Ministry of Defense 2016). Although these initiatives strengthen Danish Arctic capabilities, they amount to roughly half a percent of the total defense budget and they therefore hardly represent a pivot to the north (Rahbek-Clemmensen 2016).

Enhanced Greenlandic autonomy and voice and the opening of the Arctic have altered political–military security dynamics in Greenland in four ways: increasing Greenland's influence over Danish–American relations, introducing other great-power players into Greenland, engaging Denmark in regional diplomacy, and necessitating active uranium safeguard management.

First, while Cold War geopolitics was largely a bilateral matter between Denmark and the United States (with Denmark largely keeping the Greenlandic government and people out of the loop), Nuuk has gained a voice in the post-Cold War world, transforming the Copenhagen–Washington dyad into a Copenhagen–Nuuk–Washington triangle (Archer 2003). For instance, when the United States requested permission to upgrade its radar facilities in Thule in 2002, the negotiations were no longer a primarily Danish–American affair, as the Greenlandic government used the postcolonial heritage and the specter of wrongdoing from the Cold War to influence the process. As a result, Greenland managed to gain a guaranteed say in future upgrades (Archer 2003; Kristensen 2005). As Olesen has highlighted, this process reflects a general shift in triangular relations, as Copenhagen has begun to incorporate some of Greenland's independent interests in its interactions with the United States while functioning as a lightning rod for Greenlandic grievances (Olesen 2017).

Second, Chinese investments in Greenland have altered Denmark and Greenland's relationship with the United States. Several Greenlandic mining projects, most prominently the iron ore mine in Isua and the rare earth elements and uranium mine in Kvanefjeld, either have or are likely to attract Chinese investments (Boersma and Foley 2014, 43). Chinese companies are typically closely connected to the government in Beijing, and voices in both Denmark and the United States fear that even minor investments in the small Greenlandic economy may give China leverage that it could use to weaken the American position on the island (Danish Defense Intelligence Service 2016, 42; Henriksen and Rahbek-Clemmensen 2017). The Greenlandic government, by contrast, sees Chinese investments as a way to generate much-needed capital for its economy and uses the specter of Chinese involvement as leverage vis-à-vis Denmark and the United States. The low global prices of natural resources have thus far meant that none of these projects have become operational (C. N. Sørensen 2017), so the underlying divergence of interests has therefore remained latent, but it could lead to a clash between the three parties in the future.

Third, Denmark has become engaged in regional diplomacy and institution-building in order to enhance cooperation and diminish the risk of great-power tensions. Military tensions in the Arctic would stretch Denmark's limited Arctic capabilities and necessitate investments in High North defense as well as a strengthened American presence in Greenland. This development would, in turn, weaken Denmark's ability to demonstrate its sovereignty over the island and complicate its already strained relationship with the Greenlandic government (Jørgensen and Rahbek-Clemmensen 2009, 28–33; Rahbek-Clemmensen, Larsen, and Rasmussen 2012, 50–57).

Russia's 2007 flag-planting on the North Pole seabed led Danish policymakers to recognize that the opening of the Arctic could lead to military tensions. Denmark and Greenland invited the Arctic coastal states to the 2008 Ilulissat meeting, where they acknowledged the importance of regional cooperation and declared that regional boundary disputes should be settled in accordance with international law ("The Ilulissat Declaration" 2008; Petersen 2009; Jacobsen and Strandsbjerg 2017; Rahbek-Clemmensen 2017a; Rahbek-Clemmensen and Thomasen 2018). Denmark developed an Arctic strategy that emphasized the importance of regional cooperation and tailored Danish activities to diminish great-power tensions, which included engaging Russia, China, Japan, and the United States in regional institutions. The activities of the Danish Armed Forces became focused on signaling peaceful intensions and enhancing military and coast guard cooperation (Government of Denmark, Government of Greenland, and Government of the Faroe Islands 2011; Rahbek-Clemmensen 2017a). The Danish diplomatic effort has concurrently been complicated by the Greenlandic insistence on having a separate voice in international affairs, as illustrated by the embarrassment caused by Greenland's boycott of the 2013 Arctic Council Ministerial (Olsen and Shadian 2016).

Several recent policies illustrate this approach in action. For instance, Denmark's extensive 2014 continental shelf submission was made in accordance with international law and was coordinated with the governments of Russia and Canada (Danish Ministry of Foreign Affairs and Government of Greenland 2014). Similarly, unlike other Western countries, the Danish government was careful to keep criticisms of Russia out of Arctic forums during the Ukraine Crisis and Denmark remains skeptical of the value of an enhanced role for NATO in the region (Kristensen and Sakstrup 2016; Rahbek-Clemmensen 2017b).

Finally, the prospect of an active uranium mine in Kvanefjeld has introduced nuclear nonproliferation as a new issue in Danish–Greenlandic relations. Denmark's nonproliferation obligations, such as those deriving from the Nuclear Nonproliferation Treaty, have forced Denmark to adopt legislation on safeguards and export control for Greenland. The process has highlighted a fundamental ambiguity regarding the boundary between Denmark and Greenland's spheres of authority, as the two governments disagreed about whether the export of uranium ore concentrates is a foreign policy issue (and thus within Denmark's purview) or a resource policy issue (and thus under Greenlandic authority). A 2016 compromise, the so-called Uranium Agreement, created a new division of power, whereby Greenland accepted that Denmark has the final say over issues related to nonproliferation and export but Greenland maintains control over safety issues, such as environment regulation. In addition, Nuuk has full responsibility for licensing mining operations (Vestergaard and Thomasen 2015, 2016).

Conclusion

Greenland illustrates the enduring importance of shifting local conditions and Inuit empowerment for both civilian and political–military security. Danish sovereignty over Greenland has always been precarious, as foreign nations either challenged Denmark's position or created their own sovereign presence on the island, as the United States has done since the early 1940s. In recent decades, Greenland has become an actor in its own right; this has further complicated the civilian and political–military security challenges created by the end of the Cold War, globalization, and climate change.

Different civilian and political–military security issues have experienced different shifts. Some civilian security challenges, such as societal and economic security, have become an internal Greenlandic matter. For instance, while threats against Greenlandic identity during the Cold War were largely caused by outside forces such as American interference and Danish modernization programs, today the main threat to traditional ways of life is industrial activity, which is spurred on by the government in Nuuk. Other civilian security challenges, such as safety at sea beyond three nautical miles from the coast, remain a Danish responsibility; the expected increase in activity has necessitated a stronger Danish presence. Increased Greenlandic autonomy has also changed political–military security dynamics, as the government in Nuuk has inserted itself into issues that had been exclusively within Denmark's purview. Perhaps most importantly, the prospect of large-scale Chinese mining activity endorsed by the Greenlandic government could complicate the American presence on the island. Whereas international security was once something that happened over the heads of the Greenlandic people, Greenland has now gained its own voice.

Acknowledgments

The author would like to thank Gry Thomasen, the editors of this volume, as well as the anonymous reviewers for their helpful feedback and comments. The research for this chapter is supported by the Carlsberg Foundation.

References

Ackrén, Maria, and Uffe Jakobsen. 2015. "Greenland as a Self-Governing Sub-National Territory in International Relations: Past, Current and Future Perspectives." *Polar Record* 51 (4): 404–12.

Archer, Clive. 1988. "The United States Defence Areas in Greenland." *Cooperation and Conflict* 23 (3): 123–44. doi:10.1177/001083678802300302.

Archer, Clive. 2003. "Greenland, US Bases and Missile Defence." *Cooperation and Conflict* 38 (2): 125–47.

Berry, Dawn A. 2012. "Cryolite, the Canadian Aluminium Industry and the American Occupation of Greenland during the Second World War." *The Polar Journal* 2 (2): 219–35.

Berry, Dawn A. 2016. "The Monroe Doctrine and the Governance of Greenland's Security." In *Governing the North American Arctic – Sovereignty, Security, and Institutions*, edited by Dawn A. Berry, Nigel Bowles, and Halbert Jones, 103–21. London: Palgrave Macmillan.

Beukel, Erik, Frede P. Jensen, and Jens Elo Rytter. 2010. *Phasing Out the Colonial Status of Greenland, 1945–54: A Historical Study*. Copenhagen: Museum Tusculanum Press.

Boersma, Tim, and Kevin Foley. 2014. "The Greenland Gold Rush – Promise and Pitfalls of Greenland's Energy and Mineral Resources." Washington, DC: The Brookings Institution.

Bryld, Tine. 1998. *I Den Bedste Mening*. Nuuk: Atuakkiorfik.

Buzan, Barry, Ole Wæver, and Jaap de Wilde. 1998. *Security: A New Framework for Analysis*. Boulder, CO: Lynne Rienner Publishers.

Christensen, Svend Aage, and Kristian S. Kristensen. 2009. "Greenlanders Displaced by the Cold War: Relocation and Compensation." In *Historical Justice in International Perspective: How Societies Are Trying to Right the Wrongs of the Past*, edited by Bernd Schaefer and Manfred Berg, 111–31. Cambridge: Cambridge University Press.

Danish Defense Intelligence Service. 2016. "Intelligence Risk Assessment 2016." Copenhagen.

Danish Institute for International Affairs. 1997. *Grønland under den Kolde Krig: Dansk og Amerikansk Sikkerhedspolitik 1945–68*. Copenhagen: Danish Institute for International Studies.

Danish Institute for International Studies. 2005. *Danmark under den Kolde Krig: Den Sikkerhedspolitiske Situation 1945–1991*. Copenhagen: Danish Institute for International Studies.

Danish Ministry of Defense. 2016. "Forsvarets Fremtidige Opgaveløsning i Arktis." Copenhagen: Ministry of Defense.

Danish Ministry of Foreign Affairs, and Government of Greenland. 2014. "Partial Submission of the Government of the Kingdom of Denmark Together with the Government of Greenland to the Commission on the Limits of the Continental Shelf – The Northern Continental Shelf of Greenland." Copenhagen: Geological Survey of Denmark and Greenland.

DNV GL AS DNV GL Oil & Gas. 2015. "Marine Environmental Risk Assessment – Greenland." Høvik: BDL Newbuilding.

Doel, Ronald E. 2016. "Defending the North American Continent: Why the Physical Environmental Sciences Mattered in Cold War Greenland." In *Exploring Greenland: Cold War Science and Technology on Ice*, edited by Ronald E. Doel, Kristine C. Harper, and Matthias Heymann, 25–46. New York: Palgrave Macmillan.

Gad, Ulrik P. 2016. *National Identity Politics and Postcolonial Sovereignty Games: Greenland, Denmark, and the European Union*. Copenhagen: Museum Tusculanums Forlag.

Gerhardt, Hannes. 2011. "The Inuit and Sovereignty: The Case of the Inuit Circumpolar Conference and Greenland." *Tidsskriftet Politik* 14 (1): 6–14.

Government of Canada, Government of the Kingdom of Denmark, Government of the Kingdom of Norway, Government of the Russian Federation and Government of the United States. 2008. The Ilulissat Declaration. May 28, 2008. https://cil.nus.edu.sg/wp-content/uploads/2017/07/2008-Ilulissat-Declaration.pdf

Government of Denmark. 2009. *Lov Om Grønlands Selvstyre. Lovtidende A*. Vol. 473.

Government of Denmark, Government of Greenland, and Government of the Faroe Islands. 2011. "Strategy for the Arctic 2011–2020." Copenhagen: Ministry of Foreign Affairs.

Gramer, Robbie. 2016. "Russia's Ambitions in the Atlantic." Foreign Affairs Snapshot. September 9, 2016. www.foreignaffairs.com/articles/2016-09-09/russias-ambitions-atlantic.

Hansen, Violeta, Jens Søndergaard, Gert Asmund, Peter Aastrup, Kim Gustavson, Gabriela Garcia, Josephine Nymand, and Morten B. Larsen. 2016. "Exploitation of Radioactive Minerals in Greenland: Management of Environmental Issues Based on Experience from Uranium Producing Countries." Aarhus: Danish Centre for Environment and Energy.

Heinrich, Jens. 2017. "Independence through International Affairs: How Foreign Relations Shaped Greenlandic Identity Before 1979." In *Greenland and the International Politics of a Changing Arctic – Postcolonial Paradiplomacy between High and Low Politics*, edited by Kristian S. Kristensen and Jon Rahbek-Clemmensen, 28–37. London: Routledge.

Henriksen, Anders, and Jon Rahbek-Clemmensen. 2017. "The Greenland Card: Prospects for and Barriers to Danish Arctic Diplomacy in Washington." In *Danish Foreign Policy Yearbook 2017*, edited by Hans Mouritzen and Kristian Fischer, 75–98. Copenhagen: Danish Institute for International Studies.

Howard, John. 2011. "Fixed Sonar Systems: The History and Future of the Underwater Silent Sentinel." *The Submarine Review*. 1–12.

Jacobsen, Marc, and Jeppe Strandsbjerg. 2017. "Desecuritization as Displacement of Controversy: Geopolitics, Law and Sovereign Rights in the Arctic." *Politik* 20 (3): 15–30.

Jakobsen, Uffe, and Biritaí Dali. 2016. "The Greenlandic Sea Areas and Activity Level Up to 2025." In *Maritime Activity in the High* North – *Current and Estimated Level up to 2025*, edited by Odd J. Borch, Natalia Andreassen, Nataly Marchenko, Valur Ingimundarson, Halla Gunnarsdottir, Iurii Iudin, Sergey Petrov, Uffe Jakobsen, and Birita í Dali, 86–111. MARPA Project Report 1. Bodø: Nord Universitetet.

Jakobsen, Uffe, and Bolette Kern. 2016. "Maritime Activity Risk Patterns and Types of Unwanted Incidents. The Greenlandic Sea Areas." In *Maritime Activity and Risk Patterns in the High North*, edited by Odd J. Borch, Natalia Andreassen, Nataly Marchenko, Valur Ingimundarson, Halla Gunnarsdottir, Uffe Jakobsen, Bolette Kern, et al., 87–106. MARPA Project Report 2. Bodø: Nord Universitetet.

Jørgensen, Henrik J., and Jon Rahbek-Clemmensen. 2009. "Keep It Cool! Four Scenarios for the Danish Armed Forces in Greenland in 2030." Copenhagen: Danish Institute for Military Studies.

Juel, Knud, Gerda Engholm, and Hans Storm. 2005. "Registerundersøgelse Af Dødelighed Og Kræftforekomst Blandt Thulearbejdere, 2005." Copenhagen: Ministry for the Interior and Health.

Kristensen, Kristian S. 2005. "Negotiating Base Rights for Missile Defence – The Case of Thule Air Base in Greenland." In *Missile Defence – International, Regional and National Implications*, edited by Bertel Heurlin and Sten Rynning, 183–207. London: Routledge.

Kristensen, Kristian S., and Jon Rahbek-Clemmensen. 2017. "Greenlandic Sovereignty in Practice – Uranium, Independence, and Foreign Relations in Greenland between Three Logics of Security." In *Greenland and the International Politics of a Changing Arctic – Postcolonial Paradiplomacy between High and Low Politics*, edited by Kristian S. Kristensen and Jon Rahbek-Clemmensen, 38–35. London: Routledge.

Kristensen, Kristian S., and Casper Sakstrup. 2016. "Russian Policy in the Arctic after the Ukraine Crisis." Copenhagen: Center for Military Studies. http://cms.polsci.ku.dk/publikationer/russian-policy-in-the-arctic_kopi/.

Lidegaard, Bo. 1996. *I Kongens Navn : Henrik Kauffmann i Dansk Diplomati 1919–1958*. Copenhagen: Samleren.

Mortensen, Bent O. G. 2013. "The Quest for Resources – The Case of Greenland." *Journal of Military and Strategic Studies* 15 (2): 93–128.

Mouritzen, Hans. 2007. "Denmark's Super Atlanticism." *Journal of Transatlantic Studies* 5 (2): 155–67.

Nielsen, Henry, and Kristian H. Nielsen. 2016. "Camp Century – Cold War City under the Ice." In *Exploring Greenland: Cold War Science and Technology on Ice*, edited by Ronald E. Doel, Kristine C. Harper, and Matthias Heymann, 195–216. New York: Palgrave Macmillan.

Nielsen, Jørgen S. 2016. "Camp Century – En Iskold Gyser Om Fortidens Synder." *Information*. August 10, 2016, sec. 1.

Nielsen, Kristian H. 2016. "Small State Preoccupations: Science and Technology in the Pursuit of Modernization, Security, and Sovereignty in Greenland." In *Exploring Greenland: Cold War Science and Technology on Ice*, edited by Ronald E. Doel, Kristine C. Harper, and Matthias Heymann, 47–71. New York: Palgrave Macmillan.

Nuttall, Mark. 2013. "Zero-Tolerance, Uranium and Greenland's Mining Future." *The Polar Journal* 3 (2): 368–83.

Olesen, Mikkel R. 2017. "Lightning Rod: The US, Greenlandic and Danish Relations in the Shadow of Post-Colonial Reputations." In *Greenland and the International Politics of a Changing Arctic – Postcolonial Paradiplomacy between High and Low Politics*, edited by Kristian S. Kristensen and Jon Rahbek-Clemmensen, 70–82. London: Routledge.

Olsen, Inuuteq H., and Jessica M. Shadian. 2016. "Greenland & the Arctic Council: Subnational Regions in a Time of Arctic Westphalianisation." *Arctic Yearbook* 5: 229–50.

Petersen, Nikolaj. 2009. "The Arctic as a New Arena for Danish Foreign Policy: The Ilulissat Initiative and Its Implications." In *Danish Foreign Policy Yearbook 2009*, edited by Nanna Hvidt and Hans Mouritzen, 35–78. Copenhagen: Danish Institute for International Studies.

Petersen, Nikolaj. 2011. "SAC at Thule: Greenland in U.S. Polar Strategy." *Journal of Cold War Studies* 13 (2): 90–115.

Public Accounts Committee. 2013. "Beretning Om Danmarks Indsats i Arktis." 16. Copenhagen: Public Accounts Committee.

Rahbek-Clemmensen, Jon. 2016. "'An Arctic Great Power'? Recent Developments in Danish Arctic Policy." *Arctic Yearbook* 5: 346–59.

Rahbek-Clemmensen, Jon. 2017a. "The Arctic Turn – How Did the High North Become a Foreign and Security Policy Priority for Denmark?" In *Greenland and the International Politics of a Changing Arctic – Postcolonial Paradiplomacy between High and Low Politics*, edited by Kristian S. Kristensen and Jon Rahbek-Clemmensen, 54–69. London: Routledge.
Rahbek-Clemmensen, Jon. 2017b. "The Ukraine Crisis Moves North. Is Arctic Conflict Spill-over Driven by Material Interests?" *Polar Record* 53 (1): 1–15.
Rahbek-Clemmensen, Jon. 2020. "Arctic by Proxy – How Denmark's Bilateral Relationship to Greenland Shapes Its Arctic Policy." In *The Routledge Handbook of Arctic Politics*, edited by Anita D. Nuttall and Mark Nuttall. London: Routledge. [Forthcoming.].
Rahbek-Clemmensen, Jon, Esben S. Larsen, and Mikkel V. Rasmussen. 2012. "Forsvaret i Arktis – Suverænitet, Samarbejde Og Sikkerhed." Copenhagen: Center for Military Studies.
Rahbek-Clemmensen, Jon, and Gry Thomasen. 2018. "Learning from the Ilulissat Initiative: State Power, Institutional Legitimacy, and Governance in the Arctic Ocean, 2007–18." Copenhagen: Center for Military Studies.
Rasmussen, Mikkel V. 2013. "Greenland Geopolitics: Globalisation and Geopolitics in the New North." Copenhagen: Committee for Greenlandic Mineral Resources to the Benefit of Society.
Ringsmose, Jens, and Sten Rynning. 2008. "The Impeccable Ally? Denmark, NATO, and the Uncertain Future of Top Tier Membership." In *Danish Foreign Policy Yearbook 2008*, edited by Nanna Hvidt and Hans Mouritzen, 55–84. Copenhagen: Danish Institute for International Studies.
Rosing, Minik, Karen Hanghøj, and Per Kalvig. 2014. "Den Geologiske Baggrund for Grønlands Naturressourcer." Copenhagen: University of Copenhagen.
Sejersen, Frank. 2014. "Efterforskning Og Udnyttelse Af Råstoffer i Grønland i Historisk Perspektiv." To the Benefit of Greenland Background Paper. Copenhagen: University of Copenhagen.
Sørensen, Axel K. 2009. *Denmark-Greenland in the Twentieth Century*. Copenhagen: Museum Tusculanum Press.
Sørensen, Camilla N. 2017. "Promises and Risks of Chinese Investments in Greenland Seen from Nuuk, Copenhagen and Beijing." In *Greenland and the International Politics of a Changing Arctic - Postcolonial Paradiplomacy between High and Low Politics*, edited by Kristian S. Kristensen and Jon Rahbek-Clemmensen, 83–97. London: Routledge.
Stashwick, Steven. 2016. "US Navy Upgrading Undersea Sub-Detecting Sensor Network | The Diplomat." The Diplomat. November 4, 2016. http://thediplomat.com/2016/11/us-navy-upgrading-undersea-sub-detecting-sensor-network/.
Steensgaard, Bo M., Henrik Stendal, Per Kalvig, and Karen Hanghøj. 2017. "Review of Potential Resources for Critical Minerals in Greenland." Copenhagen: Center for Minerals and Materials.
Thorsen, Rosa. 2011. "Arktisk Kommando Placeres i Nuuk." Sermitsiaq. August 25, 2011. http://sermitsiaq.ag/node/106240.
Vestergaard, Cindy, and Gry Thomasen. 2015. "Governing Uranium in the Danish Realm." Copenhagen: Danish Institute for International Studies.
Vestergaard, Cindy, and Gry Thomasen. 2016. "New Uranium Deal between Denmark and Greenland Clarifies Competences." DIIS Comment. Copenhagen: Danish Institute for International Studies.
Wilkening, Dean A. 2004. *Ballistic-Missile Defence and Strategic Stability*. Adelphi Paper 334. London: Institute for International Strategic Studies.

16

SMALL STATE, BIG IMPACT?

Iceland's first National Security Policy

Page Wilson and Auður H. Ingólfsdóttir

In April 2016, Iceland published its first National Security Policy (NSP). The culmination of eight years of work, it re-examined the security context in which Iceland operates (Althingi 2016a)[1]. The timing and necessity of the NSP can be explained by reference to both international and domestic factors. The changing geopolitical landscape and the anticipated climate change-driven increase in all kinds of human activity in the Arctic region has motivated Iceland, like other Arctic states, to reconsider the meaning of security and articulate new goals for the area (Althingi 2011).[2]

Against this international backdrop, two major domestic events triggered the process that led to Iceland's NSP: (a) the unilateral US decision in 2006 to close its military base at Keflavik; and (b) the 2008 financial crisis, one of the early signs of what was later to become the Global Financial Crisis. These domestic factors highlighted the fact that long-held assumptions about Icelandic security, whether conceived as a narrower military-focused notion or as broader and more inclusive social concerns, could no longer be taken for granted. Thus, conditions were ripe for a fresh and comprehensive review. The aim of this chapter is to analyze the NSP's content, with a view to revealing fresh insight into Iceland's latest security stance. Before turning to this task, the chapter will first consider the wider domestic and international context from which Iceland's NSP has emerged.

Thinking about security: the Icelandic context

There are – and always have been – deep tensions in Iceland's security identity.[3] On the one hand, Iceland is a small state in geographic and demographic terms – a relatively remote island in the North Atlantic. Like other small states, its material resources are therefore limited and it must apply these limited resources to its own priority issue-areas. From this small-state perspective, it is improbable that the country would have much to contribute in practical terms to wider international concerns, and thus it must survive in a world largely of others' making. Although Iceland can and does work in concert with other small and middle-sized powers in an attempt to effect change regionally and internationally,[4] its own clout is significantly curtailed.

With respect to traditional security issues, this small-state security identity helps explain why Iceland: (a) has never maintained any armed forces of its own; (b) remained politically neutral during World War II, despite the presence of American and British forces; (c) has committed to "working against any kind of militarization of the Arctic";[5] and (d) has an international reputation for implementing and promoting peaceful values, including democracy and gender equality:[6] a reputation Iceland actively seeks to promote abroad.[7]

On the other hand, Iceland has a second security identity which belies its small-state status. Despite its resource constraints, Iceland's location and territory have proven strategically important to larger powers, as demonstrated in World War II and the Cold War. During the former conflict, Iceland provided an ideal location for basing air and naval forces in defense of the sea lanes and skies of the western and central Atlantic Ocean – key supply routes for the United Kingdom (Zabecki 1999, 1538). In the latter conflict, Iceland hosted important installations and a US military command post that contributed to tracking Soviet activities in and across the Greenland–Iceland–United Kingdom (GIUK) gap.[8] These contributions were not only directly important for the larger powers involved, but they also indirectly facilitated the creation of a wider international order that recognized Iceland's independence and preserved its own national interests. From this perspective, Iceland cannot simply be thought of as a small state. Rather, its ability to have a disproportionate impact on national, regional and international security more accurately characterizes its security identity (Kochis and Slattery 2016, 1).

Reflecting this second *big-impact* understanding of Iceland's security identity, Iceland: (a) in 1949 became a founding member of the North Atlantic Treaty Organization (NATO), the world's premier military alliance; and (b) in 1951 entered a bilateral defense agreement with the United States, legalizing the presence of the US military in Iceland and therefore also that of NATO (Ingimundarson 2007, 14).[9] At this time, Iceland's political neutrality was abandoned – a fact that, even today, sits uncomfortably with Iceland's small-state security persona. In addition, in 2003, Iceland joined the "coalition of the willing" in support of the 2003 US-led invasion of Iraq. (The White House 2003). Although the United States withdrew its troops and military hardware from Iceland in 2006, NATO air policing missions have regularly taken place there since 2008 (Pétursson 2014, 33).

Furthermore, when Icelandic and great-power interests have diverged, Iceland has demonstrated its adroitness at using these security arrangements as leverage to get its own way. For instance, during Iceland's series of so-called Cod Wars with the UK between 1958 and 1976, Iceland threatened to leave NATO unless the fishing dispute was resolved (Ingimundarson 2003, 114). Iceland also demonstrated its willingness to use the US military presence in Iceland as a bargaining chip in the fishing dispute (Ingimundarson 2003, 115). Despite the overwhelming superiority of British maritime capabilities vis-a-vis the Icelandic Coast Guard, Iceland largely achieved its goals – namely, the expansion of its fishing zones. Cold War-driven American and British concerns that Iceland might actually carry out its threats by withdrawing its security cooperation helped explain Iceland's success against the odds (Habeeb 1988, 127).

This tension between Iceland's security identities – the peace- and democracy-loving small state on the one hand versus the canny big-impact traditional security actor on the other – reflects divisions within Iceland itself. Given that the ultimate responsibility for Iceland's survival and prosperity, both domestically and on the international stage, rests with its government, it is no surprise that the executive has prioritized the latter security identity. In contrast, public opinion – and some elements within the Parliament – strongly favors Iceland's small-state identity. Recent examples of how this tension between the two security identities has played out in domestic political discourse include debates about the role of the Icelandic Crisis Response Unit (ICRU) in international peacekeeping missions[10] as well as 2016 parliamentary discussions about the NSP, during which several MPs expressed concern that it was too militarily focused (Althingi 2016a).[11]

In light of this ongoing tension, one might wonder how it was possible for sufficient consensus to be reached on the NSP for it to be passed by a parliamentary resolution (Althingi 2016a).[12] Part of the answer lies in the text of the NSP itself. Instead of resolving the tension between Iceland's security identities, the NSP largely preserves it. For instance, the "fundamental premise" underpinning the NSP is described in the following terms:

> Iceland's status as a sparsely populated island nation that has neither the resources nor the desire to maintain an army and provides for its security and defense through active cooperation, both with other countries and within international organizations.
>
> *(preamble, Para 3)*

While this tension is specific to Iceland, parallels can be drawn between Iceland's NSP and other countries' recent approaches to national security policy. These are examined in the next section.

Iceland's NSP in international context

It is useful to consider Iceland's NSP against the backdrop of other post-9/11 efforts by Western governments to bring the formulation and implementation of security policy out of the shadows and into the public domain. Prior to 9/11, detailed, open statements about national security policy were few and far between; typically, the design and execution of security policy were entrusted to a small group of high-ranking members drawn from the national political and military elite, with the populace kept at arm's length from the process. However, the changed nature of security threats highlighted by the 9/11 attacks – and in particular the growing awareness of the important contributions that ordinary citizens, various government agencies, and foreign allies can make to combat terrorism and other transnational threats – required a fresh approach (President of the United States 2002). Since 2001, the United States, United Kingdom, and Finland have released three national security strategies each (President of the United States 2002, 2010, 2015; Prime Minister's Office (Finland) 2004, 2009, 2012; United Kingdom Cabinet Office 2008, 2010, 2015); the European Union has published its own security strategy (European External Action Service 2003); and Norway and NATO have released their respective Strategic Concept documents (Norwegian Ministry of Defence 2009; NATO 2010).[13] While Iceland's first NSP took longer to materialize, it is part of this broader trend.

In contrast to the narrow, state-centric, military-oriented concept of security traditionally relied upon by state governments, the notion of security underpinning these recent security strategies is an expanded one, covering environmental, economic, health, and energy issues in addition to military matters (President of the United States 2015).This is equally true of Iceland's NSP, which addresses "global, societal and military risks" (preamble, Para 4).[14] Indeed, the extent to which Iceland has adopted this new approach to security is evident from the NSP's first stated goal:

> To ensure the protection of Iceland's broad security interests through active international cooperation on the basis of international law and with peaceful resolution of conflicts, disarmament, respect for human rights and the rule of law, gender equality, and the fight against inequality, hunger and poverty as guiding principles.
>
> *Althingi (2016b)*

Although Iceland's NSP does not explicitly prioritize certain security issues over others – claiming instead that each listed issue carries "equal weight" (preamble, Para 5) – some hierarchy is apparent from the language of the text. For instance, the NSP refers to giving "*particular* consideration to Iceland's environmental and security interests in the Arctic" (Para 2) and to ensuring that "Iceland's membership of the North Atlantic Treaty Organization (NATO) remains a *key* pillar in its defense and the *main forum* for Western cooperation" (Para 3) (emphases are the authors'). This ostensibly no-priority approach departs from the preparatory work completed by Iceland's Committee for the Development of an NSP in 2014 and from the approach employed in the American and British national security strategies.[15] In contrast, in terms of process and procedure, Iceland's creation of a national security council and its decision to review the NSP "at intervals of no more than five years" (numbered para 11) follows in the footsteps of the UK's approach to national security strategy (Her Majesty's Government (UK) 2015).

With regard to those "global, societal and military risks" confronted by Iceland, the NSP outlines a three-pronged response: (a) an active foreign affairs policy, (b) civil security, and (c) defense cooperation (preamble, Para 4). It is towards each of these areas that we shall now turn.

An active foreign affairs policy

The wider political context within which Iceland asserts its security identities is evident from various themes highlighted in the NSP. As previously mentioned, Paragraph 2 underscores "particular consideration" for Iceland's Arctic-based environmental and security interests. This priority corresponds with increased attention to the Arctic in Icelandic foreign policy over the last eight years (Ministry for Foreign Affairs 2009b; Althingi 2011). The measured language of Paragraph 2 is also noteworthy, as it highlights a shift away from the somewhat panicked tone of Iceland's Arctic Policy, which included the aims of "securing Iceland's position as a coastal state within the Arctic region" and the development of "arguments which support this objective." Since 2011, the strengthening of the Arctic Council as the main forum for Arctic affairs – supplanting the Arctic Five meeting, to which Iceland has never been invited – may have helped assuage Icelandic concerns.

Similarly, Iceland's status as a Nordic state is featured in the NSP. Paragraph 5 highlights the importance of building further Nordic cooperation on security and defense. Although the Nordic states have cooperated on a broad range of issues for decades, this cooperation generally excluded security-related topics[16]. The 2009 Stoltenberg Report, which was introduced at a meeting of Nordic foreign ministers, changed this approach by placing security firmly on the Nordic agenda (Stoltenberg 2009). The creation of Nordic Defense Cooperation (NORDEFCO) in the same year has provided a dedicated forum for Nordic states to engage more consistently in security dialogue and cooperation.

A third point to note about foreign affairs is that despite the NSP's emphasis on both regional and international cooperation, it makes no reference to the EU. This is rather odd, given the close collaboration Iceland shares with the EU on a number of international issues through the European Economic Area (EEA) agreement.[17] Although this agreement does not cover security and defense matters per se, it does cover some issues which could fall within the broader notion of security – for example, the environment, and research and development. Given the controversy in domestic politics about whether Iceland should apply for EU membership, it is possible that reference to the EU was left out to avoid language that may have threatened the NSP consensus.[18]

Civil security

The NSP's provisions concerning civil security reflect the new, wider security paradigm described earlier. Paragraphs 7, 8, and 9 all relate to different aspects of civil security. Paragraph 7 states the need to:

> Ensure that the Government's policy on civil protection and security, which is formulated by the Protection and Civil Security Council, is an integral part of the national security policy, and that consideration is given therein to threats related to climate change, natural disasters, food safety and security, health safety issues, and epidemics.
>
> *(Althingi 2016b)*

This emphasis on integrating civil security concerns into the NSP is a clear change of approach from before, when politicians usually discussed civil security and military security as separate topics. Given Iceland's reliance on its natural resources, its harsh weather conditions, and the constant danger that comes with living on an active volcanic island, civil security has always been an important topic in Icelandic politics. However, it has historically been dealt with under domestic policy and not been associated with national security. This was clearly demonstrated in 2008, when two security-related acts were passed in Parliament: one on defense matters (Althingi 2008a) and the other on civil security (Althingi 2008b). The MPs themselves frequently emphasized the need to address civil security and military security separately (Ómarsdóttir 2008, 144). The NSP takes a different approach, however, embracing civil and societal security as important components of national security. This is in line with the expanded understanding of security underpinning the previously mentioned 2009 Risk Assessment for Iceland (The Ministry for Foreign Affairs 2009a).

In addition to topics that have traditionally been part of civil security, such as threats related to natural disasters, food safety and security, and health safety issues, the NSP also lists cybersecurity (Para 8) and terrorism and organized crime (Para 9) as priorities. Both topics were discussed in Iceland's 2009 Risk Assessment. Iceland released its own cybersecurity policy in 2015, examining the individual security of internet users as well as the capacity of the state to defend itself against cyber-attacks (Ministry for Interior 2015). With regard to terrorism, while Iceland has not experienced an attack on its territory, recent attacks in several European countries ensure that terrorism remains a significant, if latent, security concern. Reflecting this, the Icelandic government announced in June 2017 that police officers would carry visible weapons during summer mass-events, including on Iceland's national day (17 June) (Kolbeinsson 2017, 1). This executive decision, taken without any parliamentary debate, does not sit easily with a populace that favors Iceland's peaceful small-state security identity[19].

A final point to mention is the inclusion of threats to financial and economic security in Paragraph 9. Such threats were not mentioned at all during the political debate over the pair of security-related laws enacted in 2008 (Ómarsdóttir 2008, 152), and the 2009 Risk Assessment only briefly refers to them. The Global Financial Crisis of 2008–2009, which led to the collapse of Icelandic banks, had put financial security on the security agenda in Iceland. This ongoing preoccupation is reflected in the NSP.

Defense cooperation

Regarding Iceland's second security identity – as a big-impact traditional security actor – defense-related issues remain an important theme within Iceland's NSP. Of its eleven paragraphs, five specifically cite defense matters.[20] As indicated above, Paragraph 3 of the NSP emphasizes the linchpin role of Icelandic membership of NATO in terms of the former's defense arrangements and as the *main* – but not necessarily *exclusive* – arena for Western cooperation. The provision goes on to point out that the nature of Iceland's participation is "on civil premises, in order to strengthen its own security and that of other NATO members." In a similar vein, Paragraph 4 stresses the need:

> To ensure that the 1951 defense agreement between Iceland and the United States continues to provide for Iceland's defense, and that cooperation between the two countries continues to be developed on the basis of the agreement, which takes account of military threats and other risks where mutual defense and security interests are at stake.'
>
> *(Althingi 2016b)*

Both of these provisions imply anxiety about NATO's role with respect to Iceland in the wake of the US decision in 2006 to close its base at Keflavik, as well as Iceland's role with respect to the alliance. To what extent are the United States and NATO meeting their responsibilities to Iceland – particularly in light of changes in the international security environment since 2006 – and vice versa? Furthermore, how is Iceland's contribution to the military alliance to be valued – given its civilian and strategic, territorial nature – in comparison with the contributions of other members, many of whom provide material support in the form of money, troops, and military assets? These sorts of questions led the commission that produced the 2009 Risk Assessment to conclude: (a) "a renewed discussion in Iceland over its position within NATO and its contribution to the Alliance is called for" (Ministry for Foreign Affairs 2009a, 12), and (b) a real need existed for clarification of "the status of the Defense Agreement ... following the departure of the US military forces and within the context of security cooperation with other countries" (Ministry for Foreign Affairs 2009a, 12). In terms of Iceland's domestic politics, by 2014, multiparty support existed for Iceland's continued NATO membership, though one party remained firmly opposed (Bailes and Olafsson 2014, 2).

Paragraph 5 of the NSP highlights an intent to further develop security and defense cooperation with the Nordic countries – an obvious step, in light of the Iceland–NATO uncertainties mentioned above. Since the establishment of NORDEFCO in 2009, cooperation among the five Nordic states has already increased in the areas of cyber-defense and airspace surveillance (EU Info Centre 2014). In this way, Iceland is banding together with other small Nordic states to pursue common interests.

Paragraph 6 focuses on the "defense infrastructure, equipment, capacity, and expertise needed both to respond to the challenges facing [Iceland] in connection with security and defense and to honor its international commitments." This provision reflects a newfound understanding of the flexibility of defense assets, which are not only about defense capability but can also be useful in nonmilitary security situations such as accidents and emergencies. Multi-use assets offer a clear advantage to small states of limited means. This realization has helped Iceland move beyond its previously oversimplified debate between hard and soft security matters (Bailes and Olafsson 2014, 3).

Finally, in pursuit of Iceland's goals of promoting disarmament and peace, Paragraph 10 outlines the intention to declare Iceland and its territorial waters a nuclear weapons-free zone, "subject to Iceland's international commitments." For the present, this aim should not be too difficult to achieve: successive decisions of US governments since 1991 have ended the deployment of nuclear weapons on ships, attack submarines, and naval air bases (Kristensen 2016). Thus, the complete breakdown in defense relations between New Zealand and the United States over the former's declaration of a nuclear weapon- and nuclear power-free zone during the Cold War is unlikely to be repeated in the current Icelandic context.

Conclusions

Iceland's first NSP can be seen as yet another contribution to the wider efforts of Western governments to articulate and hone security policy in response to the changed post-9/11 security landscape. As such, the NSP follows the trend of adopting a broadened notion of security, going beyond traditional military concerns to encompass wide-ranging topics such as environmental, economic, energy, and cybersecurity.

At the heart of the Icelandic approach to security is a tension between competing identities – the small-state identity on the one hand and the big-impact identity on the other. The NSP should be examined with this double security identity in mind. At times, this tension has manifested itself as a domestic power battle between the Icelandic executive, which favors a more traditional, strategic, *realpolitik* understanding of security, and a segment of Parliament, supported by public opinion, that prefers to think of Iceland as the quintessentially unarmed, pacifist small state.

The NSP does not try to resolve this tension. Instead, it is inclusive of both, embracing the broader security issues relevant for civil and societal security as well as traditional military and defense matters. The NSP has therefore attracted widespread support across Iceland's political spectrum. For the same reason, it is likely that the ways in which the NSP is implemented will perpetuate the tension between Iceland's security identities for some time to come.

Notes

1 The NSP passed was adopted as an act of Parliament and therefore is in Icelandic. An official translation is available at: https://mfa.is/media/Varnarmal/National-Security-Policy-ENS.pdf

2 Iceland's Arctic policy in English is available at: https://mfa.is/media/nordurlandaskrifstofa/A-Parliamentary-Resolution-on-ICE-Arctic-Policy-approved-by-Althingi.pdf

3 For a further discussion of Iceland's security identity, see (Ingimundarson, 2007).

4 Note, for example, the collective role of Nordic states as *norm entrepreneurs* in fields such as environmental policy, international development and gender equality (Ingebritsen, 2006)

5 See Iceland's Arctic Policy, para 9. What comprises militarization is not defined; one assumes that if, in the future, the US base at Keflavik did reopen by mutual agreement, it would be characterised in a different way.

6 For instance, the Icelandic parliament (Althingi) was established in 930AD, making it one of the oldest parliaments in the world, thereby cementing Iceland's long democratic credentials. In addition, the

Institute for Economics and Peace's Global Peace Index has ranked Iceland as the most peaceful state in the world since 2008, with one exception: in 2010, it came second (Institute for Economic and Peace, 2017). Furthermore, the World Economic Forum's Global Gender Gap Report for 2017 ranked Iceland first in the world for gender equality for the ninth consecutive year (World Economic Forum, 2017).

7 See, for example, the opening of the Hofdi Reykjavik Peace Centre, which bills itself as a "forum for international multidisciplinary cooperation, with an emphasis on the role of small states, cities and citizens in promoting peace" (Hofdi – Reykjavik Peace Centre, n.d.). Another example is the United Nations University-Gender Equality Studies and Training Program (UNU-GEST) postgraduate diploma, a course open to persons from developing countries, hosted by the University of Iceland (GEST, n.d.).

8 The GIUK gap refers to an area in the northern Atlantic Ocean located in the open ocean between Greenland, Iceland and the United Kingdom.

9 Ingimundarson also argues that since the 2006 withdrawal of U.S. forces from Iceland, the 1951 Defense Agreement "has been deprived of its substance."

10 Loftsdóttir and Björnsdóttir (2012) argue that Icelandic politicians deliberately downplay the military dimension of the ICRU's deployment of experts to conflict zones by characterising such acts as humanitarian and part of development cooperation in an effort to depoliticize Iceland's participation in such matters.

11 Some parliamentarians emphasized the need for a broad understanding of security. Valgerður Bjarnadóttir, the chair of the committee that was responsible for the original draft of the NSP, repeatedly expressed concern that security institutions that are cooperating with sister institutions which are part of other states' military establishment tend to want more weapons and behave more like military institutions. She emphasized the importance of keeping Icelandic security institutions such as the Coast Guard and the police force as civil institutions (Althingi 2016a).

12 In fact, all of Iceland's political parties – other than the abstaining Left Greens – voted in favour of the NSP.

13 Although the focus of these Strategic Concepts is more defense-oriented, they still consider wider security issues, such as how to define security, identifying threats, formulating responses, etc.

14 This broadening of security in the Icelandic context can first be noted in a risk assessment report published by the Ministry for Foreign Affairs in 2009. There, a group of experts – in line with international trends – explored security using a broader and more inclusive understanding of the concept than before. The Risk Assessment was also the first Icelandic attempt to map out key security risks for the nation. Prior to this, Iceland had relied on risk assessments conducted by foreign militaries (Ministry of Foreign Affairs, 2009a).

15 Iceland's Committee for the Development of a National Security Policy proposed a three-category system identifying from where threats would come, with Category 1 containing threats that "the committee feels should have priority status in terms of anticipatory measures and financing" at p. 8. The US 2015 National Security Strategy states: "We will prioritize efforts that address the top strategic risks to our interests," and then presents a list of these risks: Similarly, the UK's 2015 National Security Risk Assessment categorizes risks into three tiers on the basis of both their likelihood and impact. For a further discussion of security in the context of the UK's 2015 National Security Strategy, see Wilson (2015).

16 The different situations the Nordic states found themselves in after World War II and during the Cold War explains why there was hesitation among them to focus on conventional security topics. Efforts to set up a Nordic defense union failed when Norway, Denmark, and Iceland decided to join NATO in 1949 (Nordic Council of Ministers, n.d.).

17 The EEA agreement, in force since 1994, brings together the EU member states and three EFTA states (Iceland, Norway, and Lichtenstein) in a single, internal market. In addition to the free movement of goods, services, persons, and capital, the agreement covers cooperation in areas such as research and development, education, social policy, the environment, consumer protection, culture, and tourism (EFTA, n.d.).

18 Iceland applied for EU membership in 2009, nine months after the financial crash. From the beginning, however, the process was heavily debated in Icelandic politics and when a new government took power in 2013 the accession process was put on hold (Thorhallson, 2014, 1).

19 The announcement created some debate. Several bloggers claimed this was an unfortunate and even dangerous development (Brynjarsson, 2017).

20 In addition, reference is made to "security and defense issues" in the context of the newly established National Security Council's role (Para 11).

References

Althingi (2008a). "Varnarmálalög 2008 nr. 34". Retrieved from *Alþingistíðindin* – Web version: https://althingi.is/lagas/nuna/2008034.html.

Althingi (2008b). "Lög um almannavarnir 2008 nr. 82". Retrieved from *Alþingistíðindin* – Web version: https://althingi.is/lagas/146a/2008082.html.

Althingi (2011). "Þingsályktun um stefnu Íslands í málefnumnorðurslóða, þskj. 1148 – 337.mál". Retrieved from *Alþingistíðindin* – Web version: http://althingi.is/altext/139/s/1148.html.

Althingi (2016a). "Þingsályktun um þjóðaröryggisstefnufyrirÍsland, þskj. 1166 – 327. mál". Retrieved from *Alþingistíðindin* – Web version: http://althingi.is/altext/145/s/1166.html.

Althingi (2016b) "Parliamentary Resolution on a National Security Policy for Iceland". Retrieved from https://www.government.is/media/utanrikisraduneyti-media/media/Varnarmal/National-Security-Policy-ENS.pdf

Bailes, Alyson & Olafsson, Kristmundur Thor (2014). *Nordic and Arctic Affairs: Iceland's National Security Policy: Latest Progress.* Reykjavík: University of Iceland, Centre for Small States Studies.

Brynjarsson, Snæbjörn (2017). "Vopnuðlögregla– viðhverjumábúast?" *Stundin.* Retrieved from:https://stundin.is/blogg/snaebjorn-brynjarsson/vopnu-logregla-vi-hverju-ma-buast/.

EFTA (n.d.) "EEA Agreement". Retrieved from webpage: http://efta.int/eea/eea-agreement.

European External Action Service (2003). "A Secure Europe in a Better World: European Security Strategy". Retrieved from: https://europa.eu/globalstrategy/en/european-security-strategy-secure-europe-better-world.

European Union Info Centre (2014). "Committee for the Development of a National Security Policy in Iceland: Proposals". Retrieved from: http://eeas.europa.eu/archives/delegations/iceland/documents/press_corner/20140324_en.pdf.

Habeeb, William Mark (1988). *Power and Tactics in International Negotiations. How Weak Nations Bargain with Strong Nations.* Baltimore and London: University Press.

Her Majesty's Government (UK) (2010). "A Strong Britain in an Age of Uncertainty: The National Security Strategy". Retrieved from webpage: https://gov.uk/government/uploads/system/uploads/attachment_data/file/61936/national-security-strategy.pdf.

Her Majesty's Government (UK) (2015). "National Security Strategy and Strategic Defence and Security Review 2015". Retrieved from: https://gov.uk/government/uploads/system/uploads/attachment_data/file/478933/52309_Cm_9161_NSS_SD_Review_web_only.pdf.

Hofdi Reykjavík Peace Center (n.d.). "About us. Hofdi Reykjavík Peace Center". Retrieved from website: https://fridarsetur.is/en/about-us/.

Ingebritsen, Christina (2006). *Scandinavia in World Politics.* New York: Rowman & Littlefield Publishers.

Ingimundarson, Valur (2003). "A Western Cold War: The Crisis in Iceland's Relations with Britain, the US and NATO, 1971–1974". *Diplomacy and Statecraft* Vol 14(4), pp. 94–136.

Ingimundarson, Valur (2007). "Iceland´s Security Identity Dilemma. The End of U.S. Military Presence". *The Fletcher Forum of World Affairs* Vol 31, pp. 7–23.

Institute for Economic and Peace (2017). *Global Peace Index 2017.* Sidney: Institute for Economic and Peace.

Kochis, Daniel & Slattery, Brian (2016). "Iceland: Outsized Importance for Transatlantic Security". *Backgrounder No. 3121.*The Heritage Foundation. Retrieved from webpage: http://heritage.org/global-politics/report/iceland-outsized-importance-transatlantic-security.

Kolbeinsson, JóhannBjarni (2017). "Lögregla verður vopnuð 17.Júní. RÚV". Retrived from website: http://ruv.is/frett/logregla-verdur-vopnud-17-juni.

Kristensen, Hans M (2016). "Declassified: US Nuclear Weapons at Sea". Retrieved from: https://fas.org/blogs/security/2016/02/nuclear-weapons-at-sea/.

Loftsdóttir, Kristín & Björnsdóttir, Helga (2012). "Unpolitical Wars: Presentations of Conflict in Development and Foreign Policy Discourses in Iceland". *International Peacekeeping* Vol 19(1), pp. 35–47.

Ministry for Foreign Affairs (2009a). "A Risk Assessment for Iceland: Global, Societal and Military Factors. English Summary". Retrieved from webpage: https://mfa.is/media/Skyrslur/A_Risk_Assessment_for_Iceland_-_English_Summary.pdf.

Ministry for Foreign Affairs (2009b). "Ísland á norðurslóðum". Retrieved from webpage: https://stjornarradid.is/media/utanrikisraduneyti-media/media/Skyrslur/Skyrslan_Island_a_nordurslodumm.pdf.

Ministry for Interior (2015). "Net- og upplýsingaöryggi. Stefna 2015–2026". Retrieved from webpage: https://stjornarradid.is/media/innanrikisraduneyti-media/media/frettir-2015/netoryggisstefna_2015_april.pdf.

NATO (2010). "Active Engagement, Modern Defence: Strategic Concept". Retrieved from: https://nato.int/nato_static_fl2014/assets/pdf/pdf_publications/20120214_strategic-concept-2010-eng.pdf.
Nordic Council of Ministers (n.d.). "Before 1952". *Behind the Nordic Council*. Retrieved from: http://norden.org/en/nordic-council/bag-om-nordisk-raad/the-nordic-council/the-history-of-the-nordic-council/before-1952.
Norwegian Ministry of Defence (2009). "Capable Force: Strategic Concept for the Norwegian Armed Forces". Retrieved from: https://regjeringen.no/globalassets/upload/FD/Dokumenter/Capable-force_strategic-concept.pdf.
Ómarsdóttir, Silja Bára (2008). "Öryggissjálfsmynd Íslands. Umræða um varnarmála- ogalmannavarnalög á Alþingivorið 2008". *Stjórnmál of stjórnsýsla* Vol 4(2), pp. 133–157.
Pétursson, Gústav (2014). "Icelandic Security in a Changing Regional and Geopolitical Seascape: Limited Capabilities and Growing Responsibilities". In: Heininen L. (ed.) *Security and Sovereignty in the North Atlantic*. Palgrave Macmillan: London, 28–41.
President of the United States (2002). "National Security Strategy of the United States of America". Retrieved from webpage: https://state.gov/documents/organization/63562.pdf.
President of the United States (2010). "National Security Strategy". Retrieved from webpage: http://nssarchive.us/NSSR/2010.pdf.
President of the United States (2015). "National Security Strategy". Retrieved from webpage: https://obamawhitehouse.archives.gov/sites/default/files/docs/2015_national_security_strategy_2.pdf.
Prime Minister's Office (Finland) (2004). "Finnish Security and Defence Policy 2004". Retrieved from: http://defmin.fi/files/311/2574_2160_English_White_paper_2004_1_.pdf.
Prime Minister's Office (Finland) (2009). "Finnish Security and Defence Policy 2009". Retrieved from: http://defmin.fi/en/publications/finnish_security_and_defence_policy/2009.
Prime Minister's Office (Finland) (2012). "Finnish Security and Defence Policy 2012". Retrieved from: http://vnk.fi/documents/10616/1093242/J0113_FinnishSecurity_net.pdf/f7d0b3db-f566-4d32-af19-68a7064e24ee?version=1.0.
Stoltenberg, Torvald (2009). "Nordic Cooperation on Foreign and Security Policy". Proposals presented to the extraordinary meeting of Nordic foeign ministers in Oslo, February 9th 2009. Retrieved from webpage: https://mfa.is/media/Frettatilkynning/Nordic_report.pdf.
Thorhallson, Baldur (2014). "Europe: Iceland Prefers Partial Engagement in European Integration". Center for Small State Studies. Retrieved from: https://rafhladan.is/bitstream/handle/10802/6159/WhitePaper1.pdf?sequence=1.
United Kingdom Cabinet Office (2008). "The National Security Strategy of the United Kingdom: Security in an Interdependent World". Retrieved from webpage: https://gov.uk/government/uploads/system/uploads/attachment_data/file/228539/7291.pdf.
UNU-GEST (n.d.). "United Nations University Gender Equality Programme (UNU-GEST)". Retrieved from website: https://gest.unu.edu/en/about.
The White House (2003). "Iceland. Statement from Prime Minister Oddsson". *The White House. George W. Bush*. Retrieved from webpage: https://georgewbush-whitehouse.archives.gov/infocus/iraq/news/20030326-7.html.
Wilson, Page (2015). "Three Emerging Security Challenges for the UK". *Global Society* Vol 29(3), pp. 373–389.
World Economic Forum (2017). *The Global Gender Gap Report 2017*. Geneva: World Economic Forum.
Zabecki, David T (1999). *World War Two in Europe*. New York: Garland Publishing.

17

SECURITY PERSPECTIVES FROM FINLAND

An Arctic case

Lassi Heininen

Introduction

Geographically, Finland is located in the northernmost part of Europe, bordering Sweden to the west, Norway to the north and Russia to the east. The country also borders the Baltic Sea to its west and south. Finland is almost an island, in an economic sense, and therefore its trade, particularly exports, is heavily dependent on sea transportation, including requiring icebreakers during the winter months. Geopolitically, an important component of Finland's Cold War foreign policy was to engage in various types of international cooperation, acting at times as a mediator or interlocutor and often engaging with international organizations and agreements. Helsinki proclaimed its neutrality during the Cold War and maintained its independence despite its proximity. As an independent Nordic state, Finland has joined many international organizations since the 1950s, including the Nordic Council, the United Nations and its sub-organizations, such as the United Nations Convention of the Law of the Sea (UNCLOS), as well as the European Union, (a member since 1995), and the Eurozone. After joining the EU and adapting the joint currency, Finland is no longer fully "neutral," as it is politically and economically aligned with Europe. Finland perceives the EU as "a venue for fostering a security community, which is not an alternative to NATO, but complementary to it" (Raik et al. 2015, 7). Ultimately, Finland's decision to join the EU just after the end of the Cold War was a strategic decision, as leading policymakers later stated.

From a military-political viewpoint, Finland retains a certain degree of non-alignment, especially in regards to relations with NATO and Russia. Responsibility for national defense is held by the Finnish Defense Forces (*Puolustusvoimat*). According to the 2012 Security and Defense Policy, the main goals of Finland's security policy, which includes addressing defense development and the greater global security environment, are "safeguarding the country's independence and territorial sovereignty, guaranteeing the basic values, security and well-being of the population, and maintaining a functioning society" (Prime Minister's Office, March 2013b). Finland is also strengthening its security-political and military cooperation with other Nordic countries, particularly Sweden (also outside of NATO), within the Nordic Defense Cooperation (NORDEFCO) program (Zhilina 2013, 43–44). Finland also supports the EU's Common Foreign and Security Policy, as well as the potential formation of a joint European Union army. In recent years, there has also been deeper military integration with NATO via its Partnership for Peace (PfP) framework since Finland signed a Host Nation Agreement with NATO in 2014. As a result, it can be concluded that Finland is ready to be more fully militarily integrated into NATO, especially as a result of concerns over a resurgent Russia, and that the only piece missing is a firm political decision on NATO membership. The military relationship with the United States is also significant for Finland, given the large American role within NATO.

Finland's sovereignty is distinct, as it does not have any official disputes with other states, including within the Arctic region. The country emphasizes comprehensive security and supports international cooperation, including economic and business cooperation, as a means of increasing security in the whole of Europe, especially in Northern Europe and the Arctic. Being geo-economically dependent on foreign trade and income from exports, Finland has supported the greater liberalization of the global economy via free trade. Finland is also a modern democratic welfare state, with a strong civil society and is renowned for its education policies. Demographically, Finland is considered a small state, (population 5.5 million), with limited political weight, even from a regional viewpoint. Based on its strategic neutrality and its support for cooperation and peace, Helsinki has traditionally supported the United Nations and been a liaison and initiator, and at times a leader, in international politics for decades. Finland has achieved several foreign policy successes, such as hosting the Summit of European Security and Cooperation (CSCE) in 1975, as well as US–Russian Summits, and initiating the EU's Northern Dimension (ND) project in 1997 (Mäkinen 2014). Indeed, as a Nordic state and one of the northernmost countries of the world, the country has been active in Northern and Arctic affairs. However, even though Finland is one of the eight Arctic states, its self-identification as an Arctic country is a relatively recent phenomenon, as the first official Finnish statement proclaiming this status was only put forward in 2010 (Prime Minister's Office 2010).

Within the EU, Finland sought to bolster the Northern Dimension, one of the major external policies of the Union, which originally had an Arctic focus. The ND has also sought to create a common policy among the EU, the Russian Federation, Iceland, and Norway. Finally, Finland has also wished to turn the EU into a Global Arctic stakeholder (Prime Minister's Office 2010).

This chapter takes a non-traditional approach to security and security policy in the case of Finland, emphasizing climate change and environmental protection, as well as various types of cooperation. Thus, it aims to contribute to the discussion about the security aspects of large-scale environmental challenges and problems and also to emphasize the importance of international cooperation, confidence-building, and stability. It first describes the state of Arctic security and Finland's geopolitical context in the 2010s and redefines its security and other national interests in the Arctic region and Arctic affairs. Second, it analyzes the geopolitical, environmental, and security importance of the Arctic region to Finland. Third, the chapter discusses potential areas of confrontation and cooperation between Helsinki and other Arctic states. Fourth, it briefly examines how Finland can, individually and in concert with international security forces, promote security cooperation, reduce potential regional friction, and respond to human and environmental challenges in the Arctic region.

The state of Arctic geopolitics and security

Among the traditional and non-traditional security concerns Finland is facing in the Arctic are long-range regional pollution and rapid climate change, as well as the security of resources and how to respond to regional militarization – specifically from Russia. There are interactions among the physical impacts of climate change and economic concerns such as: the search for new Arctic Ocean sea routes due to melting sea ice; growing large-scale exploitation of hydrocarbons; increased traffic on sea lanes; an emphasis on traditional resource geopolitics; increased greenhouse gas/CO_2 emissions; and, consequently, improved offshore drilling opportunities for the petroleum and gas industry. Arctic offshore oil drilling involves significant environmental and societal risks, including potential long-term damage to both the local environment and socioeconomic activities. These new issues in resource geopolitics, driven by neoliberal globalization, together with associated challenges and problems, and the emphasis on economic activities by the Arctic states – also called the "Arctic Paradox" (Palosaari 2019) – pose a danger to the unique Arctic ecosystem. All of these issues challenge the human security of Arctic peoples, nations, civil societies, and even the traditionally defined sovereignty of the Arctic states.

It is a well-known and oft-discussed fact that the 2010s have witnessed a heightened global interest in the Arctic region due to the rapid warming of the Arctic climate and the consequent geostrategic and geo-economic potential of the energy and other resources in the region (e.g. AMAP 2017; The GlobalArctic Handbook 2019). The global impact of long-range pollution and climate change in the Arctic has been apparent for a few decades (e.g., ACIA 2004). Various forms of globalization are nothing new in the Arctic region, having been seen in the impact, in decades and centuries past, of whaling, the fur trade, polar exploration, militarization, and long-range pollution (Globalization and the Circumpolar North 2010). This global view was manifested in the Arctic Council's ministerial meeting in May 2013 in Kiruna, Sweden, when the Arctic states applied a global approach and accepted five Asian nations – China, India, Japan, Singapore, and South Korea, as well as Italy – as new observers of the Council (The Kiruna Declaration 2013), after years of wrestling with the problem of how to add more state actors to the observer roster. Switzerland was added to the observer roster at the Council's Fairbanks summit in 2017, but there were no new state observers added two years later at the Rovaniemi meeting. By the 2010s, the Arctic region had also become an integral part of global political, economic, technological, environmental, and societal changes; hence, what happens in the Arctic now has significant worldwide implications, many of which may not be positive. Within this context, the "Global Arctic" can be interpreted as a new geopolitical reality. This idea is in accordance with the policy and policy priorities of Finland, since it and the Kingdom of Denmark have specifically included a global perspective on such issues in their national Arctic strategies (Heininen 2011).

The growing global interest in the Arctic is seen in at least two different and controversial ways. First, there have been headlines, especially when energy and commodity prices were high, about a "race" to exploit Arctic resources due to rapid climate change and that a "scramble" was about to commence in the Arctic. This aspect was particularly prominent after the now-infamous 2007 Russian expedition to the North Pole, which saw the planting of a Russian flag beneath the sea ice. This event was followed by predictions of large-scale utilization of hydrocarbons and increasing traffic in Arctic sea routes, as well as the Arctic being caught in Russian–Western conflicts after the Russian annexation of Crimea in 2014 and the subsequent eastern Ukrainian conflict (Martikainen et al. 2016). The growing importance of the Arctic was partially reflected in the Arctic policies of the five littoral Arctic states (Canada, Denmark/Greenland, Norway, Russia, and the United States) in the early 2010s, which were intended to protect not only the countries' economic interests, but also their national security and state sovereignty. Second, at the same time, the

Arctic has been, and remains, geopolitically very stable and peaceful since the start of the post-Cold War period, without armed conflicts or real reasons for conflict to develop between the Arctic states (Heininen 2016). The Arctic Council has been resilient and acted as a stability-builder (see Brigham et al. 2016). The latter perspective has always been supported by Finland, as will be discussed below.

Despite a few disputes over maritime borders, such as between Canada and the United States in the Beaufort Sea, growing global interest in the region, and headlines about expected conflicts in the Arctic, Arctic stability seems to be high and resilient. Even the biggest geopolitical change, the 2009 granting of self-rule status in Greenland, was executed peacefully between the Danish government in Copenhagen and the Greenlandic home government in Nuuk. The cohesion of Arctic multilateral cooperation and the high stability of the region is an achievement that the Arctic states would not like to place at risk. That said, the Ukrainian crisis and subsequent conflict, and the developing tensions between Russia and the United States/NATO, put this stability to the test and threaten it for the first time (Heininen 2016). The Arctic states, including Finland, have agreed and have managed to "maintain peace, stability and constructive cooperation in the Arctic," as outlined by the ministerial meetings of the Arctic Council in 2015 and 2017 (The Iqaluit Declaration 2015; The Fairbanks Declaration 2017).

Post-Cold War Arctic geopolitics and security are indeed characterized by a high level of political stability, which includes region-building by nation-states, few disputes between the Arctic states, trans-border cooperation, de-territorialization of borders, and regionalization by non-state actors. Together with globalization, this means a power transformation from nation-states to supranational and subnational entities, and the delegation of authority (Ackren 2014). Stability was also strengthened at the ad hoc ministerial meeting in May 2008 in Ilulissat, Greenland, between the five littoral Arctic states. The Ilulissat Declaration 2008 was a practical way to better monitor the Arctic Ocean and the resources of its shelves, based on the United Nations Convention of the Law of the Sea (UNCLOS) without a "need to develop a new comprehensive international legal regime to govern the Arctic Ocean" (Ilulissat Declaration 2008). It also readily manifests the common interests and mutual understanding of sovereignty shared by these five Arctic states. No wonder then that in their national strategies the littoral states emphasize maritime state sovereignty and military defense, unlike the three other Arctic states (Finland, Iceland, Sweden), which do not mention sovereignty and instead emphasize international cooperation (Heininen 2011). Finland, as well as the two other non-littoral Arctic states, instead highlight the importance of the geopolitical stability and peacefulness of the Arctic as part of their national policy, as well as international cooperation in the Arctic region to decrease tension and increase stability and security.

Finland's geopolitical, environmental, and security interests in the Arctic

In its Arctic strategy (Prime Minister's Office 2013a) Finland clearly states that the Arctic region is a stable and peaceful area, adding that significant changes are taking place in the region, including climate change and increased transportation. The strategy elucidates that Helsinki respects the principles of regional sustainability, although the environment is not necessarily Finland's first priority. As noted above, Finland greatly supports international regional cooperation in the Arctic, particularly environmental cooperation and economic activities. However, it views the Arctic Council as the main intergovernmental body and platform for addressing the Arctic region. Finland is also among the member states that seek to further develop the Council and broaden its mandate.

Finland's first official Arctic strategy document (Prime Minister's Office 2010) had four substantial chapters: "Fragile Arctic Nature," "Economic Activities and Know-How," Transport and Infrastructure," and "Indigenous Peoples." It also had a specific focus on external relations: the chapter "The EU and the Arctic Region" clearly outlined Finland's policy objectives in relation to the European Union's activities in the Arctic. The government adopted an updated Arctic strategy in August 2013 (Prime Minister's Office 2013a). In addition to having the same four substantive areas as the 2010 version, the updated version is based on the government's 2012 vision of "Arctic" Finland as consisting of the following pillars of policy: Finland is an "Arctic country" and an "Arctic expert" which complies with the principles of sustainable development and promotes "international cooperation in the Arctic." In the latest updated version (Government's Strategy Session, 26.9.2016) the government states that Finland "aims to strengthen security policy stability in the Arctic and enhance the vitality of the region, in line with the principles of sustainable development." The objective of this updated version is "to ensure that Finland is a leading actor in international Arctic policy, both in the EU and globally."

During the Cold War period, the European North, and indeed the entire Circumpolar North, became militarily important for Finland as one of the major geostrategic regions for the country's defense. It was also noted in the report that "the military footprint in the Arctic region has grown. As a base with strategic weapons, the Kola Peninsula retains its importance to Russia" (Prime Minister's Office 2017, 9). The strategic-military importance of the Baltic Sea region was described as even more important for Finland, with the report stating "that military activity has intensified in the area" and a "conflict in the Baltic Sea region would inevitably impact Finland's security" (ibid., 11). Finland's sovereignty in the Arctic region, including the region of Lapland as its northernmost county, is uncontested; neither sovereignty nor national security is mentioned as a national priority of its Arctic policy. Instead, in its Arctic policy, and particularly in the areas of security and defense policy (Prime Minister's Office, March 2013b, 65–67), the Finnish government has clearly stated that it supports comprehensive security and stability based on international cooperation; recognizes the security implications of climate change; and supports international cooperation, together with economic and business interests, as a means of increasing security in the Arctic region.

Finland has no disputes with other Arctic states and has not recently made any further claims in the Arctic region.[1] However, there are environmental conflicts in Finnish Lapland, due to large-scale utilization of resources, such as mining and forestry, and land-use conflicts. The conflict partly stems from the fact that Finland has not ratified the 1989 International Labour Organisation (ILO) 169 Convention on Indigenous and Tribal Peoples, which is very important for the Sámi, an Indigenous people who live in Finland and other parts of the European Arctic. A deeper analysis (Heininen 2014; also Bailes and Heininen 2013) indicates that Helsinki's Arctic strategy (both the 2010 and 2013 versions) contains most of the features of a modern strategy document by adopting a holistic approach that includes all major indicators of national strategies. The strategy also reflects and responds to recent significant and multifunctional environmental and geopolitical changes in the Arctic region through its worldwide approach to the region. It has neither clear priorities nor priority areas, though there is an apparent preference for economic activities, including transport, infrastructure, and know-how. In slight contrast, there is also an emphasis on high geopolitical stability and general objectives for international cooperation on Arctic issues, based on international treaties and agreements.

Finland is also actively participating in the work of the Arctic Security Forces Round Table (ASFR), and it also participated in the first meetings of Arctic Chiefs of Defense, ACHODs. Finland negotiated a special border-crossing arrangement on the northernmost part of the Finnish–Russian border to stop a wave of asylum seekers from crossing into Finland. Despite this political-security aspect, Finland's long-term interests in the Arctic region focus on the environment, as the Finnish initiative for the Arctic Environmental Protection Strategy (AEPS) clearly manifests. Many of the collaborative goals of this process can be traced back to the initiatives outlined by Soviet President Mikhail Gorbachev in his famous Murmansk Speech in 1987 (Gorbachev 1987). The growing environmental awakening of the Sámi people, environmental NGOs, and some scientists and scholars, to long-range pollution, radioactive waste, and nuclear accidents in the European Arctic and Northern Seas (Heininen 2013) can also be credited with this process. During its period as chair of the Arctic Council from 2017–19, Finland stressed its commitment to environmental issues in the country's policies, which had placed environmental protection as the first priority.

All in all, Finland has sought to follow its best foreign policy traditions, reflecting that its successes in foreign policy were achieved via the promotion and enhancement of international cooperation and peace initiatives. The 1975 European Security and Cooperation Summit was often mentioned as the most important achievement, though the Finnish initiative for the AEPS, (signed at the first-ever ministerial meeting of the eight Arctic states in 1991), also called the Rovaniemi Process, was a success story spearheaded by Finland. Along with others, Finland promoted the establishment of the Arctic Council in 1996, which has become one of the best high-level regional forums in international politics (Arctic Yearbook 2016).

Potential areas of confrontation and cooperation

As described above, among the Arctic states, as well as among the Arctic Council observer countries, there is a consensus in official statements that there are no military conflicts in the Arctic – not even emerging ones. Rather, there is a high level of stability based on regional/international cooperation. Finland agrees with this stance, and firmly supports and promotes international, mostly multilateral, cooperation in the Arctic. This is much needed, given that the dangers of the grand challenges outlined earlier could impact the region despite the high level of stability in the post-Cold War Arctic and its institutionalized cooperation on environmental protection and sustainable development. The Paris Agreement from the COP21 climate change conference in December 2015 is not legally binding, and the limit of two additional degrees Celsius may be too little, too late. There also are doubts whether sustainable development is truly integrated into the national strategies of Arctic states, because they are hesitating to adopt stricter environmental regulations against the large-scale utilization of Arctic natural resources, particularly hydrocarbons, and seem unable to resist accessing these resources.

Due to its geographical location and full sovereignty within the Arctic region, Finland has the right to utilize Arctic resources and be involved when these resources, including offshore oil and gas, are exploited. On the other hand, as the initiator of the Arctic Environmental Protection Strategy (AEPS) and having redefined itself as an "Arctic expert," Finland has responsibility for environmental protection and upholding good governance in the Arctic. Finland's first Arctic strategy in 2010 can be criticized for not clearly emphasizing the environment and environmental protection as the country's first priority (e.g. Heininen 2011). Instead, the country emphasized the importance of economic activities in the region. The 2013 version (Prime Minister's Office 2013a) focused on education and research first; it ties in environment and stability, as mentioned, but concentrates on "Finland's business operations in the Arctic." The 2016 strategy has continued this, saying that the main elements of the 2013 strategy remain valid, with the document outlining Finland's desire to "achieve growth and competitiveness," respond "to the climate change and environmental protection challenges," and have "the Arctic Council and international agreements and organizations" as the main channels of influence. Thus, Finland aspires to both economic growth and environmental protection, but might not act as a leader in achieving the latter goal.

This stance can be contrasted with the 1996 Ottawa Declaration, the founding document of the Arctic Council, in which the Arctic states affirmed their "commitment to the well-being of the inhabitants, ... to sustainable development in the Arctic, ... [and] to the protection of the Arctic environment." One reason to emphasize economic activities and growth in the Arctic region is the importance of global energy security. Related to this are the growing geopolitical and economic interests in Arctic hydrocarbons, particularly for the petroleum industry, as well as the political inability of the Arctic states to adopt stricter environmental regulations that would limit or stop offshore oil drilling in icy Arctic waters. What does this mean? Can it be argued that the Arctic states, including Finland, have failed to implement the two aims and pillars of the Arctic Council: environmental protection and sustainable development? Neither of the first legally binding agreements concerning the Arctic region, the Search and Rescue Agreement, and the Arctic offshore oil and gas guidelines, do much to regulate large-scale utilization of resources. In addition, national measures for critical infrastructure protection, as part of the changes in the security environment, and measures for industrial management, such as ecosystem-based management plans, (for example, by the Norwegian government), have not minimized environmental risks.

If that is truly the case, this will mean a real, albeit "non-traditional," threat for the Arctic region and its security; this is also a potential threat for Finland. If the development of Arctic resources continues, Finland will lose its most important means of protecting its sovereignty and security in the Arctic. Could the next step be that Finland would be willing to make a difference by proposing to stop offshore oil and gas drilling in the Arctic waters? Or how might Finland, alone or in concert with international security forces, promote security cooperation, reduce the potential for friction, respond to human and environmental challenges in the Arctic, and decrease human insecurity among Sámi communities?

Finland's response to Arctic challenges

As an "Arctic country" and "Arctic expert" which "complies with the principles of sustainable development and respects the basic conditions dictated by the Arctic environment" (Prime Minister's Office 2013a, 17), Finland could do much better in practice. As a pragmatic problem-solver and expert in sustainable development that is committed to decreasing its CO_2 emissions and is looking to develop its bio-economy and alternative energy sources, Finland could again become a leader in Arctic environmental protection. In the 2013 Arctic Strategy, the main priority was economic activities in the Arctic driven by know-how, such as technology-based expertise on shipping, icebreaking, energy, and mining. "Environment" and "stability" were combined in the same section as objectives and action proposals (Prime Minister's Office 2013a, 38–41 and 57–59). Unlike this 2013 strategy, Finland's program for the Arctic Council's 2017–19 chairmanship placed environmental protection, with an aim to put recommendations into practice, as the first priority (Ministry for Foreign Affairs of Finland, October 2016). Does this mean a considerable change, or a paradigm shift, in Finland's priorities? This appears not to be the case because the environment and environmental protection have been top priorities since the Finnish initiative for the AEPS. On the other hand, so much concerning the Arctic is at stake for Finland. As a small economy facing stagnation, a decrease in exports, and challenges of competitiveness, Finland will not undertake any radical initiatives or policies, such as proposing a ban on offshore oil drilling in the Arctic.

Finland is one of the leading countries in planning and building icebreakers and other vessels for icy waters and cold, harsh climates. The country also prioritizes transport in the Arctic and actively participates in Arctic shipping. If one had to interpret Finland's aims in the Arctic and identify the country's top priority, it would be economic activities to leverage technology-based know-how and business opportunities and to sell icebreaker services, including services for offshore utilization of hydrocarbons. Indeed the updated strategy states that Finland "wishes to achieve growth and competitiveness, for example, in the 'cleantech' and bio-economy sectors via Arctic operations," of course "with due respect for the environment." Finland also supports the Sámi and emphasizes their status as the only Arctic Indigenous people within the European Union. It safeguards human security within the country, including the Sámi area. The Arctic Council is not only by and for the Arctic states, but also by and for northern Indigenous peoples, such as the Sámi in Finland. After becoming concerned about the quality of the Northern environment due to long-range air and water pollution, in the 1980s the Sámi started to push governments to cooperate on environmental protection and sustainable development in the European Arctic, including the Sámi lands. There is, however, the sensitive issue that Finland has not yet ratified the ILO 169 Convention. Thus, the next logical step would be to implement a right to self-determination and self-governance among the Sámi and to ratify the Convention.

Finland also has a long tradition of Arctic research, and makes a substantial contribution to Arctic science in many fields. Finland's scientific expertise is seen in technology (icebreaker and ship design and building, cold-climate expertise), in natural sciences, (climatology, geology, and forest research), and in social sciences and humanities, (anthropology, philology, Sámi studies, political sciences, and security studies). Finnish universities and research institutions that concentrate on Arctic research and studies have several research stations in Lapland and other parts of northern Finland, (Finland established a research station in Svalbard in the 1950s, but it is currently unused). There are also a few universities in the country which focus on Arctic studies, combining research and higher education, including the University of Lapland and the University of Oulu, which play important roles in international Arctic research. Following from this, one Finnish priority as the Arctic Council's chair was regional education, including creating sustainable development and building resilience.

Conclusions

Being a Nordic country and an Arctic state, and as a leader in international cooperation, it is natural that Finland is and has been active in Northern and Arctic affairs. In its Arctic strategy, the Finnish government clearly states that the Arctic region, though affected by significant environmental, geopolitical, economic, and cultural changes, is stable and peaceful. While recognizing and prioritizing economic opportunities and growth in the

Arctic, Finland has stated that it is committed to sustainable development and protecting the Arctic environment. Having environmental protection as the first priority during its tenure as chair of the Arctic Council, Helsinki acknowledged and respected the legacy of the Arctic Environmental Protection Strategy and sought to create programs to implement its commitments among the Arctic states.

Visualizing the Arctic within the context of globalization, and its significant multidimensional implications worldwide, has not been obvious among Arctic states. In addition, the importance of the Arctic in world politics and global governance has not yet been broadly understood, even among the Arctic states. Where some observers have emphasized new opportunities, such as the attractiveness of the Arctic as a stable and peaceful region with politically and legally innovative structures, others see new threats and bigger risks and still others view the region as a geopolitical and intellectual periphery. In this context, a worldwide, global perspective on Finland's Arctic strategy is a solid basis for promoting the geopolitical stability of, and security cooperation in, the Arctic region, as well as trying to solve the grand, mostly environmental, challenges of the Arctic. Furthermore, concerning Arctic security as well as military-security policy in general, Finland could continue its best traditions by concentrating on confidence-building measures and (nuclear) disarmament globally (although Finland abstained from voting on a United Nations resolution in December 2016 over whether to prohibit nuclear weapons), particularly in the Arctic. Finnish Arctic Strategy, as well as the country's security and defense policy, provides a sturdy foundation for active nuclear disarmament and confidence-building.

Note

1 As part of the peace treaty negotiations after World War I, the newly independent state of Finland made a claim on Petsamo, a short coastal area of the Barents Sea that became the other arm of Finland between the two World Wars.

References

ACIA. 2004. Arctic Climate Impact Assessment.

Ackren, Maria. 2014. "Greenlandic Paradiplomatic Relations." in *Security and Sovereignty in the North Atlantic*. Edited by Lassi Heininen. Basingstoke: Palgrave Macmillan: 42–61.

AMAP. 2017. *Snow, Water, Ice and Permafrost in the Arctic. Summary for Policy-makers.* Online: www.amap.no.

The Arctic Yearbook. 2016. "The Arctic Council – 20 Years of Cooperation & Policy-Shaping." *Thematic Network on Geopolitics and Security, and Northern Research Forum.* Online www.arcticyearbook.com.

Bailes, Alyson J.K. and Heininen, Lassi. 2012. "Strategy Papers on the Arctic or High North: A comparative study and analysis." *Occasional Paper of the Centre for Small State Studies.* Reykjavik: Institute of International Affairs at University of Iceland.

Brigham, Lawson, Exner-Pirot, Heather, Heininen, Lassi and Plouffe, Joel. 2016. "Introduction – The Arctic Council: Twenty Years of Policy Shaping." *The Arctic Yearbook 2016.* "The Arctic Council – 20 Years of Cooperation & Policy-Shaping." *Thematic Network on Geopolitics and Security, and Northern Research Forum*: 12–18.

The Fairbanks Declaration. 2017. *On the Occasion of the Tenth Ministerial Meeting of the Arctic Council* (11th Day of May, 2017 in Fairbanks, Alaska). Online available at www.arctic-council.org.

Gorbachev, Mikhail. 1987. "The Speech of President Mikhail Gorbachev on October 2, 1987 in Murmansk." *Pravda*, October 2, 1987.

Heininen, Lassi. 2011. *Arctic Strategies and Policies – Inventory and Comparative Study*, updated April 2012. Akureyri: The NRF & University of Lapland. (Online publication available at www.nrf.is/arctic-strategies).

Heininen, Lassi. 2013. "'Politicization' of the Environment: Environmental Politics and Security in the Circumpolar North." in *The Fast-Changing Arctic: Rethinking Arctic Security for a Warmer World.* Edited by Barry Scott Zellen. Calgary: University of Calgary Press: 35–55.

Heininen, Lassi. 2014. "Finland as an Arctic and European State." in *International Relations and the Arctic. Understanding Policy and Governance*. Edited by Robert W. Murray and Anita Dey Nuttall. Amherst: Cambria Press: 321–347.

Heininen, Lassi. 2016. "Security of the Global Arctic in Transformation – Changes in Problem Definition of Security." in *Future Security of the Global Arctic*. State Policy, Economic Security and Climate. Edited by Lassi Heininen. Basingstoke: Palgrave Macmillan, Palgrave Pivot: 12–34.

Heininen, Lassi and Southcott, Chris. Eds. 2010. *Globalization and the Circumpolar North*. Fairbanks: University of Alaska Press.

The Ilulissat Declaration. 2008. *Arctic Ocean Conference*. May 28. http://arcticcouncil.org/filearchive/Ilulissat-declaration.pdf.

The Iqaluit Declaration. 2015. "Adopted at the Ministerial Meeting of the Arctic Council in May 2015 in Iqaluit, Canada." Online available at www.arctic-council.org.

The Kiruna Declaration. 2013. "Adopted at the Ministerial Meeting of the Arctic Council on the 15th of May 2013 in Kiruna, Sweden." Online available at www.arctic-council.org.

Mäkinen, J. 2014. "Puolustajasta pelinrakentajaksi." *Ulkopolitiikka* 2014: 2, 19–23.

Martikainen, Pynnönniemi, Saari & FIIA International Affairs Team. 2016. *Russia's Changing Role in Finland's Neighbourhood*. Publications of the Government's analysis, assessment and research activities 34/2016.

Ministry for Foreign Affairs of Finland. 2016. "Exploring Common Solutions." Finland's Chairmanship Program for The Arctic Council 2017–2019.

The Ottawa Declaration. 1996. "Declaration on the Establishment of the Arctic Council." (Ottawa, Canada, 19 September 1996).

Palosaari, Teemu. 2019. "Arctic Paradox (and How to solve it). Oil, Gas and Climate Ethics in the Arctic." in *The GlobalArctic Handbook*. Edited by Matthias Finger and Lassi Heininen. Cham: Springer: 141–152.

Prime Minister's Office. 2010. "Finland's Strategy for the Arctic Region." Prime Minister's Office Publication 8/2010.

Prime Minister's Office. 2013a. *Finland's Strategy for the Arctic Region*. Prime Minister's Office Publications 16/2013.

Prime Minister's Office. March 2013b. *Finnish Security and Defence Policy* 2012. Government Report. Prime Minister's Office Publications 1/2013.

Prime Minister's Office Finland. 2016. 'Government policy regarding the priorities in the updated Arctic strategy' The Government's strategy session 26 June 2016.

Prime Minister's Office. 2017. *Government's Defence Report*. Helsinki: Prime Minister's Office Publications 7/2017.

Raik, Kristi, Aaltola, Mika, Pynnöniemi, Katri and Salonius-Pasternak, Charly. 2015. "Pushed Together by External Forces? The foreign and Security Policy of Estonia and Finland in the Context of the Ukraine Crisis." *FIIA Briefing Paper* 167. January 2015. Helsinki: Ulkopoliittinen instituutti.

Zhilina, Irina. 2013. "Security Outlook of the Arctic States and Perspectives on NATO's Involvement." University of Akureyri, Master's Programme in Polar Law. September 2013.

18
SECURITY PERSPECTIVES FROM SWEDEN

Niklas Eklund

Introduction

When Sweden assumed chairmanship of the Arctic Council for the period 2011–2013, many observers were skeptical. Not only was the organization's ability to spearhead positive steps toward economic and social development in the circumpolar sphere increasingly questioned (Koivurova 2009), but there were also misgivings about Sweden's role as a "reluctant" Arctic nation (Sörlin 2014). Before then, Sweden did not even have a specific government policy for the Arctic: one was only produced and published just as the Arctic Council chairmanship was assumed by the Swedish government (Heininen 2011). As chronicled by Nord, Sweden nevertheless contributed both to an organizational revitalization of the Council and to moving its agenda on soft security matters forward by playing on its "strength," which "was in its organizational abilities, not in its profile as an Arctic state." (Nord 2016, 171)

In examining how Swedish security perspectives intersect with Arctic affairs, it is possible to speculate that perhaps the lack of a hard security agenda in the Arctic Council ultimately contributed to Swedish success. Even to this day, the Arctic rarely if ever figures in Swedish debates on hard security. Hard security issues are framed in terms of Sweden's role in European or global affairs and, more recently, focused upon the re-emergence of Russia as a military threat. To Swedish governments, it seems, Northern Europe and the Baltic Sea area are the strategic theaters *par preference*. Ideas exist about how these relate to the Arctic as a security-political context, but they only rarely come to the fore in Swedish politics.

In the Swedish political context, the Arctic figures most prominently in discussions about climate change. The country was swept by the same re-emergence of geopolitical interest in the Arctic as other European countries, "responding to a series of media-friendly events in 2007–2008," most notably the planting of a Russian flag at the North Pole but also the "spectacularly low sea-ice minimum in 2007" (Eklund and van der Watt 2017, 87). With a long-standing tradition of involvement in different aspects of Arctic exploration and research, Sweden has continued to contribute to Arctic knowledge-building, not least in the area of climate change (Government Offices of Sweden 2011; Ministry of Environment and Energy 2016). With its two northernmost regions being part of the Barents Euro-Arctic Region, Sweden has also continued to support transnational interaction and development in the European High North. Like the Arctic Council, this organization bans high-political or national security-related issues from its agenda, but it has made significant contributions to transboundary relations between the Fennoscandian countries and Russia (Elenius 2015). Over the past decade, there has also been an upsurge in research on northern Indigenous peoples, particularly driven by an interest in the Sámi people (Sörlin 2014; Josefsen, Mörkenstam, and Saglie 2015). While both climate change and social cohesion can be seen as significant drivers of the overall political agenda in Sweden, their relationship to ideas about security nevertheless remains tenuous (Kraska 2011; Nord 2016).

The aim of this chapter is to tease out and describe the core ideas underpinning Swedish security perspectives and how these can be related to the Arctic. The chapter does not represent original research based on empirical sources, but is, rather, an effort to describe, categorize, and discuss some of the core ideas in Swedish national perceptions of security. It privileges the perspective of the state. Ideas and beliefs are brought to the fore, in time-honored fashion (Goldstein and Keohane 1993; Hall 1993; Roberts and Sutch 2012), focusing upon Swedish security politics in the first two decades of the 21st century and how these ideas relate to the potential of Arctic affairs as a decisive factor in Swedish national security. Particular attention is given to Swedish-language literature, as it is not only key to political discourse in Sweden but also probably less well-known outside the small Nordic language group. Thus, the chapter focuses on the following questions: do Arctic security considerations impact Swedish national security perceptions? If so, how?

Geopolitical framing and the preeminence of the Baltic Sea Region

Because Sweden is not a NATO member, an indication of the security orientation of the country may come from an overview of its current organizational linkages. While Sweden's military doctrine rests on a self-determined version of neutrality, which among other things precludes membership in military alliances during times of peace, the country has revamped its policy of nonalignment over the past three decades. Sweden has actively participated in NATO-led military activities, both military operations and joint military training, under the Partnership for Peace umbrella. NATO membership, nevertheless, remains a highly divisive issue in Swedish politics; an issue to which this chapter shall return in its penultimate section. In simple geopolitical terms, however, Sweden has forged closer security-political ties with Europe via the EU. This has been achieved not only through EU membership but also through the development of particularly close ties with the countries of the Baltic Sea Region (BSR).

The BSR comprises NATO member countries like Denmark, Germany, Poland, Estonia, Latvia, and Lithuania. It also includes Sweden and Finland as neutrals and, last but far from least, Russia, which during the past decades has moved, or been moved, away from security cooperation schemes with NATO and the West. The BSR is, thus, a highly complex geopolitical setting, and the Baltic Sea is well suited for submarine warfare (Elfving 2017). In recent years, Sweden has embarked on a security-political route toward reassurance among BSR neighbors, regardless of their military allegiances. An increasing number of bilateral agreements with Finland (e.g, Swedish Ministry of Defense 2018), Norway and the United States underpin this policy, which in turn flows from the pivotal 2009 Declaration of Solidarity. The Declaration states:

> Sweden will not remain passive if another EU Member State or Nordic country suffers a disaster or an attack. We expect these countries to take similar action if Sweden is affected. Sweden should, therefore, be in a position to both give and receive military support.

The Declaration does not have an explicit Arctic dimension. Furthermore, from the Swedish point of view, the "Declaration of Solidarity is not a manual for our security-policy action." (Hugemark 2012, 2) According to Elfving, the Declaration was soon forgotten and remained so until Russia annexed Crimea in 2014. Since then, Sweden has been able to reassure its neighbors and other actors of its commitment in the event of a crisis through bilateral diplomacy and agreement (Elfving 2018).

Geopolitically as well as militarily, the BSR is a patchwork of cooperative schemes, international organizations, national traditions, and preferred security solutions. This is nevertheless the main security context in which Swedish concerns and strategic initiatives are steeped. The fact that Russia not only belongs to the geopolitical setting but is also a key military actor – one with great-power status – exacerbates the geopolitical preeminence of the BSR in Swedish military security policies. It could be argued that the BSR was rediscovered and redefined by Swedish policymakers in the wake of the armed conflict in eastern Ukraine, particularly after the Russian annexation of Crimea in 2014. Pivoting from a marked preference for extraterritorial and internationalized military involvement since the early 2000s, the Swedish government chose, for example, to reinstate its military presence on Gotland, an island in the Baltic Sea, reinforcing the "temporarily forgotten" geopolitical reality of the BSR in Swedish military and security-political thought (Elfving 2017, 16). What remains unspoken is what might be termed the current reterritorialization of Swedish security policy. To what extent can Arctic security concerns be seen as separate from developments in the BSR?

Russian interest in the Arctic and the slow but deliberate build-up of military and other security-related resources there, the reopening of what used to be Soviet bases in the Arctic, and its general military assertiveness in the current decade, lead to questions about geopolitical linkages (Laruelle 2015; Tsygankov 2016). For Sweden, the interlocking of the BSR and the wider Arctic region has two major tenets. One is the fact that Russia places significant military resources aimed at the Arctic theater either in or near the BSR. Murmansk is still the home base of the Russian Northern Fleet and its strategic nuclear submarines. Russia and NATO come head-to-head not only in the Arctic but also in the BSR, particularly on the Baltic Sea via the so-called Activity Sets (Metzger and Schmitt 2012; Elfving 2017). This adds to the security patchwork of the BSR and significantly links the BSR to the broader Arctic security context (Granholm 2012). This idea of security linkages between the BSR and the Arctic is not new, either to analysts or in and of itself, and it was particularly important in Swedish security policy during the Cold War (Blunden 2009; Sakwa 2013). What is relatively new, however, is that the linkage is rarely, if ever, made in the public Swedish debate on geopolitical or military security.

Looking at the Swedish priority given to EU membership, bilateral agreements with its Nordic and Baltic neighbors, and the contours of its new reterritorialized deployment of military resources, the BSR appears as an ideational pivot. Swedish geopolitical and military security concerns radiate out from the BSR. This image is strengthened by the lack of military or high-security issues on the agendas of those Arctic organizations in which the country plays different roles: the Arctic Council and the Barents Euro-Arctic Region. Swedish involvement in regional Nordic high-security initiatives, for example NORDEFCO (Westberg 2015), may over time increase the priority of Arctic security concerns for Sweden due to Norwegian influence. However, while the attention and resources given by Swedish governments to global multilateral arenas such as the United Nations are considerable, direct, or immediate Swedish involvement in Arctic security is scant. The Swedish perspective on military security and geopolitical power projection seems firmly rooted in the BSR.

The roots of Swedish Arctic security perceptions: shifting to climate change and non-state actors

Among Swedish researchers, there seems to be agreement that current Swedish perspectives on Arctic security flow from activities immediately before and during the Arctic Council chairmanship (2011–2013). Also, it is assumed that the renewed EU interest in Arctic issues fueled Swedish activities. Three reports from the Swedish Defense Research Agency (FOI) produced between 2008 and 2010 are the ideational basis for the upsurge in Swedish attention paid to the Arctic during its chairmanship (Keskitalo 2014; Engelbrekt, Holmberg and Ångström 2015; Agrell 2016). The high profile given to Arctic issues by Sweden while it briefly held the gavel at Arctic Council meetings was not followed up by significant changes in Swedish security policy.

As observed by Keskitalo, all three FOI reports more or less leave Sweden and Swedish options out of the picture (Keskitalo 2014). In the 2008 report, commissioned by the Swedish Ministry of Foreign Affairs, the perspective is strategic, referring to linkages between Swedish security interests and developments in the wider Arctic context (Granholm 2008). Other than developments in Russia, particularly signs of change in maritime activities on the Kola Peninsula, the report describes changes in Arctic security as distant from, even external to, Swedish security concerns. Much attention is given to relations and issues among the five Arctic littoral states. In its conclusion, the document conveyed the message that developments in the Arctic are "elusive" (Granholm 2008, 4).

The 2009 report, commissioned by the same Swedish ministry, focuses specifically on the Arctic policies of Canada, Iceland, and Denmark, noting that domestic political agendas are decisive for policymakers; hence, the dynamics of Arctic development are open to different trajectories (Granholm 2009). The third and final document, a 2010 report commissioned by the Swedish Energy Agency, focuses on the growing international interest in Arctic natural resources, mainly oil and gas, against the backdrop of the warming of the global climate (Granholm and Kiesow 2010). Swedish policy makers thus chaired the Arctic Council in 2011 while acting under the assumption that Arctic affairs were driven by domestic political agendas and were aimed at mitigating the effects of global environmental change, issues of social cohesion in particular Arctic countries, or potentially balancing the interests of business and industry with Russian geopolitical interests.

Turning the ideational tables, perhaps the High Arctic profiling of Sweden that took place in 2011–2013 and the lack of a consequent follow-through can be understood in this light? In its Arctic policy, Sweden has since emphasized a modernizing, market- and non-state actor-driven political agenda for the Arctic (Government Offices of Sweden 2011). The Swedish government extols the virtues of controlled, traditional industrial development in the field of natural resource extraction, making special reference to the sustainability of modern Arctic forestry. More emphasis is given to the virtues of local and regional livelihoods such as fishing and reindeer husbandry, given that the Arctic is now defined as land and sea above the 60th parallel. In effect, a whole new developmental agenda is presented, according to which increased and modernized shipping in Arctic waters can be reconciled not only with natural resource extraction and industrialization but also with increased tourism and the development of the traditional livelihoods of Indigenous Arctic peoples. As poignantly observed by Keskitalo:

> The strategy thus highlights economic development and distances itself from the traditional frontier-related discourse on the Arctic. Furthermore, with regard to

> Sweden's aims in Arctic cooperation, the strategy supports the EU view that the Arctic should remain a low-tension area when it comes to security policy.
> *(Keskitalo 2014, 309).*

Consequently, Swedish Arctic policy continues to target areas of economic and social development. Whether the image of Sweden as an "honest broker" (Nord 2016, 139–72) still holds among the other members of the Arctic Council almost a decade after its chairmanship of the Arctic Council is an open question. What seems clear, nevertheless, is that the Swedish outlook on Arctic affairs in general and Arctic security in particular has not changed (Nilsson and Larsbrink 2013; Neretnieks 2016). Because Swedish security perceptions are in a state of major overhaul nearing the year 2020 and what one Swedish analyst has called "the beginning of an unfamiliar era" (Agrell 2016, 230), little or no change in ideas about Sweden's role in Arctic security is discernible. Territorial remilitarization is high on the political agenda, as is a continuation of bi- and multilateral approaches to security in the European High North by way of the Baltic Sea Region. Linkages to Arctic security, however, remain either tenuous or outright neglected (Engelbrekt, Holmberg, and Ångström 2015; Agrell 2016).

Approaching the Arctic by alternative agendas

As observed by Dodds and Nutall, "powerful agents of Arctic geopolitics, such as prime ministers and presidents, pick and choose where possible" (Dodds and Nutall 2016, xii). Although their reasoning is built on examples from Canadian politics, the idea that different images of the Arctic can be selected by political actors to achieve different political goals has a general appeal, which also makes it relevant in the case of Sweden. Swedish foreign policy has long been guided by ideas about free trade, multilateralism, and scientific and subnational cooperation (Bjereld 2007; Brommesson and Ekengren 2007). Membership in the United Nations went from being a contentious issue in the 1950s to becoming a cornerstone of Swedish foreign policy; membership of the European Union, which was perhaps even more contentious in the 1990s, has followed a similar trajectory (Andren 1997; Engelbrekt, Holmberg, and Ångström 2015). From their beginning as divisive political issues of Swedish adaptation to international change, over time both memberships have been integrated with the Swedish national interest, almost to the point of redefining it as an international interest.

It is therefore less surprising that Sweden chose to play the role that it did in its 2011–2013 Arctic Council chairmanship. Finding a new outlet for its wish to multilateralize Arctic affairs, the Swedish government more or less latched on to the renewed interest in the Arctic among the Nordic states and the European Commission, which began to show a serious interest in the Arctic only in 2008–2009 (Keskitalo 2014; Dodds and Nutall 2016). The Swedish agenda was, and still is, driven by an interest in desecuritization in the Arctic and by the idea that economic and scientific cooperation can take the edge off relationships driven by security (Ministry of the Environment and Energy 2016). Not being a littoral Arctic state and thus lacking a geopolitically driven Arctic interest, unlike Norway or Denmark, Sweden emphasizes global trade, climate change, and social cohesion on its Arctic agenda (Nord 2016). This spills over into an interest in Arctic sciences and scientific cooperation schemes.

Most pertinent information about how Sweden has contributed to Arctic research over the past few decades can be accessed at the Swedish Polar Research Secretariat (Karlqvist 2006). It is noteworthy, however, that the secretariat focuses on polar research in the wider sense, including Antarctica. Furthermore, polar research is emphasized in its exploratory, natural science-driven sense. This is joined to a scientific interest in economic structures and climate change, but security and politics are mostly absent from the research agenda. Academic interest in the interplay between political and social developments relevant to the Arctic has been channeled through Swedish universities, most notably through a deliberate build-up of academic capacity in Sweden's northernmost universities in Umeå and Luleå. At Umeå University, the Center for Arctic Research (Arcum) has promoted multidisciplinary research about the history and living conditions in the European High North (www.arcum.umu.se).

In recognition of its status and international scientific involvement, Arcum hosted the 9th International Congress of Arctic Social Sciences in June 2017. Looking at the publication record and the research agenda, however, Umeå University has particularly contributed to an improved understanding of the historical and political circumstances of the Sámi people (Sköld and Lantto 2000). Significant contributions have also been made to improve knowledge and understanding about transnational cooperation in the Barents Sea Region in a longer historical perspective (Elenius 2015). Overall, the Swedish research agenda in the Arctic nevertheless plays to the same tune as Swedish foreign and security policy. Discussions of whether Arctic means something in its own right are obscured by sectoral and policy-related considerations. With the exception of critical studies of the plight of the Sámi as an Indigenous people in a modern European state (Mörkenstam 2015), who define the Arctic territories of northern Sweden as a homeland, purely Arctic components of the observed phenomena remain hidden or unspoken. The same mostly unsaid assumptions about the desirability of multilateralism and subnational cooperation in government policy are made by the scientific community. Arctic security seems a long way away.

Neutrality: principled belief or potential game changer?

Sweden's 200-year tradition of military nonalignment merits particular attention in this context. Having been doctrinal for so long and being historically so closely linked with issues of war and peace in continental Europe, what bearing does it have on Sweden's role in the Arctic? As discussed above, it is important to keep in mind that nonalignment in peacetime is aimed at neutrality in a European war. The principle was self-imposed by Sweden; it does not spring from any international or legal agreement. It was steeped and honed politically over time, always with an eye to European and trans-Atlantic relations, in an era when Europe went from the great-power politics of the 1800s via the two World Wars in the 1900s to a period of relative international stability during the bipolar superpower era up until the 1980s. More than one Swedish analyst has therefore concluded that the neutrality doctrine became obsolete in the 1990s (Dalsjö 2015). At least two public inquiries in Sweden have determined that neither nonalignment nor neutrality were ever regarded as absolute by Swedish governments; rather, they were flexible foreign policy instruments by which informal alliances could be maintained (Committee SOU 1994, 11, Committee SOU 2002, 108). It is, in other words, no secret that Sweden has fostered friendly relations and military agreements with both NATO member countries, particularly Nordic members, and with NATO itself.

Considering the many economic, political, and cultural ties Sweden has, not only with its Nordic NATO neighbors but with a significant number of other NATO countries, the issue of nonalignment almost seems moot from an international perspective. Five major changes related to security that have pushed Sweden further in that direction can be discerned since the 1990s (Dalsjö 2015). As described by Dalsjö, first of all, the Baltic States regained their independence, changing the security and geopolitical structure of the

BSR. Second, the war in the Balkans produced the first great wave of refugees to hit Northern Europe; this made it easier for the Swedish government to realize that common solutions to common problems would be necessary in the still-emergent new Europe. Third, military cooperation in the Balkans made it clear to Swedish decision-makers that NATO was a factor in peacekeeping and that European partners would apply NATO standards in military activities. Fourth, Swedish EU membership came of age rapidly after Sweden joined in 1995, paving the way for internationalist outlooks and messages among Swedish political elites. Fifth, the covert cooperation between the Swedish government and NATO governments during the Cold War was publicized. Adding to this, the military restructuring of Sweden´s armed forces well into the 2010s was aimed at functionality in joint international operations (Westberg 2016).

Still, the doctrine of non-alliance and neutrality in a European war is deeply rooted in the Swedish political self-image and among most Swedish citizens. NATO membership remains a deeply divisive issue in Swedish politics. What should be a debate over the merits of the nonalignment doctrine and the potential need for adaptation to international change, has become entrenched as an ideological left–Right issue in Swedish politics. Political parties to the left of the Swedish political spectrum, such as Vänsterpartiet and Socialdemokraterna, are opposed to NATO membership, while political parties to the right, such as Liberalerna and Moderaterna, are in favor. Despite a right-wing coalition government between 2006 and 2014, during which the issue might have been moved up on the political agenda, nothing happened. The left-wing coalition in government until fall 2018 continued to nurse Sweden's strategic relationships with its Nordic neighbors, particularly with the other Nordic neutral, Finland. In the latest polls, the Swedish electorate seems more or less evenly divided on the issue of NATO membership.

NATO membership is, nevertheless, a potential game changer in how Sweden contributes to Arctic security. If Sweden departs from its long-standing security path, it would not only reshuffle the strategic situation in the Baltic Sea Region, but it would by a stroke of the pen giving Sweden a clearer, better-defined role in Arctic security. The careful balancing of formal and informal alliances with other Nordic countries, EU, and NATO countries would be cleanly replaced by a formal position in a military alliance. The question would no longer be whether Sweden should support, for example, Norwegian efforts at maintaining a balanced relationship with a militarizing Russia in the Arctic, but rather how. Russia, on the other hand, is the political ghost that keeps haunting Swedish politicians and citizens alike. While the many reasons for Sweden to join NATO and become a part of a global military alliance, thereby also gaining a distinct role in Arctic security, are easy to enumerate, there are considerably more question marks regarding the potential Russian reaction. There is strategic pressure on Sweden, as Russia's military build-up looms behind more or less veiled threats from marine and flyover incidents and, more recently, outright warnings not to join NATO (Hugemark 2012; Elfving 2014; Agrell 2016, 217–52). To reiterate, the issue is nevertheless deeply divisive in Swedish politics, which means that in 2018, it is only possible to speculate about potential futures for Swedish nonalignment aimed at neutrality in a European war.

Conclusion: regional drivers and diverging legitimacies

Geopolitical framing, political agenda-setting, and military doctrine relating to Sweden and Arctic security all belong to the world of ideas. So too does the overarching theme of security perceptions. Having looked at these ideational fields in the case of Sweden, it would be only too easy to conclude that there is no obvious rationale behind how these ideas may play out politically, singularly, or in interaction. They also entail several intriguing questions, such as whether history plays a role and, if so, how much of future Swedish Arctic policy can be attributed to it? Other ideas and areas of political interest that fall through the analytical net cast in this chapter may be of equal value to an understanding of the present. This problem of analytical delineation is not unique to the Swedish case, but rather it is typical for the conceptual worlds of security studies: There are always alternative, contending definitions of *what security* and *whose security* to consider.

What has been described and discussed, nevertheless, are some of the core ideas upon which Swedish understandings of national security pivot. The many references to the Swedish chairmanship of the Arctic Council 2011–2013 are motivated first and foremost by the upsurge of interest in Arctic affairs that swept Swedish politics and the public debate during those years. With hindsight, and given the consequent resecuritization of relations in the Baltic Sea Region, it is possible to speculate that those years, in connection with the previous interest in the Arctic shown by the EU, were a unique policy window. Highly motivated by emergent EU policies, Swedish politicians could sweep in to bring order to an organization where matters of international security were missing from the political agenda. Another reason why this point in time is interesting is that, ideationally, it is formative for Swedish politics on the Arctic. While efforts at cooperation in Arctic research and various transnational structures, most notably in the Barents Euro-Arctic Region, were already in place and securing Sweden a role in the wider Arctic context, Sweden did not have a coherent national policy for the Arctic. Regardless of how one perceives the expediency with which it was put in place in 2011, for all intents and purposes Arctic policy indicated a small shift in the trajectory of Swedish foreign policy. But again, this ideational shift was not significant in terms of security policy because matters related to Swedish national security were omitted. Also, the Swedish Arctic policy has not been amended, at least not in the five-year period immediately following the end of the Swedish chairmanship in 2013.

With a view to the potential for change in the mostly reluctant and non-security-related Swedish position in Arctic affairs, which with the possible exception of ideas about scientific exploration is a historical fact, this chapter has identified geopolitical framing, political agenda-setting, and military doctrine as the core areas in which a significant change of Swedish ideas would have to take place for any change in the country's stance in the Arctic to occur. This is not to say that the ideational aspect of political choice has exclusive explanatory value with regard to Swedish security policy, or that it somehow overshadows functional or rationalist approaches. However, as the saying goes, a journey of a thousand steps begins with an itch to move. Scratching that itch for a bit, in the case of Sweden, allows for conclusions to be drawn about more than the component parts of Swedish Arctic policy.

Swedish politics in general has a penchant for modernity and conceptual play. The effects are also visible in the areas of foreign and security policy, where the current government has opted to label its foreign policy "feminist." As argued by Swedish researchers on security, however, such labeling should not be mistaken for playfulness, a lack of severity, or, indeed, for being a testing ground for postmodern ideas (Edström 2016; Egnell 2016). On the contrary, behind the conceptual façade hides the eternal battle between constructivist and rationalist approaches to policymaking (Ångström 2015; Engelbrekt, Holmberg, and Ångström 2015). Around 2008, there was a convergence among Arctic policy drivers in Sweden. Accelerating climate change, relatively high prices on global resource markets, an emergent EU interest, and relative stability in the Baltic Sea Region all contributed to making the Arctic more interesting to the Swedish government. Finding an outlet for its need to react to these drivers, Sweden took the lead in a reorganization of Arctic diplomacy in a number of non-security-related areas, also reconstructing itself as an Arctic nation. Having found itself under pressure from different policy drivers since then, Sweden has been experimenting with its Arctic identity. The brief period during which the Arctic was high on the Swedish political agenda, however, never put a dent in the underlying rationale of Swedish security perceptions (Government Offices of Sweden 2017; Swedish Ministry of Defence 2018). The original geopolitically driven focus on the BSR and the unceasing Russian military build-up and threat paved the way for a return to time-tested ideas about territorial defense and nonalignment in the all-European context. NATO membership seems to be the only thing that could force Swedish security perceptions to become more influenced by Arctic security.

References

Agrell, Wilhelm. 2016. *Det säkra landet? Svensk försvars- och säkerhetspolitik från ett kallt krig till ett annat.* Malmö: Gleerups.

Andren, Nils. 1997. *Säkerhetspolitik. Analyser och tillämpningar.* Stockholm: Norstedts Juridik.

Ångström, Jan. 2015. "Försvarsmaktens internationella insatser: I den svenska säkerhetens eller identitetens tjänst?." In Engelbrekt, Kjell and Arita Holmberg and Jan Ångström, eds. *Svensk säkerhetspolitik i Europa och världen.* Stockholm: Norstedts Juridik.

Bjereld, Ulf. 2007. "Utrikespolitisk opinion i Sverige." In Brommesson, Douglas. and Ann-Marie Ekengren, eds. *Sverige i världen.* Malmö: Gleerups.

Blunden, Margaret. 2009. "The New Problem of Arctic Stability." *Survival* 51, no. 5: 121–142.

Brommesson, Douglas and Ann-Marie Ekengren 2007. "Sverige i världen—idag och imorgon." In Brommesson, Douglas and Ann-Marie Ekengren, eds. *Sverige i världen.* Malmö: Gleerups.

Committee SOU 1994. 11. *Om kriget kommit.Förberedelser för mottagande av militärt bistånd 1949-1969.* The Swedish Government Offices: Betänkande av Neutralitetspolitikkommissionen.

Committee SOU 2002. 108. *Fred och Säkerhet. Svensk säkerhetspolitik 1969-89.* The Swedish Government Offices: Slutbetänkande av den säkerhetspolitiska utredningen.

Dalsjö, Robert. 2015. "Från neutralitet till solidaritet: Omgestaltningen av Sveriges säkerhetspolitik efter det kalla kriget." In Engelbrekt, Kjell and Arita Holmberg and Jan Ångström, eds. *Svensk säkerhetspolitik i Europa och världen.* Stockholm: Norstedts Juridik.

Dodds, Klaus and Mark Nutall 2016. *The Scramble for the Poles.* Cambridge: Polity Press.

Edström, Håkan. 2016. "Gömd eller glömd—Realism i den svenska Riksdagsdebatten." *Statsvetenskaplig tidskrift* 118, no. 4: 529–562.

Egnell, Robert. 2016. "Feministisk utrikespolitik i teori och praktik." *Statsvetenskaplig tidskrift* 118, no. 4: 563–588.

Eklund, Niklas and Lize-Marié van der Watt 2017. "Refracting (Geo)Political Choices in the Arctic." *The Polar Journal* 7, no. 1: 86–103.

Elenius, Lars. chief-editor. 2015. *The Barents Region. A Transnational History of Subarctic Northern Europe.* Oslo: Pax Forlag.

Elfving, Jörgen. 2014. *Putin rustar Ryssland. Den ryska björnen vaknar till liv.* Stockholm: Svenskt Militärhistoriskt Biblioteks Förlag.

Elfving, Jörgen. 2017. "Norden-ett militärt lapptäcke." *Vårt Försvar* no. 4: 14–16.

Elfving, Jörgen. 2018. *Personal Communication between the Author of this Chapter and Lt.Col.* Enebyberg, Sweden: (ret) Elfving, Senior Analyst at Fingni Konsult AB on August 7 2018.

Engelbrekt, Kjell and Arita Holmberg and Jan Ångström, eds. 2015. *Svensk säkerhetspolitik i Europa och världen.* Stockholm: Norstedts Juridik.

Goldstein, Judith and Robert Keohane, eds. 1993. *Ideas and Foreign Policy. Beliefs, Institutions and Political Change.* Ithaca: Cornell University Press.

Government Offices of Sweden 2011. *Sweden's strategy for the Arctic Region.* Stockholm: Ministry for Foreign Affairs. Downloaded from www.sweden.gov.se/content/1/c6/16/78/59/55db8e0d.pdf.

Government Offices of Sweden. 2017. *Swedish Defence Commission.* Downloaded from www.government.se/government-of-Sweden/ministry of defence/defence-commission.

Granholm, Niklas., ed. 2008. *Strategiska frågor i en region i förändring.* Stockholm: Swedish Defence Research Agency.

Granholm, Niklas. 2009. *Delar av ett nytt Arktis—Utvecklingar av dansk, kanadensisk, isländsk arktispolitik.* Stockholm: Swedish Defence Research Agency.

Granholm, Niklas. 2012. "The New Arctic and the North Atlantic—Strategic Significance for Sweden?." In Hugemark, Bo., ed. *Friends in Need. Towards a Swedish Strategy of Solidarity with her Neighbours*. Stockholm: The Royal Swedish Academy of War Sciences.

Granholm, Niklas and Ingolf Kiesow 2010. *Olja och gas i ett nytt och förändrat Arktis: Energifrågans utveckling mot bakgrund av regionens strategiska dynamik*. Stockholm: Swedish Defence Research Agency.

Hall, John. 1993. "Ideas and the Social Sciences." In Goldstein, Judith and Robert Keohane, eds. *Ideas and Foreign Policy. Beliefs, Institutions and Political Change*. Ithaca: Cornell University Press.

Heininen, Lassi. 2011. "Sweden's Strategy for the Arctic Region: Priorities and Objectives." Downloaded from www.geopoliticsnorth.org.

Hugemark, Bo. 2012. "Historical Background to the Swedish Declaration of Solidarity." In Hugemark, Bo, ed. *Friends in Need. Towards a Swedish Strategy of Solidarity with her Neighbours*. Stockholm: The Royal Swedish Academy of War Sciences.

Josefsen, Eva and Ulf Mörkenstam and Jo Saglie 2015. "Different Institutions within Similar States: The Norwegian and Swedish *Sámediggis*." *Ethnopolitics* 14, no. 1: 32–51.

Karlqvist, A. 2006. *Svensk polarforskning: Ett utredningsuppdrag*. Stockholm: Vetenskapsrådet.

Keskitalo, Carina. 2014. "Sweden and Arctic Policy." In Murray, Robert and Anita Dey Nutall, eds. *International Relations and the Arctic. Understanding Policy and Governance*. Amherst, N.Y.: Cambria Press.

Koivurova, T. 2009. "The Limits and Possibilities of the Arctic Council in a Rapidly Changing Scene of Arctic Governance." *Polar Record* 46, no. 237: 146–156.

Kraska, J., ed. 2011. *Arctic Security in an Age of Climate Change*. Cambridge: Cambridge University Press.

Laruelle, Marlene. 2015. *Russia's Arctic Strategies and the Future of the Far North*. New York: Routledge.

Metzger, Johan and Peter Schmitt 2012. "When soft spaces harden: The EU strategy for the Baltic Sea Region." *Environment and Planning* 44, 263–280.

Ministry of the Environment and Energy. 2016. *New Swedish Environmental Policy for the Arctic*. Memorandum downloaded from www.government.se/4901d4/globalassets/regeringen/dokument/miljo-och-energidepartementet/pdf/160125-environmental-policy-for-the-arctic.pdf.

Mörkenstam, Ulf. 2015. "Recognition *as if* sovereigns? A procedural understanding of indigenous self-determination." *Citizenship Studies* 19, no. 6–7: 634–648.

Neretnieks, Karlis., ed. 2016. *Hotet. Mål och medel vid ett eventuellt angrepp mot Sverige*. Stockholm: The Swedish Academy of War Sciences.

Nilsson, Sven-Christer and Göran Larsbrink 2013. *Challenges and Opportunities beyond 2014*. Stockholm: The Swedish Academy of War Sciences.

Nord, Douglas. 2016. *The Changing Arctic*. Houndmills: Palgrave Macmillan.

Roberts, Peri and Peter Sutch 2012. *An Introduction to Political Thought*. Edinburgh: Edinburgh University Press.

Sakwa, Richard. 2013. "The Cold Peace: Russo-Western Relations as a Mimetic Cold War." *Cambridge Review of International Affairs* 26, no. 1: 203–224.

Sköld, Peter and Patrik Lantto, eds. 2000. *Den komplexa kontinenten. Staterna på Nordkalotten och staterna i ett historiskt perspektiv*. Umeå: Institutionen för Historiska studier.

Sörlin, Sverker. 2014. "The Reluctant Arctic Citizen: Sweden in the Arctic." In Powell, Richard and Klaus Dodds, eds. *Polar Geopolitics: Knowledge, Resources and Legal Regimes*. Cheltenham: Edward Elgar.

Swedish Ministry of Defence. 2018. *Memorandum of Understanding between the Government of the Republic of Finland and the Government of the Kingdom of Sweden on Defence Cooperation*. Downloaded from www.government.se/government-of-sweden/ministry-of-defence/defence-commission.

Tsygankov, Andrei. 2016. *Russia's Foreign Policy. Change and Continuity in National Identity*. Lanham: Rowman & Littlefield.

Westberg, Jacob. 2015. "Det nordiska försvarssamarbetets drivkrafter och utvecklingsmöjligheter." In Engelbrekt, Kjell and Arita Holmberg and Jan Ångström, eds. *Svensk säkerhetspolitik i Europa och världen*. Stockholm: Norstedts Juridik.

Westberg, Jacob. 2016. "Säkerhet utan alliansfrihet—Svenska alliansstrategiers teori och praktik." *Statsvetenskaplig tidskrift* 118, no. 4: 411–444.

PART III

Security in the Arctic through governance

19

THE ARCTIC COUNCIL

Soft actions, hard effects?

Piotr Graczyk and Svein Vigeland Rottem

Introduction

The Arctic Council is the Arctic region's central intergovernmental forum, addressing a wide range of issues revolving around the environment and sustainable development, with special focus on the effects of climate change and globalization. Although military security is explicitly excluded from its mandate, the Council plays an important role in indirectly strengthening security and stability in the Arctic. Despite not having a legally binding foundation, the Arctic Council has been successful in reconciling different interests of Arctic states, contributing to confidence building and regional cooperation (see Koivurova and Graczyk 2014).

Today, accelerating climate change in the Arctic requires great political and scientific efforts to cope with consequences of this transformation. Opening economic opportunities related to, among other factors, the extraction of natural resources and navigation, requires closer collaboration between the Arctic states on many levels. Furthermore, powerful non-Arctic actors such as China, Japan, India, and the European Union, have demonstrated a growing interest in being involved in the Council's work as observers.[i] Along with these developments, a need has arisen to adjust and strengthen key regional governance within the institution (Rottem 2017). Apart from internal institutional reform, the Council's openness to, and relation with, the outside world has become an increasingly important issue in the current debate on its shape and place in the Arctic governance architecture (Stokke 2017). Building regional security and stability in the Arctic has been, to a large extent, possible via cooperation on soft security issues, where the Arctic Council played an important role. Hard security concerns such as military operations, sovereignty and jurisdictional disputes, and geopolitical considerations are also part of Arctic politics handled outside the Council, primarily through bilateral relations. Nonetheless, concentrating on issues of common concern under the Arctic Council has also established a general and more predictable pattern of cooperation on matters beyond its initial mandate.

This chapter highlights the Arctic Council's role within this landscape, gives a brief overview of the core areas of the forum's work done in the policy and assessment realms, and argues that the Arctic Council has contributed to regional stability and security, despite being declaratively deprived any security functions. The role of the Arctic Council is examined as one that provides security in the region by acting as a forum where a wide range of Arctic issues are considered and debated, thereby enhancing regional stability. The key features that make the Arctic Council crucial for regional security and stability regardless of the lack of legal powers and exclusion of security-related issues from the forum's mandate are also discussed. Particular focus is placed on actions that are implicit in inducing improved security prospects.

Set against the backdrop of the Council's role in Arctic governance and security systems, this chapter examines the role of the Arctic Council in regional security and sovereignty discourses, even though military-related issues are *explicitly* excluded from its mandate while more controversial issues are *implicitly* banned from its agenda. We argue that the Arctic Council, while not handling security issues avowedly, has directly and indirectly contributed to improvement in certain soft security areas and has been able to influence other spheres as the source and originator of activities beyond its own mandate.

First, the chapter briefly discusses the theoretical aspects of security provided by international regimes and how these considerations relate to the Arctic Council. We identify here specific Arctic circumstances that have precluded the emergence of any type of a formal regional security regime. The second section outlines the evolution of Arctic cooperation structures into the Arctic Council with the gradually expanding scope of its interests to include security elements in broader terms, without touching upon the military security aspects. In the third part, the key means through which the Council has been contributing to alleviating threats and preserving regional stability, and thus security in the Arctic, are examined. The chapter concludes with views on how the Council's profile and policies may affect future circumpolar cooperation and security.

Theorizing the Arctic Council's security role

Before proceeding to further analysis, it is important to clarify the understanding of security within the context of the Arctic Council. The nature of contemporary challenges in the Arctic has changed significantly from high militarization and geostrategic concerns to, among others, environmental, economic, social, and human security issues. At the same time, all threats in these areas are interconnected (Buzan, Wæver, and De Wilde 1997) and stem primarily from the effects of climate change, globalization, and the internationalization of the Arctic. Over the last 20 years, civil areas of cooperation have been predominant.

Some authors have argued that "securitizing Arctic politics draws attention to the potential for conflict in the Arctic in contrast to opportunities for promoting cooperation in meeting emerging needs for governance" (Young 2011, xxvi). The argument that security may not be the most pertinent framing with which to comprehend regional challenges was raised at the dawn of Arctic cooperation in the 1990s. There were concerns that inherent difficulties in negotiations or cooperation on security issues, especially when old enemies were only just getting to know new circumstances and collaboration prospects, were still imposing (Griffiths 1992, 299). As noted by Griffiths, "a security concept appropriate to the region will have early policy relevance only if it is generated in a process that produces consensus on the problem and the implications for collective action," thus "creation and use of integrated security conception of Arctic security is decidedly unpromising" (ibid.). Others pointed out that preferably the very term *security* should be avoided in crafting regional cooperation as it could direct it onto a "wrong track … as having a strong nationalistic and militaristic burden" (Tennberg 2000, 90–91).

Given the informal nature of the Arctic Council, resembling a regime rather than an international organization (Young 1998), it is useful to revisit theoretical considerations on regime formation, especially in the security realm. Since the basic function of international regimes, (principles, norms, rules, and decision-making procedures), is "to coordinate state behavior to achieve desired outcomes in particular issue-areas" (Krasner, 1983), there is a need to identify common interests and those issue-areas in which cooperation is plausible. These are well established within the existing cooperation structures, in which the Arctic Council plays a central role, and include a wide range of issues such as environmental protection, sustainable development, or maritime safety, to mention a few. Nevertheless, it is essential to recognize emerging patterns of behavior that may potentially influence the collaborative approach. These are to be found in "national policy debates and in the international interplay between otherwise separate debates" (Griffiths 2011, 4). Such conduct, evincing a reckoning of interests, tends to lead to the creation of regimes, which in turn reinforce patterned behavior.

However, regimes in the security sphere are weak, as pure power motivations preclude them (Krasner 1983, 8). Conditions for forming a security regime include the willingness of great powers involved (it must be in their interest) to act in a more regulated environment, and conviction of the actors that "others share the value they place on mutual security and cooperation" (Jervis 1983, 176). The Arctic context, although providing possible circumstances for creation of a security regime, might not be seen as necessarily conducive for such an arrangement, which is also a reason why the Arctic Council, (and any other body), does not play this role. This context is characterized by a rather complex and comprehensive system of international institutions for multilateral cooperation on the most pertinent issues. Jurisdictional matters are managed within the existing legal framework and through bilateral negotiations. The Arctic states are not a uniform group sharing threats to countries' specific interests, or diverse threats to their common interests. In other words, their perceptions of threats to security do not always converge, and in many areas differ, which effectively precludes creation of a security regime.

The leading role of the Council is stated in Arctic states' policies and strategies towards the region. Some non-Arctic actors are also formulating official positions on the Arctic and seek actively to hold an observer status at the Council. A challenging area in this regard is the question of security and the pursuit of national interests in the region by Arctic and non-Arctic states, which are not always harmonious. Nonetheless, with a well-developed and inclusive international cooperation on civil issues based on shared knowledge and understanding, prospects for regional security are much better. As noted by Griffiths (2011), "good government is at once a precondition and a consequence of security." Hence, our argument is that the Arctic Council, along with the United Nations Convention on the Law of the Sea (UNCLOS), provides the framework for dealing with regional security issues and thus contributes to strengthening Arctic stability. As long as there are no major disputes either among the Arctic states or between Arctic and non-Arctic actors, (or they are well managed elsewhere), these two institutions play a central role, with supplementary arrangements filling gaps when needed. These initial assumptions and observations may prove useful in better understanding how the Council practically affects the security environment in the Arctic.

Avoiding security debates? Evolution of the Arctic Council's approach

During the Cold War, the Arctic was marked by the strategic military rivalry between the United States, the Soviet Union, and their respective allies. Since the mid-1980s, awareness of the environmental problems affecting the region had increased. In his famous 1987

Murmansk speech, Soviet Secretary-General Mikhail Gorbachev expressed his ambition to change the Arctic into "a zone of peace," but also to develop cooperation on the northern environment, Indigenous peoples, and research (Gorbachev 1987; Scrivener 1989). This gave an additional impetus to change the political situation in the region. In September 1989, Finland's government took the initiative and galvanized the other seven states with territories above the Arctic Circle into action to work together on environmental protection in the region, launching the so-called "Rovaniemi process." Although it was important and timely to address these issues on an international level, Finland also properly concluded that it was even more critical to keep the momentum going and to constructively respond to the Soviet bid. To institutionalize regional cooperation, even at the cost of adjustments to its scope, seemed to be the most effective way to proceed. The Finnish Initiative assumed, therefore, the creation of a collaborative structure which would first and foremost involve the Soviet Union and would tackle matters that were important and politically acceptable to all Arctic states (Rajakoski 1989, 56, Young 1998, 170).

Once established and proven to be effective, this format could then extend to other areas. After preliminary diplomatic consultations, transnational environmental problems affecting the Arctic appeared to be the least controversial issues. It was decided that the various countries' authorities with a responsibility for the Arctic environment should meet regularly. As the Finnish Ambassador Esko Rajakoski, leader of the negotiation process, later commented, at this early stage of discussion the inclusion of any additional elements with political connotations touching upon differences or disputes between the states would have determined the failure of the entire initiative (Berger and Roch 1989, 79). For Finland, the theme of cooperation, although relevant, was not as important as seeking ground for launching nonbelligerent interstate connections. Development of peaceful relations and the opportunity to discuss common problems on a regular basis with hitherto antagonistic neighbors in a highly militarized and strategically important region did have significant consequences for regional security and stability, regardless of the subject of joint endeavors. Thus, scientific cooperation on less controversial environmental and sustainable development issues provided a catalyst to initiate and maintain an ongoing dialogue that deepened the cooperation over time (cf. Nilson 1997, 4).

This undertaking came to be known as the Arctic Environmental Protection Strategy (AEPS). It was adopted along with a ministerial Declaration on the Protection of the Arctic Environment. AEPS assumed work on the six most pertinent environmental problems in the Arctic: persistent organic pollutants, oil pollution, heavy metals, noise, radioactivity, acidification. To ensure effective implementation of the strategy, the Arctic states established four programs that later became the Arctic Council's working groups: the Arctic Monitoring and Assessment Program (AMAP), Protection of the Arctic Marine Environment (PAME), Emergency Prevention, Preparedness and Response (EPPR), and Conservation of Arctic Flora and Fauna (CAFF). They also decided to meet biennially at ministerial meetings and to delegate Senior Arctic Affairs Officials (SAAOs) to supervise the activities and report to the ministers. The new structure also included observers from among Indigenous peoples' organizations, non-Arctic states, and different types of organizations.

In parallel to the Finnish Initiative, Canada also put forward a proposal building on Gorbachev's speech. The idea of creating an Arctic Council was first mentioned in 1989 by then-Canadian Prime Minister Brian Mulroney in Leningrad, (now St Petersburg), and was officially announced by Canada's Secretary of State for External Affairs, Lloyd Axworthy, in November 1990 (ACP 1991; Axworthy 2013, 13; English 2013, 158–159). The Canadian project was more far-reaching than the Finnish one and proposed the creation of a fully fledged international organization with an open mandate (including military security) and a complex institutional design (Pharand 1991; 1992; Graczyk 2011, 594–596). This proposal was met with resistance, however; the United States in particular was skeptical (Scrivener 1996; Bloom 1999). After the decisive US–Canada meeting in 1995 between American President Bill Clinton and Canadian Prime Minister Jean Chrétien, the Arctic governments agreed to organize the enterprise as an intergovernmental high-level forum. The Arctic Council is therefore a forum without a "legal personality" and not an international organization as such. The Declaration on the Establishment of the Arctic Council, (aka the Ottawa Declaration) was adopted in September 1996.

The statutes governing the Council were decided at the ministerial meeting in Iqaluit, Canada, in 1998. All decisions in the forum and subsidiary bodies were to be made by consensus. The actual work of the Council proceeds on three levels: ministerial, senior civil servant (SAOs – Senior Arctic Officials) and working groups. Task forces can be created for specific undertakings. When the Arctic states hold ministerial meetings – which constitute the highest decision-making authority and occur every second year – they tend to attract the attention of the public. In the early years, civil servants frequently represented member states at these meetings. This is no longer the case; since the 2011 ministerial meeting in Nuuk, Greenland, these meetings are regularly attended by the foreign ministers and the US secretaries of state, with the exception of the 2015 Iqaluit meeting where the Russian Federation was represented by minister of natural resources Sergei Donskoi due to Canadian–Russian tensions over the post-2014 Ukraine crises. This is indicative of the Council's increased importance as a discussion forum in recent years (and also as a launching pad for binding agreements negotiated by the Arctic states). By their declarations from the ministerial gatherings, the member states show how they would like the Council to evolve. This is where the basic policy underlying the Council's work finds expression. The participation of the American and Russian foreign ministers gives these statements further political weight.

At the official level, the SAOs convene at least twice a year. They serve as a liaison between the ministerial and working-group levels. The SAOs are senior civil servants, normally in the rank of ambassadors, empowered by their respective governments to manage and oversee the work of the Council on a daily basis. Nevertheless, most of the work is done in the working groups. They are producers of scientific knowledge whose work involves identifying, assessing, and making recommendations on the most pertinent regional issues. Such challenges include everything from mercury levels to guidelines for Arctic shipping. The working groups have been described as the powerhouse of the Arctic Council (Graczyk and Koivurova 2015, 309). Another aspect worth emphasizing in this general picture is the voluntary funding of the projects and work of the Council by the member states. This means, among other things, that the working groups must apply for funding from a variety of sources. Further, programs and projects must be approved by all member states before they can get underway, and governments can be quite selective when it comes to financing projects. The Council does not have a separate program budget. Member states' perceptions of the Council's role are thus the Council's real driving force (or counterforce).

One can subdivide the history of the Council into three periods. In the first period, from 1996 to the mid-2000s, research on Arctic pollution was at the top of the agenda, precipitated by the high levels of toxins and heavy metals appearing in the region. Much of this pollution is carried northwards by ocean and air currents. The working groups submitted, (and continue to provide), reports addressing this challenge. Their work has informed climate negotiations and international conventions on various contaminants (such as the 2013 Minamata Convention on Mercury and the 2001 Stockholm Convention on Persistent Organic Pollutants, or POPs). The working groups, such as ACAP (Arctic Contaminants Action Program) and AMAP (Arctic Monitoring and Assessment Program), continue to work on these conventions as part of their principal activity.

Climate change received greater attention in the work of the Council in the early 2000s. This was most evident in the most publicized scientific work performed under Council auspices: the Arctic Climate Impact Assessment (ACIA). According to this assessment, the Arctic is in a unique position with regard to climate change, in that the first signs of the global consequences of climate change will be observed in this region. Thus, the Council concentrated in this period on mapping the implications of global warming and on adaptation to climate change. Furthermore, limiting the emission of so-called short-lived greenhouse gases such as soot, methane, and tropospheric ozone is one of several particularly challenging items on the mitigation agenda.

In recent years the Council has nonetheless focused mainly on what can be done to adapt to climate change and to respond to the growing interest in the Council as a forum for international cooperation. This concern in particular has increased with the steady rise in activity in the North: a result of the retreating sea-ice cover. The binding agreements under the auspices of the Council include pacts on Cooperation on Aeronautical and Maritime Search and Rescue in the Arctic (the SAR Agreement) signed in 2011, and Cooperation on Marine Oil Pollution Preparedness and Response in the Arctic (the MOPPR Agreement) signed in 2013. The Arctic has also been influential on the foreign policy agendas of the Arctic states and others with a stated interest in the region. All of the Arctic states have presented Arctic strategy documents in recent years; for example, Canada's 2009 Arctic Foreign Policy sets out fairly explicitly Ottawa's views concerning the Council's future role. The Council, it says, is the key forum for collaboration on Arctic affairs, and Canada will work to strengthen the forum. This positive approach towards the future of the Arctic Council is found in Denmark as well; for example, the Danish government has argued that the Council should become a "decision-making organization."

The strategic documents of the three states without an Arctic coastline, (Iceland, Finland and Sweden), also highlight the Council as the central forum for addressing Arctic-related issues. They express their respective government's commitment to strengthening the Council's role. The Finnish Arctic Strategy from 2013 made the most far-reaching proposal to transform the Council into a treaty-based organization. Key actors have, on the other hand, claimed that non-littoral Arctic states (apart from Iceland) have taken a less active part in the work of the Council. If we look at the two great-power members, the US and Russia, they are also sympathetic to the part played by the Council. A United States presidential directive issued in January 2009 on the Arctic highlighted the key role of the Council in facilitating cooperation on Arctic issues. This was also emphasized in the United States 2013 Arctic Strategy. The positive attitudes towards the SAR and MOPPR Agreements were concrete expressions of this. Then-Secretary of State Hillary Clinton's participation at the 2011 Nuuk meeting, and her successor John Kerry's at the 2013 Kiruna meeting and the Iqaluit meeting in 2015, also testified to the importance of the Arctic in US foreign policy.

In recent years, the Russian government of Vladimir Putin has issued several documents detailing its Arctic strategy, stressing again the importance of the Council in facilitating international cooperation. Russia has long wanted to play a key role in the development of search and rescue operations in the Arctic, a concrete expression of which could be seen in their participation in the drafting of the SAR Agreement (Graczyk and Koivurova 2015, 316–317). Russia's engagement was also evident in the drafting of the oil-spill agreement. Working with others, Russia spearheaded the work that eventually resulted in the two agreements. Norway chaired the Council from autumn 2006 to spring 2009, a key period in the formulation of Norway's High North policy and Arctic strategy. Norwegian interest in the Council grew as well, with the government describing the Arctic Council as "the main multilateral forum in the North." Efforts to establish a permanent secretariat in Tromsø were also important. In the recent white paper on the High North titled *The High North: Visions and Strategy*, the government underlined its commitment to ensuring a well-functioning Council. Norway's Arctic policy, the government wrote, was developed mainly in the context of the Council.

Different governments have differing reasons for their involvement in Arctic issues. What they have in common, however, is a strong commitment to the work of the Council. Moreover, in connection with the Kiruna ministerial meeting, the question of observer status for the European Union and China headed the agenda. China and several other countries were indeed granted an accredited "formal" observer status in 2013. The EU application was "received affirmatively," but hinged upon the resolution of the dispute between Canada and the EU on the wider terms before the EU's observer status could be finally confirmed. The tense relationship between Canada and the European Union over the issue of an EU ban on seal products was the main cause for the delay, but the Canadian objection was lifted after reaching a trade agreement in September 2014. The confirmation of the EU's observer status then became hostage to the situation in Ukraine and Russian retaliatory objection. Nonetheless, the EU is an "observer in principle," with no practical difference compared to other observers, having the possibility to participate the Council's work (Graczyk and Koivurova 2015, 320). The desire for observer status on the part of the EU and China, as well as smaller powers such as Britain, France, Germany, Japan, and South Korea, demonstrates that stakeholders outside the geographically limited Arctic region have begun to perceive the region as important.

While traditionally understood security concerns could be seen as the main incentive for launching the environmental cooperation in the Arctic, state sovereignty issues were intrinsic aspects of the negotiations toward the creations of AEPS and the Arctic Council. States have actually been more focused on preserving their interests and securing existing power relations than on solving certain problems both inside and outside individual Arctic states. Nevertheless, the Finnish Initiative succeeded in bringing together all the eight Arctic nations to protect the Arctic environment, despite the context being highly influenced by security and sovereignty interests. The focal point is that the Arctic has undergone a political renaissance, the difference this time being the emphasis on cooperation rather than conflict. In this context, the Council is perceived as a relevant arena by all the Arctic states and many non-Arctic states.

Soft actions, hard effects

The question emerges whether these developments and the work of Arctic Council projects have contributed to stability, and thus indirectly to security in the region. If yes, in what manner has it happened? It is argued that the Arctic Council has three integrated key functions in this respect: (a) as an important arena creating common understandings and emphasizing common interests, (b) as the "first choice" when addressing emerging Arctic issues, and (c) correcting misunderstandings about the Arctic.

Common understandings

First and foremost, the projects and assessments undertaken by the Arctic Council have created a common understanding of issues, and thus limited the possibility of different views on the fundamentals and facts. Interaction and joint ventures have mitigated the potential for conflicts and disputes. This in turn resulted in increased predictability, which is essential to maintaining peaceful and effective cooperation. The shared consensual knowledge generated under the Council's projects provides for common understanding of phenomena occurring in the Arctic and reduces the possibility of disagreements in relation to the basic facts and perceptions of certain issues.

The Arctic Council is the only intergovernmental body covering the whole area of the Arctic. Together with the AEPS, the Arctic Council contributed significantly to the deepening of interaction and confidence building in the post-Cold War Arctic, becoming an example of a successful project to enhance regional stability and creating an innovative and sustainable model of cooperation. A practically open mandate, albeit limited in individual cases to the lack of consent to engage in certain areas, or a consensus to postpone them, allows for the initiation of projects relevant to current developments on the most pertinent issues in the region. Unconstrained exchange of views between representatives of governments and Indigenous peoples' organizations contributes to faster and more appropriate actions to solve common problems. While lacking the ability to make legally binding decisions, the Arctic Council has proven to be quite successful in resolving issues by promoting them in the relevant institutions that have such powers. Most countries in the Arctic appear to express the belief that the essential and unique mission of the Council is to deal with problems of the Arctic at a high political level. According to the most shared viewpoints between the member states, the organization should act as a decision-shaping rather than decision-making body. Nevertheless, the importance of this institution is revealed primarily through its ability to generate knowledge and encourage innovation in approaches to the issues arising from predictions about the consequences of climate change in the Arctic. This is accomplished primarily by providing guidance, best practices, and expertise to other international forums where decisions can be made. In this context, the Arctic Council should be viewed in connection with the entire regional governance framework encompassing a wide range of regional and global agreements and institutions with competence in the Arctic (Hoel 2009). Furthermore, it may be seen as the political pillar of the international architecture in the Arctic, along with UNCLOS as its legal cornerstone.

For example, the Arctic Council has established its role as a central actor in shaping regional marine-shipping governance. That is particularly meaningful when taking into consideration that almost all economic activities thought to pose the potential for conflicts in the region depend on marine transport. Although assessments are kept within the mandate of the Council, and as such do not deal with military and naval-related issues, there are certain ramifications for marine navigation rights and infrastructure with respect to security. Creation of a regional search and rescue instrument was also called for in the Arctic Maritime Shipping Assessment (AMSA) recommendations, which was a driver to complete this first-ever legally binding agreement negotiated under the auspices of the Arctic Council. The importance of the SAR Agreement, however, may be seen as going much further in terms of security, as it requires close cooperation and use of military capabilities as well as exchange of best practices and joint exercises, thus supporting confidence building and stability.

It is important to bear in mind that, in distinctive Arctic conditions, military and civil spheres are highly interdependent. Already in 2011, the top military commands from the eight Arctic states along with representatives of France, Germany, the Netherlands, and the United Kingdom, launched an annual event called the Arctic Security Forces Roundtable (ASFR) to further strengthen partnerships and collaboration among nations with strategic interests and responsibilities in the Arctic. The discussions revolved around practical matters related, but not limited to, SAR operations and the impacts of climate change on trade and economic issues. Another initiative that to certain degree can be attributed to the adoption of the SAR Agreement was the format initiated by Canadian Chief of Defense Staff General Walter Natynczyk in April 2012 at the meeting in Goose Bay, Labrador. The Meetings of the Chiefs of Defense Staff from the eight Arctic states added another forum to discuss security-related issues at the top military level. Again, the SAR Agreement was used as an argument for the need for closer collaboration. The most developed collaborative effort in this regard is the Arctic Coast Guard Forum (ACGF), established by the coast guards from the Arctic states in October 2015.

The ACGF defines itself as an "independent, informal and operationally driven organization" (ACGF website: www.arcticcoastguardforum.com/about-acgf) that is not bound by a treaty; it was created through a joint statement and thus has clearly defined areas of activity and a basis for operation, by which it fulfills the requirements of being considered an international institution. These examples demonstrate that the activities originating from the work of the Arctic Council in areas within its mandate translate directly into hard security matters. The Council can then be seen as delegating certain tasks beyond its mandate to external bodies, but still having a role in creating the context for their operation. As in many cases, hard security concerns spring from soft security issues and the Arctic Council may play a critical role in alleviating them at the earliest possible stage. Also, when almost all of these military arrangements were affected by the Ukraine crisis, (with ASFR and Chiefs of Defense Staffs suspending their relations with Russia), the Arctic Council remained a body where suspension of Russian involvement was unthinkable.

Another area in which the Arctic Council (indirectly) takes a position related to regional security is its handling of observers, namely non-Arctic states. It is fair to say that by specifying the criteria for observers the Council has also defined its place in the regional discourse on sovereignty, from which it is only a small step to regional security and stability. As stated in the criteria, applications for observer status are considered by taking into account the extent to which candidates:

> Recognize Arctic States' sovereignty, sovereign rights and jurisdiction in the Arctic. Recognize that an extensive legal framework applies to the Arctic Ocean including, notably, the Law of the Sea, and that this framework provides a solid foundation for responsible management of this ocean.
>
> *(Arctic Council 2013/2015, Annex 2)*

To a certain extent, inclusion of sovereignty issues (even if only associated with outside entities) in the Arctic Council's agenda may be perceived as an attempt to bridge the gap that opened up between the Arctic Five and the Arctic Eight in political terms after the 2008 Ilulissat Declaration (Graczyk and Koivurova 2014). The increased activity of the five Arctic Ocean littoral states has been caused by outside rather than regional factors, primarily media and experts and the EU-driven debate on an Arctic treaty or some other form of a legally binding basis for Arctic governance. What makes this point even more relevant is the nature of sovereignty issues in the Arctic, which may indicate that they are most likely to be dealt with bilaterally among the Arctic states. Inclusion of the key principles of the Ilulissat Declaration into the Arctic Council documents suggests that Arctic states have chosen to move these discussions into the Council's forum. Thus, the body can be perceived as an actor in mitigating regional sovereignty issues, at least those emerging from outside the region. Nowadays some Arctic states attach at least as much attention to sovereignty issues as to cooperation efforts. This is not to say that disputes on sovereignty questions will prevail among the Arctic countries. It becomes more and more apparent that they would rather include sovereignty issues than a regional cooperation agenda. Thus, the Council will likely also have a place in the regional discourse on sovereignty. The first step towards this was already taken in the criteria for observers.

A first choice

The Arctic Council enhances stability by its very existence and by providing the "first choice" channel for discussions on emerging Arctic issues within its mandate. This is further strengthened by a rather rigid calendar of meetings and activities as well as continued dialogue. Some Arctic states believe that the essential and unique mission of the AC is to deal with problems of the Arctic at a high political level (Vasiliev 2008). Although military security was excluded from the agenda of the Arctic Council (Declaration on the Establishment of the Arctic Council, 1996), primarily due to strong resistance from the United States (Scrivener 1996, 22), the wider concept of security has not been completely excluded from its work. Environmental, human, and energy security, even if not explicitly framed, are dealt with in the Council (Bailes 2009, 45). Moreover, the body may be seen as an institutional arrangement managing the interplay of inside and outside entities to protect the integrity of the region where Arctic and non-Arctic actors pursue their own interests.

There are still areas in which the Council's activity may contribute to improvement of security in a wide sense. They include, for instance, regional identity, harmonization of national interests, and a decision-making component in the Arctic governance and its interplay with the broader set of institutions, including security-related institutions. Despite being established on "soft law" foundations with limited financial, organizational, and regulatory frameworks, the Arctic Council is the only intergovernmental body covering the entire Arctic area. While lacking the ability to make legally binding decisions, the Arctic Council, founded as a consultative and coordinating body, has proven to be quite successful in resolving certain issues by making appropriate arrangements like task forces, or promoting the issues in relevant institutions that have such powers. Together with the AEPS, the Arctic Council contributed significantly to the deepening of interaction and confidence building in the post-Cold War Arctic, becoming an example of a successful project that enhanced regional stability, creating an innovative and sustainable model of cooperation (Heininen 2010, 279–280).

Alleviating misunderstandings

Yet another crucial role played by the Council is alleviating misunderstandings about the Arctic, especially those related to security situations in the region. It was the renewed debate over jurisdictional issues sparked by the Russian flag planted on the seabed beneath the North Pole in 2007, and the vast reduction in sea ice that enabled the media narrative of a "scramble for resources," which drew a picture of states competing over who gets to claim most of the

Arctic's safe and supposedly plentiful resources. This affected Arctic policy developments, ultimately challenging the Arctic Council. With the decreasing presence of sea ice and an increasing amount of commercial activities, it seems difficult to communicate the "Arctic message" in such a way that expresses that this is just a region that needs more solid scientific research and environmental and sustainable development measures. This is not so much a question of what the correct interpretation is as it is the reality of what is unfolding in the Arctic. The civil servants and experts of Arctic affairs have tried to convey that there is no scramble for resources or threats of military security in the Arctic. Yet, it is the perceived reality that seems to dominate the Arctic narrative much more than the things which the experts and civil servants try to tell us. The media speaks of possible military threats arising in the Arctic because of a scramble for resources, even if most experts agree that no such narrative accurately captures what is taking place in the region. Additionally, it is the perceived reality spread by the media that keeps feeding the southern constituencies and policymakers. Therefore, there is yet another important role for the Arctic Council: to include these actors as observers and to inform them about the real situation. It may serve as a platform for building common understanding with outside entities and thus alleviate their perception of the media-driven picture.

The Arctic Council acted upon these narratives and proved to be particularly important, though not always successful, in communicating to the world that there is peaceful and well-established cooperation going on in the region. Hence, the Council contributes to mitigating the perception of the Arctic as a place for potential conflict and disputes over access to natural resources and underlines common interests and understandings among the Arctic states for keeping the region stable and secure.

Conclusions

The AEPS, and to a lesser extent the Arctic Council, emerged in a highly securitized international environment. High-politics issues have been present since the very inception of (and even long before) current environmental cooperation in the Arctic, and to a large degree laid the fundamentals for this endeavor. Behind the timely idea of conservation of the environment, the AEPS and the Council were meant to mitigate controversial and security-related issues by providing regular consultations and discussions on common issues, enhancing mutual confidence and understanding and preparing the ground for deeper and more far-reaching collaboration that could spill over to other areas. Although the AEPS and the Arctic Council were not created as institutions focused strictly on security, they have nonetheless played an important role in building and ensuring regional stability and security (at least in minimizing the likelihood of conflicts). Arguably, their role in enhancing regional security in a traditional understanding of the term was inherent in the idea from the outset.

The environmental cooperation under AEPS and the Arctic Council has evolved into a kind of nerve center for the Arctic security system, a conceptual and institutional hub for other arrangements that stem from Arctic Council activities and proceed in accordance with discourses and perceptions devised and negotiated under the Council's auspices. By establishing its role as the major knowledge broker for the region and the primary forum for cooperation on: common regional consciousness for the Arctic states, non-Arctic actors involved as observers, and global public opinion, the Council has emerged as a focal point within a unique network of linkages with other, more specialized international institutions that to a large extent rely on the information and arrangements produced within it. Immunity and sturdiness displayed during the Ukraine crises, embedded in well-established structures and procedures, may be seen as the best guarantee for Arctic stability and security we have today.

The model incorporated in Arctic Council activities proved to be successful for keeping the region free from any serious threats of conflict. It may be argued that the Arctic Council operates and plays its roles more effectively when avoiding security-related discussions in its proceedings. Keeping its profile low in terms of politics and security, but high in terms of its ability to shape common perceptions and understanding through shared knowledge, seems to be serving the region and regional security well. The Council has been instrumental in preventing the creation of misperceptions and misunderstandings about the basic facts that could escalate into more serious disputes or conflicts; at least with sources in the region. It remains to be seen if it will be able to protect regional security from spillovers from outside the region.

Note

i Observer status in the Arctic Council is open to non-Arctic states, global and regional intergovernmental and inter-parliamentary organizations, and nongovernmental organizations. At the 2013 Kiruna Ministerial Meeting China, India, Italy, Japan, Republic of (South) Korea and Singapore were admitted as accredited observers. The EU, while being a *de facto* observer, (or "observer in principle"), has not been recognized as an accredited observer, first due to the dispute with Canada over the regulations on seal products, and after the resolution of this issue in 2014, due to retorsion over sanctions imposed on Russia after the Ukraine crisis.

References

Arctic Council. 2013/2015. Arctic Council Rules of Procedure. Adopted at the First Arctic Council Ministerial Meeting in Iqaluit, Canada September 17–18, 1998, Revised by the Arctic Council at the Eighth Arctic Council Ministerial Meeting in Kiruna, Sweden May 15, 2013.

Arctic Council Panel (ACP). 1991. *To Establish an International Arctic Council: A Framework Report.* Ottawa: CARC, Canadian Centre for Arms Control and Disarmament, Inuit Circumpolar Conference.

Axworthy, Thomas. 2013. "Changing the Arctic Paradigm from Cold War to Co-operation: How Canada's Indigenous Leaders Shaped the Arctic Council." Paper prepared for the Fifth Polar Law Symposium, 6–8 September 2012, Rovaniemi and Finland.

Bailes Alyson J. K. 2009. "Options for Closer Cooperation in the High North: What is Needed?" In *Security Prospects in the High North: Geostrategic Thaw of Freeze?* edited by Sven G. Holtsmark and Brooke A. Smith-Windsor, 28–57. *NDC Forum* Paper 7. Rome: NATO Defense College.

Berger, Thomas R., and Douglas Roch. eds. 1989. *The Arctic Choices for Peace and Security, Proceedings of a Public Inquiry.* Vancouver, BC: Gordon Soules Book Publishers.

Bloom, Evan T. 1999. "Establishment of the Arctic Council." *American Journal of International Law* 93(3): 712–722.

Buzan, Barry, Ole Wæver, and Jaap De Wilde. 1997. *Security: A New Framework for Analysis.* Boulder, CO: Lynne Rienner Publishers.

English, John. 2013. *Ice and Water: Politics, Peoples, and the Arctic Council.* Toronto: Allen Lane.

Gorbachev, Mikhail. 1987. Speech at the Ceremonial Meeting on the Occasion of the Presentation of the Order of Lenin and the Gold Star to the City of Murmansk, 1 October 1987, www.barentsinfo.fi/docs/Gorbachev_speech.pdf (accessed 25 May 2018).

Graczyk, Piotr, and Timo Koivurova. 2015. "The Arctic Council." In *Handbook of the Politics of the Arctic*, edited by Leif Christian Jensen and Geir Hønneland, 298–327. Cheltenham: Edward Elgar Publishing.

Graczyk, Piotr, and Timo Koivurova. 2014. "A New Era in Arctic Council's External Relations? Broader Consequences of the Nuuk Observer Rules for Arctic Governance." *Polar Record* 50(254): 225–236.

Graczyk, Piotr. 2011. "Observers in the Arctic Council – Evolution and prospects." *Yearbook of Polar Law* 3: 575–633.

Griffiths, Franklyn. 1992. "Epilogue: Civility in the Arctic." In *Arctic Alternatives: Civility or Militarism in the Circumpolar North*, edited by Franklyn Griffiths, 280–309. Toronto: Science for Peace and Samuel Stevens.

Griffiths, Franklyn. 2011. "Arctic Security: The Indirect Approach." In *Arctic Security in an Age of Climate Change*, edited by James Kraska, 3–19. Cambridge: Cambridge University Press.

Heininen, Lassi. 2010. "Circumpolar International Relations and Cooperation." In *Globalization and the Circumpolar North*, edited by Lassi Heininen and Chris Southcott, 265–304. Fairbanks: University of Alaska Press.

Hoel, Alf Håkon. 2009. "Do We Need a New Legal Regime for the Arctic Ocean?" *International Journal of Marine and Coastal Law* 24(2): 443–456.

Jervis, Robert. 1983. "Security Regimes." In *International Regimes*, edited by Stephen D. Krasner, 173–194. Ithaca, NY: Cornell University Press.

Koivurova, Timo, and Piotr Graczyk. 2014. "The Future of the Arctic Council: Navigating between Sovereignty and Security." In *International Relations and the Arctic: Understanding Policy and Governance*, edited by Robert W. Murray and Anita Dey Nuttall, 441–482. Amherst, NY: Cambria Press.

Krasner, Stephen D. ed. 1983. *International Regimes*. Ithaca, NY: Cornell University Press.

Nilson, Håken R. 1997. "Arctic Environmental Protection Strategy (AEPS): Process and Organization, 1991–97." *NPI Rapportserie*, 103. Oslo: Norwegian Polar Institute.

Pharand, Donat. 1991. "Proposal for an Arctic Council Treaty." *Northern Perspectives* 19 (2): n.p.

Pharand, Donat. 1992. "The Case for an Arctic Region Council and a Treaty Proposal." *Revue generale de droit* 2 (23): 163–195.

Rajakoski, Esko. 1989. "Multilateral Cooperation to Protect the Arctic Environment: The Finnish Initative." In *The Arctic Choices for Peace and Security, Proceedings of a Public Inquiry*, edited by Thomas R. Berger and Douglas Roche, 53–59. Vancouver, BC: Gordon Soules Book Publishers.

Rottem, Svein Vigeland. 2017. "The Arctic Council: Challenges and Recommendations." In *Arctic Governance I: Law and Politics*, edited by Svein Vigeland Rottem and Ida Folkestad Soltvedt, 231–251. London: I. B. Tauris.

Scrivener, D. 1996. *Environmental Cooperation in the Arctic: From Strategy to Council.* Oslo: The Norwegian Atlantic Committee.

Scrivener, David. 1989. *Gorbachev's Murmansk Speech: The Soviet Initiative and Western Responses.* Oslo: The Norwegian Atlantic Committee.

Stokke, Olav Schram. 2017. "The Arctic: Environmental Security or Multi-Level Governance?" In *Arctic Governance I: Law and Politics*, edited by Svein Vigeland Rottem and Ida Folkestad Soltvedt, 73–87. London: I. B. Tauris.

Tennberg, Monica. 2000. *Arctic Environmental Cooperation: A Study in Governmentality*. Aldershot: Ashgate.

Vasiliev, Anton. 2008. "Russian Policy in the Arctic and the Arctic Council." Final Report on Northern Research Forum Plenary Session "The Future of Northern Co-Operation" and Special Roundtable Discussion "The Arctic Council and Multilateral Cooperation: Reports and Articles." 5th NRF Open Assembly "Seeking Balance in a Changing North." Anchorage and Alaska, 24–27 September 2008.

Young, Oran R. 1998. *Creating Regimes: Arctic Accords and International Governance*. Ithaca, NY and London, UK: Cornell University Press.

Young, Oran R. 2011. "Foreword - Arctic Futures: The Politics of Transformation." In *Arctic Security in an Age of Climate Change*, edited by James Kraska, XXI–XXVII. Cambridge: Cambridge University Press.

20

SCIENCE DIPLOMACY AND THE ARCTIC

Rasmus Gjedssø Bertelsen

Introduction

The Arctic is a well-integrated part of the international system and of international politics, and has been so for centuries (Heininen and Southcott, 2010. The Arctic is also the hub of much scientific activity, scientific cooperation, and the use of science for foreign- and security-policy purposes (International Arctic Science Committee (IASC), 2015). Therefore, the Arctic is a useful region in which to explore and discuss science diplomacy and its applications. This chapter will discuss what science diplomacy is and how it can be used for confidence building in the Arctic and in general.

The Arctic has been an integrated part of the international system for centuries, and conflict or militarization in the region has closely mirrored conflict at the international-system level. This integration was clear during World War II and the Cold War. Today, the Arctic is also affected by the two processes of post-post-Cold War relations between Russia and the West and the rise of China and power transition from West to East. Science diplomacy in the Arctic has played, and continues to play, important and interesting roles during these conditions of conflict or tension.

Science diplomacy in the Arctic offers important and interesting lessons for general international policy and also scholarly challenges, because the cases in the Arctic where science diplomacy has played a role are generalizable situations and not solely Arctic situations. The chapter provides a historical account of the role of polar science diplomacy during the Cold War. The role of Arctic science diplomacy in (a) the current post-post-Cold War relations between Russia and the West, and (b) in adapting Arctic governance to global changes of power transition from West to East, are discussed. Post-post-Cold War Russia–West relations pose significant challenges in, for instance, the Baltic Sea Region, where science diplomacy can and should play a significant role. Power transition from West to East, especially driven by the rise of China, poses challenges around the world; hence, lessons from Sino–Arctic science diplomacy are valuable not only for developing policy, but also for advancing policy and scholarship around the role of science diplomacy in global governance under global change.

The experience of Russia–West Arctic science diplomacy under current post-post-Cold War politics demonstrates that science diplomacy can maintain relations between Russia and the West in the civilian educational and research domain.But political, defense, and commercial relations are more vulnerable to political crisis. Sino–Arctic science diplomacy offers valuable lessons on adapting regional governance to global change. It is an example of how status quo powers can integrate a power that is on the rise with less conflict.

What is science diplomacy?

Science diplomacy is the use of science to achieve a certain foreign-policy goal. In this chapter, science includes all fields of academic research, health, humanities, natural sciences, social sciences, and technology. *Science* in English often means the natural sciences, whereas it is much more useful, when discussing the foreign-policy use and role of science, to think of the German *Wissenschaft* or Scandinavian *videnskab/vitenskap/vetenskap*, which cover all areas of research. It is important to keep in mind that although science diplomacy may be a recent concept for analysis and theoretical discussion, the practice of using science for foreign-policy aims is not new.[1]

In an influential 2010 report on science diplomacy, the Royal Society and the American Association for the Advancement of Science introduced a grid of science diplomacy activities, which is very useful for discussing science diplomacy, including in the Arctic (The Royal Society and AAAS, 2010.

Science in diplomacy

Science *in* diplomacy is when science is used to inform foreign policy, diplomatic action, and diplomatic negotiations. It is common to think of science *in* diplomacy as positive-sum activities, where injecting scientific knowledge into negotiations helps to solve the common problems of mankind. An obvious example would be the work of the International Panel on Climate Change and their assessments feeding into the political negotiations at the successive Conferences of the Parties (COP) of the United Nations Framework Convention on Climate Change. The Arctic (and the Antarctic) play prominent roles in this science *in* diplomacy concerning climate change because these two regions play key roles in the global climate system and are the locations of the especially crucial ice-core climate research. The other great environmental convention of the UN is on biodiversity, where there is also a large body of scientific work inserted into these negotiations.

However, Langenhove raised the concern that applying knowledge in diplomacy can also be an adversarial and competitive zero-sum activity. Negotiations on various industrial standards hold great economic interests, and here the application of scientific and technological knowledge is competitive and potentially zero-sum. If hard security and military activities are considered a part of diplomacy, then there is a large scientific and technological component (Langenhove, 2017.

Diplomacy for science

Diplomacy *for* science is the application of diplomatic activity to support scientific activities. UNESCO is the clearest example of multilateralism in the service of science. At the regional level, the European Union makes great investments in science through the framework programs and in educational diplomacy through the Erasmus program. The Nordic countries pursue common scientific and educational purposes through the Nordforsk common research funding body and the Nordplus exchange scheme. At its Fairbanks ministerial meeting on

11 May 2017, the Arctic Council created the *Agreement on Enhancing International Arctic Scientific Cooperation*, which facilitates cross-border scientific cooperation in the Arctic and is a particularly clear example of diplomacy *for* science in the Arctic.

Science for diplomacy

Science *for* diplomacy is when scientific cooperation supports diplomacy and foreign policy. This is often the dimension of science diplomacy that receives most interest. Science *for* diplomacy can play a useful role in keeping lines of communication and dialogue open during political conflict when relations between states are strained. Science *for* diplomacy can create resilient lines of communication between parties in conflict. Such dialogue and communication can perform an important confidence-building role. This dialogue also has potentially interesting and important socialization effects on decision-makers and can create epistemic communities across political dividing lines.

This chapter will devote most attention to the science *for* diplomacy dimension as the most interesting Arctic cases for discussing science diplomacy concern such confidence building and mutual learning in epistemic communities.

Science diplomacy for confidence building: also in the Arctic

Science *for* diplomacy entails scientific cooperation across borders. As mentioned, the Arctic has been and remains a well-integrated part of the international system, so the conflict lines of the international system are also well represented in the Arctic. For the purposes of this chapter, these conflict lines were between the USSR and the West during the Cold War, and today they are between Russia and the West in the context of the Ukraine crisis, and between rising China and the Western status quo powers.

Science *for* diplomacy often entails the formation of epistemic communities, which the chapter shows can play an important role for building confidence and increasing levels of shared knowledge and understanding across such conflict lines. Epistemic communities are transnational expert communities who share and co-create knowledge and understanding about problems and acceptable solutions. Such shared beliefs about problems and their solutions can be important for international policy coordination (Adler and Haas, 1992; Haas, 1992; Haas, 2011.

Arctic science diplomacy during the Cold War: International Geophysical Year, Polar Bear Treaty, Norwegian-Soviet Fishing Commission, and the Danish National Museum

The Cold War deeply affected the Arctic for systemic rather than local reasons, which makes examples of East–West science diplomacy in the Arctic during the Cold War interesting and important cases for analyzing and discussing science diplomacy and security in the Arctic and in general. The first case to mention is the International Geophysical Year 1957–1958, which was an attempt to reanimate East–West scientific connections that had suffered seriously during the early Cold War. The International Geophysical Year was modeled after the International Polar Years of 1882–1883 and 1932–1933. Great efforts were made to shield the International Geophysical Year from being tainted by national politics. The year played a foundational role for the Antarctic Treaty System, which regulates the Antarctic, thereby keeping it out of the Cold War competition between the United States and USSR (Launius, Fleming, and DeVorkin, 2010).

The first East–West environmental Arctic treaty was the Polar Bear Protection Treaty of 1973 between Canada, the Kingdom of Denmark, Norway, the United States, and the USSR. A lesser known, but important and interesting case that laid groundwork for later better known science diplomacy in the Arctic, was the Norwegian–Soviet Fisheries Commission, which started work in 1975. Norway and the USSR (now Russia) share some of the world's most profitable cod stocks in the Barents Sea, so the two countries had a great interest in optimal co-management. The two countries did well based on both marine science and game theory, (sharing 50/50 so that stock optimization was the best way to increase one's own share). This marine science cooperation built an important Norwegian–Soviet epistemic community between institutions in Tromsø and Murmansk, which became the foundation for later and more visible science diplomacy when the Cold War ended (Jørgensen and Hønneland, 2013.

According to Arctic ethnologist and historian of studies of Arctic Indigenous peoples, Igor Krupnik, Danish Eskimology specialists, particularly those centered around the Danish National Museum in Copenhagen, played a critical intermediary role between Soviet and Western Arctic ethnology and ethnography beginning in the late 1930s and particularly during the Cold War era (Krupnik, 1998, 2016). The Danish National Museum had important Arctic ethnographic collections and forged professional lines of communication with Soviet ethnographic institutions. In the 1950s and up to the late 1980s, the USSR considered Denmark a "safe place" in multiple political dimensions for Soviet anthropologists to meet their Western counterparts. Therefore, Danish Arctic institutions played an early convening role prior to the era of *perestroika* and *glasnost* in facilitating East–West Arctic science cooperation. The important circumpolar Arctic scientific bodies were formed in the last years of the USSR; bodies such as the International Arctic Science Committee (IASC, in 1990) and the International Arctic Social Sciences Association (IASSA, also in 1990) (Krupnik, 2010, 2018).

Post-Cold War Arctic science diplomacy: AEPS, Barents Region, Arctic Council

The end of the Cold War in the Arctic was initiated by the famous speech by Mikhail Gorbachev in Murmansk in 1987, where he called for the Arctic to be a zone of peace, environmental protection, and scientific cooperation in stark contrast to the extreme levels of nuclear militarization in the region during the Cold War. Finland quickly followed these Soviet overtures with the Rovaniemi Process in 1989, which led to the adaptation of the Arctic Environmental Protection Strategy (AEPS) by the eight Arctic states in 1991 and established some of the working groups, which continue under the Arctic Council. This initiative by Finland was a clear-cut example of a small state in a very exposed position neighboring the USSR that, because of a relaxed international system, had the opportunity to use environmental monitoring, science, and protection to pursue foreign and security-policy goals (Heininen and Southcott, 2010; Heininen, 2013).

Norway followed the same path, quickly taking the initiative to establish the Barents Euro-Arctic Council and Barents cooperation in 1993. Norway pursued an ambitious High North policy towards Russia, where Norway employs the full range of educational, scientific, environmental, cultural, and economic development dimensions to develop and deepen a comprehensive relationship with northwest Russia in the strategic pursuit of a stable and predictable High North. This strategy is easily understandable in view of Norway's key foreign and security-policy interests related to its common land and sea border with the Russian Federation (before the USSR) (Hønneland, 2005, 2017). The Finnish and Norwegian initiatives are both good illustrations of how small, highly developed states in exposed geostrategic positions can employ science diplomacy, especially in the Arctic environmental field, for foreign and security-policy aims.

Canada followed up on the Finnish AEPS initiative by proposing and establishing the Arctic Council with the Ottawa Declaration of 1996. The Arctic Council's work centers on environmental monitoring, research and protection, and sustainable development through the work of its eight working groups, some of which were initiated under the AEPS. Canada is an example of a middle power, geographically distant from the dangerous USSR or Russia, which could use a relaxed international order to take on and further develop the Finnish small-state Arctic environmental science diplomacy initiative to promote itself (English, 2013).

Post-post Cold War Arctic science diplomacy and the Ukraine crisis

Two shifts in the international system are also affecting the Arctic. The first is that Russia is again a great power pursuing its interests in its surroundings (Mearsheimer, 2014. Russian and post-Soviet society went through a social, economic and political crisis that is difficult to imagine for outsiders. The dissolution of the USSR and the ensuing crisis greatly reduced Russia's power and power-projection potential. With the presidencies of Vladimir Putin and rising oil prices, Russia is returning to great-power status, although it is still well below that of the USSR. Russia lost its Central and Eastern European sphere of influence during the 1990s and early 2000s. That process came to a halt, first with the Russo–Georgian war in 2008, and on a much greater scale with the Ukraine and Crimea crises since 2014. In this struggle, Russia, the United States, the European Union, and European great powers are escalating the conflict horizontally into different regions and functional areas, with military posturing and sanctions, while continuing cooperation in other geographic and functional regions. A big question has been whether the Ukraine and Crimea crises would affect the Arctic region.

Referencing the Russian military build-up in the Arctic, some Western voices have raised concerns about Russian aggression in Ukraine and Crimea being replicated in the Arctic (Bittner, 2016). With respect to the Georgian and Ukrainian situation, Russia responded with military force to specific strategic problems in the Caucasus and Eastern Europe. Russia does not have any such strategic problems in the Arctic; hence, there is little reason to expect Russia to act with military force there. Concerning any Arctic military build-up, it is necessary to keep in mind that Russian Arctic military installations and forces had deeply deteriorated with the dissolution of the USSR, so this build-up may be a course-correction. Secondly, Russian strategic nuclear forces in the Arctic and the conventional forces protecting them are placed in the region for geostrategic reasons, and not for reasons connected to the Arctic per se.

It is, rather, the West that has escalated the Ukraine and Crimea crises horizontally to the Arctic through financial and technological sanctions against Russian Arctic offshore oil and gas developments. This horizontal escalation from the West reflects a calculated desire to punish a key sector of the Russian domestic political economy built around oil and gas rents (Rosen, 2016). In addition, Canada boycotted some Arctic Council meetings in Russia, which may have been motivated by Canadian domestic politics. The scientific and educational cooperation in the Arctic continues despite the Ukraine and Crimea crises, with some noteworthy exceptions. Both Western and Russia students and scholars seem determined to continue this cooperation, and most funding support structures continue. However, the exceptions are noteworthy.

The University of Northern British Columbia in Prince George, British Columbia, Canada, hosted the International Congress of Arctic Social Sciences in May 2014, coinciding with the Ukraine and Crimea crises unfolding. A large number of Russian scholars could not participate because Canada withheld their visa applications (Bennett, 2014). Shortly after, in August 2014, the Russian Federation Security Council hosted its annual high-level Arctic meeting in Naryan-Mar, Nenets Autonomous Okrug. This annual meeting usually gathers diplomats from Arctic states. The host of the meeting is the secretary of the Security Council, Nikolay Patrushev, former director of the FSB national security service. No Western Arctic diplomats participated in this meeting but the Security Council, together with the Northern Arctic Federal University (NARFU) in Arkhangelsk, invited foreign Arctic scholars, where I represented Denmark. In September 2015, at this meeting in Arkhangelsk, Western Arctic diplomats returned with the Danish ambassador to Moscow as the highest ranking Western official. Scholars were still invited and remain so, adding a sense of resilience to this venue in light of potential external political disruptions. However, Russia is suppressing and harassing civil society organizations that collaborate with and receive funding from abroad, including Arctic people-to-people cooperation. This policy has included demanding that the Nordic Council of Ministers' St. Petersburg Office change its status from an NGO to a foreign agent, raiding the Norwegian University Center in St. Petersburg, and expelling Norwegian and Swedish students there on visa charges. Both the Nordic Council of Ministers' Office and the Norwegian University Center have closed (Nordisk samarbeid, 2015; Helle and Randen, 2017; Hellesund, 2018; *Det norske universitetssenter i St. Petersburg*, n.d.). Suppression of transnational civil society should be seen both in the context of Russian domestic politics and foreign relations.

Despite the disruptions above, Russian–Western Arctic science (and education) diplomacy continues to play a key role in science *for* diplomacy between Russia and the other seven Arctic nations. This science and education cooperation is continuously (re)building epistemic communities of new generations of scholars and students from Russia and the West who get to know each other personally and visit each other's locations. These epistemic communities co-create a shared understanding of the Arctic, mutual positions, and interests. This science *for* diplomacy takes place parallel to the continuing national security interests in the Arctic surrounding, especially, the strategic balance of nuclear deterrence. Russian–West Arctic science diplomacy is therefore an illustration that, with sufficient mutual political will, it is possible for Russia and the West to maintain extensive scientific and educational cooperation in a region with strong and competing national security interests.

Russia and the West should keep this Arctic lesson in mind concerning, for instance, the Baltic Sea and the Baltic states, where there is more dangerous national security competition in much more restricted air and sea space with a higher risk of incidents than in the Arctic. There are marine environmental issues in the Baltic, for instance, in the vicinity of Kaliningrad and bordering two NATO countries, Poland and Lithuania, which could be explored as topics of science and education *for* diplomacy.[2]

Power transition and Arctic science diplomacy: integrating a rising China in the Arctic

The other and more important global social, economic, and political change in the international system today is the power transition from West to East driven by economic growth in Asia, especially in China. This change is also affecting the Arctic profoundly. Sino–Arctic science diplomacy plays an important practical role in these changes, with interesting policy and research lessons (Bertelsen, 2016; Bertelsen, Li, and Gregersen, 2017; Bertelsen and SU, 2018).

Asia hosts more than half the world's population, and until the 1800s it accounted for more than half the world's economic output. Asia's relative share of economic output was greatly diminished to less than 20% in the 1950s, while the West's relative share was greatly increased due to the industrial revolution, imperialism, and world wars. Asia is now reclaiming its historical share of the world economy. According to the Asian Development Bank, Asia now accounts for 34% of the world economy and will account for more than half in 2050. This development was first led by Japan's strong growth after World War II, which made Japan the world's second largest economy. China has experienced phenomenal economic growth since opening up its economy in 1978, and is now the world's second largest economy and will eventually become the world's largest economy (Asian Development Bank, 2011.

The effects of such shifts in economic power are felt around the world, including in the Arctic. The largest or most advanced Asian economies – China, Japan, South Korea, India, and Singapore – have in recent years engaged themselves in the Arctic and achieved regular observer status in the Arctic Council in 2013 (Arctic Council, 2018). China's interest in the Arctic has attracted much attention and raised suspicions (Breum and Chemnitz, 2013; Higgins, 2013). The relationship between China and Greenland in particular has caused suspicion and arguments about a special Chinese economic interest in Greenland, especially in the area of resource extraction (Lanteigne & Shi, 2019). Here it is important to keep in mind that the second largest and soon-to-be largest economy in the world can be expected to be globally engaged around the world, including in Greenland, as the United States is engaged around the world. This fact does not make China's engagement in the Arctic less strategically problematic, but it is a reminder that this engagement is a reflection of global change and not restricted to the Arctic.

Power transition is the great engine of international relations, and is extraordinarily complex and potentially dangerous. Power transition occurs when the existing hegemon, or leading power, is being caught up with, or challenged, by a rising power due to its higher economic growth. Such power transitions or attempts at power transition have caused bloody world wars (Organski, 1968 [1958]). A very rare, peaceful, power transition occurred between Britain and the US in the early and mid-1900s. China's rise relative to the United States is, therefore, cause for extraordinary concern for peace, first and foremost in East Asia (Allison, 2017) but also in other regions of the world, including the Arctic. Here Sino–Arctic science diplomacy offers interesting and valuable lessons, and perhaps opportunities.

Mere talk of Chinese investments in land, natural resource extraction, or infrastructure in the Arctic raises high levels of suspicion. Below, the chapter demonstrates how Sino–Arctic scientific collaboration is received very differently. This section lists some illustrative examples of suspicions coming from Iceland and Greenland. It is important to keep in mind that such suspicion is not unique to China or the Arctic. Power transitions always cause high levels of suspicion about the rising power. For example, Britain and France, in the early years of the 1900s, were highly suspicious of the German Berlin–Baghdad–Bahn railroad idea, which would have linked Germany over land to the Middle East, bypassing British and French naval forces (McMeekin, 2010).

An early example of suspicion of China in the Arctic was the saga of the Chinese real estate billionaire Huang Nubo and his plans to buy land in the northeastern quarter of Iceland for an ecotourism resort. Huang had personal connections to Iceland through some of the first Icelandic students to study at Peking University after China readmitted foreign students, following the Cultural Revolution in the 1970s. Huang's plans of buying an apparently desolate area in Northeast Iceland caused extreme suspicions of ulterior strategic designs on natural resources, espionage, or strategic strong points. Icelandic authorities delayed the project through various types of red tape related to the requirements of foreign entities buying land in Iceland, and eventually Huang gave up on the idea (Higgins, 2013). The strong growth in Chinese tourism to Iceland suggests that the idea may have been commercially viable, contrary to the assertions that it had to be merely politically and strategically motivated.

The main forces in Greenlandic politics have been clear about the ultimate goal of independence since the 1970s, and what is keeping Greenland back is, primarily, economic dependence on Denmark. Around 2012–2013, when world market commodity prices were high, there were high expectations in Greenland that a number of large mines could accelerate the road to independence. The most promising location was the iron ore deposit at Isua, where a British mining project development company, London Mining, owned the license, but the likely investors and suppliers of manpower would have been from China. This situation led to an exceptional crisis in Danish–Greenlandic–Chinese relations, with widespread Danish sentiments of suspicion towards China and paternalistic distrust in Greenland's handling of this matter. The then-Greenlandic Premier Kuupik Kleist gave an interview in a leading Danish newspaper, *Weekendavisen*, under the heading "Are the Chinese Worse than Other Capitalists?" The interview basically stated that investors other than Danes were preferable due to their unprejudiced approach to Greenland, unlike Danish postcolonial behavior (Andersen, 2013). The Chinese Foreign Ministry took the highly unusual step of declaring in a press conference that there were no Chinese mining activities in Greenland. The Danish journalist Martin Breum and the Greenlandic photographer and political columnist Jørgen Chemnitz wrote an op-ed in the *New York Times*, stating "Greenland does not belong to China" (Breum and Chemnitz, 2013).

A few years ago, the Danish Ministry of Defense put the abandoned and rundown former main Danish navy base at Grønnedal, Greenland up for sale. A Chinese mining company expressed interest in the location as a logistical hub in Greenland, and the Danish navy quickly discovered that it needed the location again. It was clearly too controversial for the Danish government to sell even a rundown and abandoned naval facility in Greenland to a Chinese mining company. It was also potentially too provocative towards China to sell the base to another buyer (Hannestad, 2016). Today, Greenland is planning to build or expand two to three new airports with runways capable of receiving international flights. Six construction companies were prequalified to submit offers, including the China Construction Company, which again raised great suspicion in Denmark (Breum, 2018; Matzen and Daly, 2018) and subsequently prompted the Danish government to underwrite the project itself by the end of 2018.

China's scientific engagement with the Arctic states is in stark contrast to the distrust highlighted above. China has been a member of the International Arctic Science Committee since 1996, and Mr. Yang Huigen, director of the Polar Research Institute of China, serves as one of the vice presidents of the IASC. China has been a regular observer[3] at the Arctic Council since 2013 and has access to participate in the working groups of the Council. The most structured Chinese Arctic science engagement is with the Nordic countries through the China Nordic Arctic Research Center (CNARC), which is a virtual center of eight Chinese and ten Nordic institutions at the Polar Research Institute of China (PRIC) in Shanghai. CNARC originates in Sino–Icelandic Arctic research cooperation, which was quickly and wisely elevated to a Sino–Nordic level and started in 2013. CNARC organizes an annual China Nordic Arctic Cooperation Symposium every second year in China and every second year in the Nordic countries, as well as a researcher exchange, where this author was a CNARC guest researcher in Shanghai in March and April 2016.

There are bilateral initiatives, such as the joint China–Iceland Aurora Observatory built in Northeast Iceland on the former farm Kárhóll, in the region of Huang's thwarted tourism project idea. Upon officially opening in October 2018, the facilities were renamed the China–Iceland Arctic Science Observatory, suggesting a wider scope of potential activities. There have also been bilateral Sino–American Arctic dialogues. China and Russia are increasingly cooperating in areas centered around Chinese investments in Russian Arctic energy resources, the Yamal Liquified Natural Gas (LNG) project being a prime example. Since 2016, there have been very interesting trilateral Arctic dialogues between China, Japan, and South Korea, which is especially noteworthy in light of the strained political relations between China and Japan (Bennett, 2017; Bertelsen and SU, 2018.

From a close observation of Sino–Arctic science diplomacy during the last four years, it is clear that there now exists a Sino–Arctic epistemic community of scholars and students who are familiar with each other personally and academically. There is a much higher degree of mutual understanding of positions and interests. Unlike the public outcries over possible Chinese investments in Arctic land and natural resources, science diplomacy has allowed for the Arctic states to integrate China into Arctic science and education without these public displays of distrust.

There are enormous strategic challenges and dangers surrounding power transition with the rise of China, as pointed out by Graham Allison (Allison, 2017). The lessons from the Arctic of how the Arctic states and China have used science to integrate China into Arctic institutions and build Sino–Arctic epistemic communities are therefore valuable and interesting. The Arctic lessons suggest the importance of building a foundation of scientific cooperation between China and other parties in different geographic and functional domains (Bertelsen, Li, and Gregersen, 2017, though China's domestic political system raises serious issues concerning open societies and academic freedom.

Conclusion: Arctic science diplomacy lessons for managing conflicts and transformations

Arctic science diplomacy offers interesting research and policy lessons to the wider international system. The Arctic is host to relatively intense scientific activity compared to other human activity. Arctic science is among the most expensive, after space and deep-ocean research, which encourages international cooperation. Arctic and non-Arctic states have historically used, and continue to use, scientific activities for foreign and security-policy reasons. The Arctic has been a closely integrated part of the international political, economic, and security system for centuries, and international politics and political economy in the Arctic have closely reflected the wider international system and continue to do so. Arctic science diplomacy therefore offers the opportunity to observe the use of science diplomacy in general international conflicts that are also present in the Arctic.

The Arctic was exceptionally militarized during the Cold War for geostrategic reasons, and not for local Arctic reasons. The Barents Sea was, and remains, a particularly important geostrategic location. Under these conditions, the five Arctic coastal states managed to create the Polar Bear Treaty in 1973, and Norway and the USSR initiated particularly successful joint fisheries management of the very valuable commercial fish stocks in the Barents Sea. This fisheries-management cooperation founded epistemic communities of importance for later knowledge-based cooperation in the Barents Region. Finland and Norway immediately used a less constrained post-Cold War international system to use environmental and other civilian cooperation in the Barents

Region for foreign and security-policy reasons. Canada as a middle power took these initiatives further with the founding of the Arctic Council, which includes working groups as epistemic communities.

Today, the Arctic is also affected by two dominant systemic processes: of higher-level, post-post-Cold War relations between the West and a recovering Russia; and power transition from West to East with the rise of China. The West and Russia are locked in geostrategic competition in the Caucasus (Russian–Georgian War 2008) and the Eastern Europe/Black Sea region (Ukraine/Crimea since 2014). Both sides must consider carefully whether to escalate this conflict horizontally into the Arctic, where neither side has similar geostrategic conflicts. Research and educational cooperation is generally continuing and producing epistemic communities. China is regaining its previous historical position as one of the world's largest economies, and as such has interests around the world, including in the Arctic. Potential or real Chinese investments in the Western Arctic (outside of Russia) have been received with great suspicion typical of power transitions. In contrast, research cooperation between China and the Arctic states continues to develop with increasing levels of mutual understanding and co-creation of knowledge. Sino–Arctic science diplomacy is therefore a potential lesson for building greater mutual understanding and co-creating knowledge between status quo powers and rising powers.

Notes

1 See the history-driven H2020 project Inventing a shared Science Diplomacy for Europe, www.insscide.eu. InsSciDE has received funding under the European Union's Horizon 2020 research and innovation programme (grant agreement no 770,523), 2018–2021.

2 Visit by Dean Ainius Lasas, Kaunas University of Technology, to UiT The Arctic University of Norway, 21–23 February 2018.

3 "Regular observer" is the correct form rather than "permanent observer," as any observer can lose its status if not fulfilling its tasks.

References

Adler, Emanuel and Peter M. Haas 1992. "Conclusion: Epistemic Communities, World Order, and the Creation of a Reflective Research Program." *International Organization* 46 (1, Knowledge, Power, and International Policy Coordination (Winter)): 367–390.

Allison, Graham. 2017. *Destined for War: Can America and China Escape Thucydides's Trap?*. New York, NY: Houghton Mifflin Harcourt.

Andersen, M. K. 2013. "Er Kinesere Værre End Andre Kapitalister? [Are the Chinese Worse than Other Capitalists?]." *Weekendavisen*, 2013/01/18.

Arctic Council. 2018. "Observers." *Arctic Council*, last modified 2018/01/17, accessed 07/04, 2018, www.arctic-council.org/index.php/en/about-us/arctic-council/observers.

Asian Development Bank 2011. *Asia 2050: Realizing the Asian Century*. Singapore: Asian Development Bank.

Bennett, Mia. 2014. "Reflections on the Eight International Congress of Arctic Social Sciences." *Cryopolitics*, last modified 05/28, accessed 11/21, 206, https://cryopolitics.com/2014/05/.

Bennett, Mia. 2017. "Iced Out: China, Japan, and S. Korea Hold Dialogue on the Arctic." *Cryopolitics*, last modified 2017/06/27, accessed 07/04, 2018, www.cryopolitics.com/2017/06/13/iced-out-china-japan-and-s-korea-hold-dialogue-on-the-arctic/.

Bertelsen, Rasmus Gjedssø. 2016. "Triple-Helix Knowledge-Based Sino–Nordic Arctic Relationships for Trust and Sustainable Development." *Advances in Polar Science* 27 (3): 180–184.

Bertelsen, Rasmus Gjedssø, Xing Li, and Mette Højris Gregersen 2017. "Chinese Arctic Science Diplomacy: An Instrument for Achieving the Chinese Dream?." *Global Challenges in the Arctic Region*

Sovereignty Environment and Geopolitical Balance, eds. Sara Iglesias Sanchez and Elena Conde Perez, 442–460. London and New York: Routledge.

Bertelsen, Rasmus Gjedssø and Ping Su. 2018. "Knowledge-Based Institutions in Sino-Arctic Engagement: Lessons for the Belt and Road Initiative." *Rethinking the Silk Road: China's Belt and Road Initiative and Emerging Eurasian Relations*, ed. Maximilian Mayer, 147–160. Singapore: Palgrave Macmillan.

Bittner, Jochen. 2016. "To Whom does the North Pole Belong?" *Zeit* Online, last modified 2016/04/09, accessed 11/21, 2016, www.zeit.de/politik/ausland/2016-04/arctic-russia-america-conflict-zone.

Breum, Martin. 2018. "How a Dispute Over China and Greenland's Airports Worked its Way Toward a Solution." *ArcticToday*, last modified 2018/06/30, accessed 06/30, 2018, www.arctictoday.com/dispute-china-greenlands-airports-worked-way-toward-solution/.

Breum, Martin and Jørgen Chemnitz. 2013. "No, Greenland does Not Belong to China." *The New York Times*.

Det norske universitetssenter i St. Petersburg. "Velkommen Til Nettsidene for Det Norske Universitetssenter i St. Petersburg! [Welcome to the Webpages of the Norwegian University Center in St. Petersburg!]." Det norske universitetssenter i St. Petersburg, last modified nd, accessed 07/08, 2018, www.st-petersburg.uio.no.

English, John. 2013. *Ice and water: Politics, Peoples, and the Arctic Council*. Toronto: Allen Lane.

Haas, Peter M. 1992. "Introduction: Epistemic Communities and International Policy Coordination." *International Organization* 46 (1): 1–35.

Haas, Peter M. 2011. "Epistemic Communities." *International Encyclopedia of Political Science*, eds. Bertrand Badie, Dirk Berg-Schlosser and Leonardo Morlino, 788–792. Thousand Oaks, CA: SAGE Publications.

Hannestad, Adam. 2016. "Nu Vil Kina Til at Købe Et Militært Anlæg i Grønland, Men Lars Løkke Siger Nej [Now China Wants to Buy Military Installation in Greenland, but [PM] Lars Løkke Says no]." *Politiken*.

Heininen, Lassi. 2013. "Finland as an Arctic and European State - Finland's Northern Dimension (Policy)." *International Security and the Arctic: Understanding Policy and Governance*, eds. Robert Murray and Anita Dey Nuttall, 294–319. Amherst, NY: Cambria Press.

Heininen, Lassi and Chris Southcott, eds. 2010. *Globalization and the Circumpolar North*. Fairbanks, AK: University of Alaska Press.

Helle, Birk T. and Mads. Randen. 2017. "Ni Norske Studenter Kastes Ut Av Russland – Anklager UiO for Visumjuks [Nine Norwegian Students Expelled from Russia - Accusing University of Oslo of Visa Cheating]." *Universitas*, last modified 2017/12/08, accessed 07/08, 2018, http://universitas.no/nyheter/63384/ni-norske-studenter-kastes-ut-av-russland-anklager.

Hellesund, Dag. 2018. "Kjenner Framleis Ikkje Grunnen Til St.Petersburg-Razzia [Still does Not Know Reason for St. Petersburg Raid]." *Khrono*, last modified 2018/01/03, accessed 07/08, 2018, https://khrono.no/universitetet-i-oslo-studier-razzia/kjenner-framleis-ikkje-grunnen-til-stpetersburg-razzia/205868.

Higgins, Andrew. 2013. "Teeing Off at the Edge of the Arctic? A Chinese Plan Baffles Iceland." *The New York Times*, 03/22.

Hønneland, Geir. 2005. *Barentsbrytninger: Norsk Nordområdepolitikk Etter Den Kalde Krigen ["Barents Breaking": Norwegian Foreign Policy in the North After the Cold War]*. Kristiansand: Høyskoleforlaget.

Hønneland, Geir. 2017. *Arctic Euphoria and International High North Politics*. Singapore: Palgrave Macmillan. 10.1007/978-981-10-6032-8_1.

International Arctic Science Committee (IASC). 2015. "25 Years of International Arctic Research Cooperation." *International Arctic Science Committee*, accessed 11/21, 2016, http://iasc25.iasc.info.

Jørgensen, Anne-Kristin and Geir Hønneland. 2013. "In Cod we Trust: Konjunkturer i Det Norsk-Russiske Fiskerisamarbeidet [in Cod we Trust: Trends in Norwegian-Russian Fisheries Cooperation]." *Nordisk Østforum* 27 (4): 353–376.

Krupnik, Igor. 1998. "Jesup Genealogy: Intellectual Partnership and Russian-American Cooperation in Arctic/North Pacific Anthropology. Pt.1: From the Jesup Expedition to the Cold War, 1897-1948." *Arctic Anthropology* 35 (2): 199–226.

Krupnik, Igor. 2010. *Personal Communication "Cold War Arctic Ethnography Role of Danish National Museum" to Rasmus Gjedssø Bertelsen* at the International Polar Year – Oslo Science Conference, June 2010.

Krupnik, Igor. 2016. "From Boas to Burch: Eskimology Transitions." *Early Inuit Studies: Themes and Transitions, 1850s-1980s*, ed. Igor Krupnik, 1–32. Washington DC: Smithsonian Institution Scholarly Press.

Krupnik, Igor. 2018. *Email Correspondance 2018-07-02-03 between Dr Igor Krupnik and Professor Rasmus Gjedssø Bertelsen*.
Langenhove, Luc Van. 2017. *Tools for an EU Science Diplomacy*. Brussels: Directorate-General for Research and Innovation (European Commission). 10.2777/911223.
Lanteigne, Marc and Mingming Shi. 2019. "China Steps up Its Mining Interests in Greenland," *The Diplomat*, 12 February 2019, https://thediplomat.com/2019/02/china-steps-up-its-mining-interests-in-greenland/
Launius, Roger D., James Rodger Fleming, and David H. DeVorkin, eds. 2010. *Globalizing Polar Science: Reconsidering the International Polar and Geophysical Years*. 1. Ed. New York, NY: Palgrave Macmillan.
Matzen, Erik and Tom. Daly. 2018. "Greenland's Courting of China for Airport Projects Worries Denmark." *Reuters*, last modified 2018/03/22, accessed 07/03, 2018, www.reuters.com/article/china-arctic-greenland/greenlands-courting-of-china-for-airport-projects-worries-denmark-idUSL4N1QP346.
McMeekin, Sean. 2010. *The Berlin-Baghdad Express: The Ottoman Empire and Germany's Bid for World Power*. Cambridge, MA: Belknap Press.
Mearsheimer, John J. 2014. "Why the Ukraine Crisis is the West's Fault: The Liberal Delusions that Provoked Putin." *Foreign Affairs* 93 (5 September/October): 77–89.
Organski, A. F. K. 1968 [1958]. *World Politics*. 2d ed. [rev.] ed New York: Knopf.
Rosen, Mark E. 2016. "The Arctic is the First Stop in the United States Reset with Russia." *The National Interest*, last modified 2016/11/15, accessed 11/21, 2016, http://nationalinterest.org/blog/the-buzz/the-arctic-the-first-stop-the-united-states-reset-russia-18409.
The Royal Society and AAAS 2010. *New Frontiers in Science Diplomacy: Navigating the Changing Balance of Power*. London; Washington, DC: The Royal Society; AAAS.
Nordisk, samarbeid, 2015. "Nordiska Ministerrådets Kontor i St Petersburg Kontaktat Av Åklagarmyndigheten [Nordic Council of Ministers' Office in Saint Petersburg Contacted by Public Prosecutor]." *Nordisk samarbeid*, last modified 2015/01/12, accessed 07/08, 2018, www.norden.org/no/aktuelt/nyheter/nordiska-ministerraadets-kontor-i-st-petersburg-kontaktat-av-aaklagarmyndigheten.

21
GEOPOLITICS AND INTERNATIONAL LAW IN THE ARCTIC

Bjarni Már Magnússon and Charles H. Norchi

Introduction

The condition most affecting Arctic interactions and outcomes is climate change (Norchi and Mayewski 2017 104). For the national security community, climate change is more than a condition: it is a threat (National Intelligence Council of the United States 2016). Because of the disproportionate impact of climate change on ice-covered areas, the Arctic has emerged as an important foreign policy issue and is forcing decision-makers to confront difficult questions bearing upon geopolitics and international law (Kraska 2018). On the international plane, the two are as inseparable as law is from power. Hence geopolitics is a *sine qua non* of Arctic governance and order. We appraise the frameworks and roles of international law (the *lex generalis* and the *lex specialis*) as they bear upon the power processes that maintain the public order of the Arctic.

This chapter considers the interplay of geopolitics and international law, or fundamentally, power and law as they pertain to the Arctic region. The chapter describes the broad international legal framework, the *lex generalis*. Thereafter, the chapter considers the relevant *lex specialis* including the law of the sea and, in particular, an issue that has catapulted the Arctic into the spotlight: the continental shelf beyond 200 nautical miles (nm).[1] Subsequently, select maritime boundary matters are examined, followed by Arctic territorial disputes and demilitarized zones. This section will be followed by concluding statements.

The interplay of geopolitics and international law

The term *geopolitics* designates power relationships of territorial units known as states (and increasingly, non-state actors) and the assets and resources they claim. When the exercise of geopolitical power meets the expectation of authority of the world community via state practice and/or codification, it is international law (McDougal, Reisman, and Willard 1985, 353). As stated by McDougal (1989) "[T]he term 'law' includes reference to both authority, in the sense of community expectations about the requirements of decision, and control, in the sense of actual participation in the making and enforcement of decision." In essence, geopolitics and international law focus on the same activities of states but from different angles. Geopolitics is about the power and interests of states and other actors across many arenas, including land, sea, air, and outer space. International law is the measure by which the exercise of power is legitimately deployed.

A significant portion of international law is devoted to the acquisition, modification, delimitation, and loss of space, in addition to the legality of the exercise of power vested in states. International law does not outlaw power struggles between states. It generates a pathway for states to pursue their national interests in ways considered acceptable by the international community. Examples include collective security organizations such as the North Atlantic Treaty Organization (NATO) (The Antarctic Treaty (1959). While power is indispensable to all law, international law serves to impose limits on the state exercise of power in many realms, such as the obligation to respect other states' sovereignty, the law of armed conflict, and human rights. The role of international law in the context of geopolitics is "to pronounce on the legality of particular conducts forming part of the broader agenda of geopolitical expansion and counter-expansion, as opposed to judging the propriety of broader geopolitical interests" (Orakhelashvili 2008, 155).

The media has periodically and unhelpfully portrayed High North trends as a "Scramble for the Arctic" (see, e.g. *Financial Times*, 19 August 2007). Arctic trends, including stakeholder claims and demands, have nothing in common with the geopolitical scrambles for foreign territories and resources as pursued by the European powers of an earlier historical period. The current geopolitical developments in the Arctic have very little to do with invasion, occupation, colonization (with the exception of the decolonization of Greenland), and annexation of territory, as did the late 19th century "Scramble for Africa." The popular press portrayed the Russian flag-planting of 2007 on the seabed of the North Pole in the spirit of the Scramble for Africa (see. e.g. CBC News, 2 August 2007; *The Guardian*, 2 August 2007; National Geographic News, 3 August 2007; *The New York Times*, 3 August 2007). This view is misplaced. The 1982 United Nations Convention on the Law of the Sea (UNCLOS 2017), which Russia is a party to, states clearly that "[t]he rights of the coastal State over the continental shelf do not depend on occupation, effective or notional, or on any express proclamation" (UNCLOS, Art 77(3)). In short, flag plantings on the continental shelf have no meaning in the context of international law. The flag-planting was a political publicity stunt and, as such, masterful. Perhaps more importantly, in contrast to Russia's destabilizing role in Europe and the Middle East, including its invasion of Georgia and Ukraine, Russia has largely played by the rules in the Arctic Ocean region.

The Arctic is neither the Wild West of the 19th-century American frontier nor is it the 21st-century South China Sea. As elsewhere, international law places power struggles in the region within structural limits that states generally respect, including the United States and Russia. The legal framework for the Arctic is mostly in line with the interests of the main players in the Arctic game, which makes it rational for them to respect it. Consequently, the framework is one of the variables that limit the possibility of the outbreak of armed hostilities in the region.

The legal framework

No specialized treaty applies to the Arctic such as applies to Antarctica through the 1959 Antarctic Treaty. The same rules of international law that generally apply to other regions of the world apply to the Arctic.[2] In the Arctic, as elsewhere, states are under an obligation to refrain "from the threat or use of force against the territorial integrity or political independence of any state" (UN Charter, art. 2(4)) (The Charter of the United Nations (1945) and "settle their international disputes by peaceful means" (UN Charter, art. 2(3)) (ibid.). The Law of Treaties, the law of state responsibility, the law of armed conflict, and every other branch of international law applies to the Arctic in the same manner as to other regions of the world. The prevailing view among the Arctic states, both the littoral states to the Arctic Ocean and the other member states of the Arctic Council, is that there is no need to develop a new international legal regime for the Arctic Ocean. A clear demonstration of this view is found in the 2008 Ilulissat Declaration of the Arctic 5:

> [A]n extensive international legal framework applies to the Arctic Ocean ... Notably, the law of the sea provides for important rights and obligations concerning the delineation of the outer limits of the continental shelf, the protection of the marine environment, including ice-covered areas, freedom of navigation, marine scientific research, and other uses of the sea. We remain committed to this legal framework and to the orderly settlement of any possible overlapping claims.
>
> *(The Ilulissat Declaration 2008)*

All the member states of the Arctic Council, except for the United States, are state parties to UNCLOS. On the other hand, the United States generally views UNCLOS, with the exception of Part XI on seabed mining, as reflective of customary international law, which is legally binding. Although most provisions of the Convention are regarded as customary international law and the United States views the provisions of the Convention as such (The White House 2013), the US outsider status introduces unfortunate ambiguity and causes complexities in some areas of the international law of the sea, as will be addressed below. The Clinton, Bush, and Obama administrations supported US accession to the 1982 Convention. Other U.S. stakeholders, such as the U.S. Navy and Coast Guard, U.S. fishing and shipping interests, undersea cable, mining, and oil and gas industries, as well as environmentalists, have also expressed support for the United States to accede to the Convention (Eagleburger and Moore 2007). Despite this broad support, all accession attempts so far have been unsuccessful. At the time of the writing of this chapter, the position of the current U.S. president on accession to UNCLOS is unclear.

UNCLOS is one of the most, if not the most, comprehensively applicable treaties. It is also a product of the geopolitics of the time: the Cold War. Hence, the preamble asserts that the "Convention will contribute to the strengthening of peace, security, cooperation and friendly relations among all nations." UNCLOS reaffirmed some existing well-settled areas of the law of the sea but also created new areas of law. No reservations may be made to UNCLOS unless expressly permitted by the Convention (art. 309). UNCLOS is a package deal with no option for cherry-picking among its disparate provisions, and has been called a Constitution for the Oceans (Koh 1982). Perhaps it can also be seen as the constitution for the Arctic, central to the constitutive process (Norchi 2017, 16).

One of the central purposes of UNCLOS is to define various maritime zones, including their extent and limits. It also lays out the principles and rules for navigation, including the provisions on transit passage through straits used for international navigation. The importance of navigational freedom to maritime powers and the world's merchant fleets cannot be overstated. It bears directly on geopolitics, from the exercise of sea power to the defense of coastal domains and states. This includes the Arctic Ocean and its littoral seas and straits. Since the USS *Nautilus* made the first submerged Arctic transit in 1958, the Arctic Ocean has been a transit route for submarines between the Atlantic and Pacific Oceans.

Submarine cables, which enable digital exchange and internet traffic, are the foundation of the global information network and thus critical to geopolitical communication and the use of force. They are laid on the ocean floor traversing multiple maritime zones employing Submarine Branching Units (SBUs), enabling data transmission to multiple endpoints. Submarine cables are increasingly vulnerable to threats by state and non-state actors. Submarine cables have long been deemed critical to world order and they have been long protected under international law. The 1884 Convention for the Protection of Submarine Telegraph Cables "applies outside territorial waters to all legally established submarine cables landed on the territories, colonies or possessions of one or more of the High Contracting Parties" (Convention for the Protection of Submarine Telegraph Cables 1884) UNCLOS accords rights and responsibilities pertaining to submarine cables within the law of the sea framework across maritime zones from the territorial sea to the continental shelf and the high seas. Despite widely accepted prescriptions in international law, states have been slow to enact measures to protect cable ships and submarine cables from accidental damage and attack (Davenport 2012). These legal gaps have direct effects on the geopolitics of the Arctic and beyond.

The creation of the dispute-settlement part of UNCLOS is one of the more progressive steps that international law has seen in recent decades. It has been argued that the entry into force of the Convention "is probably the most important development in the settlement of international disputes since the adoption of the UN Charter and the Statute of the International Court of Justice" (Boyle 1997, 37). UNCLOS consists of 320 articles and nine annexes. In addition, two implementation agreements have been concluded and negotiations of the third agreement recently began.

Although UNCLOS is of great importance for the Arctic, other aspects of international law are also of importance. It is pertinent to keep in mind what the preamble of the UNCLOS states: "[M]atters not regulated by this Convention continue to be governed by the rules and principles of general international law." For example, UNCLOS has in fact very little direct effect on the rules of naval and air warfare. Therefore, the law of armed conflicts continues "to be governed by the rules and principles" of The Hague and Geneva Regimes[3] in the Arctic.

The continental shelf beyond 200 nm in the Arctic

International law, with its prescriptions and mechanisms, is a helpful tool to settle disputes concerning the issues surrounding the continental shelf beyond 200 nm that have put the Arctic into the global spotlight. As noted above, one of the central purposes of the international law of the sea is to define various maritime zones, including their extent and limits. According to UNCLOS, the continental shelf extends at least to a distance of 200 nm from the baselines from which the breadth of the territorial sea is measured (art. 76(1)).[4] If a coastal state fulfills complex geoscientific criteria laid out in the Convention, it is entitled to the continental shelf beyond the 200 nm limit. The reason for the global interest in this issue lays in the fact that it is possible to explore and exploit important natural resources from the seabed beyond 200 nm. In some areas of the world, such as in the Arctic, it is necessary for neighboring coastal states to settle disputes concerning these limits. The economic, financial, and political incentives to solve such disputes are often high. Another factor is that territorial rights and natural resources have throughout history been a flammable combination that has negatively impacted peace and stability.

UNCLOS provides that information on the limits of the continental shelf beyond 200 nm from the baselines shall be submitted by the coastal state to a scientific and technical commission, named the Commission on the Limits of the Continental Shelf (CLCS or Commission). The Commission is responsible for making recommendations to coastal states on matters related to the establishment of the outer limits of their continental shelves beyond 200 nm. If the limits of the shelf established by a coastal state are on the basis of the recommendations, they are final and binding (UNCLOS, Art. 76(8)). This process is quite different from the establishment of other maritime zones, such as the Exclusive Economic Zone (EEZ), under international law, which can be established without the involvement of an international entity.

The establishment of the outer limits of the continental shelf beyond 200 nm has two main features: the establishment of the boundary line between the continental shelf and the international sea bed area[5] (the delineation of the continental shelf), and the establishment of the boundary between the continental shelf of adjacent or opposite coastal states (the delimitation of the continental shelf). These features overlap profoundly and cannot be viewed in complete isolation from each other (Lathrop 2011). The delineation process is a complex legal-scientific-technical procedure, where the CLCS plays a pivotal role in curtailing the territorial temptations of broad margin states.

The delimitation process is different from the CLCS procedure. The actions of the CLCS are without prejudice to matters relating to the delimitation of boundaries between states with opposite or adjacent coasts (UNCLOS, Annex II, art. 9). According to UNCLOS, it is for neighboring states to delimit the maritime boundaries of their continental shelves (Art. 83). The delimitation is supposed to be effected by agreement and, if not possible, within a reasonable time, resort shall be made to procedures provided for in the dispute-settlement part of UNCLOS. The Convention provides that this process shall be guided by international law as defined in Article 38 of the Statute of the International Court of Justice. The purpose of the delimitation is to achieve an equitable solution,[6] not to fulfill specific scientific and technical criteria as in the CLCS procedure.

Boundary delimitation can be defined as consisting of "drawing a demarcation line, a boundary, between two neighboring states when the geographical situation does not allow both the parties concerned to enjoy their title to its full extent" (Weil 1989, 48). What complicates this act is that many statesmen view territory as power, and loss of power as weakness. After all, borders – land or maritime – serve "to delimit the existence of a political order by means of its separation from others" (Craven 2014, 220). Most maritime boundary delimitations have been concluded by negotiations through political channels without the involvement of third parties (Antunes 2005). This applies to the Arctic, as in other regions of the world. The main reason for preferring negotiation over adjudication is that states engaged in negotiations are "able to take into account human and resource conditions that have been ignored in boundaries settled through adjudication or arbitration" (Klein 2005, 255).

In recent decades, international courts and tribunals have developed a three-stage delimitation method: the equidistance/relevant circumstances method, which is usually not only applied before international courts or tribunals but also in maritime boundary negotiations. The first step is to construct a provisional equidistance line based on the geography of the parties. The second step is to determine whether there are any relevant circumstances requiring adjustment of the provisional equidistance line that produces an equitable result. At the third and final stage in this process, an assessment is made to check whether the line results in any significant disproportion between the ratio of the respective coastal lengths and the ratio of the relevant maritime areas allocated to each party (International Tribunal for the Law of the Sea, Bangladesh/Myanmar 2012, para. 240). In such cases, courts may make equitable adjustment to the median line.

All the Arctic states abide by the above-mentioned legal framework, including the United States, though it is not a party to UNCLOS. While the Russian flag-planting attracted international attention in 2007 and sparked negative reactions, the Russians have in fact been acting in line with their legal obligations under UNCLOS. Russia actually made the first submission to the CLCS in 2001 and received the first recommendations of the CLCS in 2002. The Commission did not accept Russia's original submission because of certain flaws and asked Russia, among others, to revise the part concerning its continental shelf in the Central Arctic Ocean. Russia made a partial revised submission in 2015 for the Arctic Ocean that is currently under consideration by the CLCS. Russia's original submission covered an area that was more than 386,000 square nautical miles. The 2015 submission added a further 30,000 square nautical miles (Jensen 2016). Denmark, Norway, and Iceland have all submitted information to the CLCS. Canada made a preliminary submission to the CLCS in 2013 and is expected to make a full submission in the near future. Since the United States is not a state party to UNCLOS, it is questionable whether the CLCS would consider a submission from it. Whether the United States can establish the continental shelf beyond 200 nm based on customary international law is, however, a different question (Magnússon 2017).

It is clear from these submissions that the main complexities in the Arctic concern submarine ridges and elevations (Jensen 2016). It is also clear that because the submissions overlap profoundly, the vast majority of the outer limits of the continental shelf beyond 200 nm in the Arctic will be solved through bilateral maritime boundary agreements. All relevant parties in the Central Arctic Ocean have made so-called non-objection agreements that allow for considerations of the submission in the Arctic region before the CLCS without prejudice to future delimitation negotiations (DOALOS). The ambitious Danish submission in the Central Arctic Ocean and the more modest Russian submission overlap intensely. It is very likely that the forthcoming Canadian submission will also create a large overlap with the Russian and Danish submission. These three states will have to negotiate maritime boundaries in the future. It seems that this will not happen in the near future since Denmark has rejected Russia's call to swiftly decide a maritime boundary, insisting that the CLCS should finish its task before the states enter into boundary negotiations (Milne 2016). The wait could take years.

In short, there is very little indication that the continental shelf beyond 200 nm is causing turbulence in the international relations among Arctic states, which has a stabilizing effect on the geopolitical order in the region. In fact, the conduct of the states in the Arctic towards this issue is an example of how international law creates a pathway for states to seek their national interests in a way considered acceptable by the international community.

Maritime boundaries

The geopolitical purpose of delimitation of boundaries among states is to settle overlapping claims and thereby stabilize the expectations of national elites. Arguably, the two most important maritime boundary agreements in the Arctic region are the agreements that delimit maritime areas between NATO member states and Russia. These are the *Agreement between The United States of America and The Union of Soviet Socialist Republics on the Maritime Boundary* (Oude Elferink 1991), concluded in 1990, and the *Treaty between the Kingdom of Norway and the Russian Federation Concerning Maritime Delimitation and Cooperation in the Barents Sea and the Arctic Ocean*, concluded in 2010. The importance of these agreements cannot be overstated for the geopolitics of the region.

The 1990 United States/USSR agreement created the longest maritime boundary in the world. It is approximately 1,600 nm in length between the opposite states. In general, the boundary line follows a version of the line under the 1867 Convention by which Russia sold Alaska to the United States (Colson 2003). The boundary line extends from the Bering Strait north along a meridian through Chukchi Sea far into the Arctic Ocean and south-westward from the Bering Strait through the Bering Sea to the 167° East meridian of longitude in the North Pacific Ocean. The negotiations, which took nine years to complete, were highly political. Considerations of hydrocarbon resources and fisheries were prominent in the negotiations (Verille 1993, 450).

The United States ratified the agreement quickly. The Soviet Union, later Russia, has on the other hand not ratified it due to opposition to the outcome since the boundary line in the Bering Sea runs significantly to the west of where an equidistance line would be located. It has been pointed out that "[o]pponents of the treaty attribute this result to the weak negotiating position of the Soviet Union, which was literally disintegrating as the talks were taking place" (Byers 2013, 34). This does not mean that the parties do not respect the agreement. When signing the agreement, the two parties entered into an exchange of notes, in line with the Law of Treaties (Vienna Convention on the Law of Treaties 1969 art. 25),[7] whereby: "pending the entry into force of that Agreement, the two Government agree to abide by the terms of that Agreement as of 15 June 1990" (Oude Elferink, annexes 2 and 3). Furthermore, under Article 18 of the Vienna Convention, Moscow has a legal obligation not to defeat the object and purpose of agreements pending ratification. Moscow has observed this legal duty despite current bilateral tension over issues arising from outside the region.

The 2010 treaty between Norway and Russia marked the end of a 40-year-old maritime boundary dispute between the parties. The treaty delimits an area that can be divided into three parts. The first is at the mouth of the Varangerfjord and extends to 200 nm from the mainlands of Norway and Russia. The second area is in the middle of the Barents Sea beyond 200 nm, known as the Barents Sea Loophole. The third area is in the northern Barents Sea (Henriksen and Ulfstein 2011, 1). The treaty does not reveal much about the delimitation method except that the preamble makes reference to the provisions of UNCLOS. A joint statement made by the Russian President and the Norwegian Prime Minister a few months before the conclusion of the treaty reveals more. According to the statement, delegations from the parties recommended "a delimitation line on the basis of international law in order to achieve an equitable solution" and that the line should divide "the overall disputed area in two parts of approximately same size" (Joint Statement on Maritime Delimitation and Cooperation in the Barents Sea and Arctic Ocean 2010). The only relevant factor mentioned was the major disparities in respective coastal lengths.

The vast majority of maritime boundaries within 200 nm in the Arctic region have been delimited. Negotiations have been the main tool of dispute settlement. The only unresolved maritime boundary dispute within 200 nm in the Arctic Region is in the Beaufort Sea between the United States and Canada. Canada argues that the boundary was delimited in the 1825 treaty between Great Britain and Russia. The United States disagrees, arguing that no maritime boundary has been concluded and that the boundary should follow the median line between the coastlines of the states (McDorman 2009). Although the dispute has not been solved, it has not caused any geopolitical tension in the region. It must be noted that, while Denmark (Greenland) and Canada have not concluded a formal maritime boundary treaty in the Lincoln Sea, the two countries have reached a tentative agreement on the maritime boundary (Hartmann 2013). All other maritime boundary disputes within 200 nm have been resolved in the region.

Territorial disputes in the Arctic

There is only one remaining dispute over title to territory in the Arctic. It is the insignificant dispute concerning Hans Island. The island is a small uninhabited islet, measuring 1.3 km^2, 1,290 m long and 1,199 m wide, located in the center of the Kennedy Channel portion of

Nares Strait between Ellesmere Island and northwest Greenland that connects Baffin Bay with the Lincoln Sea. It was only in 1973 when Danish and Canadian diplomats were negotiating a 1450 nm long continental shelf boundary between Greenland and Canada that they became aware of a difference of opinion concerning title over the island. Instead of delaying their talks with this unexpected, almost inconsequential development, the negotiations simply drew the boundary line up to the low-water mark on one side of the island and continued it from the low-water mark on the other. The resolution of the treaty will have no consequences on other legal issues near the island, such as seabed or fishery rights.

One of the reasons why the dispute has not been solved is that it has caught the attention of the media and, furthermore, politicians have used it to gain electoral advantage in domestic politics. Solutions to the dispute can be found in the toolbox of international law. Byers (2013, 15) pointed out that it should be easy to solve the dispute by either drawing a straight line directly between the points where the maritime boundary line ended or by creating condominium, "in the sense that Canada and Denmark would share sovereignty over all of it."

It is possible to argue that another dispute in the Arctic has a territorial element. That is the dispute of whether the Northwest Passage and parts of the Northern Sea Route are straits considered suitable for international navigation or are internal waters. The dispute is in essence about coastal states' control over maritime areas in the Canadian Arctic archipelago and parts of the Russian coastline. Canada and Russia argue that the straits along their northern coastline are internal waters (Byers and Baker 2013). Internal waters have almost the same status under international law as territory. Foreign vessels do not generally enjoy the right of innocent passage through internal waters and domestic law applies there fully. The United States on the other hand regards the Northwest Passage and parts of the Northern Sea Route as straits used for international navigation subject to the regime of transit passage, which constrains the legislative and enforcement jurisdiction of coastal states and reduces the modalities of passage for foreign vessels (UNCLOS, Part III).

Canada's internal waters claims have been called "the most extensive maritime claims of any Arctic nation" (Kraska 2018, 547). Although the United States and Canada found a practical solution for navigation within the Canadian Arctic archipelago through the 1988 Arctic Cooperation Agreement, the dispute remains unresolved (McDorman 2009). If commercial shipping becomes a viable option in the Arctic this could become a major dispute. Consequently, it would be wise to engage in negotiations "with a view to concluding treaties on the various Arctic straits that address the unique challenges of the region" ((Byers and Baker 2013, 170).

Demilitarized areas

Although the Arctic is often presented as a peaceful area, for decades thousands of nuclear warheads and delivery systems including missiles, bombers, and submarines have been located in the region. For both Russia and NATO, the Arctic Ocean has been an important region for the deployment of nuclear-missile submarines. Given the current situation in international politics, it is unlikely that this will change in the near future. Nonetheless, it must be noted that a few international treaties contain important elements of demilitarization for the Arctic region, which impacts the geopolitics of the area. Arguably the most important are the 1971 Treaty on the Prohibition of the Emplacement of Nuclear Weapons and Other Weapons of Mass Destruction on the Seabed and the Ocean Floor and in the Subsoil Thereof, and the 1920 Svalbard Treaty.

All the Arctic states ratified the 1971 Treaty, as have all declared nuclear-weapon states apart from France. The Treaty prohibits the deployment of nuclear weapons on the seabed beyond the territorial waters (12 nm) of the member states (art. 1). This means that almost the entire seabed and subsoil of the Arctic Ocean is free of nuclear weapons. However, this does not mean that the ocean space above, and the surface of the oceans in the Arctic Ocean and nearby seas, are nuclear- weapon-free zones. Among the peace movement, the idea to establish a nuclear weapon-free zone in the Arctic has been popular. For example, since the 1960s, a discussion has regularly taken place about the possibility of a Nordic nuclear weapon-free zone (Lindahl 1988) despite the fact that three of the Nordic states (Denmark, Iceland and Norway) are member states of NATO. To make a long story short, since the Arctic Ocean is a major theater of operations for NATO and Russian nuclear submarines, unless that changes dramatically, the push to establish a comprehensive nuclear weapons-free zone in the region is destined to fail.

All the member states of the Arctic Council have ratified the Svalbard Treaty. In total, 45 states are parties to the Convention. The preamble of the Treaty states clearly that one of the purposes of it is to assure the development and peaceful utilization of the archipelago. One of the controversies concerning Svalbard has been whether the archipelago is a demilitarized area or whether it only contains elements of demilitarization. The Soviet Union, later Russia, has been the main promoter of the view that Svalbard is a demilitarized area, while Norway has been the primary advocate for the view that Svalbard is not a fully demilitarized area. Art. 9 of the Svalbard Treaty reads:

> Subject to the rights and duties resulting from the admission of Norway to the League of Nations, Norway undertakes not to create nor to allow the establishment of any naval base in the territories specified in Article 1 and not to construct any fortification in the said territories, which may never be used for warlike purposes.

The provision indicates that Svalbard is only partly demilitarized. It does not prohibit the stationing of troops or weapons, military exercises, the testing of weapons, or the hosting of NATO meetings in the archipelago. Neither does it outlaw the inherent right of self-defense, whether individually or collectively, in case of an armed attack on Svalbard. Importantly, it has been noted that the "[i]ntegration into NATO does not in itself commit Norway to the establishment of naval bases or fortifications in peacetime [...] art. 9 does not prohibit the establishment of such installations during war as part of the self-defense of Svalbard" (Ulfstein 1995, 388). The demilitarized status of Svalbard will very likely continue to be part of the controversies concerning the interpretation of the Svalbard Treaty.

Conclusion

The essential relation between international law and geopolitics is the maintenance of the public order. Ambassador David Balton observed:

> In the Arctic there is an order, but it is changing very rapidly. There is no threat of armed conflict, no terrorism, mass migration nor narco-trafficking in the region. Although nations are claiming the sea floor, there is a process to determine which part belongs to whom.
>
> *(quoted in Norchi 2017, 20)*

The Arctic region is presently stable. International law continues to contribute to that stability through treaties such as UNCLOS and other codes, customs, and mechanisms that contain power struggles in the region within structural limits that states generally respect. A good example of this is the conduct of states in their quest for the continental shelf beyond 200 nm. Despite the Russian flag-planting in 2007, Russia and the other states, which are sorting out the question of to whom does the seabed in the Arctic belong, are conducting themselves in line with international law. International law has also affected geopolitics in different ways in the region. It provides the method to draw maritime boundaries and has been helpful when states have decided to settle their maritime boundary disputes. In fact, currently no signs exist that there will be an escalation concerning an unresolved territorial or maritime boundary in the Arctic region. In addition, states have concluded treaties that have demilitarizing effects on the region. In short, the phrase "the Scramble for the Arctic" does not fully capture the interplay between geopolitics and international law in the region. International law is one of the variables that limit the possibility of the outbreak of armed hostilities in the Arctic. By clarifying common interests, encouraging and enabling the peaceful settlement of disputes, and supporting the human dignity of regional peoples, international law, in concert with geopolitics, is maintaining the public order of the Arctic.

Notes

1 1 nautical mile equals 1,852 metres.
2 Alternative ideas about the legal framework in the Arctic can be viewed in e.g. Koivurova, T., 2010. Limits and possibilities of the Arctic Council in a rapidly changing scene of Arctic governance. Polar Record 46(237), pp. 146–156.
3 The law of armed conflict is traditionally divided into two categories; Hague law and Geneva law. Hague law refers to the outcome of two conferences in 1899 and 1907. Hague law concerns the restrictions on the conduct of hostilities. Geneva law concerns the protection of victims of war and was largely laid down in four conventions in 1949 in Geneva under the auspices of the Red Cross. Two additional protocols belong to Geneva law concluded in 1977.
4 The provisions on baselines are found in Arts. 5–14 of UNCLOS
5 The international seabed area is usually referred to as the Area. Art. 1(1) of UNCLOS defines the Area as "the seabed and ocean floor and subsoil thereof, beyond the limits of national jurisdiction." The definition is a negative one "for in order to know the exact extent of the Area, one needs to know up to where exactly coastal states have extended their national jurisdiction at sea" (Franckx, 2010, p. 552). Art. 140 of UNCLOS provides that "[a]ctivities in the Area shall ... be carried out for the benefit of mankind as a whole."
6 This is also the purpose of delimitations involving the Exclusive Economic Zone (EEZ) (UNCLOS, art. 74(1)).
7 Art. 25 of the Vienna Convention on the Law of Treaties. It read: "A treaty or part of a treaty is applied provisionally pending its entry into force if: the treaty itself so provides; or the negotiating States have in some other manner so agreed."

References

Agreement between The United States of America and The Union of Soviet Socialist Republics on the Maritime Boundary (1990), 29 International Legal Materials, p. 941. Available from: https://state.gov/documents/organization/125431.pdf [Accessed 21 August 2017].

The Antarctic Treaty (1959), 402 *United Nations Treaty Series*, p. 71. Available from: http://ats.aq/documents/ats/treaty_original.pdf [Accessed 21 August 2017].

Antunes, N. (2005) Some Thoughts on the Technical Input in Maritime Delimitation. In Colson, D and Smith, R. (eds.) *International Maritime Boundaries*, Vol. V. Leiden: Martinus Nijhoff Publishers pp. 3377–3398.

Boyle, A. (1997) Dispute Settlement and the Law of the Sea Convention: Problems of Fragmentation and Jurisdiction. *International and Comparative Law Quarterly*, 46(1), pp. 37–54. Available from: doi: 10.1017/S0020589300060103 [Accessed 21 August 2017].

Byers, M. and Baker, J. (2013) *International Law and the Arctic*. Cambridge, UK. Cambridge University Press.
CBC News 2007 Russia Plants Flag Staking Claim to Arctic Region, 2 August. Available from: http://cbc.ca/news/world/russia-plants-flag-staking-claim-to-arctic-region-1.679445 [Accessed 2 August 2018].
The Charter of the United Nations (1945), 1 United Nations Treaty Series. xvi. Available from: http://un.org/en/charter-united-nations/[Accessed 21 August 2017].
Colson, D. (2003) The Delimitation of the Outer Continental Shelf between Neighbouring States. *The American Journal of International Law*, 96(1), pp. 91–107. Available from: doi: 10.2307/3087106 [Accessed 21 August 2017].
Convention for the Protection of Submarine Telegraph Cables 1884 Australian Treaty Series 1, 1901. Available from: https://iscpc.org/documents/?id=13 [Accessed 2 August 2018].
Craven, M. (2014) Statehood, Self-Determination and Recognition. In Evans, M. (ed.) *International Law*, 4th ed.. Oxford: Oxford University Press pp. 201–247.
Davenport, T. (2012) Submarine Communications Cables and Law of the Sea: Problems in Law and Practice. *Ocean Development & International Law*, 43(3), pp. 201–242. Available from: doi: 10.1080/00908320.2012.698922.
Eagleburger, L. and Moore, J. Opportunity on the Oceans. Washington Post, p. A15. 30 July 2007 Available from: http://washingtonpost.com/wp-dyn/content/article/2007/07/29/AR2007072900860.html [Accessed 21 August 2017].
Financial Times 2007 Scramble for the Arctic, 19 August. Available from: https://ft.com/content/65b9692c-4e6f-11dc-85e7-0000779fd2ac [Accessed 2 August 2018].
Franckx, E. (2010) The International Seabed Authority and the Common Heritage of Mankind: The need for States to Establish the Outer Limits of their Continental Shelf. *The International Journal of Marine and Coastal Law*, 25(4), pp. 543–567. Available from: doi: 10.1163/157180810X525377 [Accessed 21 August 2017].
The Guardian 2007 Russia plants flag on the North Pole Seabed, 2 August. Available from: https://theguardian.com/world/2007/aug/02/russia.arctic [Accessed 2 August 2018].
Hartmann, J. (2013) Canada and Denmark Reach Agreement on the Lincoln Sea Boundary. *EJIL Talk*. Weblog [Online] Available from: https://ejiltalk.org/canada-and-denmark-reach-agreement-on-the-lincoln-sea-boundary/[Accessed 22 August 2017].
Henriksen, T and Ulfstein, G. (2011) Maritime Delimitation in the Arctic; The Barents Sea Treaty. *Ocean Development and International Law*, 42(1-2), pp. 1–21. Available from: doi: 10.1080/00908320.2011.542389 [Accessed 21 August 2017].
The Ilulissat Declaration (2008). Available from: http://oceanlaw.org/downloads/arctic/Ilulissat_Declaration.pdf [Accessed 21 August 2017].
International Tribunal for the Law of the Sea (2012). Dispute concerning Delimitation of the Maritime Boundary between Bangladesh and Myanmar in the Bay of Bengal (Bangladesh/Myanmar). Available from:https://itlos.org/fileadmin/itlos/documents/cases/case_no_16/published/C16_Judgment.pdf [Accessed 21 August 2017].
Jensen, Ø. (2016) Russia's Revised Arctic Seabed Submission. *Ocean Development and International Law*, 47(1), pp. 72–88. Available from doi: 10.1080/00908320.2016.1124487 [Accessed 21 August 2017].
Joint Statement on Maritime Delimitation and Cooperation in the Barents Sea and Arctic Ocean (2010) Available from: http://regjeringen.no/upload/UD/Vedlegg/Folkerett/030427_english_4.pdf [Accessed 21 August 2017].
Klein, N. (2005) *Dispute Settlement in the UN Convention on the Law of the Sea*. Cambridge. Cambridge University Press.
Koh, T. (1982) A Constitution for the Oceans. Available from: http://un.org/Depts/los/convention_agreements/texts/koh_english.pdf. [Accessed 21 August 2017].
Kraska, J. (2018) International Security and International Law in the Northwest Passage. In Rothwell, D. and A.D. Hemmings (eds.) *International Polar Law*, Elgar Publishers, pp. 1109–1132.
Lathrop, C. (2011) Continental Shelf Delimitation Beyond 200 Nautical Miles: Approaches Taken by Coastal States before the Commission on the Limits of the Continental Shelf. In Colson, D. and Smith, R. (eds.) *International Maritime Boundaries*, Vol. VI. Leiden: Martinus Nijhoff Publisher pp. 4139–4160.
Lindahl, I. (1988) *The Soviet Union and the Nordic Nuclear-Weapon-Free-Zone Proposal*. London. Macmillan.

Magnússon, B. (2017) Can the United States Establish the Outer Limits of Its Extended Continental Shelf Under International Law?. *Ocean Development & International Law*, 48(1), pp. 1–16. Available from: doi: 10.1080/00908320.2017.1265361 [Accessed 21 August 2017].

McDorman, T. (2009) *Salt Waterr Neighbors: International Ocean Law Relations between the United States and Canada*. New York. Oxford University Press.

McDougal, M. S. (1989) Law and Peace. *Denver Journal of International Law and Policy*, 18(1), pp. 1–36.

McDougal, M. S., W.M. Reisman and A.R. Willard (1985) The World Process of Effective Power: The Global War System. In McDougal, M.S. and M. Reisman (eds.) *Power and Policy in Quest of Law. Essays in honor of Eugene Victor Rostow*, Boston: Martinus Nijhoff Publishers pp. 353–414.

Milne, R. (2016) Denmark Rejects Russia Call for Swift Talks on Arctic Rights, *Financial Times*. 12 September Available from: http://ft.com/cms/s/0/d1810bd4-77e5-11e6-97ae-647294649b28.html#axzz4K4fS2Ahf [Accessed 21 August 2017].

National Geographic News 2007 Russia Plants Underwater Flag, Claims Arctic Seafloor, 3 August. Available from: https://news.nationalgeographic.com/news/2007/08/070802-russia-pole/[Accessed 2 August 2018].

National Intelligence Council of the United States (2016) Implications for US National Security of Anticipated Climate Change. Available from: https://dni.gov/files/documents/Newsroom/Reports%20and%20Pubs/Implications_for_US_National_Security_of_Anticipated_Climate_Change.pdf [Accessed 2 August 2018].

New York Times 2007 Russians Plant Flag on the Arctic Seabed, 3 August . Available from: https://nytimes.com/2007/08/03/world/europe/03arctic.html [Accessed 2 August 2018].

Norchi, C., and Mayewski, P. (2017) The Arctic: Science, Law and Policy. *Ocean and Coastal L.J.*, 22(2), pp. 97–110.

Norchi, Charles H. (2017) The Arctic in the Public Order of World Community, 22. *Ocean & Coastal L. J.*, 22(1), pp. 5–21.

Orakhelashvili, A. (2008) International Law and Geopolitics: One Object, Conflicting Legitimacies?. *Netherlands Yearbook of International Law*, 39, pp. 155–204. Available from: doi: 10.1017/S0167676808001554 [Accessed 21 August 2017].

Oude Elferink, A. (1991) The 1990 USSR-USA Maritime Boundary Agreement. *International Journal of Estuarine and Coastal Law*, 6(1), pp. 41–51. Available from: doi: 10.1163/187529991X00261 [Accessed 21 August 2017].

Treaty between the Kingdom of Norway and the Russian Federation Concerning Maritime Delimitation and Cooperation in the Barents Sea and the Arctic Ocean (2010), 50 International Legal Materials, p. 1113. Available from: https://regjeringen.no/globalassets/upload/SMK/Vedlegg/2010/avtale_engelsk.pdf [Accessed 21 August 2017].

Ulfstein, G. (1995) *The Svalbard Treaty*. Oslo. Scandinavian University Press.

United Nations Convention on the Law of the Sea (1982), 1833 *United Nations Treaty Series*, p. 396. Available from:http://un.org/depts/los/convention_agreements/texts/unclos/closindx.htm [Accessed 21 August 2017].

Verille, E (1993) United States-Soviet Union. Report Number 1-6. In Charney, J and Alexander, L (eds.) *International Maritime Boundaries*, Vol. 1. Leiden: Martinus Nijhoff Publishers pp. 447–460.

Vienna Convention on the Law of Treaties (1969) 1155 United Nations Treaty Series 311. Available from: https://treaties.un.org/doc/publication/unts/volume%201155/volume-1155-i-18232-english.pdf [Accessed 21 August 2017].

Weil, P. (1989) *The Law of Maritime Delimitation – Reflections*. Translated from French by Maureen MacGlashan Cambridge. Grotius Publications Limited.

The White House (2013) National Strategy for the Arctic Region. Available from: https://obamawhitehouse.archives.gov/sites/default/files/docs/nat_arctic_strategy.pdf [Accessed 21 August 2017].

22
GEOPOLITICS, SECURITY, AND GOVERNANCE

Klaus Dodds

Introduction

The intersection of geopolitics, security, and governance in the regional context of the Arctic is anything but straightforward (see for example Knecht and Keil 2013). As this chapter investigates, terms such as *geopolitics*, *security*, and *governance* have attracted substantial scholarly literature in political geography, security, and international relations (IR). The function and significance of the region is not immune from scholarly conversation and dissent (Agnew 2013; Browning 2003; Neumann 1994; Paasi 2009, 2013). Political geographers in particular devote a great deal of analytical energy to considering how regions and regionalism are socially and politically constructed and embedded in a variety of spatial scales (Agnew 1994; Jones and Paasi 2013). The Arctic as a region can be considered conceptually mobile and contestable. Where the Arctic begins and ends, for example, has ramifications for how Arctic geopolitics, security, and governance are operationalized and legitimated (Albert 2016).

The chapter is structured in three main sections. Initially, the chapter considers geopolitics and how the term applies to the Arctic. The first section focuses on the idea that there might be metageographies at play that help to define, police, and discipline the Arctic as a region. As Lewis and Wigen (1997: ix) noted over 20 years ago, metageography refers to "a set of spatial structures through which people order their knowledge of the world: the often unconscious frameworks that organize studies of history, sociology, anthropology, economics, political science, or even natural history." Following this section, metageographies of the Arctic are tethered to an examination of geopolitical cultures and how they might inform and influence the discourses, practices, and performances of Arctic security.

The second section converges more explicitly on security and the sorts of shifts that have occurred from a preoccupation with the behavior and interest of states and territorial domains, to a more wide-ranging interrogation of everyday, nontraditional, and Indigenous securities. To generalize about Arctic security debates, they are now far more likely to be dominated by a medley of actors, institutions, sites, scales, and spaces. Finally, governance for the purpose of this chapter is a useful shorthand term for thinking about how the Arctic is caught up in a myriad of demands for the management of both human and nonhuman communities, ecosystems, and stakeholders that include Arctic and non-Arctic states, and intergovernmental and nongovernmental organizations, in an era of globalization and environmental change

(Heininen and Southcott 2010). The international waters of the central Arctic Ocean provide an interesting and timely example of how Arctic governance is contributing to a renewed sense that there is now a truly "global Arctic" taking shape and form.

Arctic geopolitics and metageographies of the Arctic

The manner in which the world is divided into spatial categories such as area, continent, and region is rarely innocent and certainly never devoid of legal and political circumstance. Geopolitics has at its heart a preoccupation with the politics of representing space. For the last 30 years, scholars have thought of geopolitics as capable of being distinguished between formal, practical, and popular forms of geopolitics. These are defined as the work done by universities and think tanks, political leaders and agents of the state, and mass media and public opinion, respectively. Geopolitics, under this conceptual rubric, is not simply something created by academic thinkers in either university or think tank environments. Instead, geopolitics is best thought of as something more fluid, multilocational, and interlocked with practical and popular elements. As an example, a political leader such as US President Donald Trump might articulate a plan to build a border wall (practical), the media might cover that story (popular), and analysts might thereafter analyze and speculate on the rationale and underlying logic for wall building (formal).

Geopolitics is produced by wider geopolitical cultures. To speak of a Norwegian geopolitical culture, for example, would be to identify how the country's role, identity, and mission in the world are conceptualized (Medby 2018). For example, one striking feature of contemporary Norwegian geopolitical culture is the emphasis placed on the High North. The foreword of *Norway's Arctic Strategy*, titled "Between geopolitics and social development" (2017) notes:

> The Arctic is important for Norway and for the world as a whole. Foreign and domestic policies are intertwined in the region, and people's everyday lives are affected both by high politics and by day-to-day issues. Here, people are not divided by the ice, but rather joined by the ocean. In the Arctic, our most important foreign policy priority, countries from three continents have found new ways of cooperating, based on common interests and respect for international law.

Popular geopolitical imaginaries matter because of their framing capacity (Dittmer et al. 2011). The Arctic as a space is not preformed but is subject to intervention, representation, and reproduction through particular institutional and stakeholder organizations. For example, public education is an important element in the socialization of Arcticness. Schools, media, and public information campaigns, often using maps and charts, help to articulate what might be integral to the Norwegian High North. As a geographical region, the High North as a Norwegian geopolitical culture is a region stretching from Greenland to the western margins of Russia, encompassing northern Norway and the archipelago of Svalbard (Keskitalo 2004).

This geopolitical thinking is not unique to Norway. The eight Arctic states of Canada, Denmark (Greenland), Finland, Iceland, Norway, Russia, Sweden, and the United States are active producers of Arctic identities, including geographical representations of the Arctic as a region. Using lines of latitude, such as the Arctic Circle or 60 degrees North, or simply the boundary lines of a northern state such as Alaska, Arctic imaginaries have been grounded in cartographic coordinates and geographical locations. They have been supplemented, however, by other cultural and economic factors and forces such as the presence of Indigenous and northern communities, resource projects, and military investment in "northern commands" and Arctic forces. Every Arctic state has its own distinctive investment, imaginative and material, in this Arctic-building process. There is no single Arctic state identity (Medby 2018).

Building and sustaining a distinct "Arcticness" is an ongoing project; one that is not under the control of any one particular actor or stakeholder. Arctic states are powerful producers and circulators of popular geographical imaginaries, but they are not alone. At the height of the British Empire, 18th- and 19th-century British sailors, explorers, and traders, alongside artists and novelists, were actively engaged in harvesting stories, images and objects of and from the Arctic North (Depledge 2017). There is a long history and geography to how the Arctic as a transnational space (rather than formed regions) attracted imaginative and material investment. For British expeditioners and travelers in the 19th century, the Arctic was something to pass through: a passage onto other trading and cultural worlds. There was nothing discrete about the Arctic per se. It was a space, both terrestrial and maritime, that was poorly mapped, defined, and understood. There was little appreciation that Indigenous communities were resident, and in part that ignorance was indicative of the fact that these expeditions were traveling by ship in some of the remotest parts of the now North American Arctic.

In the 20th century, the Arctic attracted not only the attention of Arctic states seeking to integrate northern homelands into their national boundaries through assimilation, infrastructural investment, and militarization, but also interest in projecting further northwards. In Canada and Russia from the 1920s onwards, military and political actors looked further north and imagined their countries projecting sector-like towards the North Pole. Using lines of longitude, governments on either side of the Arctic Ocean began to stretch their national ambitions ever northwards. Most notably, the Soviet Union sent ships, planes, and men northwards. Taming Arctic nature, conquering Arctic sea ice, and establishing infrastructure on permafrost and tundra became a leitmotif of Stalin's Soviet Union (Rowe and Blakkisrud 2014).

Arctic geopolitical ambition was hardened further by the experiences of war: imagined and real. World War II transformed the Arctic as an active wartime theater. Alaska, Russia, Northern Norway, and Svalbard witnessed German, Japanese, and Allied forces in action. Atlantic convoys traveled back and forth from the North Atlantic and the Barents Sea. Infrastructure was extended northwards, connecting the territory of Alaska to the southern provinces of Canada and the continental United States. The northern territories of Arctic states became ever-more connected to their southern constituencies through airports, sea lanes, lines of communication, and media stories about why they mattered to the war effort. New maps were produced in American newspapers, which championed a polar projection so that readers could better understand how Alaska was tied to Pacific Ocean military operations against the Japanese imperial forces.

Wartime investment and experiences of conflict in the high latitudes fueled Cold War scenarios of potential future conflict. Superpower enmity involving the United States and the Soviet Union and their respective allies radiated across the northern hemisphere. Yet, strategies took on a particular imaginative purchase in the Arctic. Precisely because the Arctic was imagined to be a barren wasteland with few settled communities, it became a productive space to fantasize about what might occur. Both the United States and the Soviet Union invested more in academic disciplines such as glaciology and oceanography as they recognized that they needed to better understand northern environments, both on land and at sea. Infrastructure such as the Distant Early Warning (DEW) system, built in the mid- to late 1950s, was intended to provide an electronic "tripwire" in the event of a possible sneak Soviet bomber attack over the frozen Arctic Ocean. Stretching from Alaska and Canada to Greenland and Iceland, the DEW was one of the most iconic manifestations of Cold War militarism. For millions of American citizens, the North was defined by images of isolated radar stations immersed in a wintery environment (Farish 2010).

However, Cold War militarism also had a biopolitical element as well (Albert and Vasilache 2018). If the United States and the Soviet Union were motivated by geopolitical rationales pertaining to the control and surveillance of their respective northern territories, they were also concerned with the regulation and control of communities and populations. As Michel Foucault (2008) noted, with the development of the modern nation-state biopolitics and geopolitics became co-constitutive of one another. Regulating territory and people in the Arctic North was a multifaceted affair, from relocating Indigenous communities to areas of strategic significance and forced assimilation to the development of prison systems (i.e. gulags in the Soviet Union), and resource–industrial development projects, which necessitated the movement of non-Indigenous people into new mining projects and resource cities across the Arctic. Military bases and associated land, sea, and aerial patrolling also carried with them particular costs to both native communities and local ecosystems, notably in places such as Thule in northwest Greenland. Thule, an American air station established in the early to mid-1950s, led to community displacement and the establishment of exclusion zones. As with the Soviet Union, large areas of the Arctic became, in effect, closed spaces where human mobility was strictly regulated.

When speaking of geopolitical cultures in the way that political geographers assert, attention is drawn to how states in particular imagine the world, spatialize it, and link it to economic, political, and cultural projects, including identity politics, knowledge, resource extraction, and physical security (Dodds and Nuttall 2016). To speak of the Canadian Arctic, the High North, and/or the Russian Arctic is to enter into a contested and complex imaginative terrain and material space that bares the traces of colonial, Cold War, and transnational histories of encounter and exchange. Nationalist myths and stereotypes on the one hand coexist with biopolitical and geopolitical interventions on the other. There is no one Arctic per se, but tracing multiple Arctic(s) is not a straightforward process or practice either, despite what might be suggested by maps.

In 2007, stories and images circulated of a Russian flag being planted on the bottom of the central Arctic Ocean. News organizations were swift to pronounce the ideological and visual significance of the event. Headlines such as "Scramble for the Arctic" were rolled out, as commentators warned that Russia was hell-bent on spatial expansionism and the domination of Arctic place (Dodds 2010; Dittmer et al. 2011). While the provenance of the flag-planting was rather more complicated than social media and headlines might attest, it unleashed an affective geopolitics of fear: a type of geopolitics that triggers forceful sentiment and feelings, which appear to supersede discourses and practices of legal and political governance. Emotions circulate, jeremiads are produced, and calls for action are issued. Canadian political leaders reassured the public that their sovereignty in the Arctic would not be imperiled. Other countries unfolded new Arctic strategies, and resource companies, Indigenous organizations, and nongovernmental organizations also released their own visions for a future Arctic.

What the flag-planting incident revealed is how febrile geographical imaginaries and practices remain. The planting of a Russian flag (as opposed to a Canadian, Norwegian or even UN flag) carried with it a particular sort of affective geopolitics in Europe and North America. It recalled not only past imperial practices such as the scramble for and colonizing of territories in Africa,

Asia, and the Americas, but also touched upon contemporary anxieties that Russia had embarked on a new project under President Putin to recover its great-power status. If the Chinese flag had been deposited alongside the Russian one, then that might also have triggered a fresh round of concern about China's great-power pretensions in the international waters of the central Arctic Ocean. The flag as a material object exemplifies that geopolitics is more than simply language and representation. The Russian flag was made of titanium and considered rust-proof, thus hinting at a quasi-permanence.

What made the flag-planting incident in 2007 even more visceral was that it coincided with a record low for Arctic sea ice. For many commentators, the Arctic appeared to be "opening up" and thus inviting more geopolitics: more flag-planting, more resource extraction, more transiting, and more strategic scrambling for comparative advantage. In this articulation, Arctic geopolitics is better thought of as an unstable assemblage of discourse, practice, performance, and affect. It is more than simply visual and cartographic. While maps and media such as film contribute to popular geopolitics of the Arctic, helping to identify, represent, and dramatize the coordinates and configurations of space, these are not sufficient. Arctic geopolitics is not reducible to frames such as "Scramble for the Arctic" or "A return to the Cold War," however popular and resilient they might be.

Arctic geopolitics comes in many shapes and sizes (for example, Tamnes and Offerdal 2014). It is integral to the everyday lives of northern residents, it is performed in an array of sites and spaces in northern and non-northern locations (which in itself might be contested), and it is animated and inflamed by affective atmospheres. National leaders demand action in the Arctic; popular media warns of others trespassing in their airspace, seascape, and landscape; and Indigenous and northern communities and organizations articulate their own demands and wishes for past, present, and future Arctic(s). Hope, fear, dread, resentment, and the like all play their part in making Arctic geopolitics affective, emotive, more than representational, and corporeal (on affective geopolitics, see Toal 2017).

Arctic security and securing the Arctic

IR scholars have been at the forefront of writing and thinking about how security and region intersect with one another (for example, Albert 2016). One area of concerted interest is the manner in which security and insecurity grapple with challenges and threats that are transnational and mobile in character. Recognizing that the world is more complex than a world of nation-states and national territories might imply, governments have invested institutional and financial energies in developing and managing responses to issues that do not respect national boundaries. These issues include pollution as well as policy challenges such as shipping and environmental management that are best handled by affected coastal states and communities in particular spaces such as the Mediterranean, the Black Sea and/or the Arctic Ocean (Ciuta 2008). This desire to avoid spillover and regional conflict influences regional security initiatives as well. Across the world, there is evidence of regional states working together to promote confidence-building mechanisms and arenas for cooperation and dialogue. The Arctic, for example, has the Arctic Coast Guard Forum, which describes its mission as:

> The Arctic Coast Guard Forum (ACGF) is an independent, informal, operationally-driven organization, not bound by treaty, to foster safe, secure, and environmentally responsible maritime activity in the Arctic. All Arctic countries, Canada, Denmark, Finland, Island, Norway, Russia, Sweden and the United States are members of the forum.
>
> *(ACGF 2018)*

What the ACGF does, moreover, is embed the idea that they are Arctic countries and that they collaborate and discuss Arctic issues, including maritime domain awareness.

It is important to consider how a region such as the Arctic is defined and what it means for the actors and institutions involved. From there, attention might then shift towards securing the Arctic and recognizing that institutions such as the ACGF play their part in disciplining and policing the Arctic region as a space for action, and as a space where some actors are considered legitimate and others are, literally, out of place. The formal role accorded to observers, for instance, makes it clear that formal membership is limited to those who are geographically proximate and acknowledged by others as the most legitimate stakeholders. The region is not a neutral geographical framework but one that is vital in determining a distinct space of operation for the ACGF. In the ACGF's listed strategic goals, the spatial extent of the Arctic is embedded in thematic priorities such as "Strengthen multilateral cooperation and coordination within *the Arctic maritime domain*, and existing and future multilateral agreements." The Arctic maritime domain is not defined formally.

The geopolitics of regions, in this case the Arctic, shapes claims to identity narratives and knowledge production. The ACGF is an exemplar of this: it identified and legitimated eight Arctic states and empowered them to collect information and develop "common solutions" pertaining to their shared Arctic maritime domain. Legal mechanisms such as the United Nations Law of the Sea (UNCLOS) help to legitimate and justify such institutional developments. The eight Arctic member states, although varied in terms of access to the Arctic maritime domain, are grouped together as part of a shared Arctic state identity-building project. One could argue that a North Atlantic state, such as the UK, is more intimately involved in the Arctic maritime domain than Sweden and Finland. Yet both Sweden and Finland have icebreakers and bring to the forum their experience of operating in ice-covered waters in the Baltic Sea. The Arctic maritime domain involves both the deployment of specialist knowledge and experience and geographical proximity.

IR studies of regions and security have undergone a degree of change since flourishing in the post-Cold War era (Browning 2003; Agnew 2013; Paasi 2013). Building on an easing of superpower antagonism, regional organizations including the EU expanded membership, pursued nontraditional security agendas, and promoted integrative mechanisms. Some scholars termed this regional and security turn as indicative of "new regionalism" and/or regional security governance. This coincided with an active engagement on behalf of policymakers and the popular media with region-building projects. Underpinning this scholarly literature was interest in the role of trust and confidence-building mechanisms and collective identity politics. In other words, how was it possible for sovereign states to pool sovereignty and develop security communities that would be willing and prepared to work together in areas of mutual interest? IR scholars focused on institution building, mechanisms of governance, and the recognition of interdependence.

Security interdependence was a watchword of regional security complex theory (RSCT). The Copenhagen School of security, in particular, interrogated the regionalization of world politics in the post-Cold War era. A decline in superpower tension was credited with allowing different forms of regional experimentation to find purchase, as neighboring states recognized that perceptions of threats tended to undergo distance-decay. For example, cross-border migration, pollution, and smuggling were considered to be of most relevance to those states closest to one another or linked through a shared watershed or maritime region. The scale and extent of regional security communities varies and can be shaped by an array of complicating factors such as past histories, shared cultural values, and patterns of economic and political cooperation. How issues and processes become securitized (or desecuritized) requires careful examination because it should not be assumed that regional security initiatives are self-evident.

However, it is not clear whether the RSCT devotes sufficient attention to how spaces, such as regional spaces, shape the identified security cultures and dynamics. Detecting a series of unacknowledged geographical assumptions implicit within IR theory, John Agnew warned nearly 25 years ago that states and regions should not be considered to be preformed spatial containers (Agnew 2013). The politics of defining and redefining is integral to any regional security project, with an array of accompanying practices. To take an Arctic example, the 1996 Ottawa Convention, which led to the establishment of the Arctic Council, purposefully excluded security from its area of remit. The official text of the agreement notes via Footnote 1 that "The Arctic Council should not deal with matters related to military security." This follows after the statement that the Council will "provide a means for promoting cooperation, coordination, and interaction among the Arctic States, with the involvement of the Arctic Indigenous communities and other Arctic inhabitants on common Arctic issues." Excluding any explicit security dimensions came after defining concepts such as Arctic states and common Arctic issues, and paved the way for nonmilitary practices such as infrastructural investment, mapping, and science to buttress state security interests.

The footnote helps bring to the forefront something important: the role of imaginative and strategic interventions. The United States and Russia were the strongest advocates of this particular form of omission. Instead, attention was devoted to environmental protection and sustainable development as mechanisms for promoting region building and regional cooperation. Notwithstanding that exclusion, the Ottawa Convention takes for granted the Arctic as a regional space defined by eight Arctic states who are identifiable because of their geographical, cultural, legal, and political entanglements and entitlements. The Arctic Council acknowledges the presence of permanent participants (Indigenous organizations such as the Sámi Council and Inuit Circumpolar Council) and non-Arctic observers, including other states and nongovernmental and intergovernmental organizations. What is clear throughout is that the interests of the Arctic states are paramount, and the Arctic region is considered to be durable and self-evident.

Arctic security is embroiled in an assemblage of social, political, cultural, and legal processes, which involve an array of struggles and competition for ideological and material resources. To examine *the Arctic* and *security* is to enter a contested terrain where both concepts are slippery and capable of accommodating multiple interpretations and interests. Does security mean something involving nation-states and their militaries working on protecting national territories and interests within and beyond the Arctic? How, as environmental, feminist, and Indigenous scholars note, does that definition coexist with alternative conceptions of security? What about the everyday insecurities faced by Indigenous women in settler-colonial states? How do we account for Arctic ecologies and nonhuman communities? Finally, how do competing conceptions of security get reproduced, negotiated and settled? For instance, resource projects involving large-scale mining, power generation, and oil and gas extraction are often contentious and bring to the fore competing stakeholders, spatial scales of governance, and visions of what the Arctic represents, such as a resource frontier, a wilderness region, and a homeland. Security can and does conjure up economic, political, military, ecological, and social and cultural agendas.

What informs and animates these competing and coexisting security projects is how space, in this case regional space, is brought to the fore. Acknowledging that there are multiple Arctic(s) at play should lead to an investigation of how the region as a spatial category is constructed and mobilized. Rather than conceptualize region as either substate and/or intergovernmental, political geographers focus more on how those regional imaginaries are shot through with power–knowledge relationships and a spatial politics of inclusion and exclusion. The Arctic is not predefined but, rather, actively generated through regional security projects, the identifying of stakeholders, common issues, and future directions.

Regional security projects are never straightforward. In the Arctic context, the 1990s and 2000s saw a flourishing of regional innovation involving multiple stakeholders. Critical geopolitics includes formal academic commenters/think tanks, practical geopolitical reasoning of governments, militaries and businesses, and popular geopolitics of media and public culture (Toal 1996, 2017). Region building is not something endogenous to particular regions either. Regional security projects can and do originate, circulate, and spread both inside and outside the regional space in question. They coexist with other initiatives such that those Arctic states involved with Arctic region building are engaged in an array of Arctic and non-Arctic activities encompassing other spatial units, including continental regions and maritime domains. How they inform one another is something that deserves more considered attention, such as Norway's membership and participation in NATO, the Nordic Council, Euro-Barents Council, EEA, Arctic Council, and the Schengen Agreement. All of these carry with them particular commitments to meanings, logics, and agencies of security.

There are thus several takeaways from this discussion of Arctic security. If security is a contested and slippery term, then linking it to a region such as the Arctic does not remove any conceptual and empirical slipperiness. If anything, it complicates further what both terms signify. There is a geopolitics to *security* and *region*; space in both cases is not a preformed container for security to be articulated and materialized. Norway's multiple membership in NATO, the Nordic Council, Arctic Council, and so on, provides a good example of how one state has to negotiate multiple regional types and security practices as a northern European, Arctic, northern-flank, associate-member state. Arctic security is about the discourses, imaginaries, and practices at play in making the thing it names possible.

Reversing the focus on Arctic security to think about how the Artcic is secured involves exploring how spatial references get articulated, performed, legitimated, and justified. How do regional security practices contribute to the organization and management of regional spaces such as the Arctic? Are some regional security practices more hegemonic than others, and do some stakeholders dominate more than others? In the Arctic region, Indigenous and northern communities would point out that militaries, energy companies, and political bodies have been pivotal in defining what counts as Arctic security and how the Arctic is secured by imposing policing, resource management plans, settlement planning, infrastructural investment, and patrolling. The social, economic, and cultural implications of this for individuals, communities, and ecologies remains a topic of considerable interest where competing claims to knowledge and understanding loom large. In many northern communities, this might take the form of arguments over how living and non-living resources such as fish, whales, and minerals should be managed and secured. The intersection between scientific and Indigenous knowledge claims has been critical to the negotiation of a secure and sustainable Arctic(s). But as with security, sustainability traffics in biopolitics and geopolitics, with implications for how territories and human and nonhuman communities are imagined, managed, and disciplined.

Arguably, the last 30 years have witnessed far greater involvement of northern and Indigenous communities in regional security and the geopolitics of securing the Arctic. From participating in national militaries, such as the Canadian Rangers in the High Arctic, to acting as substantial land and resource rights holders, northern communities have demanded consultation, social licensing, and respect via the recognition of political autonomy and legal rights as Indigenous peoples. Alaska, Canada, Greenland, and the Nordic Arctic have seen some of the most profound changes in this regard (Nuttall 2017). This process of Indigenous empowerment remains a work in progress as Indigenous peoples continue to insist that their interests, wishes, and rights are often deprioritized by Arctic states when it comes to national security planning and economic and political priority setting. In Canada, for example, former Prime Minister Stephen Harper was accused by Northerners of being more concerned with protecting national sovereignty and security in the Northwest Passage and Canadian Arctic than with addressing the everyday insecurities facing many communities in the form of poor housing, limited education and training, inadequate sanitation, costly internet connectivity, and expensive transport.

To speak of Arctic security and/or to act in the name of Arctic security is not self-evident. In the last decade, emphasis has tended to fall on traditional topics and practices such as investment in infrastructure, patrolling and policing, scrutinizing published strategies, and Arctic state behavior in the Arctic Ocean. The objects of security include airspace, seabed and maritime passages, resource blocks, extraterritorial actors, institutional structures, and organizations such as the Arctic Council. Plus, as we note below, there is a desire to insulate the Arctic from worsening relationships involving Russia in the post-Crimea era (Dodds and Nuttall 2016). However, as other scholars have reminded us, there are also human security considerations to account for in the Arctic (Gjørv et al. 2013).

Arctic governance

As a field, Arctic governance has grown exponentially since the end of the Cold War (Ingimundarson 2014). This is not to imply that the circumpolar North was previously devoid of shared governance arrangements and interstate cooperation. In the late 19th and early 20th century, examples included the International Polar Years and initiatives such as the North Pacific Sealing Convention and the 1920 Spitzbergen Treaty. In both examples, a group of states including the UK, United States, Japan, Russia, and Norway agreed on a series of living-resource conservation measures, and in the Svalbard example, a regime for demilitarization and sovereignty management. Later, in the midst of Cold War détente, five Arctic countries signed the Polar Bear Agreement, which committed the signatories to share information and cooperate on conservation. As with the North Pacific Sealing Convention, the rationale for cooperation was rooted in the transboundary mobility of the polar bear.

The ending of superpower tension in the late 1980s ushered in renewed interest in developing new forms of regional, international, and transnational cooperation. This mosaic of Arctic governance included state and non-state stakeholders, including the Northern Research Forum, International Arctic Science Committee, Arctic Environment Protection Strategy (AEPS), Barents Euro-Arctic Region, and, most significantly, the Arctic Council. Much of the literature on Arctic governance has focused on institution building, mechanisms of peace and cooperation, and the regional architecture. At the heart of this interrogation lies the intergovernmental forum, the Arctic Council, which established distinct categories of Arctic state, permanent participant, and observer.

Inspired by the 1991 AEPS, the Arctic Council's strategic mission centered on environmental protection and sustainable development. Uniquely, the category of *permanent participants* (PPs) was envisaged as a progressive intervention into the fixed architecture of territorial states and exclusive sovereignty. The PPs as a category formally recognized the Arctic as inhabited and populated by Indigenous and northern communities that experienced colonial and Cold War-era disruption and dislocation. The Arctic Council was also intended to bring together Russia and the other Arctic states in a new forum based on mutual recognition and noninterference in their respective territories (Young 2010; Rowe 2018).

Since its inception in the mid-1990s, the Arctic Council has often been credited with sustaining a form of Arctic exceptionalism. Implying that the Arctic is a spatial container that is largely immune from the prevailing dangers of global geopolitics, it is posited as an isolated, even idealized space for constructive regional governance, peaceful coexistence, and technical cooperation in areas such as environmental management, sustainable development, and maritime safety. For at least a decade, from the late 1990s to the late 2000s, it was common to read analyses that articulated a sense of Arctic governance as being insulated from the specter of military confrontation, genocidal violence, and strategic intrigue that bedeviled Southeast Europe, Africa, Asia, and Latin America. This is often referred to as *Arctic exceptionalism*.

What has arguably placed Arctic governance under new pressures has been four notable developments. First, relations between Russia and the other Arctic states have become more sensitive, as Nordic and Baltic states worry about Russian revivalism. The detention of the so-called "Arctic 30" and the Greenpeace ship *Arctic Sunrise* in 2013, followed by the annexation of Crimea and the Eastern Ukraine conflict in 2014, was followed by the imposition of sanctions against Russia by the EU and the United States. While some observers worried about conflict spillover, the net result was to generate new fears about Russian military expansionism in the Arctic and possible consequences for Arctic peace and stability. The 2017 Fairbanks Agreement on Enhancing International Arctic Scientific Cooperation has been seen as a stabilizing force and a victory for science diplomacy (Berkmann et al. 2017).

Second, commercial opportunity and resource speculation in the Arctic has encouraged newer actors to become involved. In May 2013, the Arctic Council membership approved five Asian states as observers; namely China, Japan, South Korea, Singapore, and India. For some, this appeared to herald a more global Arctic; one where extraterritorial actors were intent on shaping the present and future contours of Arctic governance (Sidaway and Woon 2017).

Third, ongoing climate change is continuing to make its impact felt on Arctic sea ice, permafrost, and the livelihoods of human and nonhuman communities, contributing to a more demanding Arctic environment. This is an Arctic that is not only making its own demands on the non-Arctic, but the non-Arctic is demanding things from the Arctic. While Indigenous peoples demand that their wishes and interests are heard and respected, nongovernmental organizations and commercial actors make their own demands regarding the exploitation and protection of the region.

Finally, Arctic states are using international legal mechanisms such as UNCLOS and the Polar Code to advance their own sovereignty–security–stewardship agendas (Jensen 2016). Canada, Denmark/Greenland, Norway, Russia, and the United States, as Arctic Ocean coastal states, remain determined to ensure that their sovereign interests extend as far as possible over the water column and seabed of the Arctic Ocean. In 2017, the Arctic Five and five other actors, including China and the European Union, agreed upon a moratorium on fishing in the central Arctic Ocean (CAO) for 16 years. Remarkably, it would have been unthinkable not so long ago to have even raised the prospect of a commercial fishery in the CAO (Norris and McKinley 2017).

Making sense of Arctic governance is becoming ever-more complicated (Young 2016). The Arctic Council works on the basis of regional agglomeration, which asserts that the Arctic states and PPs are the dominant stakeholders due to their geographical rootedness.

However, a more networked Arctic, where mobility, flow, and connection are globalizing the region, is challenging this rooted view of the Arctic. The formal regional architecture of the Arctic, including the Arctic Council, provides a limited view of Arctic governance. Arctic governance is better thought of as possessing multiple manifestations that reveal multiple stakeholders, sites, spaces, layers of interaction, issues, and challenges (Knecht and Keil 2013; Knecht and Keil 2017). The Arctic in all of this remains a polysomic and malleable term – even more so in the face of ongoing evidence that the ecologies and communities in the northern latitudes are being profoundly affected by globalizing trends in climate, resources, geopolitical competition, and technological development. Perhaps it has been helpful for many parties, state and non-state alike, to deploy a flexible geopolitical imagination, with the scope of the Arctic growing and shrinking at different political moments?

Conclusion

In January 2018, the Chinese government released its first Arctic policy document and articulated a vision of an Arctic region in which the country could take advantage of commercial, diplomatic, and scientific opportunities for exchange, while mindful of its rights as an extraterritorial state to access the international waters of the Arctic Ocean and assert rights of innocent and transit passage (Hong 2018). Beijing's Arctic policy also formally placed the Arctic Ocean within broader commercial and geopolitical framing of the Belt and Road initiative's trade routes. Emphasis was placed on flow and connection, with China as a great power eager to generate mutual advantage with partners all over the Euro–Asia macro-region in particular. When the Arctic Council was negotiated in 1996, little formal consideration was given to the idea that China, Japan, South Korea, and Singapore might one day be approved observers, whereas the European Union remains an ad hoc observer. While Arctic states will remain vigilant in defending their sovereign interests in the maritime Arctic, they have also embraced Asian state involvement in order to leverage commercial and diplomatic advantage.

Arctic governance is not solely about states and their interests. The last 30 years have witnessed Indigenous peoples on the one hand asserting their rights and interests, and on the other hand, non-state actors such as environmental organizations demanding that the Arctic be protected, saved, and/or managed. Melting ice and iconic wildlife such as polar bears and whales play their part in generating ideas and images of Arctic governance. Yet so do resource projects, traversing ships through sea ice, and pollutants seeping into northern bodies and ecosystems. When the term "global Arctic" is cited, it can helpfully challenge conceits that this particular regional (or regionalized) space is in any way isolated from the broader dynamics of geopolitics, neoliberal capitalism, and environmental disruption (Heininen 2016).

References

Agnew, J (1994) 'The territorial trap: the geographical assumptions of international relations theory' *Review of International Political Economy* 1: 53–80.

Agnew, J (2013) 'Arguing with regions' *Regional Studies* 47: 6–17.

Albert, M (2016) *A Theory of World Politics* Cambridge: Cambridge University Press.

Albert, M and A Vasilache (2018) 'Governmentality of the Arctic as an international region' *Cooperation and Conflict* 53: 3–22.

Arctic Coast Guard Forum (2018) Mission Statement URL available at: www.arcticcoastguardforum.com

Berkmann, P et al. (2017) 'The Arctic science agreement propels science diplomacy' *Science Magazine* 358 Issue 6363: 596–598. 3rd November 2017.

Browning, C (2003) 'The region-building approach revisited: the continued 'othering' of Russia in discourses of region-building in the European North' *Geopolitics* 8: 45–71.

Ciuta, F (2008) 'Region? Why region? Security, hermeneutics and the making of the Black Sea region' *Geopolitics* 12: 120–147.

Depledge, D (2017) *Britain and the Arctic* London: Palgrave.

Dittmer, J et al. (2011) 'Have you heard the one about the disappearing ice? Recasting Arctic geopolitics' *Political Geography* 30: 202–214.

Dodds, K (2010) 'Flag planting and finger pointing: the Law of the Sea, the Arctic and the political geographies of the outer continental shelf' *Political Geography* 29: 63–73.

Dodds, K and M Nuttall (2016) *The Scramble for the Poles* Cambridge: Polity.

Farish, M (2010) *Contours of the Cold War* Minneapolis: University of Minnesota Press.

Foucault, M. (2008) *The Birth of Biopolitics: Lectures at the Collège de France, 1978–1979: Lectures at the College De France, 1978–1979*. London: Palgrave Macmillan.

Gjørv, G et al. editors (2013) *Environmental and Human Security in the Arctic* London: Earthscan.

Heininen, L editor (2016) *Future Security of the Global Arctic* London: Palgrave.

Heininen, L and C Southcott editors (2010) *Globalization and the Circumpolar North* Fairbanks: University of Alaska Press.

Hong, N (2018) *China's Interests in the Arctic: Opportunities and Challenges: Examining the implications of China's Arctic policy white paper* Washington: Institute for China-America Studies.

Ingimundarson, V (2014) 'Managing a contested region: the Arctic council and the politics of Arctic governance' *Polar Journal* 4: 183–198.

Jensen, O (2016) 'The international code for ships operating in polar waters: finalization, adoption and law of the sea implications' *Arctic Review of Law and Politics* 7: 60–82.

Jones, M and A Paasi (2013) 'Guest editorial: regional world(s): advancing the geography of regions' *Regional Studies* 47: 1–5.

Keskitalo, E (2004) *Negotiating the Arctic: The Construction of an International Region* London: Routledge.

Knecht, S and K Keil (2013) 'Arctic geopolitics revisited: spatialising governance in the circumpolar North' *Polar Journal* 3: 178–203.

Knecht, S and K Keil editors (2017) *Governing Arctic Change* London: Palgrave.

Lewis, M and K Wigen (1997) *The Myth of Continents* Berkeley: University of California Press.

Medby, I (2018) 'Articulating state identity: 'peopling' the Arctic state' *Political Geography* 62: 116–125.

Neumann, I (1994) 'A region-building approach to Northern Europe' *Review of International Studies* 20: 53–74.

Norris, A and P McKinley (2017) 'The central Arctic Ocean-preventing another tragedy of the commons' *Polar Record* 53: 43–51.

Norway (2017) Arctic Strategy URL available at: www.regjeringen.no/en/dokumenter/arctic-strategy/id2550081/

Norway (2017) *Norway's Arctic Strategy: Between Geopolitics and Social Development* Oslo: Government of Norway, p. 1.

Nuttall, M. (2017) *Climate, Socity and Subsurface Politics in Greenland: Under the Great Ice* London: Routledge.

Paasi, A (2009) 'The resurgence of the 'region' and 'regional identity': theoretical perspectives and empirical observations on regional dynamics in Europe' *Review of International Studies* 35: 121–146.

Passi, A (2013) 'Regional planning and mobilization of 'regional identity': from bounded spaces to relational complexity' *Regional Studies* 47: 1206–1219.

Rowe, E (2018) *Arctic Governance* Manchester: Manchester University Press.

Rowe, E and H Blakkisrud (2014) 'A new kind of Arctic power? Russia's policy discourses and diplomatic practices in the circumpolar North' *Geopolitics* 19: 66–85.

Sidaway, J and C Y Woon (2017) 'Chinese narratives on 'one belt, one road' in geopolitical and imperial contexts' *Professional Geographer* 69: 591–603.

Tamnes, R. and K Offerdal (2014) *Geopolitics and Security in the Arctic: Regional dynamics in a global world*. London: Routledge.

Toal, G (1996) *Critical Geopolitics* London: Routledge.

Toal, G (2017) *Near Abroad: Putin, the West, and the Contest Over Ukraine and the Caucasus* Oxford: Oxford University Press.

Young, O (2010) 'Arctic Governance - Pathways to the Future' *Arctic Review on Law and Politics* 1: 164–185.

Young, O (2016) 'The shifting landscape of Arctic politics: implications for international cooperation' *Polar Journal* 6: 209–223.

23

SECURITY ISSUES IN THE SVALBARD AREA

Tobjørn Pedersen

Introduction

The archipelago of Svalbard, littoral to the Arctic Ocean, is linked to a set of traditional security issues. The islands (which belong to Norway, a member-state of the NATO alliance) raise concerns in Moscow because they sit just outside Russia's most important military bases on the Kola Peninsula (Åtland, 2014; Østreng, 1975; Pedersen, 2008b). Russian strategic assets, including aircraft, missiles, submarines, and surface vessels, would likely pass close to Svalbard en route to the Arctic Ocean, North America, and the Atlantic Ocean (Figure 23.1). Thus, the Soviet Union, and later Russia, kept a close eye on all activities in Svalbard and vigorously protested when Norway established infrastructure that could potentially serve military purposes, including an airport, research radar, and satellite ground stations (Åtland, 2014; Åtland and Pedersen, 2008, 2013). The Russian news service *Pravda* has referred to the islands as "NATO's outpost under Russia's nose" (Rivetov, 2003).

The islands also cause security headaches in Oslo (Pedersen, 2009a). The late Norwegian Prime Minister Johan Nygaardsvold was, according to his own Foreign Minister Trygve Lie, always "grumpy" when Svalbard was put on the agenda (Lie, 1958). Another former Foreign Minister, Jon Lyng, stated that *Svalbard* was the first thought that crossed his mind when his telephone rang in the middle of the night (Frydenlund, 1982). Rolf Tamnes, a history professor who headed an expert group appointed by the Norwegian Minister of Defense in 2014 to look into Norway's ability to cope with present and future security challenges, stated that "There is only one larger, potential security challenge in the High North, and that is Svalbard" (High North News, 2016).

The 1920 Svalbard (Spitsbergen) Treaty, which was signed in the aftermath of World War I and recognized Norway's "full and absolute sovereignty" over the archipelago, is subject to different interpretations. This treaty is the backdrop for disputes in the Barents Sea between Norway and other parties, notably the European Union, Iceland, and Russia. Some argue that treaty provisions that grant the citizens of all contracting parties an equal right of fishing, hunting, and mining in the islands and the adjacent territorial waters also extend beyond the 12-nautical-mile territorial limits. Norway maintains that the Svalbard Treaty has no relevance to the surrounding continental shelf or the 200-mile Fisheries Protection Zone (Pedersen, 2008a), thus rendering the maritime resources exclusive to Norway under the 1982 Law of the Sea Convention. The disputes over maritime rights

Figure 23.1 The archipelago of Svalbard

outside Svalbard have on occasion resulted in episodes that involved the use of force. Notably, in 1994, a Norwegian Coast Guard vessel fired live rounds of non-explosive grenades at a Belize-registered trawler in the Fisheries Protection Zone when the Icelandic crew refused to allow Norwegian inspectors on board in what Iceland regarded to be the High Seas. Norway has also faced blunt threats from treaty parties as well as the European Commission, which, in 2004, reserved its right to "take any action it deems appropriate to safeguard its rights and interests" in the waters surrounding Svalbard (Pedersen, 2008a: 250).

Current security issues in the area relate to three different geographical spheres: First, the Svalbard islands and their territorial waters, stretching out to 12 nautical miles from the coastlines; second, the Fisheries Protection Zone, established in 1977 by the Norwegian government, and extending up to 200 nautical miles from the archipelago; and third, the continental shelf surrounding Svalbard, a seabed area which also extends beyond 200 nautical miles from Svalbard toward the North Pole. Each of these three spheres raises different security concerns and involves different security actors. This chapter provides an overview of the security issues and actors associated with each of the three geographical spheres. Before these analyses, some background information is presented.

A brief history

The discovery of Svalbard is subject to debate. Some Russian historians suggest that Russian merchants, the *pomors*, found the islands during the 1550s, although the claim has not been convincingly substantiated (Arlov, 2003). Some Norwegians, on the other hand, have suggested that the Vikings located Svalbard, having sailed north from Iceland for roughly four days (sailing annals from 1194 include references to *Svalbardi funning*, "Svalbard found," an entry which is also the origin of the archipelago's present name) (ibid.). This claim has been ridiculed, especially by Russian historians. Undisputedly, however, the Dutch explorer Willem Barentsz came to the islands in 1596, and named the land *Spitsbergen*. This discovery was followed by a century of intensive and large-scale hunting in the area by the English, Dutch, and others, which led to the near-extinction of several species, including whales and walruses.

With maritime resources depleted, the interest of governments in the islands was marginal. During the 18th and 19th centuries, the archipelago attracted few people other than fur trappers from Russia and Norway. By the early 1900s, however, Norway took a greater interest in the islands as mineral resource exploitation proliferated. The issue of jurisdiction was raised in conferences in 1910 and 1912 by Norway, Russia, and Sweden, who discussed the prospects of governing the archipelago as a trilateral condominium (Berg, 1995). Discussions on jurisdiction in Svalbard were discontinued at the outbreak of World War I, but the topic resurfaced again during the 1919 Paris Peace Conference. At this stage, in the absence of the Russian government, Norway sought full sovereignty over the islands. The five great powers at the conference – France, Italy, Japan, the United Kingdom, and the United States – established a Spitsbergen Commission, which drafted a treaty that recognized Norwegian sovereignty but also safeguarded some of the international interests in the archipelago and its natural resources.

The Treaty Concerning Spitsbergen (hereinafter referred to as the Svalbard Treaty) was signed on 9 February 1920, and entered into force five years later. Taking on sovereignty, the Norwegian government renamed the archipelago *Svalbard*, referencing the old Viking annals, but retained *Spitsbergen* as the name of the main island. The 1925 Svalbard Act established the islands as an inseparable part of the Kingdom of Norway. The Soviet Union acceded to the Svalbard Treaty in 1935.

The Svalbard Treaty

The Svalbard Treaty is composed of ten articles. Notably, Article 1 recognizes Norway's full and absolute sovereignty over the archipelago, which include all islands between 10° and 35° East and 74° and 81° North (sometimes referred to as the Svalbard Box). Articles 2 and 3 stipulate that the nationals of the treaty parties, not the state parties themselves, enjoy the equal right of fishing and hunting in the islands and their territorial waters, equal liberty of access and entry, and the same conditions for maritime, industrial, mining, or commercial activities on the islands and in their territorial waters. Article 8 limits the Norwegian government's access to levy taxes in Svalbard. The article specifies that collected taxes and duties must be devoted exclusively to the islands. Article 9 prohibits Norway from creating or allowing the establishment of naval bases and fortifications in Svalbard, "which may never be used for warlike purposes." A total of 44 states are now parties to the Svalbard Treaty, with Latvia, Lithuania, and North Korea being the latest adopters.

A few legal scholars have taken an interest in the Svalbard Treaty and the related Mining Code, which also entered into force in 1925 and stipulated procedures for staking out and exploiting mineral claims in Svalbard. Most notably, Norwegian professors Carl August Fleischer and Geir Ulfstein have engaged in a heated debate about the application of the Svalbard Treaty to areas beyond the territorial waters of Svalbard. While Fleischer maintains that the treaty applies explicitly to the islands and their territorial waters (Fleischer, 1976, 1983, 1988), which currently extend 12 nautical miles from the baselines, Ulfstein argues that the provisions also apply to the surrounding 200-mile zone and continental shelf by analogy (Churchill and Ulfstein, 1993; Ulfstein, 1995). The latter argument has since been reiterated or developed by others (e.g. Anderson, 2009; Molenaar, 2012). Curiously, Vylegzhanin and Zilanov (2007) have launched an alternative legal interpretation, essentially referring to the maritime areas around Svalbard as the High Seas, but this viewpoint has found little support in international law (Pedersen & Henriksen 2009).

Paradoxically, the Svalbard Treaty, which settled the sovereignty issue, also gave rise to myths about the archipelago's legal status. One study argued that jurisprudence only has limited relevance if Svalbard is widely *perceived* as international (Pedersen, 2017). Treaty-related particularities of Svalbard include the existence of institutions like *Sysselmannen* (the Governor of Svalbard) and a Local Council, unlike the institutions found on the Norwegian mainland. Also, Svalbard is kept outside the Schengen Area, which makes travelling between Svalbard Airport Longyearbyen and destinations on the Norwegian mainland quite different from other domestic flights. Planes leave from international terminals and passengers must present their passports, though visas are not required. Shopping is tax-free. Coupled with the increasing share of non-Norwegians settling in Longyearbyen and the other communities in Svalbard, these hallmarks give the archipelago an international persona that may reinforce misperceptions about Svalbard being something different or separate from Norway (Pedersen, 2017). Misperceptions about the legal status pose a security challenge to the Norwegian government. They could potentially invite foreign governments to fill a perceived political vacuum and assert their influence. Hence, even perceptions about Svalbard and its legal status are of significant security concern to Norway.

Security issues on land

In the 1950s and 1960s, most Svalbard-related security issues concerned infrastructure on land. In January 1951, the Norwegian government formally included Svalbard, with Bjørnøya (Bear Island), in NATO's defense area and command structure, which was met with diplomatic protests from Moscow (Arlov, 2003). As a rule, the Soviet Union protested all measures that could potentially serve early-warning purposes and/or affect its nuclear second-strike capabilities, including plans to build airfields in Longyearbyen and Kings Bay in the 1950s, and the telemetric station at Kings Bay, in cooperation with the European Space Research Organization (ESRO), in the 1960s. On all occasions, the Soviet Union referred to Article 9 of the Svalbard Treaty, which prohibits Svalbard from being used for "warlike purposes." The Russian understanding of the provision as a demilitarization clause magnified Moscow's concerns. While in English *warlike purposes* and in French *but du guerre* are the phrases, the Russian translation, *v vojennykh tseljakh*, refers to all *military* purposes (Jørgensen, 2003), arguably a broader term than expressed by the authentic language of the Treaty. Thus, Moscow also objected to Svalbard port calls by frigates of the Norwegian Navy as well as C-130 Hercules and P-3 Orion fixed-wing aircraft of the Norwegian Air Force.

The coal mining settlements of Barentsburg and Pyramiden served as the Soviet Union's, and later Russia's, eyes and ears in this NATO territory. In the 1960s, the USSR established a helicopter base at Kapp Heer just outside of Barentsburg, equipped with military-type Mi-8 helicopters (Arlov, 2003). The helicopters were formally needed for prospecting. However, for decades, the helicopter base was allegedly also run as a military unit, which in a state of war was to seize control of the Svalbard Airport Longyearbyen, which was officially opened in 1975 (Amundsen, 2001; Arlov, 2003). This example illustrates the security concerns that Svalbard continues to raise in Moscow.

Although mining operations in Pyramiden were discontinued in 1998, Russia maintains a significant presence in Svalbard through the state-owned mining company, Trust Arktikugol and the Consulate General in Barentsburg. Over the last decade, buildings in

Barentsburg have been refurbished and the infrastructure significantly upgraded (Jørgensen, 2016). A designated government commission, the Commission on Russian Presence in the Spitsbergen Archipelago, ensures that the Russian presence in Svalbard is maintained, not only through the highly unprofitable coal mining activity but also by tourism and research (Jørgensen, 2010). In 2016, the Russian Science Center in Spitsbergen (RSCS) was officially established in Barentsburg, featuring modern laboratory facilities, observatories, and even a satellite ground station (Nikulina, 2016). Occasionally, the Russians seem to forget or defy the fact that the settlement is on Norwegian territory and under the exclusive jurisdiction of the Norwegian government. In 2008, for instance, the Russian patrol vessel *Mikula* made a surprise call to Barentsburg, without obtaining the proper diplomatic clearance from the Norwegian government in advance. The Russian government commission has also discussed the stationing of government search and rescue (SAR) capabilities in Barentsburg (Pedersen, 2017), which the Norwegian government would certainly object to.

Other nations have also established a presence in Svalbard. Government-funded and/or government-run research institutions from nations like China, France, Germany, India, Italy, Japan, Korea, the Netherlands, and the United Kingdom operate permanent research stations in Ny-Ålesund, a research village north of Longyearbyen. Its entrance decorated with solid marble guardian lions, or *shishizi*, the Yellow River Station (*Huanghe Zhan*) overseen by the Chinese Arctic and Antarctic Administration (CAA) resembles a government outpost as much as a research facility. Here, at 79°N, the Chinese and others have experimented with unmanned aerial vehicle (UAV) technology in the harsh Arctic climate and conducted research on the atmosphere, glaciers, oceans, and ecosystems. Their presence has been welcomed and encouraged by the Norwegian government, although Oslo seems increasingly determined to put international researchers in shared research facilities rather than allowing a proliferation of autonomous foreign stations in Svalbard (The Norwegian Ministry of Justice, 2016). Differences between Oslo and Beijing over acceptable scientific research projects in Svalbard flared up in March 2019 over plans by the Norwegian government to set specific parameters on what scientific activity could be conducted on the islands (Rapp, 2019).

The location of Svalbard, close to the North Pole, also makes the islands increasingly attractive for space-related infrastructure, including radars and satellite ground stations. Research radars benefit from Svalbard's immediate vicinity to the magnetic cusp at the pole, a window to interplanetary space (Rinne, 2010). Satellite ground stations, in turn, may communicate with satellites in polar orbit on every pass due to their near-pole location. Customers at the Norwegian-controlled Svalbard Satellite Station (SvalSat) include satellite owners such as the US National Aeronautics Space Administration (NASA), the US National Oceanic and Atmosphere Administration (NOAA), the European Space Agency (ESA) and the European Organization for the Exploitation of Meteorological Satellites (EUMETSAT). Some space-related infrastructure could potentially serve dual purposes. Observers, notably the Norwegian reporter Bård Wormdal, allege that the infrastructure already services non-civilian customers (Wormdal, 2011). In *Satellittkrigen* ("The War of Satellites"), an account of the relevance of ground stations in Svalbard and Antarctica to the Western military establishment, Wormdal suggested that some of the data from civilian Earth-observation satellites, environmental monitoring and weather satellites, and communications satellites might be used in military missions and operations (Wormdal, 2011).

Although Wormdal's account is highly tendentious, and his implication that any dual-purpose activity would be in violation of the Svalbard Treaty is a stretch, infrastructure in Svalbard certainly has military potential. In 2014, the Norwegian government repudiated China's plans to establish a third radar at the European Incoherent Scatter (EISCAT) facilities outside Longyearbyen. Following the Norwegian decision, the spokesperson for the Ministry of Research and Education, Anne Kristin Hjuske, explained that "The stated purpose of the facility is to conduct space research. However, the technology also has other uses" (Norwegian Broadcasting 2014).

At present, Norwegian sovereignty over Svalbard is firmly established and largely unchallenged. The Norwegian government is explicitly committed to honoring the provisions of the Svalbard Treaty, including Article 9, in its exercise of jurisdiction in the Svalbard islands and their territorial waters (Ministry of Justice 2016). At the same time, the Norwegian government seems determined to scale back its self-imposed restraints; that is, Svalbard-specific limitations in the exercise of Norwegian jurisdiction resulting from political considerations rather than treaty provisions (Norwegian Ministry of Justice 2016). A previous study concluded that Norway's grip on the islands is getting incrementally firmer as the self-imposed restrictions are eased, and that the exercise of jurisdiction in Svalbard is increasingly aligned with the exercise of Norwegian jurisdiction in the mainland (Pedersen, 2009b).

Security issues and the Fisheries Protection Zone

Following legal developments during the Third Law of the Sea Conference (UNCLOS III) in the mid-1970s, the Norwegian government established a 200-nautical mile Exclusive Economic Zone (EEZ) along its mainland in 1976 but opted for a softer, non-exclusive regime around the Svalbard islands the following year. "An exclusive zone [around Svalbard] would have caused infinite dispute and conflict," Norwegian Foreign Minister Knut Frydenlund told the public at the time (Dragnes, 1986). The fisheries resources in the 200-nautical mile Fisheries Protection Zone (FPZ) around Svalbard would become regulated, but not reserved exclusively for Norwegian fisheries. The resources would be shared by fishermen from all nations with a record of fishing in the area over the last decade, in the nondiscriminatory spirit of the Svalbard Treaty (Pedersen, 2011). The United States played an active but tacit role in mustering support for the new zone among key NATO allies, notably France, the United Kingdom, and the then-West Germany (Pedersen, 2011). The non-exclusive character of the zone would accommodate, as the US State Department put it, the Soviet Union's "strategic sensitivities in a region neighboring the Kola Peninsula and the sea lanes between the Norwegian and the Barents Sea" (Pedersen, 2011).

Still, following the introduction of the zone, Norway received numerous diplomatic notes of reservations and protests from other governments (Pedersen, 2008a). The closest allies expressed the view that they would reserve any rights they may have if the Svalbard Treaty applied to the zone. The then-Warsaw Pact members Czechoslovakia, Hungary, Poland, and the Soviet Union protested the unilateral actions of the Norwegian government, which established the zone by Royal Decree without prior consultations with the other parties to the Svalbard Treaty (Pedersen, 2008a, 2011).

The dispute over rights in the Fisheries Protection Zone did not heat up until the mid-1980s. In 1986, the Spanish government was outraged when Norway introduced nondiscriminatory quota regulations to the area based on traditional fishing, and ended the season's cod fishing for third-party states once their quota was reached. Madrid told Spanish fishermen to disregard Norwegian regulations and instructed them to continue fishing outside Svalbard (Pedersen, 2008a). Spain was partially backed by the European Community's Directorate General for Fisheries in Brussels, which asserted that the Norwegian regulations could be perceived as discriminatory (Pedersen, 2008a). As Spanish fishing continued, Norway deployed three Coast Guard vessels to the zone, keeping an additional three on standby, ready to arrest unyielding Spanish vessels (Pedersen, 2008a). Only at the last minute did the Spanish crews hoist their gear and leave the area, thus avoiding having their ships seized by force.

In 1993, the Norwegian Coast Guard was explicitly authorized to use brute force to stop what the government regarded as illegal fishing in the Fisheries Protection Zone. The first warning shot was fired in June 1993, and the following season the Coast Guard started trawl-cutting to stop what it regarded as illegal fishing. "We will take any measures necessary to stop the illegal fishing," Norway's then-Defense Minister Jørgen Kosmo proclaimed (NTB, 1994). On 5 August 1994, his words were put into action. The Coast Guard fired two live rounds of non-explosive grenades at the Icelandic-owned trawler *Hagangur II*, which sailed under a flag of convenience. The crew had resorted to small arms in the attempt to scare Norwegian fisheries inspectors from boarding the ship. In the response, two live 57-millimeter grenades penetrated the hull in the aft and brought the fishing vessel to a halt. Two more Icelandic vessels were seized during the 1994 season, turning Iceland into the most vocal critic of Norway's exercise of jurisdiction in the Fisheries Protection Zone. Iceland, acceding to the Svalbard Treaty the same year, did not, according to the Norwegian government, qualify for Northeast Arctic cod quotas in the area, since Icelandic fishers had no history of fishing there; this pronouncement infuriated Reykjavik.

In 1998, the first Russian trawler was seized for having violated fishing regulations in the Fisheries Protection Zone. However, the Coast Guard released the vessel *Novokuybyshevsk* before it reached a Norwegian port, following the prosecutor's issue of an immediate *nolle prosequi* (Pedersen, 2008a). Three years later, in 2001, another Russian fishing vessel was seized. This time, the Norwegian Coast Guard escorted the trawler *Chernigov* to the Norwegian mainland, which triggered strong reactions in Russia (Jørgensen, 2004). Moscow asserted that the maritime areas around Svalbard were regulated by "international legal norms pertaining to the high seas," outside the jurisdiction of Norway, and asked for the vessel's immediate release (Pedersen, 2008a).

Researchers, most notably Kristian Åtland, have linked Russia's responses to the Copenhagen School's concept of *securitization* (Wæver, 1995). Relevant security actors described the Norwegian exercise of enforcement jurisdiction not as attempts to manage vulnerable fish stocks and clamp down on illegal fishing outside Svalbard, but as efforts to push the Russians away from the area (Jørgensen, 2003, 2004, 2010, 2016). Several actors framed the issue as a security matter, thus warranting a response by all necessary means (Åtland and Bruusgaard, 2009; Åtland and Pedersen, 2008, 2013). Illustratively, the chairman of the Russian State Fisheries Committee, Yevgeniy Nazdratenko, urged Russian federal vessels to sink Norwegian Coast Guard vessels in the area "and do nothing to save their crew" (Jørgensen, 2003, 2004). The following season, the Russian Northern Fleet deployed a Udaloy-class destroyer to the Fisheries Protection Zone in an unprecedented maneuver to intimidate Norwegian authorities. Russia also started patrolling the area on a more regular basis with smaller government vessels, first from the State Fisheries Committee and later the Federal Security Service (FSB), to deter further arrests of Russian vessels.

Notwithstanding, on 15 October 2005, the Norwegian Coast Guard sought to arrest another Russian vessel after inspectors boarded the ship and uncovered gross violations of Norwegian fisheries regulations. However, rather than complying, the crew on the trawler *Elektron* changed its course, with the Norwegian inspectors still on board, and headed toward Russian waters. The dramatic chase for the runaway Russian vessel, which lasted for six days, featured four Norwegian Coast Guard blue ocean vessels, a jammed cannon, the scrambling of *Marinejegerkommandoen* (MJK) – a unit of the Norwegian Special Operations

Command – and low passes with both helicopters and a P-3 Orion fixed-wing aircraft. Approximately 400 Norwegian military personnel were involved in the hunt (Gramshaug, 2005). The Norwegian Minister of Defense repeatedly authorized armed special forces to board the vessel, but the operation was deemed too risky on site due to rough seas (Engebretsen-Skaret, 2012). The *Elektron* finally reached Russian territorial waters, the Norwegian pursuers yielded, and the trapped inspectors were transferred back to their vessel by Russian authorities.

The 2005 *Elektron* incident illustrated the continuous security concerns of the Fisheries Protection Zone and the potential for conflict and escalation. The Norwegian government demonstrated its resolve to use all means necessary, including military force, in an episode arising in the Fisheries Protection Zone, even if it involved a Russian vessel and related to what Russia regarded as a national interest in the region.

Since 2005, a handful of Russian vessels have been seized by the Norwegian Coast Guard in the Fisheries Protection Zone, usually followed by protests from Moscow but not by the same drama as that of the *Elektron* incident. Despite the occasional episodes, activities in the Fisheries Protection Zone around Svalbard are generally orderly and well regulated (Hønneland, 2005, 2012). Illegal, unreported, and unregulated (IUU) fishing in the area has been brought to a minimum: in part due to the harmonization of Norwegian and Russian fisheries legislation, mandatory automatic identification system (AIS) tracking equipment on all fishing vessels, and the control of catches landed in the ports of all North East Atlantic Fisheries Commission (NEAFC) members, which include Denmark in respect of the Faroe Islands and Greenland, the European Union, Iceland, Norway, and Russia.

The present amity in the Fisheries Protection Zone is founded on pragmatism, rather than the result of a communal legal understanding among nations. The arguably fragile harmony could still be disrupted, not least since rapid climate change propels the introduction of new maritime species to the area and alters migration patterns of already harvested fish stocks. At present, both herring and mackerel stocks are moving north (Spijkers & Boonstra 2017), stirring controversies among fishing nations such as the European Union, the Faroe Islands, Greenland, Iceland, and Norway as the stocks expand into the Norwegian Sea. Climate change-induced fish-stock dynamics arguably pose one of the largest challenges to the present nondiscriminatory management of the Fisheries Protection Zone and would accordingly be a concern for the Norwegian government.

Security issues and the continental shelf

Initially, in the late 1960s and early 1970s, the Norwegian government argued that Svalbard did not generate continental shelf rights. According to the official Norwegian argument, the archipelago was surrounded by shelf areas generated by, and stretching out from, the mainland (Pedersen, 2008a). This legal interpretation angered several scholars of jurisprudence and was quietly abandoned by Oslo. Today, it seems evident that the Norwegian government assumes that Svalbard, similar to other Norwegian coastal territory, generates continental shelf rights under international law (Pedersen and Henriksen, 2009; Tiller and Nyman, 2017). However, Norway maintains that the shelf is part of one continuous Norwegian continental shelf, a prolongation of Norwegian territories, including Svalbard, extending into the North Sea, the Norwegian Sea, the Greenland Sea, the Barents Sea, and the central Arctic Ocean. The argument of the Norwegian government was consolidated through the process of establishing final and binding outer limits of the Norwegian continental shelf in the mid-2000s, to which no state objected (Pedersen and

Henriksen, 2009; Tiller and Nyman, 2017). Since Norway maintains that the Svalbard Treaty provisions do not apply to the Norwegian continental shelf beyond the 12-mile territorial sea around the archipelago, it rejects any notion of a Svalbard shelf separate from the Norwegian continental shelf. In Norway's view, to do so would be as awkward and unreasonable as addressing a Hebrides continental shelf separate from the British shelf or a Franz Josef Land shelf adjacent to the Russian continental shelf (Pedersen and Henriksen, 2009).

Although most of the continental shelf areas outside Svalbard, formally defined as the *Barents Sea North* area, have not been opened for petroleum activities, legal rights here are already disputed and represent one of the most pressing controversies associated with Svalbard. Even Norway's closest ally, the United States, has identified the oil and gas reserves in the area as a matter of national interest. In 1989, Washington concluded "this would only become an active issue in the unlikely event that the [Norwegian government] offered exploration licenses in the Svalbard continental shelf" (Pedersen, 2011: 130).

The United Kingdom, another NATO ally of Norway, is perhaps the most verbal opponent of Oslo in the continental shelf issue. In 1986, London expressed the explicit legal position that the Svalbard Treaty applies to continental shelf areas even beyond the territorial seas surrounding the archipelago (Pedersen, 2008b). Three years later, a British *nota verbale* to the Norwegian Ministry of Foreign Affairs stated that the views of the United Kingdom and other parties to the treaty "should be carefully taken into account in the handling of future economic activities in the region" (Pedersen, 2008b: 244). As late as 2005, the British Government also indicated that it would see the case adjudicated if Norway did not budge. "We believe that, if this issue were ever to be referred to the International Court of Justice, our position would find strong support in international law," London stated in a diplomatic note presented to the Norwegian government (2008b: 253).

The Norwegian claim to exclusive rights on the continental shelf has also been challenged rather bluntly by the Soviet Union, and later by Russia. In the 1980s, Moscow instructed the Russian Marine Arctic Geological Expedition (MAGE) to conduct seismic mapping of the shelf areas surrounding Svalbard, disregarding the fact that Norway kept the area closed to petroleum exploration. The MAGE surveys were continued in the 2000s. Rather than confronting Moscow, the Norwegian government allowed the surveys as scientific research in accordance with the 1982 Law of the Sea Convention. However, the Norwegian government's frustrations with Russia's exploration became evident from an exchange of diplomatic notes in 2005 (Pedersen, 2006). At present, oil and gas activities are rapidly moving north and approaching the continental shelf areas surrounding Svalbard, having reached the northernmost parts of the Barents Sea south and southeast exploration areas. In August 2017, the exploration rig *Songa Enabler* drilled for oil at 74.07° (74°04′20″) northern latitude, 35.81° (35°48′25″) eastern longitude (marinetraffic.com), marginally east of the area sometimes referred to as the Svalbard Box, on behalf of the Norwegian oil company Statoil.

Another immediate issue in dispute is the management of the snow crab in the areas adjacent to Svalbard. The species is new to the area, recorded for the first time in the Barents Sea in 1996. Rachel Tiller and Elizabeth Nyman concluded that the snow crab might become "a vehicle for escalating disputes about the contested area" (Tiller and Nyman, 2017: 24). Crabs, though moving along the seafloor, are in legal terms a sedentary species, which puts them inside the same areas of jurisdiction as oil and gas. While Norway has opted for a nondiscriminatory management of fisheries resources in the water column surrounding Svalbard, i.e., in the Fisheries Protection Zone, the management of seabed resources is a different matter. Here on the continental shelf, the Norwegian government has allowed only Norwegian vessels to exploit the resources since 2015 (Øst-Finnmark District Court, 2017).

In disagreement with Oslo, in December 2016, the European Commission (which is not a party to the Svalbard Treaty) requested that the European Council issue its own snow-crab licenses to EU vessels in response to the exclusive claims of Norway. The licenses, awarded to 16 vessels from Latvia, Lithuania, and Poland the following month, covered catches around Svalbard, as if the continental shelf area were international waters under international law. On 15 January 2017, one of the vessels, the *Senator,* was seized outside Svalbard by the Norwegian Coast Guard and brought to the Norwegian mainland for further prosecution (Øst-Finnmark District Court, 2017). This incident was followed by strong reactions within the European Union. Members of the European Parliament slammed Norway for illegally interrupting EU vessels from catching snow crabs (Mon et al., 2017). Europêche, the association of national organizations of fishing enterprises in the European Union, criticized Norway for its hostile approach and asserted that the EU fishing industry would explore "other means of action," including seeing that the case be referred to the International Court of Justice (Europêche, 2017). Norway's case was significantly bolstered in the wake of a February 2019 ruling by the Norwegian Supreme Court stating that foreign seafood interests must obtain Oslo's permission before engaging in snow-crab fishing in northern Norwegian waters (Doyle and Fouche, 2019).

If the snow-crab case, which is still unfolding, were to be referred to the International Court of Justice in The Hague, it could clarify Norway's jurisdiction in the maritime areas surrounding Svalbard and determine the geographical scope of the Svalbard Treaty provisions. Hence, a decision by the international court could defuse the conflict potential in the area and would most likely be welcomed by the Norwegian government, which has little to lose. The fisheries are already managed in a nondiscriminatory manner, and the surrounding continental shelf areas remain closed for oil and gas activities, which is also nondiscriminatory and thus in the spirit of the Svalbard Treaty.

Conclusions

Svalbard remains a sensitive and contentious issue for multiple reasons. The security challenges in the Svalbard area relate to traditional geopolitics as well as to the exploitation of natural resources on land, in the 200-nautical-mile Fisheries Protection Zone, and/or on the continental shelf that surrounds the archipelago.

To Russia, Svalbard represents a strategic challenge due to its location and proximity to the Northern Fleet's bases on the Kola Peninsula as well as their most vital sea lanes of communication. Hence, Moscow remains eager to discourage all uses of the islands that may affect its strategic capabilities. The large presence of Russians in the Svalbard archipelago suggests that Moscow is still committed to keeping a close eye on Western infrastructure and uses and to deterring the Norwegian government from acting in ways that could undermine Russian interests in the greater Barents Sea area. Norwegian sovereignty over Svalbard is undisputed, but Moscow is likely to maintain a significant foothold there and to continue to pursue its interests in the archipelago by different means, some of which the Norwegian government might find unpleasant and challenging. At the same time, the Norwegian government is set to normalize its exercise of jurisdiction in Svalbard and scale back its self-imposed restrictions as a result of political considerations, rather than Svalbard Treaty provisions, which could potentially create friction with Moscow.

In the maritime areas surrounding Svalbard, the security challenges also relate to the exploitation of natural resources. In general, the Norwegian government sees national maritime industries as a provider for "a significant of Norwegian welfare and central to Norway's future" (Norwegian Ministry of Foreign Affairs 2017: 16). Approximately 37% of Norway's gross domestic product (GDP) derives from traditional maritime industries. The offshore oil and gas industry, shipping, and the seafood industry also account for two-thirds of Norway's total export revenues. Hence, to Norway, the exploration of maritime resources, as well as compliance with international law including the law of the sea, are vital national interests.

In the Fisheries Protection Zone, Norway is challenged by several nations. Some of the most notable clashes over interests in these waters include the Norwegian government and fisheries actors from the European Union, the Faroe Islands, Greenland, Iceland, and Russia. Although IUU fishing in the Fisheries Protection Zone has been brought to a minimum and most vessels observe the Norwegian management regime, dramatic episodes such as the *Hagangur II* incident in 1994 and the high-profile *Elektron* chase in 2005 demonstrate the potential for escalation and conflict. Climate change, which affects the migration of fish stocks, could potentially increase the risk of new incidents in these waters.

On the continental shelf areas surrounding Svalbard, the exploitation of natural resources is only just beginning. The snow crab, a species new to the area, is presently putting Norway's claimed exclusive rights to continental shelf resources to the test. The European Union is the main contender to Norway in the snow-crab case, which could potentially be referred by EU member states to the International Court of Justice. Norway, steadfast in its legal interpretation, is likely to welcome adjudication rather than giving in to outside pressure over these seabed resources. When the European Commission issued licenses to EU snow-crab vessels in 2016, essentially assuming jurisdiction over the continental shelf surrounding the Norwegian islands, it certainly crossed a red line which the Norwegian government is likely to enforce by all necessary means.

Lurking behind the snow-crab case is oil and gas, the multibillion-dollar industry that also affects the national interests of political heavyweights such as the United Kingdom and the United States. The sovereign rights of Norway to petroleum resources outside Svalbard equal those to the snow crab, whether they are exclusive to Norwegians or subject to the Svalbard Treaty provisions on nondiscrimination and taxation. Washington is likely to review its legal views on the Svalbard issue if and when the Norwegian government opens the Barents Sea North area for oil and gas activities. The United States and other NATO allies would have to balance potential economic interests with security concerns, as an escalation of the issue and the undermining of Norway's legal position in the area vis-à-vis Russia would affect stability in the region and ultimately have wider security implications.

References

Amundsen, Birger. 2001. *Svarthvitt.* Oslo: Mitra Forlag.

Anderson, David. 2009. "The Status under International Law of the Maritime Areas Around Svalbard," *Ocean Development &International Law* 40: 373–384.

Arlov, Thor Bjørn. 2003. *Svalbards Historie.* Trondheim: Tapir Akademisk Forlag.

Åtland, Kristian. 2014. "The status of Svalbard and its consequences for international politics," in Eckart D. Stratenschulte (ed.) *Heilsame Vielfalt? Formen differenzierter Integration in Europa.* Baden-Baden: Nomos.

Åtland, Kristian & Kristin Bruusgaard 2009. "When Security Speech Acts Misfire: Russia and the Elektron Incident," *Security Dialogue* 40(3): 333–353.

Åtland, Kristian & Torbjørn Pedersen 2008. "The Svalbard Archipelago in Russian Security Policy: Overcoming the Legacy of Fear – or Reproducing it?" *European Security* 17: 3.

Åtland, Kristian & Torbjørn Pedersen 2013. "Cold war legacies in Russia's Svalbard policy," in Gunhild Hoogensen Gjørv, Dawn R. Bazely, Marina Golovznina & Andrew J. Tanentzap (eds.) *Environmental and Human Security in the Arctic*, 17–36. London & New York: Routledge.

Berg, Roald. 1995. *Norge på egen hand 1905-1920: Norsk utenrikspolitisk historie*. Vol. II, Oslo: Universitetsforlaget.

Churchill, Robin & Geir Ulfstein 1993. Marine Management in Disputed Areas: The Case of the Barents Sea. London: Routledge.

Doyle, Alister and Gwladys Fouche 2019. *Abide by the claw: Norway's Arctic snow crab ruling boosts claim to oil Reuters*, 14 February.

Dragnes, Kjell. 1986. Fiskestriden ved Svalbard: Spanierne knuste Frydenlunds håp. *Aftenposten*, 23 August.

Engebretsen-Skaret, Sigrid. 2012. *Bruk av norske spesialstyrker i krisehåndtering - utfordringer og muligheter*. Oslo: Forsvarets høgskole.

Europêche 2017. "*EU snow crab fishermen illicitly expelled from the Barents Sea and Svalbard waters*," Press release EP 17(22): 13 March.

Fleischer, Carl August. 1976. "Svalbards folkerettslige stilling," in Arne Treholt et al. (ed.) *Norges Havretts- og Ressurspolitikk*, 139–140. Oslo: Tiden Norsk Forlag.

Fleischer, Carl August. 1983. *Petroleumsrett*. Oslo: Universitetsforlaget.

Fleischer, Carl August. 1988. *Folkerett*. Oslo: Universitetsforlaget.

Frydenlund, Knut. 1982. *Lille land - hva nå? Refleksjoner om Norges utenrikspolitiske situasjon*. Oslo: Universitetsforlaget.

Gramshaug, Katrine. 2005. "Dramatikken i Barentshavet," *I Marinen* 2(6): http://sms1835.no/arkiv/2;%206%20(2005)%20I%20Marinen.pdf

High North News 2016. *Forvarsekspert: - Vår største utfordring er Svalbard*, 16 October http://highnorthnews.com/forsvarsekspert-svalbard-er-var-storste-utfordring/

Hønneland, Geir. 2005. *Barentsbrytninger: Norsk nordområdepolitikk etter Den kalde krigen*. Kristiansand: Høyskoleforlaget.

Hønneland, Geir. 2012. *Arktiske Utfordringer*. Kristiansand: Høyskoleforlaget.

Jørgensen, Jørgen Holten. 2003. *Russisk Svalbard-politikk: Eksterne og interne forklaringsfaktorer*. Oslo: Universitetet i Oslo.

Jørgensen, Jørgen Holten. 2004. "Svalbard: Russiske persepsjoner og politikkutforming," *Internasjonal politikk* 62(2): 177–197.

Jørgensen, Jørgen Holten. 2010. *Russisk svalbardpolitikk: Svalbard sett fra den andre siden*. Trondheim: Tapir.

Jørgensen, Jørgen Holten. 2016. Den evige utopi? Gruvedrift og nasjonale interesser *Ottar* 310.

Lie, Trygve. 1958. *Hjemover*. Oslo: Tiden Norsk Forlag.

Molenaar, Eric. 2012. "Fisheries Regulations in the Maritime Zones of Svalbard," *International Journal of Marine & Coastal Law* 27: 3–58.

Mon, Francisco et al. 2017. *Question for Written Answer to the European Commission*, 5 April.

Nikulina, Anna. 2016. *Russian Science Center on Svalbard*. Presentation at UNIS, Longyearbyen 12 September. http://unis.no/wp-content/uploads/2016/11/AnnaNikulina_120916.pdf

The Norwegian Ministry of Foreign Affairs 2017. *Report No. 22 (2016-2017) to the Parliament on the Place of the Oceans in Norway's Foreign and Development Policies* https://regjeringen.no/en/dokumenter/meld.-st.-22-20162017/id2544710/

The Norwegian Ministry of Justice 2016. *Report No. 32 (2015-2016) to the Parliament on Svalbard* https://regjeringen.no/no/dokumenter/meld.-st.-32-20152016/id2499962/

Norwegian Broadcasting. 2014. *Norsk nei til Kina-radar på Svalbard*. 11 September https://nrk.no/troms/nekter-kina-radar-pa-svalbard-1.11927625

NTB 1994. *Varselskudd mot islandsk tråler,*15 June.

Øst-Finnmark District Court 2017. *Decisions in cases 17-057396MED-OSFI & 17-057421MED-OSFI*, 22 June 2017.

Østreng, Willy. 1975. *Det Politiske Svalbard*. Oslo: Gyldendal Norsk Forlag.

Pedersen, Torbjørn. 2006. "The Svalbard Shelf Controversy: Legal Disputes and Political Rivalries," *Ocean Development &International Law* 37(3-4): 339–358.

Pedersen, Torbjørn. 2008a. "The Dynamics of Svalbard Diplomacy," *Diplomacy & Statecraft* 19(2): 236–262.

Pedersen, Torbjørn. 2008b. *Conflict and Order in Svalbard Waters*. Tromsø: University of Tromsø.

Pedersen, Torbjørn. 2009a. "Endringer i internasjonal Svalbard-politikk," *Internasjonal Politikk* 67(1): 30–44.

Pedersen, Torbjørn. 2009b. "Norway's Rule on Svalbard: Tightening the Grip on the Arctic Islands," *Polar Record* 45(2): 147–152.

Pedersen, Torbjørn. 2011. "International Law and Politics in U.S. Policymaking: The United States and the Svalbard Dispute," *Ocean Development & International Law* 42(1-2): 120–135.

Pedersen, Torbjørn. 2017. "The Politics of Presence: The Longyearbyen Dilemma," *Arctic Review on Law and Politics* 8: 95–108.

Pedersen, Torbjørn & Tore Henriksen 2009. "Svalbard's Maritime Zones: The End of Legal Uncertainty?" *International Journal of Marine and Coastal Law* 24(1): 141–161.

Rapp, Ole Magnus 2019. Kina raser mot Norge, *Klassekampen*, 7 March.

Rinne, Yvonne. 2010. *EISCAT Svalbard Radar studies of meso-scale plasma flow channels in the polar cusp ionosphere*. Oslo: University of Oslo.

Rivetov, Pavel. 2003. *Shpitsbergen – forpost NATO pod nosom Rossii* [Spitsbergen: NATO's outpost under Russia's nose], *Pravda online*, 14 April. https://ssb.no/befolkning/statistikker/befsvalbard. (Accessed 5 September 2017).

Spijkers, Jessica & Wiebren Boonstra 2017. "Environmental Change and Social Conflict: The Northeast Atlantic Mackerel Dispute," *Regional Environmental Change* 17(6): 1835–1851.

Tiller, Rachel & Elizabeth Nyman 2017. "The Clear and Present Danger to the Norwegian Sovereignty of the Svalbard Fisheries Protection Zone: Enter the Snow Crab," *Ocean & Coastal Management* 137 (1): 24–33.

Ulfstein, Geir. 1995. *The Svalbard Treaty: From* terra nullius *to Norwegian Sovereignty*. Oslo: Scandinavian University Press.

Vylegzhanin, A.N. & V.K. Zilanov 2007. *Spitsbergen: Legal Regime of Adjacent Maritime Areas* trans. William Butler. The Hague: Eleven International Publishing.

Wæver, Ole. 1995. "Securitization and desecuritization," in Ronnie D. Lipschutz (ed.) *On Security*. New York: Columbia University Press.

Wormdal, Bård. 2011. *Satellittkrigen: Norsk militarisering av polområdene og verdensrommet*. Oslo: Pax Forlag.

24
ARCTIC COAST GUARDS
Why cooperate?

Andreas Østhagen

Introduction

Coast guards are a state's foremost tool for protecting sovereign rights and enforcing jurisdiction within its maritime domain. Coast guards in the Arctic, however, are few and far between. Current investment levels and equipment do not match the proclaimed goals of lofty Arctic policy documents. This has led to a so-called capability-expectations gap,[1] which has been critiqued in recent years (Brigham 2013; Funston 2014). Yet, there is more to coast guards than their immediate role as upholders of law and order at sea. They are also being utilized as platforms to initiate and scale up international cooperation between states.

An Arctic Coast Guard Forum was officially established in 2015, after years of deliberation about its potential role. Some argued that the Forum could serve as an arena for tackling security dialogue with Russia at a time when other channels were unavailable (H.A. Conley and Rohloff 2015; Grønning 2016). Others, however, worry about attaching too much significance to the Forum, hampering practical cooperation in favor of creating yet another Arctic "talk-shop" (Sevunts 2016). This speaks to the core concern of Arctic coast guards; namely, balancing performing everyday practical tasks and partaking in an increasingly complex governance system in the Arctic, while their resources are under pressure.

This chapter explains the role of Arctic coast guards in the Arctic system. Why do they matter, and why has attention turned to developing low-level pan-Arctic cooperation between coast guards? In turn, are these types of forums set up to deal with a specific problem that states are incapable of managing on their own? Or are they set up for a completely different reason, namely the promotion of cross-border dialogue and the development of amicable relations at times when the Arctic is "heating up?"

Although these two conceptions of cooperation are not mutually exclusive, they do entail somewhat different causal mechanisms concerning the purpose of international cooperation and coast guards. Is coast guard cooperation a dependent variable, a result of states' desires to cooperate to solve a number of pressing concerns in the Arctic? Is cooperation, rather, an independent variable, affecting the states partaking and shaping outcomes between them? This speaks to the heart of debates in international studies; namely the rationale for, and effects of, international cooperation in a system of states often described as based on the principle of self-help.

This chapter explores these various descriptions of low-level Arctic cooperation, examining coast guards specifically. This can in turn create better understanding of the Arctic governance system in general, as well as why the role of coast guards is on the rise in northern waters. First, the work outlines how to conceptualize international cooperation between states. Then, the chapter describes the roles of Arctic coast guards across the various Arctic countries. Thereafter, the growth in cooperative mechanisms for Arctic coast guards, with an emphasis on the Arctic Coast Guard Forum, is outlined. Finally, the chapter concludes with a debate and discussion of the role of coast guards and coast guard cooperation in the Arctic.

Conceptualizing international cooperation

International cooperation has been promoted as a measure for dealing with the challenges arising in Arctic waters.[2] Yet, a question that seems to preoccupy most scholars in international studies is, "under what conditions can we expect states to cooperate?"[3] Initially, cooperation is the product of states pursuing their self-interests. Realists in international relations theory, in particular, have limited belief in the value of cooperation, as states seek (material) power to enhance their security, at times in a relative structural power balance. Cooperation becomes a limited means to an end, with a restrained lifespan and a shallow depth (Mearsheimer 1995). Liberal institutionalists,[4] on the other hand, have more faith in states' ability to cooperate to achieve goals beyond security, as well as a belief in the effects of international cooperation (and its institutions) (Moravcsik 1997). By distinguishing harmony from cooperation and discord, Keohane argued that "[c]ooperation takes place only in situations in which actors perceive that their policies are actually or potentially in conflict, not where there is harmony" (Keohane 1984, 53–4). Discord thus provides the platform for *potential* cooperation.

How do states manage to align their policies when discord occurs? Game theory can help explain certain outcomes in the international arena, or mechanisms that could help manage the problems underlying the dynamics of different types of games (Martin 1992, 769–82; Snidal 1985). Different sets of problems require different types of organizations to manage the underlying dynamics between participating states. A collaboration game ("prisoner's dilemma") is defined by the equilibrium (each actor's first choice) being suboptimal. The solution in the international domain is thus to set up a strong organization that can enhance the "shadow of the future" and provide information about the other actors' behavior. In a coordination game (e.g. "battle of the sexes"), however, the core problem is a lack of information (lack of coordination) about the other actors' preferences, and the solution can be achieved through a simple (weak) organization performing basic coordination. A third game is what Martin (1992) termed "suasion problems," namely in situations with considerable asymmetry between actors (imagine the United States in NATO). The solution is an international organization. Finally, "assurance problems" (an example being the stag-hunt scenario) are games where the sole preferred outcome is cooperation, but actors worry about others' payoffs and actors not being rational.[5] The solution thus requires transparent agreements and limited international arrangements (Keohane 1984, 67–70; Martin 1992, 769–82; Oye 1985, 6–9).[6]

How, in turn, does cooperation translate from an initial bargaining towards an alignment of policies and interests? When states cooperate in the international system, they often cooperate within an explicit or implicit *regime*.[7] Regimes help "improve the contractual environment and thus stabilize cooperation" (Levy, Young, and Zürn 1995). More recent literature, however, provides a different take on the effects of cooperation. States' interests are not predetermined and/or based on purely goal-seeking behavior (Hopf 2002; Wendt 1999). When pursuing cooperation, states are not only constrained by their relative abilities and structural position, but they are also constrained and influenced by international norms and perceptions (Checkel 1998, 2008). Crucial to the effects of cooperation is the concept of socialization. Johnston set out the argument by stating "actors who enter into a social interaction rarely emerge the same" (2001, 488).

Particularly relevant is the notion of *epistemic communities*. Put forth by Haas (1989), it is the notion that a small issue area of international cooperation will be dominated by technical experts who not only represent their own states, but also start to share common beliefs and approaches to solving the problems at hand. Haas stated, "Regimes are not simply static summaries of rules and norms; they may also serve as important vehicles for international learning that produce convergent state policies" (Haas 1989, 377). The inclusion of *knowledge* as an explanatory variable for state behavior is crucial.

In turn, what do these various conceptions of state participation in international cooperation hold for Arctic coast guards? The key point is that they outline differing (and competing) ways of understanding *why* states cooperate on certain issues, as well as *what* effect cooperation might have on the states in return. With these pointers, a better understanding of Arctic coast guard cooperation can be pursued.

Facing a new environment

Although it is difficult to generalize across the Arctic, research points to a trend of increased maritime activity in the various Arctic regions. Most of this traffic derives from intra-Arctic shipping and destinational shipping in the Arctic itself. The trans-Arctic sea routes themselves are relatively insignificant in terms of traffic numbers, as the routes have yet to become fully operational (Borch et al. 2016; Brigham 2013; Humpert 2014; Office of the Auditor General of Canada 2014). This does not necessarily mean that all Arctic states are expecting a further increase of traffic in their maritime waters. With steady growth since the turn of the millennium, the numbers seem to have stabilized in waters around Greenland and northern Canada, while they are slightly increasing in Alaska, Russia, and northern Norway. The Danish Ministry of Defense, for example, stated that it does not expect any further dramatic increase of maritime traffic up until 2027 (Danish Ministry of Defence 2016, 31–2).

Yet, a higher number of vessels present in the north during the summer months, in tandem with increased complexity of the maritime activities undertaken, has led to a new situation for the various Arctic coastal states. Increase in traffic has the potential to increase the number of incidents that require engagement from public assets, as well as an increase in the risk of a severe emergency. The insurance company Allianz highlighted, in its annual shipping report for 2015, that there were 55 shipping incidents, termed *causalities*, in their definition of Arctic waters in 2014. A decade ago, there were just three (Allianz 2015). Similarly, the number of emergency response incidents in northern Norway alone rose by 10.5% in just one year from 2013 to 2014 (Norwegian Government and Norwegian Ministry of Foreign Affairs 2014).

This new reality has spurred demand for presence and capabilities amongst the Arctic states, whose prerogative it is to deal with these threats and provide emergency response capacity. When fisheries grow in volume, so does the need for regular fisheries inspections. Similarly, other constabulary tasks under the prerogative of police authorities demand constant presence in the maritime domain. When vessels traverse maritime borders, control of these movements is sometimes required. Such tasks are part of upholding a country's sovereignty in its own waters. At the same time, public assets are needed to respond to immediate incidents, such as the search and rescue of sailors and passengers, or environmental protection due to a spill from a vessel or a platform. Less immediate, but still in response to specific demands, are tasks related to the assistance of navigation and passage (Mitchell 2013; Østhagen 2015; Østhagen and Gestaldo 2015). The multitude of tasks is roughly outlined in Table 24.1.

When a maritime incident occurs, the first point of contact is usually the Joint Rescue Coordination Center (JRCC) located in the various Arctic countries. After contacting a JRCC, how each country responds to a given incident depends on the national structure and the capabilities available. In most instances, the military provides additional capacities and information relevant to the emergency response. After initial coordination between the civilian and military structures, coast guards are most likely the first institution tasked with handling a maritime emergency response. Yet, coast guards vary greatly across the countries in question. Each coast guard is tailor-made to the national and historic circumstances they were developed under, and they often are a result of the size of both the country itself (geographically) and its population and economy (Østhagen 2015).

The Canadian Coast Guard (CCG) is a civilian agency under the Department of Fisheries and Oceans Canada (DFO). Its core tasks are providing aid to navigation, search and rescue, and environmental protection at seas. For Arctic waters around Greenland, Denmark does not have a specific coast guard entity, as it is the Royal Danish Navy (*Søværnet*) that is responsible for providing services that normally fall to coast guards. The Icelandic Coast Guard (ICG) is a semi-military institution. It belongs to the Ministry of Justice, but as Iceland does not have a defense force of its own, the coast guard is the only public agency that is armed. The Norwegian Coast Guard (*Kystvakten*) is a part of the Royal Norwegian Navy and thus part of the Norwegian Armed Forces. Yet, the coast guard is separated from the regular navy and has a specific law regulating its mandate. The Russian Coast Guard (**Береговая охрана ПС ФСБ России**) is part of the Border Guard Service, which in turn belongs to the Federal Security Service (FSB). It has a limited law-enforcement mandate as well as military capabilities. Yet,

Table 24.1 The different types of maritime tasks/challenges becoming more prevalent in the Arctic areas.

Maritime task	*Type of task*	*Mode of task*
Constabulary tasks (*anti-terrorism, law enforcement, etc.*)	Legal	Constant & Responding
Border controls	Legal	Constant
Fisheries inspection	Legal/Environmental	Constant
Sovereignty protection (*involves constabulary tasks and border control, in addition to military actions*)	Legal/Defense	Constant & Responding
Search and rescue	Safety	Responding
Assisting passage and navigation (*including icebreaking*)	Safety	Responding
Oil-spill preparedness and response	Safety/Environmental	Responding

Source: Østhagen 2015.

its primary role is performing civilian law and order tasks as well as environmental tasks (Åtland 2015). Finally, the United States Coast Guard (USCG) is part of the US Armed Forces, but kept separate from the Navy in peacetime. Organized under the Department of Homeland Security, it has full law-enforcement authority, and considerable military capabilities that are at times utilized in the US armed mission abroad (Ostrom 2012).The various structures, as well as a simplified illustration of the civilian-military spectrum, are found in Table 24.2.

Multilateral coast guard cooperation: limitations and opportunities

As the limited maritime capabilities of coastal Arctic states came to light with the increasing national and international attention given to the Arctic, multilateral cooperation became the focal point to alleviate pressure. In 2011, the eight Arctic countries signed an agreement for search and rescue under the auspices of the Arctic Council. A similar agreement on oil-spill preparedness was signed two years later in 2013 (Arctic Council 2011, 2013). Although signs of how Arctic states are embracing multilateral cooperation, these agreements have been criticized for having limited impact in the Arctic, mainly outlining existing responsibilities and boundaries (Rottem 2014). The coast guards themselves have also pointed out that an increased number of exercises and more regular contact between practitioners are needed to operationalize the agreements (Joint Arctic Command 2013; Neffenger 2014).

As a response, the idea of establishing a dedicated forum for Arctic coast guards was proposed (H. Conley et al. 2012). Modeled on already existing forums for the North Pacific

Table 24.2 Organizations with responsibility for coast guard tasks and associated institutional structures (simplified).

Country	*Name*	*Organization*	*Civilian/ Military*
Denmark (Greenland)	Søværnet (Navy) (1. Eskadre)	Danish Defense	Military
Norway	Kystvakten (Coast guard)	Royal Norwegian Navy	Military
USA	United States Coast Guard (USCG)	Department of Homeland Security	Military*[1]
Iceland	Landhelgisgæsla (Coast guard)	Ministry of Justice	Semi-military
Finland	Rajavartiolaitos (Border guard)	Ministry of the Interior	Semi-military
Russia	Coast Guard of the Border Service*[2]	Federal Security Service (FSB)	Semi-military
Canada	Canadian Coast Guard (CCG)	Department of Fisheries and Oceans	Civilian
Sweden	Kustbevakningen (Coast guard)	Ministry of Defense	Civilian

*[1] The USCG is part of the US Armed Forces. Yet, it is dissimilar from the Navy and the Danish/Norwegian counterparts operating under Navy structures.

*[2] In Russian: Береговая охрана ПС ФСБ России

and the North Atlantic, American and Russian officials subsequently took the first steps towards the establishment of a so-called Arctic Coast Guard Forum. The Russian actions in Ukraine in 2014 halted the process, as representatives from Russia were not included in two meetings of experts hosted by Canada in Sidney, Nova Scotia. It was, however, decided that the chair of the Forum should follow the chairmanships of the Arctic Council. The next experts meeting in March 2015 was therefore held in Washington DC, and this time the Russian Coast Guard was present. The eight countries decided to push ahead, and the Arctic Coast Guard Forum (ACGF) was formally established on October 30th, 2015 at the US Coast Guard Academy in New London, Connecticut (Melia 2015).

The structure of the Forum is simple. It has a rotating chair in tandem with the chair of the Arctic Council. The heads of the coast guards convene annually, whereas working groups meet more frequently when needed. The working groups are concerned with tasks such as joint operations, asset sharing, and increased focus on exercises. It aims at developing common situational awareness between the eight members, while also coordinating with the work being done in the Emergency Prevention, Preparedness and Response (EPPR) working group under the Arctic Council.

Although there has been great interest in forming a coast guard forum for the Arctic, there are some fundamental challenges that limit which tasks the Forum can embark on. An overarching task for most coast guards is the protection of the coastal state's sovereign rights. Coast guards uphold sovereignty through a naval presence and the enforcement of national jurisdiction (Till 2004, 330–47). Fisheries inspections, for example, are an integral part of protecting a state's sovereign rights through the management of its own marine resources. This authority cannot easily be shared.

Additionally, as outlined previously, there is significant variation in structure, mandate, and capabilities between the coast guards in the Arctic. There is not one unified Arctic coast guard structure, as each coast guard is tailored to national interests, geography, and institutional cultures. The variety of mandates and structures create challenges for potential dialogue on issues of a sensitive and/or military character. Hence, an Arctic Coast Guard Forum would have to lend itself to a "lowest common denominator" approach (Østhagen 2015, 10). Moreover, effective collaboration is often dependent on a similar set of structures, with similar sizes and priorities (Diesen 2013; Valasek 2011). The geographic vastness of the Arctic is an additional challenge to effective cooperation. Arctic geography involves large maritime domains, where few incidents occur, with limited or no capabilities present. Sharing responsibility or handing over tasks to other countries is often not even an option, as states are struggling even to provide capabilities in their own Arctic maritime domains.

In addition to these challenges, the integration of Russia into an Arctic Coast Guard Forum is crucial, albeit challenging. In the Bering Sea, the Chukchi Sea, and through the Bering Strait, Russia and the United States share an extensive maritime border, settled in 1990. Similarly, in the Barents Sea, Russia, and Norway share an extensive and predominantly ice-free maritime border, settled in 2010. Finland shares a maritime border with Russia in the Gulf of Finland, albeit smaller in size and not in the Arctic. In all these border areas, cooperation with Russia on both a practical and a governmental level is essential to effectively manage straddling fish stocks and to provide environmental protection and a search and rescue response.

In the initial pre-meetings for an Arctic Coast Guard Forum, it thus became clear that Russian participation would be vital for the Forum's relevance, partly because of Russia's extensive coastline and responsibilities along the Northeast Passage and partly because of

Russia's shared maritime borders as outlined above. A possible expansion of coast guard collaboration in all these areas would be dependent on both diplomacy and cooperation with Russia. At the same time, Russia's natural place around the table led to a bumpy start for the Forum, initially postponing its launch. Sensitive information cannot be shared on the same level as between the five NATO members, or even the two NATO partners Finland and Sweden. Yet, how much the Forum will be hampered by the contemporary political situation ultimately rests on the overall relationship between Russia and the other Arctic states, and their willingness to keep this venue sheltered from the larger political environment in the Arctic and beyond. In most cases, coast guard affairs constitute so-called low politics, which states in the Arctic have so far separated from larger diplomatic affairs (Østhagen 2016).

Given the limitations listed, there are still areas where multilateral coast guard cooperation can expand. The stated purpose of the Forum is to develop the relationships between the Arctic states on a practical level to form a community focused on operational activities. In particular, the sharing of information and identification of best practices are areas of focus for the Forum. Improving maritime situational/domain awareness and sharing information are also particularly relevant. The Arctic Coast Guard Forum can also act as a platform to initiate cross-border exercises, implementing the circumpolar agreements from 2011 and 2013 (Østhagen and Gestaldo 2015).

The pooling of resources can have applicability for coast guards if the capacity created has relevance to more than one Arctic state. For tasks that require immediate response, such as oil-spill response or search and rescue, the pooling of coast guard resources could hold value and be orchestrated by the Arctic Coast Guard Forum (Østhagen 2015, 11). In addition, practical cooperation on procurement of equipment seems to be an area with great potential.[8] In the Arctic, potential is great amongst the Nordic countries as they have relatively similar force structures and operating conditions, and they are already collaborating under the umbrella of NORDEFCO[9] (Saxi 2011; Stoltenberg 2009). The same goes for the United States and Canada, which already have a closely integrated bilateral defense cooperation under the North American Aerospace Defense Command (NORAD) framework (Jockel and Sokolsky 2012).

Why cooperate?

The Arctic states and their respective coast guards are under mounting pressure. Cooperating with neighboring coast guards, formalized through the establishment of an Arctic Coast Guard Forum, can help provide some remedy to these challenges. States engage in cooperation with other states to solve problems that transcend borders. Yet, when do officials and diplomats pack their bags and leave the negotiation table? Given the development of multilateral coast guard cooperation described above, how can these efforts be best understood in conjunction with conceptualizations of *why* states cooperate? Returning to the question posed at the beginning of this chapter, are these types of forums set up to deal with a specific problem that states are incapable of managing on their own? Or are they set up for a completely different reason, namely the promotion of cross-border dialogue and the development of amicable relations?

Returning to game-theoretical conceptions of the underlying dynamics of why states cooperate, it seems clear that Arctic states are facing a stag-hunt type scenario. They are all better off cooperating, by sharing information, improving each other's capacities, and assisting in possible emergency scenarios, than not cooperating. Yet, there is concern about the states having the ability and capacity to coordinate and capitalize on this apparent potential. The ACGF thus becomes an instrument to enable cooperation, albeit with a weak/limited structure and no enforcement mechanisms.

However, it seems clear that multilateral, pan-Arctic coast guard cooperation between Arctic states was not developed to serve an immediate demand that states could not deal with on their own or through bilateral modes of cooperation. As shown, there are marked limitations to what can actually be achieved in a multilateral setting. Instead, the coast guards (and their respective states) seem to have realized the benefits of cooperation for its own sake, and avoided a focus on contentious issues. One coast guard official described the Arctic Coast Guard Forum as "[a]n area that we can work with collegially and not as adversaries" (Melia 2015).

Cooperation is thus a goal on its own, precisely because of its value beyond coordination of actions between the relevant actors. It is therefore not sufficient to argue that cooperation is just a rational response to meeting a growing challenge. Albeit a difficult endeavor to grasp the "true" motivations of states (and their officials), we can conceptualize various additional reasons for the establishment of multilateral coast guard cooperation. First, using a rationalist approach, the concept of *signaling* holds relevance to this debate. Initially introduced in international relations as it relates to game theory and games with imperfect information, signaling helps explain actions that do not initially serve a specific purpose on their own (Mock 1992; Snidal 1985).

We can conceive of Arctic states' desires to signal at two different levels, where the message in both cases is clear, along the lines of "we are taking appropriate steps to deal with a dire situation." Given the warning calls from scholars and experts concerning Arctic maritime emergency potential, in turn leading to political and public demands for government action,[10] creating multilateral forums is done to *signal* that efforts are being made to alleviate the situation.

The audience of this signal, however, varies. On the one hand, the audience is domestic, soothing public demands for action. On the other hand, the audience is international, showcasing to other countries that the Arctic states are sufficiently managing the changing environment in the north. For example, concerns over the Arctic described as lacking political governance structures voiced by some Members of the European Parliament, as well as by some Chinese officials,[11] triggered a response by Arctic governments of emphasizing and reiterating the robustness of the Arctic regime.[12] By signaling to both external and internal actors, the Arctic states are seen to be managing an issue of growing apprehension, even if there is a question of to what extent a multilateral forum alleviates actual capacity concerns.

In addition, cooperation can be conceived as having an effect beyond the coordination of policies and signaling to other actors. As Johnston (2001) and Checkel (2005) conceived it, actors partaking in international cooperation over time do not emerge the same. The role of expert communities, such as coast guard officials, in national policymaking also cannot be underestimated. Aspirations of creating an additional layer of Arctic governance through the inclusion of another expert dimension to the already complex Arctic system[13] were evident from the initial conception of the Arctic Coast Guard Forum. As was argued by a US Coast Guard Vice Admiral, "[t]he Arctic Coast Guard Forum (ACGF) … will be a unique maritime governance group" (Neffenger 2014, 42).

It is, however, too early to come to a conclusion about the long-term effects of the Arctic Coast Guard Forum. Given its recent origin and limited scope, its potential effects are difficult to measure. Still, understanding *how* such mechanisms can serve a purpose beyond policy coordination amongst partaking states can foster comprehension of why they are created in the first place. These questions therefore add another layer to an increasingly complex regional system, as the Arctic states continue to emphasize multilateral approaches to new challenges in the Arctic.

Notes

1 Coined by Christopher Hill (1993) to describe the growing expectations concerning the EU's weight as an international actor, this term holds relevance here in describing the gap between the expectations of booming Arctic maritime activity and the inability of coast guards to manage potential incidents at sea.
2 See for example Neffenger 2014 and Norwegian Government, and Norwegian Ministry of Foreign Affairs 2014.
3 The alternative formulation is "under what conditions can we expect war."
4 Or "liberal institutionalism.." As a strand of IR theorising often lumped in under the umbrella of "neoliberalism."
5 Introduced by Robert Jervis in the field of international studies (Jervis 1978).
6 For a more exhaustive overview of game theory and political studies, see McCarty and Meirowitz 2007 and Kydd 2008.
7 Krasner's characterization of a *regime* from 1982 has become the go-to definition in studies of international cooperation. He defined a regime as "a set of implicit or explicit principles, norms, rules, and decision-making procedures around which actor expectations converge in a given area of international relations" (Krasner 1982, 2). Regimes tend to, by most definitions, be more specific than international organisations and their related policy areas. Regimes are thus issue-specific, such as clean water, Indigenous rights, or sustainable fisheries.
8 On defense cooperation in general, see Biscop and Coelmont 2012 and von Voss, Major, and Mölling 2013.
9 Nordic Defense Cooperation.
10 See for example Byers 2016; Funston 2014; Ivanova 2011; and Contenta 2010.
11 See "European Parliament Resolution of 9 October 2008 on Arctic Governance" 2008 and Byers 2013, 125.
12 For in-depth studies of these efforts, see Grindheim 2009; Offerdal 2010; Keil and Raspotnik 2014; Raspotnik and Østhagen 2014; Stokke 2014a and Bekkevold and Offerdal 2014.
13 See Exner-Pirot 2013; Keil 2013; Stokke 2006, 2014b.

References

Allianz. 2015. "Safety and Shipping Review 2015." Munich. www.agcs.allianz.com/assets/PDFs/Reports/Shipping-Review-2015.pdf.

Arctic Council. 2011. *Agreement on Cooperation on Aeronautical and Maritime Search and Rescue in the Arctic.* Nuuk: Arctic Council.

Arctic Council. 2013. *Agreement on Cooperation on Marine Oil Pollution, Preparedness and Response in the Arctic.* Kiruna: Emergency Prevention Preparedness and Response Working Group.

Åtland, Kristian. 2015. *Den Russiske Kystvakten Mot 2020 – Organisering, Kapasiteter Og Operativ Virksomhet.* FFI-Rapport. Kjeller: Norwegian Defence Establishment (FFI).

Bekkevold, Jo Inge, and Kristine Offerdal. 2014. "Norway's High North Policy and New Asian Stakeholders." *Strategic Analysis* 38 (6):825–840.

Biscop, Sven, and Jo Coelmont. 2012. "Military Capabilities : From Pooling & Sharing to a Permanent and Structured Approach." *Egmont, Royal Institute for International Relations – Security Policy Brief.* September 37, pp. 1–4.

Borch, Odd Jarl, Natalia Andreassen, Nataly Marchenko, Valur Ingimundarson, Halla Gunnarsdóttir, Iurii Iudin, Sergey Petrov, Uffe Jacobsen, and Birita í Dali. 2016. *Maritime Activity in the High North – Current and Estimated Level up to 2025.* Vol. 1, 1–130. Bodø: MARPART Projects Reports.

Brigham, Lawson W. 2013. "The Fast-Changing Maritime Arctic." In *The Fast-Changing Arctic: Rethinking Arctic Security for a Warmer World*, edited by Barry Scott, Zellen, 1–17. Calgary: Calgary University Press.

Byers, Michael. 2013. *International Law and the Arctic.* New York: Cambridge University Press.

———. 2016. "Arctic Cruises: Fun for Tourists, Bad for the Environment." *The Globe and Mail*, April 18, 2016. www.theglobeandmail.com/opinion/arctic-cruises-great-for-tourists-bad-for-the-environment/article29648307/.

Checkel, Jeffrey T. 1998. "Review: The Constructivist Turn in International Relations Theory." *World Politics* 50 (2):324–348.

———. 2005. "International Institutions and Socialization in Europe: Introduction and Framework." *International Organization* 59 (04):801–826.

———. 2008. "Constructivism and Foreign Policy." In *Foreign Policy: Theories, Actors, Cases*, edited by Steve Smith, Amelia Hadfield, and Tim Dunne, 71–80. Oxford: Oxford University Press.

Conley, Heather, Toland Terry, Kraut Jamie, and Andreas Østhagen. 2012. *A New Security Architecture for the Arctic: An American Perspective*. CSIS Report, January 20. Washington, DC: Center for Strategic & International Studies (CSIS).

Conley, Heather A., and Caroline Rohloff. 2015. *The New Ice Curtain*. Washington, DC: Center for Strategic & International Studies (CSIS).

Contenta, Sandro. 2010. "Canadians Have Their Own Oil Worries." *Global Post: Canada*. www.globalpost.com/dispatch/global-green/100602/canadians-worry-about-oil-spilling-beaufort-sea?page=0,1.

Danish Ministry of Defence. 2016. *Forsvarsministeriets Fremtidige Opgaveløsning i Arktis (Future Missions of the Danish Ministry of Defence in the Arctic)*. Copenhagen, Denmark: Danish Ministry of Defence.

Diesen, Sverre. 2013. "Towards an Affordable European Defence and Security Policy? The Case For Extensive European Force Integration." In *NATO's European allies: Military capability and political will*, edited by Magnus Petersson and Janne Haaland Matlary, 57–70. Basingstoke: Palgrave Macmillan.

European Parliament Resolution of 9 October 2008 on Arctic Governance. 2008. *European Parliament: Texts Adopted*. Brussels: European Parliament. www.europarl.europa.eu/sides/getDoc.do?type=TA&language=EN&reference=P6-TA-2008-0474.

Exner-Pirot, Heather. 2013. "What Is the Arctic a Case of? The Arctic as a Regional Environmental Security Complex and the Implications for Policy." *The Polar Journal* 3 (1):120–135.

Funston, Bernard. 2014. *Emergency Preparedness in Canada's North: An Examination of Community Capactiy*. Toronto, ON: The Gordon Foundation.

Grindheim, Astrid. 2009. *The Scramble for the Arctic? A Discourse Analysis of Norway and the EU's Strategies Towards the European Arctic*. Oslo: Fridtjof Nansen Institute.

Grønning, Ragnhild. 2016. "Why Military Security Should Be Kept out of the Arctic Council." *High North News*, June 7, 2016. www.highnorthnews.com/op-ed-why-military-security-should-be-kept-out-of-the-arctic-council/.

Haas, Peter M. 1989. "Do Regimes Matter? Epistemic Communities and Mediterranean Pollution Control." *International Organization* 43 (3):377–403.

Hill, Christopher. 1993. "The Capability-Expectations Gap, or Conceptualizing Europe's International Role." *Journal of Common Market Studies* 31 (3):305. https://doi.org/10.1111/j.1468-5965.1993.tb00466.x

Hopf, Ted. 2002. *Social Construction of Foreign Policy: Identities and Foreign Policies, Moscow, 1955 and 1999*. Ithaca, NY: Cornell University Press.

Humpert, Malte. 2014. *Arctic Shipping: An Analysis of the 2013 Northern Sea Route Season*, edited by The Arctic Institute. Vol. October 20. Washington, DC: The Arctic Institute. www.thearcticinstitute.org/2014/10/NSR-Shipping-Report.html.

Ivanova, Maria. 2011. "Oil Spill Emergency Preparedness in the Russian Arctic : A Study of the Murmansk Region." *Polar Research* 30 (7285):www.polarresearch.net/index.php/polar/article/view/7285.

Jervis, Robert. 1978. "Cooperation under the Security Dilemma." *World Politics* 30 (2):167–214.

Jockel, Joseph T., and Joel J. Sokolsky. 2012. "Continental Defence: 'Like Farmers Whose Lands Have a Common Concession Line'." In *Canada's National Security in the Post-9/11 World*, edited by David McDonough, 114–136. Toronto, ON: University of Toronto Press.

Johnston, Alastair Iain. 2001. "Treating, International Institutions as Social Environments." *International Studies Quarterly* 45 (4):487–515.

Joint Arctic Command. 2013. *Sarex Greenland Sea 2013 Final Exercise Report (FER)*. Vol. 2.0. Nuuk, Greenland: Joint Arctic Command.

Keil, Kathrin. 2013. "Cooperation and Conflict in the Arctic. The Cases of Oil and Gas, Shipping and Fishing." no. April.

Keil, Kathrin, and Andreas Raspotnik. 2014. "The European Union's Gateways to the Arctic." *European Foreign Affairs Review* 19 (1):101–120.

Keohane, Robert O. 1984. *After Hegemony: Cooperation and Discord in the World Political Economy*. Princeton, NJ: Princeton University Press.

Krasner, Stephen D. 1982. "Structural Causes and Regime Consequences: Regimes as Intervening Variables." *International Organization* 36 (02):185–205.

Kydd, Andrew H. 2008. "Methodological Individualism and Rational Choice." In *The Oxford Handbook of International Relations*, edited by Christian Reus-Smit and Duncan Snidal, 425–443. Oxford: Oxford University Press.

Levy, Marc A., Oran R. Young, and Michael Zürn. 1995. "The Study of International Regimes." *European Journal of International Relations* 1 (3):267–330.

Martin, Lisa L. 1992. "Interests, Power, and Multilateralism." *International Organization* 46 (4):765–792.

McCarty, Nolan, and Adam Meirowitz. 2007. "Political Game Theory." *Politische Vierteljahresschrift* 48 (4):767–768.

Mearsheimer, John J. 1995. "The False Promise of International Institutions." *International Security* 19 (3):5–49.

Melia, Michael. 2015. "Arctic Coast Guards Pledge Co-Operation at U.S. Meeting." *CBC News: North*, October 30, 2015. www.cbc.ca/news/canada/north/arctic-coast-guards-pledge-co-operation-at-u-s-meeting-1.3296921.

Mitchell, James R. 2013. *The Canadian Coast Guard in Perspective: A Paper Prepared for Action Canada*. Vol. August. Ottawa: Action Canada. www.actioncanada.ca/en/wp-content/uploads/2013/08/Canadian-Coast-Guard-In-Perspective_EN.pdf.

Mock, William B.T. 1992. "Game Theory, Signalling and International Legal Relations." *George Washington Journal of International Law & Economics* 26:33–60.

Moravcsik, Andrew. 1997. "Taking Preferences Seriously: A Liberal Theory of International Politics." *International Organization* 51 (04):229. 10.1162/002081898550536.

Neffenger, Peter V. 2014. "Testimony of Vice Admiral Peter V. Neffenger Vice Commandant on Implementing U.S. Policy in the Arctic." *House Coast Guard and Maritime Transportation Subcommittee*, U.S. Department of Homeland Security.

Norwegian Government, and Norwegian Ministry of Foreign Affairs. 2014. "Nordkloden." In *Nordområdene Statusrapport 2014*, edited by Norwegian Ministry of Foreign Affairs. Oslo.

Offerdal, Kristine. 2010. "Arctic Energy in EU Policy: Arbitrary Interest in the Norwegian High North." *Arctic* 63 (1):30–42.

Office of the Auditor General of Canada. 2014. *Report of the Commissioner of the Environment and Sustainable Development: Marine Navigation in the Canadian Arctic*, edited by Office of the Auditor General of Canada. Vol. Chapter 3. Ottawa: Office of the Auditor General of Canada.

Østhagen, Andreas. 2015. "Coastguards in Peril: A Study of Arctic Defence Collaboration." *Defence Studies* 15 (2):143–160.

———. 2016. "High North, Low Politics Maritime Cooperation with Russia in the Arctic." *Arctic Review on Law and Politics* 7 (1):83–100.

Østhagen, Andreas, and Vanessa Gestaldo. 2015. *Coast Guard Co-Operation in a Changing Arctic*. Torono: Munk-Gordon Arctic Security Program. http://gordonfoundation.ca/publication/749.

Ostrom, Thomas P. 2012. *The United States Coast Guard and National Defence: A History from World War I to the Present*. North Carolina: McFarland & Company.

Oye, Kenneth A. 1985. "Explaining Cooperation Under Anarchy: Hypotheses and Strategies." *World Politics* 38 (01):1–24.

Raspotnik, Andreas, and Andreas Østhagen. 2014. *From Seal Ban to Svalbard – The European Parliament Engages in Arctic Matters*. Washington, DC: The Arctic Institute, March, 2014.

Rottem, Svein V. 2014. "The Arctic Council and the Search and Rescue Agreement: The Case of Norway." *Polar Record* 50 (3):284–292.

Saxi, Håkon Lunde. 2011. "Nordic Defence Cooperation after the Cold War." *Oslo Files*, Vol. March 2011. Oslo: Norwegian Institute for Defence Studies.

Sevunts, Levon. 2016. "Arctic Nations Deepen Coast Guard Cooperation." *Eye on the Arctic*, June 10, 2016.

Snidal, Duncan. 1985. "The Game Theory of International Politics." *World Politics* 38 (1):25–57. doi:10.2307/2010350.

Stokke, Olav Schram. 2006. "Examing the Consequences of Arctic Institutions." In *International Cooperation and Arctic Governance: Regime Effectiveness and Northern Region Building*, edited by Olav Schram Stokke and Geir Hønneland, 13–26. New York: Routledge.

——— 2014a. "Asian Stakes and Arctic Governance." *Strategic Analysis* 38 (6):770–783. doi:10.1080/09700161.2014.952946.

———. 2014b. "International Environmental Governance and Arctic Security." In *Geopolitics and Security in the Arctic*, edited by Rolf Tamnes and Kristine Offerdal, 121–146. London: Routledge.

Stoltenberg, Thorvald. 2009. "Nordic Cooperation in Foreign and Security Policy." *Proposals Presented to the Extraordinary Meeting of Nordic Foreign Ministers*, Oslo.
Till, Geoffrey. 2004. *Seapower: A Guide for the Twenty-First Century*. London: Frank Cass Publishers.
Valasek, Tomas. 2011. *The Case for a New Approach to about the CER Surviving Austerity The Case for a New*. Brussels: Centre for European Reform, no. April 2011.
Voss, Alicia von, Claudia Major, and Christian Mölling. 2013. "The State of Defence Cooperation in Europe." *Working Paper*. Vol. December. Berlin: Stiftung Wissenschaft und Politik.
Wendt, Alexander E. 1999. "Social Theory of International Politics." *American Political Science Review* 94:429. Cambridge: Cambridge University Press. doi:10.1017/CBO9780511612183.

25

LEGAL REFORM, GOVERNANCE, AND SECURITY IN THE RUSSIAN ARCTIC

Aytalina Ivanova and Gail Fondahl

Introduction

Security is often categorized into traditional and human domains, with the former focused more on issues of state security and the latter on individual and community security. Human security includes community/cultural, economic, environmental, food, health, personal, and political security (UNDP 1994). Many scholarly works on the evolution of security concerns in Russia, and in the Russian Arctic specifically, focus on the traditional aspects of security (e.g., Conley and Rohloff 2015; Flake 2014; Konyshev and Sergunin 2014; Laurelle 2013; Klimenko 2016; Staun 2015). In this chapter, several of the various facets of human security are discussed: economic, environmental, cultural, and political security. This work observes how human security issues are acknowledged or ignored in Russia's policy, and explores laws that address, or significantly affect, Russia's Arctic.

Expanding on coverage of economic and environmental security, this chapter attends to governance as it is practiced, including laws adopted, by sub-federal levels of government in Russia, and also notes the role of nongovernmental organizations in contributing to and lobbying for these laws as means to improve human security. It is asserted that regional legal reforms have promoted human security in the Arctic in ways not provided for in federal legislation. The examination of a wider range of Arctic-focused laws permits a look at more local visions and practices of security. The chapter also remarks on threats posed by both a failure on the part of the federal government to pass certain laws, and by proposed federal legislation that, if adopted, would weaken sub-federal laws and governance.

Law, policy, governance, and security

If policies provide objectives to influence decision-making, laws (theoretically) ensure that such objectives are met through formalizing the objectives and making them enforceable. Both policy and law reflect societal values; both reflect the spatial and temporal contexts in which they are adopted (Blomley 2014), as well as the cultures in which the respective societies feel rooted. Policies often depend on laws to be drafted in order for the stated objectives to be attained. Governance structures at various levels influence the content, adoption, and implementation of laws.

Russia's Arctic, like the Arctic regions of other states, hosts an intricate network of governance institutions, both state and non-state, at the local, regional, and national levels. It is also part of numerous international governance institutions (Wilson, Fondahl, and Hansen, n.d.). Some of these are law-generating (e.g., regional governments), while others play a key role in initiating, helping draft, and thus influencing the content and adoption of laws (e.g., the Russian Association of Indigenous Peoples of the North and its regional branches).

Security concerns of various types are expressed in the pronouncements of policies and laws. A given policy may prioritize a certain type, or types, of security issues. The passage of laws (or failure to do so), as well as their implementation, further demonstrates these prioritizations at the societal level. Law, indeed, has been one key force in creating, directing, and limiting the security of individuals and collectives in the North.

Russia's Arctic regions share some commonalities that lead to common challenges for implementing laws and providing security to the citizens, such as a harsh climate, remoteness, and sparse population density. These common characteristics in some cases have thwarted the ability of legal reforms, both national and regional, to provide for greater human security. Russia's Arctic regions are also very diverse in their economy, society, and cultural differences among different groups of the population. Under the Russian Federation's federal system, its sub-federal units (*subjects*) develop their own legislation, with differing content and at different times than federal law; however, these laws must not contradict federal law. Thus, the securities provided by law vary across space and time. The various subjects of the Russian Federation's Arctic regions have taken diverse approaches to legislation that provide for differing aspects of human security, depending on their own specific needs and legal cultures (Ivanova and Stammler 2017).

In this chapter, discussion of legal reforms and their impacts on various dimensions of human security in the Arctic is organized into economic, environmental, political, and cultural sections. However, it is important to stress that legislative reforms often affect several of these domains of security at the same time.

Economic security: living and working in the North as a risk

Two key northern policy pronouncements on the North, *Foundations of the State Policy of the Russian Federation in the Arctic to 2020 and Beyond* (Osnovy 2008) and *Strategy of Development of the Arctic Zone of the Russian Federation and Guarantees for National Security up to 2020* (Strategiya 2013), lay out Russia's priorities for and interests in the Russian Arctic. The 2008 document, the first to articulate an Arctic policy in Russia in the post-Soviet period, prioritized the use of Russia's Arctic zone for "a strategic resource base … providing for resolving objectives of social economic development of the country," (Osnovy 2008, II.4a), "maintaining the Arctic as a zone of peace and cooperation" (II.4b), "stewardship of the unique ecological systems of the Arctic," (II.4c), and "use of the Northern Sea Route for national unified transportation-communication" (II.4d). The document proceeds to outline the need for addressing ecological legacies of past industrial development, improving communications networks and transportation infrastructure, developing state governance systems for social-economic development, and improving the life of the Indigenous population. While focused on national economic development and security, its elements, if fully realized, could certainly address human security interests as several of its goals speak in a general way to such interests.

The 2013 *Strategy of Development of the Arctic Zone* proclaimed many things: social-economic development; development of science and technology; creation of modern information-telecommunication infrastructure; provision for ecological security; international cooperation; and guaranteeing military security, defense, and the protection of Russia's Arctic borders as important priorities (Strategiya 2013, §7). Its general pronouncements can be interpreted to include human security objectives. The challenge in terms of the improvement of human security in the Arctic is in the implementation of these state priorities.

The Arctic population of Russia includes numerous Indigenous peoples, Russians, and other non-Indigenous people who have lived in the area for generations, as well as relative newcomers. The latter group, arriving in the Arctic during the Soviet and post-Soviet period, makes up the majority of the population. For reasons of national security, sovereignty, and economic autarky, the Soviet Union pursued the settlement of the region, the establishment of towns and cities, and the development of resource hearths across the North. During the Soviet period, the population of the Russian North grew from approximately 3.1 million in 1939 to 9.7 million in 1989 and 7.9 million in 2016 (Fauzer 2016, p. 10). At the end of the Soviet period, slightly more than half of those living in the North had been born outside of the North, and over one-third had lived there fewer than ten years (Heleniak 2009, pp. 38, 40).

Up until the early 1950s, the Soviet Union depended to a large degree on prison labor for developing its Arctic territories. In the 1960s, as the *gulag* was phased out, the USSR expanded a program of financial incentives, initially created in the 1930s, to attract workers to the North. Centralized economic planning controlled the cost of living in the North. University graduates could be deployed for two years to northern centers in return for free postsecondary education. However, most workers had to be lured by "northern incentives," which included higher wages, earlier pension entitlement, and subsidized vacations of longer duration, as well as the ability to maintain their accommodations back home. The program, along with propaganda encouraging workers to help "build socialism" by contributing to the construction of various mega-projects, was successful. Indeed, though visualized as mostly dormitory towns for relatively temporary industrial workers, the large industrial cities brought significant numbers who then decided to stay for much longer; sometimes for the rest of their lives (Bolotova and Stammler 2010; Stammler and Khlinovskaya 2011). The current version of this program of northern incentives continues to significantly influence the entire economy, demography, and settlement structure of the Russian Arctic (Gal'tseva, Favstritskaya, and Sharypova 2017).

In the initial post-Soviet period (1990s), the state essentially abandoned the North. Food, medical supplies, and other basic needs often failed to be delivered. Continuing to subsidize life in the North for so many people was deemed simply too expensive in that time of crisis. With the introduction of capitalism under the Boris Yeltsin government, the state no longer controlled prices, making northern cost-of-living allowances insufficient for the trickle of goods that did make their way North. Goods were offered at prices extraordinarily high to those who had lived under the Soviet system. In any event, many northerners did not receive their wages on a regular basis during this period. The dire situation in the North led to the well-known consequences of mass outmigration, economic and demographic decline, abandoned industrial sites, ghost towns, and the isolation of the remaining population (Heleniak 2015; Hill and Gaddy 2003; Vitebsky and Alekseyev 2000).

Those who stayed, including the Indigenous population, increased their dependency on local foods and other products (Pika 1999). The state also abandoned much infrastructure in the North, including along the shores of the Arctic Ocean. Meteorological stations were closed, while ports, airports, and waterways received no support. The governance of the area was left, to a much larger extent than before, to regional and local governments, which led to the development of a wider variety of regimes of governance. Economic security for most northerners declined markedly.

The living situation for most northerners has improved in the last 15 years. Today, two closely related benefits programs for persons working in the Russian Far North, which replace the Soviet incentives to move north in detail but not in objective, can together amount to a salary top-up upwards of 200% for those working in the farthest northern regions of the country (Trudovoy 2001, paragraphs 317, 326). The rationale for such policies continues to be that living in the Russian Arctic is a sacrifice, given its harsh climate and the need to import almost all food and other everyday goods. These programs sustain a logic that is socially constructed by people originally not from the North. They normalize a lifestyle that entirely relies on imports from outside the Arctic.

Meanwhile, Indigenous Arctic peoples, who consider these regions home, have developed ways of life that rely much less on outside support (e.g., reindeer herding, hunting, and fishing). These people do not easily comprehend why living at home should be considered a sacrifice for which the state must compensate, although in the 1960s they also became beneficiaries of the northern wage supplements (Armstrong, Rogers, and Rowley 1978).

The level of salary supplement depends on where exactly a person lives and works, with the principle that the harsher the conditions, the higher the salary top-up. In addition to those top-ups, most state-owned or big companies also have regulations that stipulate a set of privileges for their employees and their family members, similar to those provided during the Soviet period. These include travel to any place within Russia free of charge once every two years (*l'gotnyi otpusk*), free healthcare treatments in the South (as it is considered that life in the North is unhealthy for the human organism), and housing assistance for persons wishing to leave the North after retirement (Bolotova and Stammler 2010). However, while some companies have their own policies, the state programs apply only to people who are employed in the state sector and are registered as residents in the North. Many people working in the North remain registered in their home areas and therefore do not qualify for these northern incentive programs. Likewise, the programs do not apply to those employed as fly-in, fly-out workers, a form of labor that has become increasingly popular in the Russian Arctic since the end of the Soviet period (Saxinger 2016; Stammler and Eilmsteiner-Saxinger 2010).

Recent discussions about modifying the current level of social guarantees in scale and geographical extent, entertained by the government in 2014 and again in 2017, were met with strong resistance by those who would be affected and their governmental representatives (e.g., *Informatsionnaya rassylka "Lach"* 28 (739), #15, 4 September 2018; 29(40), #18, 11 September 2018). Occasional redrawing of the boundaries of the North has included and then removed some communities from enjoying the benefits accrued due to "living in the North" (Stammler-Gossmann 2007). The 2008 state policy document *Foundations of the State Policy of the Russian Federation in the Arctic to 2020 and Beyond* called for the development of legal documents that would define more precisely the geographical boundaries of Russia's Arctic zone to "include its southern boundary" (Osnovy 2008, IV.9. c]. The latest legal definition of the terrestrial borders of the Russian Arctic comes from the Presidential *Ukaz*[1] N. 296 of 2017, with slight modification via another *Ukaz*, N.287, in 2017 (Putin 2014). Northern residents of areas near the southern boundaries of the North, including municipal leaders of these regions, often remark upon the criticality of being classified as northern for local economic security and the crises that would ensue if their regions lost such status (Fondahl Fieldnotes Fieldnotes 2016, 2017).

Meanwhile, other state policies focused on national and military security undermine human security in the North. An example is the Murmansk region, the most militarized area of Russia and indeed of the entire Arctic. After the Soviet Union imploded, Russia reduced military capacity there significantly. For example, the army division in the small border village of Alakurtti on the Russian side of the border was closed in 2009, leaving a village without an economic base. However, the municipality searched for new avenues for development, such as cross-border tourism and cooperation, and working to secure its rather questionable future by providing local economic opportunities for its residents. Then, as part of an increasingly military-focused security agenda, the army reestablished its division (number 34,667) in Alakurtti in 2014, moved 7,000 new residents there, and essentially closed the village to access by foreigners (Reevell 2017; *V Kandalakshe i Alakurtti* 2015; Voennoe 2016). At the same time, on the other side of the border the Finnish army significantly intensified military maneuver activities in Western Europe's biggest forest military exercise ground (*Rovajärven ampuma alue*), and Finnish experts again called for Finland to join NATO in reaction to Russia's increase in Arctic military operations. This concretely exemplifies the conflict between traditional war-and-peace notions of state security and human security at the individual/community level, and between central and local powers. When abandoned by the state, local-governance structures worked to diversify the local economy and cross-border cooperation; the economic security of people inhabiting Alakurtti and similar places in the Arctic was of central concern at this level. Local economic security diminished with the return to traditional state-military security considerations and the predominance of central- over local-governance concerns (Holopainen 2015; Pesonen 2018).

How measures to improve state economic security in the North as a component of national security, including the development of Arctic hydrocarbon resources and development of the Northern Sea Route, will improve individual and community security in the North remains to be seen. Key sources of income from major northern resources, such as extraction taxes and export duties on oil and gas, supply the federal budget and are not shared with the regions as much as was the case in the 1990s. The main income that the regions currently receive from extractive industries is the income tax of individuals who work there, the resource extraction tax (of which the region where the resource is extracted gets 60% as of 2018), and the property tax of organizations (Nalogovyi 2000, Chapter 26)

Downturns in Russian economy:

> will generate a disproportional negative resonance in the Russian High North, which is very vulnerable to such accumulating negative consequences. At the same time it is also obvious that the degradation of economic and social infrastructure in the Northern regions is not crucially important for the management of deepening crisis processes in Russia and so is not prioritized by the Kremlin....
>
> *(Baev 2018, pp. 121–122)*

That is, the economic (and social) security of northerners will likely be sacrificed to national economic security issues. At the same time, the deepening crisis could once again make space, as it did in the 1990s, for increased local innovation in legal reforms and governance that pays greater attention to the economic security of local residents (as per the example of Alakurrti prior to 2014). This, however, may only be true for areas that are not militarily strategic for national security.

Environmental security: remediation, protection, inattention

Recent Arctic policy has given greater lip service to concern for the environment and the need for environmental protection. The 2008 document called for the "protection of the unique ecological systems of the Arctic" as a priority (Osnovy 2008, II.5.c) while the 2013 document stated that "guaranteeing ecological security" was a priority (Strategiya 2013, 7.d). To read into the order in which priorities are listed, in both cases environmental security follows strategic resource development, but in the 2013 document it precedes military security. A draft law on the Arctic Zone of the Russian Federation, awaiting adoption by the Russian Parliament as of this writing, also listed environmental protection as its third goal in its 2016 version. Besides this draft law, there have also been suggestions to establish a Russian Ministry for Arctic Affairs Mukhin, Grinyaev, and Lavnichenko 2014). However, highly placed Russian bureaucrats, such as Far Eastern District Presidential Representative Yuri Trutnev, continue to suggest "some sort of coordinating organ" for coordinating Russian Arctic governmental affairs (Trutnev 2018).

President Vladimir Putin declared that "Russia has a special responsibility for the Arctic. One of our priorities is to keep the balance between the economic activity and the preservation of the unique environment" (Putin 2015). To what extent are these assertions fulfilled, and to what extent are northerners experiencing improved environmental security? Tokunaga (2018) characterized the current approach, as reflected in both speeches and policy documents, as one of *ecological modernization*; that is, of the development of natural resources (modernization) under strict environmental protection regulations. In reality, the focus on implementing such regulations is often negligible, if not altogether absent, due to the economic crisis, corruption, and lack of will. Most recently, environmental security may be equated in some areas with *ecological militarization*. Tokunaga stated that "Russia's environmental policies around the Arctic Sea seem to be closely linked to military-security issues in general" (Tokunaga 2018, p. 143), as cleanup projects initiated by Russian Geographical Society prepare sites for new military facilities (see Sergunin's chapter in this volume).

Also observable is the erosion of environmental (and economic and cultural) security in recent legal reforms. For instance, earlier federal legislative reforms sought to protect certain territories in the North, such as those most important to Indigenous communities, from industrial encroachment. Specifically, the federal law on Territories of Traditional Nature Use legislated for a framework establishing such areas (Russian Federation 2001). This legislation directly addressed the economic and cultural security of Indigenous communities through environmental protection provisions. Land officially designated as a Territory of Traditional Nature Use (TTNUs) is more difficult to alienate for industrial use. In the event that territory is removed from this category for development, the Indigenous community or communities using it must receive compensation, including land of equal value to their traditional activities. Corollary regional laws or legal acts have been adopted in many subjects, some well ahead of the federal law[2] (see Kryazhkov 2013b, Volume 2). These laws, both federal and regional, were demanded by, and their crafting facilitated by, the Russian Association of Indigenous Peoples of the North and its regional affiliates: nongovernmental organizations that play a critical role in governance innovations regarding Indigenous peoples in the North.

Yet, while many TTNUs were established at the local and regional level, no federal-level TTNU has yet been successfully established (Kryazhkov 2010, pp. 243ff discusses why). In 2009, the Russian government adopted a *Concept Paper on the Sustainable Development of Indigenous Peoples of the North, Siberia and the Far East of the Russian Federation*, which called for the establishment of legislation to better protect the TTNUs by 2011 (Konseptsiya 2009).

However, this was not accomplished. Instead, subsequent federal legislation eroded the strength of the original law, removing TTNUs from a broader category of "Specially Protected Nature Territories" (Russian Federation 2013, §§6, 95). A draft federal law now proposes to further restrict the range of TTNU's by permitting their registration only on one level of land jurisdiction (either federal or regional) and not across levels. Experts fear that this would lead to a domination of extractive industrial companies on TTNUs, where the Indigenous-rights holders would have to agree with other land users individually on the terms and conditions of nontraditional land use (Dmitriev 2018). It is still unclear how this would affect existing TTNUs. Some fear that the revised law would give Indigenous persons and industrial companies equal rights to negotiate land use on TTNUs, thus abolishing the original prioritization of the Indigenous traditional way of life (e.g., Murashko and Rohr 2018, pp. 41).

Political security: restricting governance options

The first *Arctic Human Development Report* (AHDR 2004) observed that Arctic residents consider "fate control" (controlling one's own destiny) as an important dimension of their well-being (AHDR 2004, p. 240). Fate control involves enjoying decision-making powers, political power, access to information, and recognition of human rights (Dahl et al. 2010). That is, experiencing increased (or decreased) fate control is linked to one's increased (or decreased) political security. Fate control for many Russian Arctic residents has decreased over the past decade as the Russian government has centralized its power.

Notably, the federal extinguishment in 2007 of several political units – the Taymyr (Dolgan-Nenets) Autonomous Okrug (AO), the Evenki AO, and the Koryak AO – decreased fate control for these subjects' respective residents. The AOs were initially created as ethnic territorial units (ostensibly) to increase the representation of the eponymous Indigenous peoples (Gogolev 2015; Slezkine 1994). Whether or not they had succeeded at that goal, the fact that they had the legislative power to pass laws that governed activities at the regional level, as well as representation at the federal level of government (each had two representatives in the Federation Council – the Russian Federal Assembly's upper house), meant that residents of these subjects, Indigenous and non-Indigenous, had a greater opportunity to exercise their voices. Now they live within much larger governmental units. The residents of the Taymyr and Evenki AOs (2002 populations of 39,786 and 17,697 respectively), joined to the Krasnoyarsk Kray, comprise a fraction of its total population (2002 population of 3,023,525) and thus have much-diminished political power. Likewise, the population of the Koryak AO in 2002 was 25,157 while Kamchatka Oblast, which subsumed it, had a population of 358,801 that year. The removal of "ethnic status" from these subjects, and their merging into larger units allowed for some streamlining in governance institutions, and perhaps thus contributed in a small way to improving political and economic security at the federal level. Yet, it significantly impacted the political security of the residents of these northern regions in a negative way. Constitutional lawyer Vladimir Kryazhkov, a leading legal expert on Indigenous rights in Russia, commented on the loss of status of these ethnic territories by saying: "As a result, a marked weakening of guarantees of social and other rights of Indigenous peoples can be observed" (Kryazhkov 2013a, p. 146).

Nongovernmental organizations (NGOs), including those working on Arctic issues and on behalf of Arctic people(s), have also lost political security, due chiefly to state legislation on funding limitations known as the "foreign agent law" (Russian Federation 2012). The law requires NGOs that engage in political activities to register as foreign agents if they receive any foreign funding. *Political activities* are poorly defined and thus widely interpretable; they include human rights and environmental protection activities (Sulandziga and Berezhkov 2017). Numerous environmental and human rights NGOs sprang up in Russia during the 1990s, accompanying the increasing democratization of the Russian political landscape. Many Russians depended on foreign support, given the dire economic situation of the 1990s. The foreign agent law provides a way for the state to control and curtail the activities of these NGOs. One such NGO that suffered this fate – the Russian Indigenous Training Center – provides legal training and other kinds of capacity building for Indigenous northerners. Northerners' political security at the individual and community level is undermined by a state policy that is ostensibly intended to improve national security.

Cultural security: Indigenous peoples' rights and security

The Russian state recognizes 40 "Indigenous numerically small peoples" of the North, and has passed a number of laws addressing various facets of the rights of these people and their security (see Kryazhkov 2013b for relevant laws). The laws only apply to those Indigenous northern peoples with populations smaller than 50,000. This provision in itself has implications for the cultural security of several Indigenous northern peoples, such as the Sakha and Komi, who are not numerically small.

A troika of federal laws at the turn of the millennium, including the Law on Territories of Traditional Nature Use noted above, established key rights for Indigenous peoples (Russian Federation 1999, 2000, 2001; see Fondahl and Poelzer 2003). Since then, other federal laws have eroded these rights. Once able to receive land allotments in perpetuity and free of charge, Indigenous collectives no longer enjoy this right. Priority access to floral and faunal resources, to hunting land and fishing sites, and access to payments from development projects that negatively affected their lifestyles and traditional activities are just some of the rights first provided by federal legislation and then eliminated by new federal laws since 2004 (Kryazhkov 2013a). The elimination of these rights has provided greater state economic security by removing hindrances from industrial development while critically diminishing securities provided to Indigenous peoples in the early post-Soviet period. Under the revised laws, Indigenous peoples have become poachers on their own homelands.

While legal reform first provided and then removed rights of Indigenous northerners, inaction at the center can also undermine, or at least fail to promote, local securities. For instance, reindeer herding is a key economic and cultural activity for over two dozen northern peoples. The federal government has been working on drafting a law on reindeer husbandry since at least 1994. Meanwhile, several northern subjects have adopted laws on reindeer husbandry[3] (Kryazhkov 2013b). These laws vary in content, with some more focused on economic security and some more focused on cultural security. An effective federal law could provide a framework to ensure that subject laws were comprehensive in their protections (e.g., dealing with economic, cultural, and environmental securities pertaining to reindeer husbandry). Of course, an ineffective federal law might constrain the securities provided to date by the regional laws, which would have to be brought into coherence with such a law.

The federal government has also been working on drafting a law on *ethnological expertise* (social and cultural impact assessment). Planned industrial projects are subject to environmental impact assessment; the ethnological expertise would also require the assessment of *social* and *cultural* impacts that such a project would have on Indigenous communities. If these were assessed as significant, the law would require plans for mitigation and/or compensation. While this law was called for in 1999 in a Law on the Guarantees of Rights of Indigenous Peoples (Russian Federation 1999, §1), it has not yet been adopted federally. Indeed, the only region to have put such a law in place is the Sakha Republic (Yakutia) (Sakha Republic 2010). Its creation came at the behest of the republican-level Association of Indigenous Peoples of the North, and involved several Indigenous legal experts (Sleptsov 2015; Fondahl Fieldnotes, August 2016). Under this law, 11 such assessments have been carried out. However, some state companies refuse to follow regional laws even when working within Sakha Republic, claiming not to be subject to republican laws given their national status (Stammler and Ivanova 2016, pp. 1229–1234). A federal law on ethnological expertise is being discussed and would theoretically be useful for ensuring that all industrial projects on Indigenous lands undergo such assessment.

It is worth noting that in the Yamalo-Nenets AO and Khanty-Mansi AO, some companies have chosen to carry out such assessments on their own, even in the absence of a law requiring it.

Where the federal government has been slow to adapt law to improve the cultural security of northern Indigenous peoples, some regions have actively pursued such legislation. Most notable are the Sakha Republic (Yakutia), the Yamalo-Nenets AO, and the Khanty-Mansi AO (Kryazhkov 2013b). For instance, the Sakha Republic passed laws concerning the nomadic family and nomadic schools in order to increase the cultural security of its nomadic Indigenous population. Yamalo-Nenets AO and Khanty-Mansi adopted laws on Indigenous folklore, and all three of these subjects have legislation supporting the languages of the Indigenous peoples within their territories. While financial restrictions and different levels of government will hamper the implementation of such laws, their adoption speaks to a progressive intent. Their adoption also speaks to the tenacity with which local and regional Indigenous NGOs (e.g., the Associations of Numerically Small Peoples) have lobbied for such laws.

Conclusion: a disconnect between legal reform and human security

Legal reform regarding economic, political, and cultural security, including Indigenous-rights legislation as well as environmental protection, characterized the 1990s and earliest years of this millennium. Such laws, adopted at the federal and regional level (with the latter often predating the former), denoted governance strategies more focused on the individual. Many of the laws passed in the 1990s were only partially implemented, due at least in part to the economic crises. In the North, it was the very dearth of federal presence during the worst of the 1990s economic crisis that gave space for regional governments, as well as NGOs of various types, to play a stronger role in pursuing regional laws and practices based on these laws that sought to improve the human security of Arctic residents. The near-abandonment of the North by the central government at this time in terms of providing services and provisions greatly decreased human security throughout the North. The conclusion is that local efforts at least lessened the impacts of this abandonment to a degree. This is especially true for northern Indigenous peoples who, in having to increase dependence on their traditional activities to survive, at the same time benefited from laws that provided some support and protection for these activities. Importantly, these were laws that Indigenous peoples played a role in drafting and for which they lobbied vigorously.

Paradoxically, the improved economic situation in the 2000s under Vladimir Putin was frequently accompanied by decreasing environmental security for northerners. This is likely due to the reinvigoration and expansion of northern industrial development while ignoring laws regarding environmental protections with impunity. In the wake of Western sanctions following the Crimean and Syrian conflicts and the resulting growing economic hardships, this trend is likely to continue. Resource extraction is prioritized over environmental protection in a contracting economy, and laws concerning the latter are regularly ignored.

Meanwhile, centralization of governance has "tightened the screws" throughout the country on lower levels of government, as well as governance practiced by nongovernmental organizations, leading to lessened political security for northern residents. This general tendency is exacerbated in the Arctic. The recent trend toward more federal laws, especially on the rights and protections of Indigenous northerners, has undermined earlier federal laws and regional laws and has diminished human securities. Human security considerations are evident in at least some of the legal reforms made by sensitive regional politicians and lawmakers who have tried to tailor polices, modes of governance, and rules to local conditions and local northern populations. The damage done by centralizing tendencies, including in legal reform, continues to be exacerbated by federal politicians having little or no experience with northern livelihoods and needs at the individual and community levels.

Notes

1 Ukaz is the name for a presidential decree or order in Russia.

2 Including (the now defunct) Koryak Autonomous Okrug (AO) (in 1992, 1997), Primorksky Kray (1993), Irkutskaya Oblast (1997), Amurskaya Oblast (2003), Khanty-AO) (2006), Sakha Republic (2006), and Yamalo-Nenets A0 (2010).

3 Including Sakha Republic (1997), Yamalo-Nenets Autonomous Okrug (AO) (1998), Nenets AO (2002), Magadanskaya Oblast (2003), Murmanskaya Oblast (2003), Khanty-Mansi AO (2004), Kamchatskiy Kray (2010), Khabarovskiy kray (2012), Krasnoyarskiy Kray (2012), Zabaykalskiy Kray (2012).

References

AHDR. 2004. *Arctic Human Development Report.* Akureryi: Stefansson Arctic Institute.

Armstrong, T., Rogers, G., and Rowley, G. 1978. *The Circumpolar North. A Political and Economic Geography of the Arctic and Subarctic.* London: Methuen and Company.

Baev, P. 2018. Examining the execution of Russian military-security policies and programs in the Arctic. In *Russia's Far North. The Contested Energy Frontier,* V.-P. Tynkkynen, S. Tabata, D. Gritsenko, and M. Goto (Eds.), pp. 113–125. London: Routledge.

Blomley, N. 2014. Learning from Larry. Pragmatism and the habits of legal space. In *The Expanding Spaces of Law. A Timely Legal Geography,* I. Braverman, N. Blomley, D. Delaney, and A. Kedar (Eds.), pp. 77–94. Stanford: Stanford University Press.

Bolotova, A., and Stammler, F. 2010. How the North became home. Attachment to place among industrial migrants in Murmansk region. In *Migration in the Circumpolar North: Issues and Contexts,* C. Southcott and L. Huskey (Eds.), pp. 193–220. Edmonton: CCI Press, University of Alberta, (CCI Occasional Publication No. 64).

Conley, H.A., and Rohloff, C. 2015. *The New Ice Curtain: Russia's Strategic Reach to the Arctic.* Lanham, MD: Rowman & Littlefield.

Dahl, J., Fondahl, G., Petrov, A., and Fjellheim, R.S. 2010. Fate control. In *Arctic Social Indicators,* J. N. Larsen, P. Schweitzer, and G. Fondahl (Eds.), pp. 129–146. Copenhagen: Nordic Council of Ministers.

Dmitriev, V. 2018. Bespridannitsu – TTP mogut vydat' zamuzh za bogatogo zhenikha – nedropol'zovatelya [A TTP may present her sub-surface resource mining fiancé a dowry]. Retrieved from www.csipn.ru/glavnaya/novosti-regionov/3908#.W8yKTWeUSEg

Fauzer, V.V. 2016. Demograficheskiy potentsial severnykh regionov Rossii [Demographic potential of the northern regions of Russia]. Presentation at the inter-regional conference "Respublika Sakha

(Yakutia) – 2030-205-: Strategiya Uspekha." Yakutsk, 36 pp, 23 December. Retrieved from src-sakha.ru/wp-content/uploads/2017/01/2-Fauzer-V.V.pdf

Flake, L.E. 2014. Russia's security intentions in a melting Arctic. *Military and Strategic Affairs* 6(1): 99–116.

Fondahl, G., and Poelzer, G. 2003. Aboriginal land rights in Russia at the beginning of the twenty-first century. *Polar Record* 39(209): 111–122.

Gal'tseva, N.V., Favstritskaya, O.S., and Sharypova, O.A. 2017. Uroven' zhizni naseleniya severnykh i arkticheskikh territoriy dal'nego vostoka Rossii [The standard of living of the population of the northern and Arctic territories of the Far East of Russia]. *Regionalnaya Ekonomika: Teoriya I Praktika* 15(1): 85–100.

Gogolev, P. 2015. On the autonomy and territorial interests of the Indigenous peoples of the North, Siberia and the Far East at the present stage. *The Northern Review* 39: 31–38.

Heleniak, T. 2009. The role of attachment to place in migration decisions of the population of the Russian North. *Polar Geography* 32(1–2): 31–60.

Heleniak, T. 2015. Arctic populations and migration. In *Arctic Human Development Report: Regional Processes and Global Linkages*, J.N. Larsen and G. Fondahl (Eds.), pp. 53–104. Copenhagen: Nordic Council of Ministers.

Hill, F., and Gaddy, C. 2003. *The Siberian Curse. How Communist Planners Left Russia Out in the Cold.* Washington, DC: Brookings Institution Press.

Holopainen, S. 2015. Suomi tarkastaa Venajan 80. Moottoroidun jv-prikaatin aseet Alakurtissa. Ilta Sanomat, 13.10. Retrieved from www.is.fi/kotimaa/art-2000001017973.html

Ivanova, A., and Stammler, F. 2017. Многообразие управляемости природными ресурсами в Российской Арктике. *Сибирские Исторические Исследования* 4: 210–225.

Klimenko, E. 2016. *Russia's Arctic Security Policy. Still Quiet in the High North?* Stockholm: SIPRI (SIPRI Policy Paper No. 45).

Konseptsiya. 2009. Konseptsiya Ustoychivogo Razvitiya Korennykh Malochislennykh Narodov Severa, Sibiri i Dal'nego Vostoka Rossiyskoi Federatsii [The Concept for the Sustainable Development of Small Indigenous Population Groups of the North, Siberia and the Far East of the Russian Federation], N. 132-r, 4 February 2009. Retrieved 20 September 2018 from http://docs.cntd.ru/document/902142304

Konyshev, V., and Sergunin, A. 2014. Is Russia a revisionist military power in the Arctic? *Defense & Security Analysis* 30(4): 323–335.

Kryazhkov, V.A. 2010. *Korennye maloschislennye narody Severa v rossisykom prave* [*Indigenous Numerically Small Peoples of the North in Russian Law*]. Moscow: Norma.

Kryazhkov, V.A. 2013a. Development of Russian legislation on northern Indigenous peoples. *Arctic Review on Law and Politics* 4: 140–155.

Kryazhkov, V.A. 2013b. *Status korennykh narodov Rossii. Mezhdunarodnye pravovye akty i Rossiyskoe zakonodatel'tvo* [*Status of Indigenous Peoples of Russia. International Legal Acts and Russian Legislation*]. Two volumes. Moscow-Salekhard.

Laurelle, M. 2013. *Russia's Arctic Strategies and the Future of the Far North.* New York: Routledge.

Mukhin, A., Grinyaev, S., and Lavnichenko, M. 2014. Ministerstvo po delam Arktiki i Severnykh Territoriy, Proekt [A Ministry of Arctic and Northern Territories Affairs, Plan]. Moscow: Tsentr Politicheskoy Informatsii. Retreived from http://polit-info.ru/images/data/gallery/0_46__po_delam_Arktiki.pdf.

Murashko, O., and Rohr, J. 2018. Russian Federation. *The Indigenous World 2018*, Part 1, The Arctic, pp. 41–49. Retrieved from www.landcoalition.org/sites/default/files/documents/resources/indigenous-world-2018.pdf

Nalogovyi. 2000. Nalogovyy kodeks Rossiyskoy Federatsii, 05.08. N 117 FZ [tax code]. Edition 03.08. 2018.

Osnovy. 2008. Osnovy gosudarstvennoy politiki Rossiyskoy Federatsii v Arktike do 2020 goda i na posleduyushchiy period [Foundations of the State Policy of the Russian Federation In the Arctic to 2020 and Beyond]. Retrieved from https://rg.ru/2009/03/30/arktika-osnovy-dok.html

Pesonen, A. 2018. Suomen Puolustusvoimien Venaja-ryhma on Venajalle mieluinen hybridivaikuttaja. Uusi Suomi, 1 January. Retrieved from http://aripesonen1.puheenvuoro.uusisuomi.fi/248475-suomen-puolustusvoimien-venaja-ryhma-on-venajalle-mieluinen-hybridivaikuttaja

Pika, A. (Ed.). 1999. *Neotraditionalism in the Russian North: Indigenous Peoples and the Legacy of Peretroika.* Edmonton: Canadian Circumpolar Institute.

Putin, V. 2014. Ukaz Presidenta Rossiyskkoy Federatsii "O sukhoputnykh territoriyakh Arkticheskoy zony Rossiyskoy Federatsii" [On land territories of the Arctic Zone of the Russian Federation]. N. 296, 2 May 2014, with modifications, Ukaz N. 287, 27 June 2017.

Putin, V. 2015. Balans mezhdu osvoeniem Arktiki i sokhraneniem ee prirody – odin is prioritetov Rossii [A balance between the development of the Arctic and protecting its nature is one of the priorities of Russia]. Opening speech at the international conference «Obespechnie bezopasnosit i ustochivogo razvitiya Arkticheskogo regiona, sokhranenie ekosystem i traditsionnogo obraza zhizni korennogo naseleniya Arktiki». Arkhangelsk. 16 September 2015. Retrieved from https://ru.arctic.ru/environmental/20150916/166106.html

Reevell, P. 2017. Russia flaunts Arctic expansion with new military bases. ABCnews, 29 April. Retrieved from https://abcnews.go.com/international,story id 47091750

Russian Federation. 1999. O garantiyakh prav korennykh malochislennykh narodov Rossiyskoy Federatsii [On guarantees of the rights of the Indigenous peoples of the Russian Federation]. Russian Federal Law. 82-F3 30 April 1999.

Russian Federation (2000) Ob obshchikh printsipakh organizatsii obshchin korennykh malochislennykh narodov Severa, Sibiri i Dal'nego Vostoka Rossiyskoy Federatsii [On general principles for the organization of *obshchiny* (communes) of indigenous numerically small peoples of the North, Siberia and the Far East of the Russian Federation], No. 104-F3, 20 July 2000.

Russian Federation. 2001. O territoriyakh traditsionnogo prirodopol'zovaniya korennykh malochislennykh narodov Severa, Sibiri i Dal'nego Vostoka Rossiyskoy Federatsii. [On territories of traditional nature use of the Indigenous peoples of the North, Siberia and Far East of the Russian Federation]. Russian Federal Law N. 49-F3, 7 May 2001.

Russian Federation. 2012. O vnesenii izmeneniy v otdel'nyye zakonodatel'nyye akty Rossiyskoy Federatsii v chasti regulirovaniya deyatel'nosti nekommercheskikh organizatsiy, vypolnyayushchikh funktsii inostrannogo agenta. [On Amendments to Legislative Acts of the Russian Federation regarding the Regulation of the Activities of Non-profit Organizations Performing the Functions of a Foreign Agent]. Russian Federal Law N. 121-FZ 20 July 2012.

Russian Federation. 2013. O vnesenii izmeneniy v Federal'nyy zakon «Ob osobo okhranyayemykh territoriyakh» i otdel'nykh zakonodatel'nykh aktakh Rossiyskoy Federatsii [On the introduction of changes to the Federal Law "On Specially Protected Natural Territories" and other legal acts of the Russian Federation]. Russian Federal Law N. 406-FZ(28 December): 2013.

Sakha Republic. 2010. Ob etnologicheskoy ekspertize v mestakh traditsionnogo prozhivaniya i osnovnoy khozyaystvennoy deyatel'nosti korennykh malochislennykh narodov Severa Respubliki Sakha (Yakutiya) [Law on the ethnologicheskaya expertiza in the places of traditional inhabitation and main economic livelihood of indigenous small-numbered peoples of the North of the Republic of Sakha (Yakutia)E]. Sakha Regional Law. 820-3 № 537-IV.

Saxinger, G. 2016. Lured by oil and gas: Labour mobility, multi-locality and negotiating normality & extreme in the Russian Far North. *The Extractive Industries and Society* 3(1): 50–59.

Sleptsov, A. 2015. Gosudarstvennaya etnologicheskaya ekspertiza Respubliki Cakha (Yakutiya) [State ethnological expertise of the Republic of Sakha (Yakutia)]. *Arktika XXI vek. Gumanitarnyye nauki* 1: 15–24.

Slezkine, Y. 1994. *Arctic Mirrors. Russia and the Small Peoples of the North.* Ithaca, NY: Cornell University Press.

Stammler, F., and Eilmsteiner-Saxinger, G. (Eds). 2010. Biography, Shift-labour and Socialisation in a Northern Industrial City/ Biografiya,vakhtovyy trud i sotsializatsiya v severnom industrial'nom gorode. Tyumen State University & Arctic Centre Rovaniemi. Online edited volume. Retrieved from. https://lauda.ulapland.fi/bitstream/handle/10024/59445/NURbook_2ed_100421_final.pdf?sequence=1

Stammler, F., and Khlinovskaya, E. 2011. Einmal „Erde" und zurück: Bevölkerungsbewegung in Russlands Norden [Round-Trip ticket, "Earth" and Back: Population Movement in Russia's Far North]. In *Osteuropa 2–3/2011. Logbuch Arktis. Der Raum, die Interessen und das Recht*, M. Sapper, V. Weichsel and C. Humrich (Eds.), pp. 347–370. Berlin: DGO.

Stammler, F., and Ivanova, A. 2016. Resources, rights and communities: extractive mega-projects and local people in the Russian Arctic. *Europe-Asia Studies* 68(7): 1220–1244. doi:10.1080/09668136.2016.1222605.

Stammler-Gossmann, A. 2007. Reshaping the North of Russia: towards a conception of space. *Arctic & Antarctic Journal of Circumpolar Sociocultural Issues* 1: 53–97.

Staun, J. 2015. *Russia's Strategy in the Arctic*. Copenhagen: Institute for Strategy at the Royal Danish Defence College.

Strategiya. 2013. Strategiya Razvitiya Arkticheskoi Zony Rossiyskoi Federatsii i Obespecheniya Natsional'noi Bezopasnosti na Period do 2020 Goda [The Strategy for the Development of the Arctic Zone of the Russian Federation and Ensuring National Security for the Period up to 2020], Approved by President Vladimir Putin, 20 February 2013. Retrieved from http://government.ru/info/18360/

Sulandziga, R., and Berezhkov, D. 2017. *Reflections on the Influence of the Current Political Development in Russia on Indigenous Peoples' Land Rights, Indigenous Peoples' Rights and Unreported Struggles: Conflict and Peace*. New York: Institute for the Study of Human Rights, Columbia University, pp. 80–95. Retrieved from https://indigenousschool.wordpress.com/2018/09/20/2017-reflections-on-the-influence-of-the-current-political-development-in-russia-on-indigenous-peoples-land-rights-by-rodion-sulyandziga-and-dmitry-berezhkov/

Tokunaga, M. 2018. Russian Arctic development and environmental discourse. In *Russia's Far North. The Contested Energy Frontier*, V.-P. Tynkkynen, S. Tabata, D. Gritsenko and M. Goto (Eds.), pp. 129–146. London: Routledge.

Trudovoy. 2001 Трудовой кодекс Российской Федерации [Labour Codex of the Russian Federation] N. 197-ФЗ, 30 December 2001 (edited 11. 10.2018). Retrieved from www.consultant.ru/document/cons_doc_LAW_34683/

Trutnev, Y. 2018. Nuzhno lomat' mental'nost chinovinkov, schitayushchikh sebya velikimi [It is necessary to break the mentality of officials who consider themselves great]. 5 July. Retrieved from www.dfo.gov.ru/trutnev/2885/

UNDP (United Nations Development Program). 1994. *Human Development Report 1994*. New York: Oxford University Press. Retrieved 17 September 2018 from http://hdr.undp.org/sites/default/files/reports/255/hdr_1994_en_complete_nostats.pdf

V Kandalakshe i Alakurtti usileny dosmotry i mery bezopasnosti [In Kandalaksha and Alakurtti the security measures were increased]. 2015. News Feed, 13 December. Retrieved from http://blogg51.ru/news-id-4433.html

Vitebsky, P., and Alekseyev, A. 2000. *Coping with Distance: Social, Economic and Environmental Change in the Sakha Republic (Yakutia), Northeast Siberia. Report on Expedition Funded by the Gilchrist Educational Trust in Association with the Royal Geographical Society, 1999*. Cambridge: Scott Polar Research Institute. Unpublished report.

Voennoe. 2016. Posle publikatsii SMI komissiya Minoborony obsledovala problemnoye zhil'ye v Alakurtti [After mass media publication, a commission of the Ministry of Defence investigated problems with housing in Alakurtti]. 18 May. Retrieved from https://xn–b1aga5aadd.xn–p1ai/2016/220462/

Wilson, G., Fondahl, G., and Hansen, K.G. n.d. Governance for arctic sustainability. Typescript (in review stage for forthcoming chapter).

PART IV

Non-Arctic states, regional, and international organizations

26

CONSIDERING THE ARCTIC AS A SECURITY REGION

The roles of China and Russia

Marc Lanteigne

Introduction

During the 1990s, when "globalization" first entered academic and policy vocabularies, it became fashionable to discuss the "death of distance" in international relations. The proliferation of modern transportation and communications technologies, the spread of industries, and the liberalization of trade have had a significant impact on the entire world. The effects of various types of globalization are increasingly visible, including in the Arctic. The suggestion that the world was becoming "flat" due to these advances gained much currency in both policy circles and the media (Friedman 2006). In the Arctic, however, the idea of a flattening political-economic system has run headlong into the stark reality of its distinct geography, even as the region has become more accessible because of ice erosion due to climate change. Globalizing forces, both positive and negative, have not left this region untouched, yet the limits of economic and other forms of globalization in the Arctic are also becoming apparent. In a region dominated by small and often isolated populations separated by great distances, as well as harsh climatic and geographical conditions, the politics of interconnectivity become much more complicated and are tempered by the realities of isolation and vulnerability.

Environmental changes in the region have opened the Arctic to more economic activity and, as a result, more security activity. Improved access to fossil fuels (oil and gas) and raw materials in the region due to ice erosion has introduced the possibility of competition between Arctic and non-Arctic states for these resources. Talk of a "Scramble for the Arctic," which dominated regional and international debates after the turn of the century (Borgerson 2013; Fairhall 2010: 15–26), became more muted after 2014 due to the collapse in global energy (including oil) and raw materials prices, which made the extraction of Arctic resources far less attractive from a financial and logistical standpoint. A number of international energy firms have withdrawn from the region or postponed ambitious extraction projects (Dlouhy 2016). However, it is unclear how long that situation will hold, given the unpredictability of commodity markets and the growing possibility that Arctic resources will become easier to obtain and transport to Southern markets. Russia, under President Vladimir Putin, now depends greatly upon the opening of its Siberian and Russian Far East (RFE) regions to fossil fuel development. Many non-Arctic states, such as China under President Xi Jinping, now view the Arctic as an economic opportunity that requires greater regional engagement: a major example being the developing Sino–Russian Arctic partnership.

Added to these issues is the re-intrusion of old-fashioned great-power politics into the Arctic, partially due to worsening relations between Russia and the West in the wake of the 2014 Russian annexation of Crimea, and ongoing fighting in the Donbas region of eastern Ukraine. Moscow, citing growing concerns about the security of its Arctic assets, has been increasing military activity in its Far Northern regions, adding personnel, opening bases, and installing new surveillance equipment (*TASS* 29 January 2016). The Russian government anticipates greater economic activity, including increased use by both Russian and international concerns of the Northern Sea Route (NSR) for shipping between Europe and Asia. These policies have alarmed the United States and its European allies. In the case of China, the government of President Xi Jinping formally added the Arctic Ocean to the list of maritime regions essential to China's Belt and Road (*yidai yilu* 一带一路) trade initiatives in 2017. In a policy statement co-written that year by China's then-State Oceanic Administration and the National Development and Reform Commission (NDRC), Beijing identified sea routes, including the NSR and potentially the greater Arctic Ocean region that would be essential for the country to develop stronger maritime trade (Xinhua, 20 June 2017). Beijing has called for a series of Arctic development projects to be developed through partnerships with local governments and economies.

A follow-up governmental White Paper on Chinese Arctic policy was published by Beijing in January 2018. The document further detailed Chinese interests in joint economic ventures in the Arctic and in incorporating the region into China's expanding Belt and Road trade networks (PRC State Council Information Office 2018). Although the paper stressed that no non-Arctic state had the right to claim sovereignty in the Arctic region, non-Arctic governments did have the right to engage in economic activities, including shipping and resource-extraction activities, in conjunction with international law. China has taken the lead among non-Arctic states in developing strong economic ties with Arctic economies throughout the region, with the intention of being considered a "near-Arctic state" (*jin beiji guojia* 近北极国家) despite its lack of polar geography. Beijing also detailed plans in early 2019 for a nuclear-powered icebreaking vessel to be added to its two conventional icebreakers, which would make China the only nation other than Russia to use such technology (Zhen 2019).

As a result of Russian, (and to a degree, Chinese), activities in the Arctic, the United States under the Barack Obama administration responded by augmenting relations with its NATO allies in the region. Initiatives included a joint US–Nordic summit in Washington in May 2016 and the announcement that the former American base at Keflavík, Iceland, which was closed in 2006, would reopen for American military activities, including local surveillance, as a result of an uptick in aerial and naval (including submarine) incursions by the Russian military. The United States also sought to develop closer relations with its NATO allies in Northern Europe to better monitor the North Atlantic, including the so-called Greenland–Iceland–United Kingdom (GIUK) Gap, to guard against threatening Russian maritime activities (Jennings 2016; The White House, Office of the Press Secretary 2016). However, the Barack Obama government also continued to pledge its support for the Arctic Council and its work in understanding and combating climate change, with the growing mistrust between Moscow and Washington greatly muted at Council meetings, including at the ministerial gathering in Iqaluit, Canada, in 2015.

During the first two years of the subsequent Donald Trump government, there was originally far less indication that the Arctic was an American policy priority. This reflected more isolationist tendencies in American foreign policy as well as more brittle relations between the Trump government and other Arctic players, including Russia and others in Europe. Relations between the United States and many NATO governments came under strain as Trump's disdain for the alliance, as well as other forms of multilateral cooperation, became more visible. In June 2017, the United States withdrew from the Paris Climate Accord and attempted unsuccessfully to overturn bans on oil and gas exploration in the Alaskan National Wildlife Refuge (ANWR). There was scant coverage of the Arctic, and no mention at all of climate change, in the US Government's December 2017 National Security Strategy paper (*Seattle Times*/AP 2 December 2017; US National Security Strategy Archive 2017). This raised the question of whether and to what degree Washington would be withdrawing from Arctic affairs, and whether other powers like Russia and China might seek to fill that gap.

Yet by early 2019, the American government had begun to look more closely at the advances Beijing and Moscow had made in the region, including the partnership between the two governments, and began to reconsider its thinking about the region. By this time, Moscow had started reopening Arctic military installations along its Arctic coastline and becoming more active in air and submarine activities in the Nordic Arctic region. China signed numerous energy agreements with Russia, most prominently the Yamal liquefied natural gas (LNG) enterprise in Siberia, which is financially supported by the China National Petroleum Corporation (CNPC) and Beijing's Silk Road Fund. The Putin and Xi governments are enthusiastic about the NSR evolving into a vital corridor for shipping and energy trade, and there is much discussion about an evolving "Ice Silk Road" (*bingshang sichou zhilu* 冰上丝绸之路), which would include economic cooperation and further infrastructure projects, becoming further integrated into the Arctic economic system (Yao 2019).

Signs of an American backlash against a Sino–Russian Arctic partnership could be seen in an April 2019 policy paper from the US Coast Guard, which pointed to China and its growing economic presence in the Arctic. It extrapolated, without evidence, that China could readily begin to deny the United States access to the Arctic Ocean. This point was echoed the following month via the US Department of Defense's annual report to Congress on the state of the Chinese military, which again painted China as a challenger in the Arctic and attempted to link, without specifics, Beijing's growing civilian research programs in the region with the potential deployment of Chinese submarines in the Arctic Ocean (US Coast Guard April 2019; US Department of Defense 2019). The most direct criticism of China's presence in the Arctic came in a magniloquent and pugnacious policy speech by US Secretary of State Mike Pompeo at the Arctic Council's May 2019 Ministerial in Rovaniemi, Finland. Pompeo chided Beijing for developing a "near-Arctic state policy," said such an approach to Arctic affairs would gain China "exactly nothing," and pointed to both China and Russia as challengers to Arctic stability. The Chinese government largely shrugged off the remarks, and later that month Shanghai hosted an Arctic Circle forum where Chinese research and regional cooperation projects were touted along with the development of the Ice Silk Road. This suggested that Beijing considered American intransigence in the Arctic as simply a nuisance to be bypassed, especially given that several other Arctic actors, including China and the Nordic region, remained interested in engaging China in the Arctic (Lanteigne 7 May 2019; Pompeo 2019).

As it has been generally accepted that the warming effects in the Arctic are considerably more acute than in other regions, including Antarctica, and that ice erosion is exposing more of the Arctic to exploration and economic activities such as mining and drilling for fossil fuels (Jouzel et al. 2013, 223–6), two conclusions can be reached regarding the Arctic as a securitized region. First, in order to understand the parameters of Arctic security and whether this region is distinct, it is crucial to include "nontraditional" elements, including economic security, in the equation alongside material security concerns such as military strategies. Second, the Arctic can and should be examined as a distinct securitized region, albeit one that is comparatively more connected to non-Arctic states. China is the prime example of this phenomenon, given its great-power status and its ongoing attempts to develop an Arctic identity to avoid being shut out of the circumpolar North's economic opening up. It may be helpful for future studies of the sociopolitical, economic, and environmental changes in the Arctic to view it as a specific security region. Security issues have become so intertwined among political actors inside and outside the circumpolar North that it becomes advantageous to study Arctic traditional and nontraditional security issues on the regional as well as state level. As will be explained, China and Russia, from different directions but also frequently in partnership, have become especially active in shaping the idea of the Arctic as a standalone security region.

How to define Arctic security?

Recent arguments have suggested that as the Arctic becomes further globalized and more economically valuable, the region faces a higher risk of becoming militarized (Huebert 2010; Palosaari and Möller 2004; Posner 2007; Rasmussen 2015). At the same time, the popular perception of the Arctic as insulated from Southern political and security issues is being increasingly challenged by higher levels of international interest in circumpolar Northern affairs and resources, as well as the tacit spillover of specific security issues into Arctic dialogues, most notably the post-2014 Ukraine crisis (Käpylä and Mikkola 2015). Much of this debate about militarization has focused on Russia, which has been strengthening its land forces and naval presence in the Arctic.

After a long period of dormancy in the 1990s due to Russia's internal economic and political weaknesses, Moscow began to reevaluate its regional strategy at least partially out of concerns that its position there was being eroded by NATO members. This rethinking on Moscow's part included drawing up new policy documents to clarify Russia's claims in the Arctic Ocean, culminating in the infamous planting of a Russian flag underneath the North Pole in 2007 (Hønneland 2016, 47–57). This action touched off debate regarding the inevitability of a regional zero-sum game for resources and prestige. Exactly how much of this activity, including the reopening of Arctic installations and increasing naval patrols in Siberia, could be classified as offensive versus defensive is subject to debate (Dobriansky 2018). An August 2015 study suggested Moscow was seeking to build an "Ice Curtain" in the Arctic, while in May 2016 a report released by the Danish Foreign Ministry recommended discussing the creation of an Arctic security forum in light of regional Russian military activities (Conley and Rohloff 2015; Ministry of Foreign Affairs Denmark 2016). Yet, a greater examination is required regarding whether those actions can be classified as offensive, defensive, or even "swaggering" – a term used in classical international security theory to describe a display of military materiel for prestige purposes rather than for a specific strategic aim (Art 1980).

The question of hard security developments in the region does not end with Russia, as the United States and Canada have also debated increasing their military position in the Far North. For example, the United States has been increasingly concerned about an "icebreaker gap" between itself and Russia that would affect its ability to project power or maintain a constant presence in the Arctic. The United States has two aging icebreaking vessels in operation, while Russia has more than forty such ships (nuclear and diesel powered), including the record-breaking heavy nuclear icebreaker *Sibir* (Сибирь), commissioned in September 2017. Russia plans to deploy a heavy icebreaker fleet of 13 vessels by 2025 (AP, 10 April 2019; RT, 22 September 2017). The ambitious plans elucidated by the Putin government for the further development of the NSR have accelerated calls by Moscow for augmented Arctic infrastructure, including ports and increased patrols.

Non-Arctic states have also, over the past decade, developed formal Arctic economic, political, and in some cases strategic policies. These include China and other East Asian states like India, Japan, Singapore, and South Korea (Lanteigne 2017b), as well as European governments. Thus, some non-Arctic states could also develop a stronger strategic presence in the Far North in relation to their economic concerns, especially Asian governments that have been looking to the Arctic as a potential source of both commodities and faster transit routes to Western markets. For example, Japan's first Arctic policy paper, released in October 2015, included a section on the importance of the Arctic to the country's national security interests (Arctic Portal 2015). It referred to Japan's traditional role as a maritime power, emphasizing that it could ill afford to ignore a potential new maritime transit corridor given its geography and that great-power competition could significantly harm economic development along the NSR.

China, while comparatively more hesitant to openly declare its strategic aims in the Arctic, has nonetheless taken a few tentative steps to frame its Arctic policy using longer-term strategic interests. In September 2015, five Chinese naval vessels made a first-ever transit of Alaska's Aleutian Islands, sending a signal about differences between China and the United States over maritime security and acting as a reminder of Beijing's interests in maintaining a circumpolar policy despite its lack of Arctic borders. Beijing has also been moving closer to Moscow in areas of Arctic strategic policy, including the first-ever inclusion of Chinese naval vessels in Baltic Sea military drills in cooperation with Russia in July 2017 (Parameswaran 2017; Ryan and Lamothe 2015). More broadly, both great powers have expressed enthusiasm about developing deeper Arctic partnerships. In a joint statement signed by Chinese Premier Li Keqiang and Russian Prime Minister Dmitri Medvedev in mid-2017, the two governments agreed to cooperate in developing the NSR into a competitive commercial shipping route, the "Ice Silk Road" (also referred to as the "Polar Silk Road") (Xinhua, 31 August 2017). The questions are whether this will require a strong security component in order to protect local interests and whether this will help China further cement its status as a great power with essential Arctic interests.

Although hard power considerations are starting to be viewed more commonly in the Arctic, it is important to place these concerns in context. The Arctic Ocean is not a typical security region, and its security conditions are also far from typical. First, the geographic realities of the Arctic are a major impediment to hard security thinking, despite the spillover of non-Arctic security issues such as US-Russian strategic differences over Ukraine. As a result, Arctic regional differences over security will likely manifest themselves via "soft" balance-of-power behavior among Arctic and non-Arctic players. This concept is normally defined as power balancing without a military dimension and is usually undertaken through organizations and regimes (Paul 2005). The geographic and demographic realities of the Arctic strongly discourage hard power balancing or militarization. There are likely to be incidents where great-power and other non-Arctic security concerns spill over into the circumpolar North. Indeed Crimea/Ukraine is arguably acting as the "Banquo's ghost" of the region, while Arctic cooperation and securitization evolves. Yet, this is still a far cry from predictions of a sharp rise in traditional military behavior in the Arctic, even if the now-delayed Arctic boom does come about in the future. The same issues confront non-Arctic states, notably China, which has been downplaying any security dimension of its Arctic policies and has instead emphasized partnerships and bilateral/regional economic and scientific cooperation.

Second, the distinct political and legal structures of the Arctic offer one of the main reasons why soft-balancing behavior is becoming the norm in regional foreign policy among both Arctic and non-Arctic governments. Even in the case of Russia, there has been a measured approach to its security policies in the North, with military developments limited to universally accepted Russian waters and a defensive stance framed as a response to the likelihood of increased Arctic sea traffic north of Siberia, including potential Chinese/East Asian cargo transit. The ongoing diplomatic wrangling over the status of the Lomonosov Ridge, an underwater feature that partially bisects the Arctic Ocean and which has been claimed by Canada, Denmark/Greenland, and Russia as part of their continental shelves, has been difficult to resolve but has so far been viewed as a legal puzzle rather than a hard military one (Oliphant 2015).

Another example is the status of the Northwest Passage (NWP) in Northern Canada, which Ottawa considers an internal sea route but other actors, such as the United States and the European Union, view as international waters (O'Rourke 2016). During the 2019 Pompeo speech in Rovaniemi, Canadian claims to the NWP were referred to as "illegitimate," causing a diplomatic spat with the Justin Trudeau government in Ottawa. China inserted itself into this dispute in April 2016, when its government, while steering clear of commenting on the sovereignty question, announced that it was seeking to make future use of the NWP for maritime shipping in order to reduce time and fuel costs for cargo vessels traveling from China to the North American East Coast and the greater Atlantic Ocean. In August of the following year, China's main icebreaker, the *Snow Dragon* (*Xuelong* 雪龙) made its first-ever complete transit of the Northwest Passage, further underscoring Chinese interests in the waterway as a new emerging shipping route (Fife and Chase 2017; Peng 2016). Yet, as with the Lomonosov Ridge issue, there is little possibility that these disagreements could prompt a military response.

Third, the Arctic region's security concerns reflect the growing interest in the region from non-Arctic actors. There is great sensitivity about gatecrashing among some Arctic governments, especially Canada and Russia, which have traditionally been wary about their polar sovereignty, as more non-Arctic states have increased their diplomatic presence in the Far North in response to its emerging economic potential. This has especially been the case with China, which joined the Arctic Council as a formal observer in 2013 and is the largest of the non-Arctic states to have developed a distinct set of Arctic policies. China's rising power and its status as the second-largest global economy have meant that its Arctic strategies have been under more scrutiny than those of other observers. However, the potential of the Ice Silk Road has warmed Moscow considerably to the idea of China as an Arctic player. In addition to energy projects, Beijing is also interested in developing infrastructure, including rail links, ports, and communication lines that would connect China with Europe via Siberia and the RFE. Chinese shipping interests are eager to take advantage of the sea routes north of Siberia for faster maritime transit between Asia and Europe (Lanteigne and Shi 2018; Suocas 2018; Zhou 2019).

Beijing therefore has to walk a delicate political line with Russia, ensuring that Chinese interests match Moscow's as much as possible and not giving the impression that it is seeking to challenge the sovereignty of the Arctic Eight states.[1] Thus, China is stressing the opening of avenues for economic cooperation with Russia in the Arctic, especially given Western sanctions on the Putin government, as well as opportunities for educational and research cooperation. For example, one of the many announcements that came out of the April 2019 International Arctic Forum in St Petersburg, hosted by Putin himself, was the creation of a China–Russia Arctic Research and Development Center, which would act as a nexus for further joint cooperation between the two great powers in scientific realms (Shirshov Institute of Oceanography 2019).

Chinese policy in the Arctic has been largely based on attempting to maneuver between two unacceptable outcomes. One is that China pushes too hard to be included in Arctic affairs, resulting in ostracism and suspicion, especially from established Arctic powers like Russia and the United States. The other is that China's Arctic policies become too passive and the country falls victim to a "blueberry pie" (*lanmei pai* 蓝莓派) scenario in which the Arctic is cut up among the eight Arctic states, leaving non-Arctic governments like Beijing with limited access. Therefore, China has been acting as a "norm entrepreneur," promoting the concept of the Arctic as an international space that should be receptive to outside partnerships. This allows Beijing to develop a stronger presence in the region without being subject to power balancing (Lanteigne 2017a). As Arctic and non-Arctic great powers begin to brush up against each other in the region more frequently, policies have been more consistent with soft-balancing diplomatic behavior and have focused on nontraditional security concerns rather than zero-sum, hard power strategies. This does not necessarily mean, however, that the Arctic is removed from securitization trends. Both increased attention to the development of Arctic resources by regional and global actors and the intrusion of Southern security concerns into mainstream Arctic affairs are possible. Much of this debate, however, centers on how the Arctic is perceived as a region.

Regionalism processes: where does the Arctic fit?

"Regionalism," referring to the process of cooperation and identity building based on geographic contiguity, experienced a renaissance of sorts at the end of the Cold War. Many regions were "set free" by the end of bipolar rivalry, which had bisected regions, including Asia and Europe, into Soviet and Western camps (Hurrell 2007, 131). The same can be said of the Arctic, where Cold War tensions prevented it from being considered a single region as long as Russia and the West were military and ideological adversaries. With the Cold War's end, discussion and debates about the Arctic as a single region became possible. Although some institutions, such as the Arctic Council, were created as formal regimes to encourage intraregional dialogue and problem-solving, much of the post-Cold War region building in the Arctic fell into the category of functional cooperation (Fawcett 2004). This meant the creation of limited-scope agreements in specific areas, including the environment, civil defense, and human security, which involved different state and sub-state actors. Climate change in the Arctic, which has affected all of its areas, has further cemented the perception of what has been called a "we-feeling" (Deutsch et al. 1957). This underscores the Arctic as a region facing distinct nontraditional security challenges as a result of altered environmental conditions.

Regions as political actors are often studied using variations of three approaches: materialist, ideational, and behavioral (Katzenstein 2005). The *materialist* method is the most mainstream of the three, as it looks at hard geography, such as the benefits of land versus sea power, and the benefits a state may gain from its location (Till 2013, 3, 23–6). Using a materialist approach to the study of regionalism in the Arctic is straightforward. There are differing interpretations about the boundaries of the Arctic, schemes that replace the Arctic Circle with geographic and climate features such as tree-lines, isotherms, and permafrost, as well as political considerations (Keskitalo 2007; Wheeler 2010, 4–7). Nonetheless, there is little disagreement over which states are Arctic; while exact boundaries remain open to interpretation, it is possible to study the Arctic as a single region despite this ambiguity. However, with diminishing ice in the Arctic Ocean, more and more Arctic geography on land and sea is becoming accessible and economically viable for both Arctic and non-Arctic actors. This will affect local populations as well as governments, adding to the role of security in defining the region.

The second approach, employing *ideational* methods, focuses on how politics and markets shape perceptions of regions and their behavior. While regions are often created by political cooperation or rivalry, trade can also create regional identities. The Arctic Council was created in 1996, followed by the development of Track II (sub-governmental) organizations, such as the Arctic Circle conference in Reykjavík; its spinoff forums in cities including Shanghai, Singapore, and Québec City; and the Arctic Frontiers event in Tromsø. These have all contributed to deepening the political regionalization of the Arctic, especially by welcoming nongovernmental actors such as academics, Indigenous organizations, and specialists into the process. The development of Track II Arctic organizations has also allowed non-Arctic states, including China, to more effectively join debates about environmental changes, governance, and avenues of cooperation between Arctic and non-Arctic actors (Lanteigne 2018).

However, the Arctic Council has also codified the distinct status of the Arctic Eight as the primary state actors in the region. Regional regimes like the Council were heavily influenced by joint environmental concerns, which could be discussed once the Soviet Union began opening up to international dialogue in the late 1980s (Stone 2015, 23–39). The realization that the Arctic was facing specific environmental stresses, ranging from ice erosion, to greenhouse gases, to black-carbon effects, added to the developing "we must stick together" perception that underscored the Arctic as a specific region. Although no region in the international system exists in isolation, another definition of the Arctic as a region has been how non-Arctic actors have entered the region. As a result of environmental changes in the Arctic, several non-Arctic states have added the region to their lists of international priorities. One illustration of this phenomenon is the growing number of observers in the Arctic Council. As of the start of 2019, there were 13 formal governmental observers in the Council, including China, with other governments, including the European Union, seeking to gain that status.[2]

A looming question in Arctic political and strategic affairs is whether the current legal system, including the Council, can stand up to the growing level of international interest in the Arctic. Many Arctic watchers worry about so-called *black swans* in the region, referring to unpredictable events that can have far-reaching effects. The question of a possible collision between the Arctic's growing internationalization and the current parameters of Arctic governance is more of a *gray rhino* question, meaning a visible challenge that is not given enough attention until the situation becomes critical (Taleb 2007; Wucker 2016). Again, China has found itself at the forefront of this debate. Although Beijing had yet to release a formal white paper on Arctic policy, a six-point plan announced in October 2015 called for identifying the rights and responsibilities of non-Arctic states and for a multitiered approach to Arctic governance (Zhang 2019). The Ice Silk Road may be a manifestation of this idea. Beijing has been especially concerned about its place as a primary actor in the Arctic, with policy papers and speeches over the past decade referring to the country as a near-Arctic state as well as an "Arctic stakeholder" (*beiji lihaiguanxguo* 北极利害关系国) (People's Daily 22 March 2013; SIPRI 2012; Xinhua, 23 March 2013). These point to China's great-power status as well as connections between climate change in the Arctic and recent alterations to weather patterns and pollution in China (Hernández 2017).

The third approach to the study of regions, connected to the second but less rigid in scope, is a *behavioral* method, whereby regions are studied as constantly being shaped and defined in terms of their structure and their identities through day-to-day politics. Since the Arctic region has moved from relative global obscurity to far-higher visibility since the 1990s, many actors, including Indigenous populations, local governments, state governments, and regional regimes, all contribute to the definition of the Arctic. With the Arctic boom delayed indefinitely due to the fall in the prices of fossil fuels and commodities, the focus has largely shifted back to climate change and development. However, that does not diminish the question of Arctic security, as the Chinese and Russian examples have underscored. Therefore, it remains timely to contemplate the Arctic not only as a distinct region but as one being shaped by security concerns from both within and without.

Conclusions: is the Arctic now a security region?

Just as it is important not to overstate the role of hard security in current Arctic affairs, it would also be a mistake to define the Arctic through what some international security theorists have termed *asecurity* – an absence of security concerns – which would be a form of Arctic exceptionalism. The opening of the Arctic as a result of environmental change means that the region will become increasingly securitized through economics and resource diplomacy. The interconnectedness of these security concerns has prompted the need to study Arctic security using a regional level of analysis.

One option in defining the Arctic as a security region would be to use the model of "regional security complexes" (RSCs), which are "a set of units whose major processes of securitization, desecuritization, or both, are so interlinked that their security problems cannot reasonably be analyzed or resolved apart from one another" (Buzan and Wæver 2003, 44). The units involved in such studies are commonly but not always states, given the rise of multilateral organizations and other non-state actors in the international system. Commonly studied RSCs include Europe, East Asia, and the Middle East, where security concerns among the states that comprise these regions are so homogeneous that it is effective to examine these concerns on a regional as well as a state level (Diez 2005). As Buzan and Wæver's original studies of RSCs argued, such configurations are rarely static and can often be altered by political decisions and manipulation (Buzan and Waever 2003, 93–100).

However, the RSC concept is difficult to translate to the Arctic. The original work on the concept does not extend these regional complexes into the Arctic region. The Arctic Ocean is not commonly incorporated into the proposed global network of security complexes. Instead, the large space between the North American, European, and Post-Soviet RSCs in the circumpolar North is left blank, essentially a strategic *tabula rasa* rather than a security complex. The initial study briefly addressed this omission by suggesting that, in rare cases, RSCs do not coalesce because the units involved are weak and more preoccupied with domestic affairs than regional ones. Thus, the Arctic was seen as a rare case of a "null set," a place where the conditions for the development of a security complex were simply not present (Buzan and Wæver 2003, 64). Certainly, the Arctic can be defined as a coming together of different sub-regions, and it is possible to discuss the North American, Nordic, and Russian Arctic as distinct units.

Yet, climate change in the Arctic; developing regional security policies, including those of Russia; and rising international interest in the Arctic as a space of growing strategic importance from outside actors, such as Beijing, has opened up the question of whether the region should be now be considered securitized. Is there a distinct security identity on the regional level and, if so, should the Arctic be considered as a separate RSC? Because the political and economic linkages in the Arctic are weaker than in other parts of the world – again due to geography – perhaps no RSC exists at all. There is no agreed-upon measure of when a region becomes an RSC, and what the catalysts are for such a transformation to occur. However, given the growing number of traditional and nontraditional security issues that have appeared in the Arctic over the past few decades, it is fair to say that the Arctic has arrived in terms of being classified as a distinct region in the area of security studies and policymaking. The cases of Russia and China in the Arctic, and the responses of other actors such as the United States, are strong indicators that this transformation is well underway.

The composition and structure of the Arctic as a security region will be quite different from others, but the ongoing convergence of strategic concerns suggest that the Arctic will eventually be studied as a security region. The examples of Russia, a great power seeking to place its own distinct stamp on the Arctic as a security concern, and China, an outsider trying to become an insider through a multilayered policy approach to create an Arctic identity regardless of its geography, explain why the Far North is indeed an individual, distinct security region. Future Arctic studies should therefore be prepared to better factor in this regional level of analysis to understand how and why power politics has affected so many areas of the Arctic's governance and security thinking.

Notes

1 Referring to Canada, Denmark (Greenland), Finland, Iceland, Norway, Sweden, Russia and the United States.

2 As of late-2019, the observer governments in the Arctic Council were China, France, Germany, India, Italy, Japan, the Republic of (South) Korea, the Netherlands, Poland, Singapore, Spain, Switzerland and the United Kingdom.

References

Art, Robert J., 'To What Ends Military Power?,' *International Security* 4(Spring 1980): 4–35.

Borgerson, Scott G., 'The Coming Arctic Boom- As the Ice Melts, the Region Heats Up,' *Foreign Affairs* 76(July/August 2013): 76–89.

Buzan, Barry and Ole Wæver, *Regions and Powers: The Structure of International Security* (Cambridge and New York: Cambridge University Press, 2003).

'China's Arctic Policy,' *State Council Information Office of the People's Republic of China*, 26 January 2018, http://english.gov.cn/archive/white_paper/2018/01/26/content_281476026660336.htm.

Conley, Heather A. and Caroline Rohloff, 'The New Ice Curtain: Russia's Strategic Reach to the Arctic,' *Centre for Strategic and International Studies (CSIS)*, 27 August 2015, http://csis.org/files/publication/150826_Conley_NewIceCurtain_Web.pdf

'Danish Defence and Diplomacy in Times of Change: A Review of Denmark's Foreign and Security Policy,' *Ministry of Foreign Affairs of Denmark*, 1 May 2016, http://um.dk/en/foreign-policy/danish-defence-and-diplomacy-in-times-of-change/.

Deutsch, Karl W., et al. *Political Community and the North Atlantic Area: International Organization in the Light of Historical Experience* (Princeton: Princeton University Press, 1957).

Diez, Thomas. 'Turkey, the European Union and Security Complexes Revisited,' *Mediterranean Politics 10*(2)(July 2005): 167–180.

Dlouhy, Jennifer A., 'Big Oil Abandons $2.5 Billion in U.S. Arctic Drilling Rights,' *Bloomberg*, 10 May 2016, www.bloomberg.com/news/articles/2016-05-10/big-oil-abandons-2-5-billion-in-u-s-arctic-drilling-rights.

Dobriansky, Paula J., 'A Cold War in the Arctic Circle,' *Wall Street Journal*, 1 January 2018.

Fairhall, David, *Cold Front: Conflict Ahead in Arctic Waters* (Berkeley: Counterpoint, 2010).

Fawcett, Louise, 'Exploring Regional Domains: A Comparative History of Regionalism,' *International Affairs* 80(3)(May 2004): 429–446.

Fife, Robert and Steven Chase, 'Chinese Ship Making First Voyage Through Canada's Northwest Passage,' *Globe and Mail*, 31 August 2017..

Friedman, Thomas L., *The World is Flat: The Globalised World in the Twenty-First Century* (London and New York: Penguin Books, 2006).

'Full Text: Vision for Maritime Cooperation under the Belt and Road Initiative,' *Xinhua*, 20 June 2017, http://news.xinhuanet.com/english/2017-06/20/c_136380414.htm

Hernández, Javier C., 'Climate Change May Be Intensifying China's Smog Crisis,' *New York Times*, 24 March 2017.

Hønneland, Geir, *Russia and the Arctic: Environment, Identity and Foreign Policy* (London and New York: I. B. Tauris, 2016).

Huebert, Rob, 'The Newly Emerging Arctic Security Environment,' *Canadian Defence and Foreign Affairs Institute* (March 2010), https://d3n8a8pro7vhmx.cloudfront.net/cdfai/pages/41/attachments/original/1413661956/The_Newly_Emerging_Arctic_Security_Environment.pdf?1413661956.

Hurrell, Andrew, 'One World? Many Worlds? The Place of Regions in the Study of International Society,' *International Affairs 83*(1)(January 2007): 127–146.

'Japan's Arctic Policy (*Provisional English Translation*),' *Arctic Portal*, 21 October 2015, http://library.arcticportal.org/1883/.

Jennings, Gareth, 'NATO Looks to Poseidon to plug GIUK Gap Against Russian Submarines,' *IHS Jane's Defence Weekly*, 11 February 2016, www.janes.com/article/57898/nato-looks-to-poseidon-to-plug-giuk-gap-against-russian-submarines.

Jouzel, Jean, Claude Lorius and Dominique Raynaud, *The White Planet: The Evolution and Future of Our Frozen World* (Princeton: Princeton University Press, 2013).

Käpylä, Juha and Harri Mikkola, 'On Arctic Exceptionalism: Critical Reflections in the Light of the Arctic Sunrise Case and the Crisis in Ukraine,' Finnish Institute of International Affairs, FIIA Working Paper (April 2015).

Katzenstein, Peter J., *A World of Regions: Asia and Europe in the American Imperium* (Ithaca and London: Cornell University Press, 2005).

Keskitalo, Carina, 'International Region-Building: Development of the Arctic as an International Region,' *Cooperation and Conflict* 42(2)(2007): 187–205.

'Keynote Speech by Vice Foreign Minister Zhang Ming at the China Country Session of the Third Arctic Circle Assembly,' *Ministry of Foreign Affairs of the People's Republic of China*, 17 October 2015, www.fmprc.gov.cn/mfa_eng/wjbxw/t1306858.shtml.

Lanteigne, Marc, '"Have You Entered the Storehouses of the Snow?" China as a Norm Entrepreneur in the Arctic,' *Polar Record* 53(2)(March 2017a): 117–130.

Lanteigne, Marc, 'Walking the Walk: Science Diplomacy and Identity-Building in Asia-Arctic Relations,' *Jindal Global Law Review* 8(1)(April 2017b): 87–101.

Lanteigne, Marc, 'The Growing Role of "Track II" Organisations in the Arctic,' *Over the Circle*, 23 May 2018, https://overthecircle.com/2018/05/23/the-growing-role-of-track-ii-organisations-in-the-arctic/.

Lanteigne, Marc, 'The US Throws Down the Gauntlet at the Arctic Council's Finland Meeting,' *Over the Circle*, 7 May 2019, https://overthecircle.com/2019/05/07/the-us-throws-down-the-gauntlet-at-the-arctic-councils-finland-meeting/

Lanteigne, Marc and Mingming Shi, 'China Stakes Its Claim to the Arctic,' *The Diplomat*, 29 January 2018, https://thediplomat.com/2018/01/china-stakes-its-claim-to-the-arctic/.

'National Security Strategy 2017,' *National Security Strategy Archive*, December 2017, http://nssarchive.us/wp-content/uploads/2017/12/2017.pdf.

O'Rourke, Ronald, 'Changes in the Arctic: Background and Issues for Congress,' *Congressional Research Service CRS Report* 7-5700 19 January 2016.
Oliphant, Roland. 'Russia Claims Resource-Rich Swathe of Arctic Territory,' *The Telegraph*, 4 August 2015.
Palosaari, Teemu and Frank Möller, 'Security and Marginality: Arctic Europe after the Double Enlargement,' *Cooperation and Conflict* 39(3)(September 2004): 255–281.
Parameswaran, Prashanth, 'China, Russia Launch First Military Drills in Baltic Sea,' *The Diplomat*, 26 July 2017, https://thediplomat.com/2017/07/china-russia-launch-first-military-drills-in-baltic-sea/.
Paul, T.V. 'Soft Balancing in the Age of US Primacy,' *International Security* 30(1)(September 2005): 46–71.
Peng, Yining 'China Charting a New Course,' *China Daily*, 20 April 2016, www.chinadaily.com.cn/china/2016-04/20/content_24679000.htm.
People's Daily, '积极参与北极合作' ('Active Participation of Arctic Cooperation'), *People's Daily*, 22 March 2013, http://world.people.com.cn/n/2013/0322/c1002-20874313.html.
Pompeo, Michael, 'Looking North: Sharpening America's Arctic Focus – Remarks, Michael R. Pompeo, Secretary of State, Rovaniemi, Finland, May 6, 2019,' *US Department of State*, 6 May 2019, www.state.gov/secretary/remarks/2019/05/291512.htm.
Posner, Eric, 'The New Race of the Arctic,' *The Wall Street Journal*, 3 August 2007.
Rasmussen, Anders Fogh, 'The Arctic: A Place Apart,' *Harvard International Review*, 25 May 2015, http://hir.harvard.edu/the-arctic-a-place-apart/.
'Russia Launches "World's Biggest & Most Powerful" Nuclear Icebreaker,' *RT*, 22 September 2017, www.rt.com/business/404227-russia-worlds-biggest-icebreaker/
'Russia Reinforcing Permanent Troops Group Deployed in Arctic- Defence Minister,' *TASS*, 29 January 2016, http://tass.ru/en/defense/853149.
Ryan, Missy and Dan Lamothe, 'Chinese Naval Ships Came Within 12 Nautical Miles of American Soil,' *Washington Post*, 4 September 2015.
Seattle Times/Associated Press, 'Senate Votes to Open Up Alaska's Arctic National Wildlife Refuge to Oil Drilling,' 2 December 2017, www.seattletimes.com/seattle-news/environment/senate-opens-up-alaskas-arctic-national-wildlife-refuge-to-oil-drilling/.
Shirshov Institute of Oceanography, 'Россия и Китай начнут совместные исследования в Арктике' ['Russia and China Will Begin Joint Research in the Arctic'], *Russian Academy of Sciences*, 10 April 2019, https://ocean.ru/index.php/novosti-left/novosti-instituta/item/1311-rossiya-i-kitaj-v-arktike
SIPRI, 'China Defines Itself as a "Near-Arctic State"', *Stockholm International Peace Research Institute*, 10 May 2012, www.sipri.org/media/pressreleases/2012/arcticchinapr.
Stone, David P., *The Changing Arctic Environment: The Arctic Messenger* (New York: Cambridge University Press, 2015), 23–39.
Suocas, Janne, 'China Pledges $10bn to Silk Road, Arctic Projects in Russia,' *GB Times*, 13 June 2018, https://gbtimes.com/china-pledges-10bn-to-silk-road-arctic-projects-in-russia
Taleb, Nassim Nicholas, *The Black Swan: The Impact of the Highly Improbable* (London and New York: Allen Lane/Penguin, 2007).
Till, Geoffrey, *Seapower: A Guide for the Twenty-First Century* Third edition (New York and London: Routledge, 2013).
'United States Coast Guard, Arctic Strategic Outlook,' *US Coast Guard*, April 2018, https://assets.documentcloud.org/documents/5973939/arctic-strategic-outlook-apr-2019.pdf.
US Department of Defense, 'Annual Report to Congress: Military and Security Developments Involving the People's Republic of China,' May 2019, https://media.defense.gov/2019/May/02/2002127082/-1/-1/1/2019_CHINA_MILITARY_POWER_REPORT.pdf.
'US-Nordic Leaders' Joint Statement,' *The White House, Office of the Press Secretary*, 13 May 2016, www.whitehouse.gov/the-press-office/2016/05/13/us-nordic-leaders-summit-joint-statement.
'Vladimir Putin Boasts of Growing Nuclear Icebreaker Fleet as he Outlines Russia's Ambitious Arctic Expansion Plans,' *Associated Press*, 10 April 2019.
Wheeler, Sara, *The Magnetic North: Travels in the Arctic* (London: Vintage, 2010).
Wucker, Michele, *Gray Rhino: How to Recognise and Act of the Obvious Dangers We Ignore* (New York: St Martin's Press, 2016).
Xinhua, '专访:中国愿为北极地区可持续发展作出贡献 (Interview: China Willing to Contribute to Sustainable Development in the Arctic),' *Xinhua*, 23 March 2013, www.gov.cn/jrzg/2013-03/23/content_2360686.htm

Xinhua, '"钢铁丝路"与"冰上丝路"：锻造中欧贸易新通道 [The "Steel Wire Road" and the "Ice Silk Road": Forging the New Channel of Sino-European Trade]', *Xinhua*, 31 August 2017, http://news.xinhuanet.com/fortune/2017-08/31/c_1121579721.htm.

Yao, Zhang, 'Ice Silk Road Framework Welcomed by Countries, Sets New Direction for Arctic Cooperation,' *Global Times*, 7 April 2019, www.globaltimes.cn/content/1144928.shtml.

Zhen, Liu, 'Could China's "Experimental" Ship be the World's Biggest Nuclear-Powered Icebreaker?', *South China Morning Post*, 20 March 2019.

Zhou, Laura, 'Russia Seeks Chinese Support in Developing Arctic Shipping Routes, Promising Long-Term Gas Supplies in Return,' *South China Morning Post*, 18 April 2019.

27

JAPAN AND ARCTIC SECURITY

Wrenn Yennie-Lindgren

Introduction

Japan has a long history of Arctic engagement, which over the past decade has developed at a faster and more integrated pace than ever before, especially in the political field. In 2009, Japan applied for observer status to the Arctic Council (AC) and commissioned its icebreaker *Shirase* for polar research. The following year, the Ministry of Foreign Affairs (MOFA) established an Arctic Task Force. In 2011, a Japanese shipping company sent a vessel through the Northeast Passage for the first time. Two years later, in 2013, Japan appointed its first Arctic Ambassador, drafted an Ocean Policy that included the Arctic, and was granted observer status at the Arctic Council's Ministerial Meeting in Kiruna, Sweden. In late 2015, the Japanese Cabinet Office released Japan's first Arctic Policy and elevated Japan's science diplomacy initiatives on the Arctic region. This Policy came to fruition 95 years after Japan's first encounter with Arctic politics, when it was one of the original signatories to the Spitsbergen (Svalbard) Treaty (1920), and nearly 25 years after Japan established a research station on Svalbard (1991). Japan's deeper involvement in Arctic issues has coincided with the entrance of other Asian states, at both formal and informal levels, into Arctic affairs (Solli et al. 2013).

These recent notable developments have all informed Japan's perception of how challenges and opportunities in the Arctic region will unfold. They have also provided ample opportunity for Japan to further define its identity as a maritime state that is engaged in Arctic affairs and to outline Japanese priorities, contributions, and interests in the region. While Japan acknowledges its status as a non-Arctic state, it still manifests interest and involvement in the security and safety of the High North. This chapter focuses on what Arctic security means to Japan and how Japan handles the security dimension in its three-spoke approach to the Arctic, involving economic, political, and scientific factors. The chapter favors a broad definition of security, in which traditional and nontraditional security issues are both given weight. In the Arctic context, traditional security issues have focused on military defense, particularly on the protection of national borders and maritime and nonmaritime sovereignty claims, while nontraditional issues have been more concerned with economic, cultural, social, and environmental issues (Greaves and Lackenbauer 2016). Concern about nontraditional issues became more pronounced in the post-Cold War period with the onset of globalization.

As these two security lenses came to coexist on a global level, security framings in the Arctic underwent notable, albeit gradual, change. In today's Arctic, security can be just as much about military threats as it can be about icequakes or mental health issues affecting Arctic populations. This chapter considers Japan's Arctic security lens, which shares many features with the eight Arctic states – Norway, Sweden, Denmark, Finland, Iceland, Russia, Canada, United States) – but is less focused on traditional security matters. Although Japan's Arctic Policy does not deny a traditional type of security framing, in practice Japan's approach to the High North emphasizes sustainability and nontraditional security aspects, especially environmental issues related to climate change.

The chapter begins by addressing the changing understandings of what Arctic security entails. What are the historic and contemporary understandings of Arctic security? It then embarks on a discussion of Japan's three-pronged approach to the Arctic, involving political, scientific, and economic features, demonstrating how security fits into traditional and nontraditional, and into national and international levels. How does Japan convey its position as a non-Arctic state concerned about security developments in the Arctic? This analysis is based on recent statements and activities stemming from Japan's official Arctic Policy (2015), as well as developments in the political, research, and business sectors since 2008. The chapter concludes that, while traditional security issues in the Arctic are not the explicit framing of Japan's Arctic Policy and engagement, they do play an implicit role both on paper and in practice.

Changing security understandings in the Arctic

The Cold War was a major divide in how security in the Arctic is understood and framed. Before and during the Cold War, its conception was largely embedded in the Arctic architecture as a matter of national security and sovereignty (Greaves and Lackenbauer 2016). However, as the pace of globalization picked up in the post-Cold War era, a broader and deeper conception of security developed in the Arctic. Conventional ideas about security were extended by the advent of nontraditional security challenges, which arise primarily out of nonmilitary sources, are often transnational in nature, and threaten the survival and well-being of people and states (e.g. climate change, natural disasters, food shortages) (Caballero-Anthony 2007). This conceptual expansion affected the framing of Arctic security as well, broadening it from being largely about sovereignty issues to being increasingly linked to humans and their environment (Bailes 2015). The greater understanding of and concerns about nontraditional issues affecting the Arctic on several levels: economic (e.g. sustainable development), social (e.g. mental health risks), environmental (e.g. climate change) and cultural (e.g. Indigenous communities' livelihoods) gradually resulted in new mappings of the security landscape in the Polar North. The years following the end of the Cold War were also a time when the Arctic came to be reframed as a location for cross-border cooperation, with the establishment of governance structures like the Arctic Council (Wilson Rowe 2018: 3). This development created spaces and encounters for discussing Arctic security issues.

It would be misleading, however, to give the impression that there is one cohesive understanding of what Arctic security is or entails. The Arctic is not a single holistic place (Greaves and Lackenbauer 2016) but is rather a diverse environment where the interests of various groups – littoral states, Indigenous peoples, non-Arctic states, etc. – meet. Arctic security is thus difficult to generalize about given the various national and non-national understandings of what security entails and how it should be framed. Using the word *security* can itself be ambiguous, as its general connotation points to traditional security matters. Some have proposed a reframing that would shift the discourse from "Arctic security" to "Arctic stewardship," thus emphasizing sustainability over national security (Griffiths 2011). The argument is that if a certain degree of sustainability in the Arctic environment is not managed, then national security becomes a non-issue (see Young 2011: xxxvi). Since Japan's first encounter with the Arctic, when it became a signatory of the Svalbard Treaty in 1920, security issues in the region have undergone great change with regard to how they are framed, understood, and addressed. What does Arctic security mean to Japan and how is it actualized in its three-spoke Arctic engagement?

Japan's three-spoke Arctic engagement

Over the past decade, the pace of Japan's Arctic engagement has increased in the political, economic, and science sectors. Ohnishi (2014) described Japan's Arctic Policy evolution as developing from a period of less-strategic *involvement* in the 1990s to concerted, tactical *engagement* from the 2000s to the present, outlining the three pillars of Japan's Arctic engagement: diplomacy, science, and business (Ohnishi 2015). Japan's veteran status in Arctic engagement has allowed Tokyo access to the region's fast-developing scientific, economic, and political architecture. It has genuine and growing political and economic interests as well as long-standing scientific interests in the Arctic, but also recognizes that these interests are best addressed via long-term strategies in the region. Of the five Asian states engaged in Arctic politics, Japan has the longest tradition in the region and has maintained its reputation for making positive contributions by mobilizing and upgrading its diplomacy, business undertakings, and science activities in recent years. These activities often involve dialogue concerning security factors (see Figure 27.1) and have been paralleled by the Government of Japan's development of more formal strategies in three broad policy areas: ocean policy, science and technology diplomacy, and Arctic policy (Ohnishi 2016).

Japan's burgeoning Arctic diplomacy (2009–present)

The political pillar of Japan's Arctic engagement is arguably the most comprehensive, as it often encompasses scientific and economic engagements. The four Japanese ministries tasked with the coverage of Arctic issues – the Ministry of Foreign Affairs (MOFA), the Ministry of Education, Culture, Sports, Science and Technology (MEXT), the Ministry of Land, Infrastructure and Transport (MLIT), and the Ministry of Economy, Trade and Industry (METI) – have upgraded their engagement on topics relating to Arctic politics, science, and business by activating bilateral, trilateral (i.e., Japan–China–ROK), and multilateral (e.g. the Asia–Europe Meeting (ASEM)) channels to develop and communicate a more formal national strategy concerning Arctic affairs. The Headquarters for Ocean Policy, headed by the Prime Minister and established in 2007, serves as the coordinating body for Japan's Arctic Policy. Both hard and soft security issues are addressed through diplomacy on Arctic-specific, (e.g. search and rescue in the Northern Sea Route), and Arctic-encompassing, (e.g. freedom of the seas, climate change) issues.

The recent political momentum for Japan's Arctic engagement began in 2009 with Japan's decision to apply for observer status in the Arctic Council, an initiative largely led by MOFA (Ohnishi 2016) and likely part-motivated by the applications of other Northeast Asian states (Jakobsen and Lee 2016). Japan's application was bolstered by internal developments such as: the establishment of an Arctic Task Force (2011), the appointment of

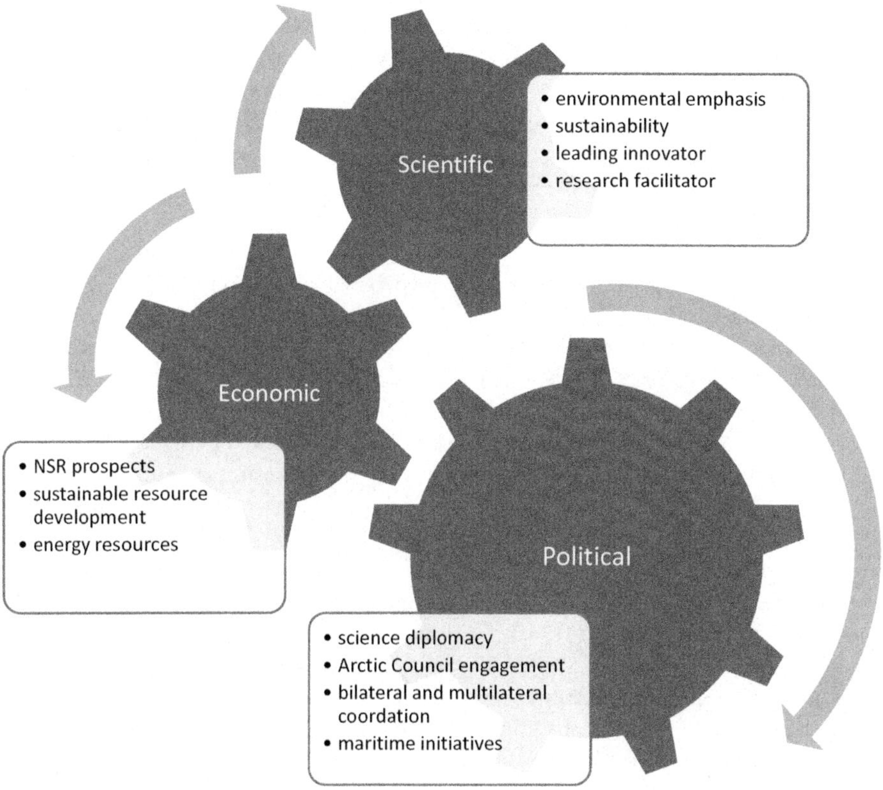

Figure 27.1 Japan's three-spoke Arctic engagement and security factors

an Arctic Ambassador (2013), and Arctic-related measures at the Cabinet level laid out in the Basic Plan on Ocean Policy (2013) – a document that emanated from the Headquarters for Ocean Policy at the Prime Minister's Office, but which was the product of cross-ministerial coordination on issues. Japan was granted observer status at the Council's ministerial meeting in Kiruna, Sweden in 2013, along with China, South Korea, Singapore, India, and Italy.

In the years following Japan's successful bid, Japanese engagement with Arctic issues continued to increase. The Government of Japan (GOJ) assessed its Arctic-related activities with the intention of seeing where they stood and where they could develop. This period of information and resource collection emanated into a formal Arctic Policy after MOFA proposed the idea of a Japanese Arctic Policy at an intergovernmental meeting on ocean issues. The Policy took approximately one year to formulate and was released rather abruptly at the 2015 Arctic Circle in Reykjavík. Given its purpose of implementing the specifics of Japan's Arctic engagement, the Policy paper stood out for its linkage of Arctic affairs, including economic, environmental, and institutional issues, to national security interests.

Although the Arctic is not a major priority in Japan's foreign policy, recent administrations, especially the Shinzō Abe government, have actively elevated and enhanced Japan's international visibility, status, and influence. Japan's Arctic engagement has been part of this effort. The 2017 edition of Japan's *Diplomatic Bluebook* (外交青書, *gaikōseisho*), an annual policy statement published by MOFA, describes a Japanese foreign policy that "takes a panoramic perspective of the world map" (MOFA 2017b). This perspective covers Japan's immediate neighborhood – Asia and Oceania – as well as North America, Latin America, Europe, the Middle East, Russia, and Africa, and has also extended its coverage to include developments in Japan's Arctic activities. With an explicit reference to security, the *Diplomatic Bluebook* acknowledges that the Arctic is an area of great resources but that the region faces challenges relating to the impact of human activity on the environment:

> Environmental changes in the Arctic, caused by global warming (melting of sea ice, permafrost, ice sheet, and glaciers, etc.) have brought about new opportunities to the international community, such as utilization of the Arctic Sea Routes and resource development. On the other hand, it has also posed various challenges, such as the acceleration of global warming, its negative impacts on the vulnerable environment of the Arctic, and potential changes in the international security environment, resulting in mounting attention by the international community.
>
> *(MOFA 2017b: 280)*

Beyond the *Diplomatic Bluebook*, Japan's scientific presence on Svalbard and engagement in the Arctic is frequently underlined in Japanese ministry documents. For instance, the Arctic was mentioned in the GOJ's 2013 Basic Plan on Ocean Policy, which emphasized sea resource development (MOFA 2013). The updated 2018 Ocean Policy, which has shifted its focus to "comprehensive maritime security," for the first time included Arctic Policy as one of its main measures (Cabinet Office 2018). In addition to government documents, the Japanese media has demonstrated an increased interest in the topic, often publishing on environmental issues and resource extraction in the Arctic and the opening of the Arctic to non-Arctic states.

While no concrete initiative has been framed, related to hard or soft security in Japan's Arctic Policy, there are three specific initiatives: (a) research and development, (b) international cooperation, and (c) sustainable use. Each of these broadly addresses security through the promotion of collaborative research, political dialogue, and the development of a sustainable Arctic environment. Within the political realm, international cooperation is emphasized. Prime Minister Shinzō Abe, who before reassuming the prime ministerial role in December 2012 was the chair of Japan's nonpartisan Arctic study group, has elevated discussion of Japanese interests in the Arctic at bilateral and multilateral summits as well as at domestic political fora.[1] At the Asia–Europe Meeting (ASEM) meeting in October 2014, Abe held an inaugural summit with the Nordic Baltic Eight countries (NB8 – five Arctic states included), at which polar research was an agenda item. At this meeting, it was agreed that the Arctic was an area of "high potential" but also one that is environmentally fragile and would require cooperation on various issues (MOFA 2014). Japan emphasized the importance of collaboration in Arctic research and highlighted its interests in pursuing collaboration by utilizing Japan's scientific technology.

In addition to discussing and promoting Japan's Arctic engagement within multilateral settings, the topic has received increasing attention domestically. Nevertheless, attention to Arctic issues is still relatively limited compared to Japan's Antarctic initiatives, which engage in many more activities and benefit from more resources. The increased political focus on the Arctic can be attributed to a stronger lobby from the Ocean Policy Research Institute (OPRI),[2] a think tank and lobbying organization for the Japanese shipping and manufacturing industries, which has conducted research on the Arctic, specifically on the feasibility of the Northern Sea Route (NSR) as a transport route. After being granted Arctic Council Observer status in 2013, the GOJ set up an inter-ministerial committee on the Arctic (Liaison Committee among Ministries and Agencies on Various Issues Related to the Arctic). In January 2014, the Ocean Policy Research Institute began a new project with MLIT – one of Japan's most active ministries on Arctic issues – and MEXT to look into the construction of a new icebreaker for Arctic observation. Japan's *Shirase* icebreaker is owned by the Japanese Self-Defense Forces, and so, due to legal restrictions, is only able to act as a supply vessel. Hence, this vessel is deployed primarily in the Antarctic.

Japan's Arctic research initiatives

Japan positions itself as a maritime state with an extended polar research tradition that is able and willing to make important contributions to Arctic scientific cooperation. The country had an early start in the Arctic as one of only 14 countries that recognized Norway's sovereignty over the archipelago of Svalbard when it signed the Spitsbergen Treaty in 1920. Japan began conducting polar research, primarily in the Antarctic, in 1957 and reinforced its scientific interests by establishing Japan's National Institute of Polar Research (NIPR) in 1973 (Ohnishi 2016: 173). In 1990, Japan formally became part of the Arctic research community when it joined the International Arctic Science Committee (IASC) and also launched NIPR's Center for Arctic Research. A year later, in 1991, it established its Ny Ålesund research center on Svalbard.

According to the GOJ, the primary aim of Japan's Arctic engagement is to understand and protect the natural environment. This is reflected by Japan's strong and long-standing scientific engagement in the region. Creating a sustainable environment and combating climate change are at the forefront of Japan's Arctic policies and scientific research activities (MOFA 2018a). As expressed in the government's Arctic Policy:

> Japan is called upon to recognize both the Arctic's latent possibilities and its vulnerability to environmental changes, and to play a leading role for sustainable development in the Arctic in the international community, with foresight and policy based on science and technology that Japan has advantage in order to achieve sustainable development [*sic*].
>
> *(Kantei 2015a)*

Japan conducts research on a number of natural science topics, such as ocean acidification. In working to elucidate the impact of ocean acidification on marine ecosystems, Japan has deployed its research vessel *Mirai* to the Arctic Ocean and has also conducted a series of underwater survey exercises, utilizing the autonomous underwater vehicle (AUV) *Urashima*. The *Urashima* is an autonomous robot for deep-sea exploration that was developed by the Japanese Agency for Marine-Earth Science and Technology (JAMSTEC). Japan launched a project for developing an Arctic Navigation System and is working to develop a new AUV capable of conducting surveys under the harsh conditions of the Arctic Ocean. In addition to ocean acidification, Japan has conducted cutting-edge research on greenhouse gas observations in high-latitude regions including the Arctic, focusing on black carbon and methane, and has contributed to the Arctic Council working group on Arctic Monitoring and Assessment Program (AMAP).

The Japanese government has manifested its commitment to promoting research and collaboration on a sustainable Arctic environment through international initiatives that showcase advanced Japanese technologies and also more general Arctic engagement. For instance, in October 2014 the Innovation for Cool Earth Forum (ICEF), an annual international forum that assembles experts from the public, academic, and business sectors, was established. It features Japanese innovation in the energy and environmental fields. Japan has also hosted large international conferences and summits, such as the annual Arctic Science Summit Week (ASSW) in 2015, which was an occasion for scientists, students, policymakers, and other professionals from all over the world to facilitate research efforts by coordinating, collaborating, and cooperating in various areas of Arctic science. In 2015, the Arctic Challenge for Sustainability (ArCS), a four-and-a-half-year project funded by MEXT, was launched to:

> elucidate the changes in the climate and environment, clarify their effects on human society, and provide accurate projections and environmental assessments for internal and external stakeholders, so that they can make appropriate decisions on the sustainable development of the Arctic region.
>
> *(ArCs 2017)*

In 2017, MOFA hosted a Japan Night at the high-level Arctic Circle meeting in Reykjavík, featuring Japan's Arctic research alongside Japanese entertainment and cuisine. In November 2020, Tokyo will hold the inaugural Arctic Circle Japan Forum, which will coincide with The Third Arctic Science Ministerial Meeting, to be co-hosted with Iceland.

In his keynote speech at the 2018 Arctic Circle, former Japanese Foreign Minister Tarō Kōno introduced the idea of an "Ideal Arctic," comprised of three elements: (1) understanding and responding to the mechanism of environmental changes at an international level; (2) pursuing sustainable economic activities that respect the Arctic's livelihood; (3) ensuring the rule of law and promoting international cooperation in a peaceful and ordely manner (MOFA 2018b). Foreign Minister Kōno expressed Japan's will and determination to cooperate with Arctic stakeholders in realizing the common vision and to engage actively in rule-making in the region and emphasized that Japan attached importance to the scientific aspect (MOFA 2018c). Furthermore, at the June 2019 meeting at the Headquarters for Ocean Policy, the main coordinating body for Japan's Arctic Policy, Prime Minister Abe urged the acceleration of Japanese research on the Arctic, especially concerning the utilization of the Arctic Sea, and recognized the growing importance of the Arctic as "the next frontier" (Kantei 2019). Given the country's reputation for high research standards and technology leadership, the Arctic is an arena where Japan has made and will continue to make significant scientific contributions.

Northeast Asian trilateral engagement on Arctic issues

Japan's increased political engagement in the Arctic has in part been instigated by the growing attention paid to the Arctic by its regional neighbors, China and South Korea. In 2015, the three countries established a trilateral high-level dialogue on Arctic issues that coincided with the broader Japan–ROK–China trilateral meeting. The high-level dialogue took place for the first time in April 2016 in Seoul and later in June 2017 in Tokyo, June 2018 in Shanghai, and June 2019 in Busan. The Arctic trilateral brings together the countries' respective delegations led by Arctic Ambassadors and Special Representatives as well as the Trilateral Arctic Expert Group

(TAEG), which facilitates trilateral cooperation by identifying areas of mutual interest (MOFA Korea 2019). The aim of the dialogue is "to engage in further discussions to address common challenges over the Arctic with a particular focus on measures to strengthen scientific cooperation among the three countries in order to contribute to the efforts of the international community" (MOFA 2017a). The 2017 dialogue's joint statement emphasizes nontraditional aspects of Arctic security, in particular the environmental impact of climate change in the Arctic:

> The Arctic is experiencing environmental and climate change faster than any other part of the world. These significant changes present the international community with both urgent challenges and opportunities. Climate change is affecting the vulnerable Arctic ecosystems, the livelihoods of local inhabitants and indigenous communities on a global scale, while the melting of ice brings new opportunities such as natural resources and marine fisheries in the Arctic as well as the opening of sea routes. In particular, it is indispensable for the international community to ensure the protection and preservation of the fragile marine environment of the Arctic Ocean, and maintain peace, stability, and constructive cooperation based on a rule-based maritime order.
>
> *(MOFA 2017a)*

The entrance of new actors and interests into the region has given the Arctic a profile that the field of international relations might frame as a geopolitical power struggle. Empirical studies show, however, that among the East Asian observer states, the Arctic is not a playground for traditional power politics (Solli et al. 2013). Although the Asian states have done little to coordinate their Arctic Policy initiatives among themselves, their approach to Arctic politics has largely focused on the same issues. They are interested in economic opportunities and environmental issues: primarily climate change and other issues that lend themselves to cooperative scientific research. In addition to developing Japan's own domestic scientific capabilities and competence, Japan's research efforts often promote joint research with Arctic and non-Arctic states. In 2015, NIPR reorganized its Arctic Environment Research Center to enhance international collaborations. NIPR has also signed memorandums of understanding with numerous international counterparts, including the Korean Polar Research Institute (KOPRI) and the Polar Research Institute of China (PRIC).

Although Japan is one of the most scientifically advanced and experienced Asian countries in the field of Arctic research (perhaps even more advanced and experienced than South Korea or China), its research activities are hindered by its lack of icebreaker capabilities. This barrier to research has led to inter-Asian collaboration between Japan and other non-Arctic states in the Arctic. For instance, Japanese researchers joined South Korea's polar research expedition on the Korean scientific icebreaker *Araon* in 2012. In this way, the Arctic has become a place where Asian states can seek out scientific research alliances with their regional neighbors. There is opportunity in the Arctic for cooperation and collaboration among states where historical rivalry, war memories, and territorial disputes plague their bilateral relations.

The Northern Sea Route

While China's presence and economic interests in the Arctic have arguably been covered the most in international media in recent years, especially since 2013 (see Lanteigne 2017), the involvement of other East Asian states has also increased. Although economic motives have been cited in the media as Japan's primary interest in the region, shipping routes from the High North to Japan have been deemed unprofitable in the short- to mid-term by commercial actors. Equipment is costly, risk is high, and efficiency is debatable. Representatives of major Japanese shipping companies have stressed the lack of profitability and cost savings associated with the route. However, shipping companies are closely monitoring developments and regularly assess the NSR's viability as a transport route. Russian law requires that users have their own icebreakers (Japan does not at present) and potential tariffs involved in the route are unclear. Furthermore, there are infrastructure challenges, such as not enough refuge ports, that need to be overcome before the route can be deemed economically attractive. In Japan, business and industry initiatives often play a critical role in motivating government efforts. As one interviewee explained during a discussion of the viability of the NSR as a shipping passage for Japan, "the business community comes first. If they have the demand, the government will pave the way."[3]

Government actors, such as Japan's Arctic Ambassador and MLIT, the lead ministry on issues relating to the NSR, are also interested in the route and seek to evaluate and monitor its commercial viability, particularly as it relates to energy security and liquefied natural gas (LNG) transportation from Norway and Russia. While traditional security concerns have a modest to nonexistent place in Japanese public thinking about the Arctic (Solli et al. 2013), Japan's energy security concerns are actively debated. Japan is an energy-hungry country that relies on imports for over 80% of its energy needs, so it is understandable that there is interest. In the post-Fukushima environment, the country is seeking to diversify its mix of energy sources and is likely to rely less on its traditional suppliers in the Middle East and more on energy resources within the Asia–Pacific area (Yennie-Lindgren 2018). In light of this, energy sources in the Russian Arctic and the possible development of new petroleum fields in the Arctic are of interest to Japan.

Japan and Arctic security: the nexus of national and international concerns

The traditional versus nontraditional security divide is important for understanding how Japan approaches security in the Arctic, as is the framing of Arctic security versus Arctic sustainability. Although Japan primarily emphasizes nontraditional Arctic security issues, it remains interested in traditional security concerns. Japan identifies as a maritime nation and has actively used this identity to further its Arctic activities and to promote and engage in important political discussions revolving around the United Nations Convention on the Law of the Sea (UNCLOS) and the International Maritime Organization's (IMO) Polar Code. As a country that relies on sea lines of communication and has multiple territorial disputes of its own (e.g. Senkaku/Diaoyu islands with China, Takeshima/Dokdo with South Korea, and Northern Territories/Kuril islands with Russia), Japan is an especially staunch supporter of international frameworks related to sovereignty issues (Yennie Lindgren and Lindgren 2017). Japan recognizes UNCLOS as the fundamental legal framework for the Arctic and believes that upholding it as well as the Ilulissat Declaration is important for Arctic security. For Japan, Arctic security is viewed as a long-term issue, while safety issues, namely safety for operators, search-and-rescue missions, and oil-spill response, have been the predominant short-term focus (Ocean Policy Research Foundation 2012).

With this backdrop to Japan's comprehensive interests in the Arctic, Japan's Arctic Policy was drafted in 2015. While the Policy emphasized nontraditional security issues, the traditional features of Japan's ideas about Arctic security were also explicitly outlined, with national security being one of the seven Arctic issues comprising Japan's basic perspective (Kantei 2015a). The Policy's paragraph on national security links domestic concerns to the international sphere by emphasizing risks in the Arctic that could concern non-Arctic states, such as Japan:

> There is a risk that factors such as opening of new shipping route(s) [sic] and the development of natural resources may become a cause for new friction among states. It is important to prevent moves to strengthen (the) military presence in the region from leading to tension and confrontations. At the same time, while recognizing that these developments may become factors that change the international security environment, not only in the Arctic but for the surrounding states including Japan, it is necessary to pay close attention to moves by the states concerned and also to promote cooperation with the Arctic and other states.
>
> *(Kantei 2015a)*[4]

This part of the Arctic Policy, which was penned by Japan's ministries that focus on foreign affairs and defense, was added to the document in part due to concern about the Russian military build-up in the region and how it could affect Japan's sea area (Bering Sea and Sea of Japan).[5] Military developments in Japan's surrounding waters occupy a large part of Japanese security thinking, as they could affect access to both existing and future sea lanes (Hyodo and Kanda 2015; Lanteigne 2017).

In May 2012, Russian President Vladimir Putin issued an armed forces modernization and improvement decree that aimed to boost naval presence, especially in the Arctic and the Far East. Since the decree, Russia has been intensifying its sea power at both ends of the NSR (across the northern coast of Russia from the Arctic Ocean to the Sea of Okhotsk) with its strategic interests of securing the sea route and developing the region's natural resources in mind (Hirose 2016; Hyodo 2014). This development has been cautiously followed by Japan, as it not only concerns its territorial dispute with Russia over the Northern Territories (Hoppo Ryodo), which are located along the NSR, but also access to the sea lanes and economic resources, such as energy, that are vital to the Japanese economy (Yennie-Lindgren 2018).

The GOJ in particular has been following Russian military activity around Matua Island (part of the Kuril islands/Northern Territories), which was previously occupied by Japan and could become a focal point for Russian airpower in the future (Hyodo in Fukumoto 2017). Japan's Arctic Surveillance Force, operating under the Maritime Self-Defense Force, is responsible for monitoring developments in the Arctic waters around Japan. There have been calls for deeper cooperation between Japan and the United States – its security ally – when it comes to monitoring and responding to increased activity and power projection in the Arctic (see for instance Asari 2012; Kaneda 2012). Japan further seeks to reinforce cooperation between the Japanese Coast Guard (JCG) and its counterparts in Arctic states to promote a rule-based martime order in the Arctic (MOFA 2018b). Recent analysis forecasts that Japan's increased maritime activities in the Arctic will likely translate into more military activity and naval operations in the waters around northern Japan (Jakobson and Lee 2016: 133). The widening scope of Russia's military polar operations and capabilities has instigated a more strategic-minded approach to the Arctic by not only Japan but also other Asian states involved in the Arctic, namely China and South Korea (Jakobson and Lee 2016: 130). Japan recognizes that Arctic security issues often encompass bilateral security matters and thus considers the Arctic Ambassadorship to be a position that is complementary to Japan's engagement on security issues within both Arctic dialogues and bilateral relations.[6]

The inclusion of a paragraph on national security issues and concerns about the safety and viability of international cooperation in the Arctic demonstrates that traditional security is still part of Japan's Arctic Policy. However, when contextualized in the broader security situation that Japan faces, such a framing is neither alarmist nor surprising. Rather, it can be argued that Japan's Arctic Policy is relatively less security-oriented than are other Japanese foreign policy debates, such as over North Korea's nuclear program and ballistic missiles (Lindgren 2018). National security and the Russian military build-up are neither the priority issues for Japan in the Arctic nor the focus of Japan's nine-page Arctic Policy paper, only a single paragraph of which refers to national security. Japan's Arctic priorities are aligned with its areas of strong competency, namely science and technology and recognition of the fragile Arctic environment. When Japanese academics and experts discuss and present on Japan's Arctic Policy in international fora, nontraditional issues are usually emphasized and traditional security concerns are less in focus.[7] Environmental issues, particularly those related to climate change, are the crux of Japan's Arctic Policy, security understanding, and approach. Thus, nontraditional or soft security issues take priority in Japan's Arctic activities and engagement.[8]

Conclusion

There are various understandings of what Arctic security issues (both traditional and nontraditional) consist of and how they should be prioritized and addressed. The post-Cold War shifts from a sole focus on state-level security to individual-level security and from maritime sovereignty issues to maritime sea-life protection issues due to climate change have resulted in a common understanding that both traditional and nontraditional issues make up the Arctic security environment. Security and sustainability should not be understood as static but rather as moving targets, temporally and thematically, that have undergone notable change as the world has globalized.

As Japan has upgraded its Arctic profile in recent years by becoming an observer in the Arctic Council (2013) and releasing its first Arctic Policy (2015), it has taken a more explicit stance on security issues affecting the Arctic region. The clause on national security in Japan's Arctic Policy acknowledges that changes in the remote Arctic space can have international implications. Japan's approach to Arctic security is guided by a combination of traditional and nontraditional concerns, yet ultimately nontraditional and environmental issues remain at the forefront of its Arctic policies and activities. Although shipping opportunities through the Northern Sea Route and natural resources motivated the development of its Arctic Policy, Japan recognizes the significant challenges that the changing Arctic environment, its flora, and people face (e.g. climate change, Indigenous peoples' livelihoods, and migratory birds). Japan primarily aims to contribute to the region's sustainability through political, economic, and scientific endeavors.

It is often said that the Arctic is a meeting place for different parts of the globe. This is true, however the countries from each of these regions meet on different terms and in different capacities. For Japan, this capacity has primarily been, and will likely remain in the short term, largely scientific, but with time and the necessary conditions it could develop into a more economic role. Although Japan's Arctic political engagement has increased significantly in recent years, given the imminent security challenges it faces in its immediate neighborhood (e.g. territorial disputes with China, South Korea, and Russia, and the nuclear issue on the Korean peninsula), and domestically in terms of its economic and demographic security, Arctic security issues by themselves do not rank high on Japan's overall foreign policy agenda. Nevertheless, there is notable synergy between Arctic security issues and broader, high-priority foreign policy issues (e.g. freedom of the seas, peaceful coexistence, environmental sustainability) that will continue to dominate Japanese dialogue and activity. Tokyo's current approach to Arctic security remains cautious, forward-looking, and linked to broader security developments in its immediate neighborhood and beyond.

Notes

1 For instance, in 2016 the multi-ministry Science Diplomacy Study Group within the Japanese Government held two sessions on the Arctic.
2 Formerly known as the Ocean Policy Research Foundation (OPRF).
3 Interview with bureaucrat, MOFA, Tokyo, June 2015.
4 In the Cabinet Office's simultaneous launching of the Arctic Policy, Prime Minister Abe gave a similar explanation for the reasoning behind the policy, stating "Rapid environmental change in the Arctic in recent years is causing environmental problems on a worldwide scale, such as global warming; making the Arctic Sea Route and resource development possible; and bringing about changes in the security environment. These issues pose new challenges for the international community that are deeply relevant to Japan's national interests" (Kantei 2015b).
5 Interview with bureaucrat, MOFA, Tokyo, June 2015.
6 For example, Mr. Keiji Ide, Japan's former Ambassador in Charge of Arctic Affairs, is a Russian and Chinese specialist and also led the 2018 "Russia Year in Japan," an initiative aimed at further strengthening bilateral relations.
7 Author's observation made from Arctic Frontiers 2016, Japan–Norway Arctic Science Week 2016, various meetings and interviews with informed Japanese academics and bureaucrats.
8 Interview with bureaucrat, MOFA, Tokyo, June 2015.

References

ArCs. 2017. "About ArCs," Arctic Challenge for Sustainability Website. www.arcs-pro.jp/en/about/.

Asari, Hideki. 2012. "Recommendations for Japan's Diplomacy: 'Arctic Governance and Japan's Diplomatic Governance Project'" in *Arctic Governance and Japan's Foreign Strategy (Hokkyoku no gabanansu to nihon no gaikou senryaku)*, JIIA Report. www2.jiia.or.jp/en/pdf/research/2012_arctic_governance/08e-recommendations.pdf

Bailes, Alyson J.K. 2015. "Wider Security Angles" in Juha Jokela (ed.) *Arctic Security Matters* (ISS Report No. 24, June) (Paris: European Union Institute for Security Studies): 69–74.

Bailes, Alyson J.K. 2016. "Security in the Arctic: Definitions, Challenges and Solutions" in Jakobson, L. and N. Melvin (eds.) *The New Arctic Governance* (Stockholm: Stockholm International Peace Research Institute): 13–40.

Caballero-Anthony, Mely. 2007. "Nontraditional Security and Multilateralism in Asia: Reshaping the Contours of Regional Security Architecture?" Policy Brief, The Stanley Foundation. www.stanleyfoundation.org/publications/pab/pab07mely.pdf.

Cabinet Office. 2018. "Outline of the Third Basic Plan on Ocean Policy." May. www8.cao.go.jp/ocean/english/plan/pdf/plan03_gaiyou_e.pdf

Fukumoto, Tatsuya. 2017. "Northern Territories Part of Russia's Arctic Strategy." *Yomiuri Shimbun*. 10 January.

Greaves, Wilfrid and Whitney Lackenbauer. 2016. "Re-Thinking Sovereignty and Security in the Arctic." *Arctic Deeply*. 23 March. www.opencanada.org/features/re-thinking-sovereignty-and-security-arctic/.

Griffiths, Franklyn. 2011. "Arctic Security: The Indirect Approach" in James Kraska (ed.) *Arctic Security in an Age of Climate Change* (Cambridge: Cambridge University Press): 3–20.

Hirose, Yoko. 2016. "Recent Russian Movement Over the Arctic Circle: Focusing on the Trend of China." in Japanese: 「北極圏をめぐる近年のロシアの動き：中国の動向に注目して」) *International Situations* 86: 75–88.

Hyodo, Shinji. 2014. "Russia's Strategic Concerns in the Arctic and Its Impact on Japan- Russia Relations." *Strategic Analysis* 38(6): 860–871.

Hyodo, Shinji and Hidenobu Kanda. 2015. "Global Efforts on Issues Concerning the Arctic: Implications Regarding Security." *Boei Kenkyusho Kiyo [NIDS Security Studies]* 17(2): 61–95.

Jakobson, Linda and Seong-Hyon Lee. 2016. "North East Asia Eyes the Arctic" in L. Jakobson and N. Melvin (eds.) *The New Arctic Governance* (Stockholm: Stockholm International Peace Research Institute): 111–146.

Kaneda, Hideaki. 2012. "The Arctic Ocean and Japan's Self Defense" in *Arctic Governance and Japan's Foreign Strategy (Hokkyoku no gabanansu to nihon no gaikou senryaku)*, JIIA Report 1–15. www2.jiia.or.jp/en/pdf/research/2012_arctic_governance/04e-kaneda.pdf.

Kantei. 2015a. "Japan's Arctic Policy." 16 October. www.research.kobe-u.ac.jp/gsics-pcrc/sympo/20160728/documents/Keynote/Japan_Arctic%20_Policy.PDF

Kantei. 2015b. "Prime Minister Shinzō Abe held the 14th Meeting of the Headquarters for Ocean Policy at the Prime Minister's Office, Headquarters for Ocean Policy." 16 October. http://japan.kantei.go.jp/97_abe/actions/201510/16article1.html

Kantei. 2019. "General Ocean Policy Headquarters Holding Status." (*Sōgō kaiyō seisaku honbu kaisai jōkyōı*), 18 June. www.kantei.go.jp/jp/singi/kaiyou/kaisai.html

Lanteigne, Marc. 2017. "Walking the Walk: Science Diplomacy and Identity-Building in the Asia-Arctic Relations." *Jindal Global Law Review* 8(1): 87–101.

Lindgren, Petter Y. 2018. "Advancing the Role of Social Mechanisms, Mediators, and Moderators in Securitization Theory: Explaining Security Policy Change in Japan." *Asian Security* 1–22 doi: 10.1080/14799855.2018.1445895.

MOFA. 2013. "Basic Plan on Ocean Policy." April. www.kantei.go.jp/jp/singi/kaiyou/kihonkeikaku/130426kihonkeikaku_e.pdf

MOFA. 2014. "Summit Meeting with the Nordic-Baltic 8 (NB8)." 17 October. www.mofa.go.jp/erp/we/page23e_000349.html

MOFA. 2017a. "The Second Tri-lateral High-level Dialogue on the Arctic." 8 June. www.mofa.go.jp/files/000263104.pdf

MOFA. 2017b. *The Diplomatic Bluebook 2017*. 15 September. www.mofa.go.jp/files/000290287.pdf

MOFA. 2018a. *The Diplomatic Bluebook 2018*. 20 September. www.mofa.go.jp/files/000401236.pdf

MOFA. 2018b. "Speech by H. E. Mr. Tarō Kōno, Minister for Foreign Affairs of Japan at the Arctic Circle 2018." 19 October. www.mofa.go.jp/files/000410409.pdf

MOFA. 2018c. "Extraordinary Press Conference by Foreign Minister Tarō Kōno." 19 October. www.mofa.go.jp/press/kaiken/kaiken4e_000560.html.

MOFA Korea. 2019. "The Fourth Trilateral High-Level Dialogue on the Arctic." 27 June. www.mofa.go.kr/eng/brd/m_5676/view.do?seq=320574

Ocean Policy Research Foundation. 2012. "Developing a Japan Policy towards the Arctic Ocean." March. www.nccj.or.jp/wordpress/wp-content/uploads/2013/02/Developing-a-Japan-Policy-towards-the-Arctic-Ocean-OPRF.pdf

Ohnishi, Fujio. 2014. "Japan's Arctic Policy" in Oran R. Young, Jong Deog Kim and Yoon Hyung Kim (eds.) *The Arctic in World Affairs*. Korea Maritime Institute (Honolulu: East-West Center): 188–206.

Ohnishi, Fujio. 2015. "Does the Sun also Rise in the Arctic? Three Pillar's of Japan's Arctic Policy." *The Arctic Yearbook*. www.arcticyearbook.com/commentaries2015/161-does-the-sun-also-rise-in-the-arctic-three-pillars-of-japan-s-arctic-policy.

Ohnishi, Fujio. 2016. "Japan's Arctic Policy Development: From Engagement to a Strategy" in Leiv Lunde, Yang Jian and Iselin Stensdal (eds.) *Asian Countries and the Arctic Future* (Singapore: World Scientific): 171–182.

Solli, Per Erik, Elana Wilson Rowe and Wrenn Yennie Lindgren. 2013. "Coming into the Cold: Asia's Arctic Interests." *Polar Geography* 36(4): 253–270.

Wilson Rowe, Elana. 2018. *Arctic Governance: Power in Cross-Border Cooperation* (Manchester: Manchester University Press).

Yennie Lindgren, Wrenn and Petter Y. Lindgren. 2017. "Identity Politics and the East China Sea: China as Japan's 'Other'" *Asian Politics & Policy* 9(3): 378–401.

Yennie-Lindgren, Wrenn. 2018. "New Dynamics in Japan-Russia Energy Relations 2011–2017." *Journal of Eurasian Studies* 9(2): 1–11.

Young, Oran R. 2011. "Arctic Futures: The Politics of Transformation" in James Kraska (ed.) *Arctic Security in an Age of Climate Change* (Cambridge: Cambridge University Press): xxi–xxvii.

28
SECURITY ASPECTS IN EU ARCTIC POLICY

Adele Airoldi

The beginnings

Security issues were part of the first manifestation of EU attention given to the Arctic region. In 1993, the European Commission, along with the Nordic countries and Russia, was one of the original signatories of the Barents Euro–Arctic Council (BEAC). Financed by the partners, it focused on cross-border cooperation between Russia and neighboring regions in Norway, Sweden, and Finland. Fostering good relations with Russia was the key element for Norway. This encouraged the participation of the EU, which was at that time negotiating the accession of the same three states.

In 1995, with the accession of Finland and Sweden, the EU acquired northern territories and, crucially, a border with Russia. Finland, already the initiator of international environmental cooperation in the Arctic, strongly promoted the creation of the Northern Dimension policy (ND) after its accession. The ND, involving a broad area from Greenland to northwest Russia to the Baltic states, was created in 1999 with clear soft security intentions: to foster good relations with the Baltic countries and northwest Russian regions, and to counteract environmental risks, particularly nuclear contamination originating from Russia. A so-called Arctic Window in the ND, introduced at the prompting of Denmark/Greenland, was more specifically geared to higher-latitude areas; it received sporadic attention.

In 2006 the ND was revamped, accentuating its political character, into a joint policy with four equal partners: the EU (which by then included the Baltic states), Russia, Norway, and Iceland. It is an expression of the four "common spaces" on which the bilateral EU–Russia relationship was being built: economy/environment; freedom, security, and justice; cooperation on external security; and research, education, and culture. The Arctic and sub-Arctic areas of Europe are its priority areas. The ND is implemented through partnerships that co-finance projects. The environmental partnership remains important and successful and has been followed by partnerships in the areas of health, transport, and culture. The ND has evolved into a general umbrella for the other northern cooperation regional councils: Barents, Baltic, Nordic, and Arctic. Like BEAC, it is a success story despite funding difficulties which are a consequence of the Ukraine crisis.

Security issues deriving from climate change prompted the development of an embryonic EU Arctic policy. A paper on climate change and international security submitted to the European Council in 2008, by the High Representative for the Common Foreign and Security Policy and the Commission, identified, inter alia, potential threats to international security in the Arctic region originating from climate change, such as disputes over territorial claims, access to resources, and new trade routes. It recommended the development of an EU Arctic policy "based on the evolving geo-strategy" of the region to safeguard relevant EU interests. The paper echoed considerations already developed in the 2007 Integrated Maritime Policy for the EU, which recognized that the intensification of maritime activities was leading to user conflicts and environmental deterioration. It recommended that the EU create a report on strategic issues relating to the Arctic Ocean.

The slow development of the EU's Arctic policy

There is no formal document setting out firm, legally binding principles for the EU's engagement with the Arctic. Rather, there has been a series of political pronouncements by EU institutions that, for over a decade, and with different accents, concreteness, and precision, has elaborated on possible and desirable roles for the EU in the Arctic.[1]

A European Parliament Resolution on Arctic governance in October 2008 suggested that, given the risk of conflict over changes in the Arctic, the Commission pursue negotiations for an international treaty for the protection of the Arctic, inspired by the Antarctic Treaty. In the wake of the May 2008 Ilulissat Declaration by the Arctic Five, the suggestion was misinterpreted as an expression of the political will of the EU and raised a general furor. It continues to be quoted as an example of the EU's undue interference in the Arctic, notwithstanding subsequent repeated reassurances by all institutions, including Parliament, that the EU would support no such initiative.

The first Communication on the Arctic by the Commission – November 2008's "The EU and the Arctic region" – aimed at "providing the basis for a more detailed reflection" that might ultimately lead to a "first layer of an Arctic policy for the EU." This remains the most concrete and articulate EU text on Arctic issues. It set out EU interests and suggested actions grouped around three main policy objectives: (a) promoting and preserving the Arctic in unison with its population, (b) promoting sustainable use of resources, and (c) contributing to enhanced Arctic multilateral governance.

These goals were later endorsed in substance by the European Council and Parliament. They were reaffirmed, albeit in modified forms and with different emphases, in subsequent pronouncements.

With respect to governance, the Commission underlined that no new legal instrument was needed to ensure security and stability, strict environmental management, and sustainable and equitable use of resources in the region. There already was an extensive international legal framework, particularly the UN Convention on the Law of the Sea (UNCLOS), which could be developed to enhance cross-border cooperation.

Reacting to the Communication, the Council's 2008 and 2009 conclusions accented the EU's responsibilities and interests. They stressed that the EU's policy approach to Arctic issues should be based on multilateral governance and on maintaining the Arctic as an area of peace and stability.

In 2011, the Parliament adopted a long and ambitious Resolution on a sustainable EU policy for the High North. It stressed the need for a united and coordinated EU Arctic policy that would clearly define EU priorities, potential challenges, and strategy. In a second round of pronouncements in 2012, the Commission and the High Representative (HR) submitted a joint Communication on developing a EU policy towards the Arctic region, based on the concepts of "knowledge, responsibility, and engagement." The Communication took stock of the achievements in the EU's Arctic-relevant policies and underlined the EU's potential contribution to international Arctic cooperation (a softening of the previously used "multilateral governance") and sustainable and peaceful developments in the region.

Nearly two years later, in March 2014, the Parliament's "Resolution on the EU Strategy for the Arctic" addressed all aspects of relevant policies at length. It reiterated calls for a coherent strategy and action plan for the EU in the Arctic. The Resolution focused on socioeconomic and environmental issues, so as to ensure legitimacy for the EU's Arctic engagement. In May 2014, the European Council adopted conclusions that noted the growing strategic importance of the Arctic region and invited the EU to enhance its contribution to Arctic cooperation. It also requested proposals for the further development of an integrated and coherent Arctic policy. It is clear that by 2014 the three institutions continued to regard Arctic policy as a work in progress.

Latest developments

Both European Parliament and Council had invited the Commission to develop a more coherent and forward-looking framework for the EU's Arctic policy. Several politically significant factors appeared to require such an overhaul. These were: renewed efforts to arrive at an ambitious agreement on climate change (COP21 in Paris – December 2015) in a field where the EU traditionally played a leading role; the increasing prominence of Arctic issues on the international scene, attracting important new actors such as China; the need to ensure coherence with the several national Arctic policy documents issued by EU Member States (Arctic and non-Arctic); and last but not least, the new tension between the EU and Russia following the Ukrainian crisis.

The global strategy for the European Union's foreign and security policy

The Arctic fits into the general strategic framework for foreign and security policy that was being elaborated at that time. The new Global Strategy submitted by the HR in June 2016, "Shared Vision, Common Action: A Stronger Europe," set out the EU's core interests and principles for engaging in the world.

The Strategy argues for a stronger EU to counteract instability and security threats, including disruptions induced by climate change. The Strategy recommends using different policies and instruments, both soft and hard power, as well as autonomy and multilateralism to counteract those threats. It further indicates that external action needs to be responsible and concentrated foremost in Europe and the surrounding regions. It needs to be "joined-up" across Member States and the EU and involve both the internal and external dimensions of EU policies, particularly for security issues. One priority for external action indicated by the Strategy is support for "cooperative regional orders," which "offer states and peoples the opportunity to better manage security concerns, reap the economic gains of globalization, express cultures and identities more fully, and project influence in world affairs" as the EU's own experience had shown.

The Strategy indicates "A Cooperative Arctic" is one place where the EU would invest in a cooperative relationship:

> With three Member States and two European Economic Area members being Arctic states, the EU has a strategic interest in the Arctic remaining a low-tension area, with ongoing cooperation ensured by the Arctic Council, a well-functioning legal framework, and solid political and security cooperation. The EU will contribute to this through enhanced work on climate action and environmental research, sustainable development, telecommunications, and search & rescue, as well as concrete cooperation with Arctic states, institutions, indigenous peoples and local communities.
>
> *(European Commission 2012)*

It is clear from this text that the EU does not envisage a role for itself regarding hard security issues in the Arctic. It expresses the hope that the main political actors involved, the Arctic States, will continue the peaceful cooperation they have maintained and respect international law. The EU's contribution would be on soft security issues, in cooperation with all relevant actors. This openness and commitment to cooperation is confirmed in the section on the European Security Order. After reaffirming that only full respect for international law by Russia would bring a substantial change in EU–Russia relations, the Strategy underlines EU–Russia interdependence and pledges to engage with Russia to discuss disagreements and cooperate when the EU's and Russia's interests overlap. The Arctic is explicitly mentioned as one area for such "selective engagement," together with climate, maritime security, research, and cross-border cooperation – the most important fields for EU–Russia interaction in the Arctic area.

Selective engagement on issues of interest to the EU is one of the five guiding principles of EU policy towards Russia, as supported by the EU's Foreign Affairs Ministers on 14 March 2016 and re-confirmed on 16 April 2018. Another principle – support for people-to-people relations and civil society in Russia – is also relevant for EU cross-border cooperation with Russia in northern areas.[2]

The latest EU Arctic policy documents

The joint Communication, "An integrated European Policy for the Arctic," submitted by the Commission and HR in April 2016, aligns with the Global Strategy by stressing the global political dimension. For the first time the term "policy" is used, rather than the previous periphrasis implying work in progress. When presenting the Communication, the HR stressed that the Arctic is important to the world environmentally, socially, and economically. It also emphasized that the region is crucial in terms of regional and global security and remains a strategic component of the EU's foreign policy. The three priority areas indicated in the Communication: climate change and safeguarding the Arctic environment, sustainable development in and around the Arctic, and international cooperation on Arctic issues correspond broadly to previous documents.

While climate change and environmental protection remain the prime movers and declared purposes of EU presence in the Arctic, the introduction to the Communication makes it clear that the focus of EU Arctic policy must be on "advancing international cooperation in responding to the impacts of climate change on the Arctic's fragile environment, and on promoting and contributing to sustainable development, particularly in the European part of the Arctic."

The primacy of international cooperation and the reference to the European part of the Arctic are probably meant to reassure the Arctic partners about the limits of the EU's ambitions. The Communication lists issues, policy responses, and proposed actions for the three priority areas. Large-scale scientific cooperation is seen as the main catalyst for arriving at a common understanding in the search for solutions to emerging risks. Elements new to this document include a greater focus on the European Arctic regions, a certain shift in attention from oil and extractive industries to investments and capacity-building, more innovative and sustainable forms of development (such as information technology and cold-climate technologies), and the enhanced participation of Arctic stakeholders.

This Communication, with its expressed aspiration to guide EU actions in coming years, does not really respond to the Council's request for a coherent and integrated policy – the coherence aspect already having been dropped in its title. This was in fact a near-impossible task, given the variety of EU actors and policies involved[3] and the very different levels of interest the Arctic elicits among EU institutions and Member States. It has been observed that the Communication remains, like previous Communications, "an overview of the EU's Arctic-relevant policies and actions," with the primary purpose not to streamline such policies and actions but "to communicate the scope of the EU's presence in the region, to show that the Union has an appropriate understanding of the situation in the region and to state overall principles that the EU commits to follow" in its activities. The key audiences are Arctic States and EU Member States (Stepien and Raspotnik 2016).

Regarding security issues specifically, a thorough analysis of Arctic security matters was made in 2015 with a view to contributing to the Communication (Jokela 2015). However, the Communication addresses aspects of security only in a general, implicit way. The lack of clear support for a more active EU role in Arctic security is noted in a study on EU Arctic policy in regional contexts that was requested by the Parliament and discusses, inter alia, a possible role for the EU in Arctic security (Stang 2016, 21). The Council in its June 2016 Conclusions emphasized that the EU's reinforced engagement in the region through an ambitious and well-coordinated policy would be important from a foreign and security policy angle, and confirmed the potential for a significant EU contribution to Arctic regional or multilateral cooperation.

The Parliament, which had previously called for a "strategy," was, as usual, bolder in responding to the Communication in March 2017. It issued another very long Resolution that emphasized environmental and external policy aspects. One of the rapporteurs indicated that the main goal of EU Arctic policy was to keep the Arctic as a low-tension area despite renewed Russian military activity in the region, although the role the EU could play to defuse potential security challenges (see, for instance, paragraphs 26 and 27 of the Resolution) is probably overstated.

The EU in the Arctic context

The continuing cautious approach to Arctic geopolitics is probably due to the desire not to jeopardize the place the EU has gained in the Arctic context by taking erratic actions that might lead to considerable expenses, including financial costs related to its Arctic-related research and cooperation programs. Furthermore, the EU has to atone for two different original sins, long-remedied but still casting a shadow: the presumed aspiration to an Arctic Treaty and the perceived lack of sensitivity to Arctic Indigenous peoples, due mainly to the infamous 2009 trade ban on seal products, with its dire consequences for some of those peoples. Suspicions about EU attitudes are still present and surface from time to time.

An example of EU difficulty in the Arctic context is the long and ongoing saga of the EU's admission as an Observer to the Arctic Council (AC). Its application, first presented by the Commission in 2008, faced open opposition from Canada (due principally to the seal products ban). When Canada dropped its objections, the EU's application was received affirmatively in 2013 under certain conditions, a final decision being deferred pending consensus among AC ministers. Further complications, including a WTO ruling favorable to the ban, were overcome, but the deterioration of EU–Russia relations brought overt opposition from Russia. The EU is presently a de facto Observer, with a standing invitation to attend the Arctic Council sessions at all levels and participating in many AC activities, but it does not enjoy full Observer status.

The EU saw participation in the AC as a token of importance and political clout in the Arctic, and its admission as an Observer was supported by all the other AC members. However, beyond the declared opposition, a broad uneasiness about an enhanced EU role can be detected, including among Permanent Participants. The special nature of the EU in the international context and the complicated division of competences between the EU and its Member States are difficult to grasp and integrate into the AC's construction and operation. The EU has competence – exclusive or shared with Member States – in many policies pertaining to the Arctic. It has exclusive competence for the conservation of marine biological resources under the Common Fisheries Policy. Competence is shared with Member States, to different degrees, for environment, fisheries, transport, energy, regional development, tourism, and civil protection. Generally, external competence mirrors internal competence, with implications for positions taken in international negotiations. The 1994 European Economic Area (EEA) Agreement extends in principle to Iceland and Norway (except for Svalbard). The EU legislates on Arctic-relevant areas, such as the environment, energy, tourism, and civil protection (Koivurova et al. 2011)

Three AC members are also EU Member States, two are EEA states, and more and more EU Member States have become Observers: at the last count seven, namely France, Germany, Italy, Netherlands, Poland, Spain, and the UK (although the latter may be changing due to the 2016 Brexit vote for the UK to leave the EU). Switzerland, which is part of the European Single Market and the Schengen Agreement, also joined the AC as an Observer in 2017. Thus, the EU increasingly risks being the elephant in the room. Of the AC/EU members, Finland has consistently recognized and advocated for an EU role in the Arctic. Sweden is more tepid, while Denmark appears sometimes to see the EU as a hindrance to its ambition to play a leading role in the Arctic[4] and as the originator of Denmark's problems with Greenland, particularly on matters relating to the exploitation of natural resources. The Arctic policy documents produced by the EU Member State Observers in the AC support the legitimacy of the EU's role in the Arctic, but they are, in general, relatively subdued, except perhaps for France, in supporting an enhanced EU Arctic role.

Security aspects in the main Arctic: relevant EU policies

The EU addresses soft security issues in some of its policies that are relevant to the Arctic.

Climate change and environmental security

Climate policy is first and foremost among these. The EU fully recognizes the nexus between climate change and Arctic security and stability. The EU's concrete and diplomatic efforts for effective mitigation and adaptation policies, at the European and global level, can be regarded as its most important contribution to Arctic security issues. The Arctic region is furthermore noted as a priority area in the 7th EU Environment Action Programme 2014–2020, whose main objectives are to protect natural capital, promote a green economy, and safeguard citizens from environment-related risks. EU activity in the reduction of environmental pollutants, both at the EU and international level, is of particular importance in the Arctic context. A comprehensive analysis of the EU perspective on environmental issues relating to the Arctic is found in a report by the European Environment Agency (European Environment Agency 2017).

Maritime security

Security issues in the maritime Arctic, the origin of the EU's interest in the region, continue to be a focus of attention for both environmental and economic reasons – the EU Member States account for a large part of the world's merchant fleet. Conscious of the increasing pressure on world oceans, the EU adopted a Maritime Security Strategy in 2014. It addressed both internal and external aspects of maritime security, which was understood as "a state of affairs in the global maritime domain in which international law and national law are enforced; freedom of navigation is guaranteed; and citizens, infrastructure, transport, the environment, and marine resources are protected." Arctic waters are mentioned in the Maritime Strategy as an area of particular attention, as possible new transport routes and the exploitation of Arctic natural and mineral resources would pose environmental challenges that should be managed with the utmost care in cooperation with partners. Respect for rules and principles and multilateralism, including cooperation with NATO and with third countries, are integral elements of the Strategy. An agenda for international oceans governance, adopted in 2016, addresses security issues in the Arctic region in similar terms.

The 2016 Arctic Joint Communication refers to the measures for effective stewardship of the Arctic Ocean that were advocated in the Maritime Strategy. It recommends that the EU take a proactive negotiating position in relevant UN fora on climate change and environmental issues, (e.g., on the establishment of marine protected areas and conservation and sustainable use of biodiversity in the high seas) as well as on emerging challenges such as maritime safety and sustainable resource management. It also reaffirms the need to continue to ensure and promote peaceful rule-based governance in the Arctic through recognition of and support for existing legal frameworks, in particular UNCLOS. The EU already has extensive regulations that are relevant to soft security in the maritime Arctic. These cover pollution from ships, rules for ship inspection, port state control, and the use of EU ports. It has pledged support for the implementation and improvement of the International Maritime Organization (IMO) Polar Code and contributes to Arctic Council activities on marine oil pollution, black-carbon reduction, and search and rescue (including cooperation between respective coast guard institutions).

The EU's role as a global maritime security provider, promoting maritime multilateralism and the rule of law at sea, was underlined by the Council in its 19 June 2017 Conclusions on maritime security. The Council highlighted that cooperation with countries in the Arctic region in the framework of the Arctic Council is an EU priority and that it should explore more significant engagement in the Arctic region. It stressed, inter alia, the importance of respecting the right of innocent passage in territorial seas and the right of transit passage through straits as reflected in UNCLOS, thus touching lightly on a potential source of conflict in Arctic waters: the Northwest Passage and the Northern Sea Route are expected to become increasingly navigable as ice melts. The 2016 joint Arctic Communication, unlike previous documents, had been silent on this point.

Possible future conflict over fishing resources that are moving northward to the high seas of the Arctic Ocean because of climate change appears to have been defused by a legally binding Agreement to prevent unregulated high seas fisheries in the Central Arctic Ocean. This was initiated by the five Arctic Ocean coastal states and signed in December 2017 by those five states, four other major fishing powers (China, Iceland, Japan, and South Korea), and the EU (by virtue of the latter's exclusive external competence in this regard). The Agreement will prevent commercial fishing in the Arctic Ocean's international waters for at least 16 years while scientific research is conducted to learn more about the situation. The possible creation of a regional fishing management organization after that time is left open.

Energy security

Energy became a recognized EU policy area after the oil crises of the 1970s and early 1980s. Since then, ample supplies and modest prices have kept energy policy at second-tier status. In 2006, when Russia briefly interrupted the delivery of gas to Ukraine, the question of *security of supply* was pushed to the top of the EU agenda, where it continues to be regarded as a priority issue. By then, Russia had become one of the biggest oil and gas exporters – with production coming increasingly from its Arctic territories – and Europe offered a convenient market. This led to a perception of EU dependence.

Those fears do not appear completely justified. Oil is traded in a global market, aiming at the lowest cost of transport and refining. The EU offers a cost-effective outlet for Russian production, but as long as other sources of supply continue to be available there are no significant security-of-supply issues. Interdependence is greater with Russian gas, as that trade is overwhelmingly via pipelines and around one-third of the gas supplied to the EU comes from Russia. However, the boom in liquefied natural gas (LNG) production worldwide is making gas more of a globally traded commodity; several LNG terminals have already been built in the EU. As Russia expands its LNG production in the Arctic, it is turning to the East (particularly China) to diversify its customers. However, it remains largely dependent on EU demand, and sanctions are affecting its capacity to develop offshore production in the Arctic. In conclusion, security of supply appears for the time being a lesser problem for the EU than security of EU demand is for Russia. Fears remain, however: strengthening the resilience of the EU, inter alia, on energy security, is one of the five principles that guide EU policy towards Russia. The considerable involvement of EU companies in the development of Russian Arctic resources, present in the Arctic policy documents of some EU Member States, is a security problem of a different order.

The 2016 Joint Communication has language on environmental security in energy production. The EU underlines its commitment to working closely with all stakeholders to promote the adoption of the "highest security standards of major accident prevention and environmental control" and pledges to share its "regulatory and technological best practice" with international partners in the region. The Communication is less vocal than previous ones on oil and gas activities. This may be due to the fact that previous expectations of an Arctic oil and gas bonanza have been dampened by the evolution of the markets and the recognition of the difficulties involved in their exploitation. It can also be attributed to a desire not to appear as overly interfering with crucial Arctic partners, not least important energy suppliers such as Norway, which strongly objected and lobbied against strict regulatory standards for offshore oil and gas exploration in the Arctic.[5] The 2016 Communication insists, with the blessing of the Council, on a pledge to work to facilitate energy efficiency and renewable energy solutions.

Greenland

When Denmark joined in 1973, the EU acquired a vast Arctic territory: Greenland. Most Greenlanders opposed EU membership, or rather the implications of the EU fisheries policy, which would have given EU Member States more access to Greenland waters. In 1982, Greenland withdrew from the EU, to which it remains linked by different forms of partnership. In connection with the renewal of the partnership agreement for 2014–2020, the EU recognized the geostrategic position of Greenland and provided for the possibility of enhanced dialogue on Arctic issues. The EU showed interest at that time for cooperation in the extraction of raw materials, particularly strategically important rare earths. A 2012 letter of intent on this subject has however not been followed by any action, as concerns about the availability of rare earths have abated.

Present-day sources of agitation in Greenland and Denmark include minerals extraction and transport development projects involving China and others, as well as the ever-present problems, including environmental security issues, linked to the US military presence in North Greenland, specifically the US Air Force Base at Thule. These do not directly involve the EU, particularly as Denmark opted out of the Permanent Structured Cooperation on Security and Defense (PESCO).

Conclusions

An Arctic policy has not yet gained a proper place in the EU. Since the beginning, the Arctic was the object of only sporadic interest at both the institutional and Member-State level, with the exception of Finland, without whose constant initiative and drive the EU would probably not have arrived at the level of Arctic policy it now has. It is legitimate to think that both hard and soft security considerations have continued to influence Finland's attitude.

The slow pace at which the EU Arctic policy has advanced and the repetitiveness of its various pronouncements prove that the Arctic is not considered sufficiently relevant to the EU to be a priority. Paradoxically, the only issue with clear Arctic focus that was able to stir emotions in European citizens and governments, and was elevated to the level of legislation – the ban on the trade of seal products – resulted in an Arctic backlash against the EU.

While several EU policies affect the Arctic, the EU continues to behave as an outsider, if not an interloper. Hence, its cautious attitude to controversial issues; the constant repetition of allegiance to international legal order, and, as in the Global Strategy; and the vision of an Arctic at most only partially affected by external tensions, where conflict can be solved through international cooperation.

In this situation, hard security issues in the Arctic – where the EU has little competence – are, and will probably continue to remain, conveniently in the background. Geopolitical implications and security aspects were only hinted at or, perhaps more accurately, intentionally avoided, in the pronouncements of EU institutions, except to a certain extent the Parliament, which is less constrained by considerations of political opportunity and by the need to present a united front to the outside world. The focus has been on the neutral merits of EU action for and in the Arctic. The largest EU expenditure directly benefiting and involving non-EU partners has been research – principally on climate change and its consequences. The focus has also been on environmental protection; maritime issues, particularly pollution prevention and maritime safety; cooperative or supportive action; and financing cross-border regional cooperation.

It has been observed that due to insufficient political attention and ambition, and the insufficient and fragmented knowledge and treatment of Arctic issues, the Arctic remains "somewhat of a 'blind spot' in the EU's overall strategic outlook" and that the EU should focus on participating in soft security institutionalization processes, which are the basis for international relations in the Arctic (Fert-Malka and Kekkonen 2017).This is not likely to happen in the short or medium term. The EU is faced with a number of existential issues – Brexit, outside immigration, and the emergence of populisms – that threaten its core security rather than its Arctic periphery.

Notes

1 The acts setting out the EU position on Arctic issues are Communications submitted to the European Parliament and the Council of Ministers – the first by the European Commission and the subsequent ones, following changes in the EU's institutional structure, jointly submitted by the Commission and the High Representative for Foreign Affairs and Security Policy/Vice President of the Commission. Communications represent the views of the submitters on a given subject with accompanying suggestions for action (including, though not in this case, legislative proposals). The Council reacted each time with Conclusions, which express the unanimous political agreement by Member States on the subject and invite further consideration or action. Parliament's Resolutions, adopted by majority, usually but not necessarily reacting to a Commission's act, aim to give political impetus to a legislative or political process and invite action on certain issues.

2 In fact, EU–Russia cross-border people and business cooperation in Arctic zones under the 2014–2020 EU budgetary exercise has continued, largely unaffected (Kolarctic and Karelia programmes).

3 A variety of actors deal with Arctic issues in the EU institutions. The EEAS, which recently created a post of Ambassador for the Arctic, appears to have the general lead. It shares work with the Commission, whose leading service is DG MARE, which is responsible for maritime affairs but deals also with other aspects, including dialogue with Arctic Indigenous peoples. In the Council, Arctic issues at a general level are examined by the Working Party on Eastern Europe and Central Asia (COEST), showing the strong focus on relations with Russia. In the Parliament, all EU's northern policies (Arctic, Barents, and Northern Dimension) are part of the competence of the Delegation for relations with Switzerland, Iceland, Norway, and the EEA.

4 Denmark is the only state that has both an Arctic Ocean coast and is an EU Member State. It was the principal sponsor of the Arctic Five format derived from the Ilulissat Declaration.

5 Already in 2013, a rather inoffensive formula in EU Directive 2013/30 on the safety of offshore oil and gas operations, by which the Commission was "to promote high safety standards for offshore operations at international level, particularly in the Arctic," led Norway – an EEA State and therefore in principle applying EU environmental legislation – to choose not to apply the directive in its territory. Intense lobbying prevented the insertion in the 2017 Parliament Resolution of a call for a blanket ban on offshore drilling in the Arctic waters of the EU and EEA.

References

EU-Arctic until 2014

Airoldi, Adele. 2008. *The European Union and the Arctic: policies and actions*. Copenhagen: Nordic Council of Ministers.

Airoldi, Adele. 2010. *The European Union and the Arctic: main developments July 2008–July 2010*. Copenhagen: Nordic Council of Ministers.

Airoldi, Adele. 2014. *The European Union and the Arctic: developments and perspectives 2010–2014*. Copenhagen: Nordic Council of Ministers.

European Commission. 2012. "High representative of the European Union for Foreign Affairs and Security Policy, 26 June 2012." *Joint Communication to the European Parliament and the Council – Developing A European Union Policy towards the Arctic Region: Progress since 2008 and Next Steps*. http://eeas.europa.eu/archives/docs/arctic_region/docs/join_2012_19.pdf

EU-Arctic post-2014

EU–Arctic policy

https://eeas.europa.eu/arctic-policy/eu-arctic-policy_en
NB the texts of relevant documents can be found under the heading "A short introduction"
https://eeas.europa.eu/headquarters/headquarters-homepage/20956/arctic-short-introduction_en
https://ec.europa.eu/maritimeaffairs/policy/sea_basins/arctic_ocean_en

EU foreign and security policy and related subjects

https://europa.eu/globalstrategy/en/global-strategy-foreign-and-security-policy-european-union
https://eeas.europa.eu/delegations/russia/35939/european-union-and-russian-federation_en
https://eeas.europa.eu/headquarters/headquarters-homepage/347/northern-dimension_en
www.barentscooperation.org/en

Arctic-relevant EU sectoral policies

Environment Agency. 2017 *The Arctic environment.European perspectives on a changing Arctic.* EEA Report No.7/2017. www.eea.europa.eu/publications/the-arctic-environment
https://ec.europa.eu/maritimeaffairs/policy/maritime-security_en
https://ec.europa.eu/maritimeaffairs/policy/ocean-governance_en

Other references

Fert-Malka, Morgane, and Kekkonen, Alexandra. 2017. "Optimizing EU influence on Arctic affairs." *Arctic Yearbook*, [online] Briefing Notes. www.arcticyearbook.com/briefing-notes2017

Jokela, Juha, ed. 2015. *Arctic security matters.* Paris: EU Institute for Security Studies. [online]. www.iss.europa.eu/content/arctic-security-matters-0

Koivurova, Timo, Kokko, Kai, Duyck, Sebastien, Sellheim, Nikolas, and Stepien, Adam. 2011. "The present and future competence of the European Union in the Arctic." *Polar Record* 48(4): 361–371.

Stang, Gerald. 2016. *EU Arctic policy in regional context.* European Parliament. www.europarl.europa.eu/RegData/etudes/STUD/2016/578017/EXPO_STU(2016)578017_EN.pdf.

Stepien, Adam and Raspotnik, Andreas. 2016. "The EU's new Arctic communication: not-so-integrated, not-so-disappointing?" *ArCticles – Arctic Centre Papers.* University of Lapland. www.arcticcentre.org/blogs/The-EU%E2%80%99s-new-Arctic-Communication-not-so-integrated,-not-so-disappointing/ne2t4glg/65469626-3128-4ae2-96e3-c38b75cf387d.

29

NATO, THE OSCE, AND THE ARCTIC REGION

European security organizations and the High North

Benjamin Schaller and Horatio Sam-Aggrey

Introduction

Discussions about Arctic governance and governmental organizations usually center on the work of the Arctic Council (AC). Over the years, the AC's selective approach to security[1] and the Arctic states' reluctance to adequately address hard security issues in the region has been controversial among policymakers and researchers. Skeptics of a more comprehensive approach to security in the region point to the Arctic states' history of peaceful dispute-settlement and cooperation, (Ebinger and Zambetakis 2009; Tamnes and Offerdal 2014; Humrich 2015; Knecht 2015). Proponents of a more comprehensive approach argue that the region's geostrategic importance has made the Arctic an important arena for competing geopolitical interests (Borgerson 2008; Blunden 2009; Huebert 2010; Sale and Potapov 2010). Since new tensions between Russia and the West have emerged due to the conflict in and around Ukraine, scholars have not only devoted increased attention to the question of NATO's role in the region (Holtsmark and Smith-Windsor 2009; Conley 2014) but they have also looked for lessons learned and inspiration from other regional security arrangements, such as the Organization for Security Co-operation in Europe (OSCE) (Bailes 2009; Conley and Melino 2016; Schaller 2018b).

This chapter sheds light on some of these discussions in order to gain a clearer picture of the current role, perceptions, and prospects of a stronger role for NATO and the OSCE in the Arctic security context. More specifically, it explores the role that the Arctic plays in the organizations' policy and strategic thinking, the factors that guide and constrain their approaches to the region, and to what extent both organizations might in the future play a stronger role in the region. To this end, the chapter first reviews the most relevant aspects of the Arctic security environment. This overview will be concise and focus on the most relevant aspects. Then the chapter will discuss the roles, approaches, and relevance of the Arctic region for NATO and the OSCE, before concluding with comparative reflections and remarks.

Arctic security: a short background

Security in the Arctic has always been multifaceted, ranging from the traditional notion of security to human, environmental, energy, and other dimensions. Climate change has increased access to natural resources, in particular oil and gas, and hopes for the opening of lucrative shipping routes. This has yielded significant opportunities and challenges to the Arctic security environment.

Over the last 11 years, the Arctic states have developed a strong and close level of cooperation in order to address many of these nontraditional threats to security,[2] particularly through the AC. Examples include agreements for responding to oil spills and coordinating search and rescue (SAR) operations in the region (Le Mière and Mazo 2013, 110–112; Rottem 2016).

At the same time, the state of military security in the High North is much less uniform. Not only does the Arctic not have a forum specifically dedicated to addressing military security issues,[3] but the Arctic states are also members of different defense and security arrangements. Five of them (Canada, Denmark, Iceland, Norway, and the United States) are members of NATO. Sweden, Finland, and Russia participate in NATO's Partnership for Peace (PfP) Program. Russia is a member of the Collective Security Treaty Organization (CSTO). Sweden and Finland cooperate with their Nordic partners Denmark, Iceland, and Norway in the framework of the Nordic Defense Cooperation (NORDEFCO).

While relations between Russia and the West have cooled in recent years, overall military presence and activities in the Arctic continues to be small in scale and far below Cold War levels (Wezeman 2016, 22). What is often overlooked is that the harsh Arctic climate places demands on military equipment and personnel operating in the region. This makes large-scale military operations costly, so military modernization and procurement plans usually proceed slowly or are even completely called off (Hilde 2013, 146; Wezeman 2016, 22; Schaller 2018b, 217).

NATO and the Arctic - new old realities at the Northern Flank?

NATO was founded in 1949 as a defense alliance of 12 states, including the Arctic states of Canada, Denmark, Iceland, Norway, and the United States. From its beginning, the Arctic has been of particular strategic importance for NATO (Archer and Scrivener 1982; Lindsey 1989; MccGwire 1990; Åtland 2011; Le Mière and Mazo 2013, 82–83). This section explores factors that make the Arctic of particular strategic importance to the alliance, followed by a concise summary of the current security situation on NATO's Northern Flank and an assessment of NATO's role in the High North.

The geostrategic importance of the Arctic for NATO

NATO members are spread over two continents and geographically separated by the North Atlantic Ocean, so controlling and ensuring reinforcements across the Atlantic in case of "an armed attack against one or more of them in Europe or North America" (Article 5, North Atlantic Treaty 1949) has always been of paramount importance for the alliance. NATO's collective defense is, inter alia, ensured by strategically located air bases in the High North, such as Naval Air Station Keflavík in Iceland or Thule Air Base in Greenland, and also by monitoring and controlling the waters between Greenland, Iceland, and the United Kingdom: the so-called GIUK Gap, through which vessels of the Russian Northern Fleet need to pass before entering the North Atlantic Ocean (Archer and Scrivener 1982; Lindsey 1989; Petersen 1990, 48–49; Åtland 2011, 270).

Since the route over the Arctic Ocean is the shortest distance between the former Soviet Union and the North American continent, the Arctic has also played an important role in the nuclear deterrence strategies of the two opposing military blocs. Most of Russia's strategic nuclear missiles, air defense systems, and strategic-missile submarines are stationed in the Russian Arctic, mainly on its northwestern Kola Peninsula. Various radar installations in the Arctic, as well as the United States' and Canada's North American Aerospace Defense Command (NORAD), were established to provide early warning and air defense against Russian bombers and missile systems (Lindsey 1989; Åtland 2011, 269; Le Mière and Mazo 2013, 82–83). Their common security concerns and strategic location for early detection and reconnaissance led the United States, Canada, Denmark, Iceland, and Norway to join forces in their national defense and become founding members of NATO in 1949.

NATO and the Arctic - limited and ad hoc engagement in the absence of a collective strategy

Despite the downsizing of military presence and activities by all Arctic states in the immediate post-Cold War period, the Arctic has not lost its strategic importance for the alliance. The Arctic Ocean continues to be largely covered by thick layers of ice, so the GIUK Gap remains an important maritime bottleneck for monitoring Russian vessels leaving the Barents Sea and entering the North Atlantic Ocean. Nuclear-capable ballistic-missile submarines still operate underneath the Arctic ice cap, the Barents Sea continues to be a testing ground for military forces and new equipment, and the Russian Northern Fleet still constitutes the country's largest and geostrategically most important naval force (Åtland 2011, 267; Rosamond 2011, 15; Conley and Rohloff 2015, 76–88; Bailes 2016, 17–18; Wezeman 2016, 22). Nevertheless, the Arctic states have been able to maintain exceptional levels of multilateral cooperation and preserve the region as a low-tension area, even in times of increased geopolitical tensions (Wezeman 2016, 21–22; Klimenko 2016, 36).

In recent years, the trend of decreasing military presence and activities in the Arctic has been slowly reversed. While this trend started in the late 2000s with a comprehensive analysis of the geopolitical consequences of climate change (Le Mière and Mazo 2013, 86–87; Wezeman 2016, 21–22), it is hard to ignore the fact that the deterioration of NATO–Russia relations over the crises in Ukraine and Syria have accelerated this trend and also noticeably affected security relations in the High North (Conley and Rohloff 2015, 112; Käpylä and Mikkola 2015, 12–17). Since 2014, NATO members have noted an increase in Russian air and submarine activities in the area (Conley and Rohloff 2015, 81–83; Sonne 2016), testing the alliance's responsiveness and resolve. Also, the increased build-up of Russian military infrastructure and capabilities in the Arctic has spurred new security concerns, particularly among Northern European NATO allies, raising once again questions about the appropriate role of the alliance in the High North (Østhagen et al. 2018).

However, NATO allies have been unable to agree on a collective response to the changing Arctic security environment. While Norway regularly advocates for a stronger NATO presence in the area, Denmark, the United States, and Canada have repeatedly voiced their reservations, emphasizing the importance of regional cooperation over military deterrence. Canada has so far blocked any mention of the Arctic in official NATO documents (Le Mière and Mazo 2013, 125–127; Conley 2014, 55; Bergh and Klimenko 2016, 43–45; Østhagen et al. 2018, 164). At the Strasbourg-Kehl NATO summit in 2009, for example, Canada argued that it did not see a role for NATO in dealing with the softer security challenges in the Arctic. Since then, any NATO policy explicitly dealing with the Arctic has been at a standstill (Østhagen 2016, 5; Haftendorn 2011, 341–342). This skepticism vis-à-vis stronger NATO involvement in the region is shared by the nonaligned European NATO partners, Sweden and Finland, both of which fear that a stronger NATO presence in the region could trigger a strong response from Russia and potentially lead to an escalation spiral that could drag the entire region into an arms race and a dangerous security dilemma (Le Mière and Mazo 2013, 126).

The institutionally separate NATO Parliamentary Assembly (NATO PA),[4] which brings together parliamentarians from across the alliance to influence NATO decision-making, has so far been the most vocal advocate for a stronger NATO role in the Arctic region. In a recent draft report, the PA highlighted the fact that climate change has wider security implications, with profound strategic implications for the alliance, noting that "the re-emergence of the Arctic on the international agenda and possible spillover of tension between Russia and NATO allies, as well as China's increasing engagement, could make the Arctic an arena for strategic rivalry" (NATO PA 2017, 1). This requires NATO "at the very least, [to] have the capacity and resources to monitor and consider developments in the Arctic" (NATO PA 2017, 10).

In the absence of a collective strategy in the High North, most NATO allies rely on other, mainly bilateral, security arrangements and have decided to review their own national strategies and military capabilities in the Arctic region. In 2011, Denmark adopted a special Arctic strategy; in 2012, it merged its military assets in the High North into a new joint Arctic Command (Wezeman 2016, 7–8). Since 2006, Norway has regularly invited NATO allies and partners to train in winter conditions during the military exercise series named Cold Response (Wezeman 2016, 11). In summer 2018, Oslo announced that it would increase the number of US Marines based in Norway from 330 to 700. The additional forces would be stationed further north, in Inner Troms, close to the Norwegian-Russian border (Forsvarsdepartementet 6/12/2018).

Despite the absence of a dedicated regional strategy, it should be highlighted that the European High North has not been completely absent from NATO's agenda. For example, to reassure allies against a more aggressive Russian military posture, NATO ships are more frequently seen in the waters and ports of Northern Norway. NATO's Allied Command Transformation (ACT) is conducting scientific research off the coast of Iceland to boost the alliance's submarine-detection capabilities (Allied Command Transformation Public Affairs 2017). NATO and Russia are both stepping up their military exercises and maneuvers in the region (Bentzrød 2015; Conley and Rohloff 2015, 80–83). One of the preliminary highlights on NATO's side was the second edition of its high-visibility Trident Juncture exercise, which took place in October–November 2018 in Norway (Forsvaret 2018).

Apart from its traditional state-based military security agenda, NATO also recognizes that its mandate is linked to nontraditional security concerns, most notably the impact of climate change.[5] However, NATO's involvement in soft security issues in the Arctic has so far been limited and ad hoc. The alliance has sponsored several SAR exercises (Bailes 2016, 34), organized expert seminars and workshops devoted to the role of NATO in tackling emerging challenges in the Arctic such as climate change, and is funding research projects and workshops on topics related to environmental security in the Arctic and its impact on regional and global security dynamics (Berkman and Vylegzhanin 2013).

The Arctic: a role for NATO in the future?

Because the alliance seems focused on finding adequate responses to the security challenges on its eastern and southern borders and on sending a strong signal of allied cohesion, it seems highly unlikely that it will try to tackle the internally controversial issue of an allied strategy towards the Arctic region any time soon. For now, it appears that Arctic NATO members appreciate the alliance's potential support in the Arctic region, to the extent that it is also compatible with their regional political and economic interests. It can therefore be expected that the alliance will for now maintain its low profile in the region, while occasionally reassuring its allies on the Northern Flank (Le Mière and Mazo 2013, 155; Hilde 2014, 159; de Sitter 2015, 408; Østhagen et al. 2018, 166).

However, the continuance of this approach will largely depend on the further development of NATO–Russia relations, which have considerably deteriorated over the crises in Ukraine and Syria. Should relations stay tense or even deteriorate further, and Russia continue to step up its military procurement and infrastructure plans in the region, the opposition to a stronger NATO presence in the region might become less vocal (Østhagen et al. 2018, 166). From a long-term strategic perspective, it will be interesting to observe to what extent the increasing maneuverability of naval forces in the region as a consequence of climate change will affect the planning and thinking of military strategists in Brussels and Moscow. As the latest report of the NATO PA concludes: "As the strategic relevance of the High North increases in the future, the Arctic littoral states of the Alliance, and indeed all Allies, can ill afford to postpone an evaluation of NATO's approach to the region indefinitely" (NATO PA 2017, 10). However, without a specific triggering event or a general paradigm shift, such a major strategic adaption is unlikely to take place soon.

The OSCE and the Arctic security environment

Originating from the Conference on Security and Co-operation in Europe (CSCE), the Organization for Security and Co-operation in Europe (OSCE) is a child of the early-1970s period of political détente during the Cold War. Unlike NATO, the OSCE became a broad and inclusive security forum that brought together the members of both opposing military blocs, as well as militarily nonaligned states from the wider Euro-Atlantic area, to discuss a wide variety of issues across the entire security spectrum. Today, the OSCE counts 57 participating States in North America, Europe, and Asia; all Arctic states have been part of the organization since its beginning (OSCE 2016).

This section provides a short overview of the mandate and decision-making bodies of the OSCE. Afterwards, it explores how the Arctic features in the OSCE's three security dimensions: politico-military, economic and environmental, and human.

The OSCE: the structure and mandate of a comprehensive European security organization

After the Helsinki Final Act in 1975 and the Paris Charter in 1990, the CSCE became slowly institutionalized (e.g., it became permanently based in Vienna, establishing a formal secretariat and permanent institutions). It was officially renamed the OSCE in 1994 (OSCE 2016, 3), but it has preserved much of its former conference character. For example, the organization does not have an official legal personality, so its consensus-based decisions are politically but not legally binding, members are still referred to as *participating States* (pS), and every year the organization's chairmanship rotates to a different pS (OSCE 2016).

The OSCE follows a comprehensive approach to security in its area of jurisdiction. This means that the organization, unlike the Arctic Council, covers aspects of security across the entire spectrum, ranging from traditional politico-military security to environmental and economic security, all the way to human security, holding that each dimension affects the others (OSCE 2016, 5). With the increasing importance of nonmilitary threats to security, and renewed tensions between East and West, the organization's comprehensive approach to security seems more relevant today than ever before.

Formally, OSCE summits, bringing together the heads of state or government of all participating States, are the organization's highest decision-making body. However, de facto, the annual OSCE Ministerial Council at the foreign ministerial level acts as the central decision-making body, as heads of state or government summits take place on an irregular basis (OSCE 2018b). Beyond the ministerial council, OSCE pS also meet weekly at the ambassador level in the Permanent Council (PC), which includes the three informal subsidiary bodies that cover the three OSCE security dimensions (politico-military, economic and environmental, and human) (OSCE 2018a). The pS also meet at the Forum for Security Co-operation (FSC), an autonomous decision-making body with a separate chairmanship (rotating three times a year) that deals exclusively with issues related to military security and stability in the OSCE area (OSCE 2011).

In addition, the OSCE PA, comprising legislators from all OSCE pS, offers recommendations and issues resolutions on pertinent issues. The Personal Representatives assist the Chairperson-in-Office on issues such as gender, youth, or nondiscrimination. Furthermore, there are three so-called OSCE-related bodies: the Joint Consultative Group (JCG), which discusses all issues related to the Treaty on Conventional Armed Forces in Europe (CFE); the Open Skies Consultative Commission (OSCC), which covers aspects related to the aerial transparency and confidence-building regime of the Open Skies Treaty (OS); and the Court of Conciliation and Arbitration (OSCE 2016, 7). The OSCE structure and organization is further explained in Figure 29.1.

How does the Arctic feature in the OSCE's comprehensive security approach?

As with NATO, the Arctic does not feature prominently on the different OSCE agendas. This is hardly surprising, considering that the agendas of the various OSCE bodies are set by the respective chairmanships. Apart from recurring agenda items, for example the preparations of the Annual Security Review Conference (ASRC) or the Human Dimension Implementation Meetings (HDIMs), pS usually use the regular meetings to inform or raise awareness about topics, security issues, and regions that are of particular interest to them (OSCE 2018a).

In this regard, several Arctic states have occasionally used the platform provided by national statements in various OSCE bodies to, inter alia, raise awareness about the security situation in the High North (Efjestad 10/22/2015), inform other pS about military exercises in the area (OSCE-FSC 2013a, 2013b, 2014), or to highlight other events of particular importance to the region such as Sámi People's Day (Johansen 2/9/2018). However, as is common in the OSCE, these statements have remained purely declaratory in nature.

In the politico-military security dimension, the Arctic only seems to be a peripheral region to the OSCE (Bailes 2009, 35). For example, the existing arms control regimes and Confidence and Security-Building Measures (CSBMs) of the OSCE mainly focus on land and air forces on the European continent, so only the land territories of the European High North are covered by their regulations (Schaller 2018b, 223). Furthermore, many provisions of these documents still reflect the political, military, and technological realities of the early 1990s and are increasingly unable to provide sufficient levels of transparency and

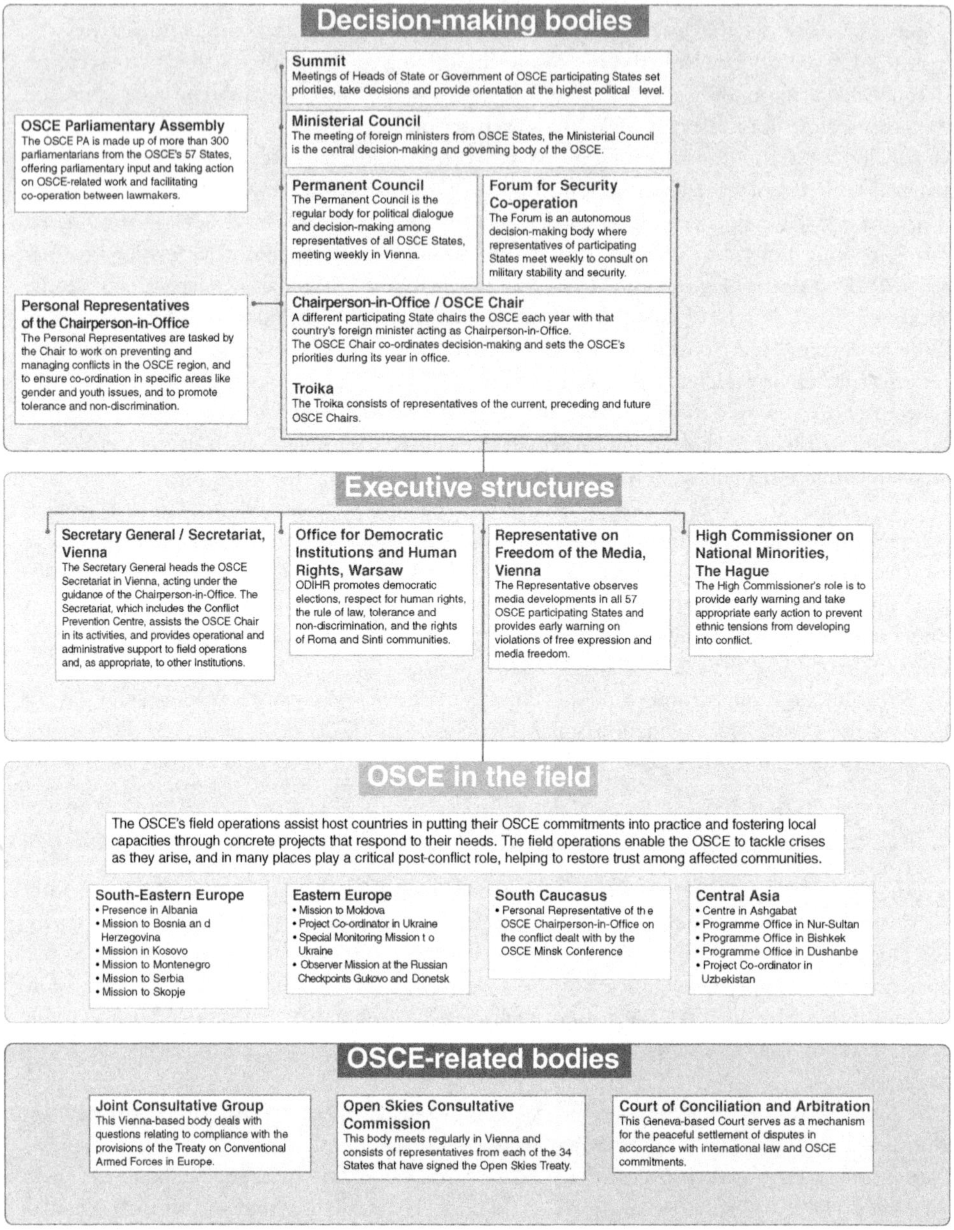

Figure 29.1 OSCE structure

predictability in the currently tense political climate (Tiilikainen 2015, 25; Koivula 2017, 119; Schaller 2018a, 116).

While climate-related security risks and environmental security have gradually become more important in the work of the OSCE (Hardt 2017, 177), the OSCE has been largely dormant when it comes to going beyond raising awareness of the nexus between climate change and security-related issues in the Arctic. One of the few exceptions was a 2009 project to study the possible security implications of climate change for the OSCE region, develop regional scenarios, and help identify how the OSCE could contribute to mitigating these challenges. The OSCE's inadequate attention to the Arctic is also apparent regarding the issue of energy security. In 2006, 2007, 2009, and 2013, the OSCE Ministerial Council passed decisions to enhance dialogue on energy security among OSCE pS, to promote awareness regarding the protection of critical energy infrastructures from potential terrorist threats, and to strengthen dialogue and cooperation on energy security in the OSCE area (OSCE Ministerial Council 12/5/2006, 11/30/2007, 12/2/2009, 12/6/2013). While these did not focus specifically on the Arctic region, one could at least argue that the decisions implicated the Arctic in many ways, given the region's current and future role in the global energy market.

So far, the OSCE PA has been its most active body regarding Arctic security issues. In 2005, the PA organized its first conference that was specifically focused on the environmental and security challenges faced by Arctic states (OSCE PA 2005). The norm-setting advisory body has sought through various resolutions to highlight the security implications of climate change on the Arctic security environment and the world as a whole (OSCE PA 7/10/2010; OSCE PA 7/3/2013). In particular, the PA's Istanbul Declaration acknowledged the need for strengthened cooperation in the fields of environmental and civil security, in light of changing conditions in the Arctic (OSCE PA 2013). In 2015, the PA appointed Norwegian parliamentarian Ola Elvestuen as its first Special Representative for Arctic Issues. The mandate of the Special Representative includes raising awareness and promoting cooperation on Arctic issues within the PA, maintaining contact with and following up on the work of the OSCE and other international organizations that deal with the Arctic region, monitoring the situation in the Arctic region, and reporting to the PA and to the President on relevant developments (OSCE PA 12/16/2015). In his 2017 report, Elvestuen noted that "the challenges for the Arctic area are geopolitical, environmental and economic, and human rights-related" and that these challenges "cut across all dimensions of human security that the OSCE covers" (2017, 1). Beyond the challenges for environmental and economic security, he also highlighted the social challenges for Indigenous communities trying to preserve their livelihoods and culture given increased extraction of resources in the High North (2017, 2–3).

Once again, it appears that the main hindrance to greater OSCE involvement in the Arctic is the lack of consensus among OSCE pS, most vividly expressed by Canada's position. At a meeting on Maritime and Inland Waterways Cooperation in the OSCE area in 2008, the head of the Canadian delegation to the OSCE expressed the country's opposition to stronger OSCE involvement in the Arctic due to the "effectiveness of existing mechanisms and limited organizational expertise [of the OSCE] in this area" (Delegation of Canada to the OSCE 5/21/2008).

An Arctic role for the OSCE?

In light of the increasing relevance of Arctic security issues beyond the area's regional boundaries, and considering that all Arctic states are also pS in the OSCE, the question arises: what role might the OSCE play in the future? These considerations are particularly relevant when recalling that regional security bodies, such as the AC, do not cover the whole spectrum of security issues and dynamics.

For example, in these times in which both NATO and Russia are stepping up their military programs and activities and the risk of unintended escalation seems ever-present, a substantial update of existing arrangements, maybe even a separate set of Arctic CSBMs that would increase the transparency of military deployments and activities could help maintain the stable security situation in the High North (Wezeman 2016, 23; Conley and Melino 2016, 17–19; Schaller 2018b, 226). However, the AC specifically excludes military security issues from its agenda. While the political climate is currently not ripe for any progress on arms control negotiations, the issue of including the Arctic in existing arms control frameworks will certainly be raised during future discussions between OSCE pS.

The OSCE has many opportunities for increasing its Arctic engagement via its economic and environmental security dimensions. The OSCE has a long tradition of promoting regional cooperation on environmental security issues, as manifested by its work addressing climate-related security risks in Eastern Europe, Southeastern Europe, the South Caucasus, and Central Asia (see the Environment and Security (ENVSEC) Initiative for more information: OSCE 2018c). The human security challenges in the Arctic seemingly fit well into the organization's comprehensive security approach and the OSCE's expertise as an established and inclusive forum for dialogue.

As these examples highlight, there is significant potential for an enhanced OSCE role in Arctic security issues. However, given the current lack of a political consensus for greater involvement of the OSCE in Arctic issues, and considering the organization's limited financial resources, it is unlikely that the OSCE will take a stronger role in the Arctic anytime soon.

NATO, the OSCE and the Arctic region: comparative reflections and concluding remarks

This chapter assessed the extent to which the Arctic is featured in the day-to-day work of NATO and the OSCE, focusing on both organizations' policies, strategies, and internal debates. It might seem odd to compare the approaches to the Arctic of two very different security organizations. However, upon a second look, many commonalities – in particular with regard to the factors that constrain their efforts in the Arctic region – come to light.

First, it is evident that neither NATO nor the OSCE as organizations have a dedicated Arctic strategy or a collective approach to address traditional or nontraditional security issues in the region. The main reasons seem to be a lack of political consensus and the hesitancy of some Arctic states to open the region to any third party. Since both organizations are consensus-based, their agendas are ultimately set and defined by the lowest common denominator of the national interests of their members. So far, the most vocal opponents of a stronger role for either organization in the Arctic are Canada and Russia. In the case of Canada, this has less to do with the country's position towards these organizations and, as most scholars agree, more to do with sovereignty concerns in the High North, such as the disputed legal status of the Northwest Passage and unresolved border issues with Denmark and the United States. Because of these concerns, Canada has not only blocked any concrete steps towards a bigger role for the two organizations in the High North, but for the same reasons it has blocked the EU's application for observer status on the AC several times.

Second, due to the region's long history of cooperation in a challenging and sometimes even inhospitable climate, as well as the common economic interests at stake, there seems to be a common preference for keeping other national actors and governmental and security organizations out, or at least relegating them to an observer's seat. In other words, some other Arctic states might feel quite comfortable with Canada's strong opposition against external involvement in the area. It is, for example, hard to believe that Russia, and also military nonaligned Sweden and Finland, would be keen to see a stronger NATO involvement in the region, which would carry the risk of disrupting the current atmosphere of cooperation and could trigger an unintended spiral of escalation in the region.

Third, even though both organizations maintain a low profile in the area, they have, so far, both taken modest steps towards a larger involvement in security issues in the region, most notably in the area of climate change and environmental security. While the OSCE focuses more broadly on the implications of climate change across all security dimensions, NATO focuses on the military conception of security and military cooperation among its member states (e.g. SAR, disaster response, maritime safety, and the protection of critical infrastructure). Similar observations are also true regarding human security, in which the OSCE, furthermore, has the comparative advantage of a comprehensive approach to security and an equal role for Russia at the negotiating table.

Fourth, the most vocal advocates for a stronger NATO and OSCE role in the region are the organizations' parliamentary assemblies. Both have been particularly active in highlighting the security implications that changes in the Arctic security environment might have for the core mandate of both organizations and they have taken steps to keep the issue active and visible on their agendas. However, both assemblies mainly have a norm-setting advisory function and, given that they consist of representatives from the national parliaments, their position may not always reflect the position of their respective governments.

Finally, in light of growing tensions between Russia and the West and the increasing impact of Arctic security issues beyond the region, it remains to be seen to what extent the strong opposition of some Arctic states against an enhanced role for NATO and the OSCE in the region can be upheld. This seems particularly relevant in the field of military security, considering that regional bodies like the AC are by mandate unable to respond to security challenges in this field. However, the OSCE, with its comprehensive security approach and long tradition as an inclusive forum of dialogue, seems to have many opportunities to increase its Arctic engagement, not only in the economic and environmental security sphere, but also when it comes to military transparency and confidence-building. However, in the end, both organizations will only be able to be as strong in the region as the Arctic states allow them to be. In attempting to bring together different national positions, it is important to keep in mind that in the security sphere there is not just one but many "Arctics": perspectives change from actor to actor and from security sphere to security sphere.

Notes

1 The mandate of the Arctic Council specifically excludes military security from its agenda. (Arctic Council 9/19/1996, p. 2).

2 Traditionally, state-based security pertained to interstate relations and was mainly of a military character, as threats came in the form of external aggression by other states. As states became more secure, especially after the Cold War, this security did not necessarily extend to state populations, giving rise to a number of new security threats and concepts (e.g., Buzan et al. 1998; Hoogensen Gjørv 2018).

3 As a response to Russia's annexation of Crimea and its role in the conflict in and around Ukraine, Western countries have suspended all practical military cooperation with Russia, including the meetings of the Arctic Chiefs of Defence Staff, the Arctic Security Forces Roundtable (ASFR), and several joint military exercises in the region Käpylä and Mikkola (2015, 13). The newly established Arctic Coast Guard Forum (ACGF) is not directly affected by these sanctions as it consists of a mixed composition of civil, military, and paramilitary coast guards Arctic Coast Guard Forum.

4 The NATO Parliamentary Assembly is an interparliamentary organization that brings together legislators from NATO member countries to consider security-related issues of common interest and concern. Since the 1980s, it has assumed additional roles by integrating into its work parliamentarians from NATO partner countries in Europe and beyond.

5 In its 2010 Strategic Concept for the Defence and Security of the Members of NATO, the alliance acknowledges that: "key environmental and resource constraints, including health risks, climate change, water scarcity and increasing energy needs will further shape the future security environment in areas of concern to NATO and have the potential to significantly affect NATO planning and operations" NATO (2010, Para. 15).

References

Allied Command Transformation Public Affairs (2017): Charting the Arctic Sea's Changing Environment. Available online at www.act.nato.int/charting-the-arctic-sea-s-changing-environment, checked on 8/11/2018.

Archer, Clive; Scrivener, David (1982): Frozen Frontiers and Resource Wrangles: Conflict and Cooperation in Northern Waters. In *International Affairs* 59 (1), pp. 59–76. DOI: 10.2307/2620158.

Arctic Coast Guard Forum (ACGF) Available online at www.arcticcoastguardforum.com/, checked on 5/17/2018.

Arctic Council (9/19/1996): *Declaration on the Establishment of the Arctic Council.* Ottawa Declaration.

Åtland, Kristian (2011): Russia's Armed Forces and the Arctic. All Quiet on the Northern Front? In *Contemporary Security Policy* 32 (2), pp. 267–285. DOI: 10.1080/13523260.2011.590354.

Bailes, Alyson J. K. (2009): Options for Closer Cooperation in the High North. What Is Needed? In Sven G. Holtsmark, Brooke A. Smith-Windsor (Eds.): *Security Prospects in the High North: Geostrategic Thaw or Freeze?* Rome: NATO Defense College (NDC Forum Paper, 7), pp. 28–57.

Bailes, Alyson J. K. (2016): Security in the Arctic: Definitions, Challenges and Solutions. In Linda Jakobson, Neil Melvin (Eds.): *The New Arctic Governance.* Oxford: Oxford University Press (SIPRI Research Report, no. 25), pp. 13–40.

Bentzrød, Sveinung Berg (2015): Både Russland Og Norge Viser Styrke I Nord. In *Aftenposten*, 3/17/2015 (Online). Available online at www.aftenposten.no/norge/i/O9RA/Bade-Russland-og-Norge-viser-styrke-i-nord, checked on 3/5/2018.

Bergh, Kristofer; Klimenko, Ekaterina (2016): Understanding National Approaches to Security in the Arctic. In Linda Jakobson, Neil Melvin (Eds.): *The New Arctic Governance.* Oxford: Oxford University Press (SIPRI Research Report, no. 25), pp. 41–75.

Berkman, Paul Arthur; Vylegzhanin, Alexander N (2013): *Environmental Security in the Arctic Ocean. Promoting Co-operation and Preventing Conflict.* Dordrecht: Springer Netherlands; Imprint; Springer (NATO Science for Peace and Security Series C: Environmental Security, 75).

Blunden, Margaret (2009): The New Problem of Arctic Stability. In *Survival* 51 (5), pp. 121–142. DOI: 10.1080/00396330903309899.

Borgerson, Scott G (2008): Arctic Meltdown. The Economic and Security Implications of Global Warming. In *Foreign Affairs* 87 (2), pp. 63–77.

Buzan, Barry; Wæver, Ole; de Wilde, Jaap (1998): *Security. A New Framework for Analysis.* 12th reprint. Boulder, CO: Lynne Rienner.

Conley, Heather A. (2014): A Role for NATO in the Arctic? In Ann-Sofie Dahl, Pauli Järvenpää (Eds.): *Northern Security and Global Politics. Nordic-Baltic Strategic Influence in a Post-unipolar World.* 1. publ. London: Routledge (Routledge global security studies, pp. 54–64.

Conley, Heather A.; Melino, Matthew (2016): *An Arctic Redesign. Recommendations to Rejuvenate the Arctic Council.* A Report of the CSIS Europe Program. Center for Strategic & International Studies (Ed.). Washington, DC: Center for Strategic & International Studies.

Conley, Heather A.; Rohloff, Caroline (2015): *The New Ice Curtain. Russia's Strategic Reach to the Arctic.* Center for Strategic & International Studies (Ed.). Washington, DC: Center for Strategic & International Studies.

Delegation of Canada to the OSCE (2008): *Closing Statement at the 16th Meeting of the OSCE Economic and Environmental Forum. EEF.DEL/45/08. Maritime and Inland Waterways Co-operation in the OSCE Area: Increasing Security and Protecting the Environment.* Prague: OSCE Economic and Environmental Forum, 5/21/2008.

Ebinger, Charles K; Zambetakis, Evie (2009): The Geopolitics of Arctic Melt. In *International Affairs* 85 (6), pp. 1215–1232. DOI: 10.1111/j.1468-2346.2009.00858.x.

Efjestad, Svein (2015): *Statement by Mr. Svein Efjestad, Policy Director, Ministry of Defence of Norway, at the 800th Meeting of the Forum for Security Co-operation*. FSC.DEL/195/15. Vienna: OSCE. Forum for Security Co-operation, 10/22/2015.

Elvestuen, Ola (2017): *Report of the Special Representative for Arctic Issues*. Vienna: OSCE PA.

Forsvaret (2018): Trident Juncture 18. Forsvaret. Available online at https://forsvaret.no/en/exercise-and-operations/exercises/nato-exercise-2018, updated on 8/1/2018, checked on 8/10/2018.

Forsvarsdepartementet (6/12/2018): *Det Amerikanske Marinekorpsets Øving Og Trening I Norge*. Oslo. Available online at www.regjeringen.no/no/aktuelt/det-amerikanske-marinekorpsets-oving-og-trening-i-norge/id2604216/, checked on 8/10/2018).

Haftendorn, Helga (2011): NATO and the Arctic: Is the Atlantic Alliance a Cold War Relic in a Peaceful Region Now Faced with Non-military Challenges? In *European Security* 20 (3), pp. 337–361. DOI: 10.1080/09662839.2011.608352.

Hardt, Judith Nora (2017) *Environmental Security in the Anthropocene*. Routledge: Assessing Theory and Practice.

Hilde, Paal Sigurd (2013): The "new" Arctic – The Military Dimension. In *Journal of Military and Strategic Studies* 15 (2), pp. 130–153.

Hilde, Paal Sigurd (2014): Armed Forces and Security Challenges in the Arctic. In Rolf Tamnes, Kristine Offerdal (Eds.): *Geopolitics and Security in the Arctic. Regional Dynamics in a Global World*. London: Routledge (Routledge Global Security Studies), pp. 147–165.

Holtsmark, Sven G.; Smith-Windsor, Brooke A. (Eds.) (2009): *Security Prospects in the High North: Geostrategic Thaw or Freeze?* Rome: NATO Defense College, (NDC Forum Paper, 7).

Hoogensen Gjørv, Gunhild (2018): Human Security. In Paul D. Williams, Matt McDonald (Eds.): *Security Studies. An Introduction*. 3rd ed. Milton: Taylor and Francis, pp. 221–234.

Huebert, Rob (2010): *The Newly Emerging Arctic Security Environment*. Canadian Defence & Foreign Affairs Institute (Ed.). Calgary: Canadian Defence & Foreign Affairs Institute.

Humrich, Christoph (2015): Sicherheitspolitik Im Arktischen Rat? Lieber Nicht! In *S+F* 33 (3), pp. 23–29. DOI: 10.5771/0175-274X-2015-3-23.

Johansen, Henning Hj (2018): *Statement on the Occasion of the Sámi People's Day*. PC.DEL/160/18. Vienna: OSCE. Permanent Council, 2/9/2018.

Käpylä, Juha; Mikkola, Harri (2015): *On Arctic Exceptionalism. Critical Reflections in the Light of the Arctic Sunrise Case and the Crisis in Ukraine*. The Finnish Institute of International Affairs (Ed.). Helsinki: The Finnish Institute of International Affairs (FIIA Working Paper, 85).

Klimenko, Ekaterina (2016): *Russia's Arctic Security Policy. Still Quiet in the High North?* Stockholm International Peace Research Institute (Ed.). Stockholm: Stockholm International Peace Research Institute (SIPRI Policy Paper, 45).

Knecht, Sebastian (2015): Die Mär Vom Kalten Krieg. Wie Geopolitische Paradigmen in Den Internationalen Beziehungen Im Arktisraum (re)produziert Werden. In *S+F Sicherheit Und Frieden* 33 (3), pp. 121–126.

Koivula, Tommi (2017): Conventional Arms Control in Europe and Its Current Challenges. In Tommi Koivula, Karariina Simonen (Eds.): *Arms Control in Europe. Regimes, Trends and Threats*. Helsinki: National Defence University (National Defence University Series 1, Research publications, No. 16), pp. 113–132.

Le Mière, Christian; Mazo, Jeffrey (2013): *Arctic Opening. Insecurity and Opportunity*. London: Routledge (Adelphi, 440).

Lindsey, George (1989): *Strategic Stability in the Arctic*. International Institute for Strategic Studies. International Institute for Strategic Studies (Ed.). London: Potomac Books Inc (Adelphi papers, 241).

MccGwire, Michael (1990): Strategic Interests in the Arctic Ocean. In Edgar Dosman (Ed.): *Sovereignty and Security in the Arctic*. London: Routledge, pp. 24–40.

NATO (2010): *Active Engagement, Modern Defence*. Lisbon.

OSCE (2011): *What Is the Forum for Security Co-operation?* Vienna.

OSCE (2016): *What Is the OSCE?* Vienna.

OSCE (2018a): Permanent Council. Vienna. Available online at www.osce.org/permanent-council, updated on 8/9/2018, checked on 8/10/2018.

OSCE (2018b): Summits. Vienna. Available online at www.osce.org/summits, updated on 8/9/2018, checked on 8/10/2018.

OSCE (2018c): Environment and Security (ENVSEC) Initiative. Available online at www.osce.org/secretariat/ENVSEC, updated on 8/10/2018, checked on 8/11/2018.
OSCE – FSC (2013a): Journal of the 710th Plenary Meeting of the Forum for Security Co-operation. Vienna (Journal of the Forum for Security Co-operation, FSC.JOUR/716/Corr.1).
OSCE – FSC (2013b): Journal of the 717th Plenary Meeting of the Forum for Security Co-operation. Vienna (Journal of the Forum for Security Co-operation, FSC.JOUR/723).
OSCE – FSC (2014): Journal of the 747th Plenary Meeting of the Forum for Security Co-operation. Vienna (Journal of the Forum for Security Co-operation, FSC.JOUR/753).
OSCE Ministerial Council (12/5/2006): Decision No. 12/06 - Energy Security Dialogue in the OSCE. MC.DEC/12/06.
OSCE Ministerial Council (11/30/2007): Decision No. 6/07 - Protecting Critical Energy Infrastructure from Terrorist Attack. MC.DEC/6/07.
OSCE Ministerial Council (12/2/2009): Decision No. 6/09 - Strengthening Dialogue and Co-operation on Energy Security in the OSCE Area. MC.DEC/6/09.
OSCE Ministerial Council (12/6/2013): Decision No. 5/13 - Improving the Environmental Footprint of Energy-Related Activities in the OSCE Region. MC.DEC/5/13.
OSCE PA (2005): *Tromsø Sub-Regional Conference.* Tromsø: The High North - Environment, Security and Co-operation. OSCE PA.
OSCE PA (7/10/2010): *Oslo Declaration of the OSCE Parliamentary Assembly and Resolutions Adopted at the Nineteenth Annual Session.* Oslo: Oslo Declaration.
OSCE PA (7/3/2013): *Istanbul Declaration and Resolutions Adopted by the OSCE Parliamentary Assembly at the Twenty-Second Annual Session.* Istanbul: Istanbul Declaration.
OSCE PA (12/16/2015): *Norway's Elvestuen Appointed OSCE PA Special Representative for Arctic Issues.* Copenhagen. Available online at www.osce.org/pa/209921, checked on 8/10/2018).
Østhagen, Andreas (2016): *A Quick Start Guide to 21st Century Security in the Arctic.* Washington, DC: The Arctic Institute.
Østhagen, Andreas; Levi Sharp, Gregory; Sigurd Hilde, Paal (2018): At Opposite Poles: Canada's and Norway's Approaches to Security in the Arctic. In *The Polar Journal* 8 (1), pp. 163–181. DOI: 10.1080/2154896X.2018.1468625.
NATO PA (2017): NATO and Security in the Arctic. With assistance of Gerald E. Connolly (Report, 172 PCTR 17 E rev.1 fin).
Petersen, Charles C (1990): Soviet Military Objectives in the Arctic Theatre and How They Might Be Attained. In Edgar Dosman (Ed.): *Sovereignty and Security in the Arctic.* London: Routledge, pp. 41–67.
Rosamond, Annika Bergman (2011): *Perspectives on Security in the Arctic Area.* Copenhagen: Dansk Institut for Internationale Studier (DIIS Report, 9).
Rottem, Svein Vigeland (2016): The Arctic Council in Arctic Governance. The Significance of the Oil Spill Agreement. In Linda Jakobson, Neil Melvin (Eds.): *The New Arctic Governance.* Oxford: Oxford University Press (SIPRI Research Report, no. 25), pp. 147–173.
Sale, Richard; Potapov, Eugene (2010): *The Scramble for the Arctic. Ownership, Exploitation and Conflict in the Far North.* 1. Frances Lincoln edition. London: Frances Lincoln Limited Publishers.
Schaller, Benjamin (2018a): Back to the Future? Revisiting Military Confidence-Building in Europe. In *S+F (security and Peace)* 36 (3), pp. 115–120.
Schaller, Benjamin (2018b): Defusing the Discourse on "Arctic War." The Merits of Military Transparency and Confidence- and Security-Building Measures in the Arctic Region. In Institute for Peace Research and Security Policy at the University of Hamburg (Ed.): *OSCE Yearbook 2017. Yearbook on the Organization for Security and Co-operation in Europe (OSCE).* With assistance of Pál Dunay, Adam Daniel Rotfeld, Andrei Zagorski, Ursel Schlichting, Graeme Currie. Baden-Baden: Nomos (OSCE Yearbook, 23). pp. 213–226.
de Sitter, Maarten (2015): NATO & the Arctic. In Lassi Heininen, Heather Exner-Pirot, Joël Plouffe (Eds.): *Arctic Yearbook.* Iceland: Northern Research Forum hosted by the University of Akureyri, pp. 408–409.
Sonne, Paul (2016): Russia Upgrades Military Prowess in Arctic. In *Wall Street Journal, Eastern edition* 2016, 10/5/2016.
Tamnes, Rolf; Offerdal, Kristine (Eds.) (2014): *Geopolitics and Security in the Arctic. Regional Dynamics in a Global World.* London: Routledge (Routledge global security studies).
Tiilikainen, Teija (Ed.) (2015): *Reviving Co-operative Security in Europe through the OSCE.* Helsinki: OSCE Network of Think Tanks and Academic Institutions, checked on 2/22/2018.
Wezeman, Siemon T. (2016): *Military Capabilities in the Arctic. A New Cold War in the High North?* Stockholm: Stockholm International Peace Research Institute (SIPRI Background Paper).

PART V

People, states, and security

30
INDIGENOUS PEOPLES

Wilfrid Greaves

Introduction

In the last decade, there has been a proliferation of research on Arctic security policy and discourse. Following Soviet leader Mikhail Gorbachev's watershed Murmansk speech in 1987, perceptions of the Arctic began to shift from that of a military theater to a "zone of peace" characterized by confidence-building measures through inter-state cooperation, inclusion of non-state actors in regional governance, economic growth, and environmental protection. A new understanding among Arctic states and peoples that different Arctic futures were possible opened conceptual space for novel and critical ideas and practices to emerge about the very meaning and nature of security within the region. The 1990s and 2000s saw an explosion of political, social, economic, and scientific activities that had been precluded by Cold War tensions, including a web of new and revamped institutions of sub-state, transnational, and regional governance, most notably the Arctic Council. In the past decade, academic and policymaking interest in Arctic security issues has been sustained by the intersection of two transformative forces: economic globalization and anthropogenic climate change that have substantial effects around the globe. The most dramatic effects have been seen in the circumpolar region.

In response to these changing structural forces, circumpolar states have revised and updated their Arctic foreign and security policies. While Arctic states are broadly aligned in terms of identifying the defense of territorial sovereignty, responsible natural resource management, peaceful management of inter-state disputes, and adaptation to climatic and environmental changes as central to their regional security interests (Heininen 2012), the issue of security has become complicated. First, heightened interest in the economic viability of the Arctic's abundant natural resources has stoked fears that competition over territory or resources could erode or even break down the still-evolving system for regional cooperation (Åtland 2014; Borgerson 2008, 2013). Though downplayed by other observers (Greaves 2012; Keil 2014), the possibility of conflict has become a central theme of recent Arctic security analysis and scholarship.

Second, such concerns have been exacerbated by the deterioration of diplomatic relations between Russia and the West. This deterioration is due to the Russian invasion and annexation of Crimea in 2014, support for non-state militia groups in eastern Ukraine, and interference in the domestic political and electoral processes of Western allies, including the United States, United Kingdom, Germany, and France. While these geopolitical factors originated outside the Arctic, they affect cooperation between Russia – the largest and single-most-important Arctic state – and its circumpolar neighbors, five of which are members of NATO. A loss of trust or worsened relations due to activities in other parts of the world risks undermining the support for Arctic regional cooperation that appeared so promising in the 1990s and first decade of the 2000s. It also demonstrates the fundamental point that the meaning of security in the Arctic is malleable. States and other actors continue to redefine the nature of Arctic security according to geopolitical, economic, and ecological developments arising both within the region and affecting it from outside.

Typically overlooked within discussions of Arctic security is its relationship with the region's Indigenous peoples. Historically, Arctic Indigenous peoples were negatively affected by actions taken by circumpolar states to protect their national security interests. However, the post-Cold War decline in concern over conventional or unconventional conflict, combined with the establishment of new institutions that increased Indigenous representation in Arctic politics, created opportunities for Indigenous political actors to articulate and pursue their interests in new ways. It became possible to frame long-standing and emerging challenges to Indigenous peoples and communities as central to overall conditions of security for the region and its inhabitants. In response, new or renewed concerns rose to the fore within discussions of Arctic security. These concerns include poverty and economic underdevelopment; Indigenous culture and language loss; chronic social and health ills such as addiction, suicide, and domestic violence; the impacts of extractive industrial projects; transboundary pollutants; marine and ecosystem health; and the increasingly rapid and acute effects of climate change.

While some Indigenous Arctic actors deliberately articulated their most pressing concerns as security issues in an attempt to mobilize a greater state response, often framed as *human security* to appeal to the foreign policy values of middle powers such as Canada and Norway, deeper questions about the conceptual compatibility of typically state-centric concepts such as security with Indigenous ontologies have been largely unexamined. As such, there has been a problematic dual movement with respect to research on Indigenous peoples and Arctic security: the conceptual widening and deepening of security has allowed for the inclusion of human and environmental security issues of great importance to Indigenous peoples to finally register within Arctic security discourse (Greaves 2012, 2016a; Hoogensen Gjørv et al. 2014). But underlying questions about the relationship between security and colonialism, Indigenous and non-Indigenous ways of knowing, and Indigenous and non-Indigenous forms of political authority have largely gone unexamined. Meanwhile, the material conditions of life for many Arctic Indigenous peoples remain challenging, as the ongoing processes of climate change, economic modernization, and cultural assimilation continue to undermine and displace Indigenous peoples and traditional lifestyles (Poppel 2015).

This chapter provides an overview of Indigenous peoples and security in the Arctic. First, it outlines the diverse contexts and contemporary status of Arctic Indigenous peoples. It then examines the relationship between Indigenous peoples and the fields of international relations and security studies, focusing on the Arctic but also identifying commonalities with non-Arctic Indigenous peoples. This section explains the relationship between Indigenous identity and the specific kinds of threats facing Indigenous peoples – namely the unequal relations of power and authority that exist between Indigenous peoples and the non-Indigenous societies and institutions of the states in which they now reside – and the ontological relationship between Indigenous peoples and land. These two factors, possession of a nondominant identity within their respective political contexts and having their identities and well-being inherently tied to specific ecological systems, produce unique security issues for Indigenous peoples and particular challenges in adequately responding to those issues that threaten their survival and well-being. The chapter concludes with an overview of security issues facing Indigenous peoples across the circumpolar region.

Indigenous peoples and politics in the Arctic

Indigenous peoples in the circumpolar region exhibit typical and atypical traits for Indigenous peoples in contemporary global politics. On the one hand, they are historically colonized populations who no longer exercise full authority over their traditional lands. They also retain continuity with precolonial practices and social organization, due in part to the relatively recent experiences of colonization by many Arctic Indigenous peoples, especially in North America. On the other hand, most of the Arctic states are democratic political systems with strong rule of law, social welfare systems, and greater legal protections for Indigenous rights than most other countries with Indigenous populations. As discussed below, Arctic Indigenous peoples enjoy some of the highest qualities of life and greatest degrees of political autonomy of any Indigenous peoples in the world. Arctic Indigenous peoples have also organized themselves politically into groups that sometimes challenge the preferences of their state governments; even, as in Russia, when faced with the possibility of overt political repression, violence, or retaliation. Thus, overall, Arctic Indigenous peoples enjoy a high degree of political freedom, while also experiencing material conditions and political nondominance within settler-colonial political contexts that curtail their political agency (AHDR 2004; Larsen and Fondahl 2014).

While debates over indigeneity and identity remain relevant in the circumpolar region (Corntassel 2003; Gausset, Kenrick, and Gibb 2011; Guenther et al. 2006), by virtue of their distinct structures of political representation, Arctic Indigenous peoples are more clearly identifiable than elsewhere. By definition, they comprise the Indigenous peoples living in Arctic territories under the sovereignty of the eight circumpolar states (Canada, Denmark/Greenland, Finland, Iceland, Norway, Russia, Sweden, and the United States). Drawing on one widely employed definition of indigeneity, the *Arctic Human Development Report* defined Indigenous peoples as:

> Those peoples who were marginalized when the modern states were created and identify themselves as Indigenous peoples. They are associated with specific territories to which they trace their histories. They exhibit one or more of the following characteristics: they speak a language that is different from that of the dominant group(s); they are being discriminated against in the political system; they are being discriminated against within the legal system; their cultures diverge from that of the remaining society; they often diverge from the mainstream society in their resource use by being hunters and gatherers, nomads, pastoralists, or swidden farmers; they consider themselves and are considered by others as different from the rest of the population.
>
> *(Csonka and Schweitzer 2004: 46)*

Numbering approximately 500,000 of the 4 million total inhabitants of the circumpolar region, Indigenous peoples form an overlapping ring of transboundary societies surrounding the Arctic Ocean. A majority of these live in Russia, which also has the greatest diversity of Indigenous peoples with over 41 different groups, including the Chukchi, Evenki, Khaka,

Khanty, Nenet, Tuvan, and Yakut peoples. Aleuts inhabit the easternmost Russian region of Kamchatka and the Aleutian Islands. Mainland Alaska is home to Athabaskan, Gwich'in, and Inupik (Alaskan Eskimo) peoples, whose territories cross the border into the Yukon and Northwest Territories in northern Canada. However, a majority of the Indigenous population in the Canadian Arctic are Inuit, who form large majorities of between 80% and 90% in the territory of Nunavut and in neighboring Greenland – a self-governing polity under Danish sovereignty. Sámi comprise the entire Indigenous population of northern Norway, Sweden, and Finland, with a small number also on the Kola Peninsula in northwestern Russia (Dubreuil 2011). While now rooted in the social and political structures of their respective states, the sociological boundaries of Arctic Indigenous peoples are not consistent with the colonial borders imposed upon them. Indigenous peoples are living reminders of precolonial patterns of occupancy and land use in the circumpolar region; they maintain ongoing kinship and social relationships that transcend sovereign boundaries.

Indigenous peoples are central to political institutions and social organization across the circumpolar region. Indeed, one of the key features of post-Cold War Arctic politics is the establishment of devolved forms of Indigenous self-government exercising a range of political authority. Greenlanders first achieved home rule from Denmark in 1979, then self-rule in 2009 following a Yes vote of 75% in a nonbinding referendum. Since then, the Greenlandic legislature has assumed control over all areas of public policy except for foreign policy and defense. Inuit in Canada exercise self-government over four land-claim areas that account for 35% of Canada's total land area: Nunatsiavut, Nunavik, Nunavut, and the Inuvialuit Settlement Region. Alaskan Indigenous peoples were incorporated into Native Regional Corporations by the US government in 1971, but have also found representation as the majority population of the North Slope Borough and other self-governing municipalities in Alaska.

In Fennoscandia, the Sámi have separate parliaments in Norway, Sweden, and Finland that serve advisory and quasi-policymaking roles for their respective national governments on issues related to the Sámi people. In Norway, the passing of the Finnmark Act in 2005 gave Sámi in that country a legislated role in the co-management of large swathes of land in northern Norway comprising part of their traditional territory of Sápmi. Lastly, following the dissolution of the Soviet Union in 1993, the Russian Federation established various ethnic republics that also provided some representation for Indigenous peoples residing in the far north and eastern regions of the country.

In addition to their significant degrees of self-government, political autonomy, or elected representation within their respective states, Indigenous peoples have been central to regional governance through their active participation in the establishment and activities of the Arctic Council. Founded in 1996 to provide a dedicated forum for regional dialogue and cooperation, the Council owes much of the impetus for its creation to the activism of Indigenous leaders and advocacy groups. Since the 1970s, Indigenous peoples across the Arctic established nongovernmental organizations such as the Inuit Circumpolar Conference (later Inuit Circumpolar Council), Inuit Tapirisat of Canada (later Inuit Tapiriit Kanatami), and the Sámi Council to lobby on their behalf to southern-based national governments. Historian John English (English 2013: 95) credits these organizations with the eventual success of the Arctic Council negotiations:

> Voices that were silenced in the fifties became audible in the sixties, eloquent in the seventies, and powerful and influential later. The colonized now came to the colonial capitals no longer as subjects but as actors shaping their times and the lives of their people.

Six groups were formally incorporated into regional governance through their inclusion as Permanent Participants on the Arctic Council: the Aleut International Association, the Arctic Athabaskan Council, the Gwich'in Council International, the Inuit Circumpolar Council, the Russian Association of Indigenous Peoples of the North (RAIPON), and the Sámi Council. As the first body to grant Indigenous peoples formal status with rights to membership and participation approximating that of the Member States, the Council provided Indigenous peoples with representation at the premier forum for regional cooperation. English (2013: 298) argued "it is a mark of the historic change that the growing prominence of the Arctic Council with its Indigenous participants means that many rules will now be set not only in imperial southern capitals but often by northern peoples."

The emergence of Indigenous voices as a potent political force has substantially altered politics in the circumpolar region (Tennberg 2010). English's analysis of the Arctic Council's origins affirmed the conclusions of other scholars like Oran Young (2005) that it is partly through the efforts of Indigenous peoples that the Arctic has developed from a "region of peripheries" into a coherent region of its own. Timo Koivurova and Leena Heinämäki (2006: 104) even suggested that Indigenous peoples have become so key to regional politics that they collectively exercise a de facto veto over the decision-making processes of the Arctic Council. Although they continue to reflect the significant differences of opportunity afforded by their respective historical experiences and contemporary circumstances, Arctic Indigenous peoples have been at the forefront of advancing the political interests of Indigenous peoples and their inclusion in organizations and forums previously reserved for states.

In this respect, Arctic politics reflects the achievements of "global indigenism" as an Indigenous social movement based on identifying indigeneity as a legitimate basis for collective rights and political representation (Niezen 2003). The adoption of the United Nations *Declaration of the Rights of Indigenous Peoples* in 2007, the creation of the UN Permanent Forum on Indigenous Issues, and domestic initiatives that recognize and offer reparations for colonial wrongs all signify the contemporary reemergence of Indigenous peoples as important political actors. However, the terms of this inclusion remain constrained by the interests and actions of settler-colonial states and the international institutions over which they exhibit significant influence.

Although "the most egregious expressions of colonialism have been discredited [...] what remained untouched are those 'colonial agendas' that have had a controlling (systemic) effect in privileging national (white) interests at the expense of Indigenous rights" (Maaka and Fleras 2005: 12). Despite the progress that has been made by settler-colonial governments and legal authorities in terms of acknowledging and respecting Indigenous rights and titles, the relationships between Indigenous peoples and national governments remain structured by the dominance of settler-colonial values, institutions, and interests. Though more empowered than ever before, and more so than most Indigenous peoples elsewhere in the world, even in the Arctic, Indigenous peoples lack the power to control their own collective futures.

Indigenous peoples and security

There is universal agreement on the centrality of Indigenous peoples to the new forms and functions of Arctic regional politics. However, Indigenous peoples have generally been absent from the academic fields of international relations and security studies (Epp 2000;

King 2017; Shaw 2002), with some notable exceptions. Neta Crawford's (1994) study of the Iroquois Great Law of Peace is an example of a security regime that generated important discussions about indigeneity and international relations (Bedford and Workman 1997; Crawford 2017). Postcolonial approaches to security have examined Indigenous peoples as sovereign nations with distinct cosmologies, political systems, and diplomatic practices (Beier 2005, 2007, 2010, 2016), and as experiencing specific harms associated with military activities, such as nuclear testing in the southwestern United States (Laffey and Nadarajah 2016). Other recent scholarship examined the problems Indigenous politics create for the foreign policies of settler states (Lackenbauer and Cooper 2007), Indigenous peoples as threatening the interests of settler-colonial states (Bland 2014), and the governmental tactics of criminalization, surveillance, and police and paramilitary violence that are used against them (Bell and Schreiner 2018; Crosby and Monaghan 2012, 2016; Pasternak et al. 2013; Proulx 2014). Although it has been common in the post-Cold War period for "nonstate units [to] claim security interests of their own," including Indigenous peoples who "definitely have their own specific security problems" (Eriksson 1995: 271–278), even critical perspectives that explore the security interests and ontologies of subaltern groups in the Global South overlook Indigenous peoples within the Global North or their relation to security (Barkawi and Laffey 2006).

However, the recent boom in studies of Arctic geopolitics and security, combined with the unique salience of Indigenous peoples to circumpolar politics, means that Arctic Indigenous peoples' security has received greater attention than Indigenous peoples in other parts of the world (Greaves 2016a, 2016b; Nickels 2013; Smith 2010). However, there are still limitations to this small but growing literature on the international dimensions of Arctic Indigenous peoples, including an emphasis on international law, particularly following promulgation of the UN *Declaration on the Rights of Indigenous Peoples*, and an uneven empirical focus on different subparts of the Arctic region. For instance, while Indigenous peoples in Canada, Sámi in Scandinavia, and Greenlandic Inuit are widely discussed (Abele and Rodon 2007; Lawrence 2014; Loukacheva 2007; Shadian 2010, 2014; Smith 2010), there is little discussion that positions Alaska Natives or the so-called small numbered peoples of the North, Siberia, and Far East in Russia in terms of security or international relations. The explicit exclusion of "matters related to military security" from the mandate of the Arctic Council may also have directed scholars of Arctic governance and Indigenous peoples away from pursuing security research, even when pertaining to unconventional security issues (Greaves 2013).

Moreover, Arctic security discourse and practices have come at the direct expense of Indigenous peoples, and their negative effects manifest in both ideational and material forms. Ideationally, the very concept of security possesses a Eurocentric genealogy, and an applied history that is inseparable from the establishment of Westphalian forms of sovereignty and the global expansion of European power through processes of conquest, colonization, and imperial expansion (Rothschild 1995). On this basis, concepts such as security and sovereignty, which are central to the Westphalian understanding of modern, Western, politics, are not only limited in their capacity to reflect Indigenous worldviews, but their use by analysts and governments risks imposing forms of neocolonialism. This potential has been identified, for instance, with the application of human security theory to understand the challenges facing Indigenous peoples in the Arctic. Whereas some scholars have argued for the applicability of human security due to its emphasis on non-state human referent objects and nonmilitary forms of security threats (Greaves 2012; Hoogensen Gjørv et al. 2009, 2014; Hossain et al. 2016), others have rejected the concept as a form of "virtuous imperialism"

(Hoogensen Gjørv 2014) that fails to capture the specific qualities of Indigenous peoples, particularly their relations with nonhuman actors and the land (Griffiths 2008). While human security has become quite widely applied to the Arctic, the concern among some observers is that this "result[s] in the violent imposition of modern modes of thought upon fundamentally unmodern expressions of human being, and the tragic loss of the opportunity to explore an alternative form of life" (Bedford and Workman 1997: 91). If Indigenous worldviews are defined in contrast and opposition to the modern, Eurocentric modes of thought that accompanied colonization, then analyzing contemporary Indigenous peoples through the lens of historically powerful concepts that have been employed to oppress them only furthers the structural violence inflicted upon Indigenous peoples.

Materially, Indigenous peoples have been negatively affected by the policies through which Arctic states have pursued their own national security interests. Indigenous leaders identified militarization of the Arctic during the Cold War as coming at the direct expense of Indigenous peoples through the damage to humans and wildlife caused by chemical pollutants and contamination, low-flying military aircraft, and the construction of military facilities such as air bases and radar stations in ecologically sensitive environments (Erasmus 1986; Simon 1989). At times, Indigenous peoples were also manipulated in order to assert sovereignty over Arctic territory or state authority over Indigenous communities. For example, in the 1950s the Canadian government deceptively relocated Inuit families thousands of kilometers north of their previous communities in order to serve as "human flagpoles" in support of Canada's Arctic sovereignty claims (Makkik 2009; Tester and Kulchyski 1994). In the 1950s and 1960s, Inuit in Canada were also subjected to the mass slaughter of their sled dogs by federal and provincial police in order to reduce Inuit mobility and essentially force them into permanent settlement (Croteau 2010; QIA 2010).

However, in a different sense, security for Indigenous peoples is undermined by the very fact of settler-colonialism as a historical and ongoing process that constituted the existence of circumpolar states and produced them as politically sovereign over Arctic territories. The security of modern states, particularly in the New World of North America, but also in northern Fennoscandia and the Russian Far East, was premised on the subordination or elimination of non-European-descended peoples. Though experiences of colonialism varied considerably across the region, all Arctic states except Iceland can be characterized as having engaged in colonial relations of power and dominance over the Indigenous populations who live in territories that have been incorporated into their states. While there is no question of a colonial history in the case of Canada, Greenland, and the United States, the same is increasingly recognized of the Nordic states, which historically avoided such a characterization (Fur 2006; Naum and Nordin 2013).

For centuries, Sámi people in Scandinavia were at the center of great power competition between Denmark, Norway, Sweden, and Russia over control of the Scandinavian interior (Greaves 2018a). This foreshadowed the "post-imperial sovereignty games" that would later occur between the Nordic states and their Arctic colonial possessions (Adler-Nissen and Gam 2014). In Russia, Siberia has been called "Russia's North Asian colony," (Forsyth 1992) and the processes and techniques of colonial conquest, territorial acquisition, and Indigenous subjugation resembled those in the Americas and elsewhere (Bassin 2004). The Stalinist period was particularly difficult for Soviet/Russian Indigenous peoples, as state violence was endemic and many people were forced to assimilate to the communist national identity and abandon distinct Indigenous linguistic and cultural traditions that were thought to weaken the unity of the proletariat and the Soviet Union (Josephson 2014). Thus, across the Arctic, security and well-being for Indigenous peoples has been harmed not only by actions taken by states in the assertion of their Arctic sovereignty, but also by the superimposition of those states over the Indigenous peoples and governance systems that already existed on Arctic territories.

The common outcome has been the production of contemporary Arctic societies in which Indigenous peoples are structurally subordinated to the authority of non-Indigenous peoples and institutions. This structural position of Indigenous peoples within settler-colonial societies produces conditions of insecurity rooted in the assertion of non-Indigenous forms of political authority over Indigenous peoples and territories that are distinct from those of Indigenous people (Greaves 2016a, 2018b). Thus, the two most important factors for the production of Indigenous peoples' insecurity are their political and social subordination relative to the majority European or European-descendant populations of their countries, and their "ontological relationship to land [...] that the nation-state has sought to diminish through its social, legal, and cultural practices" (Moreton-Robinson 2015: 15–20). The relationship of Indigenous peoples to specific lands makes degradation of the environment through industrial pollution, land-use changes, and other modern practices directly threatening to Indigenous practices, culture, and identity: "Cultural survival, identity and the very existence of Indigenous societies depend to a considerable degree on the maintenance of environmental quality. The degradation of the environment is therefore inseparable from a loss of culture and hence identity" (Cocklin 2002: 159).

While there is neither a universal Indigenous identity, nor are all Indigenous peoples' interests defined in the same way, there are common characteristics and experiences that constitute Indigenous peoples *as* Indigenous. Indigenous peoples are distinct from other groups of people precisely because of the ongoing experience of colonization and dispossession resulting from the coercive imposition of non-Indigenous systems of power and value by people originally from somewhere else. The distinct security issues that Indigenous peoples in the Arctic face are rooted in this distinctiveness from the majority populations and dominant institutions of the societies they inhabit.

Circumpolar Indigenous peoples' security issues

What, then, constitute security issues for Indigenous peoples in the Arctic? While the literature on Arctic security is considerable, and research on Indigenous peoples and security has grown and continues to develop, there is still relatively little scholarship where the two overlap. What research does exist, moreover, is unequally representative of the total circumpolar region, and is further limited by the distinct linguistic, academic, and policymaking communities of different parts of the Arctic. However, on the basis of current research, some conclusions are possible. First, notwithstanding Indigenous critiques that have been made of academic discourses of the current Anthropocene age (Sundberg 2014; Todd 2015), some Indigenous political actors employed security language to characterize the existentially threatening nature of contemporary global conditions of environmental crisis. Most threats confronting Indigenous peoples today are directly linked to the degradation of complex human–animal–ecological–cultural systems on which Indigenous identities and interests are based. For instance, Inuit and other Arctic Indigenous peoples, particularly in Canada but also transnationally through the Inuit Circumpolar Council, have operationalized security in terms of the direct and indirect effects of human-caused environmental change on their Arctic homeland, cultural identity, and political and social autonomy (Greaves 2016a, 2016b).

Even where disagreement exists over the relative "security-ness" of some of these claims, the severe impact of climate change on Inuit survival is indisputable (Smith and Parks 2010). This significant concern over the harmful effects of industrial pollution and environmental damage on Indigenous peoples is echoed in the security discourse employed by sub-Arctic Indigenous communities in northern Canada, who are experiencing threats to human health, air and water quality, country foods, and hunting game as a result of bitumen mining, leaks from oil pipelines and tailing ponds, and the contribution of oil and gas extraction to global climate change. Sámi people in Norway share similar concerns over the impacts of natural resource extraction, particularly energy projects, and climate change, on their abilities to maintain their economic and cultural practices (Greaves 2016a; Hossain 2016). While there is no unitary Indigenous conception of what security means, there are clear similarities across different Indigenous peoples with respect to what is considered threatened. Common concerns include the ecological vitality and survival of Indigenous peoples' traditional territories, and the Indigenous cultural and subsistence practices developed over many centuries that rely upon them.

Though harder to ascertain, evidence for Indigenous peoples in Russia appears consistent with that from elsewhere in the Arctic. Available English-language research suggests that Russian Indigenous peoples also frame their survival and well-being in terms of the environment–culture nexus, particularly with respect to the negative impacts of hydrocarbon resource extraction. Populations in the Russian Arctic experience worse quality-of-life indicators than the general public, with Indigenous people even more prone to poor health and poor well-being than non-Indigenous inhabitants (Hild and Stordahl 2004). Structural changes in Russian politics during the 1990s restricted the ability of regional or autonomous governments to address these trends. In addition to the reduction of certain powers and the elimination of sovereignty claims for northern republics within the Russian Federation, natural resource revenues were redirected towards Moscow, depriving regional governments of the income necessary to support social services (Maj 2012). A long period of coexistence prior to the 1990s between industrial activities and traditional livelihoods such as subsistence hunting, gathering, and reindeer herding may have masked the fact that environmental damage from the Soviet period, lax regulation and monitoring during *perestroika* and the economic liberalization of the 1990s, and a steady increase in extractive activities since 2000 have severely degraded the ecological foundations of Indigenous cultural and economic practices. Fondahl and Sirina (2006), for instance, detailed Indigenous concerns over the construction of the Eastern Siberian-Pacific Ocean Pipeline, identifying the focus of the local Evenki people on the potential for a pipeline spill to contaminate the Lake Baikal watershed. The link between environmental degradation and indigeneity is clear in the expression of local people's security concerns:

> While Evenki were very concerned with the environmental dangers a pipeline rupture would pose to their homelands and subsistence activities, they also expressed apprehension regarding other issues [...] These included increased competition with pipeline workers for local subsistence resources such as game, fish and wild food plants; increased forest fires [...] the desecration of sacred places important to the Evenki for cultural purposes; disturbing reindeer migration routes; [and] decreased access to resources due to a pipeline cutting through their territory.
>
> *(Fondahl and Sirina 2006: 62)*

Kirsti Stuvøy's research on the relationship between oil extraction and human security in the Komi Republic, though not exclusive to Indigenous people, similarly finds that while the oil industry is linked with the degradation of people's health and personal security, "people's security is contested locally, and also that there are gender differences in the assessment of the role of oil and security in regard to local livelihood" (Stuvøy 2011: 17). While Indigenous communities sometimes support extractive activities due to the benefits for local employment and investment, they appear to be always aware of the damage caused to the environment and to activities that rely upon it, such as fishing and reindeer herding.

As such, similar to elsewhere in the Arctic, Indigenous peoples in northern Russia have sometimes challenged the growth of extraction occurring on their traditional territories, though the limited autonomy of Indigenous organizations calls into question their ability to effectively make security claims against the economic interests of the Russian state. In several republics and autonomous regions of northern Russia where hydrocarbon extraction is prevalent, Indigenous associations are financed by regional governments, resulting in correspondingly "little space for individual or collective agency from below" to further Indigenous interests (Stammler and Forbes 2006: 56). The Russian Association of Indigenous Peoples of the North (RAIPON), a Permanent Participant on the Arctic Council, has also experienced direct interference by the Russian government. In August 2012, RAIPON joined other Indigenous groups in demanding a ban on oil extraction on traditional land-use areas of the Arctic continental shelf, and intended to raise the issue at the Arctic Council meeting scheduled for May 2013.

The draft statement for this meeting recognized the Arctic as a "homeland – a vulnerable environment in need of protection" in order to protect the rights of its Indigenous inhabitants (George 2012). This resulted in RAIPON's suspension by the Russian government due to an "alleged lack of correspondence between the association's statutes and federal law" (Axworthy 2013). Writing shortly after RAIPON was suspended, political geographer Mia Bennett (2012) observed "the Russian government is likely 'concerned' because RAIPON may be viewed as obstructing attempts to extract more and more resources from Siberia." RAIPON Vice President Rodion Sulyandziga suggested something similar when he stated:

> RAIPON is one of the last barriers to companies and states to the extraction of these resources and [it is] easier to use force, using selective justice, so as not to distract the extra energy, time and resources to negotiate with Indigenous [peoples].
>
> *(Quoted in Bennett 2012)*

The suspension provoked an international outcry, including a unanimous statement by the Arctic Council calling for RAIPON's reinstatement, which may have contributed to the Russian government's decision in March 2013 to restore RAIPON's legal standing (George 2012). However, this episode demonstrates the vulnerability of Russian Indigenous peoples to political repression, and may reflect broader tensions between the interests of the Russian state and of Indigenous peoples in the Russian North. It also suggests that in Russia, too, Indigenous peoples identify environmental issues that undermine their capacity to practice subsistence lifestyles on their traditional land base as being of the utmost importance to their survival and well-being.

Conclusion

As the Arctic has changed in recent decades, so too has the meaning of security for the region and its inhabitants, including Indigenous peoples. Today, Arctic security is deeply contested, with different actors articulating distinct, often contrasting understandings of what is to be secured, from what, and by which means (Greaves and Lackenbauer 2016). While Arctic governments have principally pursued state-centric conceptions of security defined around territorial sovereignty and defense and maximizing the economic benefits of natural resource extraction, Indigenous peoples across the region identify their security as being threatened by the direct and indirect effects of climate change, natural resource extraction, and cultural assimilation. To this end, self-government or self-determination are perceived as necessary in order to provide Indigenous communities with the political autonomy necessary to pursue their own security interests that are perceived as distinct from those of the non-Indigenous majority populations of Arctic societies.

As such, the relationship between Indigenous peoples and security in the Arctic, as elsewhere, is defined by the inherent differences between Indigenous and non-Indigenous peoples. The conditions of relative insecurity experienced by Indigenous peoples are derivative of their experiences of colonization and political subordination to others. As Indigenous peoples across much of the Arctic achieve greater control over land use and other policy areas in their traditional territories, their capacities to pursue their security may increase. However, nowhere have Indigenous peoples achieved complete self-determination, or freed themselves from the political constraints of non-Indigenous governance systems and sovereign states. Moreover, given that Indigenous conceptions of security are deeply tied to protecting the natural environments of their territories, and since that environment is transforming dramatically and rapidly as a result of global climate change in addition to local resource extraction and other activities, Arctic Indigenous peoples will continue to experience distinct and acute forms of insecurity. Their security in the future will thus remain tied both to developments within, and far beyond, the Arctic region.

References

Abele, Frances and Thierry Rodon. 2007. "Inuit Diplomacy in the Global ERA: The Strengths of Multilateral Internationalism." *Canadian Foreign Policy Journal* 13 (3): 45–63.

Adler-Nissen, Rebecca and Ulrik Prad Gam. 2014. "Introduction: Postimperial Sovereignty Games in the Nordic Region." *Cooperation and Conflict* 49 (1): 3–32.

AHDR. 2004. *Arctic Human Development Report*. Akureyri: Steffanson Arctic Institute.

Åtland, Kristian. 2014. "Interstate Relations in the Arctic: An Emerging Security Dilemma?" *Comparative Strategy* 33 (2): 145–166.

Axworthy, Thomas S. 2013. "Op-ed: Russia Turns Back the Clock." *Embassy Magazine*. January 9. Accessed at http://gordonfoundation.ca/news-item/622.

Barkawi, Tarak and Mark Laffey. 2006. "The Postcolonial Moment in Security Studies." *Review of International Studies* 32 (2): 329–352.

Bassin, Mark. 2004. *Imperial Visions: Nationalist Imagination and Geographical Expansion in the Russian Far East, 1840–1865*. Cambridge: Cambridge University Press.

Bedford, David and Thom Workman. 1997. "The Great Law of Peace: Alternative Inter-Nation(al) Practices and Iroquoian Confederacy." *Alternatives* 22 (1): 87–111.

Beier, J. Marshall. 2005. *International Relations in Uncommon Places: Indigeneity, Cosmology, and the Limits of International Theory*. New York: Palgrave.

Beier, J. Marshall. 2007. "Inter-national Affairs: Indigeneity, Globality, and the Canadian State." *Canadian Foreign Policy Journal* 13 (3): 121–131.

Beier, J. Marshall. 2010. "At Home on Native Land: Canada and the United Nations Declaration on the Rights of Indigenous Peoples." In *Canadian Foreign Policy in Critical Perspectives*, eds. J. Marshall Beier and Lana Wylie, 175–186. Toronto: Oxford University Press.

Beier, J. Marshall. 2016. "Critical Interventions: Subjects, Objects, and Security." In *Contemporary Security Studies*, 4th ed. ed. Alan Collins, 108–121. Oxford: Oxford University Press.

Bell, Colleen and Kendra Schreiner. 2018. "The International Relations of Police Power in Settler Colonialism: The 'Civilizing' Mission of Canada's Mounties." *International Journal* 73 (1): 111–128.

Bennett, Mia. 2012. "Why did Putin Suspend Key Russian Indigenous Group?" *Alaska Dispatch*. November 24. Accessed at www.alaskadispatch.com/article/analysis-why-did-putin-suspend-key-russian-indigenous-group.

Bland, Douglas L. 2014. *Time Bomb: Canada and the First Nations*. Toronto: Dundurn.

Borgerson, Scott. 2008. "Arctic Meltdown: The Economic and Security Implications of Global Warming." *Foreign Affairs* 87 (2): 63–77.

Borgerson, Scott. 2013. "The Coming Arctic Boom: As The Ice Melts, the Region Heats Up." *Foreign Affairs* 92 (4): 76–89.

Cocklin, Chris. 2002. "Water and 'Cultural Security'." In *Human Security and the Environment: International Comparisons*, eds. Edward A. Page and Michael Redclift, 154–176. Northampton: Edward Elgar.

Corntassel, Jeff J. 2003. "Who is Indigenous? 'Peoplehood' and Ethnonationalist Approaches to Rearticulating Indigenous Identity." *Nationalism and Ethnic Politics* 9 (1): 75–100.

Crawford, Neta C. 1994. "A Security Regime Among Democracies: Cooperation Among Iroquois Nations." *International Organization* 48 (3): 345–385.

Crawford, Neta C. 2017. "Native Americans and the Making of International Society." In *The Globalization of International Society*, eds. Tim Dunne and Christian Reus-Smit, 102–121. Oxford: Oxford University Press.

Crosby, Andrew and Jeffrey Monaghan. 2012. "Settler Governmentality in Canada and the Algonquins of Barriere Lake." *Security Dialogue* 43 (5): 421–438.

Crosby, Andrew and Jeffrey Monaghan. 2016. "Settler Colonialism and the Policing of Idle No More." *Social Justice* 43 (2): 37–58.

Croteau, Jean-Jacques. 2010. *Final Report of the Honourable Jean-Jacques Croteau, Retired Judge of the Superior Court, Regarding the Allegations Concerning the Slaughter of Inuit Sled Dogs in Nunavik (1950–1970)*. Accessed at http://caid.ca/FinCroRep2010.pdf.

Csonka, Yvon and Peter Schweitzer. 2004. "Societies and Cultures: Change and Persistence." In *Arctic Human Development Report*, 45–68. Akureyri: Steffanson Arctic Institute.

Dubreuil, Antoine. 2011. "The Arctic of the Regions: Between Indigenous Peoples and Sub-National Entities – Which Perspective?" *International Journal* 66 (4): 923–938.

English, John. 2013. *Ice and Water: Politics, Peoples, and the Arctic Council*. Toronto: Penguin.

Epp, Roger. 2000. "At the Wood's Edge: Towards a Theoretical Clearing for Indigenous Diplomacies in International Relations." In *International Relations: Still an American Social Science? Towards Diversity in International Thought*, eds. Robert M.A. Crawford and Darryl S.L. Jarvis, 299–326. Albany: SUNY Press.

Erasmus, George. 1986. "Militarization of the North: Cultural Survival Threatened." In *Information North*. Calgary: The Arctic Institute of North America.

Eriksson, Johan. 1995. "Security in the Barents Region: Interpretations and Implications of the Norwegian Barents Initiative." *Cooperation and Conflict* 30 (3): 259–286.

Fondahl, Gail and Anna Sirina. 2006. "Oil Pipeline Development and Indigenous Rights in Eastern Siberia." *Indigenous Affairs* 2 (3): 58–67.

Forsyth, James. 1992. *A History of the Peoples of Siberia: Russia's North Asian Colony 1581–1990*. Cambridge: Cambridge University Press.

Fur, Gunlög. 2006. *Colonialism in the Margins: Cultural Encounters in New Sweden and Lapland*. Leiden and Boston: Brill Academic Publishers.

Gausset, Quentin, Justin Kenrick, and Robert Gibb. 2011. "Indigeneity and Autochtony: A Couple of False Twins?" *Social Anthropology* 19 (2): 135–142.

George, Jane. 2012. "Arctic Officials Call for Reinstatement of Russian Indigenous Org." *Nunatsiaq News*. November 15. Accessed at www.nunatsiaqonline.ca/stories/article/65674arctic_council_calls_for_russian_indigenous_orgs_return/.

Greaves, Wilfrid. 2012. "For Whom, From What? Canada's Arctic Policy and the Narrowing of Human Security." *International Journal* 67 (1): 219–240.

Greaves, Wilfrid. 2013. "Canada, Circumpolar Security, and the Arctic Council." *Northern Public Affairs* 2 (1): 58–62.

Greaves, Wilfrid. 2016a. "Arctic In/Security and Indigenous Peoples: Comparing Inuit in Canada and Sámi in Norway." *Security Dialogue* 47 (6): 461–480.

Greaves, Wilfrid. 2016b. "Environment, Identity, Autonomy: Inuit Perspectives on Arctic Security." In *Understanding the Many Faces of Human Security: Perspectives of Northern Indigenous Peoples*, eds. Kamrul Hossain and Anna Petrétei, 35–55. Leiden: Brill.

Greaves, Wilfrid. 2018a. "Colonialism, Statehood, and Sámi in *Norden* and the Norwegian High North." In *Human and Societal Security in the Circumpolar Arctic: Local and Indigenous Communities*, eds. Kamrul Hossain, José Roncero Martín, and Anna Petrétei, 100–121. Leiden: Brill.

Greaves, Wilfrid. 2018b. "Damaging Environments: Land, Settler Colonialism, and Security for Indigenous Peoples." In *Environment and Society: Advances in Research,* ed. Jaskiran Dhillon, 9 (Special Issue on Indigenous Resurgence, Decolonization, and Movements for Environmental Justice): 107–124.

Greaves, Wilfrid and P. Whitney Lackenbauer. 2016. "Arctic Sovereignty and Security: Updating Our Ideas." *ArcticDeeply.org*. Accessed at www.arcticdeeply.org/op-eds/2016/03/8825/arctic-sovereignty-security-updating-ideas/.

Griffiths, Franklyn. 2008. "Not that good a fit? 'Human security' and the Arctic." *Arctic Security in the 21st Century*. Conference Report Co-convened by The Simons Foundation and the School for International Studies, Simon Fraser University. Vancouver: Simon Fraser University.

Guenther, Mathias, Justin Kenrick, Evie Plaice, Trond Thuen, Patrick Wolfe, Werner Zips, and Alan Bernard. 2006. "Discussion: The Concept of Indigeneity." *Social Anthropology* 14 (1): 17–32.

Heininen, Lassi. 2012. "State of the Arctic Strategies and Policies – A Summary." In *Arctic Yearbook 2012* Lassi Heininen, Heather Exner-Pirot and Joël Plouffe eds., 2–47. Akureyri: Northern Research Forum.

Hild, Carl M. and Vigdis Stordahl. 2004. "Human Health and Well-being." In *Arctic Human Development Report*, 155–168. Akureyri: Steffansson Arctic Institute.

Hoogensen Gjørv, Gunhild. 2014. "Virtuous Imperialism or a Shared Global Objective? The Relevance of Human Security in the Global North." In *Environmental and Human Security in the Arctic*, eds. Gunhild Hoogensen Gjørv, Dawn R. Bazely, Maria Goloviznina, and Andrew J. Tanentzap, 58–80. New York: Routledge.

Hoogensen Gjørv, Gunhild, Dawn Bazely, Julia Christensen, Andrew Tanentzap, and Evgeny Bojko. 2009. "Human Security in the Arctic – Yes, it is Relevant!." *Journal of Human Security* 5 (2): 1–10.

Hoogensen Gjørv, Gunhild, Dawn R. Bazely, Maria Goloviznina, and Andrew J. Tanentzap, eds. 2014. *Environmental and Human Security in the Arctic*. New York: Routledge.

Hossain, Kamrul. 2016. "Securitizing the Arctic Indigenous Peoples: A Community Security Perspective with Special Reference to the Sámi of the European High North." *Polar Science* 10 (3): 415–424.

Hossain, Kamrul, Gerald Zojer, Wilfrid Greaves, José Miguel Roncero, and Michael Sheehan. 2016. "Constructing Arctic Security: An Inter-Disciplinary Approach to Understanding Security in the Barents Region." *Polar Record* 53 (1): 52–66.

Josephson, Paul R. 2014. *The Conquest of the Russian Arctic*. Cambridge: Harvard University Press.

Keil, Kathrin. 2014. "The Arctic: A New Region of Conflict? The Case of Oil and Gas." *Cooperation and Conflict* 49 (2): 162–190.

King, Hayden. 2017. "The Erasure of Indigenous Thought in Foreign Policy." *OpenCanada.org*. July 31. Accessed at www.opencanada.org/features/erasure-indigenous-thought-foreign-policy.

Koivurova, Timo and Leena Heinämäki. 2006. "The Participation of Indigenous Peoples in International Norm-Making in the Arctic." *Polar Record* 42 (221): 101–109.

Lackenbauer, P. Whitney and Andrew F. Cooper. 2007. "The Achilles Heel of Canadian International Citizenship: Indigenous Diplomacies and State Responses." *Canadian Foreign Policy Journal* 13 (3): 99–119.

Laffey, Mark and Suthaharan Nadarajah. 2016. "Postcolonialism." In *Contemporary Security Studies*, 4th ed. ed. Alan Collins, 122–138. Oxford: Oxford University Press.

Larsen, Joan Nymand and Gail Fondahl, eds. 2014. *Arctic Human Development Report: Regional Processes and Global Linkages*. Akureyri: Steffanson Arctic Institute.

Lawrence, Rebecca. 2014. "Internal Colonisation and Indigenous Resource Sovereignty: Wind Power Developments on Traditional Saami Lands." *Environment and Planning D: Society and Space* 32 (6): 1036–1053.

Loukacheva, Natalia. 2007. *Arctic Promise: Legal and Political Autonomy for Greenland and Nunavut.* Toronto: University of Toronto Press.

Maaka, Roger and Augie Fleras. 2005. *The Politics of Indigeneity: Challenging the State in Canada and Aotearoa New Zealand.* Dunedin: University of Otago Press.

Maj, Emilie. 2012. "Internationalisation with the use of Arctic Indigeneity: The case of the Republic of Sakha (Yakutia), Russia." *Polar Record* 48 (246): 210–214.

Makkik, Romani. 2009. "The High Arctic Relocations." In *Naniiliqpita*. Fall. Iqaluit: Nunavut Tunngavik Incorporated. Accessed at www.tunngavik.com/documents/publications/Naniiliqpita%20Fall%202009.pdf.

Moreton-Robinson, Aileen. 2015. *The White Possessive: Power, Property, and Indigenous Sovereignty*. Minneapolis: University of Minnesota Press.

Naum, Magdalena and Jonas M. Nordin, eds. 2013. *Scandinavian Colonialism and the Rise of Modernity: Small Time Agents in a Global Arena*. New York: Springer-Verlag.

Nickels, Scot, ed. 2013. *Nilliajut: Inuit Perspectives on Security, Patriotism, and Sovereignty*. Ottawa: Inuit Tapiriit Kanatami.

Niezen, Ronald. 2003. *The Origins of Indigenism: Human Rights and the Politics of Identity*. Berkeley: University of California Press.

Pasternak, Shiri, Sue Collis, and Tia Dafnos. 2013. "Criminalization at Tyendinaga: Securing Canada's Colonial Property Regime through Specific Land Claims." *Canadian Journal of Law and Society* 28 (1): 65–81.

Poppel, Birger, ed. 2015. *SLiCA: Arctic Living Conditions – Living Conditions and Quality of Life among Inuit, Saami and Indigenous Peoples of Chukotka and the Kola Peninsula*. Copenhagen: Nordic Council of Ministers.

Proulx, Craig. 2014. "Colonizing Surveillance: Canada Constructs and Indigenous Terror Threat." *Anthropologica* 56 (1): 83–100.

QIA. 2010. *Qikiqtani Truth Commission Final Report: Achieving Saimaqatigiingniq*. Iqaluit: Qikiqtani Inuit Association.

Rothschild, Emma. 1995. "What is Security?" *Daedalus* 124 (3): 53–98.

Shadian, Jessica. 2010. "From States to Polities: Reconceptualizing Sovereignty through Inuit Governance." *European Journal of International Relations* 16 (3): 485–510.

Shadian, Jessica. 2014. *The Politics of Arctic Sovereignty: Oil, Ice, and Inuit Governance*. New York: Routledge.

Shaw, Karena. 2002. "Indigeneity and the International." *Millennium: Journal of International Studies* 31 (1): 55–81.

Simon, Mary. 1989. "Security, Peace and the Native Peoples of the Arctic." In *The Arctic: Choices for Peace and Security*, ed. Thomas R. Berger, 36–67. Vancouver: Gordon Soules.

Smith, Heather A. 2010. "Choosing Not to See: Canada, Climate Change, and the Arctic." *International Journal* 65 (4): 931–942.

Smith, Heather A. and Brittany Parks. 2010. "Climate Change, Environmental Security, and Inuit Peoples." In *New Issues in Security #5: Critical Environmental Security: Rethinking the Links Between Natural Resources and Political Violence*, eds. Matthew Schnurr and Larry Swatuk, 1–18. Halifax: Centre for Foreign Policy Studies.

Stammler, Florian and Bruce C. Forbes. 2006. "Oil and Gas Development in Western Siberia and Timan-Pechora." *Indigenous Affairs* 2 (3): 48–57.

Stuvøy, Kirsti. 2011. "Human Security, Oil and People: An Actor-Based Security Analysis of the Impacts of Oil Activity in the Komi Republic, Russia." *Journal of Human Security* 7 (2): 5–19.

Sundberg, Juanita. 2014. "Decolonising Posthumanist Geographies." *Cultural Geographies* 21 (1): 33–47.

Tennberg, Monica. 2010. "Indigenous Peoples as International Political Actors: A Summary." *Polar Record* 46 (238): 264–270.

Tester, Frank and Peter Kulchyski. 1994. *Tammarniit (Mistakes): Inuit Relocation in the Eastern Arctic, 1939–63*. Vancouver: UBC Press.

Todd, Zoe. 2015. "Indigenizing the Anthropocene." In *Art in the Anthropocene: Encounters Among Aesthetics, Politics, Environment and Epistemology*, eds. Heather Davis and Etienne Turpin, 241–254. London: Open Humanities Press.

Young, Oran. 2005. "Governing the Arctic: From Cold War Theater to Mosaic of Cooperation." *Global Governance* 11 (1): 9–15.

31

HUMAN SECURITY, EXTRACTIVE INDUSTRIES, AND INDIGENOUS COMMUNITIES IN THE RUSSIAN NORTH

Florian Stammler, Kara K. Hodgson, and Aytalina Ivanova

Introduction

Russian law classifies a large swath of the country as the Russian "Far North" (Дальний Север) and equivalent territories (hereafter called the "Russian North") – see Figure 31.1. This region holds the majority of the natural resources that form the mainstay of Russia's national economy, and is populated by approximately 10 million people (Fauzer 2016). Approximately 1.45 million of this population would be classified as Indigenous by international law,[1] and many members of these Indigenous groups continue to live traditional livelihoods centred around reindeer herding and subsistence activities such as hunting, fishing, and berry-picking.

Territories highlighted in dark grey are considered to be completely within the legal classification of "the Russian Far North and equivalent territories." Left to right, they are the Republic of Karelia, Murmansk Oblast', Arkhangelsk Oblast', Republic of Komi, Nenets Autonomous Okrug, Khanty-Mansi Autonomous Okrug-Yugra, Yamalo-Nenets Autonomous Okrug, Krasnoyarsk Kray, Republic of Sakha (Yakutia), Chukotka Autonomous Okrug, Magadan Oblast' Kamchatka Kray, and at the bottom, Republic of Tyva and Sakhalin Oblast.' Territories highlighted in lighter grey are considered to be partially within the legal classification of "the Russian Far North and equivalent territories." Left to right, they include the Perm Kray, Tyumen Oblast', Tomsk Oblast', Republic of Altai, Irkutsk Oblast', Republic of Buryatia, Chita Oblast', Amur Oblast', Khabarov Kray, and Primor Kray. Source: Federal State Statistics Service, www.gks.ru/bgd/regl/b08_22/IssWWW.exe/Stg/kart.htm

The majority of the total population, approximately 8.5 million, migrated to the Russian North in search of economic opportunities in extractive industries (EI). For non-Indigenous EI workers, who either relocated to the North or commute there, EI is a source of economic security. EI migration began in the 1920s at the beginning of the Soviet regime. Many of the cities in the Russian North were built especially for these incomers. As such,

Figure 31.1 The Russian Far North and equivalent territories

many have developed emotional and symbolic attachments to the extractive industries and the Northern communities where they live and/or work (Bolotova & Stammler 2010). Their livelihoods continue to depend on employment opportunities from the EI sector. This has caused tensions between the needs of those who migrated in and those who have been there for centuries, maintaining traditional livelihoods.

This tension is exacerbated by conflicting mindsets about the Russian North. Many EI workers, especially recent incomers, disregard the traditional lifestyles that Indigenous peoples have maintained for millennia. A colonial mentality exists in the EI communities that the Russian North was "built with their own hands under extreme conditions and with the spirit of 'pioneers'," (Saxinger 2015, 89). In this way, for those who were there before EI opportunities arrived, these industries became a threat to the security of their communities. Many locals even see it as an invasion which brings more problems than benefits. Complicating the matter is the fact that some Indigenous people have secured employment in the EI sector as a means to supplement or even replace their traditional livelihoods. Thus, EI can be simultaneously a threat and a source of security for Indigenous people. Many want employment, but at the same time they want to reduce the industry-related threats to their communities' security.

Embracing the concept of human security "from the bottom up," this chapter analyses the influence of industrial development in the Russian North on the human security of those residents in areas of extraction, whose ancestors lived there before the industries came. It poses the question: in what ways are Russia's Indigenous peoples not only experiencing everyday human insecurity, but also producing human security for themselves? This chapter highlights three different categories of measurable threats to the human security of Indigenous communities from EI activities: demographic marginalization, environmental pollution, and disruptions to the traditional way of life. It then highlights a less measurable but arguably important threat: that of the alienation of people from their land and their cultural values due to broader socioeconomic changes driven by EI development. Examples from two case studies illustrate how, even in a political environment that favours industrial development over Indigenous rights, individuals, and groups still manage to carve out niches of security for their communities. The cases also document the precariousness of these niches; despite significant efforts by state agencies on various levels and by industrial companies in their social and environmental performance, threats to human security continue to endanger entire livelihoods in the Russian North.

The chapter is divided into four parts. The first part discusses the evolution of the human security concept. The second part provides an overview of the current political and economic landscape regarding Russian extractive industries and Indigenous peoples. The third part introduces the above-mentioned categories of threats. Finally, examples will be provided that demonstrate how Russia's Indigenous groups produce security for their communities in response to the threats discussed, using two regional cases from the Russian North: that of the Sakha and Evenki people in the Republic of Sakha (Yakutia) or RSY, and that of the Nenets people in the Yamalo-Nenets Autonomous Okrug (YNAO).

Conceptual considerations: (critical) human security

The human security concept is a useful prism through which to analyze the relationships between EI and Indigenous peoples in the Russian Arctic. The United Nations Development Program (UNDP), in its watershed 1994 *Human Development Report*, first introduced the concept of human security. It was a novel approach that acknowledged that *security* means something different to ordinary people than it does to traditional security studies scholars. To some experts in academic and political circles, security has been equivalent to national or military security that protects the interests of the state. The aim of the human security perspective, on the other hand, is to help ordinary people minimize the insecurities they experience in their everyday lives. The UNDP categorized seven different areas of (in)security: economic, food, health, environmental, personal, community, and political security (United Nations Development Programme (UNDP) 1994).

Although all of the categories are interdependent, the classifications of significance here are those of "economic security" and "community security." Economic security involves ensuring that people have an assured basic income or access to a social safety net. Insecurity in this category can manifest as, for example, unemployment, underemployment, and/or precarious employment. It also comes through inadequate, or a total lack of, government-sponsored social safety-net programs. Economic insecurities can result in such drastic conditions as poverty and homelessness (United Nations Development Programme (UNDP) 1994, 25–26). Community security involves protecting the sense of belonging and support that people receive from membership in a group, which helps to provide the group with a common identity and set of values. The size of the community can be as intimate as a family unit or as encompassing as an entire ethnic society. Insecurity in this category can come in violent forms, such as ethnic clashes, or in more subtle forms, such as restrictions on the movement of people or livestock. Indigenous groups were specifically highlighted as vulnerable in this category (United Nations Development Programme (UNDP) 1994, 31–32). In this chapter, the concept of community is understood as a term for people who reside in one of our two case-study regions in areas impacted by the extractive industries. Being a member of a community in this sense does not mean that one lives in the same village, shares the same ethnic sense of belonging, or speaks the same language. "Community" in this sense refers to people who share a common set of interests related to the impact of industry in their area, and they interpret impacts along common lines.

Since its unveiling, the concept of human security has been contentious. One of the more salient debates in the human security literature concerns the role of the state. In its original conception, human security was designed to shift emphasis away from the state as the object in need of being secured and to place the focus on the individual instead. However, this spawned a debate regarding operationalization. Some scholars have argued that the state can be a source of insecurity for individuals and that non-state actors are equally, if not better, positioned to ensure human security. Other scholars have claimed that states are often the actors with the best mechanisms for delivery.

The latter position involves two assumptions. First, it assumes that the state in question is developed, strong, and amenable to such a task. This led to accusations from critics that the concept had been co-opted by Western/Global North states for use in their foreign and development policies toward non-Western/Global South states (Duffield & Waddell 2006; Chandler 2008; Hoogensen Gjørv 2014). Secondly, it assumes that individuals in Northern states do not experience such insecurities. Studies have shown that often-marginalized groups, such as women and Indigenous people, in Northern states have been particularly vulnerable to a combination of insecurity categories (Slowey 2014; Irlbacher-Fox et al. 2014; Stuvøy 2014). This, in turn, has led to calls for a realignment of the concept with its original intent: a focus on the everyday security of everyday people and communities. In other words, the focus should be on human security "from the bottom up," or "security [as it] is understood from within the context from which it is identified and experienced" (Hoogensen Gjørv 2014, 59). Human security "from the bottom up" has been applied to a handful of analyses regarding Arctic Indigenous groups, such as Aboriginal groups in Canada (Slowey, 2014), Indigenous women in

Alaska (Sweet 2013), and the Sámi people in the Barents region (Hossain et al. 2017). It has also been applied to the context of the Russian North in two cases: one case study of women's centres (Stuvøy 2010) and one case study of the Komi-Izhma people (Loginova 2018). Given the diversity of peoples and situations in the Russian Arctic, this chapter seeks to contribute to the expansion of contextualized analysis of the human security of Arctic Indigenous groups in the Russian North.

The Russian context

Natural-resource development has been declared a national priority in multiple successive policy documents on the Russian Arctic (see Segunin's chapter in this book). Revenues from extractive industries are the principal source of hard currency income for the Russian economy. Approximately three-quarters of Russia's exports in 2017 consisted of extracted natural resources, the majority of which came from hydrocarbons (OEC n.d.). In 2018, Russia was the world's second-largest producer of gas and third-largest producer of crude oil (BP 2019). Most of the production takes place in western Siberia, but there is growing production coming from the Russian Arctic, including RSY and YNAO. In addition to hydrocarbons, Russia also produces a vast array of metals and precious minerals.

The Russian state is actively involved in many of the country's industrial enterprises. It has controlling ownership in major corporations such as Rosneft and Gazprom, the country's largest oil and natural gas companies, respectively. Thus, the state has a vested interest in maximizing natural-resource extraction, production, and exportation. This creates conflicts over access to, and priorities for, land use. On the one hand, the federal Russian state and EI companies seek to maximize revenues in the interests of private and national economic security. On the other hand, Indigenous and local residents of the Russian North rely on surface resources for their basic human security needs. Recent scholarship on Arctic communities has corroborated the notion that security for many Arctic inhabitants is threatened by rapid economic development, the erosion of cultural traditions, and land-use conflicts (Hossain et al. 2017). Due to the large imbalance of power between the two groupings, it can be reasonably argued that the federal state in Russia serves more as a source of insecurity than security for the latter group.

Threats to human security by extractive industries

The presence of industrial extractive operations in areas traditionally occupied by Indigenous groups generates conditions for a variety of potential threats. Some of these threats are possible to quantify using specific proxies as mentioned in the following categories. However, as this chapter argues, only when the cumulative nature of these threats is taken into consideration, combining both quantitatively discernible and qualitatively experienced threats, can a more accurate picture about the influence of extractive industries on the lives and cultures of Russia's Northern ethnic groups be provided. Threats are organized into these next four categories.

Demography

The first threat is demographic marginalization. Since the overwhelming majority of Russia's Northern population has migrated to the region, Indigenous groups are often outnumbered in their homelands, thereby having their voices and control over their ancestral lands diluted. This process is well documented by Arctic demographers

(Bogoyavlenskiy 2010). It is, however, of major importance to analyze the administrative structure of the area in detail. Often the non-Russian population is marginalized in larger territorial units, while they still form a significant portion of the population in particular municipalities, whereupon they have some influence on local political processes and decision-making.

Environment

The second threat is environmental degradation. During the Soviet era, environmental degradation was considered an affliction of "bourgeois development and social and political conditions in the capitalist world," (Peterson 1993, 12). With the assumption that the socialist project was superior to bourgeois capitalism, Soviet officials disregarded environmental considerations for industrial development programs. Many current industries have inherited both the degradation and the dismissive mentality that is the Soviet legacy to the environment. To be sure, industries have been held more accountable for their environmental and social performance in the post-Soviet era. For example, environmental impact assessments are mandatory for industrial development projects. Yet, despite improvements through increased accountability and advances in technology, EI activities still exert a negative impact on the environment. The main reported damages are land pollution caused by industrial products, including oil spills, leftover materials and rubbish during the construction period, chemical contamination of water, tailings of mining operations, air pollution from dust, and flaring from processing plants. These sources of insecurity of the Indigenous people cause contamination of reindeer pastures, hunting and fishing grounds, groundwater, and eventually the sources of food on which Indigenous communities rely. These impacts have been extensively studied throughout the Russian North since the 1990s, both by state ecological monitoring teams and by scholars (Wiget & Balalaeva 1997; Moiseenko et al. 2006; Stuvøy 2011; Walker et al. 2011; Kumpula et al. 2012). Usually the damage is greatest during the construction period of industrial infrastructure, such as roads, railroads, pipelines, and the actual extraction sites.

Traditional way of life

The third threat is disruptions to the way of life of herders, hunters, fishers, and gatherers. Russian law specifies these four activities as the main traditional occupations carried out by Northern Indigenous peoples (Zadorin et al. 2017). Disruptions to these activities have been extensively documented by anthropological and interdisciplinary research (Wilson 2003; Fondahl & Sirina 2006; Stammler & Wilson 2006; Forbes et al. 2009; Degteva & Nellemann 2013; Wilson & Stammler 2016). Typical impacts of such disruptions include reduced access to hunting and herding grounds, changes in wildlife and domestic animal migration routes, and environmental degradation as a result of industrial construction and the accompanying infrastructure, such as roads.

Alienation of people and the land

The three already mentioned threats can be quantified to some extent; for example, by measuring pollution levels or measuring percentages of Indigenous population by area. However, a major long-term threat to the human security of Indigenous communities in the Russian North is more intangible. This threat is the psychosocial consequences that can be caused by alienation from one's land. One of the ways in which Indigenous people have been alienated from their traditional lands is through the damage and displacement caused by pollution. Another is through *sedentarization*. Sedentarization was an official policy carried out together with collectivization as part of the Soviet modernization campaign, started under Josef Stalin and continued up to the rule of Leonid Brezhnev. During Soviet times, there were state targets for the transfer of nomadic peoples to a sedentary way of life. This created a feeling of insecurity for many Indigenous persons, and the subsequent danger of losing self-confidence, independence, and pride (Vitebsky & Alekseyev 2015). One quote by a Nenets informant illustrated this feeling particularly well:

> Being put into a house with four concrete walls, solid, which do not breathe, was for me like being put into prison. Every time I come to the village, I feel I can't breathe. I stay for 10 days in the house, and then I need to go out to the tundra again.
>
> *(A. Serotetto, FS field notes 2006)*

Towards the end of the Soviet Union, only a small minority of the Russian Northern Indigenous peoples still lived nomadic lives. In the current post-Soviet era, some sedentary decision makers have stated that they consider the settling of nomads to be a positive outcome for industrial development. Industries in the North need to expand their operations into ever-more remote territories and nomadic people, with their extensive land-use practices, are potential competitors for territory. Settling them in villages gives the state and industry the ability to claim the formerly pastoral land and the possibility to boost their reputations by launching welfare programs for the former nomads. The problem is that, after physical sedentarization, the problems of cultural alienation remain, and social and psychological adaptation to a sedentary life is in many cases unsuccessful (Vitebsky & Alekseyev 2015).

"Alienation from the land" as a threat category can be quantitatively measured using proxies such as numbers of people sedentarized, amount of land lost to traditional livelihoods, or percentage of Indigenous language command per ethnic group. However, these proxies taken separately cannot provide a full account of the psychosocial impact of alienation. It is the cumulative nature of all the threats that influences behaviour and life trajectories. Alienation can cause a chain of successive situations: sedentarization can leave Indigenous people ill-prepared for an immobile or even urban lifestyle, a lack of appropriate capacity and education, an increased vulnerability to substance abuse, deteriorating health due to lack of movement and unhealthy diet, and a loss of cultural pride and resilience (Larsen et al. 2010; Larsen & Fondahl 2014). In Russia, quantification is one of the main challenges in the implementation agreements between companies and representatives of Indigenous groups (Novikova 2016). How should people be compensated for damages such as loss of language, self-confidence, and livelihood?

Nevertheless, despite such intimidating circumstances, Indigenous communities still have agency, however limited, to produce security for themselves and their communities in a variety of ways. The cases below illustrate three of the ways Indigenous communities have utilized their agency: by creating regional-level laws, by arranging individualized benefit-sharing agreements, and by adapting the traditional lifestyle to contemporary realities.

Case studies

In this section, we provide examples of how Indigenous groups in two regions have worked to ensure some security for their communities. It is important to clarify that Russia deviates from international law in its definition of *Indigenous*. The Russian definition is numerically based, as opposed to utilizing international principles based on "those who were there first." Thus, groups that would be considered Indigenous under international law are divided into two main categories under Russian law. The first category is *titular nations*, which have population sizes larger than 50,000 and which, during the Soviet period, were granted territorial administrative units of their own in which they kept and continue to keep a certain level of regional political control. There are currently 21 such titular nations within the Russian Federation. The second category is called the *Indigenous small-numbered peoples of the North, Siberia and the Far East* (hereafter, SNPs), which by law can have no more than 50,000 people in their groups in order to qualify (Donahoe et al. 2008; Zadorin et al. 2017). Of the two categories, Russian law considers only SNPs to qualify as "Indigenous." For the purposes of maximum inclusiveness and good faith representativeness, we utilize the international principles of *Indigenous*.

Republic of Sakha (Yakutia)

The ethnic Republic of Sakha (Yakutia), or RSY (Республика Саха (Якутия)), is Russia's largest administrative unit and is located in the Far Eastern District of Russia. It is also the ancestral homeland of the Sakha people, who belong to the Turkic language group. Their origin is debated, but they most likely migrated to the territory of current Yakutia in the Middle Ages (Keyser et al. 2015). Approximately 49% of RSY's population, or 467,000, are ethnic Sakha. In addition to the titular Sakha, the Republic is home to over 40,000 residents from 31 of the officially registered SNPs (FSSS 2010, 130–1). Many members of SNPs, such as the Evenki, continue to engage in traditional reindeer herding, hunting, fishing, and gathering activities.

RSY is abundant in natural resources, and EI is the backbone of the Republic's economy. South Yakutia, in particular, holds 10% of the world's coal reserves, 20% of Russia's gold deposits, and the Elkon uranium deposits, which are considered the largest in Russia (VIMS 2018). However, all these deposits lie on the territories of Evenki and Sakha herders, hunters, and gatherers. This situation has put them in competition for territory with other land users (Stammler & Ivanova 2016). These communities had already had negative experiences with the EI sector when the East-Siberia Pacific Ocean (ESPO) oil pipeline was constructed in 2007. The pipeline's route crossed through the traditional territory of the Evenki. Migration routes of hunted animals, as well as pastures for domestic reindeer herds, were disrupted. Despite laws stipulating that environmental and social impact assessments were to be conducted, the tight construction deadlines did not allow for them to be completed on time (Fondahl & Sirina 2006; Ivanova 2007).

Thus, industry representatives did not substantively address the concerns and needs of the wider Evenki community (Yakovleva 2011). This led to protests and legal action by the RSY regional government, which was convinced that it was necessary to strengthen legislation to prevent future such incidents from occurring. This resulted in Russia's first and only Law on Anthropological Expert Review. The anthropological expert review is a "scientific study of the impact to the Indigenous habitat of small-numbered peoples and upon their socio-cultural development caused by changes" (Zakon 2010). This Republic-level law is serving as a blueprint for a potential federal-level law (see Ivanova & Fondahl, this volume). The presence and implementation of laws like this forced industry actors, such as Gazprom, take local and Indigenous concerns into consideration when planning projects such as the Power of Siberia (Сила Сибири) gas pipeline in 2012.

Measures like this are designed to create better conditions for the human security of local and Indigenous inhabitants. However, in practice, many anxieties and insecurities remain among the Indigenous populations of these areas. First, the content of the law reduces the Indigenous populations to the role of victims, as opposed to agents in the process. In practice, the reviews are carried out mainly with the goal of compensating Indigenous inhabitants for the damage incurred, not with the intention of *preventing* damage from occurring. Moreover, the reviews are sometimes carried out without the participation of competent anthropological experts. These shortcomings led experienced experts such as Novikova (2017) to criticize the RSY law and its implementation and call for improvements on the federal level. Secondly, even though all requirements by the law may be met, it is very hard to control the quality of how these requirements are met. For the Power of Siberia Pipeline, for example, documentation on the environmental impact assessment of the Yakutian part of the pipeline is accessible online, but contains almost no information about the importance of the ecosystem for local economies and cultures. However, what can be seen from this documentation is that borders of protected areas have been changed for the purpose of pipeline construction (Diem 2014, 160). This shows that industry needs can overrule environmental or social concerns, affecting the human security of local residents.

In turn, the Republic has reacted to this pressure by updating legislation that protects Indigenous lands as "territories of traditional nature use of regional significance" (*Zakon* 2015), placing more hurdles to alienation of such lands for uses other than Indigenous economies. Nonetheless, the Indigenous population still has a clear sense of being marginalized amidst big industry and state interests, and the future of their nomadic livelihood is anything but secure. Moreover, especially after the sanctions that many Western countries imposed on Russia, Central and East Asian markets have become more significant. This is evidenced by the 2016 declaration of South Yakutia as a "territory of accelerated socioeconomic development" (TASED) (*Postanovlenie* 2016). TASEDs are federally designated zones where regulations are simplified and tax incentives are offered to attract investment and more rapidly develop industrial projects. Development plans for the South Yakutia TASED include the construction of a hydroelectric power station, natural gas and chemical production plants, as well as a uranium, a coal, and two iron ore mines. It remains to be seen how well regional laws will be respected and implemented throughout the project.

Yamalo-Nenets Autonomous Okrug

The Yamalo-Nenets Autonomous Okrug (Ямало-Ненецкий автономный округ), or YNAO, was named after the Indigenous Nenets people who have occupied the territory since the first millennium. The Nenets have been a reindeer-herding people for centuries and a significant proportion of the population continues to maintain the nomadic reindeer-herding lifestyle (Zen'ko 2012, 1417–1418). The region is currently home to almost 523,000 people, of whom less than one-seventeenth (approximately 30,000) are Nenets (Federal State Statistics Service (FSSS) 2010, 110–111). The Nenets are only the third-largest group in YNAO, following ethnic Russians and Ukrainians (Heleniak and Bogoyavlensky 2014, 88). Thus, Indigenous demographic marginalization is steeper in YNAO than it is in RSY, where the titular nation has more demographic representation and holds more political power. In this situation, individuals and communities have sought different ways to enhance their human security, two of which – agreements and adaptation – are highlighted later.

YNAO holds the country's largest natural gas reserves and has been Russia's principal natural gas-producing region since the 1970s. During the Soviet era, companies were considered to be a "total social institution" (Humphrey 1998) that were responsible for all social matters of the population in the area of their operations. All citizens, be they incomers for industrial development or local nomads, played a role in socialist enterprises. The tundra and forest were conceived as giant "open-air meat factories" (Vitebsky 2005) and local reindeer herders became state employees whose job was to provide local meat for company workers. Although not without significant disruptions and consequences, the traditional occupation of the Nenets was integrated into the Soviet economic model.

The situation changed drastically after the collapse of the Soviet Union. Privatization meant that companies were no longer legally responsible for the social welfare of their employees or the local communities in which they operated. However, in reality, many Russian corporations simply superimposed the norm of "corporate social responsibility" (CSR) onto the old Soviet "total social institution" system that continues, in a more limited fashion, to exist throughout Russia. Thus, many communities, Indigenous and non-Indigenous alike, turn to the industries to mitigate threats and violations that EI has caused to their human security. The most common solution is a benefit-sharing agreement, wherein a company agrees "to return part of the income generated through the resource extraction activity back to the community and Indigenous peoples in a monetary or non-monetary form" (Tulaeva & Tysiachniouk 2017, 2). Such arrangements are a common and popular practice for EI companies around the world, and Russia is no exception.

In the Russian context, two predominant types of benefit-sharing arrangements have evolved. The first involves the company entering into a collective contract with the municipality where the extractable resources are located. The second involves an individualized agreement between the company and specific communities directly impacted by EI operations. Scholars and Indigenous politicians alike have debated which arrangement is more reliable and equitable. Individual agreements are known to increase inequality, while in collective agreements the benefits do not always reach those who have to bear most of the costs (Garipov 2014; Henry et al. 2016; Stammler & Ivanova 2016). In YNAO, the former arrangement is dominant. All of its municipalities today have agreements with EI companies on the socioeconomic development of their territories. These agreements are not binding by law. They resemble impact–benefit agreements and are usually confidential in detail, but they form an important development booster for the municipalities.

As an alternative, or in addition to formal arrangements, personal networks and informal agreements have long been accepted as normal means of accomplishing objectives on which many activists continue to rely. For example, the location of one of the Yamal megaproject's extraction sites threatened nomads' access to all of their summer pastures and would have forced all affected nomadic families to relocate to villages. This situation was avoided due to the intervention of two key Nenets activists who sidetracked a Gazprom official during a smoke break, whereupon they voiced their concerns. As a result, an agreement was made to construct a chain of corridors and passages for humans and animals around the field (see maps in Kumpula et al. 2012, pp. 1056–1061, FS field notes 2012, 2013, 2014).

These examples of both formal and informal agreements highlight the precarious situation in which many Indigenous people in Russia find themselves. Formal agreements do not necessarily result in a feeling of greater security for Indigenous people. The first reason is that the municipalities themselves are largely responsible for determining how the benefits they have received (usually capital) will be distributed. Many municipalities opt to develop their settlements, which mostly benefit the sedentary population. The remaining nomadic population benefits the least from such industry payments, although they are the ones who have to bear much of the negative consequences. The second reason is that most agreements are compensation-based, which involves calculations for damages that have already occurred. Thus, the focus is diverted from preventing damage from happening in the first place.

Finally, benefit agreements in the Russian context continue to replicate the power imbalances that were inherent in the Soviet system. The original intent behind benefit-sharing agreements was to increase local participation in the decision-making processes for industrial development. However, CSR in Russia still resembles the paternalistic Soviet-style command-and-control system, wherein state-controlled industries deliver charity and social benefits in a top-down manner onto a recipient community that has little to no opportunity to participate in the decision-making process (Stammler & Ivanova 2016). On the other hand, informal agreements can be beneficial, when the right people meet at the right time and state their concerns in the right way. However, if any of the necessary conditions are missing, there is generally no recourse.

A second, more individualized approach through which members of Indigenous groups have produced niches of security is through adaptation. Recent research has highlighted the high adaptive potential of Indigenous people to cumulative changes (Hovelsrud et al. 2010) and the resilience of Indigenous cultures such as those on Yamal (Forbes et al. 2009). Here, we highlight three different examples of such adaptation: reindeer herding as a business, Indigenous people's employment in EI, and the evolution of sedentary village culture.

First, there is the story of commercial reindeer meat production. During the Soviet era, reindeer herds were collectivized into state-run farms. In the post-Soviet era, these farms have chosen to enter the competitive international meat market. In the late 1990s the Yamal Peninsula region launched an initiative to get its reindeer meat certified for export into the European Union. The Yamal'skie Oleni municipal company rose to the challenge. As a result of being able to export its products, the company was able to pay reindeer herders a higher price for their meat, use more of the animal for intensive processing, and pass on some of the export revenue back to the nomadic producers of the meat (FS field notes 2002, 2012, 2013, 2014). This case has been used as a model for the resilience of reindeer herding as a nomadic livelihood as something of which Indigenous people can be proud.

Next, we highlight the employment of Indigenous workers in EI. Since the turn of the millennium, two big industrial developments were pushed forward on the Yamal Peninsula: Gazprom's Yamal megaproject and the Yamal LNG project, a liquefied natural gas venture which is managed by a consortium of the three international partners: Total, Novatek (a private Russian company, partially owned by Gazprom), and the China National Petroleum Corporation. This acceleration in industrial development on the Yamal Peninsula has left the Indigenous population with increased insecurity and anxiety about the future. In recent years industrial companies such as Gazprom have increasingly invested in educating Indigenous candidates, so some Indigenous individuals have chosen to seek employment in the EI sector to supplement their nomadic livelihoods. Nenets Gazprom workers have subsequently been able to function as an informal link between the industry and reindeer-herding families. Workers have claimed that the fly-in/fly-out work regime suits their needs because it allows them to have a full-time paid job and still spend half of the time in the tundra and be part of a reindeer-herding life (FS field notes 2013). Such a form of adaptation has been controversial. Doubts remain among both Indigenous workers as well as managers in industry; firstly whether employment is for the better or worse of the Indigenous society, and secondly whether the herders and hunters can get used to a kind of work and schedule that is alien to their own livelihood on the land (FS and AI field notes 2013, 2018).

Finally, we turn to the example of the evolving village cultures. While for some the transition to a sedentary lifestyle has resulted in psychosocial trauma, for others living in a village does not mean solely abandoning one's culture. Rather, a new sedentary culture has evolved among those who live in town (Lyarskaya 2001). Village culture is considered to be an addition, not a replacement, to the traditional lifestyle of the nomads and many nomads nowadays switch between two worlds. Among the Nenets, this occurs according to the general principle that innovations in society are incorporated as additions rather than replacements of old techniques or patterns (Stammler 2005).

Conclusion

This chapter explored the nexus between the human security of the people in the Russian North and the development of extractive industries in their homeland. Russia's Indigenous people face a substantial power imbalance vis-à-vis the federal state and state-controlled EI companies, which overwhelmingly favor the latter. The power imbalance renders them vulnerable to four main categories of threats to the security of their individual and collective livelihoods: demographic marginalization, environmental degradation, disruptions to traditional ways of life, and psychosocial consequences of alienation from the land. Utilizing case studies in two different regions, we provided three examples of security production: the creation of regional-level laws, the signing of individualized benefit-sharing agreements, and adaptation by the fusion of traditional lifestyles with contemporary realities. Each of these solutions is problematic in their own way, however, each example illustrates how Indigenous groups use what agency they possess to produce niches of security, however precarious, for themselves and their communities.

In conclusion, for industry employees of non-Indigenous and non-local origin, the presence of EI may well increase their sense of security. For those Indigenous peoples with a direct connection to the land, industry brings insecurity due to disturbance and territorial expansion, in spite of material benefits. However, examples of successful regional legal activity or Indigenous agency on the ground to shape relations with the extractive industries have shown that Indigenous people are not solely victims of industrialization. They can also be agents for increasing their own human security in settings that fit their own regional and cultural framework, as shown in the examples of the RSY and the YNAO.

Note

1 In particular, Article 1 of the International Labor Organization's Convention 169 provides the most specific of definitions for *Indigenous* as "peoples in independent countries who are regarded as indigenous on account of their descent from the populations which inhabited the country, or a geographical region to which the country belongs, at the time of conquest or colonisation or the establishment of present state boundaries and who, irrespective of their legal status, retain some or all of their own social, economic, cultural and political institutions." The spirit of "those who were there first" is also evidenced in the 2004 Arctic Human Development Report, which classifies as *Indigenous* those "peoples who were already established at the time people of European tradition came to the North" (p. 21).

References

Bogoyavlenskiy, D. (2010) 'Russia's Indigenous peoples of the North: a demographic portrait at the beginning of the twenty-first century,' *Sibirica* 9(3), pp. 91–114.

Bolotova, A. and Stammler, F. (2010) 'How the North became home. Attachment to place among industrial migrants in Murmansk region,' in Huskey, L. and Southcott, C. (eds.) *Migration in the Circumpolar North: Issues and Contexts*. Edmonton: Canadian Circumpolar Institute Press, pp. 193–220.

BP. (2019) *BP Statistical Review of World Energy 2019*. 68th ed. Available at: www.bp.com/content/dam/bp/business-sites/en/global/corporate/pdfs/energy-economics/statistical-review/bp-stats-review-2019-full-report.pdf (Accessed: 22 July 2019).

Chandler, D. (2008) 'Review essay: human security: the dog that didn't bark,' *Security Dialogue* 39(4), pp. 427-438.

Degteva, A. and Nellemann, C. (2013) 'Nenets migration in the landscape: impacts of industrial development in Yamal Peninsula, Russia,' *Pastoralism: Research, Policy and Practice* 3(1), pp. 15. [online]. Available at. doi:10.1186/2041-7136-3-15

Diem Scientific Production Firm. (2014) *'Magistralnyi Gazoprovod «Sila Sibiri» [The "Power of Siberia" main gas pipeline]*. Available at: https://docplayer.ru/26020631-Magistralnyy-gazoprovod-sila-sibiri.html (Accessed 22 July 2019).

Donahoe, B., Habeck, J.O., Halemba, A. and Sántha, I. (2008) 'Size and place in the construction of indigeneity in the Russian Federation,' *Current Anthropology* 49(6), pp. 993–1020.

Duffield, M. and Waddell, N. (2006) 'Securing humans in a dangerous world,' *International Politics* 43(1), pp. 1–23.

Fauzer, V.V. (2016) 'Demograficheskiy potentsial severnykh regionov Rossii [Demographic potential of the northern regions of Russia]'. Presentation at the inter-regional conference "*Respublika Sakha (Yakutia) – 2030-205-: Strategiya Uspekha.*" Available at: src-sakha.ru/wp-content/uploads/2017/01/2-Fauzer-V.V.pdf (Accessed 22 July 2019).

Federal State Statistics Service (FSSS). (2010) '*Naseleniye natsional'nosti i vladeniyu russkim yazykom po sub'yektam Rossiyskoy Federatsii* [Population by nationality and acquisition of Russian language, by subjects of the Russian Federation],' in *Vsyerossiyskaya perepis' naseleniya 2010 [All-Russian Federation Census 2010]*, pp. 29–141. Available at: www.gks.ru/free_doc/new_site/perepis2010/croc/Documents/Vol4/pub-04-04.pdf (Accessed 31 July 2018).

Fondahl, G. and Sirina, A. (2006) 'Rights and risks: Evenki concerns regarding the proposed Eastern Siberia-Pacific Ocean pipeline,' *Sibirica* 5(2), pp. 115–138.

Forbes, B.C., Stammler, F., Kumpula, T., Meschtyb, N., Pajunen, A. and Kaarlejärvi, E. (2009) 'High resilience in the Yamal-Nenets social–ecological system, West Siberian Arctic, Russia,' *Proceedings of the National Academy of Sciences* 106(52), pp. 22041–22048.

Garipov, R. (2014) 'Extractive industries and Indigenous minority peoples' rights in Russia,' *Nordisk Miljörättslig Tidskrift/Nordic Environmental Law Journal* 1, pp. 67–75.

Heleniak, T. and Bogoyavlensky, D. (2014) 'Arctic populations and migration,' in Larsen, J.N. and Fondahl, G. (eds.) *Arctic Human Development Report: Regional Processes and Global Linkages*. Copenhagen: Nordic Council of Ministers, pp. 53–103.

Henry, L.A., Nysten-Haarala, S., Tulaeva, S. and Tysiachniouk, M. (2016) 'Corporate social responsibility and the oil industry in the Russian Arctic: global norms and neo-paternalism,' *Europe-Asia Studies* 68(8), pp. 1340–1368.

Hoogensen Gjørv, G. (2014) 'Virtuous imperialism or a shared global objective? The relevance of human security in the global North,' in Hoogensen Gjørv, G., Bazely, D.R., Goloviznina, M. and Tanentzap, A.J. (eds.) *Environmental and Human Security in the Arctic*. London: Routledge, pp. 58–74.

Hossain, K., Zojer, G., Greaves, W., Roncero, J.M. and Sheehan, M. (2017) 'Constructing Arctic security: an inter-disciplinary approach to understanding security in the Barents region,' *Polar Record* 53(1), pp. 52–66.

Hovelsrud, G.K. and Smit, B. (eds.) (2010) *Community Adaptation and Vulnerability in Arctic Regions*. Dordrecht: Springer.

Humphrey, C. (1998) 'The Domestic mode of production in post-Soviet Siberia?' *Anthropology Today* 14(3), pp. 2–7.

Irlbacher-Fox, S., Price, J. and Wilson Rowe, E. (2014) 'Women's participation in decision making: human security in the Canadian Arctic,' in Hoogensen Gjørv, G., Bazely, D.R., Goloviznina, M. and Tanentzap, A.J. (eds.) *Environmental and Human Security in the Arctic*. London: Routledge, pp. 203–230.

Ivanova, A. (2007) 'The price of progress in Eastern Siberia: problems of ecological legislation and political agency in a Russian region,' in Kankaanpaa, P., Ovaskainen, S., Pekkala, L. and Tennberg, M. (eds.) *Knowledge and Power in the Arctic: Proceedings from a Conference in Rovaniemi*. Rovaniemi: Arctic Centre Reports 48, pp. 61–69.

Keyser, C., Hollard, C., Gonzalez, A., Fausser, J., Rivals, E., Alexeev, A.N., Riberon, A., Crube´zy, E., and Ludes, B. (2015) 'The ancient Yakuts: a population genetic enigma,' *Philosophical Transactions of the Royal Society B* 370: 20130385 [online]. doi:10.1098/rstb.2013.0385

Kumpula, T., Forbes, B.C., Stammler, F., and Meschtyb, N. (2012) 'Dynamics of a coupled system: multi-resolution remote sensing in assessing social-ecological responses during 25 years of gas field development in Arctic Russia,' *Remote Sensing* 4(4), pp. 1046–1068.

Larsen, J.M. and Fondahl, G. (eds.) (2014) *Arcic Human Development Report: Regional Processes and Global Linkages*. Copenhagen: Nordic Council of Ministers.

Larsen, J.M., Schweitzer, P. and Fondahl, G. (eds.) (2010) *Arctic Social Indicators - A Follow-Up to the Arctic Human Development Report*. Copenhagen: Nordic Council of Ministers.

Loginova, J. (2018) 'Achieving human and societal security in oil producing regions: a Komi-Izhma community perspective from Pripechor'e, Russia,' in Hossain, K., Martín, J.M.R., and Petrétei, A. (eds.) *Human and Societal Security in the Circumpolar Arctic*. Leiden and Boston: Brill, pp. 191–211.

Lyarskaya, E.V. (2001) 'Kul'turnaya assimilyatsiya ili dva variant kul'tury [Cultural assimilation or two variations of culture],' in Bayburin, A.K.and Kolosova, V.B. (eds.) *Antropologiya, Fol'kloristika, lingvistika [Anthropology, Folklore, Linguistics]*. Vol. 1. St. Petersburg: European University of St. Petersburg, pp. 36–55.

Moiseenko, T.I., Voinov, A.A., Megorsky, V.V., Gashkina, N.A., Kudriavtseva, L.P., Vandish, O.I., Sharov, A.N., Sharova, Yu. and Koroleva, I.N. (2006) 'Ecosystem and human health assessment to define environmental management strategies: the case of long-term human impacts on an Arctic lake,' *Science of the Total Environment* 369(1–3), pp. 1–20.

Novikova, N. (2016) 'Who is responsible for the Russian Arctic? Co-operation between Indigenous peoples and industrial companies in the context of legal pluralism,' *Energy Research & Social Science* 16, pp. 98–110.

Novikova, N.I. (2017) 'Etnologicheskaya ekspertiza v Rossiyskoy Federatsii: pravovye osnovaniya I perspektivy dlya korennykh narodov [Anthropological expert review in the Russian Federation: legal foundations and perspectives for Indigenous peoples],' *Arktika XXI vek. Gumanitarniye nauki [21st Century Arctic. Humanitarian Sciences]* 3(13), pp. 4–20.

Peterson, D.J. (1993) *Troubled Lands: The Legacy of Soviet Environmental Destruction*. Boulder: Westview Press.

Postanovleniye Pravitel'stva RF ot 28 December 2016 № 1524 "*O sozdanii territorii operezhayushchego sotsial'no-ekonomicheskogo razvitiya 'Yuzhnaya Yakutiya'*" [*Decree of the Government of the Russian Federation No. 1524 "On the creation of the 'South Yakutiya' territory of advanced socio-economic development," 28 December 2016*]. Available at: www.garant.ru/products/ipo/prime/doc/71479334/

Saxinger, G. (2015) '"To you, to us, to oil and gas" –The symbolic and socio-economic attachment of the workforce to oil, gas and its spaces of extraction in the Yamal-Nenets and Khanty-Mansi Autonomous Districts in Russia,' *Fennia-International Journal of Geography* 193(1), pp. 83–98.

Slowey, G. (2014) 'Aboriginal self-determination and resource development activity: improving human security in the Canadian Arctic?' in Hoogensen Gjørv, G., Bazely, D.R., Goloviznina, M. and Tanentzap, A.J. (eds.) *Environmental and Human Security in the Arctic*. London: Routledge, pp. 187–202.

Stammler, F. (2005) 'The obshchina movement in Yamal: defending territories to build identities?' in Kasten, E. (ed.) *Rebuilding Identities: Pathways to Reform in Post-Soviet Siberia*. Berlin: Reimer, pp. 109–134.

Stammler, F. and Ivanova, A. (2016) 'Resources, rights and communities: extractive mega-projects and local people in the Russian Arctic,' *Europe-Asia Studies* 68(7), pp. 1220–1244.

Stammler, F. and Wilson, E. (2006) 'Dialogue for development: an exploration of relations between oil and gas companies, communities, and the state,' *Sibirica* 5(2), pp. 1–43.

Stuvøy, K. (2010) 'Human security research practices: conceptualizing security for women's crisis centres in Russia,' *Security Dialogue* 41(3), pp. 279–299.

Stuvøy, K. (2011) 'Human security, oil and people: an actor-based security analysis of the impacts of oil activity in the Komi Republic, Russia,' *Journal of Human Security* 7(2), pp. 5-19.

Stuvøy, K. (2014) 'Human security and women's security reality in Northwestern Russia,' in *Environmental and Human Security in the Arctic*. Hoogensen Gjørv, G., Bazely, D.R., Goloviznina, M. and Tanentzap, A.J. (eds.) *Environmental and Human Security in the Arctic*. London: Routledge, pp. 231–249.

Sweet, V. (2013) 'Extracting more than resources: human security and Arctic Indigenous women,' *Seattle University Law Review* 37, pp. 1157–1178.

Tulaeva, S. and Tysiachniouk, M. (2017) 'Benefit-sharing arrangements between oil companies and Indigenous people in Russian Northern Regions,' *Sustainability* 9(8), pp. 1326. [online]..doi:10.3390/su9081326

United Nations Development Programme (UNDP). (1994) *Human Development Report 1994*. New York: Oxford University Press.

Vitebsky, P. (2005) *The Reindeer People: Living with Animals and Spirits in Siberia*. Boston and New York: Houghton Mifflin.

Vitebsky, P. and Alekseyev, A. (2015) 'Casting timeshadows: pleasure and sadness of moving among Nomadic Reindeer Herders in North-East Siberia,' *Mobilities* 10, pp. 518–530.

Vsyerossiyskiy nauchno-issledovatel'skiy Institute Mineral'nogo Syr'ya immeno N.M. Fedorovskogo (VIMS). (2018) *Informatsionnaya spravka o sostoyanii mineral'no-syr'evoy bazy tvyordykh poleznykh iskopayemykh RS(Ya). [Information Sheet on the state of the mineral-crystalline base of minerals in RS(Y)].* Available at: http://vims-geo.ru/documents/207/Yakutia_03072018.pdf (Accessed: 22 July 2019).

Walker, D.A., Forbes, B.C., Leibman, M.O., Epstein, H.E., Bhatt, U.S., Comiso, J.C., Drozdov, D.S., Gubarkov, A.A., Jia, G.J., Kaarlejärvi, E., Kaplan, J.O., Khomutov, A.V., Kofinas, G.P., Kumpula, T., Kuss, P., Moskalenko, N.G., Meschtyb, N.A., Pajunen, A., Raynolds, M.K., Romanovsky, V.E., Stammler, F., and Yu, Q. (2011) 'Cumulative effects of rapid land-cover and land-use changes on the Yamal Peninsula, Russia,' in Gutman, G. and Reissell, A. (eds.) *Eurasian Arctic Land Cover and Land Use in a Changing Climate.* Dordecht: Springer, pp. 207–236.

Wiget, A. and Balalaeva, O. (1997) 'National communities, native land tenure, and self-determination among the Eastern Khanty,' *Polar Geography* 21(1), pp. 10–33.

Wilson, E. (2003) 'Freedom and loss in a human landscape: multinational oil exploitation and the survival of reindeer herding in north-eastern Sakhalin, the Russian Far East,' *Sibirica* 3, pp. 21–47.

Wilson, E. and Stammler, F. (2016) 'Beyond extractivism and alternative cosmologies: Arctic communities and extractive industries in uncertain times,' *The Extractive Industries and Society* 3(1), pp. 1–8.

Yakovleva, N. (2011) 'Oil pipeline construction in Eastern Siberia: implications for Indigenous people,' *Geoforum* 42, pp. 708–719.

Zadorin, M., Klisheva, O., Vezhlivtseva, K. and Antufieva, D. (2017) *Russian Laws on Indigenous Issues: Guarantees, Communities, Territories of Traditional Land Use: Translated and Commented.* Rovaniemi: University of Lapland.

Zakon Respubliki Sakha (Yakutiya) "Ob etnologicheskoy ekspertize v mestakh traditsionnogo prozhivaniya i traditsionnoy khozyaystvennoy deyatel'nosti korennykh malochislennykh narodov Severa Respubliki Sakha (Yakutiya)" ot 14 aprelya 2010 goda № 3 № 537-IV [*Law of the Republic of Sakha (Yakutiya) "On anthropological expert review in areas of traditional residence for and traditional ways of living by Indigenous small-numbered peoples of the North in the Republic of Sakha (Yakutiya)," No. 3 No.537-IV, 14 April 2010*]. Available at: http://docs.cntd.ru/document/895252453

Zakon Respubliki Sakha (Yakutiya) ot 13 iyulya 2006 goda № 370-3 N 755-III "O territoriyakh traditsionnogo prirodopol'zovaniya i traditsionnoy khozyaystvennoy deyatel'nosti korennykh malochislennykh narodov Severa Respubliki Sakha (Yakutiya) (s izmenyeniyami na 28. 05.2015") [*Law of the Republic of Sakha (Yakutiya) from 13 July 2006 No. 370-3 N 755-III "On territories of traditional nature use and traditional ways of living by Indigenous small-numbered peoples of the North in the Republic of Sakha (Yakutiya) (with changes on 28. 05.2015)"*]. Available at: http://docs.cntd.ru/document/802070067

Zen'ko, A. (2012) 'Nenets,' in Nuttall, M. (ed.) *Encyclopedia of the Arctic.* New York: Routledge, pp. 1417–1420.

32

THE ROLE OF INDIGENOUS LOCAL KNOWLEDGE (ILK) IN ENHANCING INDIGENOUS SECURITY IN THE MACKENZIE VALLEY, NORTHWEST TERRITORIES, CANADA

Horatio Sam-Aggrey

Introduction

The late 20th century witnessed significant social, economic, and environmental changes in the Arctic (Noble and Hanna 2015). Increasing energy and mineral resource extraction, the opening of new transportation routes, and the impacts of climate change (Burkett 2011; Prowse et al. 2006) have ushered in a period of interrelated political, economic, social, and ecological changes in the Circumpolar North. Sustaining Arctic and subarctic ecosystems and livelihoods of northern Indigenous peoples are becoming a challenge in the face of increasing resource development (Parlee, Sandlos, and Natcher 2018).

Mining projects generate employment and promote the development of much-needed regional infrastructure, but these activities also cause local environmental damage and unintended social consequences, resulting in significant adverse effects for local communities. For example, while diamond mines are of critical importance to the economy of the Northwest Territories (NWT), Canada, they also have significant adverse impacts on the local and regional environment (Davison and Hawe 2012; Shigley et al. 2016). Mining operations in the Mackenzie Valley of the NWT are located on important caribou migration routes and near calving grounds, where caribou females are most sensitive to human disturbance (Parlee, Sandlos, and Natcher 2018). The areas in which these mines are located are also used for traditional hunting by the Dene First Nations.

In the NWT, changing climatic conditions, coupled with the additional stress of increased industrial development activities, have led to a decline in caribou populations (Vors and Boyce 2009). The decline of this species has implications for caribou hunting practices and thus for the culture, identity, and traditional ways of life of communities in the Mackenzie Valley. As competition over land use and resources continues to intensify, caribou management and its relationship with other land uses has gained prominence (Schneider et al. 2012). Given the importance of caribou to the cultural identity and socioeconomic well-being of many northern societies, balancing caribou management with natural resource management (NRM) within the existing social and political landscape is important for ensuring sustainable development in the North. Meaningful Indigenous participation in NRM is key to the success of any such endeavor.

The concept of human security, first introduced by the United Nations Development Program (UNDP) in its 1994 Human Development Report, broadened the concept of security from one that focused on military security aimed at protecting the interests of the state, to one that focused on the daily insecurities faced by individuals (UNDP 1994). The UNDP categorized seven different areas of (in)security: economic, food, health, environmental, personal, community, and political (UNDP 1994). Although all of the categories are interdependent, this chapter is informed mainly by the categories of environmental security, food security, and community security.[1] Arctic Indigenous peoples have expressed concerns over the threats posed by industrial development and climate change to their food security, traditional knowledge, traditional ways of life (community security), and health (health security) (Cameron 2012; Greaves 2012; ICC Canada 2012; Kuhnlein et al. 2014; Sejersen 2015).

Historically, Indigenous peoples have relied on Indigenous local knowledge, or ILK,[2] to guide their interaction with natural resources and their environment and to manage wildlife. Developed through an accumulation of location-specific observations and knowledge, the detailed ILK on caribou by Indigenous peoples has been transmitted from one generation to another over time. However, the meaningful integration of Indigenous peoples and their knowledge systems in environmental governance regimes, such as the environmental assessment process, continues to be the exception rather than the norm (Johannes 1993; Noble and Hanna 2015). Usher (2000) noted that in the Canadian context, environmental assessment is the "most structured and visible" of the policy arenas involving ILK. This makes environmental assessment regimes a suitable process for a focused study of ILK incorporation in resource management in the Northwest Territories.

Although environmental assessment systems are widely criticized for not adequately considering Indigenous peoples and their knowledge systems (Noble and Udofia 2015), environmental assessment systems in Canada's North may be the exception. Governance arrangements set a broader context that impacts the ability of ILK to influence NRM processes such as environmental assessment. Hence, the relationship between ecological systems stewardship and ILK cannot be discussed without considering the legal status of Indigenous nations as distinct sovereigns within wider nation-states (Ranco et al. 2011). Indigenous governance systems play important roles in defining and implementing programs to mitigate the negative impacts of resource extraction (Grijalva 2011).

In the northern regions of Canada, because of Comprehensive Land Claims Agreements (CLCAs), legislative, regulatory, or policy requirements have been instituted to ensure that the ILK of Indigenous people are included in resource management (Usher 2000). Current environmental assessment regimes in the North require that developers incorporate ILK into project reviews, including in the NWT (Mackenzie Valley Resource Management Act (MVRMA) 1998), and in the Yukon (Yukon Environmental and Socio-economic Assessment Act (YESA Act) 2003). In Nunavut, the Nunavut Land Claims Agreement similarly requires the assessment of the potential impacts of proposed developments in the Nunavut Settlement Area, considering both ILK and scientific methods.

The overarching goal of this chapter is to explore the role of ILK in environmental governance in the Mackenzie Valley. Specifically, this chapter examines the mechanisms through which ILK is deployed or incorporated into resource co-management systems in the Mackenzie Valley of the Northwest Territories, with the goal of enhancing Indigenous security. The chapter seeks to answer the following questions. What role does ILK play in environmental governance in the Mackenzie Valley? What roles do Indigenous governance structures play in facilitating the collection and inclusion of ILK in decision-making related to environmental governance?

The remainder of the chapter is presented in four sections. The second section discusses the importance of caribou to the security of Indigenous peoples in the Mackenzie Valley, the potential role of ILK in mitigating the negative impacts of mining, and the statutory and political context within which ILK is implemented. This is followed by the study methodology and findings of the research. The final section discusses some important outcomes of the study and provides concluding statements.

Literature review

The population of the Bathurst caribou herd, a species strongly linked to the cultural identity and socioeconomic well-being of Indigenous peoples in the Mackenzie Valley, has declined from roughly 450,000 in the mid-1980s to about 20,000 in 2018 (Government of the Northwest Territories ND). While it can be argued that the decline in the population of the caribou is negatively impacted by factors such as climate change, cyclical factors, and predators, the location of diamond mines on migration routes and calving grounds does not help the recovery of the species.

Caribou meat is a major source of food in northern diets. According to surveys undertaken by the Centre for Indigenous Peoples' Nutrition and Environment, the Dene people derive between 5% and 30% of their diet from traditional food (Lambden et al. 2006). Caribou meat is also rich in nutrients like protein and iron, which would otherwise be lacking in Indigenous diets due the steep price of store-bought meat. While the monetary value of caribou consumed for subsistence has not been precisely calculated, it is likely to run into the tens of millions of dollars per year (Tesar 2007). This is what it would cost for people to replace the caribou meat in their diets with expensive meat shipped up from southern Canada and to replace the other economic benefits generated by the caribou hunts.

The highest consumption of caribou meat is in remote communities and among the elderly (Lambden et al. 2006). For example, due to the remoteness of the four Tłįchǫ communities within the Bathurst range (Behchoko, Gameti, Wekweeti, and Whati), any food that cannot be hunted, trapped, gathered, grown, or fished must be flown in or driven by truck over treacherous winter roads. Shorter, milder winters can make these roads less dependable. These issues raise questions of food security – a critical component of Indigenous security in the Arctic (ICC Canada 2012; Kuhnlein et al. 2014).

Caribou are more than a source of nutrition and income. The harvesting, preparation, and sharing of the species are important cultural activities. Caribou are also highly valued for their hides, as caribou skin is commonly used for clothing and for shelter. All these activities are central to the sustenance of Indigenous cultures and knowledge, and a reduction in the abundance of caribou has consequences for traditional hunting practices, thereby negatively affecting community security.

In view of the decline in caribou herds, the role of ILK in improved land-use decision-making across the Bathurst caribou's herd range is increasingly taking center stage. Bridging

Indigenous and scientific knowledge in environmental governance systems is increasingly viewed as pivotal to mitigating the "wicked problems" related to balancing the interests of traditional practices and industrial development (Dale and Armitage 2011; Uprety et al. 2012).

Northern Indigenous peoples who have had to deal with the vicissitudes of barren-ground caribou populations are arguably among those with the greatest insights about how to cope with ecological complexity (Berkes 2008; Uphoff 1998). For example, Indigenous elders and leaders possess knowledge that provides alternative explanations of when and why the "caribou do not come," presenting alternatives to scientific models on calf recruitment and predation. ILK has contributed to environmental research and management by improving baseline data on species and ecological processes (Ferguson et al. 1998, Mallory et al. 2003), and by providing insights that can be used to develop alternative resource-management systems (Berkes 2008; Turner, Ignace, and Ignace 2000).

Recognition of the importance of engaging Indigenous peoples and their knowledge systems in environmental governance regimes, such as environmental assessment, is not new (Johannes 1993). Although many resource-management systems across southern Canada are subject to increasing criticism for their limited inclusion of ILK, the inclusion of ILK and the recognition of its value along with Western science in decision-making processes is one of the cornerstones of natural resource co-management arrangements in Canada's North (Nadasdy 1999).

ILK, comprehensive land claims agreements, and environmental assessments

In Canada, the rise in the use of ILK in resource management can be traced mainly to developments in the political and judicial recognition of Indigenous rights. The entrenchment of Aboriginal and Treaty rights in the Canadian Constitution Act of 1982 by way of Section 35 has resulted in increased attention on the content and substance of these rights, particularly as they pertain to NRM. The Supreme Court of Canada's 1973 decision in Calder v. British Columbia (AG), (1973) SCR 31 recognized the possibility of a form of "Aboriginal title"[3] existing in parts of Canada where it had not been extinguished by treaties. Given that most of northern Canada, and most of British Columbia, were not subject to "historic treaties," the Government of Canada responded to this court decision with its Comprehensive Land Claims Policy in 1973 (Alcantara 2013). This policy was designed to yield "modern treaties" in all those parts of Canada not covered by historic treaties.

The first modern treaty was the James Bay and Northern Québec Agreement, signed in 1975 between the federal government and the Cree and Inuit of Québec in response to the construction of a hydroelectric development complex (Rynard 2000). This agreement included the establishment of a co-management regime, whereby the Cree and Inuit of Québec would partner with government representatives in equal numbers on management boards in relation to such areas as environmental assessment and wildlife management. Since the James Bay and Northern Québec Agreement, 25 CLCAs have been signed between Canada and Indigenous groups (Government of Canada n.d.). Many of these modern treaties are in the northern territories of Canada and, like the James Bay agreement, these CLCAs also ensure Indigenous participation in environmental assessments and resource management through the establishment of co-management boards.

Environmental assessment is broadly defined as a process for identifying, predicting, evaluating, and mitigating the biophysical, social, and other relevant effects of development proposals before major decisions and commitments are made (Noble and Hanna 2015).

Environmental assessment is the point in the decision-making process that offers the greatest opportunities for stakeholders, such as local residents, municipal governments, and First Nations to influence the outcome of a project (Noble 2016), and it sets out the standards for managing impacts over the lifecycle of a development.

The environmental assessment process in Canada's northern territories is based on a co-management approach, rooted in the legal and cultural frameworks of CLCAs. Each territory has its own regulatory regime, administered under a variety of regional boards, responsible for various management processes including wildlife, water, and environmental assessment. These boards are referred to as *co-management boards* because they are made up of equal representatives of Indigenous community and non-Indigenous government representatives. They function as decision-making bodies that are responsible for the day-to-day management of resources in their settlement areas, though in many cases the Minister of the Environment (federal or territorial) retains ultimate decision-making authority.

Several researchers have highlighted the important role that northern co-management boards play in facilitating the use of ILK for resource management (Manseau, Parlee, and Ayles 2007; Pinkerton 1989). White (2009) noted that these boards represent the best opportunity for imbuing public, non-Indigenous governmental institutions with traditional knowledge. Others assert that the boards often lead to a change in the power dynamics, which is critical in the linking of state and Indigenous knowledge systems (McCay and Acheson 1987; Pinkerton 1989). However, not everyone is convinced about the utility of the approach of combining ILK with science in resource-management processes. Several scholars note that the two knowledge systems are "incommensurable" (Nadasdy 2003) because knowledge requires experience and the fundamental experience of Indigenous peoples is drastically different from the scientific context. Hence, combining the two systems is unproductive and only serves to maintain the subordinate position of ILK (Nadasdy 1999). Other scholars have also argued against reformatting ILK into databases for the benefit of scientists and policymakers, arguing that such processes deprive ILK of its dynamic and integrative aspects and remove it from its central context (Agrawal 2002; Fenge and Funston 2009; Stevenson 1996). Spak (2005) and Nadasdy (1999) concluded that ILK is often used merely as supplementary data to fill the information gaps of resource biologists.

Methodology

The case

The Northwest Territories – total population approximately 44,000 as of 2019 – is home to some 20,860 Indigenous peoples, accounting for about 50.7% of the territory's total population. The majority of Indigenous persons reside in small communities (Statistics Canada 2017). Population density is also very low in this region. There are three settled land claims in the Mackenzie Valley: the Gwich'in (1992), the Sahtu (1994), and the Tłı̨chǫ (2005) CLCAs. While each land claim is different, these agreements generally cover ownership, use, and management of land, environmental management, and resources. They also clarify how renewable and nonrenewable resources will be owned and managed, and how and by whom resource development will be managed and regulated. As part of the agreements covering these CLCAs, the Government of Canada was required to establish a network of co-management boards to form an integrated system of resource management. Consequently, the Mackenzie Valley Resource Management Act,[4] (MVRMA) was enacted in 1998 to implement the federal government's land claim obligations to the Gwich'in and the Sahtu peoples. The law was amended in 2005 to accommodate the Tłı̨chǫ Agreement, and again in 2013 with the Northwest Territories Devolution Act. The MVRMA implements the environmental assessment sections of the CLCA.

The MVRMA co-management boards

The MVRMA established three types of independent co-management boards to run the various stages of the EA and regulatory processes (Table 32.1). The boards created by the MVRMA are as follows:

Regional land-use planning boards (LUPBs)

LUPBs are tasked with developing regional land-use plans that define where and under what conditions resource development activities may take place, and what land will be set aside from development.

Mackenzie Valley Land and Water Boards (and its regional sub-panels)

The Land and Water Boards (LWBs) are responsible for preliminary project screenings and have the authority to issue, amend, suspend, and renew land-use permits and water licenses throughout their respective settlement areas. The Mackenzie Valley Land and Water Board (MVLWB) is responsible for project screening and issuance of land-use permits and water licenses in unsettled land claims areas and transboundary projects in the whole of the Mackenzie Valley.

The Mackenzie Valley Environmental Impact Review Boards (MVEIRB)

Environmental Impact Review Boards are responsible for environmental assessment of proposed developments and for creating panels to conduct Environmental Impact Reviews (EIR) if necessary. Based on the findings of its assessment, this board makes recommendations to the responsible NWT Minister on whether a proposed development proceeds to regulatory review or not.

Co-management boards in the Mackenzie Valley play a facilitating role in the use of ILK in environmental assessments and wildlife co-management (Kendrick 2003). This is partly due to the legal requirements in the MVRMA and the provisions of the CLCAs. Sections 115.1 and 60.1 (b) of the MVRMA require that the MVEIRB and the MVLWBs, respectively, to consider any traditional knowledge (in addition to scientific information) that is presented to them (MVRMA 1998), thereby placing ILK on a par with other scientific data – at least in principle.

Table 32.1 Boards established under the MVRMA.

Preliminary Screening and Regulating; Permitting Land and Water Boards	*Environmental Assessment and Impact Review Boards*	*Land-Use Planning Boards*
Mackenzie Valley Land and Water Board Gwich'in Land and Water Board Sahtu Land and Water Board Wekheezhi Land and Water Board	Mackenzie Valley Environmental Impact Review Board	Sahtu Land-Use Planning Board Gwich'in Land-Use Planning Board

Study design

The main data collection methods employed in this case study were semi-structured interviews and a review of available documents and literature. The interviews in this study augmented some of the issues identified in document analysis and the literature review process. A total of 14 semi-structured interviews were conducted with members of the co-management boards (the MVEIRB, the MVLWB, the Wek'èezhìı Land and Water Board (WLWB), the Wek'èezhìı Renewable Resources Board (WRRB), and the Tłįchǫ Government. The research questions and goals drove the respondent selection (purposive sampling). Depending on the respondents, the topics included the role of ILK in the decision-making process, and the role of Indigenous governments in promoting the use of ILK by the boards. The typical interview lasted between 50 minutes to one hour. The interviews were recorded and transcribed. The interview schedule consisted of about ten open-ended questions, depending on the respondents' role in the co-management process.

In addition to interviews, the study relied on a review of the literature on the role of ILK in resource management. The types of documents reviewed included legislative frameworks, CLCAs, co-management board policies and guidelines on ILK requirements, land-use permits and water licenses issued to developers, formal statements in public hearing processes, Environmental Assessment Reports, and formal letters from the boards to project proponents. The documents were reviewed for provisions on ILK or evidence of incorporation of ILK in project management activities.

Findings: the incorporation of ILK during the lifecycle of mines

The incorporation of ILK in the environmental assessment phase

The environmental assessment process conducts a thorough assessment of the environmental and social impacts of a project on an area or community. During environmental assessments, the MVEIRB determines whether the project impacts are significant, and whether the mitigation measures are sufficient. The board assesses both the significance of impacts and the significance of public concern. As a consequence of the requirements for extensive consultation and consideration of ILK by proponents at this stage, the environmental assessment process has built-in mechanisms to ensure a detailed collection and incorporation of ILK. The MVEIRB's Traditional Knowledge Guidelines (2005) provide guidance on the board's general expectations with respect to ILK for all stages of an environmental assessment (MVEIRB 2005, 14). The guidelines also explicitly state that the board uses ILK to help identify the issues to be addressed in the environmental assessment (MVEIRB 2005, 23–24).

Evidence from the study suggests that public hearing sessions are important avenues for communities to volunteer substantial ILK. Information, including ILK, provided in these meetings can and has had concrete effects on the environmental assessment process. For example, in response to community concerns based on ILK about the environmental footprint of the proposed Jay-Cardinal Pipe Project footprint identified during the environmental assessment, Dominion Diamond[5] amended its application and removed the Cardinal Pipe portion from the project entirely, thereby minimizing the impact of the proposed project on the area (MVEIRB 2016).

After the environmental assessment is completed, the board produces a recommendation and the Minister makes the formal decision. If the MVEIRB determines that there will not be significant adverse impacts, the project is recommended for approval. If the board believes otherwise, then the project is either recommended for approval with mitigation measures or the MVEIRB can send a project to the EIR screening phase if it deems the project impact will be very significant. Evidence suggests that the MVEIRB uses its power to impose mitigating measures on projects as a means to ensure the use of ILK in environmental governance. For example, as part of Measure 6–1 (road mitigations for caribou impacts) for the Jay Pipe project, Dominion is required to use traditional knowledge when designing programs for the monitoring of caribou responses to roads and waste-rock piles during the operations phase. These measures are taken into account by the LWBs when proponents apply for land-use permits and water licenses.

The incorporation of ILK in the regulatory (pre-operations) phase

The LWBs are responsible for permitting and licensing developments in the post-environmental assessment phase. To facilitate its work, the MVLWB produced a number of guidelines and policies, which not only guide their regulatory functions, but have also served to elevate the role of ILK. For example, when an application for a land-use permit or water license is submitted after the environmental assessment, the LWBs look for evidence of the proponent's pre-application engagement with the community. LWB policy and guidelines require the proponents to show the modifications that were made to their applications based on feedback received from affected communities; otherwise, the application is not considered complete (MVLWB 2013, 2014)

Once the board is satisfied with the pre-application engagement, there is a 12-month-long extensive engagement process with the community. Technical workshops and consultations with communities are held, during which ILK may be brought forward by the communities and be considered by the proponent. Stakeholders and interested parties present interventions before the board and ask questions of each other. The board may then ask the developer to modify their applications to reflect the contributions of the parties.

In issuing the licenses, the LWBs may impose *conditions* on the licenses of the developers. Conditions are legally binding provisions that proponents are required to follow in order to maintain their license. For example, a condition included in the amended[6] Land Use Permit of Dominion Diamond's Ekati Mine requires the company to seek the advice of Aboriginal elders on the location, design, and operation of caribou crossings on the Jay Road, esker crossing, and waste-rock storage area egress ramps, to limit the impacts to caribou (WLWB 2017a).

This condition was the result of a technical intervention by the Tłı̨chǫ Government, who argued that eskers (*what'àa*) are important to the caribou because they use them as trails to migrate and escape from heat and pests. The Tłı̨chǫ Government also argued that the waste-rock storage area would increase sensory disturbance during its construction and be a permanent barrier to caribou movement, hence the need for the proposed waste-rock storage area with its egress ramps to be planned and constructed based on ILK (MVLWB PR#531, 4–6). Similarly, in 2017, in response to an intervention by the Tłı̨chǫ Government during the review of Dominion Diamond's application for amendment of its water license,[7] the WLWB imposed a new condition requiring the developer to report all recommendations based on ILK received, describe how the recommendations were incorporated into their reports, and provide justification for any recommendations not adopted (WLWB 2017b).

Based on an analysis of the co-management boards' documents detailing the ILK-related interventions and recommendations of the Tłı̨chǫ Government during the regulatory process, it is evident that the recommendations of the Tłı̨chǫ Government carry immense weight and have significantly impacted mitigating measures and the licensing and permitting conditions issued by the MVEIRB and the WLWB. The co-management boards clearly take into account evidence based on ILK that is put forward by the Tłı̨chǫ Government.

The incorporation of ILK in the operations phase

At present, the effects-monitoring phase is perhaps the stage with the most significant incorporation of ILK in the mining life cycle. In the Tłı̨chǫ area, the Aquatic Effects Monitoring Program (AEMP)[8] and the Wildlife Effects Monitoring Plan (WEMP)[9] stand out as important mechanisms for the inclusion of ILK in the operations phase of mines.

The objective of the AEMP is to identify changes occurring in the aquatic environment that may be caused by mining activities. As part of this program, which is usually at a seasonal camp near the mine site, fish are caught, cleaned, inspected, cooked, and tasted by elders and community members to determine whether there are any differences in taste of the fish from one period to another or from one location to another. ILK holders and fish biologists also examine the fish for signs of deformities and parasites. For example, in a test done in August 2012, the group noted that many of the lake trout fish had mild fin erosion, a result that differed from results observed five years earlier (in 2007) when almost no fish had fin erosions (Rescan 2013). Water is inspected, sampled, boiled, and tasted during these camps. The LWBs use both ILK and Western scientific data and information to adequately evaluate the effects of mining on the aquatic environment and set effluent quality criteria to ensure that water quality standards are met.

The goal of the WEMP is to develop, implement, and monitor mitigation strategies so that the mine does not significantly adversely affect wildlife in the receiving and surrounding environment. With respect to caribou, some of the specific goals of WEMP include identifying the composition of caribou groups moving through the study area, documenting the annual timing of caribou movements through the study area to compare temporal trends in migration patterns, collared caribou monitoring, and to determine whether caribou behavior changes in proportion to distance from the mine. Elders and holders of ILK are regularly invited to the site to participate in monitoring programs and to share their knowledge about caribou behavior, diet, health and body condition, and migration movements. ILK is used to interpret the results of caribou and habitat surveys and to provide ways of preventing or reducing impacts to wildlife (Golder Associates 2016).

During site visits to the Ekati Mine, elders identified high ridges and sharp rocks along the edges of site roads as potential barriers and hazards to caribou movement. ILK has been used to construct caribou crossings to allow caribou to cross with greater ease (Rescan 2011). These crossing ramps have been constructed using crushed rock (six inches or less in size) so that the side slopes of the road are flatter and provide easier walking for caribou (Golder Associates Ltd 2016). Hence, ILK has been useful in enhancing road mitigation.

One major finding of this study is the lack of a formal mechanism to track the implementation of ILK provided to developers by elders. This is particularly important given the nonspecific nature of the boards' ILK-related license conditions. While the developers may implement the ILK recommendations, without a formal tripartite monitoring mechanism (involving the ILK holders, the developers, and the LWBs) there remains the question of how the community knows how many of said recommendations were implemented? Evidence from this study reveals that there are different perceptions among the players about whose responsibility it is to track the implementation of specific ILK recommendations. This has left a major gap in the system regarding the implementation of ILK.

Discussion and conclusion

The impacts of rapid climate change and intensified industrial development pose a formidable threat to the traditional livelihoods of Indigenous peoples in the Arctic. The ability of Indigenous communities to maintain their culture is being jeopardized (community security). The Bathurst caribou herd is the only herd of all the barren-ground caribou herds in Canada to have fallen steeply to very low numbers (GNWT n.d.). Given the importance of this species to the security of the Dene people, the rapid decline of this herd has been a source of worry and tension among Indigenous peoples and their governments in the Mackenzie Valley. Hence, the co-management boards in the region have created robust and institutionalized mechanisms for ensuring a substantial incorporation of ILK related to caribou and other species in the resource-management process in the region.

Much of the boards' focus has been on identifying and mitigating the impacts of mining on the caribou. However, a careful assessment of the nature of the ILK that are incorporated under the AEMP and the WEMP programs illustrates that the tangible aspects of ILK (for example, ILK about the type and numbers of caribou presently and formerly in particular areas) are more likely to be incorporated into management practices than the intangible aspects of ILK (for example, Indigenous worldviews on caribou).[10] Manseau, Parlee, and Ayles (2007) asserted that by contributing different values and perspectives, ILK can broadly influence management objectives. It is safe to conclude that the incorporation of Indigenous values and beliefs about caribou in the Mackenzie Valley co-management system is less apparent. Hence, legitimate questions can be raised about the influence Indigenous peoples have on developers' caribou management objectives.

Western scientific management plans break down data into smaller elements to understand whole and complex phenomena, while ILK is holistic in nature, with all elements of a phenomenon viewed as interconnected. ILK often includes a preference for observations and management options that are based on multiple interrelated ecological or socioecological variables and taken at fine-grain temporal and spatial scales (Kendrick 2003). The AEMP and WEMP focus on separate aspects of the fragile northern ecology (aquatic and wildlife issues respectively), and it is unclear what degree of coordination exists between the two programs at the implementation phase. While the nature of this study precludes the construction of a definitive conclusion on whether Indigenous values are accounted for in the Effects Monitoring Programs, anecdotal evidence suggests that these values do not influence developers' management plans. This brings to the fore the question of the long-term usefulness of these ILK initiatives. This finding lends some credence to the claims made by some researchers that ILK is used to fill science gaps rather than used in its cultural or spiritual context as an alternative way of knowing (see Nadasdy 1999; Spak 2005).

The Mackenzie Valley co-management regime is unique because of the strong Indigenous influence in the critical phase of determining the significance of impact of developments using ILK. The wide range of procedural opportunities for Indigenous peoples to volunteer ILK during the environmental assessment and post-environmental assessment phases has facilitated this. Contrary to skepticism on the part of some researchers about the usefulness of the boards' "Western and rational bureaucratic consultation processes" (Ellis 2005; White 2009), evidence from this study suggests that these engagement procedures (such as public hearings) are generally able to overcome cultural barriers to yield substantive ILK related to caribou. ILK volunteered during public sessions has made some significant impacts on the outcomes of decisions in the Mackenzie Valley. This has contributed to enhanced Indigenous security in the region.

The elevated role of ILK in resource management in the Mackenzie Valley region cannot be divorced from the positive political opportunity structures that have facilitated the recognition of Indigenous rights to self-determination, first through constitutional protections and then the CLCAs. Via a complex web of governance arrangements created by the MVRMA, the boards institutionalized the role of ILK in the project life cycle. This governance arrangement has also led to a vertical redistribution of power through processes of the devolution of powers, and the regionalization of some processes (Hooghe and Marks 2004). Indigenous governments have been beneficiaries of the vertical dispersion of power by the co-management system. The significant role played by the Tłı̨chǫ Government in promoting the use of Tłı̨chǫ knowledge in resource management exemplifies the importance of Indigenous agency in the co-management process. One reason for the strong influence of the Tłı̨chǫ Government in the regulatory process was that while the MVRMA provides clear provisions for consulting Indigenous peoples, it is fairly vague regarding the implementation of the ILK provisions of the Act (MVRMA 1998). Therefore, the CLCAs and the Indigenous governments can and do influence the implementation of provisions of the legislation.

The past 20 years have witnessed a significant growth in the policy framework regarding ILK in the NWT. With the MVRMA, the territory has taken important steps towards substantive incorporation of ILK in its environmental governance regimes. Evidence suggests that the influence of ILK on the operations phase of mining is increasing. Despite skepticism about the nature of ILK incorporated into the process, the Mackenzie Valley co-management system is at the forefront of the drive to incorporate ILK to enhance the security of Indigenous peoples in the Canadian North.

Notes

1 It is worth noting that these forms of insecurity are linked to other types of insecurities such as political, economic, health, environmental, and personal security.
2 Indigenous local knowledge (ILK) is also sometimes referred to as "Traditional ecological knowledge" (TEK), or Traditional knowledge (TK). The use of ILK in this thesis is meant to reflect the shift toward the use of the term in recent academic literature.
3 This decision was driven by the Nisga'a peoples' push for recognition of their legal rights to their land.
4 This region corresponds generally to the ancestral lands of the Dene peoples located within the boundaries of the Northwest Territories.
5 Dominion Diamond owns the Ekati Mine (Canada's first diamond mine), situated approximately 200 kilometers south of the Arctic Circle in Canada's Northwest Territories. The Jay Pipe (an open pit mine) is an expansion of the Ekati mine which would extend Ekati mine's life to 2033.
6 The amendment was needed to accommodate a new road at the mine site.
7 In an intervention during its Closing Argument, the Tłı̨chǫ Government recommended that Dominion Diamond include justification of why any recommendation coming from ILK holders is rejected.
8 The Aquatic Effects Monitoring Program (AEMP) at the Ekati Mine is a requirement specified in the mine's Class A water license (W2009L2-0001) (WLWB 2014). Wek'èezhìi Land and Water Board (WLWB). 2014. Wek'èezhìi Land and Water Board Water License #W2012L2-0001. Yellowknife, NWT, Canada.
9 A Wildlife Effects Monitoring Plan (WEMP) was established as a result of the Environmental Agreement signed on January 6, 1997 by BHP Diamonds Inc., and the Governments of the Northwest Territories and Canada (BHP 1998). BHP (BHP Diamonds Inc.). 1998. the Environmental Agreement signed on January 6, 1997 by BHP Diamonds Inc., and the Governments of the Northwest Territories and Canada. Prepared by BHP Diamonds Inc., Yellowknife, NWT, Canada.
10 See Usher (2000) for more information on categories of ILK.

References

Agrawal, A. 2002. "Common Resources and Institutional Sustainability." In *The Drama of the Commons*, eds. E. E. Ostrom, T. E. Dietz, N. E. Dolšak, P. C. Stern, S. E. Stonich, and E. U. Weber 41–85. Washington, DC: National Academy Press.

Alcantara, C. 2013. "Setting the Stage: The Context of Modern Treaty Negotiations in Canada." In *Negotiating the Deal: Comprehensive Land Claims Agreements in Canada*, ed. C. Alcantara 14–32. Toronto: University of Toronto Press. Retrieved from www.jstor.org/stable/10.3138/j.ctt2tv2c8.6.

Berkes, F. 2008. *Sacred Ecology: Traditional Ecological Knowledge and Resource Management*. London: Taylor and Francis.

Burkett, V. 2011. "Global Climate Change Implications for Coastal and Offshore Oil and Gas Development." *Energy Policy* No 39 (12), 7719–7725. DOI: 10.1016/j.enpol.2011.09.016

Calder v British Columbia (AG). (1973) SCR 313.

Cameron, E. S. 2012. "Securing Indigenous Politics: A Critique of the Vulnerability and Adaptation Approach to the Human Dimensions of Climate Change in the Canadian Arctic." *Global Environmental Change* No 22 (1), 103–114.

Statistics Canada. 2017. "Northwest Territories and Canada." Census Profile. 2016 Census. Statistics Canada Catalogue no 98-316-X2016001. Ottawa. Released November 29th 2017. Retrieved from www12.statcan.gc.ca/census-recensement/2016/dp-pd/prof/index.cfm?Lang=E (accessed November 1, 2018).

Dale, A. and D. Armitage. 2011. "Marine Mammal Co-management in Canada's Arctic: Knowledge Co-production for Learning and Adaptive Capacity." *Marine Policy* No 35 (4), 440–449. DOI: 10.1016/j.marpol.2010.10.019

Davison, C. M. and P. Hawe. 2012. "All That Glitters: Diamond Mning and Tłı̨chǫ Youth in Behchokǫ̀." *Arctic* No 65 (2), 214–228.

Ellis, S. C. 2005. "Meaningful Consideration? A Review of Traditional Knowledge in Environmental Decision-making." *Arctic* No 58 (1), 66–77.

Fenge, T. and W. B. Funston 2009. *Arctic Governance: Traditional Knowledge of Arctic Indigenous Peoples from an International Policy Perspective*. Retrieved from www.arcticgovernance.org/arctic-governance-traditional-knowledge-of-arctic-indigenous-peoples-from-an-international-policy-perspective.4667262-142902.html

Ferguson, M. A. D., R. G. Williamson and F. Messier. 1998. "Inuit knowledge of long-term changes in a population of Arctic tundra caribou". *Arctic* 51, 201–219.

Golder Associates Ltd. 2016. "Wildlife Effects Monitoring Plan. For the Ekati Diamond Mine." *Prepared for: Dominion Diamond Ekati Corporation*. Retrieved from www.enr.gov.nt.ca/sites/enr/files/ddec_wildlife_effects_monitioring_program_december_2016.pdf

Government of Canada (Aboriginal Affairs and Northern Development Canada). 1998. *The Mackenzie Valley Resource Management Act (MVRMA)*. Communications Branch. Government of Canada, March 2007. Accessed 15 October 2018.

Government of Canada (Crown-Indigenous Relations and Northern Affairs Canada. n.d.) "General Briefing Note on Canada's Self-government and Comprehensive Land Claims Policies and the Status of Negotiations." Retrieved from www.aadnc-aandc.gc.ca/eng/1373385502190/1373385561540

Government of Northwest Territories (GNWT). Department of Environment and Natural Resources (n.d.). "Bathurst Herd." Retrieved from www.enr.gov.nt.ca/en/services/barren-ground-caribou/bathurst-herd

Greaves, Wilfrid. 2012. "For Whom, From What? Canada's Arctic Policy and the Narrowing of Human Security." *International Journal* 67(1), 219–240.

Grijalva, J. M. 2011. "Self-determining Environmental Justice for Native America." *Environmental Justice* No 4 (4), 187–192.

Hooghe, L. and G. Marks. 2004. "Contrasting Visions of Multi-Level Governance." In *Multi-Level Governance*, eds. I. Bache and M. Flinders 15–30. Oxford: Oxford University Press.

ICC Canada. 2012. *Food Security across the Arctic. Background Paper of the Steering Committee of the Circumpolar Inuit Health Strategy*. Ottawa: Inuit Circumpolar Council - Canada.

Johannes, R. E. 1993. "Integrating Traditional Ecological Knowledge and Management with Environmental Impact Assessment." In *Traditional Ecological Knowledge. Concepts and Cases*, ed. J. T. Inglis 33–39. Ottawa: International Program on Traditional Ecological Knowledge, International Development Research Centre (IDRC).

Kendrick, A. 2003. "Caribou Co-management and Cross-cultural Knowledge Sharing." Ph.D. Thesis, University of Manitoba, Winnipeg, Manitoba.

Kuhnlein, H. V., Berkes, F. et al. 2014. *Aboriginal Food Security in Northern Canada: An Assessment of the State of Knowledge*. Ottawa: Council of Canadian Academies.

Lambden, J., Receveur, O., Marshall, J. and H. V. Kuhnlein. 2006. "Traditional and Market Food Access in Arctic Canada is Affected by Economic Factors." *International Journal of Circumpolar Health* No 65 (4), 331–340.

Mackenzie Valley Environmental Impact Review Board (MVEIRB). February 1, 2016. "Report of Environmental Assessment and Reasons for Decision." Dominion Diamond Ekati Corp. Jay Project EA1314-01. Retrieved from http://reviewboard.ca/upload/project_document/EA1314-01_Report_of_Environmental_Assesment_and_Reasons_for_Decision.PDF

Mackenzie Valley Environmental Impact Review Board (MVEIRB). 2005. *Guidelines for Incorporating Traditional Knowledge in Environmental Impact Assessment*. Yellowknife: MVEIRB. Retrieved from www.mveirb.nt.ca/reference_lib/guidelines.php

Mackenzie Valley Land and Water Board (MVLWB). June 1, 2013. "Engagement and Consultation Policy." Retrieved from https://mvlwb.com/sites/default/files/documents/wg/MVLWB%20Engagement%20and%20Consultation%20Policy%20-%20May%2015.pdf

Mackenzie Valley Land and Water Board (MVLWB). October, 2014. "Engagement Guidelines for Applicants and Holders of Water Licences and Land Use Permits." Retrieved from https://mvlwb.com/sites/default/files/documents/wg/MVLWB%20Engagement%20Guidelines%20for%20Holders%20of%20LUPs%20and%20WLs%20-%20Oct%202014.pdf

Mallory, M. L., Gilchrist, H. G., Fontaine, A. J. and J. A. Akearok. 2003. "Local Ecological Knowledge of Ivory Gull Declines in Arctic Canada." *Arctic* No 56, 293–298.

Manseau, M., Parlee, B. and G. B. Ayles. 2007. "A Place for Traditional Ecological Knowledge in Resource Management." In *Breaking Ice: Renewable Resource and Ocean Management in the Canadian North*, eds. F. Berkes, R. Huebert, H. Fast, M. Manseau and A. Diduck 141–164. Calgary: University of Calgary Press.

McCay, B. J. and J. M. Acheson. 1987. "Human Ecology of the Commons." In *The Question of the Commons. The Culture and Ecology of Communal Resources*, eds. B. J. McCay and J. M. Acheson 1–36. Tucson: The University of Arizona Press.

Nadasdy, P. 1999. "The Politics of Tek: Power and the 'Integration' of Knowledge." *Arctic Anthropology* No 36 (1/2), 1–18. Retrieved from www.jstor.org/stable/40316502.

Nadasdy, P. 2003. "Re-Evaluating the Co-Management Success Story." *Arctic* No 56 (4). DOI: 10.14430/arctic634

Noble, B. 2016. "Learning to Listen: Snapshots of Aboriginal Participation in Environmental Assessment." Technical Report, MacDonald-Laurier Institute.

Noble, B. and K. Hanna. 2015. "Environmental Assessment in the Arctic: A Gap Analysis and Research Agenda." *Arctic* No 68 (3), 341. DOI: 10.14430/arctic4501hawe

Noble, B. and A. Udofia. 2015. *Protectors of the land: Toward an EA Process that Works for Aboriginal Communities and Developers*. Ottawa, ON: MacDonald-Laurier Institute.

Parlee, B., Sandlos, J. and D. Natcher. 2018. "Undermining Subsistence: Barren-Ground Caribou in a 'Tragedy of Open Access'." *Science Advances* No 4, 2. DOI: 10.1126/sciadv.1701611

Pinkerton, E., ed. 1989. *Co-operative Management of Local Fisheries. New Directions for Improved Management and Community Development*. Vancouver: University of British Columbia.

Prowse, T., Wrona, F., Reist, J., Gibson, J., Hobbie, J., Lévesque, L. and W. Vincent. 2006. "Climate Change Effects on Hydroecology of Arctic Freshwater Ecosystems." *AMBIO: A Journal of the Human Environment* No 35 (7), 347–358. DOI: 10.1579/0044-7447

Ranco, D. J., O'Neill, C. A., Donatuto, J. and B. L. Harper. 2011. "American Indians and the Cultural Dilemma: Developing Environmental Management for Tribal Health and Well-being." *Environmental Justice* No 4 (4), 221–230. DOI: 10.1089/env.2010.0036

Rescan. 2011. "Ekati Diamond Mine 2010 Wildlife Effects Monitoring Program." Prepared for BHP Billiton Diamonds Inc., Yellowknife, NWT, Canada.

Rescan. 2013. "Ekati Diamond Mine: 2012 Aquatic Effects Monitoring Program Part 1 – Evaluation of Effects." Prepared for BHP Billiton Canada Inc. Yellowknife, Northwest Territories: Rescan Environmental Services Ltd..

Rynard, P. 2000. "Welcome In, But Check Your Rights at the Door. The James Bay and Nisga'a Agreements in Canada." *Canadian Journal of Political Science* No 33 (2), 211–243. Retrieved from www.jstor.org/stable/3232963.

Schneider, R., Hauer, G., Dawe, K., Adamowicz, W. and S. Boutin. 2012. "Selection of Reserves for Woodland Caribou Using an Optimization Approach." *PLoS One* No 7, 2. 10.1371/journal.pone.0031672

Sejersen, F. 2015. *Rethinking Greenland and the Arctic in the Era of Climate Change. New Northern Horizons*. New York and London: Routledge.

Shigley, J. E., Shor, R., Padua, P., Breeding, C. M., Shirey, S. B. and D. Ashbury. 2016. "Mining Diamonds in the Canadian Arctic: The Diavik Mine." *Gems and Gemology* No 52 (2), 104–131. DOI: 10.5741/GEMS.52.2.104

Spak, S. 2005. "The Position of Indigenous Knowledge in Canadian Co-Management Organizations." *Anthropologica* No 47 (2), 233–246. Retrieved from www.jstor.org/stable/25606238.

Stevenson, M. G. 1996. "Indigenous Knowledge in Environmental Assessment." *Arctic* No 49 (3), 278–291.

Tesar, C. 2007. "What Price the Caribou?" *Northern Perspectives* No 31 (1), Spring 2007, 1–3.

Turner, N. J., Ignace, M. B. and R. Ignace. 2000. "Traditional Ecological Knowledge and Wisdom of Aboriginal Peoples in British Columbia." *Ecological Applications* No 10, 1275–1287.

United Nations Development Programme. 1994. *Human Development Report 1994: New Dimensions of Human Security*. Retrieved from http://hdr.undp.org/sites/default/files/reports/255/hdr_1994_en_complete_nostats.pdf

Uphoff, N. 1998. "Community-Based Natural Resource Management: Connecting Micro and Macro Processes and People with Their Environments." Paper presented at the International Workshop on Community-Based Natural Resource Management, Washington, DC.

Uprety, Y., Asselin, H., Bergeron, Y., Doyon, F. and J. F. Boucher. 2012. "Contribution of Traditional Knowledge to Ecological Restoration: Practices and Applications." *Écoscience* No 19 (3), 225–237. DOI: 10.2980/19-3-3530

Usher, P. J. 2000. "Traditional Ecological Knowledge in Environmental Assessment and Management." *Arctic* No 53, 2. DOI: 10.14430/arctic849

Vors, L. and M. Boyce. 2009. "Global Declines of Caribou and Reindeer." *Global Change Biology* No 15 (11), 2626–2633. DOI: 10.1111/j.1365-2486.2009.01974.x

Wek'èezhìi Land and Water Board (WLWB). May 29 2017a. "Land Use Permit (LUP) W2013D0007, Dominion Diamond Ekati Corporation (DDEC), Condition #58." Retrieved from http://registry.mvlwb.ca/Documents/W2013D0007/Ekati%20Jay%20Project%20-%20Land%20Use%20Permit%20-%20May%2029_17.pdf

Wek'èezhìi Land and Water Board (WLWB). July 6, 2017b. "Water License 2017 W2012L2-0001 (Amendment to incorporate Ekati Jay Project), Part B Condition 16." Retrieved from http://registry.mvlwb.ca/Documents/W2012L2-0001/W2012L2-0001%20-%20Ekati%20-%20Water%20Licence%20-%20Amendment%20-%20Jay%20Development%20-%20RFD%20and%20Recommendation%20to%20Minister%20-%20May%2029_17.pdf

White, G. 2009. "Cultures in Collision: Traditional Knowledge and Euro-Canadian Governance Processes in Northern Land-Claim Boards." *Arctic* No 59 (4). DOI: 10.14430/arctic289

33

GENDER AND INTERSECTIONAL APPROACHES TO SECURITY IN THE ARCTIC

Gunhild Hoogensen Gjørv, Embla Eir Oddsdóttir, and Fern Wickson

Understanding the everyday threats that people encounter, why they encounter these threats, and how their perceptions of threats are influenced by endogenous and exogenous factors (including their own gender; the gender of others; their resulting place in their community; and the possible advantages or disadvantages of their ethnicity or race, their sexual orientation, their economic status, and their age) is a complicated and challenging task. Different people may experience different threats based on the social/cultural environment in which they find themselves, along with their economic opportunities (or lack thereof). These combine and result in the degree to which people have access to food, water, health services, shelter, and education. Who they are determines their access to political and social rights within and beyond their community. If we take seriously Cicero's classical departure point that the concept of security is about freedom from fear and worry, then people's lives are very much at the crux of what security is.

Arctic communities, due to their remote locations, heavy dependence upon natural resources, and lack of economic alternatives, are particularly vulnerable to changes in the natural environment and to political and corporate decisions. The quotes capture the sense of the annihilation of a community when "someone else" (in this case a mining company) chooses to shut down its operations. The decisions of industries and governments – be they local, national, or in other countries – affect people's lives constantly: in many instances people feel their very existence is at stake. Also, experiences of insecurity are not uniform across populations. Men and women are often affected differently by security threats, be they physical, economic, or environmental. The closing of a mine in a Northern community disproportionately affects men with regard to economic and employment security, as well as influencing their perceived role as breadwinners in their communities (Hoogensen and Rottem 2004, Miller 2004). Differences also arise according to ethnicity and race, sexual orientation, age, and socioeconomic status. Indigenous peoples' experiences of the relations of domination and struggles for self-determination, which are further affected by gender expectations and relations, continue to be interrogated (Kuokkanen

2019). Rates of domestic violence have been linked to gender and the additional challenges of identifying with a marginalized ethnic group – a combination that has been proven to affect many Arctic communities (Kinnon 2014).

Do people's lives matter to Arctic security? The varieties of ways in which security in the Arctic can be conceptualized are extensive, as demonstrated throughout this volume. They range from narrow state- and military-based security orientations to wider and broader accounts that include environmental and human security. In many cases, these security perceptions initially appear to be easily separable into different levels of analysis (international, state, societal, and individual), but on closer examination these distinctions are harder to maintain. Environmental security, particularly as it relates to climate change, transcends borders and assumptions about what is inside and outside of these borders. Climate change and environmental security therefore impact international or global security, as shown in the attempts by governments to sign and ratify global agreements to mitigate climate change and reduce its causes worldwide (Klare 2007, United Nations/Framework Convention on Climate Change 2015). Climate change's effects on national security include increasing access to waters that were previously inaccessible due to ice (Holland 2014). It is arguable, however, that climate change negatively affects human security – the actual survival and existence of communities – to a greater degree. People are already leaving what they know behind, due to melting permafrost destroying homes and livelihoods or by falling victim to sea-level rise (Goldenberg 2013, Milman 2019). Intertwined with these struggles for security – which is a very social and political experience – is gender. Gender and intersectional approaches to security question our assumptions about how we "know" security and are intimately connected with how security is defined, what is prioritized, and who decides.

Whose security matters?

Arctic state security remains largely stable at the regional level, but the human insecurities experienced by many Indigenous groups, as well as by refugee and migrant populations, continue. The complex relationships between Arctic states and their peoples have often been marginalized and colored by the glow of "exceptional" perspectives, notably the concept of Arctic exceptionalism. Such exceptionalism relies on a continued prioritization of state-centric security analysis and identity construction, which leaves no practical and analytical space for human insecurities within and related to Arctic states and their policies. Despite increased antagonistic rhetoric, Arctic states are still not perceived as threatening each other, or as threatened by any other entities. Often, however, this sense of state security does not transfer to all relevant actors, at least not equally to all people.

This question relates directly to issues of human security in the Arctic (see Chapter 6), but one of the challenges about human security is a tendency to universalize the human experience. This often results in rendering intangible the power dynamics and dominant/nondominant relationships between groups of people or individuals (Hoogensen and Stuvøy 2006). This is often still the case when speaking generally of human security in relation to the Global North or Global South, where relatively un-nuanced assumptions about human security still dominate. Global Northern peoples are often assessed under broad umbrella matrices that do little to recognize vastly different human security experiences. When generalizing Global North experiences using data that largely reflects dominant populations, the human security outcomes appear to be literally "on top of the world." As of 2019, all eight Arctic states were ranked highly in the United Nations Development Programme

(UNDP) Human Development Index (HDI), ranging from the top of the "very high human development" category (Norway at #1) to the bottom of the same category (Russia at #49) (UNDP 2018). The numbers start to change, however, when gender inequality is taken into account: while the Nordic states remain in the top 10ten Canada drops in rank by almost double (from #10 to #18) and the American gender-equality ranking drops to #43 from an overall HDI ranking of #11. The US ranking keeps close company with Russia, which drops to #52 when gender equality is accounted for. The indicator for gender illustrates one qualitative understanding of who has security and in which countries, expanding the divide between the Arctic states. The 2016 Human Development Report, "Human Development for Everyone," notes that development measures show progress across the globe, but certain groups of people are being left out. Indigenous peoples, refugees and migrants, and ethnic minorities are left furthest behind (UNDP 2016).

Gender, human security, and the Arctic

The everyday security and insecurity that permeate people's lives have been of concern to various scholars and policymakers for decades. Human security has been included on many policy agendas since the early 1990s; although its relevance has been questioned (Owen and Martin 2010), it has retained staying power (United Nations 2019). A number of scholars have made significant efforts to place human security concerns on the overall security agenda of both states and the international community.

Security is very much dependent upon the context in which it is experienced and understood. Over time, security has been imagined and reimagined in the Arctic context, but only in the past 15 years has there been an exploration of how the concept of human security might translate into an Arctic context (Hoogensen Gjørv and Bazely 2014). Human security has been, and continues to be, challenging. This so-called human dimension (as if security otherwise has little to do with people) is either seen as only complementing state security (UNDP 1994) or in direct conflict with it (Rubenstein 2017). Feminist and gender security studies have been engaging and informing security debates for well over 25 years, and the strong empirical foundation of this work has been very useful in informing human security debates (Blanchard 2003). Some of this scholarship has tried to open up the concept of security in general, and human security in particular, as a site of intersectional engagement for local, national, and international actors and practices. Human security in the Arctic requires a critical understanding of local actors and practices; the role of patriarchal institutions; and ways of resisting oppression, colonialism, or violence in local communities. This prioritization of a *critical* human security perspective contrasts with the demands of the dominant so-called classic and masculinist geopolitics, which attempt to direct attention away from the security of Arctic communities toward militarized concerns of the state, even though the marginalization of human security can nevertheless affect the abilities and practices of states (Newman 2010, Dixon 2015, Tyner and Henkin 2015).

Traditional notions of security are exclusive, largely involving the state, its military, and its border security. Security in this sense is an elite concept in which only a select group of state actors may participate, the rationale being that security is about state survival. This traditional notion of security has historically – particularly during the Cold War – been applied when security was concerned with military exercises or the protection of the state through military means, especially the potential use of nuclear weapons. Thus a narrow and exclusive concept appears, in which the state is considered the primary unit to be protected.

Security studies as a discipline, especially those branches that rely heavily on materialist approaches, has long been acknowledged as male-dominated. It has been the territory of the *big boys*, of male academics, militaries, and political authorities, although this is gradually changing (Hanson 2018). As long as the myth remains that state security is paramount as high politics, state security is assumed to trickle down and encompass all other security needs (Hoogensen and Rottem 2004). So it is often difficult to resist the exclusion of other dimensions of security, including human security. Significant empirical evidence – or even just casual observation – demonstrates, however, that human beings continue to find ways to provide security and survive even in weak states like Venezuela or so-called failed states like Afghanistan (Vastapuu 2017). When a state fails to provide security for its population, non-state actors often try to provide a form of security for a particular group of people or a particular region (Stuvøy 2009). Security is operationalized on multiple levels despite this very powerful state-centered discourse.

The failure of states can be reflected in the way in which a state has created insecurity for other actors while striving to provide its own security. The extermination or assimilation of populations in the name of state security has a long history (Rensmenn 2009). Hence, the state as such is not integral to the survival of other actors. At times the state can be more of a threat than a source of security for certain people, as exemplified by the colonial practices of genocide and eradicating Indigenous peoples and their cultures (Hossain 2016). In the name of security, states have sought military domination within their own territories or between states. The tremendous harm this always causes is often weighed against the benefits accrued to state security. Insofar as state security and the military have played an important role in providing security to the peoples of that state, women have frequently been excluded, as one's gender is considered integral to one's capacity to provide security.

Many scholars have increasingly rejected or challenged these notions of state security, in part because of its military connotations, not least with regard to the legacy of the Cold War (Tickner 1992, Booth 2007, Buzan and Hansen 2009, 2010). At the end of the Cold War this notion of state security – particularly its military association – was challenged because it did not adequately reflect the emerging realities that had long been suppressed behind a militarized form of security. After the Cold War, in the 1990s, alternative dimensions of security developed and challenged traditional notions of security. Environmental security – turning away from exploitation towards preservation – was one of those dimensions. It took the view that the environment is significant for human survival (Greaves 2016, Hoogensen Gjørv 2017b). The notion of human security also re-emerged, viewing security from the position of the individual and recognizing that the security of a state does not necessarily mean adequate or any security for all groups of people or individuals within the state.

The concept of human security is complex and dynamic. It includes environmental, human, political, economic, food, and health, as well as security of identity or sense of community – all of these factors combined are essential for future security (UNDP 1994, CHS 2003). The concept of human security has thus been criticized for being rather all-encompassing. A central challenge in the Arctic context is that the human security concept was designed, implicitly if not explicitly, to be largely employed by Northern states and then exported to the South. In far too many instances the concept has been employed as a form of virtuous imperialism, implying the marginalization of democratic voices and the dominance of Northern states over the recipients of assistance (Hoogensen Gjørv 2014).

Security is not exclusively a concept to be used by states. A comprehensive approach to security includes a democratic approach, whereby state perspectives compete and cooperate with other voices when prioritizing values for the future. This is part of why gender and female security studies have been attracted to the concept of human security: it provides avenues for democratizing the notion of security, making audible the voices and needs for survival that are not necessarily relegated to the state.

Identities matter

Identity has been argued to be central to the understanding of security (McSweeney 1999). Indeed, identity is often characterized as a fact about someone or something, something easily identifiable or observable that can be used to indicate difference or similarity to another person or thing. In international relations and security studies, identity has been used to "explain cooperation (or lack thereof) between states, foreign policy choices, and the rise of security problems or threats beyond purely rationalist paradigms" (Agius 2013: 243). Identities have been treated as static units or static opposites or binaries: a state, entity, or person is one thing or another. Alternatively, however, identities have been understood as discursive, allowing for multiple identities based on the ways in which identity is produced, reproduced, and represented.

Understanding security in general relies on comprehending the relationships between actors and the values and practices they exercise with regard to certain perceptions of survival, now and in the future (Hoogensen Gjørv 2017b; see Chapter 6). While security discourses are still heavily dominated by military and state security perspectives, increasing attention has been directed, not least in Arctic contexts, toward the roles and impacts of non-state actors and perspectives within discourses of human and societal security (Hossain 2016, Hossain and Zojer 2017). Indeed, the inclusion of non-state actors' perspectives challenges many of the more reductionist approaches to security, which rely on a static, universal definition about the identity of the state. The same cannot be said of non-state actors, which embody multiple complex and dynamic identities that range from human social variations such as ethnic groups, genders, and races, etc. to corporations, individuals, and even artificial intelligence. However, state-based approaches have been used even on the non-state level to "neutralize identity through assumptions of the Universal Man" (Hoogensen and Rottem 2004: 156).

Understanding diverse and complex security perspectives, and the role of identity within these perspectives, requires analytical tools that are adequate to the task. A critical step towards a more complex analytical approach was the incorporation of the concept and practice of intersectionality, which recognizes that universalizing, homogeneous methods and practices were often inaccurate and harmful to research. Universalizing methodologies restrict what is considered scientifically legitimate and thus limit potential research questions, not least across the social and natural sciences. Certain circles within the social sciences and humanities, and more specifically security studies, have already begun to break through reductionist and limited (static) approaches. Feminist and gender security studies have long assumed that individuals and their communities are security actors, functioning alongside traditional tools of security such as states and their militaries. More importantly, these non-state security actors are often found to be functioning in the absence of state actors.

These approaches claim that narrow or state-based security narratives "limit how we can think about security, whose security matters, and how it might be achieved" (Wibben 2011). Feminist scholarship has been groundbreaking for security perspectives that adopt a people-centered approach, taking their starting point from the bottom up. However, scholars of intersectionality have noted that definitions of gender equality and understanding of gender constructions for all societies were grossly inadequate because of their tendency to also universalize a particular gendered, racialized, ethnic, class-based experience that dominated the focus of feminist discourses. Intersectional analysis scholars purport that the three waves of feminism were fueled by the experiences of generally White, middle-class, European, or Western women. These experiences did not speak to the gendered norms, practices, or experiences of people of color, Indigenous persons, or non-White-centric ethnicities and cultures, or to those with differing experiences based on age, class, sexuality, and ability.

Coined by Kimberlé Crenshaw in the late 1980s (Crenshaw 1991), the term *intersectionality* was designed to critically assess the intersection of race, gender, class, and other identity categories that have been regularly produced and reproduced in different contexts. Intersectional analysis makes visible how identity has been produced and used to expand, reinforce, or reduce power. At its core it has a "non-positivistic, non-essentialist understanding of differences among people as produced in on-going, context-specific social processes" (Marfelt 2016: 32). Crenshaw (1991) has noted that the intersectional approach has been subject to a backlash that accuses it of exacerbating identity politics and being responsible for further fragmenting societies along identity lines. The relevance of identity to how we understand the world has thus been discredited in some circles, creating further resistance to understanding the role of identity in security. Such accusations reflect what we examine below: systems of trust have often relied upon, and been studied through, the normalization of an assumed identity-free universal man (Yuval-Davis 2011). When challenged however, the universal man is exposed as reflecting the identities of those with power in a given society (e.g., affluent, White, male, able, heterosexual) (Carasthatis 2014). Those not representing these normalized identities become threats to that system of trust. Indeed, for that system to survive, distrust of the other identity is imperative. As agents of security, states can try to build or maintain institutional trust through particularized distrust – building towards the racialized, gendered, classed "other."

Gendered knowing and understanding

The world is given through our methods of studying it. (Salter and Mutlu 2013: 3)

A central argument for employing gender and intersectional lenses to research, not least that which informs our understanding of security, is to be able to expose our biases regarding whose perspectives are included and whose are not. This is why, for example, a certain degree of common purpose can be found between gender and feminist approaches and human security. Thinking critically about how we understand security leads to the question of "Whose security?" At the same time, the question of "Who decides?" has been increasing in part due to, as well as independently of, feminist and gender security approaches (Booth 1991, Tickner 1992, Buzan et al. 1998, Peoples and Vaughan-Williams 2010, Singh 2017, Parashar et al. 2018). This trend has been somewhat slower to develop within Arctic security studies research, as well as in the general Arctic research that is often used to inform security perspectives (Hoogensen Gjørv and Bazely 2014, Greaves 2016, Hoogensen Gjørv 2017b). Recently, there have been multiple initiatives taking place to increase gender and intersectional awareness in Arctic research – not just within social sciences, but also in the natural sciences. These projects include the Gender in the Arctic IASSA Working Group,[1] Women in the Arctic and Antarctic,[2] and Plan A: Gender is not Plan B in the Arctic.[3] At the 2019 Arctic Science Summit Week (ASSW) in Arkhangelsk, the International Arctic Science Committee (IASC) approved the cross-disciplinary activity, "Gender in Polar Research: Gendered Fieldwork Conditions, Epistemologies and Legacies," which was supported by four of the five working groups focusing on cryospheric, marine, terrestrial, humanities, and social sciences.[4] The importance of interdisciplinary approaches, and of sharing insights across research areas and spectrums, cannot be overstated, particularly for the Arctic. The impacts of the interactions between environmental and human spaces are felt acutely in this region. Policies designed for, or including, the region – either as specifically "Arctic" or as part of the geopolitics of states globally – all impact local communities. At times, local communities also impact regional, national, and international policies (McIver 1997, Koivurova and Heinämäki 2006, Stammler and Ivanova 2017).

However, the struggles of research informed by gender and intersectionality that have implications for security policy are ongoing. In 2016, an article about Arctic glaciology, "Glaciers, Gender, and Science: A Feminist Glaciology Framework for Global Environmental Change Research" (Carey et al. 2016), made the headlines of national and international mainstream news sites precisely because it was attempting to explore gendered understandings about science. The authors of the article argue that science does not take place in a vacuum but rather in a social and political world that has influenced the development of what is considered to be the legitimate gathering of data and creation of knowledge. They argue that the natural sciences, including glaciology, have not been immune to social and political norms; thus, they examine these norms and their influences in light of the research that has been done within feminist and gender studies. The authors discuss the influences of the social and political on knowledge development in science, not just in how it is conducted but also how it is used and granted legitimacy within decision-making arenas. Glaciological knowledge continues to be highly relevant for predicting and planning for potential scenarios based on melting and moving ice, including commercial transport, military maneuverability, and claims over territory versus international space. The role of ice features as an economic and national security concern in the 2016 US Department of Defense (DoD) Arctic Strategy (DoD December 2016). The US National Ice Center, combined with the US Naval Ice Center, employs "satellite imagery to global ice analyses and forecasts" in a joint agency "to support customers with global, regional, and tactical scale interests."[5] In other words, science and security are, and have been, tightly linked together in the Arctic. Although the article can and should be discussed and criticized, it touched on a linkage that has often been under-discussed: the connections between the concept of security and the understanding, roles, and use of science and scientific data in the broader political and social world. Science and national security have been mutually supportive.

The sociopolitical shaping of science, particularly of science conducted to help inform and guide policy, is not a new or even necessarily a controversial idea. Indeed, how social and political forces work to shape and construct scientific knowledge has been the focus of an entire discipline of study known as science and technology studies (STS). Understanding how these shaping forces can be gendered and contain colonialist biases is also recognized within this field as a legitimate, relevant, and illuminating pursuit, as can be seen through the emergence of subfields such as feminist technoscience, feminist STS, and postcolonial feminism. Stating that science is shaped by social and political forces, and can therefore also be influenced by gender and colonialist biases, is not the same as saying that "anything goes" or that the natural sciences do not provide reliable or real knowledge about the world. Rather, it highlights that there are many different ways to interrogate natural phenomena in order to build knowledge. The questions we ask, the methods we employ, and the interpretations we draw from what we see can all be affected by individual, disciplinary, and sociopolitical interests, values, norms, and beliefs.

The article received immediate and enormous attention for an academic work, and by mid-2019 had registered 2,103 mentions in monitored news articles, blogs, and tweets (among other media outlets) since its publication in January 2016.[6] Many of the immediate references to the article were negative, claiming that the peer-reviewed article was "batshit,"[7] "nonsense in the humanities,"[8] and "gobbledygook."[9] The article was shamed as being potentially a hoax, a waste of American taxpayers' money (the project was funded by the US National Science Foundation), full of postmodern jargon, unclearly written, and proof that the "social sciences and humanities have gone functionally insane" (Schneider 2016). Media outlets misleadingly summarized the article in their headlines as an attempt to make glaciers feminist, or claiming that glaciers were sexist.[10] The well-known US news and commentary magazine *The Atlantic* sought to put the article in its place by comparing the paper on feminist glaciology to "this more serious one on murderous prairie dogs" (Meyer 23 March 2016). The article attempts to address traditional views of local Indigenous peoples regarding glaciers, whereby they note that there are "firm taboos against 'cooking with grease' near glaciers that are offended by such smells. … Cooked food, especially fat, might grow into a glacier overnight if improperly handled" (Carey et al. 2016: 781).The article's attempts to include Indigenous perspectives were potentially worthy of critique both with regard to a lack of adequate context for the claims made, and discussion about the ways in which Indigenous narratives can have multiple metaphoric or other forms of relevance rather than just the literal. However, the critiques instead just targeted literal interpretations of the claims made rather than interrogating further what these claims might mean. This led to such comments as: "Indigenous people are portrayed as believing batshit ideas about how grease 'offends' glaciers" (footnote 2), and "the authors denigrate those skeptics who dismiss the effect of cooking grease on glacial advance" (footnote 3).

The vast majority of this firestorm of responses can be seen as a pushback against gender and feminist analyses (and by extension, all intersectional perspectives). The feminist glaciology paper highlights how masculinist and colonialist interests and actors have largely dominated the field of glaciology and thereby narrowly shaped the questions, methods, and narratives in play. It was particularly significant to note that little to none of the public critique which followed the feminist glaciology article's publication was aimed at the authors' presentation of how science, and in particular glaciology, has been used by the national security community in the United States.

In the article, the authors highlighted four strands of investigation that can allow for the perception of masculinist and colonialist biases in glaciological knowledge, and thereby open a space for alternative approaches to knowledge generation that would be framed more by feminist and postcolonial interests, theories, and ways of thinking. The feminist glaciology framework presented in the article is primarily focused on helping people see the present biases, which, given the blizzard of negative responses, may indeed have been a very necessary first step that many privileged White males from Western industrialized nations still seem to resist taking. However, significant work remains to be done to clearly articulate the feminist alternative in terms of exactly what types of research questions and methods might be pursued by postcolonial feminist glaciologists. What questions, for example, might feminist and postcolonial scholars wish to ask within glaciology and how might their investigations look different? What might it mean to have a glaciology not dominated in its shape by questions of national security, military maneuverability, new territorial claims, or the exploration of the economic opportunities of extractive industries such as mining and drilling for oil and gas?

Conclusion

Ongoing intersectional and gender research work would recognize and embrace the presence of diverse worldviews. How to integrate these into knowledge creation or grant them legitimacy in current global environmental and security policy domains are challenges that require further articulation, experimentation, and elaboration if intersectional interdisciplinary research and policy development is to truly advance. Here we may learn from work taking place in the field of biodiversity conservation. The challenges associated with integrating the natural and social sciences, as well as Indigenous and scientific knowledge, to create advice for global environmental policy is a significant goal of the Intergovernmental Platform for Biodiversity and Ecosystem Services (IPBES).[11] One lesson to be drawn from this work is the need to direct particular attention towards the restructuring of deeply rooted power relations if other forms of knowledge are to be granted legitimacy in policy arenas.

Many of the issues highlighted in the feminist glaciology paper are not at all specific to that particular field. Instead, they are issues that apply to environmental change and security research far more broadly. To enable environmental-change research to actively embrace the value of adopting feminist and postcolonial approaches to research (in terms of the people engaged, the questions asked, the methods employed, and the interpretations drawn from observations), it may be worth considering the importance of research that helps create transformational change not only by playing the role of policy informant, but also by informing, inspiring, and creating affect and action within particular communities and civil society. Change needs to come from both the bottom up and the top down. Perhaps the one-dimensional focus on having research inform policy can be seen as another legacy of masculinist approaches that have always been oriented towards the top in hierarchies of power. If so, science and perceptions of security may be better served by giving active focus and attention to research that is rooted in community-level relations. Such research can better inform and affect change.

Notes

1 See https://gender-arctic.jimdo.com
2 See https://womeninthearcticandantarctic.ca
3 See www.genderisnotplanb.com
4 See https://iasc.info/working-groups/2015-11-27-09-11-10/activities
5 US National Ice Center: www.natice.noaa.gov/index.html
6 See Sage Publishing Article Metrics: https://sage.altmetric.com/details/4984272/peer-reviews
7 Blog: Debunking Denialism. https://debunkingdenialism.com/2016/12/06/why-postmodernist-glaciology-is-pseudoscientific-bigotry
8 Blog: Why Evolution is True. https://whyevolutionistrue.wordpress.com/2016/03/13/postmodern-glacier-professor-defends-his-study-says-it-was-misunderstood-it-wasnt
9 Editorial: New York Post Editorial Board. http://nypost.com/2016/03/08/feminism-and-icebergs-a-new-low-in-climate-science
10 See Sage Publishing Article Metrics "news outlets." https://sage.altmetric.com/details/4984272/news
11 See www.sciencedirect.com/science/article/pii/S1877343517300040

References

Agius, C. (2013). "Performing Identity: The Danish Cartoon Crisis and Discourses of Identity and Security." *Security Dialogue* **44**(3): 241–258.

Blanchard, E. M. (2003). "Gender, International Relations, and the Development of Feminist Security Theory." *Signs: Journal of Women in Culture and Society* **28**(41): 1289–1312.

Booth, K. (1991). "Security and Empancipation." *Review of International Studies* 17(4): 313–326.

Booth, K. (2007). *Theory of World Security*. Cambridge, Cambridge University Press.

Buzan, B. and L. Hansen (2009). *The Evolution of International Security Studies*. Cambridge, Cambridge University Press.

Buzan, B. and L. Hansen (2010). "Beyond the Evolution of International Security Studies?." *Security Dialogue* **41**(6): 659–667.

Buzan, B., O. Wæver and J. de Wilde (1998). *Security: A New Framework for Analysis*. Boulder and London, Lynne Rienner Publishers.

Carastathis, A. 2014. "The Concept of Intersectionality in Feminist Theory," *Philosophy Compass* 9(5) (May): 304–314.

Carey, M., M. Jackson, A. Antonello and J. Rushing (2016). "Glaciers, Gender, and Science: A Feminist Glaciology Framework for Global Environmental Change Research." *Progress in Human Geography* **40**(6): 770–793.

CHS (2003). *Human Security Now*. New York, Commission on Human Security.

Crenshaw, K. (1991). "Mapping the Margins: Intersectionality, Identity Politics, and Violence against Women of Color." *Stanford Law Review* **43**(6): 1241–1299.

Dixon, D. (2015). *Feminist Geopolitics: Material States*. Farnham, Ashgate and Routledge.

DoD (December 2016). *Report to Congress on Strategy to Protect United States National Security Interests in the Arctic Region*. (D. o. Defense). Washington, DC, US Department of Defense.

Goldenberg, S. (2013). An Alaskan Nightmare: America's First Climate Change Refugees: The Yup'iks of Newtok are Desperate to Leave Their Village before it Disappears under the Waves. *The Guardian*. www.theguardian.com/environment/interactive/2013/may/13/newtok-alaska-climate-change-refugees

Greaves, W. (2016). "Securing Sustainability: The Case for Critical Environmental Security in the Arctic." *Polar Record* **52**(267): 660–671.

Hanson, R. (2018). "Ethnographies of Security: Pushing Security Studies beyond the Bounds of International Relations." *Qualitative Sociology* **41**(2): 135–144.

Holland, A. (2014). "National Security in a Rapidly Changing Arctic: How a Lack of Attention to the Arctic Is Harming America's Interests." *Georgetown Journal of International Affairs* **15**: 79–88.

Hoogensen, G. and S. V. Rottem (2004). "Gender Identity and the Subject of Security." *Security Dialogue* **35**(2): 155–171.

Hoogensen, G. and K. Stuvøy (2006). "Human Security, Gender and Resistance." *Security Dialogue* **37** (2): 207–228.

Hoogensen Gjørv, G. (2014). Virtuous imperialism or a shared global objective? The relevance of human security in the global north. *Environmental and Human Security in the Arctic*. G. Hoogensen Gjørv, D. R. Bazely, M. Goloviznina and A. J. Tanentzap (Eds.). London and New York, Routledge.

Hoogensen Gjørv, G. (2017a). Finding gender in the Arctic: A call to intersectionality and diverse methods. *The Interconnected Arctic - UArctic Congress 2016*. K. Latola and H. Savela (Eds.). Springer Polar Sciences.

Hoogensen Gjørv, G. (2017b). Tensions between environmental, economic, and energy security in the Arctic. *Northern Sustainabilities: Understanding and Addressing Change in a Circumpolar World*. G. Fondahl and G. Wilson (Eds.). Cham and Switzerland, Springer International Publishing.

Hoogensen Gjørv, G. and D. Bazely, Eds. (2014). *Human and Environmental Security in the Arctic*. London, Routledge.

Hossain, K. (2016). "Securitizing the Arctic Indigenous Peoples: A Community Security Perspective with Special Reference to the Sámi of the European High North." *Polar Science* **10**(3): 414–424.

Hossain, K. and G. Zojer (2017). "Rethinking Multifaceted Human Security Threats in the Barents Region: A Multilevel Approach to Societal Security." *Juridica Lapponica* **2** (University of Lapland).

Kinnon, D. (2014). *Engaging Inuit Men and Boys in Ending Violence against Women and Girls: A Gender-Based Analysis*. Ottawa, Pauktuutit Inuit Women of Canada.

Klare, M. T. (2007). "Global Warming Battlefields: How Climate Change Threatens Security." *Current History* **106**(703): 355–361.

Koivurova, T. and L. Heinämäki (2006). "The Participation of Indigenous Peoples in International Norm-making in the Arctic." *Polar Record* **42**(221): 101–109.

Kuokkanen, R. (2019). *Restructuring Relations: Indigenous Self-Determination, Governance, and Gender*. Oxford, Oxford University Press.

Marfelt, M. M. (2016). "Grounded Intersectionality: Key Tensions, a Methodological Framework, and Implications for Diversity Research." *Equality, Diversity and Inclusion: An International Journal* **35**(1): 31–47.

McIver, J. (1997). "Environmental Protection, Indigenous Rights and the Arctic Council: Rock, Paper, Scissors on the Ice." *Georgetown International Environmental Law Review* **10**(1): 147–168.

McSweeney, B. (1999). *Security, Identity and Interests: A Sociology of International Relations*. Cambridge, Cambridge University Press.

Meyer, R. (23 March 2016). The Struggle of Clear Climate Communication. *The Atlantic*. New York and The Atlantic. www.theatlantic.com/science/archive/2016/03/the-struggle-of-clear-climate-communication/474987/?utm_source=yahoo

Miller, G. E. (2004). "Frontier Masculinity in the Oil Industry: The Experience of Women Engineers." *Gender, Work and Organization* **11**(1): 47–73.

Milman, O. (2019). Climate Crisis: Alaska Is Melting and It's Likely to Accelerate Global Heating. *The Guardian*: International Edition. www.theguardian.com/environment/2019/jun/13/climate-crisis-alaska-is-melting-and-its-likely-to-accelerate-global-heating

Newman, E. (2010). "Critical Human Security Studies." *Review of International Studies* **36**: 77–94.

Owen, T. and M. Martin (2010). "The Second Generation of Human Security: Lessons from the UN and EU Experience." *International Affairs* **86**(1): 211–224.

Parashar, S., J. A. Tickner and J. True, Eds. (2018). *Revisiting Gendered States: Feminist Imaginings of the State of International Relations*. Oxford, Oxford University Press.

Peoples, C. and N. Vaughan-Williams (2010). *Critical Security Studies: An Introduction*. London, Routledge.

Rensmenn, L. (2009). "Genocidal Politics: Rethinking Crimes against Humanity in Global Perspective." *Journal of Contemporary History* **44**(4): 753–766.

Rubenstein, R. E. (2017). State security, human security, and the problem of complementarity. *Rethinking Security in the Twenty-First Century: A Reader*. E. D. Jacob (Ed.). New York, Palgrave Macmilln.

Salter, M. B. and C. E. Mutlu, Eds. (2013). *Research Methods in Critical Security Studies: An Introduction*. London and New York, Routledge.

Schneider, J.-M. (2016). Why an Article about 'feminist Glaciology' in a Major Geography Journal Has Been Its Top-read Story for Months. *National Post*. Toronto, National Post. http://nationalpost.com/news/world/heres-why-an-article-about-feminist-glaciology-is-still-the-top-read-paper-in-a-major-geography-journal/wcm/1abc7402-e01e-4e99-b030-e60fd759cf6e

Singh, S. (2017). "Gender, Conflict and Security: Perspectives from South Asia." *Journal of Asian Security and International Affairs* **4**(2): 149–157.

Stammler, F. and A. Ivanova (2017). "Resources, Rights, and Communities." *Europe-Asia Studies* **68**(7): 1220–1244.

Stuvøy, K. (2009). *Security under Construction: A Bourdieusian Approach to Non-state Crisis Centres in Northwest Russia*. PhD, University of Tromsø.

Tickner, A. (1992). *Gender in International Relations: Feminist Perspectives on Acheiving Global Security*. New York, Columbia University Press.

Tyner, J. and S. Henkin (2015). "Feminist Geopolitics, Everyday Death, and the Emotional Geographies of Dang Thuy Tram." *Gender, Place, and Culture* **22**(2): 288–303.

UNDP (1994). *Human Development Report 1994: New Dimensions of Human Security*. New York, United Nations Development Programme.

UNDP (2016). *Human Development Report 2016 – Human Development Is for Everyone*. New York, United Nations Development Program.

UNDP (2018). "Human Development Reports."

United Nations (2019). "Human Security at 25: Builidng on Its Contribution to Achieve the SDGs."

United Nations/Framework Convention on Climate Change (2015). *Paris Agreement*. Paris and United Nations, s. C. o. t. Parties.

Vastapuu, L. (2017). *Hope Is Not Gone Altogether: The Roles and Reintegration of Young Female War Veterans in Liberia*. PhD, University of Turku.

Yuval-Davis, N. (2011). *The Politics of Belonging: Intersectional Contestations*. London: Sage.

Wibben, A. (2011). *Feminist Security Studes: A Narrative Approach*. London, Routledge.

34
FOOD SECURITY ACROSS THE CIRCUMPOLAR REGION

Kamrul Hossain, Thora M. Herrmann, and Dele Raheem

Introduction

Food is one of the most fundamental elements for everyday life. It is not just a commodity for physical consumption; it also offers emotional and cultural sustenance for people at large, and within their communities. Traditional food habits have crucial value for the population in a given region. Hence, traditionally produced foods remain a vital component of healthy diets and well-being of the people. The scarcity of nutritious and healthy foods to fulfill dietary needs in Arctic communities results in numerous risks. These risks pose security concerns, given that the concept of security is today broadened to include various dimensions of threats, such as threats to access to, and the ability to afford, safe, secure, and healthy food. It is within this context that this chapter offers an understanding of food security in the regional context of the Arctic. In order to promote food security, it is crucial to better understand the food systems that exist in the Arctic.

This chapter therefore highlights the specific character of the Arctic, where the rapidly changing socio-environmental and climatic conditions led to a gradual replacement of traditional local foods by imported food. Such replacement leaves Arctic communities with various health-related problems. On the other hand, imported foods are frequently not affordable to many in the region, often due to transportation costs. The insufficiency of food supply and increased contamination of traditional food due to the rise in human activities, coupled with increased reliance on increasingly unaffordable imported foods, offer a contradictory premise in relation to the food security of Arctic communities.

It is in this context that this chapter addresses the following critical questions. What are the drivers of food (in)security in the Arctic? What are the resulting cumulative impacts for Arctic residents and communities? Finally, what measures may well be recommended to promote food security in the Arctic?

Arctic food security and food sovereignty: an integrated theoretical framework

The conceptual framework presented in this section provides a platform for understanding the interconnections between the Arctic socio-ecological systems and food security, including food sovereignty. The framework provides a direction in which to assess food security in the Circumpolar North.

Food is a basic need, and remains vital for human fulfillment and survival. The enjoyment of one of the most fundamental human rights, the right to life, is dependent on access to food. The right to food is also directly related to other human rights; for example, the right to health, right to a healthy environment, right to water, and right to culture. Food is also an element around which community cohesion, identity, and culture develop. Arctic communities are the best examples to elaborate on the understanding of food security, to the extent that the concept of security is redefined by moving away from an exclusively state-centered and militarized geopolitical discourse to a more humanistic definition (Heininen and Nicol 2007). This paradigm shift was best introduced and fostered by the 1994 United Nations Human Development Report (HDR), which introduced the concept of human security, allowing for the sustained protection of individuals and communities at the subnational level. The concept of human security has been described as a way to protect the vital core of all human lives in ways that enhance their freedoms and fulfillment (CHS 2003). Food security in the Arctic, as it connects the comprehensive human security approach from various dimensions, such as community culture, health, and environment, plays a vital role in relation to the maintenance of a sustainable society (Hossain *et al.* 2018:6).

The UN Food and Agricultural Organization (FAO) endorsed a general definition of food security in 1996. It suggested that food security exists "when all people, at all times, have physical, social, and economic access to sufficient, safe and nutritious food that meets their dietary needs and food preferences for an active and healthy life" (2:49). This food security definition consists of four pillars: availability, accessibility, utilization, and food-systems stability. The availability of food is determined by the physical quantities of food that are produced, stored, processed, distributed, and exchanged (FAO 2008). Food availability not only looks at traditional and local food perspectives, but includes imported foods as well.

According to Sage (2014:709–710) accessibility is a measure of the ability to secure entitlements, which are defined as the set of resources (legal, political, economic, and social) that an individual requires to obtain to access to food. In terms of accessibility to traditional foods, the issues surrounding their safety must also be discussed. Food utilization refers to the appropriate nutritional content of the food and the ability of the body to use it effectively; in other words, the safety and social value of food. Hossain et al. (2018:16) state that:

> Lastly, food-systems *stability* concerns the removal of uncertainty and promotion of an effective, constant, and balanced supply determined by the temporal availability of and access to food (FAO 2008). As long as these four main pillars are fulfilled, a population or individual is said to be *food secure*.

Food remains important to both the Indigenous and non-Indigenous population of the Arctic, through use, consumption, and sharing. Yet, the Arctic region has witnessed drastic changes in these four pillars. Although these four pillars provide a conceptual framework that is now widely recognized in the understanding of food security, some scholars and Indigenous peoples' organizations suggest that it is inadequate because it fails to represent all interests in the securitization of food. They claim that the current concept of food security relies merely on the assessment of monetary access to market food, disregarding their need for consumption of traditional foods harvested from the land Egeland and Harrison

2013:17). Therefore, many have argued that the consumption and the stability of access to country food should be taken into account when defining food security for Indigenous peoples (Egeland *et al.* 2009; Schanbacher 2010). Given the presence of distinct groups of peoples living in the Arctic region, their food sovereignty (which empowers the communities themselves to choose and promote their food practices) is key.

Food security is integrated within the concept of food sovereignty, defined in the 2007 Nyéléni Declaration (Via Campesina 2007) as "the right of peoples, communities, and countries to define their own agricultural, labor, fishing, food and land policies which are ecologically, socially, economically and culturally appropriate to their unique circumstances." This definition also includes small and medium-sized production enterprises, calling for respect for inhabitants' own cultures, and it underlines the diversity of peasant farming, fishing, and Indigenous forms of agricultural production.

This integrated approach to food security and food sovereignty highlights the importance of production and the harvest of traditional/country foods (Pimbert 2009). According to Hossain et al. (2018:3), this is clearly relevant in the context of the Arctic, where harvesting traditional/country foods by both local and Indigenous communities "requires a stronger protection mechanism into which their voices need to be integrated." This is the condition needed to become a food-secure Arctic. Therefore, the issue of food sovereignty is key to ensuring food security. Changing access to, availability of, quality of, rights over, and the ability to use traditional food resources has implications for nutrition, well-being, identity, and culture. A range of interacting components, feedbacks, and drivers within the food system have significant impacts on food security and food sovereignty in a society (see Figure 34.1) by impacting communities' vulnerability (Wesche and Chan 2010).

Source: adapted from Ingram J., Ericksen P. and Liverman D. (Eds.) 2010. Food Security and Global Environmental Change, London, Earthscan

Drivers of food security: connectivity and cumulative impacts for Arctic communities

Colonialism and socio-economic changes caused major impacts on Arctic communities food system and related well-being (Martin 2003; Myers *et al.* 2005; Sheehy *et al.* 2015). These events accelerated a drastic diet transition away from local, nutrient-rich country foods towards a more market-based diet (Counil *et al.* 2011; Nuttall *et al.* 2005; White *et al.* 2007). This has been linked to an increase in obesity, diabetes, and cardiovascular disease in many Arctic communities (Van Oostdam et al. 2005).

Food insecurity is further exacerbated by climate change. Since 1979, the Arctic region has warmed at about twice the global rate (IPCC 2013) and reached new record levels during 2016. But during the first half of 2019, several parts of the Arctic, including Alaska, Greenland, Northern Canada and Siberia also saw higher-than-average temperatures with some records again being broken (Sun *et al.* 2018; NOAA 18 July 2019). Arctic local and Indigenous communities are particularly impacted by climate-driven changes, as they often rely on climate-sensitive Arctic ecosystem resources (Nancarrow and Chan 2010) for their nutrition, health, well-being, economic livelihoods, and cultural identity (Ford 2009). Implications for food security are significant, as climate change alters diversity, abundance, and the distribution ranges of key-food animal species such as caribou (Ford and Pearce 2010; Ford and Beaumier 2011). Vegetation ranges and phenological stages of medicinal plants, berries, and aromatic plants are shifted (Cuerrier *et al.* 2015). Numerous studies have documented how climate change makes it more difficult to engage in land-based activities

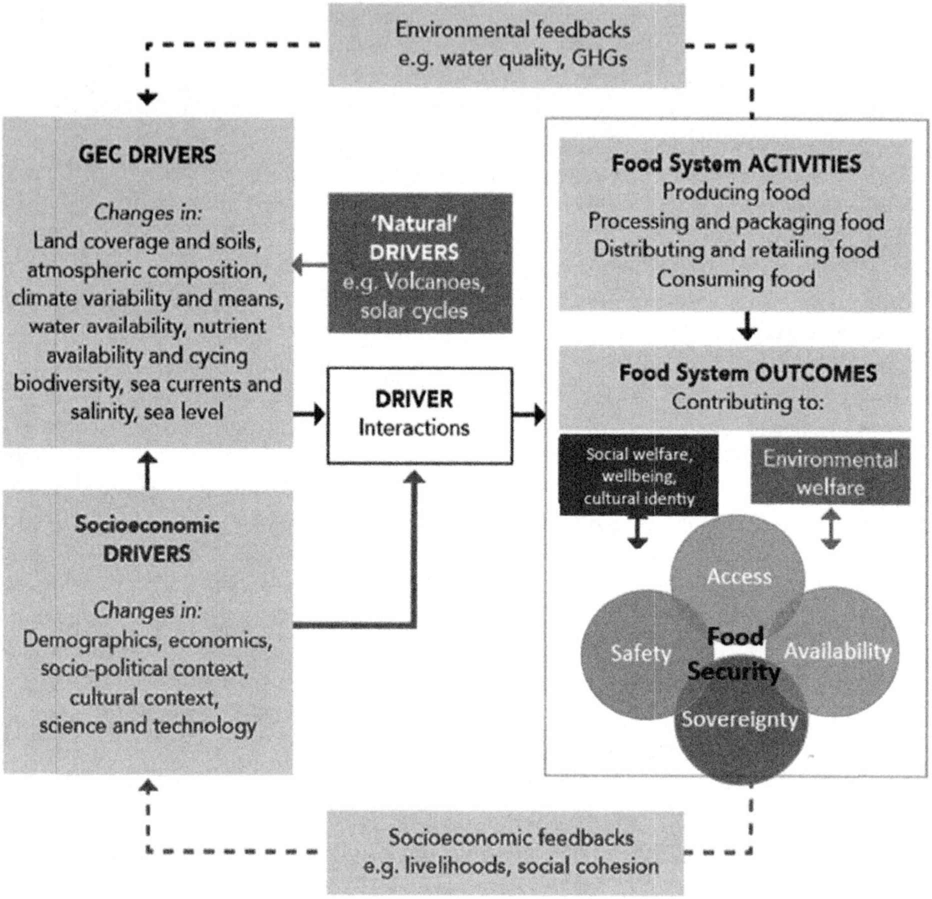

Figure 34.1 The interactions and complexity of the food system

(Nickels *et al.* 2005; Pearce *et al.* 2009; Ford and Pearce 2010). Thawing permafrost may also disrupt food-storage infrastructure (Lamoureux *et al.* 2015). Many communities are changing traditional harvest practices to adapt to these changes (Pearce *et al.* 2015; Ford *et al.* 2016).

Studies from Northern Canada highlight that climate change is community-specific and affects the country food harvest in both positive and negative ways (Nancarrow and Chan 2010). The northward-moving trend of new species as a result of warming may present new subsistence species and new hunting opportunities, as is being observed with moose and beaver in the Inuvialuit Settlement Region, Western Arctic, Canada (Wesche and Chan 2010).

Climate change has been identified as a main driver of increased extractive industry development (e.g. mineral, oil and gas exploration and extraction, and forestry) across the Arctic region (AMAP 2007; ICC 2011). Food security becomes a key issue of concern related to extractive industry development in the Arctic, especially considering how animal and plant species and country food access may be affected (NAHO 2008). Thus, the resulting disturbances from infrastructure (e.g. roads, railways, power tracks) associated with extractive industrial development on key subsistence food species, such as reindeer or caribou, are broad and vary across subspecies, space (winter and summer grazing areas), and time – including seasons (e.g. pre-calving, calving season) or phases of mining activity. They can encroach upon migration paths and fragment or destroy habitat (Herrmann *et al.* 2014). In the northwestern Russian town of Nikel, pollution has had a drastic effect on local wildlife and other food sources such as berries and mushrooms (Hansen 2016). Amongst the Sámi and Nenets in the Arctic-Barents region, forestry has a significant impact on food security, as summer and winter grazing areas used for reindeer husbandry have been heavily exploited (e.g. destroying lichen or tree-hanging lichen) (Sandström *et al.* 2012).

The presence of contaminants in traditional food sources presents a key issue of concern for Arctic communities (Donaldson *et al.* 2010). Persistent organic pollutants (POPs) are widely found in the Arctic ecosystem (Braune *et al.* 2015). Most of these environmental contaminants that impact food quality are transported to the Arctic over long distances via atmospheric currents, through water systems, and, to a lesser extent, by migratory species from regions further south (AMAP 2017). The Arctic is a sink for global pollutants transported into the region from distant sources (Peeken *et al.* 2018).

Contaminants are stored and concentrated in animals' fatty tissues and organs (bioaccumulation) and they bio-magnify up the food chain traditional food species of plants, fish, birds, and marine mammals are the highest sources of exposure to POPs (Van Oostdam *et al.* 2005, cited in Council of Canadian Academies 2014:137). In the Canadian Arctic, for example, Inuit show levels of exposure to mercury that exceed international safety guidelines (Tian *et al.* 2011, cited in Council of Canadian Academies 2014:138). Traditional food systems in northern Europe have shown high levels of lead and cadmium in plant ash, fish, sea mammals, birds, water, and soil levels (Kuhnlein and Chan 2000; Kirk *et al.* 2012). The Arctic Monitoring and Assessment Programme (AMAP) warned that exposure to environmental contaminants through a traditional diet remains one of the greatest risks to human health in the Arctic (AMAP 2015). This highlights the importance of global approaches to contaminant reduction. Three international agreements address the issue of contaminants in the Arctic: the Stockholm Convention on Persistent Organic Pollutants, the UN Economic Commission for Europe's Convention on Long-Range Trans-boundary Air Pollution, and the UN Environment Programme's 2017 Minamata Convention on Mercury. According to Friedrich (2018, para 24): "Recent studies have witnessed that the levels of many POPs have decreased in the Arctic, reflecting their ban in the last decades under the Stockholm Convention or previous national or international regulations" (Kirk *et al.* 2012). However, continued research is required to monitor health effects of emerging food contaminants in the Far North.

The right to food and food sovereignty, and the broader governance context in the Arctic

Food is one of the fundamental human rights, linking not only individuals' right to life but also the right to culture and the right to land (Hossain *et al.* 2018). Various scholars (Eide 2005; Damman *et al.* 2008; Kirchner 2015), Indigenous peoples' organizations (ITK and ICC 2012), and the international community (e.g. FAO) recognize food security as a critical human rights issue. The Declaration on the Rights of Indigenous Peoples (UNDRIP; UN 2007) provides several articles that are relevant to tackling food security. Articles 3, 26.2, and 32.1 recognize Indigenous peoples' rights to the resources and territories they have traditionally occupied, and the right to develop these lands according to traditional ownership or use. Food security of Arctic residents is not only shaped within legal instruments and norms, but is also embedded in institutional structures, in policy tools, and in governance regimes. One prominent example is the EU's post-2009 Seal Ban Regulation, an instrument that has had adverse impacts on Inuit livelihoods in both Canada and Greenland (Hossain 2013).

Arctic governance is represented at a high level by the consensus-based forum of the Arctic Council (AC), which includes eight Arctic member states and six Arctic Indigenous Peoples' organizations as Permanent Participants (Ottawa Declaration 1996). In relation to food security, the AC, through its Protection of the Arctic Marine Environment Working Group, recognized Indigenous peoples and their reliance on the ocean and marine environment for subsistence in the Arctic Marine Shipping Assessment Report (2009). More recently, the Sustainable Development Working Group and the Arctic Monitoring and Assessment Programme produced a report on food- and water-security indicators in the Arctic as they relate to health (Nilsson and Evengård 2015). The AC, however, has not yet focused on the conservation and management of targeted food species. Only recently (2016) has the Sustainable Development Working Group of the AC mandated an international research project on the opportunities and constraints to the commercialization of wild foods in the Arctic.

Governance of food security needs to embrace regional characteristics, both in regard to legislation as well as policy documents (Hossain *et al.* 2018). One of the intergovernmental forums at an interregional level is the Barents Euro-Arctic Council (BEAC), which includes Denmark, Finland, Iceland, Norway, Russia, Sweden, and the European Commission (Arctic Portal 2017). While a concrete focus on projects targeting food security is still absent at the BEAC, the actions undertaken to promote regional identity, culture, and history as well as inclusion of Indigenous peoples (e.g. Sámi , Nenets and Veps) within the cooperation framework makes this body a relevant instrument for tackling food security.

Governance achieved by cooperation between Arctic Indigenous Peoples' organizations places the strongest emphasis on food security and food sovereignty. For example, in 2015 the Inuit Circumpolar Council – Alaska identified food security as a top priority and created a framework to understand the issue from an Inuit perspective:

> We are speaking about the entire Arctic ecosystem and the relationships between all components within; we are talking about how our language teaches us when, where and how to obtain, process, store and consume food; we are talking about the importance of dancing and potlucks to share foods and how our economic system is tied to this; we are talking about our rights to govern how we obtain, process, store and consume food; about our Indigenous Knowledge and how it will aid in illuminating these changes that are occurring.
>
> *(Inuit Circumpolar Council – Alaska 2015:8)*

The report provided a framework for understanding all the components of Inuit food security, and thus a food security lens with which to understand the Arctic. Similarly, the Inuit Circumpolar Council – Canada and Inuit Tapiriit Kanatami in their Inuit and the Right to Food report (ITK and ICC 2012:7) stated that "for Inuit the ability to harvest country food is also an essential prerequisite in attaining the right to food," and called for a national Inuit strategy on the Right to Food (ibid:10).

In Canada, according to the Council of Canadian Academies (2014:148), a panoply of rights and benefits linked to food security, such as access to and ownership rights over wildlife and plant resources, are covered by land claims agreements; for example, the James Bay and

Northern Québec Agreement (1975) and the Nunavut Land Claims Agreement (1993). Yet, questions have been raised about whether the state has met its obligations under these agreements, and how well these agreements respect Indigenous peoples' human rights (Dalton 2006; MacIntosh 2010, cited in Council of Canadian Academies 2014). Co-management agreements are another policy tool relating to food security. International agreements, such as the Agreement on the Conservation of Polar Bears set out a harvesting-rights regime based on the principles that Inuit are users of wildlife.

At the community level, numerous community-led initiatives create innovative responses to food security and enhanced food sovereignty. For example, community-based monitoring programs of food species are crucial to informing government, industry, and agencies about any impacts on wildlife and plants (Gérin-Lajoie *et al.* 2018). Several communities in Arctic regions have started local food production through small-scale northern agriculture. For example, the Inuit community of Kuujjuaq in the Eastern Canadian Arctic started a greenhouse project, which has the potential of providing more cost-efficient, local, and fresh sources of food to Inuit families (Lamalice *et al.* 2016).

References

AMAP (Arctic Monitoring and Assessment Programme). 2007. *Arctic oil and gas.* AMAP, Oslo, Norway.

AMAP. 2015. *Human health in the Arctic.* Arctic Monitoring and Assessment Programme (AMAP), Oslo, Norway, vii + 165 pp.

AMAP. 2017. *AMAP assessment 2016. 'Chemicals of emerging Arctic concern.'* Arctic Monitoring and Assessment Programme (AMAP), Oslo, Norway, xvi + 353 pp.

Arctic Portal 2017. http://arcticportal.org/arctic-governance/arctic-cooperation. [Accessed 3 June 2018].

Braune, B., J. Chételat, M. Amyot, T. Brown, M. Clayden, M. Evans, A. Fisk *et al.* 2015. "Mercury in the marine environment of the Canadian Arctic: review of recent findings." *Science of the Total Environment* 509: 67–90.

CHS (Commission on Human Security). 2003. *Human security now: final report.* New York.

Council of Canadian Academies. 2014. *Aboriginal Food Security in Northern Canada: An Assessment of the State of Knowledge,* The Expert Panel on the State of Knowledge of Food Security in Northern Canada, Council of Canadian Academies, Ottawa.

Counil, É., M.-J. Gauthier, and E. Dewailly. 2011. "Alimentation et santé publique dans les communautés des inuit du nord du Québec: vers un changement de paradigme?" In J. G. Petit, Y. B. Viger, P. Aatami, and A. Iserhoff (Eds). *Les Inuit et les Cris du Nord du Québec.* Presses de l'Université du Québec, Québec (QC): 237–253.

Cuerrier, A., N. D. Brunet, J. Gérin-Lajoie, A. Downing, and E. Lévesque. 2015. "The study of Inuit knowledge of climate change in Nunavik, Québec: a mixed methods approach." *Human Ecology* 43, no. 3: 379–394.

Dalton, J. 2006. "Aboriginal title and self-government in Canada: what is the scope of comprehensive land claims agreements?" *Windsor Review of Legal Social Issues* 22, 29–78.

Damman, S., W. B. Eide, and H. V. Kuhnlein. 2008. "Indigenous peoples' nutrition transition in a right to food perspective." *Food Policy* 33, no. 2: 135–155.

Donaldson, S. G., J. Van Oostdam, C. Tikhonov, M. Feeley, B. Armstrong, P. Ayotte, O. Boucher *et al.* 2010. "Environmental contaminants and human health in the Canadian Arctic." *Science of the Total Environment* 408, no. 22: 5165–5234.

Egeland, G. M., G. Charbonneau-Roberts, J. Kuluguqtuq, J. Kilabuk, L. Okalik, R. Soueida, and H. V. Kuhnlein. 2009. "Back to the future: using traditional food and knowledge to promote a healthy future among Inuit." In *Indigenous peoples' food systems: the many dimensions of culture, diversity, environment and health.* Food and Agriculture Organization of the United Nations, New York, www.fao.org/3/a-i0370e/i0370e02.pdf. [Accessed 7 May 2018].

Egeland, G. M., Harrison, G. G. 2013. "Health disparities: promoting indigenous peoples' health through traditional food systems and self-determination." In H. V. Kuhnlein, B. Erasmus, D. Spigelski, B. Burlingame (Eds). *Indigenous peoples' food systems and well-being: interventions and policies for healthy communities*. Food and agriculture Organization of the United Nations & Centre for indigenous peoples' nutrition and Environment, Rome: 9–23.

Eide, W. B. 2005. *From food security to the right to food*. Food and human rights in development. (Vol. 1), 67–97.

FAO. 2002. *The state of food insecurity in the world 2001*. Rome. Retrieved November 4, 2019, from: www.fao.org/3/y1500e/y1500e04.pdf.

FAO (Food and Agriculture Organization of the United Nations). 2008. *Climate change and food security: a framework document*. Rome.

Ford, J. D. 2009. "Vulnerability of Inuit food systems to food insecurity as a consequence of climate change: a case study from Igloolik, Nunavut." *Regional Environmental Change* 9, no. 2: 83–100.

Ford, J. D., and M. Beaumier. 2011. "Feeding the family during times of stress: experience and determinants of food insecurity in an Inuit community." *The Geographical Journal* 177, no. 1: 44–61.

Ford, J. D., and T. Pearce. 2010. "What we know, do not know, and need to know about climate change vulnerability in the western Canadian Arctic: a systematic literature review." *Environmental Research Letters* 5, 014008.

Ford, J. D., E. Stephenson, A. C. Willox, V. Edge, K. Farahbakhsh, C. Furgal, S. Harper *et al.* 2016. "Community-based adaptation research in the Canadian Arctic." *Wiley Interdisciplinary Reviews: Climate Change* 7, no. 2: 175–191.

Friedrich, D. (2018, February 1). "The problems won't go away: Persistent Organic Pollutants (POPs) in the Arctic." 4 November 2019, www.thearcticinstitute.org/persistent-organic-pollutants-pops-in-the-arctic/.

Gérin-Lajoie, J., T. M. Herrmann, G. A. MacMillan, E. Hébert-Houle, M. Monfette, J. A. Rowell, T. Anaviapik Soucie *et al.* 2018. "IMALIRIJIIT: a community-based environmental monitoring program in the George 1 River watershed, Nunavik, Canada." *Ecoscience* 25, no. 4: 381–399.

Hansen, M. 2016. "Heavy metals in food from the Norwegian, Finnish and Russian border region." Norwegian Institute for Air Research, Tromso, Norway. Presentation at "Seminar on Globalization and Food security in the Barents region." Rovaniemi, Finland. August, 16, 2016.

Heininen, L., and H. N. Nicol. 2007. "A new northern security agenda." In E. Brunet-Jailly (Ed). *Borderlands: comparing border security in North America and Europe*. University of Ottawa Press, Canada: 117–164.

Herrmann, T. M., P. Sandström, K. Granqvist, N. D'Astous, J. Vannar, H. Asselin, and N. Saganash. 2014. IMALIRIJIIT: A community-based environmental monitoring program in the George 1 River watershed, Nunavik, Canada. *Ecoscience*. "Effects of mining on reindeer/caribou populations and Indigenous livelihoods: community-based monitoring by Sámi reindeer herders in Sweden and First Nations in Canada." *The Polar Journal* 4, no. 1: 28–51.

Hossain, K. 2013. "The EU ban on the import of seal products and the WTO regulations: neglected human rights of the Arctic Indigenous peoples?" *Polar Record* 49, no. 2: 154–166.

Hossain, K., D. Raheem, and S. Cormier. 2018. *Food security governance in the Arctic-Barents region*. Springer International Publishing AG, Cham: 141.

Huntington, H. P., P. Kankaanpää, S. Baldursson, A. L. Sippola, S. Kaitala, and C. Zöckler. 2001. "Arctic flora and fauna: status and conservation." *Conservation of Arctic Flora and Fauna*.

ICC (Inuit Circumpolar Council). 2011. *Circumpolar Inuit declaration on resource development principles in Inuit Nunaat*. ICC, Nuuk.

Ingram, J., P. Ericksen, and D. Liverman (Eds). 2010. *Food security and global environmental change*. Earthscan, London.

Inuit Circumpolar Council – Alaska. 2015. "Alaskan Inuit food security conceptual framework: how to assess the Arctic from an Inuit perspective." Technical Report. Anchorage, AK.

IPCC. 2013. "Summary for policymakers climate change 2013: the physical science basis." In T. F. Stocker *et al.* (Ed). *Contribution of Working Group I to the Fifth Assessment Report of the Intergovernmental Panel on Climate Change*. Cambridge University Press, Cambridge and New York: 1535pp.

ITK and ICC (Inuit Tapiriit Kanatami, Inuit Circumpolar Council – Canada). 2012. *Inuit and the right to food: submission to the United Nations Special Rapporteur on the right to food for the official country mission to Canada*. ITK & ICC, Ottawa.

Kirchner, S. 2015. "Climate change effects on snow conditions and the human rights of reindeer herders, forthcoming." *Pace Environmental Law Review* 33, 1.

Kirk, J. L., I. Lehnherr, M. Andersson, B. M. Braune, L. Chan, A. P. Dastoor, D. Durnford *et al.* 2012. "Mercury in Arctic marine ecosystems: sources, pathways and exposure." *Environmental Research* 119: 64–87.

Kneeshaw, D. D., M. Larouche, H. Asselin, M.-C. Adam, M. Saint-Arnaud, and G. Reyes. 2010. "Road rash: ecological and social impacts of road networks on First Nations." In M. G. Stevenson and D. C. Natcher (Eds). *Planning co-existence: Aboriginal considerations and approaches in land use planning*. Canadian Circumpolar Institute Press, Edmonton, AB: 169–184.

Kuhnlein, H. V., and H. M. Chan 2000. "Environment and contaminants in traditional food systems of northern Indigenous peoples." *Annual Review of Nutrition* 20, no. 1: 595–626.

Laird, B. D., A. B. Goncharov, and H. M. Chan. 2013. "Body burden of metals and persistent organic pollutants among Inuit in the Canadian Arctic." *Environment International* 59, 33–40.

Laird, B. D., A. B. Goncharov, G. M. Egeland, and H. M. Chan. 2013. "Dietary advice on Inuit traditional food use needs to balance benefits and risks of mercury, selenium, and n3 fatty acids–3." *The Journal of Nutrition* 143, no. 6: 923–930.

Lamalice, A., E. Avard, V. Coxam, T. Herrmann, C. Desbiens, Y. Wittrant, and S. Blangy. 2016. "Soutenir la sécurité alimentaire dans le Grand Nord: projets communautaires d'agriculture sous serre au Nunavik et au Nunavut." *études/Inuit/Studies* 40, no. 1: 147–169.

Lambden, J., O. Receveur, and H. V. Kuhnlein. 2007. "Traditional food attributes must be included in studies of food security in the Canadian Arctic." *International Journal of Circumpolar Health* 66, no. 4, 308–319.

Lamoureux, S., D. L. Forbes, T. Bell, G. K. Manson, A. C. A. Rudy, J. Lalonde, M. Brown *et al.* 2015. "Chapter 7. The impact of climate change on infrastructure in the Western and Central Canadian Arctic." In G. A. Stern and A. Gaden (Eds). *From science to policy in the Western and Central Canadian Arctic: an Integrated Regional Impact Study (IRIS) of climate change and modernization*. ArcticNet, Québec City: 300–341.

MacIntosh, C. 2010. "Developments in Aboriginal Law: The 2009–2010 term: the year when treaties became contracts." *52 Supreme Court Law Review* 2d, no. 1: 1–24.

Martin, T. 2003. *De la banquise au congélateur. Mondialisation et culture au Nunavik*. UNESCO et Presses de l'Université Laval, Paris et Québec: 202 p.

Myers, H., H. Fast, M. K. Berkes, and F. Berkes. 2005. "Feeding the family in times of change." In F. Berkes, R. Huebert, H. Fast, M. Manseau, and A. Diduck (Eds). *Breaking ice: renewable resource and ocean management in the Canadian north*. University of Calgary Press and Arctic Institute of North America, Calgary: 23–45.

NAHO. 2008. *National Aboriginal Health Organization (NAHO) final report: roundtable discussion exploring community-based responses to resource extractive development in Northern Canada*. NAHO, Ottawa.

Nancarrow, T. L., and H. M. Chan. 2010. "Observations of environmental changes and potential dietary impacts in two communities in Nunavut, Canada." *Rural Remote Health* 10, no. 2: 1370.

Nickels, S., C. Furgal, M. Buell, and H. Moquin. 2005. *Unikkaaqatigitt: putting the human face on climate change. Perspectives from Inuit in Canada*. Joint publication of the Inuit Tapiriit Kanatami, Nasivvik Centre for Inuit Health, Changing Environments at Université Laval and the Ajunnginiq Centre at the National Aboriginal Health Association, Ottawa.

Nilsson, L. M., and B. Evengård. 2015. "Food security or food sovereignty: what is the main issue in the Arctic?" In B. Evengård, J. N. Larsen, and Ø. Paasche (Eds). *The new Arctic*, 1st ed. Springer International Publishing, Switzerland: 213–223.

NOAA. 2019. "Assessing the global climate in June 2019: warmest June on record for the globe, record-low Antarctic sea ice extent." *National Oceanic and Atmospheric Association*, 18 July 2019, www.ncei.noaa.gov/news/global-climate-201906.

Nuttall, M., F. Berkes, B. Forbes, G. Kofinas, T. Vlassova, and G. Wenzel. 2005. "Hunting, herding, fishing and gathering: Indigenous peoples and renewable resource use in the Arctic." In C. Symon (lead editor), L. Arris, and B. Heal *Arctic climate impact assessment*. Cambridge University Press, New York: 649–690.

Ottawa Declaration. 1996. *Declaration on the establishment of the Arctic Council*, https://oaarchive.arctic-council.org/handle/11374/85. [Accessed 3 June 2018].

Pearce, T., J. Ford, A. C. Willox, and B. Smit. 2015. "Inuit traditional ecological knowledge (TEK), subsistence hunting and adaptation to climate change in the Canadian Arctic." *Arctic* 68, no. 2: 233–245.

Pearce, T. D., J. D. Ford, G. J. Laidler, B. Smit, F. Duerden, M. Allarut, M. Andrachuk *et al.* 2009. "Community collaboration and climate change research in the Canadian Arctic." *Polar Research* 28, no. 1: 10–27.

Peeken, I., S. Primpke, B. Beyer, J. Gütermann, C. Katlein, T. Krumpen, M. Bergmann, L. Hehemann, and G. Gerdts. 2018. "Arctic sea ice is an important temporal sink and means of transport for microplastic." *Nature Communications* 9, no. 1: 1505. DOI: 10.1038/s41467-018-03825-5.

Pimbert, M. 2009. *Towards food sovereignty*. International Institute for Environment and Development, London.

Sage, C. 2014. "Impacts of climate change on food accessibility." In B. Freedman (Ed). *Global environmental change. Handbook of global environmental pollution, vol 1*. Springer, Dordrecht: 709–715.

Sandström, P., C. Sandström, J. Svensson, L. Jougda, and K. Baer. 2012. "Participatory GIS to mitigate conflicts between reindeer husbandry and forestry in Vilhelmina Model Forest, Sweden." *The Forestry Chronicle* 88, no. 3: 254–260.

Schanbacher, W. D. 2010. *The politics of food: the global conflict between food security and food sovereignty*. ABC-CLIO, Santa Barbara.

Sheehy, T., F. Kolahdooz, S. E. Schaefer, D. N. Douglas, A. Corriveau, and S. Sharma. 2015. "Traditional food patterns are associated with better diet quality and improved dietary adequacy in Aboriginal peoples in the Northwest Territories." *Canada Journal of Human Nutrition and Dietetics* 28, no. 3: 262–271.

Sun, L., D. Allured, M. Hoerling, L. Smith, J. Perlwitz, D. Murray, and J. Eischeid. 2018. "Drivers of 2016 record Arctic warmth assessed using climate simulations subjected to factual and counterfactual forcing." *Weather and Climate Extremes* 19: 1–9.

Tian, W., G. M. Egeland, I. Sobol, and H. M. Chan 2011. "Mercury hair concentrations and dietary exposure among Inuit preschool children in Nunavut, Canada." *Environment International* 37, no. 1: 42–48.

UN General Assembly. *United Nations declaration on the rights of indigenous peoples: resolution / adopted by the general assembly*. 2 October 2007, A/RES/61/295, available at: www.refworld.org/docid/471355a82.html [accessed 4 November 2019].

Van Oostdam, J., S. G. Donaldson, M. Feeley, D. Arnold, P. Ayotte, G. Bondy, L. Chan *et al.* 2005. "Human health implications of environmental contaminants in Arctic Canada: a review." *Science of the Total Environment* 351: 165–246.

Via Campesina. 2007. "Nyéléni declaration. Sélingué, Mali: 'Forum for food sovereignty'," https://nyeleni.org/spip.php?article290 [Accessed 1 June 2018].

Wesche, S. D., and H. M. Chan. 2010. "Adapting to the impacts of climate change on food security among Inuit in the Western Canadian Arctic." *EcoHealth* 7, no. 3: 361–373.

White, D. M., S. Craig Gerlach, P. Loring, A. C. Tidwell, and M. C. Chambers. 2007. "Food and water security in a changing Arctic climate." *Environmental Research Letters* 2, no. 4: 045018. DOI: 10.1088/1748-9326/2/4/045018.

35

THE WIDENING SPECTRUM OF ARCTIC SECURITY THINKING

Gunhild Hoogensen Gjørv and Marc Lanteigne

This book has sought to explain why, and how, the debates about security in the Arctic not only need to be examined on many different levels – ranging from the individual to the regional and indeed the global – but also from a variety of different disciplines beyond 'the usual suspects', meaning political science and military studies. It is increasingly clear that a central departure point in any discussion about Arctic security is how "Arctic" is actually defined and understood. Though there is a geographical connection between territories and oceans in this region located in the northernmost part of the northern hemisphere, differences quickly begin to arise. The region as a whole is considered to be stereotypically very cold, but temperatures are often quite diverse; for example, parts of the European Arctic have extensive foliage, and may experience winters and summers similar to that of the lower-latitude, temperate zones in Canada. Other parts of the Arctic have scarce foliage and appear barren by comparison. From a demographic viewpoint, while the dominant populations in the North American Arctic (Canada and the United States, as well as Greenland) are Indigenous, the European and Russian Arctic regions have predominantly non-Indigenous populations. Also, urbanisation differs across the Arctic, from small villages and towns separated by enormous distances with few or no roads, to larger cities that may be within reasonable driving distances from each other. To what degree can we speak of the region as unified with regard to security perspectives?

As this book illustrates, there are many different "Arctics," and many different perspectives which need to be better understood. Some general trends do impact how the eight Arctic states and their diverse peoples understand security. State-centric security perspectives, and the question of hard power or hard security, are certainly not absent from this particular equation. Some commentators argue that military issues in the Arctic, which were significantly deprioritized after the end of the Cold War, have come to dominate again. Others have maintained that while hard power interests never actually left, various other security perspectives are also making themselves felt – many of which are directly connected to climate change. The retreat of ice in much of the Arctic and sub-Arctic regions has prompted concerns over the growing number of political, economic, social, and developmental effects in the Far North and louder calls for climate change action, including via a youth movement sparked by Swedish climate activist Greta Thunberg.

Numerous warning bells about Arctic climate change, including mass wildfires across much of the Arctic, including Alaska and Siberia, in the middle of 2019 (Lanteigne 2019a; Watts 2019); accelerated losses of permafrost and glaciers being measured throughout the Arctic (Welch 2019); and rising average temperatures through the region (NOAA 2019), are becoming more common now. As with numerous other parts of the world which are also experiencing climate change effects, the central question is to what degree the human response should be mitigation or adaptation? Regarding the former, how best to accomplish this? In terms of the latter, what exactly are we preparing ourselves to adapt to, and when? Tendencies to gravitate to classic geopolitical posturing between Western powers and Russia and China, replicating traditional security concerns, can soon become overshadowed by the effects of climate change; so much so that traditional security concerns pale by comparison and cooperation will have to dominate for reasons of global survival.

Perspectives of Arctic security demonstrate that we need to see beyond state-centric threat configurations. Today's threats both transcend states – such as climate change – or are components within and/or across states, such as sub-state or non-state actors from extremist movements identifying with far right, far left, white supremacy, "incel"/toxic masculinity, nationalist, or religious politics. The result is competing security narratives from state-centric, classic geopolitical fixations to non-state and "beyond state" narratives where threats and solutions are equally distanced from individual state capacities and require global input and actions.

Indeed, this book demonstrates that a comprehensive security framework is necessary to better understand the ways in which different perceptions of security interact, and perhaps conflict, between state, human, societal, and international security perspectives. The Arctic constellation of states and non-state actors provides good examples of this as the threats upon, as well as impacts of, climate change and interlinked environmental security issues (including reduced biodiversity and environmental degradation) move well beyond and across borders. Yet, at the same time, they compete with economic and energy security narratives which rely upon continued fossil fuel production and use, all of which are in turn either subordinated to, or dependent upon, state-centric defense-posturing security narratives (Hoogensen Gjørv 2017). These narratives are not givens, but reflect political choices, and therefore increased awareness about how these chosen narratives operate and their related consequences is crucial to the future of the Arctic region as well as the globe.

For example, a common theme among current studies of the Arctic, including its security questions, is that the region is "opening up." The obvious interpretation of this idea is that the the "south" has increased access to the Arctic via land and sea as a result of previously ice-locked geography now becoming accessible for the purposes of economic development, communications, and transportation. Yet the concept of opening goes well beyond that to include knowledge sharing and regime-building, as well as growing instances of security "spillover" into the Arctic from different directions. The Arctic Council, which remains the most prominent regional institution, had the luxury in its first decade of existence to remain detached from much global discourse and to keep hard security matters at arm's length. Today, with 13 non-Arctic governments sitting as observers in the Council, and with more probably wishing to join; and with the growing economic presence of non-Arctic states, ranging from China to Australia to Saudi Arabia (Humpert 2019), engaging the Arctic economically, the definition of an Arctic state is currently in transition. The caustic statement by US Secretary of State Mike Pompeo, at the Council's May 2019 Ministerial meeting, that "there are only Arctic States and Non-Arctic States. No third category exists," (Pompeo 2019) not only reflected an outdated approach to Arctic regional governance, but to use the American expression, it was a day late and a dollar short. Arctic politics, and security thinking, have expanded well beyond the Arctic states themselves, and trying to move that process backwards is an unlikely endeavour at best.

Thus, one question which is appearing is whether the growing array of security questions will result in new forms of state and sub-state dialogue on the subject. This process has been made more challenging by the still-frigid diplomatic relations between Russia on one side and the United States and its NATO allies on the other, as well as a growing shift in US Arctic policy since 2017 towards downplaying human security and climate change and instead painting the region as an arena-in-waiting for great-power brinkmanship. These developments may not only serve to decrease security in the Arctic as a whole, but also threaten to marginalize considerable security concerns on other levels, especially in regard to Indigenous persons, the environment, economic development, and socio-economic questions.

As the Arctic gains increasing international attention, we may be seeing a form of "revenge of the state," as numerous Arctic and non-Arctic governments begin to more openly vie for attention and access. The government of Russia has focused much of its evolving economic policies on building up its Arctic regions – a process which has included closer engagement with the world's largest non-Arctic state, China. The United States has seen its Arctic policy swing wildly between attempts to take the lead in addressing regional climate change challenges under Barack Obama, to hard realist, anti-environmentalist, and transactional methods under Donald Trump, with the other six Arctic states trying to walk a delicate line between the two regional giants while also questioning how the changes in the Arctic will affect their politics and finances. Numerous non-Arctic states have also sought to enunciate their Arctic policies using different methods, with some pointing to their scientific and exploration prowess (Britain, France, Germany, Italy, the Netherlands); others towards their maritime expertise (Japan, Singapore, South Korea); and another focusing on the Brobdingnagian economic and policymaking weight which it can bring to bear in the Arctic (China). The Arctic clubhouse is getting more crowded, but what does that mean for the actors actually in the Arctic itself?

The possibility of an Arctic scramble for resources which was the subject of much speculation when the region began to be seen as a potential economic powerhouse faded in the face of dropping commodity prices and the realization of the logistical challenges still facing many nascent extractive industries in the region (Kuersten 2015). At the same time, regional agreements including the Polar Code, bans on fishing in the Central Arctic Ocean, and the slow but steady moves towards an agreement to proscribe heavy fuel oil in the Arctic (George 2019) demonstrate further progress towards multilateral solutions to current and looming security challenges.

Yet even today there are still signs that the tendency to view the Arctic as an open space, with resources, and even lands, ready for the taking, stubbornly persists. There was much surprise and bemusement, in August 2019, when news reports surfaced that US President Trump had been discussing, more than once, an American purchase of Greenland from Denmark on strategic and economic grounds (Salama et al. 2019). The notion not only demonstrated a complete lack of knowledge about Greenland's legal status (as of 2009, Greenland attained self-rule within the Danish Kingdom, including the right to self-determination) but also a blithe disregard for the interests of the nation's 57,000 inhabitants. The prospect was immediately dismissed by Danish Prime Minister Mette Frederiksen as "absurd" – a comment which caused a temporary diplomatic rift with Washington (Lanteigne 2019b; Olsen 2019).

The initial responses from various quarters to the whole "buy Greenland" idea were also telling, and provided much insight into the idea that the Arctic is still seen by some policymakers as a *tabula rasa* despite all of the progress made in the past few decades in developing and augmenting various regional political and legal structures. In one 2019 commentary by a Republican US Senator, the long history of American land purchases was pointed to (Cotton 2019), ignoring the fact that these transactions took place well before the advent of the modern international legal system, specifically ignoring the lands' actual inhabitants and jingoistically assuming that Greenlanders would be overwhelmingly supportive of falling under US dominion, despite a long and painful history which many other overseas US territories faced, and some still face (Immerwahr 2019). In another piece by a former Danish Prime Minister, Greenland was painted as an inanimate bridge between Danish and American strategic interests at a time when China and Russia are viewed as threatening the Arctic's regional order (Rasmussen 2019). Again, the interests of Greenlanders were elbowed aside, and the article illustrated a long-standing paternalistic view of Greenland as being too small and vulnerable to conduct its own diplomacy.

One lesson that one can take away from this episode is that although the notion of the US buying an Arctic nation outright reflects another example of the solipsistic and at times benighted approach to foreign policy under the Trump administration, this is also a sign that the identity of the Arctic as separated from "traditional" hard security concerns is quickly eroding, or never existed in the first place. As one Greenland specialist stated, Trump's views reflect an overall growth in American interests towards Greenland, and the whole of the Arctic, out of the view that the region is becoming more directly linked to emerging US security concerns (Breum 2019). It can also be argued that current American, and to a degree Russian and Chinese, activity in the Arctic reflects an emerging vote of no confidence in regional security cooperation.

We have different, sometimes competing, visions of security in the Arctic. Military actors, including NATO, continue to focus on the enemy threat that could potentially arise, not least through geopolitical developments. The emphasis on the "Arctic exceptionalism" narrative that focuses on cooperation and dialogue in the Arctic, particularly through scientific innovation and resource development (hence "low tension" perspectives) is favoured in many Arctic political circles. Simultaneously however, other security perspectives operate, not least the diverse human security perspectives across the region regarding the ability of Arctic states to maintain a sense of community and survival of identity, particularly amongst Indigenous groups. Combined with this is the economic security of Arctic communities: both Indigenous and non-Indigenous. Complicating these security perspectives are the impacts of climate change on communities – eroding coastlines, melting permafrost, and the movement/reduction/extinction of central species of flora and fauna – with regard to community sustainability and survival.

Thus, if "the Arctic" has a unified message to send about security, it is the unavoidability and importance of understanding a complex environment that informs an intricate web of security perspectives operating at a given time. Such an approach has a greater chance of demonstrating the wisdom and necessity of cooperative measures for ensuring global security in the long term.

References

Breum, Martin. 2019. "Why President Trump's Idea of Buying Greenland Is No Joke," *High North News*, 29 August, www.highnorthnews.com/en/why-president-trumps-idea-buying-greenland-no-joke.

Cotton, Tom. 2019. "We Should Buy Greenland." *The New York Times*, 26 August, www.nytimes.com/2019/08/26/opinion/politics/greenland-trump.html.

George, Jane. 2019. "The Push to Phase out Heavy Fuel Oil in the Arctic Continues," *Arctic Today*, 27 February, www.arctictoday.com/the-push-to-phase-out-heavy-fuel-oil-in-the-arctic-continues/.

Hoogensen Gjørv, Gunhild. 2017. "Tensions between Environmental, Economic, and Energy Security in the Arctic." *Northern Sustainabilities: Understanding and Addressing Change in a Circumpolar World*. G. Fondahl and G. Wilson. Cham, Springer International Publishing, pp. 35–46.

Humpert, Malte. 2019. "Why Saudi Arabia is Looking to Enter the Arctic with an Investment in Russian LNG," *Arctic Today*, 20 March, www.arctictoday.com/why-saudi-arabia-is-looking-to-enter-the-arctic-with-an-investment-in-russian-lng/.

Immerwahr, Daniel. 2019. *How to Hide an Empire: A History of the Greater United States* (New York: Farrar, Straus and Giroux).

Kuersten, Andreas. 2015. "The Arctic Race that Wasn't: Hyperbole, Imaginaries, and the North Pole," *Foreign Affairs* 20 August, www.foreignaffairs.com/reviews/2015-08-20/arctic-race-wasnt.

Lanteigne, Marc. 2019a. "Arctic Heatwave: The Fire This Time," *Over the Circle*, 27 July, https://overthecircle.com/2019/07/27/arctic-heatwave-the-fire-this-time/.

Lanteigne, Marc. 2019b. "Greenland: The United States' Fantasy Island," *Over the Circle*, 23 August, https://overthecircle.com/2019/08/23/greenland-the-united-states-fantasy-island/.

National Centers for Environmental Information – National Oceanic and Atmospheric Association, 2019. "Global Climate Report –July 2019," www.ncdc.noaa.gov/sotc/global/201907.

Olsen, Jan M. 2019. "Danish PM: Trump's Idea of Buying Greenland is 'Absurd'," *Associated Press*, 19 August, www.apnews.com/37da8cbadb39488d87154ce820da43c2.

Pompeo, Michael R. 2019. "Looking North: Sharpening America's Arctic Focus," *US Department of State*, 6 May, www.state.gov/looking-north-sharpening-americas-arctic-focus/.

Rasmussen, Anders Fogh. 2019. 'Greenland Should Unite the US and Denmark – Not Divide Them,' *The Atlantic*, 29 August, www.theatlantic.com/ideas/archive/2019/08/greenland-should-unite-us-and-denmark/596959/?fbclid=IwAR1pkDhDqTue0omIS5DugjTJOHaO_rbf0Adxc1fbxnkIgAb0PXW8GxJ_3wo.

Salama, Vivian, Rebecca Ballhaus, Andrew Restuccia and Michael C. Bender. 2019. "President Trump Eyes a New Real-Estate Purchase: Greenland," *Wall Street Journal*, 16 August.

Watts, Jonathan. "Arctic Wildfires Spew Soot and Smoke Cloud Bigger than EU," *The Guardian*, 12 August 2019. www.theguardian.com/world/2019/aug/12/arctic-wildfires-smoke-cloud.

Welch, Craig. "Arctic Permafrost is Thawing Fast. That Affects Us All," *National Geographic* (September 2019), www.nationalgeographic.com/environment/2019/08/arctic-permafrost-is-thawing-it-could-speed-up-climate-change-feature/.

INDEX

Page numbers in *italics* denote a figure and those in **bold** a table

Printed in Dunstable, United Kingdom

78097182R00259